A FAMILY HISTORY

Part Two

A Personal Tribute to Samuel Rayner Kopecky
1945-2001

Sam Kopecky
(co-authored by Pam Kopecky)

Order this book online at www.trafford.com
or email orders@trafford.com

Most Trafford titles are also available at major online book retailers.

© Copyright 2012 Sam Kopecky.
All rights reserved. No part of this publication may be reproduced, stored in a retrieval system, or transmitted, in any form or by any means, electronic, mechanical, photocopying, recording, or otherwise, without the written prior permission of the author.

Printed in the United States of America.

ISBN: 978-1-4251-8671-5 (sc)

Trafford rev. 03/16/2012

www.trafford.com

North America & international
toll-free: 1 888 232 4444 (USA & Canada)
phone: 250 383 6864 • fax: 812 355 4082

For Sam
. . . my husband and best friend for 20 years

The Existence of Love

I thought that your death
Was a waste and a destruction,
A pain of grief hardly to be endured.
I am only beginning to learn
That your life was a gift and a giving,
And a loving left with me.
The desperation of death
Cannot destroy what has been given.
I am learning to look at your life again
Instead of your death and your departing.

Marjorie Pizer
(Contributed by John Clark)

FOREWORD

The volume of work that Sam has produced in such difficult circumstances—which would deter more able-bodied people—makes writing the foreword to this book a daunting task, so to do justice to it, 'tis important for me to return to my cultural roots and write from my heart.

I first met Sam approximately two years ago and he was then already paralyzed and confined to his bedroom with advanced terminal cancer, more often than not suffering from the on-going pain, nausea and other side effects of his illness. His gracious wife Pam asked if I would like to read what Sam was writing about and I reluctantly agreed because I did not want to become involved in what was a family affair, but I did not want to offend her. I am so pleased that I did agree as I found it so interesting. Through his book, I got to know Sam so well, I feel I have known him all my life.

The reason I was so interested in writing the foreword for this book is because Sam, in writing about his grandparents, and tracing the history of the Kopecky family from Moravia and into Texas, and the subsequent development of the Kopecky and Willis union, made me realize that Sam was writing it and telling it the way we as Maori would tell it. Yesteryear, this year, and next year are all seamless. It is not for me to judge the academic value, or indeed the quality of Sam's work, but as a member of the Maori race I pay my respects to a man who would have been a great orator if he was Maori. His courage, his integrity, his discipline and perseverance need to be recognized and acknowledged. In knowing Sam through his writing I have no doubt in my mind Joe and Golda Kopecky knew that Sam, their grandson, was indeed a Kopecky.

I believe that indigenous people throughout the world, all practice what we call whakapapa (tracing one's genealogy), and the next step, which Joe and Golda certainly practiced, was what we call whanaungatanga (what you would call family 'getogethers'). The next stage is what we call nga ritenga (that is, discovering our similarities and what we have in common). And for the Maori people we have another practice which we call nga rereketanga (which means recognizing our differences, respecting them for what they are and above all, realizing that is what makes you unique). It is your uniqueness which will propel you into whatever the future holds for you. Know where you came from, know where you are, and you will know where you are going.

In all humility I thank his gracious wife for asking me to write the foreword to Sam's work of love and in agreeing to do so, in paying my respects to a man who by his sheer courage earned my unequivocal and ultimate respect, I knew I would have to do it from my heart and with my tears.

Tena koutou, Tamihana Te Winitana.

Footnote: The late Tamihana Te Winitana was one of the New Zealand Maori people's most respected orators and scholars, who originally became involved with Sam and I as a guest staying at our lodge, while working on the Hauraki Maori Treaty of Waitangi Claims. He became a close friend of our family, and he and I both read this story together, in installments—"hot off the press"—as Sam wrote it. I believe his support and encouragement, and belief in the importance of this Kopecky family history, was a key factor in Sam's dedication to the completion of this project—Pam Kopecky.

PREFACE

(Sam's words—based on excerpts from *'A Family History—Moravia to Texas'*)

. . . It was from this time on, after I lived with my grandparents, that I got to know them and my folks better when I began to know who they were, and more about them. Little did I know this joy would be short-lived for in the next few years, so many changes would take place that it wouldn't seem like the same family. It would also be the start of my life's journey. It would be years before I would know or even realize, what my family's past had been, in full. It wasn't until after I started losing my grandparents and parents that it started to hit me on how much they had meant to others, and me.

It was before Dr. Joe's death in February 1977, after I had lived and grown up with he and Golda for several years, that he gave me the first volume of his *'Letters'*, and his diary in which he had written some stories . . . I never knew why he gave these records to me. I can only guess that he might have hoped with time, I would settle down enough to appreciate his gift, and see to it that it was brought together and shared. Maybe his hopes will come to be and we will learn something from our past family history.

I decided—with Pam's nudging—that while I had time I would try to put some of this family history together in some sort of order. After spending well over a year trying to gather various information on our family history and background, it becomes more and more apparent to me that in many ways we are just like many other families in a number of respects. In other ways we are not. I am still working on a lot of the Kopecky history and stories. I hope it will give you a better idea of who you all are, and who I am, after it is done. A number of stories are entertaining, some have lessons in them to all of us, and some help us understand why we are like we are. I sometimes think we all need reminding that we have a lot to be proud of when it comes to who and what we are. So this is your reminder for now.

If I have learned anything from this, it is that I don't have the answers. I don't think any one of us does. We all get our feelings hurt and we let what we want get in the way at times. I sometimes think it comes down to the fact that each of us must decide on how they want to live their lives and what their priorities are.

If it is the family, then where is the line between caring and interfering? When are we trying to run each other's life? This has had disastrous results in our past more than once. I have tried to keep a lot of this out of my second book but both sides do need to be told if a true picture is to be given. If we decide to only worry about number one, then when does this attitude become detrimental to the family and its members? Is it when we use them for our own advantage and gain, at another's cost? This has also had devastating effects on our family.

As society and times change, the family will change in how it takes its place and shapes itself in the future. From a one-income family, to a two-income family to just get by, for many of us is but one change. What others will we need to make in the future? What outside influences have done to us over the generations is another consideration. We have not always managed well. Religion—from one extreme to another—drugs, alcohol, and new social attitudes in tolerance, or lack of it. Our family is made up from the individuals that are in it. It is up to them to decide if they want to be part of the family and contribute to it by being a help. Is it up to the family to protect those in it, from those that want to hurt it and destroy it? I think that when we cross the line from being an individual to starting a family, we take on many new responsibilities and obligations that are to be put ahead of ourselves. Why should the other members suffer and contend with the consequences because another member

puts themselves before their promises and obligations. Or is the family an outdated idea and it should be every man for himself with the winner taking all?

It seems to me it would be nice to have a family that was supportive in all circumstances. One that you knew would help in any way they could—be it a kind word, a place to stay, a job, money, or care in old age. I guess we must first overcome each of our own problems first . . . or do we just need to try to understand and help, with no strings attached?

I am sure the hope, at first, was that we would learn from our mistakes in the past and not make them again. I can only hope so. But, as I was once told, don't kid yourself; you will make mistakes again . . . they will just be new ones. With this in mind maybe we can start to learn to try and be a little kinder.

[In his own autobiographical preface] Dr Joe expressed hope that we might learn from our previous mistakes and recognize some of our faults. In doing this we must talk of our failures and admit our mistakes. By doing this, maybe we will learn.

If any apologies were needed for writing this autobiography, Dr Joe wrote in his 1937 diary, there were several that occurred to him that seemed adequate to justify the undertaking. The first, he said, was the record's historical value for his descendants, which should mirror the opinions and viewpoints of men of his times in regard to the issues of their era. His narrative should also throw some light on the handicaps and struggles of the children of Czech immigrants to Texas during the last third of the XIX Century. Not only his children, but Americans generally, should know that the Anglo-Saxons were not the only pioneers and builders of the State, he wrote.

This record should be of some service to his descendants in still another, more intimate respect, he added. "The discussion of my reactions and adjustments to the problems and situations I had to face is bound to bring out certain characteristics and personality traits that I have fallen heir to and which, being hereditary, are likely to crop out in my own descendants. To be forewarned is to be forearmed," he observed. "If my descendants early in life, learn to identify some of the traits that run in our family as weaknesses and infantilisms, rather than as virtues; and if they strive to eradicate these from their own personality makeup—or at least modify them that they may be useful rather than harmful qualities—they may avoid some of the handicaps and disappointments of my own life, and so may lead better adjusted, more contented, and more useful and successful lives," he concludes.

In telling the stories and reading about times that have gone by, we have an opportunity to look at how those before us overcame obstacles. We can also see how they reacted to events and society around them. They were after all just people, like you and me. Sometimes they laughed, sometimes it was sad; sometimes you can see the humor in it. It resembles life itself a lot.

I hope the efforts of all those before us are not wasted. I hope we can all learn something from this project. If so, then I think it was a project well worth having done.

Sam Kopecky 2001

Introduction

After almost five years, I am finally ready to complete the second *'Family History'* book Sam wrote during his long three-year battle with cancer. On completion of *'A Family History—Moravia to Texas'* (which ended with 'After the War 1920-1960'), at the end of 2000, Sam then continued on to write about his own lifetime, just as his grandfather had done before him. As his death approached in mid-2001, Sam suddenly stopped writing one day and told me that since I knew the rest of the story I could finish it for him. (I don't think he wanted to reach the end—in any sense.) But having read some of the earlier chapters as he wrote them and felt his pain, I knew I could not tackle this project until I had begun to heal myself and was again strong enough to go further on this journey of closure with him. Having moved house three times now since leaving our lodge (in December 2004) where we had spent the previous 13 years living and working together, I have become increasingly aware that I cannot—literally—keep carrying all this hurt and sadness around with me any longer. I know I can never move any further on in finding my own life now until I have really felt, and worked through, all that accumulated pain. I must finally stop, literally, living with it all and while I have been given the time and space to work on these words of Sam's, finally let them go, in order to find those steps toward a new life.

As an (originally undiagnosed) dyslexic, Sam's writing ability has always amazed me. I have not edited his words. I feel that—as he would say—"If it ain't broke, don't fix it". Therefore, they remain exactly as he wrote them . . . unflinchingly honest and without apology. Sam was always a very honest man but I felt that the sense of his own impending mortality made him even more so. And this second book in particular, seemed to be cathartic. He finally found peace and learned to forgive himself and everyone else, in order to let go of all the accumulated pain of his past. Recognizing that his previous inability to do so had made life difficult both for himself and those closest to him, I suspect he hoped that this might be his (intended) lesson for others in his family to not also wait until the end of their lives to find this same sense of peace.

I have always felt privileged to have shared the long journey of Sam's illness and death. He was not a patient 'patient' and it was never easy but it was an unforgettable time in my life that I know now, will never really end. A large part of that life-changing experience though, was the role that you all played, as Sam's Kopecky family, in supporting us with your unquestioning faith—in life and death—throughout this first long terminal illness of your third Texan generation. This combination of faith, trust and grace, mixed with sadness and laughter, along with heartfelt love, sharing and support, sustained Sam, Amanda and I through it all. This whole episode made me realize what having a family is really about—as I suspect many who have married into the Kopeckys have also discovered. But I am not sure that you all even realize how rare and special this gift is, as I believe that most families do not have this absolute inherited sense of who they are. Being part of a very small New Zealand family (which, to quote Mary Beth's analogy, "Suffers from the curse of being normal"), I had never before experienced anything like it. I felt the loss of the Kopecky family too when Sam died, and now realize it has made me finally really search for my own sense of who I really am. I also found I had to write through my pain to do this in order to finally find peace.

I know that Sam's story, as such, should end where he left off writing it (at Chapter 86), for whatever reason he decided to do so at the time. While I was loath to get back on this emotional treadmill, this book has 'haunted' me since Sam's death, as—in spite of my own misgivings about the possible repercussions of some of his words—it did not feel right for me to not follow his wishes. In spite of my reluctance to bare his soul, he had already gone too far for me to turn back and so to do less and be politically correct now, would not be to keep faith with Sam and would devalue all that he had done. But I also could not just drop this painful and emotionally-charged autobiography into your midst without at least trying to mitigate its effects with some more positive recollections—all of which I tried to restrict to topics he had already raised within his second *'Family History'*. I have also tried to balance the rights of others involved in his life, as he did, with the material he had left me to edit. Since I cannot finish his story in the way that he wrote it, instead I have chosen to write about the end of his life and his legacy using both your (emailed) words and Sam's, as my own tribute to you all, in much the same way—albeit with updated technology—that Dr Joe and Golda told their earlier story. I could have gone in many directions with this closing but have chosen to focus on selecting the relevant emotional/spiritual content of these accumulated messages that had especially touched me, rather than the physical/medical side of all this material that, between us both, we had retained. While incomplete, collectively these words paint a real picture of this family, and its nephew, brother, cousin, father, grandfather and husband that we all loved—even if we didn't always understand him. I have learned so much about Sam through his words that I hope convey to you, as they do to me, how much he also loved us, his family. I have tried to find the positive that always exists within any negative. If anyone can take Sam's message of facing up to whatever life hands them and deal with it as he did, our work on this will have all been worthwhile.

All these words of ours and their humor, have made me again both laugh and cry. Written from my heart and through my tears, this labor of love is now my gift to the Kopecky family for all that they have done for me. I have learned so much from you all, and am just so proud to have known—and been made to feel like a part of—this amazing and uniquely special family, through this time. You all helped show me the difference between religion and spirituality—as an action and a practice, and not just a concept. The Kopecky family helped give me that sense (to quote Mary Beth again) "Of being upheld by familial presences and prayers, on both sides of the veil"—a feeling I have become aware of again now as these familial presences have once more 'gathered' around me while I have been working on these words. So much seems to have happened in all our lives since this time. Many of the people that were part of this journey have now also passed on; and there have been many changes in our world over the intervening years. I am sad that there is now such a distance between us . . . although, as Sam's daughter, Amanda will always be the link between us that can never be broken. Hopefully, we will be able to spend some time together again in the not-too-distant future, when we hope to resolve all the unfinished lodge issues that still surround us, so we can finally reorganize our lives and move on as Sam always tried so hard to help us do. We love and miss you all.

A Maori friend of our own family here (who also passed on just days after doing so), wrote something for me once when I was replying to an email from Sam's son, Craig, informing me that he had been selected for a cardiology fellowship at Walter Reed Medical Centre. It was about 18 months after Sam's passing and I was struggling to find the words to tell Craig that his father would have been so proud of him . . . while knowing with his Kopecky heritage, he would also have said that with this family medical tradition, it was the least of his expectations. Tom wrote out the following for me to send Craig so he would have a better understanding of what I was trying to say but as he also died at this time, I never passed it on as originally intended. It now seems relevant and appropriate to include his words to you all in this context . . .

Tapu Wae

Tapu wae
Tapu wae
Tapu wae haruru
Tapu wae ra ki ta matikara
Ki nga topito o te ao e
Tapu wae ki te wai I runga
Tapu wae ki te wai I raro
Haruru ara nga tapu wae Tipuna
Kowhai mai ra I nga tapu wae Tipuna
Ki te tinatatanga o nga Tipuna

Listen to the footsteps of your forbears
Harken to the thunderous sounds they make
Follow your heart that points the way
To the very ends of the earth if you must
Your spirit will always bind you to earth and sky
The ancestral footprints are so well marked
Follow them to where they lead you
Even when they finally lead you to where
They are all waiting for you

(Tupoutahi Tamihana Te Winitana—March 2003)

The foreword Tom wrote for Sam's first book in 2001 also seems to belong in this second one—especially so, since I have just discovered that, in his first book, because of humility, Sam had edited out some of the tributes to himself! These words really were written from Tom's heart and through his tears as I witnessed when he dictated them to me as I sat at my computer. I also saw how deeply his unanticipated heartfelt words touched Sam who they rendered uncharacteristically speechless. I always felt so humble to be part of this uniquely intense friendship between these two remarkable men, who, I have no doubt, are working together again now.

Pam Kopecky 2005

July 2008

More than two years after I wrote this, I am still struggling to finish this story that continues to bind me so closely to Sam. I thought I was ready to do so then but now, I guess, I finally have to accept the fact that I may never feel like it is complete . . . and just let it go. It is time for me to bless and release it, in order to finally find those steps towards a new life.

In spite of the fact that the lodge sale issues had still not been settled, I could not keep waiting to get on with our lives and so I went back to Texas late last year, in an effort to try to reconnect with Sam's family in order to find more closure. Unfortunately, I could not afford to take Amanda too and while I could not see everyone I had hoped to, it was a 'turning point' for me in terms of renewing my resolve to work on finishing up these books for Sam.

However, it was also a very painful journey in terms of rediscovering just how much we have both lost. But we will both be back there again, together, whenever our circumstances make it possible again to do so.

April 2011

I am slowly beginning to accept that our lives may never settle again now. Our never-ending saga seems to have a life of its own. But it is now Amanda's 21st birthday and my gift to her from her father, has to be to share this milestone with him by finally giving him back to her in the only way I can.

Amanda, reading your father's words will help you to know and understand him as you were not given enough time to do. They will also prove to you just how truly we were loved.

October 2011

The tenth anniversary of 9/11 has just passed and was yet another 'wake up' call for Amanda and I, that life goes on—even though we may not be ready for it to. This event happened just days before Sam's passing and so it was a shock for us both to realize we had also reached the tenth anniversary of his death.

The world as we knew it has changed so much during these intervening years, with so many changes within our own immediate—and wider—family, that it is difficult to even know how to try and reconnect now.

But this manuscript must be a start because until we let go of these remnants we are still clinging to, we will remain tied to the past . . . lost and unable to move on with our lives. Having both now been forced to make the decision that we do not want the rest of our lives to be unhappy, we have agreed that it is time to allow ourselves to find happiness again, as Sam always wanted for us.

As difficult as it has proved for me to let all this go, I have no doubt that if we now free Sam to finally move on, he will come back to us more strongly than ever.

Contents

CHAPTER 1

JOE WILLIS KOPECKY

Joe W., or J.W., was Joe Willis, Dr. Joe's and Golda's oldest child and my father. He was born in El Campo on the 17th of February 1921. His sister, my Aunt Mary, was born on the 26th of June 1926 in Galveston. I know relatively little about his younger days. I know when he was about 12 or so, a dog bit him when they lived in San Antonio. They didn't find the dog and he had to have rabies shots. He told me it was a series of something like 21 of them, one a day, in the stomach. By the end of the series, they had to hold him down it hurt him so much.

He was exposed, on somewhat of a regular basis, to the Kopecky clan and had definite feelings towards most of them. He never said much about any of them except he seemed to be fond of Jerome and Ludma

One time in Houston, during his days at Rice, he went to a party in the Rice Hotel and couldn't get into the room where most of the party was going on. As the story goes, he went to the room next door, climbed out the window and went along the ledge to the room next door. This was a number of stories up. I don't know if he was drinking when he did this. I almost hope so. I hope he wouldn't do something like that sober.

Ludma had some sort of rifts with my Aunt Mary along the way, who, even in later years, suggested we leave her alone. When I lived with my grandparents, Dr. Joe would talk to some of his brothers and sisters from time to time, especially Ludma. I guess it was because he felt he should still watch over his baby sister and provide her with some advice—regardless of whether she wanted it or not. I think some of her adventures did not help his attitude. I can remember he would be on the phone and the next thing you would hear his voice getting louder and louder, usually in Czech at this stage, then you would hear the receiver slammed down. I would look at Golda; she would shrug her shoulders and say, "must be talking to Ludma".

C.W.'s oldest son was Sam Loy Kopecky, who was killed in a plane crash during a landing attempt during his pilot training in 1943. He was my Dad's favorite cousin after whom I was named. Cyril's second and only other child was Jack, born 9 Sept. 1927 in Rowena, Texas. When we were going to Corpus Christi with Dr. Joe once, we stopped in Beeville and saw Jack for a few minutes. He was a lab technician for a medical outfit. It seems he was in the process of getting a divorce. This was not a very popular thing to do and Dr. Joe seemed somewhat irritated about the whole idea at the time. At the turn of the millennium I heard that Edith, his mother, was still alive in Rowena and was 100 years old.

My Dad, J.W. as most people called him, went out for football, once, he told me. He didn't like being hit and decided he preferred the band and social events. He learned to play the clarinet while in high school and developed a deep love for music. He had his favorite kinds of music but enjoyed most types—blues, jazz, classical, swing, pop, and later liked Elvis and lots of the other popular groups.

He made very good grades and Dr. Joe wanted him to go to Harvard. But my Dad wanted to go to Rice and stay closer to his part of the country. This caused a conflict but he eventually won. Golda told me that a number of times when issues would come up with my Dad she usually took care of them. Sometimes it was just easier and not worth a battle with Dr. Joe. One such time was when J.W. had apparently been partying and drinking and on the way home had a minor accident with the car, and was taken to the police station. When the phone rang she answered it and went to the station. The episode was dealt with and Dr. Joe didn't know the full extent of what had happened. I know that as far back as I can remember,

Golda and Dr. Joe kept separate rooms. This was evidently due to her heart condition since, after giving birth to Aunt Mary, it was strongly recommended she not have any more children. In later years he always went to bed very early, about 8 PM, and got up early, about 5 AM

J.W. was a soft spoken, easy going, sort of a person. He usually would not show his anger. He was all in favor of getting along and I don't think he really cared who was driving the bus as long as it was peaceful. I can remember him studying at times, when I was very young; this must have been when he was finishing his Internal Medicine and Cardiology. He was extremely well educated and had virtually a photographic memory. My mother, Beulah, would tell me how he would read over his notes and textbooks and just about be done with his studying. Just as well, as it seems that during this time (when in Galveston), too much of his time was taken up going out to eat, or to a club, or having some of the Rayner relatives over when they visited and drank beer. Sometimes the Rayners would even go down to the medical school when he was working on his cadaver or doing other duties. My mother told me how on one such occasion, she and her folks dropped in to see him. He was working on a cadaver at the time and eating a chocolate bar. He offered his mother-in-law a bite of the candy bar. She almost got sick. I don't think they went there to visit him again.

He went to school at the University of Texas Medical School in Galveston, where Dr. Joe had gone, and later taught. J.W. never liked people who acted like show-offs and tried to put something over on someone else all the time. One such fellow medical student finally became more than J.W. could tolerate. Seems he was always having a little chat with the nurses and showing off to them, usually at someone else's expense. One day when they were working on their cadavers and he was listening to the bragging again, he had an idea. He went over to a large Negro cadaver and removed a much larger than average penis from its body. He then had a friend distract the other fellow as he came up behind him and discreetly attached it to the bottom of his lab coat with a pin. As he walked down the hall to go and have his little chat with the nurses his new appendage dangled behind him. Before he knew it, all the nurses were in hysterical laughter. J.W. felt that if he wanted to act like one all the time, why not remove all doubt and show him for exactly what he was. The head of the Medical School was not amused and expelled J.W. for desecrating a cadaver. Out of consideration to Dr. Joe, he was reinstated after paying $100 for damages and apologizing. He told me the latter was the truly hard part.

Dad met my mother Beulah Rayner while he was attending Medical School. When she was in her early teens she and her sisters did some vaudeville performing in Galveston. Later on she worked in an office as a secretary doing short hand and typing. I don't know exactly how they met but I do know my mother enjoyed going out—be it a club, dancing, or eating. My Aunt Mary told me when she met my mother she thought Beulah was one of the most beautiful women she ever knew. She had a deep sort of voice, stemming back to damage that had been done to it when she was little and had diphtheria. Aunt Mary told me she almost worshipped Beulah.

Beulah Elizabeth Rayner (Kopecky)

J.W., Beulah and Mary Kopecky

Beulah was a definite distraction for my father and this did not please Dr. Joe at all. He felt the most important task at hand was for J.W. to get through medical school and complete his specialty. J.W. was spending much more time courting Beulah and spending time with her, than Dr. Joe thought he should. I think that this lack of co-operation was just one of many items that eventually led to some hard feelings in the years to come.

After Dad finished up in Galveston, he went to San Antonio and Brooke Army Hospital. He was there from January 1946 through December 1947. When he was discharged from the regular army he went in the reserves and was in the reserves until April 1953. My understanding was that he was happy with the idea of being a general practitioner and it was Dr. Joe who insisted he continue on, to become a specialist in Internal Medicine and Cardiology. Dr. Joe paid an allowance to my parents to help increase their income during this period. After Dad was out of the army and was ready to settle in San Antonio in private practice, Dr. Joe purchased a house and gave it to them as a late wedding present. (He also purchased and gave a house to my Aunt Mary.)

When my father was ready to go into private practice he had a place waiting for him. Dr. Joe was getting up in years (early 60's) and was concerned about the future for J.W. Several years before, he started a practice with Dr. Leon Kopecky in the Nix Professional Bldg. They had their own laboratory and shared staff, nurses, bookkeeper, and receptionist. The idea was when J.W. was ready to go into private practice he would go into a partnership with Dr. Joe, and all three of them would share the expenses and facilities. If something happened to Dr. Joe, Leon was to help J.W. get started by having him come into the office with him.

Dr. Joe had the fame, and respect of the medical community. This helped give Leon acceptance in the medical community. I was always told he was actually no kin to our family. I have never found any links. At times he was referred to as a cousin, an uncle and even a brother. This got to the point of being an irritation to my father. When he would get irritated by someone asking him, he would respond by telling them "I'm the son, Dr. Joe is my father, so Leon must be the Holy Ghost". He always felt, even though Dr. Leon was a good capable doctor, he took advantage of the situation and if someone wanted to associate him with the famous Dr. Joe, he didn't do anything to discourage it. J.W. was sure this put many a dollar in Leon's pocket, just by going along with what the person was thinking. I know myself, in later years, I was always coming across people who had thought for many years that Leon was the son, or the brother, or whatever relationship they had fallen into, and no one had ever corrected them.

This arrangement, in my opinion, was one of the major factors that produced problems in the years to come that destroyed several relationships. My grandfather was ready for J.W. to come on the scene and take over some of the load and a number of the patients as soon as possible. In the agreement, they would pool their incomes, pay their share of all expenses out of it and then split the balance on a percentage basis. I don't know the exact amounts but over the years my father's percentage grew as the family grew and my mother would still complain at times that her allowance wasn't enough to run the house on. Dad worked a lot of hours and took all of the after hours' calls. He took all emergency calls for both himself and Dr. Joe. If someone needed to go out at night, it was Dad.

When an afternoon off came (they usually closed Thursday afternoon), Dad was the one on call. When the weekends came, it was again Dad that was on call. I know my grandfather was getting old and had served his years but it was just too much for J.W. to work all the time and not have any time off—never knowing when the phone might ring and he would have to go.

When my father and mother decided the house was not large enough they had a contractor add on a playroom and a screened-in porch area, as well as a new garage. This was the house on Harrison that Dr. Joe had purchased. It was in the Alamo Heights school district where I started my schooling and we stayed until about 1954.

I can remember playing with a few of the neighborhood kids and the maid taking us on walks to Olmos dam but I don't remember very much about being with my folks. It was during these early years we would go to the ranch with my grandparents. We spent a lot of time with them at the ranch and other times we would get to go over to their house and spend the night.

By 1954 the family had grown some more and now was up to 5 children, and a maid that was to help look after us. This was when my parents decided to buy a larger house on Wyndale and sell the house on Harrison. It seems now like it happened almost overnight but as I remember it was actually over several months that the deal was worked out.

Kopecky family—Back Row: Tom, Sam, Joe;
Front Row: Beulah Ann, Charlie, Beulah (our mother)

It seems the house was custom built for someone and was to be used as a model show home for awhile in a new subdivision. When the original deal fell over, the builder was anxious to find another buyer as he had to carry the cost of this new house out of his pocket. At the time it was the latest. All brick, cedar shingle roof, multiple bathrooms with more than one sink, kitchen with built-in oven, dishwasher, and disposal, and central heating and air-conditioning! This was one of the first times I can remember Dr. Joe was not pleased with my parents. He felt they had a perfectly good house that was paid for, so why get in debt? The new house was around $30,000—about three times the price of an average house at that time. After the house on Harrison was taken in trade the balance was around $20,000. The deal was completed and we moved into our new home and a new era.

The change brought us into a new neighborhood, a new school district, and a greater distance to my grandparents' house. I think Dad felt if he had to be on call all the time, then why not be comfortable and enjoy the environment you were trapped in. He never liked the heat and with this new house having central air-conditioning, he kept it cold enough to hang meat during the middle of summer. Mom was proud of the new house since it had a formal living room and dining room, besides the everyday living areas. She could now furnish and decorate two rooms the way she wanted and put them off limits to all the kids. We were happy with more bedroom space and a workshop area that was in the garage that had been left unfinished. This made a play area that was inside, yet noise and a little dirt didn't matter.

My father never went hunting very much. Occasionally he would go dove hunting and only very rarely did he go fishing. I was told he did not like shooting deer and liked cleaning them even less. I was told this went back to when he was young and his father tried to take him hunting and have him help clean a deer. I don't know how much truth is in this.

Once Joe W. was married to my mother, the Rayner family would come up and they would go to the ranch. This was mainly during the summer. Only a handful of times in later years did Uncle Lloyd and Uncle Denny go hunting at Boerne. In the days when this was all new, it seemed they enjoyed going to fish and get away from town. All of us kids thought it was great fun to have cousins to play with.

Golda in front of smokehouse with Joey and Tuffy

Joe W. Jr and Dr Joe

Dr Joe with Joe Willis Jr (Joey), my older brother

Joe W, Dr Joe, Beulah (centre) at Boerne

The relationship between the Kopeckys and the Rayners changed over the years. As time passed, the Rayners quit going to the ranch. It seems there were hard feelings that developed from several sources of irritation. One I picked up on was that Dr. Joe felt that no one, with the exception of Uncle Denny and Uncle Lloyd, did anything to take care of the place or help keep it picked up and tidy. He found my Uncle Freddy, then in his late teens, disrespectful and more than a handful with his lack of behavior. I know he held my other grandparents, Nana and F.H., responsible, as he felt they did nothing to control him and yet Nana was involved on a state level with the Parent Teachers Association. Dr. Joe would comment she should stay home and raise her own first. I think he also had some hard feelings toward F.H. since he did not serve in World War. I. [F.H. came to Galveston from England at the age of 20 in 1920.] I do know that after the accidental shooting death of my Aunt Jerry, Uncle Freddy's first wife, in the late 1950's, the mixing and visiting of the two families was non-existent and Dr. Joe kept his distance from them. He was very fond of Aunt Jerry and talked about how much help she was out at the ranch, and was one of the few that would pitch in. He was truly sorry when he heard she was gone.

We went down to the coast from time to time but not very often. My parents sometimes sent us and we would stay with my grandparents for several weeks at a time when we would have a chance then, to see the relatives.

For several years Uncle Freddy, my mother's brother, had a filling station franchise, which F. H., his Dad, put the money up for. He also had a bar once, as I remember. I remember he had a Shell station on the main road into town that he went bust in. He let his friends have a job and run it for him and they stole him blind. He later had a Texaco on the Boulevard across from the sea wall. One summer Joe and I went down to Galveston and stayed with them some, and worked in his station. He had a new '58 Ford Fairlane 500 that was red and black, the latest thing. While we were working that summer, he had a call out one day from the Police to come and pull a car out of the surf with his tow truck. It was a new '58 Chevrolet Impala 2 door Coupe that had been stolen in Houston from Mike Persia Chevrolet, driven to Galveston and run out into the Gulf. The insurance company paid him to try and wash the car out, flush all the fluids from the motor and transmission etc., and try to save it. It was a light metallic blue color and covered in chrome. We tried to help him wash it; I can still smell that new car smell it had on the inside. He later told us the insurance company sold it to the wrecker's yard as it just had too much that was ruined by the salt water.

It was later that same year the unfortunate death of Aunt Jerry took place. The morning my mother came in to tell me that Aunt Jerry was dead, I already knew. It came to me in a dream that night and I told her I already knew. Jerry was Cherokee Indian and was known to have a temper, be on the jealous side, and unable to control her drinking at times. She was home with the two little girls they had, Cynthia and Elizabeth, and was waiting for Uncle Freddy to come home. He kept a handgun in the house since he brought the daily proceeds home. On this particular night he came home late, she had been drinking and had already gone to bed. When he came into the bedroom the noise he made woke her. She had the handgun and fired at him, he called out for her to stop, said who he was and that he was not a burglar. She did not seem to respond and he ended up wrestling with her in the bed, trying to take the gun from her. The gun went off and the shot hit her and was fatal. The police had an investigation and the new D.A., trying to make a name for himself, charged him with murder. F.H. hired one of the top lawyers out of Houston for a reported sum of $100,000. The trial did show she had been drinking, more than one shot was fired and at the end, the jury found him not guilty. The feelings were that it was all a tragic mistake.

With Joey, my older brother, and I, being the two oldest male grandchildren, we constantly went with my grandparents to the ranch. My Aunt Mary's two oldest children were girls, Mary Beth and Susie. The next two were boys, Billy and Tommy. With the age difference, Joey and I were the spoiled ones for years. My Uncle Gene, Aunt Mary's husband, was kind to us and sometimes he would come to the ranch on his own during deer season. Dr. Joe would then tell us where to direct him or where we should go to hunt. I think at times some of the relatives got sick of us being the chosen ones. We did have to earn our stripes and it was years before we were allowed to go hunting with him, much less on our own. He wanted to be sure we were not only good shots but knew how to be safe as well. This included handling the gun, the shot animal, getting in and out of the blind and the bush, and not getting in one another's way and getting shot. We absolutely must know what we were shooting at and once we fired, we must make sure the animal was dead. He always had us bleed the animal and when we went to do this we had to be extremely careful. He told us many a story about how the dead deer got up, and with his horns and hooves tore the hunter to pieces. He even introduced us to a man in Boerne that had been hurt in just such a way.

It was at the end of deer season one year when he let me know we had very little deer meat for the family as very few of us had gone hunting that year. He always paid for the processing into meat and sausage, and for the storage. He told me he also had about 20 doe permits as the female population was out of control. Uncle Gene and I went to the ranch with the tags and permits. During the day and early part of the evening we killed about 5 or 6 deer. I never got so tired of the blood and guts, and cleaning, as I did that time. It was during my university days that I ate so much deer meat it just about put me off of it and hunting both, for the rest of my life.

It was after this, in the 1960's, that Dr. Joe sold the ranch. It was a shock to the entire family. We never thought he was even thinking about it. It was just a time when we were all busy with other things in our lives. It was one of those things that would have far-reaching effects on the family.

He sold it for what seemed to be a good price back then—$100,000 for 200 acres—but turned out to be peanuts in only a matter of a few years. The last time I heard about it was from Mary Beth in the 1990's, who had seen that it had been subdivided into an exclusive neighborhood with estates rather than lots. They were selling for something like a million dollars per estate. Dr. Joe felt like the ranch was not being used and the upkeep was too much for him and Golda. It happened so fast that we were all surprised. It just happened to be one of those times when we were busy with school, new families, jobs, and friends. It's time was going to come around again—it was just one of those unfortunate things that sometimes happens. We all knew it was something that none of us could ever replace. Whether or not we could have run and enjoyed it as a group, is something none of us will ever know. Maybe this is something he feared from his past experiences from years before, and felt it was going to be an impossible task. A task that might even cause more hard feelings in the family and a result that he did not want to see.

After this, it was a problem for most of the family members to have a place to go to get outdoors. I was partly lucky, from the standpoint that I did have a place to go—my father-in-law's ranch. He first had a place near Bandera, Texas. It was not very large, about 100 or so acres, but a very nice place with a stream running through it. Later he purchased a place near Yancy or D'Hanis, Texas, of about 2,000 acres. One of the advantages of the second place was that it had much larger deer and a very large stock tank, almost a small lake, which had lots of good fishing.

It was during this time that my Uncle Gene, while working for my then father-in-law Cecil Tindall, met some of the people who had places at Yancy. One such man was Jimmy Holeckman. He had the general store and a small ranch as well. He would allow day shooters during dove season at his place and would charge per head per day. It was one of the few times I can ever remember that Uncle Gene, my father and I went day hunting for doves together at Yancy. Uncle Gene borrowed a couple of shotguns and I got one from Dr. Joe. We placed ourselves around the edge of the stock tank and waited for the doves to fly in. We had an ice chest with a few soft drinks and a few beers. In the early afternoon the doves were few and far between. As the day went on, a few other hunters showed up and took positions around the edge of the tank. As the late afternoon approached, the doves started coming in on a regular basis. We would fire at them as they flew over, the birdshot would rain down on the opposite side of the tank and sound like raindrops as it hit the water. At times the bird would hit the ground at almost the feet of the person opposite you. Sometimes the opposite hunters' shot would rain down around you. One of the other hunters, an older fellow, seemed to be having a bit of a hard time. You could watch him shoot and see the feathers fly but never really saw the bird fall. We also noticed that from time to time we would hear a 'ker-plunk' in the water.

After the day was about over, we were visiting with some of the others and as we talked to this one older man that had such poor luck, we found out he had borrowed the gun from a friend. The friend had just returned from hunting where you had to hunt deer with a shotgun and slugs. Instead of birdshot, the shells would have a large lead chunk that would spread on impact. This would not carry far in the brush when deer hunting and would pose less of a threat to other deer hunters than a rifle. We discovered that not only had he taken his friend's gun but also his shells that were with the gun. No wonder we only saw feathers fly and hear the 'ker-plunk' in the water; he was shooting slugs! We had between us about a dozen and a half birds that we took home, and called it a day.

It was a good day out and we had a lot of fun. It was not the ranch and it was only one of only a few such experiences that happened in the years to come. I think we were all looking and trying to find an elusive substitute for something we knew we could never replace. Times had changed and we were gradually learning to accept it. We would learn over time, that the time would be spent separately in small groups in different locations, instead of one meeting place that was common for all of us to come to and share.

The end of the days at the ranch was more than the end of an era for us. It was the end of the one thing that held us together. After this, we did drift away in our own different directions.

This is getting ahead of my story. I guess that is the way it is. It is towards the end of Dr. Joe's and Golda's story, yet at the start of mine where I start to notice and pay attention.

I'll need to back up and start back in Galveston where I did. In fact it is funny how we have all seemed to go back to Galveston for the beginning of our stories. It was a place that did play a part in all of our lives.

CHAPTER 2

STARTING FROM GALVESTON

I can remember pieces here and there when we lived in Galveston and I was young. I can remember having my tonsils removed. I can remember slipping out of the house with my brother Joey and walking on the oyster shells in the alleyway and going to my Aunt Jeannie's house. We also used to run down the alleyway chasing the truck that was fogging the neighborhood with DDT. There was also a time when a storm hit and my grandfather, F.H., came over and it took both my father and him to push the door closed because of the high wind.

When I was about 4 years old, Joey and I always found it more interesting at either my Aunt Jeannie's or my grandparents' house, so we decided to pay an unexpected visit to my grandmother. My grandmother, Nana as we called her, was having a bridge party at her place and my mother was invited to attend. I remember they were all dressed up, and Joey and I were instructed to stay home. As the day went on, it became too much for us and we took off to find out just exactly what was going on. We figured if it was a party, and at Nana's house, they were sure to have some goodies—and if we went to the back door we should be able to cash in. Joey and I slipped out and walked the several blocks. We walked down the driveway to the gate that was across it and climbed over the gate as it was locked, and knocked at the back door.

Beulah Jeanette Rayner, aged 40

Papa—F.H. Rayner

Much to our surprise, we were not greeted with open arms. As I remember, the lady that answered the door summoned Nana. She was not happy but gave us some candy or something and was in the process of telling us to go, when my mother, who must have just heard what was going on and was deeply embarrassed, appeared at the door in a rage. Joey and I took off running for the gate that was across the driveway, as she chased us telling us to get home and waving one of her shoes in her hand. Joey got over the gate first and as I was just clearing the top she gave me a swat and I went over, landing on my shoulder. I knew it hurt and that something was wrong but this was not the time to look for sympathy. So we ran as fast as we could. After we went a couple of blocks we sat down on the curb to catch our breath and enjoy some of the spoils. It was then that I knew I really hurt. I don't remember much about eating the spoils. I was in pain and afraid I was going to be in even more trouble when my mother got home. When she arrived, she was very angry and only because she could see I was in pain, she backed off and sent us to our room to wait for Dad to get home. I didn't know what to expect and after he examined me he told my mother I had a broken collar bone. He pulled my shoulders back and put a bandage on in a figure 8 and explained how it would take some time to heal and that it would hurt some for awhile.

This was my first broken bone. It was an accident and the first time I could remember being scared. It was the fear of the unknown. I didn't know what had happened to my shoulder and what to expect. I didn't know what to expect from my parents. I just didn't know. I think in a funny sort of way, it was a wakeup call. It made me, for the first time, question what was going on around me and how I fitted into the scheme of things. I wasn't aware of it in those words at the time but I do remember that strange cold, alone, afraid, sort of feeling that stayed with me for days.

It was after this Joey and I were put in a nursery school, a day school, for part of the day. This lasted only about a week. We went about late morning and were picked up after our afternoon nap. The so-called school was a house that had a fence around it and about a dozen or so kids attended it. We each had our own mat from home to take our nap on, or sit on when we were told to do so. This was about the extent of the activities. We were given a juice drink—grapefruit, no less. Why someone would give grapefruit juice to a kid, is beyond me. I don't remember any other activities but I do remember when preparing to have lunch, we were to go to the bathroom and wash our hands. The line was long so the teacher would have some use the basin, some the bathtub, and some the toilet. After several days of dodging the toilet line, I was finally forced in it. I was unhappy and refused to wash my hands in it. When we went home that day I told my parents about what happened. They talked to the teacher and after that we never went back.

Some of the other things we started when we were very young and lived in Galveston, we carried on after we moved to San Antonio. Each time we went back to Galveston to visit, we had to do some of the same things over and over. I think kids are creatures of habit sometimes and certainly like repetition. Playing store and going crabbing were two such things.

When Dad had time off we would usually go over to my grandparent's house. Sometimes we would go to the beach. At my grandparents we would play store out back, and sometimes we would talk F.H. into playing his movies for us. To play store we would have to get money from them and go to the corner store to load up on a variety of candy. We would then set up shop and try to sell it to each other. This is where the movies would come in really handy if we could get the cousins to come over. F.H. collected films just like they had at the theatre. He had Abbot and Costello, Laurel and Hardy, W.C. Fields, Woody Woodpecker, Mighty Mouse and many more. He also had music with the Mills Brothers, as well as a few with fan dancers. The films went back in some cases, to the previous versions of Mighty Mouse and Woody Woodpecker. He had a number of these spliced on large reels that would play for well over an hour. As the evening would get going we would all be eating our fill of candy and soda pop, and wanting to be on the floor in front of the screen. It wouldn't take long and half the kids would be asleep. F.H., with my father encouraging him, would then slip on a short film—one of the fan dancers. As soon as the music usually started, Nana would call out "F.H.! Freddy! You better not have that on with those kids in there!" There was not much to it, if the truth be known. The blonde danced with these big feather fans that she kept covered with and when she did a turn, at best, a glimpse of a body suit could be seen. I think it was more the thought of it that was the problem. Nevertheless, as years went by, this was one activity we enjoyed . . . even years later when they would come up to San Antonio in July for my mother's birthday to visit. We had F.H. bring up his equipment and reels of films, just so we could enjoy it all over again. The only change was that Nana would count how many scotches F.H. had. He would always carry around his glass half full, so when that voice called out "F.H. is that the same drink?"; he would call out "Yes dear." He never finished it. He would just add a little to it along the way.

When we went to the beach we would usually go crabbing, and would try and get Uncle Lloyd to go. He seemed to know the places to go and would give a hand. He showed us, when we were older, how to take the horse meat we purchased at the store, attach it to a long string, and then to a stick long enough so that when it was driven into the sand it would stick out of the water that was about waist deep. We would then put out about 3 or 4 such lines, and go and play. We would build our sandcastles on the beach and play in the surf. Then about every 10 or 15 minutes we would take the crab net (a net about the size of a basketball net on the end of a stick), and wade out to check the lines. We would ever so slowly pull in the string with the fingers of one hand as we got ready with the net in our other hand. As the bait got closer and lifted off the bottom, you could feel a little tug from the crabs pulling on the meat. When you thought they were close enough to put the net under to lift them up, you took the hand with the net and in one motion, did just that. Once you got used to it, it was easy and sometimes you would get more than one crab at a time. We would then run to the beach and tip them out into a tin wash tub that had water in it. One time we had such luck we caught almost a wash tub full of crabs. As fast as we could go in and out, we had crabs. Blue ones, red ones, and rock crabs. Uncle Lloyd said that was the time he took us to East Beach and the crabs were running. Joey kept saying this is a crazy place, a crazy place, and kept on bringing in the crabs. From that time on, that spot was known as the "crazy place."

As we got older and made return trips to Galveston, we did find new pleasures. On the beach an amusement park would be set up with rides and games. It was very similar to what we knew from going to the Kendall County fair with Dr. Joe and Golda. We also enjoyed going out to eat. This was something that I think was originally F.H.'s idea. I suspect he had some complaints about overwork and wanted some relief. Joey and I actually found it such a novelty and treat, we actually looked forward and enjoyed it. We even got to the point we both had favorite restaurants picked out that we liked to go to. Being on the coast, a large number of places had some sort of seafood platter. I still think some of the best seafood platters I ate during my life were in Galveston when I was a kid.

Another pastime—other than playing on the beach and in the surf—as we grew older, was going to the piers that went out into the gulf. They had shops, restaurants, movie theatres, and some had amusement rides and games. A few years after we first were old enough to go out on the piers, a number of them were damaged or destroyed by hurricanes. That was the end of that.

A number of these trips were made by just Joey and I. I think my folks wanted a break from us and so during the summer they would buy tickets on Eastern Airlines, and we would fly to Houston from San Antonio. I can remember several trips on the Constellation that took about 45 minutes to Houston. Being small kids we got to see the pilot and by the end of the flight we had the sick bags full of everything free we could find. In those days, besides the bags of peanuts and candy, the pouches in the seats in front of you also had several sample packs of cigarettes that had about 5 cigarettes in them. We would take all this and any brochures, pamphlets, etc., feeling like we had made a great haul. We kept the candy and turned in the rest to the folks as a present. We never had any problems with the aircrew, as I am sure they were glad to see the last of us.

Summer and our trips always seemed very short. The next attempt at getting us out of the house some was when I was again sent to a nursery school. This was back in San Antonio; I think Joey had just started regular school. It was in conjunction with the Methodist Church in Alamo Heights. They had activities as well as some attempt to stimulate the children. I remember we had crafts where we made something out of clay, painted it and they fired it, and then we gave it as a gift. I made a frog with an open mouth so when it was on a dresser you could put pins and buttons and things in its mouth. I knew what it was but I always had to tell everyone. I think my work may have been a bit abstract.

I can remember that I didn't know any of the other kids and I wanted to win approval from the teacher. This was about the time aluminum foil was coming on the scene. Each day during our lunch break the teacher would pick one of the children out and they would give her an idea for a story or something. As we ate our lunch the teacher would then tell us a story. A number of the children over a period of time, brought her fruit wrapped in aluminum foil. She would take this from the child, keep the foil, give back the fruit, and tell a story as the child would sit by heror give recognition to the child for helping with the story for that day.

I talked my folks into letting me take her an apple wrapped in foil. I knew this would work and I would get noticed. That day when lunchtime came, I held my hand up with the apple and pushed for her to call on me. I got her attention but instead of a story and recognition, she put me down in front of the class. I don't remember her exact words but it was to the effect that the foil-covered fruit had been done enough, that I needed to be more original, and should go sit down. The way in which she did it embarrassed me to no end. I never wanted to go back after that. In fact that is the main thing I remember about attending that school—humiliation and embarrassment.

I started my regular schooling at Cambridge Elementary in Alamo Heights. I can still remember I didn't have a clue on what was going on. I am not sure if I even knew what school was about. I became frustrated and when some of the other kids gave me a hard time, I would just hit them. I walked to and from school, about a mile or so through the neighborhood. Across the street from the school on the way home were a couple of shops. One was a bakery where you could buy a loaf of French bread that was hot and fresh for 10 cents. I could eat a whole loaf before I got home. Next to that shop was a corner store with candy and all the usual stuff.

It was during a recess one day when I was at school, that I can remember I looked up and saw something bright in the sky. I can remember this happened a couple of times. One time it was in the shape of a cigar and another time it was like two rings one on top of the other, separated a bit with the top one off to the side just a little. I didn't tell anyone back then except for a schoolmate I was playing with. I think I knew no one would believe me—besides I didn't know what I saw either.

I was once given a pink slip at the end of school one day and told to take it home to my parents. I didn't know what it was and was quite proud to have something to take home to them for once. This was a slip telling them I was not doing well in school, had been bad, and they wanted a conference.

I was given some medication and was not told what it was for, and told to take some each day at lunch. Being a friendly sort of a person and a good friend, I shared this medication with some of my schoolmates who wanted to try some also. The school didn't like this and we all ended up in the office again. Next they decided I needed to wear some corrective glasses for awhile. I wore them some at home but wouldn't have been caught dead with them on at school. Later they said they did their work and I didn't need to wear them anymore.

I still didn't know what was going on. I didn't understand school and the homework was a real problem. Dad tried to help me with it once. He could not understand me and I couldn't understand him. It ended up in a fight and crying, and was a total disaster. It was some time after this that I was placed with a private tutor after school, several days a week.

The lady would sit down with me with her books and explained she was going to teach me to read. She was going to teach me to read by using phonics. The school had started, several years before, teaching reading by sight. This was one of the main reasons I was doing so poorly in school—I couldn't read. I don't remember how long I went but it was after we moved to Wyndale in 1954 that they stopped the private lessons. It got me going again but I had still not caught up with the other kids. To top it off, they were experimenting with speed-reading when I first went to Northeast Elementary. They had a machine that would flash words up on a screen and eventually flash sentences and parts of sentences. I didn't last long in that class that was trying it.

The first year we lived on Wyndale I went to school in the old building out on the highway. This new school district was growing fast and could not keep up with facilities. They had makeshift classrooms and not enough teachers. The first class I was put in created real problems for me. We were to read an assignment in class and answer the questions. Then the teacher would call around and ask questions. Other times the teacher would call your name and you would take over reading out loud where the other student left off. I never finished answering the questions because I was so slow in reading the assignment. When I was to read to the rest of the class, between being embarrassed at standing up in front of them and having to struggle with each word, this became a nightmare for me. My attitude again became a problem and anytime a schoolmate wanted to tease me over this, he usually found himself on his back with a bloody nose or a busted lip to take care of.

After some additional conferences with the principal I was placed in another class. It was a special education class. It was the class for dummies. Some of the kids were several years older, some could hardly write their names, and some made me look like a scholar. The good news was that the teacher, for the first time, seemed to care about the kids in her room and was trying to figure out how each one of them could be helped—if they could be helped. Mrs McLeod was the one that helped get me turned around and going again.

She didn't get upset when she found me writing my lines while holding 4 pencils at the same time. (This was when you were told to write "I will not talk in class", 100 times, for talking.) I found I could do 4 lines at a time so it didn't take long to do my 100 lines. After that she just increased the number of lines. She also gave us some individual attention and assignments. I think she was the first to note that I was not stupid and that I was not trying to give everyone a hard time on purpose. After a year in her class she had me almost up to the level I needed to be. I still was a slow reader and still am to this day. When I was taught to read, it was with a very high rate of comprehension but slow. My spelling and other parts of "English" have always suffered. The good part was that for the first time in my life I was getting good marks, and starting to enjoy school and my subjects.

CHAPTER 3

EARLY DAYS AND AUTOMOBILES

Early days for me were the 1950's—in the automobile awareness category. For whatever reason; maybe boys just like cars and hot rods. My older brother Joe and I would look at *'Hot Rod'* magazine and think of all the things we would like to do. The advertisements were full of ideas, and parts to modify and beef up motors and vehicles. To us, the idea was not such a distant dream as it may have been for others.

I am not sure of the first time we started to learn to drive but it was out at the ranch with our grandfather. As I remember, Joe went first and with time, I was also allowed to get behind the wheel. It seems to me that it was around the time my grandparents had a 1954 Oldsmobile 88 and a 1952 Chevrolet. Before that, I remember a black car of my grandmother's, I think a Chevrolet—about a 1948 type—with the large fenders and chrome. I remember that one because one weekend I rode with her to the ranch, and on the road between Boerne and the ranch it decided to break down. It seemed to me to be a long time before someone came along, and then for a mechanic to come from town to get us going again. It was a fuel pump or such. Of course, with the ranch not having a phone, we could not contact Dr Joe and by the time we were getting to him, he was on his way to find us.

It was after that weekend as we left the ranch, that my grandmother took the old side road that went from the gate to the county road. It was rough and normally we didn't use this one. It went along the bush line by a fence next to an open field. Late in the day you would sometimes see deer coming out on it. We went along this way slowly and quietly, looking for deer. I didn't see anything at first and then she said to me "Look at that". I still didn't see anything. Then it was pointed out to me—not deer . . . the sunset! We stopped and sat for several minutes and watched the sunset in its reds, yellows and various colors. I think this was the start of my long fascination with the color and beauty in sunsets. As time has gone on, I must have tried to put on movie film, slides and photos, a thousand sunsets. It was not long after this that the old black car was replaced.

Over a period of time our driving skills improved and besides driving around the ranch roads, we were allowed to drive on the county roads to the highway, then the highway to the ranch. My grandfather would chew tobacco sometimes as we drove and by his efforts we acquired distinctive racing stripes down his side of the vehicle. If you were in the back seat you learned to keep your window up. His encouragement and comments as we drove, pointed out some of the dos and don'ts. As someone would speed by us he would yell "son of a bitch! . . . hell isn't half full yet!" We were told not to speed or drive without due care. (We were also told not to use his commentary, especially at our age, although we would sometimes have to a bit of a chuckle to ourselves). We drove for several years on main roads without a license because we were not old enough to get one. In town we were allowed to take the car up to the store to pick up the odd item and of course would go for the spin around the block to show off to our friends, even though we were to come straight back. Traffic did not seem as bad in those days as I now consider myself lucky not to have been in an accident, or stopped, for several years.

Along the way the idea came up that an old used car should be purchased for the ranch and left there for use. This would be used to go around the old roads, and up and down the cliff road to the creek below. A deal was struck with a dealer in Boerne for a 1948 Plymouth 4-door sedan. It had running boards and doors that opened in what I called backwards, in the back. (The handles were in the middle of the car and the rear doors would open from the middle to the back). This was a far cry from a hot rod to us but we felt it was our car–and a car was a car! We would race up and down the dirt roads on the ranch, and as we approached the house area we would slow down and act like nothing was going on.

As time went on, several of our so-called friends would go with us out to the ranch for the weekend. A couple of these friends were actually friends of Joe's and were older. They were just that much older that they would sometimes influence us in our attitudes and behavior. Joe wanted to take the air cleaner off and paint a few stripes on the car. It would sound more like a hot rod. Some of these ideas I am sure came from our friends. One weekend a couple of them went with us; and after fishing and going back to the ranch house, my grandmother was going to cook the fish for us and prepare dinner. It was then realized that we were out of several items including bottles of drinking water, tomato catsup, and a few other odds and ends.

As we all liked to go in the car, we all said we would go to town and be back before dinner could get cold. We were off! The old dirt county roads not only went around bends but also up and down hills that would leave your stomach at the top of each hill if you went fast and almost lifted off. We made it to town in a flash and purchased our items and headed back. It was my turn to drive. It was dark by now and we were wasting no time getting back. As we got to the dirt road and the hills, all I could hear was faster, faster. As I wanted to impress, I complied.

About only a mile or two from the gate was a sweeping curve on the dirt road. As I entered the curve I realized I was going too fast and started to slide. Not knowing really what to do, we all held on. As we slid across the road and through a fence, we thought it was over. Then we hit the trunk of a cut-off tree. It caught the car in the side, just below were the two doors opened on the frame. It bent the frame and the side of the car in, and flipped us over so we ended up on our side. As we rolled over, the catsup, bottles of water and the rest of the groceries, flew around the inside of the car, smashing and making a mess. The headlights still worked and the steam from under the hood could be seen in them as we came to rest.

We all climbed out and checked with each other to see how we were. Amazingly we were all okay. No real injuries. A few small cuts and bumps. Then we got really stupid. We tried to roll the car over but realized it had gone all the way over to where it was on the other side of the tree trunk and we could not move it. Then the idea was that we would tell the grandparents we had a couple of blowouts and that this was what had caused the accident. Then came the idea that we would tell them a coyote or such ran out, and I swerved to miss it and lost control. (This was so I wouldn't have to admit to driving too fast.) For whatever reason, the decision was made to use part of the blowout story as well as the animal, and our friend cut the tire with a knife in the sidewall!

Just as we started walking back, here came a car. They had started looking for us. We relayed our story and they looked at the car. Not much could be done at night so we all headed back to the ranch. Several hours later, in what seemed like the middle of the night, a car drove up and two men got out and banged on the door. After several minutes my grandparents came over to where we were and started asking questions. Who was driving? What happened? It was supposed to be someone driving with a license—like Bill. So Bill said he was driving and didn't worry too much about it. In those days, accidents and tickets didn't mean much in terms of a fine or insurance rates. Seems the two men were Texas Highway Patrol and came across the wreck on the side of the road. The license number led them to the ranch. The wet interior of the car with catsup and water and broken glass made them wonder if someone had been hurt. They talked to Bill and my grandparents, and then left.

Early 1950's model automobile

The car was towed to Boerne and the next day my grandfather went to check on things as the rest of us all returned to town. We all started to worry. We hadn't considered the police being involved or what might happen. A week or so went by and the car was towed out to the ranch to be left to rest in peace. It wasn't worth fixing. Some time went by and an air of disgust came over the incident. A few comments were made. Blowout? Looks like a knife or something cut the side of the tire.

Joe decided to see if he could get the old thing going and after several weekends of work, he removed the damage fenders, pulled it out on the side some, and refilled the oil and water. The exhaust was broken from the accident so it sounded more like a hot rod, or shot rod as the case may have been, but it ran! You could hear it coming from a mile away. This lasted for awhile but was considered to be on the dangerous side and it was later replaced with a 1953 Ford 2 door—a car Joe helped pick out. A car that could be made to look like a hot rod with some work. I always felt like he blamed me for the loss of the car, as if it was his, and until it was replaced there was a grievance. We were allowed to take the car to the house in town where Joe could work on it some before it was to be returned to the ranch. (It had a bad universal joint, so had a tendency to drop the drive shaft from time to time.)

It wasn't until sometime after that this that I felt alright again. Things weren't and never would be the same. I must have asked myself more times than I could count . . . why did you listen to them saying "Faster, faster"? Why did you go along with the blowout story? They know you lied! Why? What if someone would have really been hurt bad? The gloss of this time had come to an end. I knew from then on I would be responsible for what I said and did, and suffer my own consequences. I would not end up in a situation like this again. I might make mistakes but they would be of my own doing and choosing; not those of others—either by influence, and most certainly not lying.

CHAPTER 4

FROM HARRISON TO WYNDALE

When we were young children we always seemed to have a maid looking after us. It seems to me my grandfather may have even suggested it as he may have felt my mother could use the help and extra rest.

The main ones I remember were Minerva when we lived on Harrison, and Marguerite after we moved to Wyndale. Minerva took care of Joey and I, from about the time we first moved to San Antonio. She would tell us stories and rock us while we sat on her lap. We would go for walks with her and we would, later on, even go to the zoo with her. She seemed older and like an adult to us but years later I found out she was only 16 years old when she first went to work to take care of us.

She had a big scar across the top of her foot. When I asked her what had happened she told me that when she was little she would work out in the cotton fields. Her whole family would work in the field and some of the younger children like her would hoe, while others picked the cotton and did whatever else needed to be done. It wasn't very exciting and whenever anyone heard a plane flying over, they would stop and look up in the sky to try to see it. One day, for whatever reason, she decided to play a trick on her brother. She told him she could see a plane. He tried and tried but couldn't see anything. She had him move over a little more and a little more so that he might be able to see it. All of a sudden he started jumping and running around. She had very carefully moved him over into the middle of a big red ant bed. She laughed and laughed as she watched him dance around. He didn't find any humor in all of this and took after her with his hoe. He eventually let her have it across the top of her foot and cut it down to the bone and opened up a large section of flesh—thus the scar. She didn't seem bitter. In a funny sort of way she felt she deserved what she got even though she did feel he paid her back in spades.

She showed us another scar on the back of her leg, which was from a burn. She told us how she had backed into the heater they had and burned her leg. For treatment she told us they took fresh cow's manure and applied it over the area. We were sure she was having us on this time so we asked our folks. They didn't say much as I remember, so we asked Paw, Dr. Joe. He said they very likely did. A number of such home remedies were used like this when you lived on a farm. He had never tried it but had heard of such things before. We didn't question her about this anymore.

As we grew up and become old enough to go out with her, she took us where she could. We didn't realize that she was not allowed to take us just anywhere. It was on such outings that words eventually came up such as nigger and Negro. Back at this time the politically correct words were Negro or colored, with Negro gaining in popularity. Minerva taught us such things as "Eenie meanie miney mo, catch a nigger by the toe, if he hollers make him pay, $50 dollars every day". She also explained to us that it was not nice to call someone a nigger, as these were not nice people. One day when we were out with her, a colored man was acting the fool towards her and she tried to get rid of him. I think, looking back, he may have been drunk. She became very angry and had some words with him, and did finally get rid of him. She came back over to us and in a very angry voice pointed at him and told us "That's a nigger boys, that's a nigger."

She was always good with all of us kids but eventually she had to go her own way. She had a boyfriend who drove a big truck and he would come by and see her sometimes at the house on Harrison. I can remember my folks didn't think much of him but they eventually went away together and moved to California. We heard from Minerva from time to time over the years, up to about the mid 70's. She found out she couldn't have children so she ended up opening a nursery school in the Watts District of Los Angeles. During the riots, her nursery school was burned down.

My grandma, Golda, also took us on many an outing. She took us on our birthday or when school was about to start, out shopping for shoes and clothes. It became a major source of new clothes for us each year. We were actually allowed to pick our own and get what we liked.

For many years she would take us to the museum in San Antonio. We really enjoyed it and may have accidentally learned something. She also took us to the zoo, the alligator gardens, the Chinese sunken gardens, and the Alamo. As time went on (and I am sure it was from her), it appeared to become acceptable for Minerva to also be allowed to take us to some of these places—especially the zoo.

During these years of school I was still getting into fights. I was going to Cambridge Elementary at the time. I wouldn't take anything off the other kids and I got to the point fairly early on that I didn't like seeing some of the kids picking on another kid. One of the first fights I got into trouble for, was for just such an incident. I knew how it felt to be made fun of and I felt like these smart kids were no good, and I didn't want them for friends. When, one day after school, I found a couple of them ganging up on another boy they were making fun of, so I decided to step in. When it was over the two other boys had a few bruises and I had a sprained hand.

When I got home my mother took me over to Golda's. No one else was home yet and she wanted to have someone look at it. Golda put it in some water to soak and my mother began to yell at me and give me a hard time. Golda very politely suggested that maybe I shouldn't have gotten into a fight but whatever the other two boys got, they deserved. This may not have been the best influence on me but it sure made me feel better.

After that I was in the odd scrape here and there until we moved to Wyndale. It was like you had to start all over since you were the new kid on the block. It didn't take long for some of the kids to find out I wouldn't take anything off anyone. After I was moved into my remedial class I found a number of kids that were getting picked on and this gave me someone to watch out for, as well as an excuse to let off some of my pent-up anger. It didn't take but about one fight and a couple of threats, to get the word around to leave us dummies alone.

One year, after we moved to Wyndale, Nana and Papa came up for my mother's birthday, July 3rd, as they did for a number of summers. They decided to take us to the zoo for a day out. We had been a number of times but always enjoyed the trip—and besides we could help show them around.

As the day progressed it got hotter and hotter. We finally got around to the area with the monkeys, chimps, and other such animals lived. It was partly in the shade with benches, so we took a rest. Some of the monkeys were in cages and some were out on Monkey Island. F.H. decided he was going to have a chat with one of them in the cages near where we were. This one was putting on a show of his own for about a dozen people standing around. As the little crowd grew closer and the people spoke to him he put his hand out and, even though they shouldn't have, they gave him peanuts. Some of the folks were making fun of him and having a good laugh. I guess he took exception to this because as quick as you could say it, he put his hand behind himself, did his business in it, and then slung it out over a large portion of the crowd. F.H. was lucky from the standpoint that he only had it on his shirt, while some of the others needed to go wash their faces. This ended the day at the zoo but poor F.H. was teased well into the night about his souvenir.

This was also the start of the era of shopping malls. North Star Mall was new and the latest thing in malls. Houston had its new malls and Nana would make trips to check them out but for some reason they all liked North Star. Each trip required them to make at least two or three visits to the mall before they could go back to Galveston. Nana shopped year round and had a dropdown staircase in the hall that went up into her attic. It was full of new items she purchased and had put away for birthdays, Christmas, weddings, and any other event that might require a gift. (This may have also been the dawning of the 'born to shop' as well.)

Nana was now vice-president of the PTA (Parent Teachers Association) at a state level. She would go to Austin and other cities for meetings on a regular basis. I think she may have been the one who gave my mother a nudge to get involved in the PTA. Up to this time I can only remember my mother doing a couple of craft sort of things. She would buy some sort of expensive figures made of china and then paint them. They would then be polished and the color would be sealed in. She did several of these but I can only remember being told to leave them alone. Another time she did a mosaic tile pattern on the top of a coffee table. It was very interesting to see how it was actually done.

I don't know if this had anything to do with it or not but about this time I was into building models. Cars, ships, airplanes and boats mainly. I enjoyed doing something with my hands and feeling like I had accomplished something. The glue and paint was the kind you have to keep away from kids nowadays. I don't think it hurt me but then, I only used it to make models—I didn't put a bag over my head. I even made a model Boy Scout soapbox racer, out of wood. You had to shape it, build it and then race it. I won first place in my den but it didn't get any further than that. I was proud of the trophy and my models. I had talked Mom into letting me get the rails, brackets and hook-in shelves to put up in mine and Joey's room.

I don't think Joey liked this idea very much—or maybe it was just the time for when you don't get along with your brother. It seemed pretty much from the time we moved to Wyndale on, we spent most of our time fighting each other or just not getting along. This model stuff was an irritation and eventually we had an invisible line down the middle of the room and everything was to be just so. I still built models on and off for a few years but it was a problem when they always seemed to be getting broken.

My mother was starting to take interest in the local school PTA and not only became a member but was elected onto the active part at the local school level at Northwood Elementary. Joey and I were past this but Tom was just finishing, and Charlie and Beulah Ann still had to go through this school.

She started getting out to a few of the meetings, and she and Dad had decided they would go out to eat on Thursday afternoons on his afternoon off. I, in the meantime, had decided to get a job—a paper route.

Over the next couple of years all of our relationships changed dramatically. Mother wanted help in cleaning up the kitchen and various other help around the house. I pitched in and did help, especially after she offered to pay me. This gave me some of the extra money I needed. Joey and I had convinced our folks to buy us a couple of mopeds—small motorcycles with not enough power to get out of their own way. This was how I did my paper route—that is, when the mopeds were working. My route went all the way over to Cementville (a local community at the cement plant), and half of our local neighborhood. As luck would have it, one of the head boys that was leading the mobs of kids up and down the streets in Cementville, was an old acquaintance of my right hand, going back to Cambridge.

They all decided it would be great fun to pick up the papers I delivered to the houses or if they couldn't do that, then pelt me with rocks as I made my rounds. I tried to ignore this for the first few days but saw this was not going to work. I stopped and told one of his friends walking down the road, to tell Wa King I would meet with him the next day at 4:30 at the end of the road. The next day he and about a dozen of his helpers showed up. He laughed and wanted to know what I was going to do about it. I explained to him I was only trying to do my job and the past was the past. Besides, if this didn't mean anything to him, I would be glad to hold him responsible for everything that happened and that every time something did happen, I would come after him and take it out on him. He agreed it was time to put the past where it belonged.

I learned a lot doing my paper route. How cold it was at 4 o'clock on Saturday and Sunday mornings during the winter, and how the general public treated other people. Some would call in complaints if the paper was 5 feet off the porch. This would not only require us to take them another paper in person but we would get a fine from the paper against what we made. The biggest introduction was to dead beats. I never knew so many people tried to beat their paperboy out of what was owed them.

It became a major battle trying to get the money in each month. It took more time to collect the money than anything else did. I would have to make multiple trips back to the same house time and again to try and get paid. Every excuse in the world was given from "I don't have any money on me today" to "I am sure we paid you for several months last time". I had to pay for all the papers each month and if I didn't collect the money, then it was out of my pocket. This was the major reason (along with the Mopeds breaking down all the time) why, after about a year, I gave up my paper route. It might be worth pointing out that the worst payers I had were in the middle class area—not in Cementville.

I had previously tried my hand at some other part-time jobs. It was usually working for my grandparents or parents doing odd jobs. These were not easy jobs when it came to Paw. One time, out at the ranch, he offered us the job of cutting down cedar tree seedlings. He would pay a few cents for real small ones, then 5 cents for about the size of a little finger and on up to 25 cents each for those that were about the size of a man's thumb. The area around the house needed clearing at the ranch and Joey and I went to it. We were disappointed to find out it took a lot of the small ones to make a dollar even though they were very quick to do. We then decided to try the big ones since it only took 4 of them to make a dollar. The next thing we learned was that by the time the cedar tree seedlings were up to that size they were very tough and hard to cut. It would take us sometimes 15 to 20 minutes working as hard as we could to finally cut or tear through one of these larger ones. We put in a morning's work and were ready for inspection from Paw. He was actually quite generous as he ended up giving us both a couple of dollars for our efforts. I am sure that is what we were paid for, not the results. We agreed that maybe we would spend the rest of the weekend playing and maybe take on some other job another time.

I had already by this time started to become aware of girls . . . still to be kept at an arm's length and not sure how to talk to them at all. My mother, for whatever reason, came up with the idea we should go to dancing lessons at Bud Nash Studios. I was very reluctant at first and did not want to go—for one reason, I couldn't dance. I was assured that this was what everyone was going for.

You had to dress up and wear a coat and tie. You had a nametag on a piece of string tied to your sleeve. The first few times I went I was scared to death and could see that a lot of the kids had been going for awhile and could already dance. Being forced to get a partner and start to learn dance steps, made me meet and get to know some of the girls. I realized that a number of them would be going to the same school as me next year—the first year of Junior High School. This opened a door for me from the standpoint that I made not only new friends but also those of the opposite sex. I would start to spend more time trying to go over to their houses after school and become more social and be more involved with other students at school.

This awareness helped me make the rest of the transition from the old school and friends, to the new one. I had previously played little league baseball for two years but it was time for me to switch to pony league (the older group), or do something else. I had started to become interested in football previously, and had played flag football during school recess and sometimes after school. Starting into Junior High was the first chance I had, to go out for and play with a team that was being trained and coached like a football team.

This new school year was going to start me in a different direction—not only with the chance to play football but also for the first time, I felt like I was going to be on the inside . . . instead of being on the outside looking in.

CHAPTER 5

ONE'S OWN DEVICES

As part of my growing up was for me to be left to my own devices at various times, I found it necessary for me to take matters into my own hands if I wished to achieve my objectives. Just why or how it started I no longer remember. What I do remember is that we were given an allowance of about $5 per week—which back in those days was not bad but not nearly enough. To help supplement this, I would do the odd job around the house including cutting the lawn, cleaning the kitchen, or painting the fence. I even had the paper route for awhile as an after school job . . . but that is another story.

During the time after the Ford was returned to the ranch, my brother Joe and I had gone together and purchased a hot rod of sorts. It was one he found through some friends, that was in pieces. The friend had started to try and put this one together but decided, for whatever reason, not to and wanted to sell it–in the box so to speak. It was a 1933 Ford 3—window coupe body on a frame that had been modified. It had no motor but all of the exposed front springs and such were chrome-plated. We talked our folks into allowing us to purchase it and move it into the front part of the garage. This caused the problem of one of the cars then having to be left outside.

We didn't see this as a problem since on the other side of the wall, was an unfinished room just large enough for the car to fit in front to back, as soon as we knocked the wall out. We knew nothing of 'structure' in those days, and proceeded to remove the wall and make an opening. It was fortunate for us that the supports were out of the way and the opening we made was only an area that had been partitioned off. We assured our folks everything was fine and we were ready to build our perfect car.

I never knew a car was made of so many pieces. As we started to make our list of what we needed and wanted, it became apparent we needed a lot more money. This was the main reason for all those various jobs. The folks were good as from time to time when we ordered parts, we would give them the money, they would write the check and send the order. If we had been helping and were only a few dollars short, they would pitch in and we would get our next little batch of parts. This worked well with the exception that at this rate, it was going to be a very long time before it ever saw daylight again.

Then we had a stroke of luck. A friend of my father's had a 1950 Oldsmobile that he was going to trade in to a local dealer when one day they were visiting, and Dad told him about our car with no motor. Dad's friend had been known to celebrate on a regular basis and consequently his poor old car had more hits on it than Joe Lewis. This did nothing for its value. He offered it to us for the motor. This was an early V8 motor with overhead valves! We were over the moon. We drove the car around the neighborhood and terrorized everyone in sight for several weeks. One of our favorite tricks was to go fairly fast, turn the key off with the car in low gear and coast past someone standing by the roadside. Just as we passed we would turn the key back on and BOOM! The car would backfire through the gasoline build-up in the muffler. I don't know where Joe learned this trick but it was great fun—even though it did nothing for the muffler. I didn't know people could jump so high! We were told to park it before we ended up in trouble as we still had no driver's license at this time. This worked to our advantage however. We wanted to have the motor modified; cam, solid lifters, larger pistons and all those things done to it before we tried to put it in. The folks wanted the car off the street.

A few houses down the street lived a neighbor that had an auto parts and machine shop business. As part of the solution, Dad offered to see what could be worked out with him if we would get rid of the car and get it off the street. We made a list of what we wanted to have done and all seemed fine until we found out the neighbor would not remove the motor, much less get rid of the body. Then of course there was the problem of how you are going to mount the motor in the Ford—much less to the standard transmission.

In the hot rod magazines they sold adapter kits for motor/transmission combinations, so this was not a problem. All the rest was. So, not knowing what else to do, we started calling around to auto repair and auto yards. After numerous calls we found one that was interested in our job. We drove out to the far east side of San Antonio not knowing any better. This area of town where this operator had his location was about 90% black. We grew up in a house with black maids and over the years, neither parents nor grandparents ever expressed any form of discrimination or bigotry. So to us it was business as usual and we were unaware of any need to take any extra care or precautions.

The establishment was not what we expected as it was a combination of a pig farm (the smell hit you first) in the country, with a wrecker's yard that had about 25 cars in it—most in a state of leftover pieces. The work area in the middle was an open-air barn with several men sitting around—most likely waiting for their next victim as we soon learned. The idea was that we would take them the hot rod and the Oldsmobile. They would remove the motor and put it in the hot rod, with an adapter. We would pay them $50 and they would also keep the Oldsmobile for parts. The job would take a few weeks, as they were busy. We were happy! We paid them the $50 and handed over the keys and the vehicles. This is where I started to get my real education at the School of Life Class 101. This is the school they never tell you about but I'll promise you, you will learn more, and it can teach you and cost you more than any university.

Hot rod with the motor in it

You guessed it. Weeks turned into more weeks, then into several months. We made several trips out to his place and he always had a reason or a story. His helper was going to make the adapter then quit. He ordered one but it got lost in the mail. He liked us so much, if he could have more time he would do some fix'n on it for free before he gave it back. We finally had enough and with great determination went to see him one more time. We were getting to the point we didn't know what he was up to or if the hot rod would even be there. He finally had the motor sitting on the ground but nothing done. But much to our surprise he had an adapter plate for it, so he could finally mount it. We then agreed that if he could just get the motor in the hot rod with the transmission, we would get it out of his yard and be on our way. We returned that next weekend to retrieve our vehicle only to find that is just what he did. Getting it in the vehicle was about all you could say. Then he asked for more money! As I remember we paid him something like an extra $10 and were glad to do it, just so we could get our vehicle back and be on our way.

Our neighbor then sent his truck to our place with a lift, and loaded the motor and took it to his shop. A couple of weeks later he sent it back to us. It had been run through the vats to boil it out, modified, and repainted. It was like a new motor. We were ready for our next stage and of course more money.

Somehow during all of this, it fell to me to be in charge of keeping track of the finances. It was always up to me, it seemed, to get that extra we needed. Be it to ask Dad, or get the extra little job. I usually was able to save part of my allowance each week and put some away or earmark some for our next batch of parts.

It was during this time that we had a maid working for my folks to help with the household and keep an eye on us whenever they went away. Her name was Marguerite. We were to keep our rooms tidy and make our beds; the rest was up to her. She was in about her early 20's and whenever the folks were not around she would turn the music up loud and dance as she did the housework. She always seemed to be running short on money before each payday. She came to me one day and wanted to borrow money until payday. At first I was not sure about this but then she offered to pay me back with interest! This sounded good, as we always needed money. We soon had a deal and it became a regular thing for her to be borrowing $5 or $10, and paying me back at the end of the week with $6 or $12. After awhile I think she felt this was getting a bit old and although she did it, she did not seem overly happy.

My parents did not go away on many trips and if they did, it was usually only for a few days to a medical convention. On one such occasion when they were away, Marguerite was to stay over and take care of us. She, of course, was not to have company while they were away. One night after we had gone to bed and been asleep for awhile, I woke up to a noise. I didn't know what it was so I got up to investigate. Our room was next to the family den room with the sofas and TV. As I opened the door to see what the noise was, out of the corner of my eye I saw this jumping/wrestling motion in the light of the TV. Much to my surprise it was Marguerite and her boyfriend. They had a blanket and must have fallen asleep watching TV and fallen part way off the sofa. They were in a big hurry pulling the blanket up, although I didn't know why as they both looked quite hot. After a few moments, I turned and left the room. A little later Marguerite came to check on me. After some discussion we both decided it would be to our mutual benefit if she took back over making my bed and that some things were better left untold. Besides, I didn't want to lose my loan business.

It was after this and after I moved into live with my grandparents, that I had an opportunity to have some fun with Alma and Irene—two of the maids that had worked for my grandmother Golda for years. Over the years my grandmother had help so she could get rest during the day due to her heart condition. Alma did the housework and Irene had moved from helping in the kitchen to mainly doing ironing.

It was at the point, with years having gone by, that when lunchtime came it was up to my grandmother to fix them lunch and wait on them as their health was not much better than hers. Sometimes she would help some with the housework so they would get finished for the day—or even put off some of the ironing until next week. They became more than hired help and even with the frustration they caused at times, Golda could not consider letting them go. They were truly on the 'plantation plan' and had a place for life. At times as she helped them finish the day she would express, "I have nothing against slaves, I think everybody should own at least one". (I think she felt she was it. She told me how as a child she was told of those that had worked off their debt only to find they had no place to go.)

They were both good natured and easily amused. It had become my job to take them to the bus stop on the main street about 3 miles away at the end of the day. This would allow them to catch the bus that went straight back, with less transfers. They always seemed to get a new energy at the end of the day as they got ready to go home. They would gather their things, change their shoes, put on their hats and get their bags. They would then gather by the kitchen area by the back door and let me know they were ready. They would usually call out to me "Master Sam, we is ready". I guess this came from the times that were rapidly disappearing.

We would all go out and get in the car. They always, automatically, got in the back. Early on, Alma made a fatal mistake. She expressed to me that she feared two things; going fast and missing her bus. I think the feeling of speed always seems more from the back seat—especially so, if you are much older. As we left the house one day, in what I considered plenty of time, Alma said to me "I sure do hopes I don't miss catch'n my bus". Something about this got hold on me and the Devil made me do it. I no sooner got them in the car and we were off! Instead of going the usual 25 to 30 miles per hour to make her happy, we wound it up to a breathtaking 35 to 40 miles per hour.

"Master Sam! Master Sam!" I could hear from the back. "Oh Lord'y!" she would exclaim as she grabbed her bag and held it tight. "Don't worry Alma, I'll get you there in time for your bus in one piece. Just hold on!" About that time, she would start laughing and laughing with repeated "Master Sam! Master Sam!" thrown in, as she tried to catch her breath. In a matter of minutes we were at the bus stop with time to spare. From that first time on, all I had to do was mention speeding up or checking to see if she thought we had plenty of time and I could hear that nervous laughter starting up. I found it more fun to tease and keep her in suspense than actually doing anything.

When they did retire, it was the end of an era. In the early years the maids did become part of the family. The families worked with each other and had a respect for each other. They would share over the years, some of their family experiences and tragedies. As many things have changed over the years, this has as well. Not only are 'domestic servants' virtually no longer around but they are also highly unfashionable. Part of this comes undoubtedly from economics but also from a lack of mutual understanding of the job and the true relationship that used to exist in many of these cases. In today's world of employee/employer relationships based strictly on remuneration and contracts, this is an era that, as my grandmother would say, is gone with the wind.

CHAPTER 6

WYNDALE TO LAMONT

The first year I went to junior high school it was still located across the road that separated it from the high school. You had, in effect, the two schools next door to each other with a 6 year student age spread. On the junior high side, you rode the bus or rode to school in the car driven by one of your parents. On the high school side, a lot of the kids had their own car to drive to school and it was the place to be. With the overcrowded facilities, the classes had to share with each other until the new junior high was completed (a couple of years away yet).

During these years—more so during my junior high years—I still managed to get into fights. I managed to break my right hand and had to have it in a cast for 6 weeks once, just as our 6 weeks tests were starting. I remember I didn't get into trouble that time because the other kid had a bad reputation and had started it with me. I took my test even though I had trouble writing with my hand in a cast. The good thing that came out of this was when my algebra teacher and one of the others told me they were sure I would use it as an excuse not to take the test. When I did take the test, it totally turned them around towards me from then on.

My anger was still inside me and was not getting any better because of what was going on at home. I had started with football at the start of the new school year. Practice was always after school as the coaches had us work out, as well as try to teach us plays and what they wanted us to do. With school starting at the end of August the temperature at practice time was still at least in the 90's. By the end of practice and a quick shower, it was usually getting dark about the time we finished. My mother was to pick me up after practice. At first it wasn't too bad. A few times the coach had us a little later than usual and this didn't sit well with Mom. She wanted me to phone but there were no public phones. Then it started getting to the point I didn't know if she was just running late to get me or she had forgotten about me, or what. A number of times I had to walk home after practice. This was several miles from the school to the house. After a number of these episodes I started trying to catch a ride, at least part way, with some of the other kids.

During this time—especially on Thursdays when they went out to eat—Mom and Dad would start drinking to excess. It gradually got worse and worse. I would get my extra duty money by cleaning the kitchen and by sometimes helping get things for the younger kids. Sometimes it was as simple as taking the car and driving about a mile to the corner store to pick up a few items.

My mother never had a problem with giving us a few good swats, if she felt we needed it, along the way. By now, however, her anger would get out of control with us when she had been drinking heavily. She would give us a few licks with the belt in the old days. Now it was more likely to turn into a thrashing. Sometimes it would be a coat hanger if nothing else was available, or she would throw things—usually the nearest thing at hand. This included full glass quart milk bottles.

When it would get to this stage I would usually take the coat hanger or belt away from her and close the door to my room to keep her out. When she was like this no one, not even Dad, could control her. You would just have to wait to the next day. Sometimes she wouldn't remember all of what happened. Sometimes she would give you money out of her purse for jobs or the store and then the next day she was sure one of us just took it.

Dad would get very quiet and just sit by the phone and watch TV. As this continued on, she even started accusing him of possibly seeing another woman, or at least liking another woman. I now realize that she was a jealous person and over the years she drove some of their friends away with either her anger and drinking, or because of her jealousy. From knowing Dad both then and later on, I can assure you he never even considered another woman for he was still in love with this one. He just didn't know what to do with her . . . much less another one.

It was very unfortunate but as time went on, the fights and arguments became even more frequent. One night after a Thursday outing it became extremely bitter. I was truly unsure of what was going to happen as my mother was so angry. She had started hitting Dad and throwing things at him. He was in no condition to defend himself as he could hardly even stand up. We decided to call grandma Golda. She came over on her own after about 15 to 20 minutes. This did get them to settle down after awhile but created a whole new set of problems.

It seems that, even though we were unaware, this drinking and possibly the jealousy problem had surfaced before in the past. Golda wanted to help and wanted to keep the lid on things as much as possible which is why she left Dr. Joe at home. She was assured everything was okay and she could return home. After she left we caught hell for having called her. My mother especially, did not want this to be known about by my grandparents.

Things did not get better in the long run. Even though we would sit around the coffee table in the den and visit about school, what girl are you seeing now, and some other somewhat superficial topics, down deep was still a time bomb.

I started remembering some of the things that had happened years ago and I had forgotten about them. One time when we were staying in Galveston at Nana's house, Uncle Freddy came in during the middle of the night drunk. He was yelling and throwing things and when F.H. tried to get him to stop, he started pushing him around and saying he was going to kill him if he didn't get out of his way. Mom tried to get him to sit down at the kitchen table with her and talk to her. In the meantime they called Uncle Lloyd to come over and try and help. They got him to sit at the table and talk, and have a few drinks. After several hours everything settled down.

In the past, at Harrison, I could remember some yelling but not much more. Now I was wondering just how big a problem this was. We would get along for a few weeks, then I might ask for some extra money and everything would come undone. We would argue about how I wasn't any help and I would point out how much money they wasted on stuff to drink. Then the fight would begin.

I don't know if it was Mom or Dad's idea to take us out to eat with them. I think it was a way to try and get along, and get to know each other better. At first I can remember Joey going along and then later it was mainly just me. You see, what happened was not a lot of fun. It would all start out very nicely at 'La Lousianne Restaurant'. I would have a shrimp cocktail and if I had been good, a champagne cocktail as well. Then I would usually have a steak or lobster, followed by an ice cream parfait that had several mint-type liqueurs poured over it. I really enjoyed it and sometimes we would actually have a conversation. They even started letting me drive them home.

Unfortunately, it didn't always stay this way. Sometimes Mom would get on her high horse and everything was wrong. The steak, according to her, was over-cooked and she would demand another one. She would want more to drink, and get louder and louder. Dad would keep drinking and I think he was hoping he would melt away into the chair. The next trick was to get them out of the restaurant and into the car. Usually at least one of them could halfway walk, while the other had to be almost carried. The waiters would help and I guess it was because they were good customers over the years, they overlooked many an episode.

Round two would start once we were home. Most of the time they would want something else to drink and the fighting would start. This has always been difficult for me to try to understand. As I previously mentioned I felt that continually being on call and on duty all the time was a recipe for disaster. This along with a thick atmosphere between my mother and Dr. Joe only added to the complications.

Sure enough, sooner or later it was going to happen. My Dad had some calls from some of the duty nurses about orders he had left for patients or they wanted to know what to do because something had changed. Some of them reported to the hospital board that they had suspected he had been drinking heavily when they spoke to him. This may not have come up if he hadn't such an intolerance for what he felt was incompetence. When he felt a problem had come up because of incompetence he let them have it in no uncertain terms on how he felt about it. He left himself wide open because he had been drinking when he expressed himself and put the nurses down. His drinking as such was not the problem as long as he was still competent in performing his duties. It only became an issue because of him telling the nurses off. I never knew of any incident where a patient was compromised. However, with his behavior in question he was put on probation once for a period of time because of just such an incident with the nursing staff. I think this did not help his relationship with Dr. Leon or Dr. Joe as they felt it reflected on them as well. This again added to the pressure and problems.

One night when he was in the process of getting undressed for bed he slipped on a throw rug on the vinyl floor and fell. He landed on top of his leg and broke it in several places. It was broken in such a way that the doctor had wanted to try to avoid putting pins in it to hold it. He set it in a cast and had him stay in bed for almost 2 months at the house. He even had a portable x-ray machine sent to the house to check on how the leg was doing so he wouldn't have to move it any more than necessary. It did heal and he went back to work. He had always had trouble with his legs and this didn't help. He would walk with almost a falling gait when he was in a hurry—even when he hadn't had anything to drink at all.

Mom became angrier and drank even more. She would take things out on any one of us for no reason at all. Most of the time we didn't even know what she was going on about. She would just tell us how sorry we were . . . and go on from there. Dad would drink and hide from everything, in his own little world. Between having too much to drink and bad legs, sometimes on the way to bed you could hear him take a fall and hit the walls. He was forever scratching his bald head and having to try and cover it up so he could go to work.

This went on for a couple of years during which time we became more independent. Joey and I had our hot rod car project and I played football. We talked our folks into considering buying us a car. We actually would have been happy with a used car but didn't know enough to ask or how to look for one. Next door to the restaurant there were a couple of car dealers. One was a Chrysler Plymouth dealer and up the road was an Edsel dealer. Dad purchased an Edsel and it really was a pretty good car but with all the publicity it got, it didn't stand a chance. A couple of years later he bought a Chrysler Windsor station wagon with everything on it and traded in the Edsel. My mother then felt it was time for her to have a new car as she was driving a 1954 Buick Special, about 6 years old. She got her way and got a new Plymouth Fury station wagon.

It was the relationship with this auto dealer that gave them the idea of a new little Simca. I think it was a car from Sweden—about like a VW beetle in size. We were used to slipping the Edsel out and going to the drag strip. It had a 390 cubic inch V8 motor and would do about 90 miles an hour in the quarter mile. Joey had put an exhaust cutout underneath the car so we could open it up when we went to race. He would usually do the mechanical stuff and I was the one who would do the driving. He always said I had a touch for it but I wonder if he didn't want to be in the clear if something went wrong. We could both see a Simca just would not be the same sort of beast to be driving around in. I started looking around at cars and car yards, and talking to my folks to try to bring them around.

One day I decided to stop in the Chevrolet yard on the Austin Highway. I asked what they had that was not too much money but new, as my folks had decided a new car would be less trouble. The salesman said they had a close-out model that was a new car with very little equipment. It was a Bel Air 2 door sedan with a 348 cu inch V8 and a 3 speed standard transmission, and that was about it, except for the AM radio. This was just what we were looking for—a Chevrolet with V8 and standard transmission. My folks could hardly believe that is what we wanted. No power steering, no air conditioning, standard transmission. Well Dad was happy and in the matter of a couple of days, the car was ours. I think it was probably more than the Simca but I don't know for sure. It was our new pride and joy. Now we just had to share.

We did things together with the car and did a lot of driving around. I was still doing my football, and was playing both offence and defense, and the specialty teams. At the end of the second season in an extra game, when I was tackled, I ended up on the bottom of a stack with three guys on top of me. This resulted in a broken collar bone and broken shoulder. I was one of the fastest kids at the school but it would be the next year before I decided what I was going to do. I had made other new friends and was elected to serve on the Student Council—and held the post of Parliamentarian all the way through the end of High School. It was as if, in some ways, Joey and I were getting further and further apart. I was getting more involved with these sorts of things and a whole new group of friends. He was going his own way with his own friends.

I used the Chevrolet a number of times and on a number of dates. But it seemed to me we were, more often than not, wanting to use it at the same time and I found myself usually using the Plymouth Fury instead. I was lucky because Mom would let me take her car when the other one was unavailable. A station wagon was not the hottest car going but it was better than no car and that counted for a lot.

The relationship I had with my mother during this time was a real love/hate sort of relationship. One week she would be wanting you to go to eat with them and talk about getting a new car for you and your brother, and then the next she would be calling you every name in the book and trying to hit you with anything she could put her hands on. This was something I tried to put out of my mind and spend as much time away from the problem as possible. I would do some of my homework at home, some at school and some at a friend's house. It just depended on how things were going at the time and where it was safe to be.

It did finally get to be too much. It was partly the embarrassment when friends would come over. You never knew what state things might be at and if you were not careful, all hell could break loose. I felt sorry for Dad and felt he needed someone to watch out for him and be his friend. I wasn't sure what to do about Joey and the car, and we finally agreed I would take the hotrod as mine and he would keep the year-old Chevrolet for his. Not bad. It finally ended up in one of those bitter all-out sort of confrontations between my mother and me, one more time. Previously, Grandma Golda told me if things got too bad I could always come and stay with them. I think she knew sooner or later it would come to this, as I was not about to keep taking it from my mother and keep my mouth shut. When I called Golda she was a little hesitant at first but after talking to Dad, she came after me. I think she was thinking a weekend away would help sort things out. I did talk to Golda—and also explained that Mom had told me "Fine . . . go . . . and don't ever come back". And then I said "Fine . . . I'll never speak to you again". It probably saved us both from each other at the time. So I moved in with my grandparents on Lamont and it was, in fact, two years before I ever spoke to my mother again. This was after Dad came in to see me one day at the house and asked me to please call her and talk to her—if not for me, then for him. I did this, and we spoke on and off from then on.

It was a big move for me. I wasn't sure myself if it was going to work. It wasn't until we established the house rules, and got accustomed to each other and what was expected, that the atmosphere settled down and a happy routine developed that would then take me all the way through high school and up to my first marriage.

CHAPTER 7

THE RAYNERS

This is my mother's side of the family. The family background and history on the Rayner side of the family was unknown to me up to about my teen years—and even then it wasn't until much later a lot of the blanks were filled in. I knew my grandmother, Nana, had lived in an orphanage and some of her family was killed in the 1900 hurricane that devastated Galveston. She had some relative that went back to the Civil War or something, who my mother had shown me a picture of. F.H., Papa, was originally from England. That was about all I knew for a long time. It was later that with the help of Aunt Jeannie and my sister Beulah Ann, a lot of the information was passed on to me.

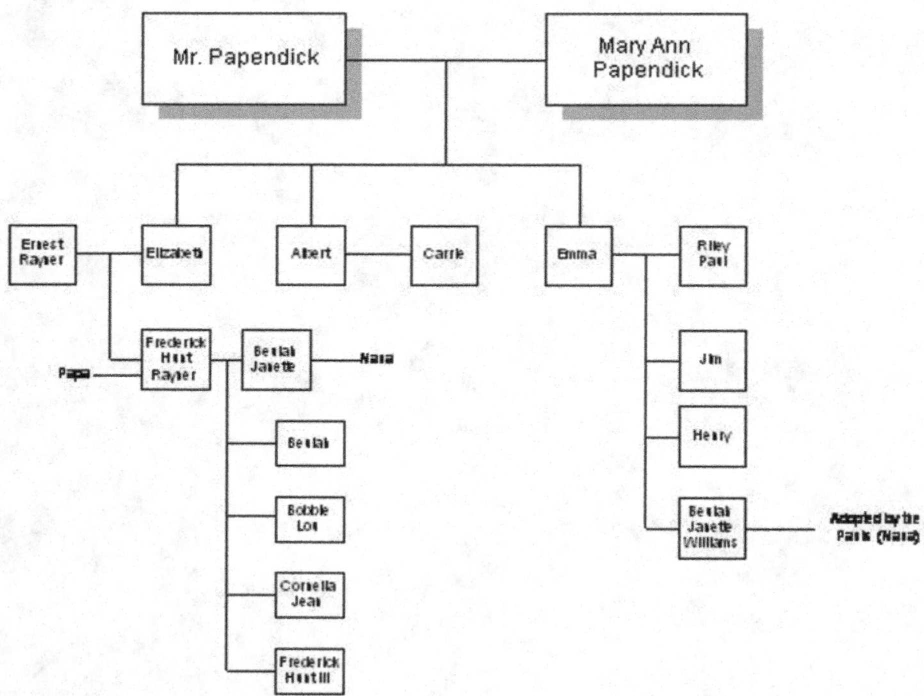

The Rayner Family Tree

The above family tree should help and make it easier to follow what had happened in the family. As you see Nana is located in two places on the tree—one on the other side from Papa.

Mr Cushman married Cornelia Jefferson. They came from somewhere in Jefferson County (the Beaumont area). The Jefferson's were supposed to have been a prominent family in that area and Jefferson County was supposed to be named after them. Sometime after 1884 but before 1900, they moved to Galveston to live. They lost one daughter, age 17, in the 1900 storm in Galveston. Their remaining children were Robert, Joseph, Bella, and Clara Onetta. Clara was born in Jefferson County in 1884. Mrs. Cornelia (Jefferson) Cushman is buried in the Catholic Cemetery on 61st street in Galveston.

Charlotte Saunders Cushman was an actress and supposedly was a Northern spy during the Civil War. Charlotte Cushman was a famous actress during that time period and the picture of her in the book *'The Blue and the Grey'* (a history of the Civil War), was the one my mother used to show me when I was growing up. It had a short piece about her being a spy but she was never executed as each time they asked her for a request for a last meal, she would order strawberries as part of it, since she was allergic to them. They wouldn't execute a person when they were ill and so eventually she was set free. She was an Aunt of Robert, Joseph, Bella and Clara.

Clara Onetta Cushman married a Mr Williams. They had one child Beulah Jeanette Williams, my grandmother, Nana. She was born in Galveston on September 14, 1903. They were divorced a few years later. Mr. Williams was killed during a robbery somewhere in Louisiana. He lived over a grocery store and hearing a noise downstairs, went to investigate and was shot by the robber. He had planned to go back to get Beulah Jeanette and take her with him. Clara had remarried and had other children. Beulah Jeanette was now about 5 years old.

Nana as child, holding baby

Beaulah Jeanette at about age 12

Clara had married Charles Pugh and they had 5 children. They were Robert, Margarette, Cornelia, Marvin and Albert. Before the last child was born they separated. Charlie was a drinker and this caused problems. He worked on the fishing boats and most of the time he did not bring his pay check home. Mrs. Clara Pugh, along with her mother Mrs Cornelia Cushman, ran a boarding house in Galveston for the men who worked on the railroad. Even with this, Clara was still having a very hard time making ends meet. It was during this period that Clara placed both Beulah Jeanette and Margarette in the Lasker Home for homeless children in Galveston.

Clara was just unable to support all the children. She always intended to get the two girls back as soon as she could. At that time, in about 1915, you had to sign a consent form agreeing to adoption before the home would take the children in. Before she could get the children back, Beulah Jeanette was adopted by Riley and Emma Paul of Galveston.

Margarette was adopted by a couple that lived in Sealy, Texas. No one saw Margarette again until after she was fully-grown and both of her adopted parents had died. She returned to Galveston to look for her family and was reunited with them. Margarette had married a Bill Hintz and they lived in Columbus, Texas.

Emma Papendick and Riley Paul, Nana's adoptive parents

Clara Onetta Cushman (Williams)—Beulah Jeanette Willims' (Nana's) mother

Clara divorced Charles Pugh and later remarried a Mr. Anton Nyberg. They had 4 children—Clarence, Blanche, Evelyn and Raymond. Clara Onetta Nyberg died in 1967 at the age of 83. She is buried in Grace Memorial Cemetery in Hitchcock, Texas.

This is how Beulah Jeanette ended up in the Lasker Home for homeless children in Galveston, and being adopted by Riley and Emma Paul. You see when you look at the family tree, that Emma Paul was Frederick Hunt Rayner's aunt. She had left England years before.

Going back to the family tree now and starting with the Papendicks [I should point out that over the years a lot of the Christian names have become unknown for sure], Mr. Papendick married Mary Ann, who became Mary Ann Papendick. Her family had owned a gentlemen's tailor shop in London, England. He had come from Denmark and was about 6 feet 6 inches tall. Mary Ann was on the short side at only 4 feet 11 inches tall. They must have made an interesting-looking couple. The exact number of children they had is a bit uncertain. However, they did have Albert, Emma and Elizabeth.

Emma had a broken love affair and immigrated to the United States, although the year and route she took is uncertain. She married a man from Shreveport, Louisiana, a Mr Riley Paul. They had two boys, Jim and Henry. Later they adopted Beulah Jeanette Williams from the Lasker home in Galveston, when she was about 12 years old. It was shortly after this they moved to Hitchcock. Mr. Paul tried his hand at farming but he was not successful and they moved back to Galveston.

Meanwhile back in England, Elizabeth Papendick, Emma's sister, married Ernest Hunt Rayner and they had one son, Frederick Hunt Rayner, my grandfather. He was born November 26, 1900 in Ipswich, England. After about two years they divorced. Elizabeth moved back to London to live with her folks. She worked in the tailor shop and Frederick was raised by his grandmother, Mary Ann Papendick.

Somewhere around 1917–1918, Elizabeth remarried. She married a Mr. Will Harrold. They had one daughter, Marjorie. She married Sidney Stephens and they had four sons—Martin, Eric, Raymond and Paul. They immigrated to Australia by ship and landed in Freemantle, Australia about January 8, 1967. Martin had emigrated to Australia a few years earlier. When last heard of, they lived in Sydney. Marjorie may still be alive as she was born around 1920. Elizabeth Papendick Rayner Harrold died in July 1967 at the age of 88, one month after her birthday. F. H., my grandfather, had some letters from Elizabeth in which she makes reference to some of the others—and possibly the children of Albert and Carrie, his uncle and aunt (Albert being Elizabeth's brother).

Carrie and Albert Papendick

Frederick Hunt Rayner immigrated to the United States in 1920 or 1921. He came in through Ellis Island and then went by boat to Galveston where he was going to live with his Aunt Emma, his mother's sister. This is where he met his aunt's adoptive daughter, Beulah Jeanette. Beulah Jeanette was working for the Western Union and F.H. was working for Kempner Cotton Co., when they were married May 17, 1922 in Eaton Chapel in Galveston. So, in this way, my mother's great aunt was also her grandmother by adoption. My mother and the family always called her Aunt Paul, strangely enough. After Mr Paul died, Aunt Paul lived with F.H., Nana and the family for a number of years. Emma and Riley Paul are both buried in Shreveport.

When F.H. came to Galveston from England after the First World War, one of the first jobs he was able to get was with the Kempner Cotton Co. They owned the docks in Galveston—which was almost the whole bay side of the developed area. He started off as an office boy and over the years worked his way up to Vice President of the company.

They had four children, my mother being the oldest. They were Beulah Elizabeth, Bobbie, Jeannie and Freddy Jr. I don't really know a lot about them when they were growing up. I know Mom and her sisters tried a little vaudeville. I know about the episode when it was agreed that Nana would do all the driving. Other than that, it is mainly when they were older or we were around as kids and watched what was going on.

Beulah, Jeannie, Bobbie Rayner

I can remember various times when we would stay with them that F.H. would get up in the middle of the night to make phone calls. He was calling Japan and trading cotton. From my understanding, at one time he had a seat on the exchange in New York for trading or something. He also at one stage was very heavily involved in cotton trading with Mexico. He was even offered a position with the companies in Mexico if he would go to work with them. He had a strong feeling of loyalty to Kempner as he had worked most of his life for them. He worked directly with Mr Kempner Sr. and ran the company with him. In about 1954, the company decided to have a party to recognize his efforts. Mr. Kempner didn't always take care of details and as the story goes, F.H. ended up picking up the bill for the party that was given to honor him!

Kempner Cotton Co. party for F.H. From left to Right: Nana, F.H. Jr, Jeannie, Lloyd, Bobbie, Denny, Beaulah, F.H.Rayner

After Mr Kempner Sr. retired or died, his son took over. He hated running the company and didn't like working. For several years he had F.H. continue on to run the company. One of the large shipping companies out of Houston wanted to buy Kempner out—both his business and his holdings in Galveston as well.

They knew it would mean that most, if not all, of the employees would end up being unemployed if the buyout was agreed to. The other company had plans to move most of the business to Houston and use the Houston Ship Channel. The offer was finally too much for Kempner Jr. and he sold out. Almost overnight many of the employees found themselves without a job. This included F.H. He was an executive in his 60's. No one wanted to hire him as he was getting old and had been on a high salary. He did some sort of part-time bookkeeping work for awhile as I remember, and that was about it. Kempner Jr., like so many others, had no loyalty to their employees or to the people who had built and run their company for them. F.H. received no retirement package—not even a gold watch and a thank you from the son. You could tell this hurt him even though he tried not to show it.

F.H. had some investments and some money saved but this had suffered over the years when he had to help Uncle Freddy out a number of times. He and Nana had built a new house in Hitchcock and they still had the house in Galveston that Uncle Freddy lived in. I don't know if Freddy paid them for the house or not.

Uncle Freddy was known to be involved in the numbers business, as they called it. He was a bookie. My understanding was he was pretty heavily involved and did this for years. He lived for many years in the house he grew up in and when we went to see all the relatives before we left for New Zealand, he was still living in that house. He had lived there so long, almost all of his life, that when he would leave there he would back across the street into the vacant lot and then drive away. One day when he went to do this, he backed his car into the neighbor's house. When they asked him what happened, he told them it was their fault as it had been a vacant lot for years and no one asked him if they could build a house there. And he drove off. He evidently forgot . . . he had backed this way all his life.

Uncle Denny, Aunt Bobbie's husband, was in the U.S. Navy in World War II and was part of the group that built the hangers for the aircraft that dropped the atomic bomb on Japan. He was always what seemed to be very angry. He was very strict with his kids and I have always wondered if this wasn't child abuse. It must have come close to it. To this day he is still strict and from what I've been told, wealthy and tight.

Uncle Lloyd, Aunt Jeannie's husband, has always been somewhat of the family favorite. In fact they both are. They have always worked hard, tried to help when they could and were always good friends to the family. Lloyd worked for the electric company, Houston Power and Light, for as long as I could remember. They always had to be careful with their money and Aunt Jeannie was in charge of saving and investing. Uncle Lloyd played the guitar and at one stage played with some of the boys. I think he wanted to give it a try for a living but Aunt Jeannie worked this out with him over a period of time. I think he was good enough—at least back then he was as good as most around that sang country. When the family would get together or we would get him to come and see us, we always wanted him to play and sing. We would all join in and have a good time. I am sure when we were older, the few beers we had didn't hurt our singing any—or at least it made it sound better to us.

He put up yard lights for my grandparents on Lamont and helped with other little projects whenever he went to the ranch. I think this is one reason he was always welcome. One year when he came up when we lived on Wyndale, he let me and Joey take his '55 Chevrolet for a run and go up to the store. We pushed it too hard and one of the valve lifters hung and caused damage to the motor. He had it fixed and they went back. I always felt bad about it as I knew they didn't have a lot of extra money. It was a few years later, after I was married, that my Dad called me up and wanted me to see what they had in used cars at Tindall's place. He wanted to do something for Lloyd and Jeannie. They had come up and the car they had was not doing very well. Dad ended up buying about a two-year-old Grand Prix and giving it to them. They really seemed happy and Dad was glad he could finally do something for them. When my grandmother Golda died, they were the only ones that came up to her funeral from the coast. They said the reason they did was because she was one of the nicest people they had ever met.

F.H. and Nana both, in later years, needed medication and help. Dad always did what he could on free advice and consultation, and provided free drug samples when he could. Later, when I had my drugstore, they told me they didn't want things for free. I would charge them cost and mail things to them. They paid me when they could and always paid. When Dad could get other drug samples I could use, I would give credit to them on their bill, to try and help out. Later, when my mother was very sick and stayed with them in Galveston, again we did what we could. They never asked for any additional help or told us it was a financial strain.

F.H. died on March 26, 1977 and Nana died on July 4, 1979. They were both buried in Grace Memorial Cemetery in Hitchcock. I was fortunate to have seen both of them not long before they passed away. I went down for Nana's funeral and my Dad went with me. My mother, Beulah, had already died August 29, 1975, prior to their deaths.

It was after this that the family—Dad, Joey, Tom, Beulah Ann, Charlie and me—were contacted by the Rayner side of the family. It seems, according to them, that the financial strain was heavy on F.H. and Nana and "they" had helped over the years and during their illnesses, with the expenses. During this time they didn't want to bother us. Now they thought it would be only fair if we would sign over to them Beulah's one-fourth share of the estate of her parents. We were shocked but all agreed that if they needed it that bad, they were welcome to it. But needless to say, this has left a sore spot between the two families to this day.

CHAPTER 8

LAMONT

When I first moved into Lamont neither Grandma Golda nor I were sure what we were getting into. Although we had always gotten along, we weren't sure it would be the same, trying to live in the same house day in and day out. I had already previously had a run-in with my other grandmother, Nana, about a year or two before. This came to a head when evidently my mother had told her what a terrible child I was and how horridly I had behaved. When I started to tell my side about the drinking and fighting, she didn't want to hear it and we ended up having words. This was something I couldn't imagine happening between Golda and I.

The situation was different between me and my grandfather. He was dictatorial in the way in which he dealt with me and I didn't like it. I did respect him but with time it did get to the point I would argue with him. When I was little I would usually do as he said—although as most little boys do, I had been known to ignore direct instructions. Once when Joey and I were playing outside at Lamont we decided to go down by the fishpond. The pond was about 3 to 4 feet wide, about 6 to 8 feet long and 2 feet or so deep. It was off limits. I was riding a tricycle that was at their house and it was decided I should ride the tricycle into the pond. I can remember the water was cold and out of nowhere Paw appeared. He pulled the tricycle out with one hand and after he had removed me from the pond, he took me by my right ear and led me on the tips of my toes up to the house. I just knew my ear was going to come off at any moment. It did hurt. That was about the only time I can ever remember him doing anything to me. I know both he and Golda had no problem with the idea of giving a few good swats but for the life of me, I can't remember ever being given any.

Paw was always good to me. He spent a lot of time with us at the ranch teaching us to fish and hunt. At times when we were in town, he would take us out to the airport to watch the planes and play on the game machines. This was back when you could be just on the other side of a wire fence from the planes as they started up the prop driven-type engines. The noise was loud and the wind from them was almost strong enough to blow you over. When we were older—in elementary school and early junior high—he would sometimes call and ask who wanted to go with him on a consultation. This was when he was going to be flying in a private plane down to Mexico or the border, to see a patient. H.B. Zachary was one of his patient's and with his not wanting anything to happen to Dr. Joe, he would tell him to call anytime and he would have one of his pilots fly him down in one of his planes. It was an experience landing on the dirt roads and the fields on the ranches.

It was also during these years, that several times he and Golda drove us down to the border town of Loredo for the day. These were some experiences I don't think I'll ever forget. He really liked Mexico and he liked talking to the people in Spanish. It would open the door for you when you spoke their language. We would walk the streets and look in all the shops. We would usually have lunch in one of the nice cafe-restaurants but the main thing to us was the shopping. So many items made of glass, metal, silver, out of coins, out of almost anything. I remember I wanted a string puppet one time, of a little Mexican man. He bought it for me and I played with it all the way home. I was so proud of it; I had to show it to the other kids and my folks. So, you see, we spent a fair amount of time around each other and we did get along.

However, I did find early on that Paw saw things very black and white . . . about when to study, when to talk on the phone and where I should be. Going back to when we first were given grades in school, he always wanted to see them and would pay us so much for each A, each B, and so on. Unfortunately I didn't exactly get rich in the early days although I got my share later on. Golda, perhaps after having the experience of raising my father, saw that it was going to take a different approach with me. Very early on, she explained to me she would work with me on what I wanted to do, as long as I did several things for her the way she wanted them done. I was to keep my grades up, stay out of trouble and let her know what was going on—and above all, I was not to ever lie to her. As long as I did this, she would let me take her car to go out on dates, drive around at night, take a day off from school every now and then, and talk on the phone more than I should. She also gave me an allowance of about $5 a week, as well as a little extra sometimes.

The car was to be kept clean by me and the service up to date. All I had to do was book it in for maintenance and let her know when the gas was getting low and she would fill it up. Later, I could take it to the station we usually went to and charge it. I always liked a clean car and on average I washed it at least 2 to 3 times a week. Since most of my friends could not go out on school nights, I wasn't worried about driving the streets most nights. Friday nights were usually one night I did want, and usually got the car. Saturday and Sunday were the problem as they usually went to the ranch on Saturday morning and didn't come back until about 5 PM on Sunday. I could still go out for awhile after they came home but it was a school night.

I went with them to the ranch some of the time at first, and once every now and then, later on. I was getting to the point I was much more interested in girls and the social side of school. This was my focus and plans for dates and dances on weekends were usually first in my mind. I had only about one, or maybe two, good friends through high school. I was lucky to have that many. A lot of people that are so-called friends are usually users and after something. It sounds cynical but when you look back at it over the years, it is usually true.

I had a number of short-term friends over the years at school and you saw them year in and year out. One guy I had spent a lot of time with since early junior high, was always borrowing a few dollars off me. He rarely paid it back. As I became more active at school we had less to do with each other and after I turned him down a few times on money, we really didn't see much of each other. At one stage he spent so much time at the house on Wyndale you would have almost thought he lived with us. He enjoyed going places and doing things with us and always enjoyed sharing whatever we had—that is, until the money ran out.

Another friend I had was about a year older than I was and he was in the same grade but had fallen behind a year in school early on. His father was in the army and they had moved around a lot which had caused some of his problems. He had settled down (if he had been a problem) by the time I knew him. We were both a bit more serious than some of the other kids–even though you might find it hard to believe when some of the stories were told about us acting the fool at times. His parents were fairly strict and had set rules for him that he had to follow. If he didn't he was usually put on restriction and grounded. His Dad was a sergeant as I remember and was strong enough and large enough to persuade him to see things his way if they had a difference of opinion. John Dietle was his name and years later he was my best man. He was probably the only true male friend I can remember having. He was polite, considerate and had manners. When he came over to the house he would pick up after himself and offer to help. The grandparents liked him and he was always welcome. Years later when I talked to him and he found out Golda had died, he almost cried.

We never got in trouble when we were together. We drove around a lot and listened to the radio, and talked about all our troubles. We would go to the food drive-in places and sometimes sit there for over an hour, just talking and watching who was out and about with whom. We double dated a few times and went to a few dances and parties but most of the time we were together we just spent it visiting with each other, and getting away from everyone else.

When I moved in with my grandparents I kept it very quiet at first. I had moved to another school district and even though my parents still lived in the district, it could have become a problem (mainly in sports). The schools were funny about eligibility and any time they thought they had something on a kid at one of the other schools, they would turn him in and try and get him disqualified from playing on the team. This is one reason I quit football. I had already that year gone to summer camp and was all but guaranteed a position on the junior varsity team with better than even prospects of playing varsity from the next year on. I had started the school year still on the team and plans to continue on. After I had moved to my grandparents and the subjects I had signed up for—which included more science and math—started to give out our homework assignments, I realized it was going to be very difficult, if not impossible, for me. I was also interested in the social side of school life and this was also going to take up part of my time. So without talking to anyone, I went and turned in my equipment and quit the team.

The next thing I knew, I had one of the coaches calling me out of class for a conference. They were absolutely shocked. I had been playing the last couple of years with the same kids that I was to play with again. All of them were top players and they had already figured me as part of their plans. I didn't tell them the truth about what was going on, I just told them about the extra studying I needed to do and that my grades concerned me. They then offered to help tutor me if I needed help and wanted me to come back. I didn't. If I remember rightly, 3 of the kids I played with got scholarships (2 went to Arkansas and one to Baylor) and one kid a year older went to Texas A&M. About a week after this, the track coach came to see me. I had been timed before in football and during a school program on fitness. He told me he knew he could get me a scholarship in track at Texas Tech if I would run track and was interested. I hated running and only did so when I needed to. I told him "Thanks but no thanks". These are always some of the things you look back at years later and wonder 'what if'. It may have amounted to nothing . . . something I'll never know.

John Dietle and I became good friends and he was one of the few that knew I was living with my grandparents. He could, on rare occasions, get the family car for a date or on a Saturday night to go somewhere. I only remember it was an old car of some sort. The real pride and joy was his father's car which could be used only on special occasions—a Cadillac that was about 6 years old. I would supply the car for things we wanted to do—usually Sunday night through Friday night. He would supply the car when he could, on the other times. Later on, in the case of a real difficult situation, I would sometimes take my grandparents to the ranch and drop them off and go back for them the next day (on Sunday). This was a bit dangerous considering their age and if anything happened to one of them, the other one would have had to walk about 2 miles to the nearest phone.

Sometimes, especially if the weather was bad, they would stay home and I could have the car almost all weekend. So, all in all, it was not a bad arrangement and sometimes when I didn't have a car I would just stay home and watch TV or talk on the phone. Sometimes Joey would come by with some of his friends but as time went on we went our own way and saw less of each other.

We had spent some time previously driving around together and had gone out in the country to a place called 1320 where they would drag race at night. [1320 being the number of feet in a quarter mile—the distance they raced.] The cops didn't like this and would try to catch the kids. Not very long after we had become acquainted with this place, Double Eagle Drag Way opened not far from there. It was a racetrack set up on private property for drag racing, paved strip, lights, safety equipment and everything. This is where the Edsel and the Plymouth Fury went for their outings. The Chevrolet had made a couple of trips but the hotrod was the one we were building for the strip. Joey and some of his friends would come over to work on the car on weekends sometimes and one time after we had it running, it caught on fire and almost burnt up because of a fuel leak by the motor.

I spent a lot of time cleaning it up again and buying new fuel lines, and we got it back to where it was again. It would start and it went around the block. The noise was terrific since it was running straight exhaust and consequently couldn't be run for very long. One of Joey's friends wanted to buy the hotrod from me and after awhile I decided it would be best to sell it. I think we agreed on something like $300 or $350. I am not sure if he gave me $50 when he picked it up or not. I do remember for sure that he never gave me a cent after that. The motor alone was worth more than that, and the body and frame should have sold for $300 but then it was not everybody's cup of tea. Joey told me that Edgar had taken the motor out and put it in his '48 Pontiac. He had been told it was a real screamer and he had been racing it from the stoplights on the Austin Highway where everyone drove up and down to be seen. Seems one night he was racing and he blew the motor up. That is why he wasn't very interested in paying any money to me and used this as a built-in excuse. Another early lesson I should have learned sooner, about friends and money.

I settled into a routine and found if I usually did my homework after I first came home from school it worked out better. Golda would take me to school and pick me up after school. I was usually the one allowed to do the driving. When we would get to the house and go inside, we usually would have a cup of coffee and a couple of cookies along with, more often than not, a conversation about the day or whatever else we wanted to talk about. A lot of times it was school, assignments, other kids or what was coming up. Sometimes we talked about the family or what some of my plans might be but very little, as at that time, I wasn't sure myself. I knew that it was most likely going to be science-related, so my studies were aimed at university with a science and math background. By late high school I had finally found myself taking advanced science and math courses although I was still struggling with "English". In fact, after one of the math courses I had passed with a good grade, I decided not to take any more advanced classes. It wasn't because you had more homework; it was because you could make it through the course and still not have any idea of what was going on. I felt like I had missed part of my building blocks for my math in the future.

After our talks I would sit at the dining room table and do my homework. Golda would be just through the doorway in the kitchen, preparing dinner. This way we could still talk to each other and I could ask her questions and get help without being under her feet.

My father would bring Dr. Joe home and drop him off—usually between 4:30 and 5:00. He would come in with his afternoon daily papers and sit at the end of the table where he had both his lamp and magnifying glass that he used to help him read. Sometimes we would visit a bit but usually he would read the news and I would do my homework. When the evening news came on TV we usually went into the living room and watched it. About this time Golda would have dinner ready and we would pull out our TV dinner tables and eat as we watched the news and programs in the early part of the evening.

After about 8:00 o'clock, Dr. Joe was ready for bed and would head upstairs. He did try at one stage to help me with my homework when I was taking Spanish. It was mainly to fulfill a requirement for two years of a foreign language to get into university. He had always had a knack for foreign languages and wanted to help me. So for awhile when he would get home, we would go into the living room and try to do my lessons. This turned into a disaster. I was having a hard time with the subject and didn't understand it very well. When I tried to speak it, my accent and pronunciation was so bad that Dr. Joe would throw his hands up in the air and tell me not to speak it to someone or I would insult them as it was so bad. We would both become frustrated and angry. It was at this time that Golda would step in, and suggest I try it on my own and practice more at school.

Golda helped me with "English", and my essays and spelling. Dr. Joe did help me but it was usually later on in biology and health when I had to write papers and he would then read them over to give me suggestions. This worked out because the main thing was the report cards that came out every 6 weeks. As long as the grades were up we all got along.

At times I didn't have a lot of homework and I would find myself visiting with grandma Golda in the kitchen while she cooked. One day when we were visiting she started showing me more and more tips about cooking. She told me she felt like it might be something that would come in handy for me. At first I think she was thinking of me being home on my own on weekends. Later on, I think she thought it was more than just that. I am not sure but she was right—it came in handy for me in the years to come.

CHAPTER 9

THE NEW CAR

When I first moved in with my grandparents they had only one car, a '58 Buick. It was my grandmother's car, as Dr. Joe had to quit driving and had previously sold his '59 Chevrolet Impala. His eyesight had gotten to the point it was hard for him to see, due to the cataracts. One day when he was coming home and was in downtown traffic at a stoplight, a lady stepped out from the sidewalk just as the light changed. She claimed he went against the light and hit her. Some of the witnesses said she stepped out against the light and walked into his car just as he was starting to go through the intersection. The insurance company settled out of court as it was only a bump and a bruise but then informed him they would no longer insure him.

He looked at alternatives—including posting $15,000 dollars with the State, as that was the minimum required liability amount to carry at that time. This was not very practical because if he was in an accident, the first thing that would happen is the person would sue the doctor for all they could get. He knew it was only a matter of time with his eyesight anyway, so he gave up driving. From then on Golda, and later I, were his chauffeurs. He did have cataract surgery later on to help his vision but I don't think he felt it was good enough to take up driving again.

I started pushing early on, for him to consider buying me a car. I looked in the newspaper to find out prices of different models that I thought I might like and he might consider. I presented him with a range of used vehicle prices including a '57 Chevrolet Bel Air, a '58 Ford—and then proceeded to give him every reason in the world why this was a good idea. In short, he summed it up with NO! Too much money and it would interfere with my schoolwork. This was an ongoing saga for a number of months until I knew I was getting nowhere and Golda told me to drop it as it wasn't going to happen. She left me to it for awhile. I think she knew I needed to give it a try and get it out of my system as, until then, I wasn't going to listen anyway.

It must have been at least 6 months after this, maybe longer, that one day as we sat at the table, he brought up the subject of cars. What did I think of this kind or that? Just a few short exchanges and then he dropped it. I was getting my hopes up and having some good daydreams. Unfortunately Mom and Dad were still continuing on with their drinking just as they had been when I left. Consequently some days Dad didn't go to the office. One day as I was driving Dr. Joe home after picking him up from the office, he told me he wanted to look at some cars. The Buick was past the depreciation time for income tax and since he used it for work and had it available for calls, he needed to replace it.

Previously, I had been with him years before when he purchased the '59 Chevrolet. He had stopped in several times at Eperson Motors in Boerne and tried to make a deal with Mr Eperson, for cash. He always paid cash for everything. He said he had learned as a kid how hard it was living in debt and once you got out of it, you should never get in it again. In fact he felt like if you couldn't pay cash, you couldn't afford it until you saved for it. The day we picked up the Chevrolet he asked Mr. Eperson if he was sure that was the best he could do. They talked a few minutes, and then he reached in his weekend khaki pants' pocket and pulled out a handful of paper money. He then proceeded to count the money out on the hood of the car. He finished up the paperwork and we drove off in his new car.

This time he wanted to surprise Golda and we were to do the shopping and not let her know. Uncle Gene, Aunt Mary's husband, was working for Cecil Tindall at Tindall Pontiac as office manager. He had gone to work for him after he left Charles Orsinger Buick in about 1959. The move was only about 8 blocks up the street on San Pedro. Uncle Gene had helped him buy the Buick in 1958 and consequently Dr. Joe decided to see if he could help this time. One day after school, he had me drive over and see Uncle Gene at the dealership. Uncle Gene had the Buick appraised and we looked at several models, and he gave me several prices and brochures to take back to Dr. Joe.

Pontiac, since about 1959, had started to become more popular and was trying to appeal to the younger set. Their new wide track campaign and flash coupe models were among the most popular. I had no problem with a Pontiac as long as it was a coupe and not a 4-door sedan or station wagon. My grandparents had bought 4 door models, as they were much more practical for them to use. I showed Paw the brochures and the figures. We talked about it and I tried to get him interested in the coupes. I told him they had a Bonneville Coupe (top of the line model), on the showroom floor that was a sort of blue-green and the interior was various shades of blue. He liked blue and wanted a blue car.

For as long as I could remember when the weekends came, Dr. Joe would switch off. He would put on his weekend clothes which consisted of khaki pants, big outdoor boots and maybe a flannel or khaki shirt. He usually didn't shave on weekends and he could start to look a little rough. He always enjoyed his beer and if he had one open he would sometimes put it into his big khaki pants pockets for safe keeping and take it along with him. On one such a day he had me drive him over to see this car I had told him about. We walked into the showroom to look at the car and not a soul came over to talk to us. I went over to the window at the counter and had them let Uncle Gene know he had someone to see him. As we looked at the car, Dr. Joe and Uncle Gene talked price. He then reached in his pocket and pulled out a handful of paper money and he counted out the money on the trunk of the car. He signed some papers and I was instructed to come back the first of the week and it would be ready to pick up. After this he was ready to go. He had a sip of his beer and he told me "Vamanos"—let's go.

The looks on the faces of the salesmen that watched from a distance as the money was counted out, were priceless. This poor old man that no one would so much as say hello to, just paid cash for the car. I think Uncle Gene got a kick out of it as well. I think as I look back at it, he must have already talked to both Golda and Uncle Gene before we went over. He already had a price for how much he needed for that one–unless he just took plenty—and the only other question was whether he and Golda could live with a 2-door coupe. He could only decide that once we were there and he could see it in person, to try getting in and out of it. If he felt it wasn't acceptable we could have always looked at some of the other vehicles and we didn't. Maybe this was a concession to me since I couldn't have my own car—at least it would be one I liked. I like to think they did it on purpose to try and give me a little something I liked as well.

The next week I picked up the new car and we were all happy. This was a new '61 Pontiac Bonneville Coupe and was the new model for about a year. It was my pride and joy as well. In fact the family joked about the fact that it was a wonder the car had any paint left on it as I was constantly washing and waxing it. They set up a charge account at the dealership so, as the service intervals came up, I could make arrangements to take the car in and have the maintenance done. This had to be done after school or on Saturday mornings. This was not very convenient and a few times I skipped school. Other times I would take the car and set up an appointment. They would then have the car picked up and delivered back later. They would hook a 3-wheel motorcycle on the back bumper and one man would run around picking up and dropping cars off to customers. Most of the time things went well and were just fine.

It was during this time on one of my visits for service after school that I went in to see Uncle Gene. The girl that was the service cashier was attractive and someone I had not seen before. I finished with the service department, took the car and parked it outside. I had some business with Uncle Gene and visited with him for a few minutes and asked who she was. He said it was the owner's daughter, Cecile Tindall, and that she sometimes worked after school as cashier. She was going to Robert E. Lee high school and was about a year older than me. He then got up and said to come with him. He took me around the corner to the cashier and introduced me to her. This was my introduction to what was to later become my first wife.

After this I hung around the cashier's station when I went to get the car serviced. It was almost to the point I felt someone was going to tell me to leave her alone so she could work. I got to know a number of other people at the dealership as well, as time went on. When summer came that year I saw her at times at one of the drive-in food places on San Pedro. As I got to know her better I ended up getting her phone number and started calling her and eventually asked her out on a date. This actually took some time and was over a number of months.

Dr. Joe and Golda were happy, and I was happy. My grades were good and I was staying out of trouble. I was not one to get into trouble much by then anyway; it was mainly only the odd fight, and they had become few and far between by now. I was happy to drive either one of them anywhere they wanted to go in our new car.

It was during this time I drove grandma Golda up to Graham, Texas, to see her brother who was in the hospital. We made the trip out to the old homestead and she showed me around and told me the stories relating back to her childhood.

Dr. Joe was having me pick him up, when necessary, after work. This gave Golda a break as she was taking him to work each morning at about 6 o'clock. Sometimes he would want to see an old patient of his on the way home and I would take him to make what I would describe as a social house call. I remember one, a Mrs. Riebe, a Russian, who would make breads and pastries and have us come by and pick them up. One was a bufta (I'm not sure of the spelling); sort of a bread with dates or something in it, that required an acquired taste. Her efforts were always appreciated even though we had been unable to get accustomed to the taste of many of her products. We shared them around the family and any of the neighbors that were interested. As soon as the previously initiated saw us coming they would call out "Mrs. Riebe, bufta!"

It was actually nice to see that a number of his old patients still considered him more than a doctor; a friend. This was something I was able to see by being with him both when I was younger and again when I was older, driving him on calls or consultations. One time when I was about 6 years old or so, he took Joey and I into a jewellery shop in Boerne so he could see the jeweler for a moment. As he went over to see the man, he saw him coming and started falling all over himself to greet Dr. Joe and thank him for coming by. He spent a little time with the man and did whatever he needed to do while Joey and I looked through the cases at all the watches and just stared at them. When they finished and we started to leave the shop the jeweler said stop. In broken English he told Dr. Joe and us that we had been such good boys he wanted to give us something. He started to unlock what seemed to be the backside of the case that had the watches in it and in a flash in my mind, I just knew the old man was going to give me a pocket watch for my very own! As he finished unlocking whatever it was behind the counter, he lifted and placed a box on top of the counter and reached inside it. He said "Here boys"—and handed us each a nickel (a five cent coin). I felt really stupid and unappreciative. I have never figured out why I thought I was going to get such a gift and have never forgotten how I felt so stupid. Here was an old man trying to be nice to a couple of kids who really weren't owed anything and yet I expected something way out of proportion when I was told he was going to give me a gift. Maybe I was the born optimist.

I had gone on a couple of calls with my father when I was very young but usually sat and waited in the car. One exception was when he called on a very old lady, a Mrs. Rubenstein, who I guess must have been at least 90 at the time. She was an old Russian and both Dr. Joe and my father had looked after her. She heard one of the children was in the car and wanted me to come in so she could meet me. It was the first time I had ever met anyone that old and she was so sick she was almost nothing but skin and bones. She was nice and after we visited a few minutes we left. After she died she left an amethyst ring to my mother—which she later gave to Joey's first wife. It was supposed to have come from the Russian Czar's family from back when Mrs Rubenstein still lived in Russia. Again, it was nice to see that some of the patients of both my father and grandfather considered them more than just their doctor.

I drove Dr. Joe on some consultations to Gonzales, Texas, as well as other outings. For me it was a treat to get to drive the new car and any excuse was fine with me. Little did I know at that time just how much I would be driving this car over the next couple of years.

CHAPTER 10

CECILE

On one of the first dates I had with Cecile, I took her out to eat at a restaurant. My father had previously offered me the use of his charge account at 'La Louisianne Restaurant'. I made arrangements and took her to this restaurant. We had the three courses and I remember the bill at the end of the evening was just over $100. That was a lot of money back then for a table of two but everything was fine and nothing was ever said to me about it. In fact, as a present to me one time, my folks offered to let me take another couple as well and they would again pick up the bill. This I did later on.

We started seeing each other a lot after this and were on the phone almost all the time. Our relationship was not always smooth and we had a number of misunderstandings. At times either one of us might be a bit jealous or not sure exactly what was going on. We were going to different schools and the time we spent with each other was mainly on weekends or during the summer.

By the time the second summer came around that we knew each other (the summer of '62) we were both crazy about each other. When I say crazy I mean we both acted crazy at times as well. I would have arguments with my grandfather as he felt I was spending too much time with her and getting too serious. She was older than I was and he was not overly fond of Cecil, her father. I had already heard rumors that he was a real lady's man but dismissed it as I found him very friendly and he seemed to be nice to me. I would eat dinner at their house several times a week, which gave us a chance to get to know each other.

At times when he had our misunderstandings it would get to the point we would break up. It would usually be over being jealous or being possessive. I was possessive and she would get jealous at times, just as I would. As I remember, every time we broke up she was the one who wanted to call it quits; this did not help me feel very secure in our relationship. One time it was so serious and no matter how hard I tried to see her she wouldn't, that Henry, her brother, got involved and talked to her. He got her to see me and we started going together again.

John, my friend, would talk to me when we would drive around sometimes. He felt the relationship was getting me tied up in knots and was not sure it was the best thing for me to continue "chasing her" as he put it. We had some words ourselves about this and he eventually dropped the subject. As I spent more time with Cecile I saw less of him and my other schoolmates.

I stayed active in the Student Council and school activities that were carried out mainly during the daytime. This enabled me to be free during the evenings to either talk to or see Cecile. We knew during that school year that led up to the summer of '62, that it would be her last school year in town as she would be moving to Austin to attend university in the fall. I wanted to make the most of the time we had left with each other and spend every possible moment we could with each other. It was very uncertain to me just exactly what would happen when she moved and this caused a great amount of anxiety.

She was to go to Austin and start university as a business major. This was with the idea that she would eventually go to work for her father and help with the bookkeeping at the dealership. This made me very nervous as I felt the extra distance would be just one more obstacle.

As we started into the summer we were both nervous about the coming fall. I wanted to prove I was committed to the relationship and I wanted her to prove the same. So, I asked her to run off with me and get married in Mexico. We could run down to Laredo and go across to Nuevo Laredo on a Saturday afternoon and be back early that evening and no one would even know we had gone. This way we would be married to each other and would each know the other was committed to the relationship. At first she didn't want to do this. She said mainly because of her folks. As we talked more and more about it, we agreed we would get married the next year anyway after I graduated from high school. She could have her big wedding then, be married twice, and we would all be happy.

Finally on July 7, 1962, we ran off to Nuevo Laredo, Mexico and got married. We got back early that Saturday evening and no one even suspected. This was the beginning of a very difficult year.

We both knew we had to keep it a secret so it wouldn't get back to our folks or back to the school. Back in the early 60's, high schools were known to expel married students. I don't know if they were afraid it was contagious or would just corrupt the whole student body. Cecile lived in a student boarding house at one stage and later in a school dormitory. Again, the possibility of being asked to leave, existed if they found out she was a married student.

When school first started that fall, her parents would drive her back to Austin. They would usually ask me to go with them and later they would allow me to drive. I think they wanted to make sure I was a safe driver because early on, they allowed me to drive her back to Austin on my own on Sunday nights.

I would call her long distance several times a week to see how she was getting on as well as writing her almost every day. When the phone bills started coming in it was made clear to me that I would have to pay for my calls out of my allowance. This limited how often and how long I would talk to her while she was in Austin. Each day after school now I sat at the table and would write a letter. Then I would walk to the end of the block and mail it. It had a 5 PM pick up so if I did this first thing after school, she was sure to get it the next day.

When I was having disagreements with Dr. Joe—a lot of times about Cecile and the amount of time we spent together—I would find myself writing to her expressing my anger about him. The only good that came out of this was I got the anger out of my system without taking it out on him or anyone else. Cecile and I still had disagreements and our arguments sometimes went back and forth in the letters, sometimes on the phone and other times later on, I would drive up to Austin to see her in person.

Golda would let me leave in the early evening as long as I came back as soon as I could. Some nights the curfew was 10:00 PM and on weekends it was something like midnight or 1:00 AM at the student dormitories. It was an hour and a half each way, so some nights I wouldn't get home until 2:30 in the morning.

Sometimes the misunderstandings would be over something that a simple explanation could take off. One time I was upset because she admitted she had gone out a couple of times with a guy. Then she explained he was helping her with one of her subjects and had been introduced by a friend. By having seen him a couple of times during the week, no one suspected she was married and according to her, he did help her with her subject.

By the time the school year was almost over, the two-year-old model Pontiac had over 60,000 miles on it. This was done while I still attended school during the daytime. I must have gone to Austin five times a week. Dr. Joe purchased another Pontiac before the school year was over. It was a '63 Pontiac Bonneville coupe, a dark blue that was almost black, with a white interior. I had spent so much time having the car maintenance done at the dealership (plus one part-time job doing filing one time), that I knew almost everyone at the dealership in every department.

My parents liked Cecile and her family. They had no reason not to like them. When they decided it was time to switch cars they asked me to help, as they wanted to buy Pontiacs as well. This started a long line of car purchases that lasted for years and accounted for about 10 new cars by 1968. Over the years, the family (including my brothers) purchased around 30 cars—between new and used. At one point, after Joey quit school, he went to work at the dealership and became a GM-trained mechanic, before he was drafted into the army.

Joey had dropped out of school and run off to marry a girl, Susan Elkins. The family was upset about him not finishing school. He had taken things like shop in high school and always liked mechanics. He took training and worked at the dealership and later for Southwest Auto Research. Joey and Susan had a little boy, Joe III, who died when he was only a few months old while staying at my parents' house. The cause of death was cot death. This devastated the family. I was still living with my grandparents at the time and can still remember when Dr. Joe came into the room where Golda and I were, to tell us the news. He broke down and started crying. Joey and Susan had a rocky relationship but they had another child later on, John. She ended up running off with another man, divorced Joey and then notified the draft board that his marital status had changed and he was now eligible for the draft. He was drafted into the army and became a tank mechanic and was sent to Vietnam.

As the school year came to an end and my graduation approached, the subject of university came up again. I had applied to a number of schools and was accepted by most as well. I had been talking to both my folks and grandparents about it. It was around this time I told them that Cecile and I wanted to get married.

Dr. Joe was very upset. He told me it was a big mistake to get married before I had any education and training. I had no job. I had no way to take care of a family and if I did, I wouldn't be able to go to school. We argued and yelled at each other for many an hour but this made me even more determined. Golda did not agree with me but did not get upset with me either. My parents were surprisingly supportive. Cecil and Elizabeth were more at the stage where they wanted to try and talk us either out of it or at least to wait. Cecil tried to ask me where I thought we were going to get enough money to live on, much less be able to afford to buy the kinds of things and clothes Cecile was accustomed to. We went over the price of dresses—some $50 and others as much as $100—and everything else.

Eventually, after much discussion they agreed. As I remember, the folks talked it over with each other, as well as with the grandparents. I really don't know why they finally gave in. I can only guess they figured she was of age and already could do what she wanted, and that as I was so hard-headed I wasn't going to back down. So they might as well make the best of it and try to be supportive.

Graduation day came for me and the plan was I would go to the municipal auditorium with my grandparents. Go to the staging area, put on the robe, go through the ceremony and then when it was over, change and catch a ride back to my grandparents' house with Cecile. They wanted to have a little party and give me a few little gifts to congratulate me on my first graduation. So much for plans.

After the ceremony I went outside the main entrance and looked around. I waited and waited. No one was there. It seemed like at least an hour went by when all of a sudden Cecile drove up. She said she didn't realize I was to ride back with her so she went on to the party and left me behind. They all had a big laugh about it and said they could just picture me standing there, looking around with no one in sight. I failed to see any humor in it and was very upset. It reminded me of the old days of waiting. I was hurt to have been so easily forgotten.

Once the question of marriage was settled, the families were all supportive. Dr. Joe was supportive and from that day on, only had praise for Cecile. He had taken out insurance education policies on each of the grandchildren, to mature when they turned 18. He gave us, or I should say Cecile, the check for $2,000. For some reason he always felt the women should handle the money, so when he gave money to Joey, Tom, or me he would always give it to the wives. This would be enough to furnish our first house we had later on—the kitchen dinette, the living room sofa, chairs, tables, lamps, bedroom suite with bed, chest of drawers and dresser, and more—with money left over. It was good down-the-middle-type quality furniture at that time.

The plan for the first two years was for me to go to San Antonio Junior College where it would be less expensive to go. We would have the support of home by living in San Antonio as she could work for her father at the dealership. I was sure that once things settled down I would be able to get a part-time job as well. As long as we were together, that is all that mattered to me. I knew things would be tight and we wouldn't have much until I got out of school. I was sure we were in it together. I didn't realize our plans had already been changed. She had become pregnant in May.

Plans were made and the date was set for the wedding, July 7, 1963. The same date, July 7, which we had been married on the year before. Later Cecile told me she had told her mother that we had run off to become married the year before. I don't know if that influenced her much or not as she never said anything to me about it.

Cecile and Elizabeth, her mother, had been going to the Lutheran Church in Alamo Heights next to Alamo Heights High School for the last couple of years. I had gone with them on a number of occasions and later Cecile and I went on our own at times, on Sunday. We agreed that we would get married at that church as I was just as happy with that as the Episcopal Church in Alamo Heights by T.M.I.

The wedding was to be the big one she wanted and the reception was to be held at Oak Hills Country Club after the wedding. I don't remember how many guests were invited but it had to have been in the hundreds—between all the people both families invited. Doctors, lawyers, other auto dealers, businessmen and anybody who counted, seemed to have been invited.

We had the usual announcements in the paper, as well as the engraved invitations sent out. The stores were listed where all the usual "suggested gifts" by the bride could be found. The china pattern that we picked out, the silverware pattern and so on. We ended up getting, as I remember, a complete setting for 6—both china and silverware—with bits and pieces of china and silverware for up to 8 place settings.

When all the gifts were in we had multiples of items; toasters, blenders, and the like. We also received towels and sheet sets, flatware sets, and lots of other items for setting up house. It saved us a fortune no doubt and gave us a head start.

After the wedding and the reception we left, and drove John Dietle, my best man, back to Louisiana. We stayed at his parents' house that night and the next day. We saw a little of the area and then had to get back to our new life in our apartment on Magnolia street, about a mile or so from the college. I had to get back to school and she had to get back to work. She also had to write thank you notes to all the folks we had received gifts from. The girl in charge of the register and gifts wrote on the cards what each person had given us, so it was going to take a long time to write and drop a note in the mail to each and every one to say thank you. I didn't know just how long it was going to take until later on. She never did send a single thank you note.

CHAPTER 11

LIVING TOGETHER

When we started living together our rent was $65.00 a month for a furnished apartment. Canned goods on sale at the store were 10 cans for $1. Sugar was 19 cents a pound. Cecile was getting paid about $250.00 a month for a 40-hour week. At first she was able to keep the company car she had been driving but we were told this was going to come to an end.

I walked home from school after class and did my homework before she got home from work on most days. Sometimes when I had a lot of homework it would take me into the evening to get it done. Cecile's morning sickness seemed to start almost as soon as we moved into the apartment. She had an extremely severe case of it and at times was almost unable to go to work, much less do anything around the place.

Cecil had tried to get Henry to go to San Antonio Junior College. He wanted him to get a better education as he had only just made it through high school. He offered him an allowance and a Mercedes Benz 300SL if he would go (he had the Mercedes franchise as well at the time). Cecil even asked me if I would help tutor Henry in his classes if he could get him to go. I told him yes but no matter what he did, he couldn't get him to go. It may have been just as well for me since I found myself busy enough as it was.

Cecile tried to cook although she had very limited experience. One time she tried to make a coffeecake to surprise me. I gave it a try and found it didn't taste bad at all. I did have one question—what were the little black crunchy bits in it? She said "Coffee . . . the book said to put in one cup of coffee when you make it". It was a good try. As time went on I helped when I could and did some of the cleaning. The one job I got to hate was cleaning out the refrigerator. We hated to throw leftovers out so we did what most folks do. Put them in the refrigerator and wait for them to turn color, grow some sort of growth, develop an awful smell and then throw them out. I made an almost fatal mistake one time when I opened the lid on a pot that had been rice with cinnamon and, I think, a little sugar. I don't know what it had turned into but it almost got the best of me. I couldn't face this mixture again for years.

I started looking for a part-time job in the paper as we both felt we needed a little more money with a baby on the way. I got a job that was part-time with a company doing sales in the evening and on Saturday. It was the Cory Coffee Company's Flavor Seal Division. We made appointments to see people in their home and gave them a free coffee maker—a very good one that I used for years myself. For this they were to allow us to show them the home products we offered. This was mainly stainless steel cookware that had cast iron on the inside and an air gap between the layers—a product that is still copied today. We also offered a Melamine (plastic) dinnerware that was unbreakable and dishwasher-safe, as well as knives and other products. This could be for those getting married or for those who wanted the best. Of course we offered the pay by the month plan as well.

After I learned the products and the company demonstration I was turned out into the field with some of the leads that had come into the company from customers. We were to always ask for referrals and the more they gave us, the more free gifts the person got. If any of their leads bought from us too, then they were entitled to even more. I had a few sales and a few failures. Most of all, Cecile and the family did not like me out at night or on Saturdays selling. But my parents liked the product so much they bought us a set of the products as a gift, and another set for Joey and Susan. The product was top quality but maybe a little on the high priced side which made it difficult for a lot of people to be able to buy it.

We were also looking for a place closer to the school that would cost us less money and yet give us a little more room. Joey and Susan told us that the other side of the duplex they lived in was coming up for rent. It was near the school, had a yard and a shared garage. It was larger and cost, as I remember, about

$50 per month. The place was run down and you had to put books under one end of the bed to level it. It wasn't ideal but we felt it would clean up, so we moved in.

Cecil had a fit. He said he wouldn't let his daughter live in such a place or such an area. I don't think that was all of it. I don't think he liked the idea of us living next door to, and being around, my brother. They never seemed to get a long around each other and there was always an atmosphere.

We didn't live there long. After only a couple of months Cecil came to us and said he had been working on a surprise for us. He claimed he had been trading up a used car for us for a long time. He had traded for an old Chevrolet, fixed it up, sold it, took the money put it in another one and did it again, and so on, down at the dealership. He had a chance to trade the car for the equity in a house on Sprucewood, near North Star Mall. We went with him and found that he had traded for the house and was having a friend of his (Palmer Painting) paint the inside of it before we were to move in. We took over the existing G.I. (previous) military loan at 4 ½ % interest, with payments of $90 per month.

He wanted me to give up the part-time job and said it wasn't necessary. Cecile and I were to make the best of it as our first house. We bought the furniture for it out of the savings and set up house. It had a fenced-in back yard, a carport, and two bedrooms—or three if you counted the back room that was to be a den or a study—two bathrooms, a living area, breakfast-eating area and a kitchen. The house had panel heating in the centre of the house and two window air conditioners—one in the living area and one in the back bedroom. One thing Cecile wanted to do as a treat, was to fix up our bedroom. She had a decorating company in town make custom drapes for our room and install new carpet in it.

The house was in a convenient location for family but not for school. We were about halfway between my grandparents and her folks. We were only a few blocks off Loop 410, which was convenient to get to my folks' house. When Sam Jr. was born 10 February 1964, everything changed again for us. My parents and grandparents came by to see Sam and gave him some presents. My mother gave a present for Cecile (she did this again when we had our other children later on, as well), a diaper service. This sounds strange but saved many an hour. All you had to do was put solids in the toilet and swish the diaper out, and then they all went into a container that had a bag and deodorizer. The man came by and exchanged clean ones for dirty ones. They had been washed and run under UV light. These were cotton cloth and not the disposable kind that are available today.

Cecil had Elizabeth Cornelius, the assistant office manager at the dealership, go out and buy a bassinet and presents. He and my mother-in-law brought these over to the house to give them to us. I must admit he was excited about Sambo. Those first number of weeks we had lots of visitors and lots of gifts. I think Cecil had taken each and every one of his friends in hand and brought them by at least once. Again, we didn't have to buy hardly a thing for the new baby.

The doctor, Dr. James Carter, was a friend of my father's and with me being a student, he didn't charge us anything. The hospital was about $150 back then and that was it. Dr. Carter was the doctor for Cecile for all the children and even after I was out of school only charged us what the insurance paid. Regular office calls later on were only a nominal charge at the time. Dr. C. Nau was the kids' pediatrician and again only charged us nominal rates. He also was a friend of my father.

Previously we had given up her company car. For awhile we drove a new car off the lot with the speedo disconnected but had to get it back on the lot when they had what they called a floor check. The company that held the papers and loaned the money for the new cars would come by and see if they were all accounted for. The law was changed later (after this time) on altering odometers and the penalty was so stiff it put a stop to it for all the major dealers. Before this, they had a box that connected to the odometer and would run at about 120 M.P.H. backwards and would take the miles off. This came in handy for cars with a few hundred or a couple of thousand miles you needed to take off.

It was at the point that this was getting to be a problem. Next thing we knew, Cecil informed us he had managed to trade up another car to the point that he had a nice '62 Pontiac Grand Prix that was ours. It was a nice car and took the problem of switching out all the time off our shoulders.

On the home front at my folks' house, Tom, my younger brother, had gone off the rails previously and was a known dope addict. He would go off and act crazy at times, breaking all the windows out in his room and threatening to hurt my parents. I was called at times and had to go over to the house to get things settled down again. Tom and I had a fight with each other from time to time as it was the only way to control him. Once they called Joey and me and told us he had taken one of the cars and run away. We found out from one of his friends that he was heading for Arkansas. Cecile and I loaded Sambo in his bassinet in the back seat of the Grand Prix and headed out, following Joey and Susan. We drove most of the night and by dawn caught up with him. He was to ride back with Joey, and Susan was to drive my folks' car back. I was there in case it took both of us to get him to give up and go home.

As luck would have it, on our way back, when we got to Texarkana we had to stop at a red light. When it changed, Joey was in front and went first. Just as he turned, a car on the inside lane ran the red light and hit him broadside. No one was hurt but the car had a lot of damage. After a couple of hours we were on the road again and made it home. This was just one of the times I would be called about such things at night in the years to come.

By the end of all of this I was about at the end of my rope—with school, the lack of money, everything. I wanted to make some money and get away from the teachers for awhile. I had a couple of teachers that had given me a hard time. One was my first year German teacher. I needed two years of a foreign language (German or French) if I was to be a science major. The first day in class he spoke in German and continued to do so for the entire semester. When I took the final I was sure I had passed, even if not by much. He had a note up by the posted grades asking several students to see him. I went to see him and he explained to me what a hard life he had being a German Jew in the camps and had shown us the number on his arm before, in class. He claimed he wanted to try to help me and told me he would give me a D if I didn't take any more German at the school. I told him that would not do me any good, as I needed more. So he then helped me out by giving me an F and told me I could take the final again. I did and made a B with much less trouble the second time. I don't know if it was because I took it again, or the teacher. The second teacher wasn't as demanding and spoke in both English and German when he taught the class.

I had made my way through English, some of my math, science, and language courses. I had taken open and closed book tests, after hours' tests and timed tests. I needed a B average for the work I had done—which I didn't have—or I needed at least 54 hours and a C average to transfer my work. I needed another semester of work to be over 54 hours. I wasn't sure what I even wanted to do anymore. I could see Cecil and Henry making money and having fun. I don't think I was jealous, I just wanted to have some money to do things and not have to worry about it all the time.

I decided I was going to drop out of school for awhile and make a few dollars while I tried to decide what I wanted to get my degree in. My father and grandfather had already told me they didn't think I should go into medicine. That put me off even trying, although at times I had been considering it. I think they felt I would never get through all the politics involved. They told me that the changes with more government interference were going to change the face of how medicine was practiced so that it wouldn't be worth doing anymore. The new social plans for Medicare with approved suppliers and amounts were on their way in.

I had started to look for a job in the paper when Cecil offered me a job at the dealership. He first put me in the Service Department as a service adviser. I was to get to work by 7 and write up the customer tickets on the cars and then follow the car's progress through the day. If the customer needed to be called for permission for repairs or if problems came up, it was up to the adviser to call and take care of it. From the years of taking the car in for maintenance I was familiar with the routine and knew a lot of the people I was to work with. The service department had two full-time advisers and the service manager, Val Luckett, who would also write tickets when needed.

The advisers were to also sell service and repair jobs when needed. They also faded a lot of heat from unhappy customers. The advisers didn't get paid any commission on warranty tickets but they did on customer-pay jobs. I learned early on that the regular advisers were very protective of what they considered their customers or their jobs—mainly customer-pay ones. I didn't seem to have this problem when it was warranty work tickets I was writing. One day I had a customer who had been calling me on and off for what seemed like all day, giving me a hard time about when his car was going to be ready. I wasn't in a very good mood by late in the day when he called again, so I just put the phone down on the desk and called out to the dispatcher trying to find out about the job. He snapped back, wanting to know why I needed to know so badly. I then proceeded to call out to him "The asshole is on the line again; I need to tell him when it will be ready". That was my first lesson on either using the hold button on the phone or placing your hand over it. Val and Cecil smoothed it over with the customer and I had my first lecture.

They put me into warranty claims processing and light bookwork. I learned how to read the repair orders and code the claims so they would be paid. I got pretty good at it and at times was caught up enough to help with some of the other books. Uncle Gene had me list some of the invoices in a book or check off some, in others. At the time it didn't mean a lot to me as it was looking at only a small piece of the puzzle. I remember looking at the invoices from one outfit that was constantly coming in for a lot of money and it surprised me. One day Cecil came in and saw me working on one of the ledgers. He called Uncle Gene over and told him he never wanted me to work on or look in any of the books; he didn't care what they were. He was hot. That was the end of that. I don't know if he was afraid I might see something or afraid I might get an idea of how much money he made. I don't know.

It was after that I was sent to the Used Car Department. I was to learn the ropes from Harvey Harper, the manager, and the salesmen. What an experience. He was called Ali Baba and his 40 thieves by some of the other dealers on San Pedro. I liked the department and got to know Dick Purvis, Harry Hyman and Bud Treadwell. I also had the opportunity to know some other salesmen named Frank and Edgar, as well as a number of others whose names I can no longer remember. But each had a little something to teach. Again not everything I learned was about selling cars—some were lessons in life itself.

CHAPTER 12

USED CARS

When I first started at Used Cars working and learning under Harvey Harper, I knew absolutely nothing. This included both how to sell and what was going on in the real world. It was an eye opener for me. Over the years a lot has changed and a number of the practices are now even against the law. Some were even against the law back then.

I was to get familiar with the cars in stock as one of my first lessons. As I was to share an office with the other salesmen, I had to get along with them and hope they would also show me the trade. They told me they took turns on waiting on people who came on the lot but if they had previously been working with a prospect, then that was their customer and they would wait on them. The first thing I was to do was to visit with the customer and get them to decide on which car they wanted to try and deal on. If the other salesmen, or Harvey, felt things were not going as they should and a change in salesman would possibly help, then they would call out that Dr. Turner was calling for you on the phone. This was telling you to introduce the prospect to the other salesman, usually as the assistant manager, and let them take over to try and sell them. Once I had the prospect settled on a car, I was to take them into the office and sit them down, then they would help me on what to do next. Other than that, they said to sit back, keep my mouth shut and watch.

Watch I did. The weekend advertising hit the papers and we were running a $19 down sale. We had lots of interest on our selected cars and those who came in were quite keen on buying under our special terms. As long as they had reasonable credit, $19, furniture and blood, they had a chance. I watched a couple of the other salesmen at first and then I tried to help a customer. He picked out his car and we then proceeded to go into the office to sign him up.

He didn't have much money but he and his wife had a home and they owned their furniture. I relayed the information to Harvey, and Harry Hyman was standing by and offered to help. They said good, "We will get him to the blood bank, hock his sticks, double dip him and send him home". I said "What?" Harry said to watch him. I introduced Harry to my customers and he proceeded to explain to them how much he wanted to help them get the car they wanted. He said to them they must work with him and if they did as he said, they would have the car they wanted without having to come up with a lot of cash they didn't have. As they visited they talked about how much a month they could afford for a car payment.

He got them to raise the amount per month up to something like $90 per month after they had started at $80. He later told me the main thing was to find out if they could, and would, go up to an amount that was close to what was needed to make a deal at that stage. Then tell them you would try for them but it depended on how much money you could get for them.

If they didn't have the $19, you would take them to the blood bank down the street and get them to sell a pint of blood to raise that part of the money. This was to get them to commit to their vehicle. Then you would have them fill out two credit applications—one for H.F.C., (Household Finance Corporation in the mall), who would make personal loans to people and use their furniture as collateral. It seems the manager at the branch was ambitious and had worked out a deal with Cecil and Harvey to loan money for down payments—even though they weren't to do that when a main company like G.M.A.C. was financing the car. It was a personal loan H.F.C. was making and the manager didn't know or care what the people did with the money. The first credit check was usually by H.F.C. and unless the people were an extremely bad credit risk, they would loan the customer the money. We then knew how much we could get for a down payment.

We would then call in the deals to the main finance organizations on Monday morning. Harvey would split up the stack of applications into several stacks and give them to several of the experienced salesmen. Sometimes the amounts phoned in were different than that on the deal. They were called in higher than agreed to, in case the finance company qualified the applicant and wanted more money down or cut back the amount they would agree to carry on the car.

In those days you phoned the application in to the company and read it out. As soon as this was done, the salesmen would switch stacks with each other and call them into the next finance company. At that time they used National Bank of Commerce, Pacific Finance and G.M.A.C. (General Motors Acceptance Corporation). The idea was that sometimes, if one of the applicants had poor credit at the credit bureau Retail Merchants Association and was turned down by say G.M.A.C., then you would call Pacific Finance to try and push them for an answer. If you hit it right, the file may be out and they would have no report—good or bad—and the company would sometimes take a chance and approve the application. This was something that happened almost every week.

Once the finance company had agreed to an amount to finance and for how long, you knew what you could get from them and how much a month it would be for the customer. You then did your math. The amount financed at both places, the money you could get from both companies, and the total of the two monthly payments were all taken into consideration. Sometimes you had a deal and sometimes you had a little more work to do.

At times the amount from the two finance companies would be enough to make a deal but the two payments when added together would be more than what was agreed. Say in the case of my man, it might add up to $100 per month. You would have the customer come in to pick up his car and then remind him you told him you would try—which you did—you just didn't get to where he wanted to be. You were able to get him the vehicle he wanted with no money out of his pocket—which he didn't have—however, the payments were a little higher. In this case ONLY $10 per month or about 33 cents a day more than he had hoped for. A lot of the time the customer would agree and you would do the papers and everyone was happy. But sometimes you would get a customer that just wouldn't budge.

When the customer dug his heels in, it usually took an experienced salesman to get the customer to agree. It was a matter of knowing what kind of customer you had—whether they were proud, just angry, unreasonable, or what the real obstacle was. Some, you only had to remind them that you were helping them, as they were the ones with no money who should be glad of the help—if not, then they could go and get their help somewhere else. This would work for some. Others just wanted to have a fit and make sure they couldn't buy it for less—and then they would agree to the higher payment and take the car home. I can't think of a time some sort of (at least) compromise wasn't reached. It might be as simple as giving them a G.W. Warranty for no extra charge to try to make it up to them. The G.W. Warranty was good for 24 months or 24,000 miles. You would get 15% off parts and labor on any repairs done in the company's shop or other shops that honored the G.W. Warranty.

G.M.A.C. supplied finance books that had rate charts. The amount financed could be looked up on the appropriate rate chart—with or without credit life insurance. The older the car, the higher the interest rate and the shorter the time they would finance it for. One of the first things Harvey did was have me bring him a rate book. He opened it up and found the chart at 24% interest with credit life insurance included. He then removed the rest of the pages and tossed them into the trashcan. He handed me back the book with only the one chart and said "Here is your book. Use only this one and it will keep you out of trouble."

I found out what he meant as time went on. If you weren't careful when working a deal with a client, you could either get on the wrong rate or start so low the customer would try and cut you back to where you would have no place to go. The client really didn't know what the car was worth; he just knew he should be able to get a lower price than what was offered to him and that if he didn't have the price improved by a large amount, then he was sure he was being taken advantage of.

One thing I needed to learn was whether the client was really a cash buyer or a payment buyer. Most of the customers we got were payment buyers. They might say the amount for the car was too much but what they really wanted to know was how much a month–that is what they were going to pay. If you knew which kind of customer you were dealing with, then you could talk to them in what really counted; monthly payments. This is where you needed to know how to use the rate chart. You would try to get them to agree to how much a month for so many months. Then you would work the numbers and see how much money the finance company would give you for that model for that many months. If you used a high chart you had more room and money to work with. The real rate might be 14% and they would finance the car for 30 months. The customer might cut your amount and agree to a lesser amount. The amount might work at a lower interest rate—the rate the finance company charged. Harvey explained to me that when a customer agreed to say $100 per month for 30 months, then they could care less how the interest and principal were split, he was still going to pay $100 per month for 30 months.

I was starting to get an understanding of the basics about this time. I was watching the lot one day when a man walked on and started looking at a couple of cars. I asked one of the other salesmen if it was his turn and he said not to worry about it, I could have the man. I waited on the man and he was easy going, asked lots of questions, and went over the car in great detail. It was a Pontiac that had only about 6,000 miles on it and was about 7 months old. He asked me why the people traded it in. I told him I didn't know but they must like Pontiacs because they bought another one and we had taken this one in trade. He must have spent three hours looking at several cars but kept coming back to the Pontiac. We went for a test drive and he looked it over again. Finally he sat down in the office, lit his pipe and said he wanted to make a cash offer.

I took out a work sheet and wrote up his offer and took it to Harvey. I thought we had a deal and was feeling good but Harvey turned it down. I almost fell over. He came back with a price almost as high as where we started. He told me to tell the man it was hard to find a car like that. It was less than a year old with only 6,000 miles and a new one would cost him at least a couple of thousand more. This was my first cash customer, I had to learn how to work and sell a cash buyer. This back and forth went on for about 20 or 30 minutes. We even went out and looked at the car again. I pointed out to him it still had some factory warranty left on it in case anything was wrong and I like to think this is what made him buy. It was after this he agreed to the last counter offer. We did the paper work and he wrote out a check for the car. He drove off and seemed to be happy.

I went to take the deal to Harvey and all the salesmen burst out laughing. I asked what was so funny. They explained to me the man had been in at least 20 times before and had spent hours and hours and never bought. They were not going to waste any more time on him. He was oriental (Chinese) and he smoked a pipe. In the car business Orientals and pipe smokers are two customers that most salesmen run from. They take a lot of time and drive you crazy before they ever buy. Here I was, didn't know any better, went out and waited on him, and sold him a car. A Chinese oriental pipe smoker, my first cash sale. They also told me it was funny to them that he had picked that car out. We had just put it on the lot the day before. It had been in a wreck and that was why the people traded it in. He was so particular yet when he bought, it was a car that had been in an accident.

I asked Harvey why he had me go back and forth so many times to try and get more money for the car if it had been wrecked. He said first of all it had been repaired and a good job at that if he didn't pick it up. Then he asked me what makes a good deal. I said the one that makes a lot of money. He said no. He said "I'll tell you why we went back and forth and what makes a good deal. It is when both parties feel they have done well, they are both happy, and the car is sold". That was so true. In years to come I saw many an unhappy customer that bought a car as cheap as anyone ever could and they still complained they had been taken. They hadn't been worked so they would feel they had not done well and thought they had been taken.

It didn't take long for some of the finance companies to catch on that Harvey was borrowing down payments for customers. The finance companies wanted the customer to have some of their own money in the vehicle and lower payments so as to lessen the chance of repossession. This type of sale was soon stopped and in the years to come, a statement was included on G.M.A.C. contracts that the down payment didn't come from borrowed money. In a way Harvey was helping those with very little money. He had come up with a way to help get them get into in a car they otherwise would not have been able to buy.

Not everything that was done at the used car lot was something you wanted to talk about. One man would come by each week and put your favorite numbers on the odometer of any car in about 10 to 30 minutes, depending on the model. Some of the salesmen were those who gave salesmen their reputations. As my old friend once said about politicians and men in general . . . bait a trap with either women or money and you are liable to catch most anything. Money and women were the focus of many a salesman.

One fellow, a young, not bad-looking sort of guy, was very hyper. He played the guitar in a band and was always walking around tapping on the walls and tables. He fancied himself as sort of a ladies' man. Sometimes he would get a solo Mom in, trying to buy a car, and he would spend half his time trying to make a deal with her if she wanted a lower price. I was surprised to find out that several times a month he would negotiate a discount in the back office on the desktop. I was very naive. The whole thing came out in the open one day and that is when the others told me what was going on.

One day, a young Negro woman was in and Bud was trying to sell her a car. It seems she had been in before but her credit was bad and the finance companies had turned her down. He took her to the back office and put a piece of paper over the window on the door. After a few minutes a few noises and bumps were heard. About that time one of the other salesmen ran to the door and called out to Bud that a big black man was coming and he looked mad. About that time the man came in the front door and wanted to know where his wife was as she was supposed to be seeing someone about a car and he wanted a few words with him. About that time you could hear some noise in the back. The man ran to the door and pushed it open. The woman was still in the office but Bud had climbed out the window. He was heading for a car and planning to take the rest of the day off.

Harry Hyman, an older heavy-set man who had gout, was the opposite. He was the one that was a charmer, the one you felt sorry for, the one you wanted to help but it always was the same; money. He was always short of money; behind on his bills and forever trying to borrow money. He was nice to me and even showed me some of his personal tricks. I didn't approve of them and refused to use them. What he would do is sell a payment buyer—after lots of back and forth—with something like $81.56 per month. He would give the customer copies of paper work with no payments on it, and other paper work, but not a copy of the finance contract. He would then change the one to say a four, or a seven or a nine. It depended on what he felt he could get away with. When the customer got the payment book in the mail, some would question the amount. Others just remembered 80-something and let it go. If they questioned it he would ask them to check their copy which, of course, they didn't have. He would get them to come down and he would show them the copy in the office that the customer had signed which had the amount of say $87.56 per month. An increase of $6 per month on 30 months would make a difference of $180 on the carry back or about $45 more in commission for him. We did all of our own contracts then so this was easy for him to do. He didn't do this all the time but management turned their heads as they didn't want to know about it. I later heard of some really bad ones. They would change the number of months from say 30 to 36. When the customer would question it they were told it was a mistake . . . they would take care of it; just tear up the last six payment coupons and put them in the trash. They would then hope the car was traded in before it was paid off and the guy wouldn't have a clue how much was still owed on it.

Once they took a customer's car keys and threw them on the roof. No one knew what had happened to his keys after his trade-in was appraised. They were sure they gave them back. Then they would convince the customer to take the car he had been looking at home. They were sure the manager would approve the deal on Monday. They wanted him to show it off to all of his friends and make him feel like the car was his. When he came back on Monday he was informed the manager turned the deal down. They needed more as his car just wasn't worth as much as they hoped. He would then say "But I've already shown all my friends". And they knew they had him then. He didn't want to look like his credit had been turned down or that he couldn't afford the car after all. Sure enough, the guy would agree to more.

The dealership was sort of a gross dealership. A true gross dealership tried to get all they could on every deal. Some of these were the worst type of car dealers around. A volume dealership was more interested in moving lots of vehicles at any price as long as they made money—no matter how little. They figured between the factory rebates and never turning down a deal, they would make more in the long haul. Years later I worked for just such a dealership.

The customer did win sometimes, if you want to put it that way. I had one customer who traded his old car in and we gave him a good price for it. He was a cash buyer but had a few things to do and couldn't change cars for a couple of days. He came in late just before we locked up a couple of nights later to pick up his car. The next day we went to start up his car and move it to the back of the lot when we heard an awful noise. The motor had a bad rod in it and was worth a lot less. I knew it wasn't like that when we appraised it. Yet when we contacted him he said it was fine when he parked it. I felt something was funny and I knew I should have checked the car when he dropped it off that night at closing. Years later I found out that he had spent those couple of days switching in a dud motor he had taken out of it several months before.

Another time, one of the salesmen made a deal with a trade-in that was originally appraised for a top price. When the car was ready to turn in the next day, it was rough. It had the same license plate number as the car appraised, same color, same make, and a few thousand more miles. Did the salesman write down the wrong mileage or just what did happen? The customer had two cars that looked the same. He switched license plates when he was trying to make a deal. He put them back on the correct car when he traded it in and the rough one was the one he turned in. The salesman only wrote down the license number. He didn't write down the 13-digit vehicle identification number on the dash you could see that could not be removed. After that, all appraisal slips had to have the V.I.N. number and the car had to be checked before the deal was complete and the people could go.

Laws were changed over time and new methods were tried. Customers would remove or destroy the catalytic converters on the cars when they first came out. Then when they went to trade them in would complain bitterly about being appraised for as much as $1,500 less than a car with no problems. It had become law for the dealer to make sure any cars he sold were up to compliance on emissions. If they weren't, they could be in for very heavy fines. The same for odometers; triple damages. [Three times the amount involved; if the car was $10,000 then you were up for $30,000.] When in doubt, the car was appraised on the basis of unknown mileage and the customer would have to sign a statement stating the same. If they wouldn't, we wouldn't trade. The penalty was just too great to take a chance.

CHAPTER 13

NEW CARS

After getting my feet on the ground in Used Cars and getting to know some of the other salesmen, I started falling into some of the same traps many salesmen do. I would size up the customer from across the lot and decide he couldn't buy or that his credit wouldn't be any good. I only wanted to wait on the buyers. 'Cherry picking', as it was called, was not good business. No one can tell for sure, across a lot, if the person can buy or not. I should have remembered this from watching the salesmen when my grandfather purchased his last car.

I started to get this way after I got so smart from seeing the other guys doing it and having them push these people off on me so they would be free if a buyer came on the lot. Other habits included listening too much to the other guys moaning. After awhile you started to get in a rut and believe it yourself. Your luck was bad. I might as well take a break and go get a cup of coffee. All sorts of mind games that would get you off the lot or in such a state you couldn't give a car away. In almost every sales force I have seen, at least one guy specializes in doing this to the other salesmen. He stays up and happy, and waits on the customers and makes the sale. He keeps the rest of the sales force in a state of turmoil and away from customers. It took me a long time before the lights came on. I trusted my fellow salesmen more than I should have.

Harry Hyman was always supporting me by telling me what to do and how to do it. But he also worked on my mind a bit just like the others. He would encourage me to take a break and go to coffee at "Bobs", about half a block away. We would walk to the coffee shop as we had no coffee facilities at the car lot, take a break and visit with some of the other salesmen. Salesmen from the other dealerships and used car departments would come in to visit, as well. They were from Orsinger Buick, Gunn Oldsmobile and a number of independent used car lots. Cecil and his friends would be in the coffee shop about half the time and he didn't seem to like me coming in when he was there. Usually whoever was doing okay would pick up the tab for the coffee and pay for everyone at the table. It was only a few dollars but it added up, day in day out.

Harry got himself in a bind one day and he was going to be evicted or something, and was begging for help even more than usual. I felt sorry for him and remembering how he had tried to help me, I decided after talking it over with Cecile, to loan him the money. It was a couple of hundred dollars. This time I drew up an agreement on a piece of paper and typed it out. I was getting smarter—or so I thought. As time passed and a couple of paydays came and went, he didn't pay me a dime. He had been selling but always claimed the money was already owed to someone for something. It finally got to the point I told him I would have to file a small claim against him in the small claims court. I learned then a person with bad credit didn't care. The claim was only a piece of paper and they had no credit anyway. Cecil found out about this (I think from Cecile) and he called me in. He got the money from Harry and gave it to me. He had basically told him to pay it or look for another job.

He then told me not to be so stupid—I couldn't afford it. He was right. The next part of the conversation was about how my sales had fallen off. He felt I was spending too much time at the coffee shop for one thing and Harvey said I wasn't waiting on the customers like I had been. I told him I would try. I also admitted to him that the one thing I didn't like about used cars was selling those I felt weren't very good or might have problems. The used cars were checked over and only obvious problems were fixed—and then only as cheaply as they could get by with. However, I understood that you couldn't spend a fortune on every car and make it over or you would go broke. The mechanical warranties and breakdown insurance plans weren't around at this time. At least the new cars had a new car warranty and so this wasn't a consideration.

I had been allowed to sell our car and buy another one the company had traded for from time to time . . . something the others were not allowed to do. The original idea was to build up to a new car. The first car we put on the lot was the '62 Grand Prix. A few days after it was on the lot, it was stolen. We came to work one day and found the chains had been driven over and broken. The police found the car a few days later. The radio, tachometer, and tires and wheels had been taken off and stolen. The insurance company paid to put it back as it was but the scratches on the dash and body weren't fixed as they said it was a used car and the scratches may have already been there.

We got a good price for the car when it sold and I bought a '59 Chevrolet Impala coupe and had it fixed up. Tom, my brother, saw the car and wanted it. My parents helped him buy the car and he was happy for awhile—that is, until he wrecked it. It was around this time that his driving was extremely bad. He was on the dope a lot and this did not improve his driving skills. Over about a 2-year period he went through 4 cars that I can remember. He had married a girl, Andrea Arquette, early on and dropped out of school. Her uncle was Charlie Weaver who played an old man on a hit TV series about that time, 'Mr Peepers'. Andrea and Tom had a little boy, Tommy. She tried to get him to settle down and help him but at this stage he was wild and wouldn't listen to anyone, so they ended up getting a divorce.

Over this period of time I fixed up and sold several cars. Another one was a car that had belonged to a teacher I had for English in high school. The car, a '62 Pontiac, was very plain but had low mileage. The bad thing was that as she parked it outside under a tree, the paint job was shot. She was also larger than the average person and so the seat cover and carpet on the driver side was worn completely out. I learned my lesson on this one. I fixed it all up–new paint, new carpet, and new seat cover. I just did get our money out of it when I finally sold it and considered myself lucky. As an old car man told me along the way, "Sam, you can't shine shit".

It was after the Harry episode and my sales being just so at the used car lot that Cecil decided I should come up to the main store and sell new cars. I could learn from the salesmen up there and he could keep an eye on me. He didn't want me going to the coffee shop several times a day. This would slow me down as it was several blocks and I would have to find a car and drive—besides I wouldn't have anyone to go with. I think Cecil liked it better when I wasn't in the coffee shop. He was known by almost everyone that came in . . . and all of the waitresses.

New cars were a different game. You still had to get the customer to pick out a car but it would always keep coming back to price. All the dealers had new cars and with two Pontiac dealers in town since about 1960, it wasn't easy with lots of competition. The selling and the customers were different from used cars. I had a lot to learn on selling again.

The gloss was starting to wear off for me. Henry was in New Cars and of course since he went to work and wouldn't go to school, the name of the company had changed to Tindall & Son Pontiac. This was okay by me; in fact a lot of the time Henry wasn't there. He was busy trying to get his hunting equipment ready to go for the season, or if it was during the season, he was gone hunting. He and Cecil, each year, would get a deer lease and the dealership would pay for it. This was part of the entertainment expense each year. Some of the good customers and friends would be taken out hunting. The rest of the time it would be Henry and his friends and rarely, some of the family.W

When Henry was at the dealership he would be in charge of telling anyone he could, what to do. He would also do a silly thing that was, I guess, to get attention or show that he could do what he wanted to you. He would take his thumb and middle finger and pop you with it. He did it hard and it would hurt. If that wasn't bad enough he would do it to you either on your nipple on your chest through your shirt or he would do it to you on the front of your pants where he guessed the end of your penis was. The more anyone complained the more he did it. This was a game of his he did for years—even when I worked for them again later in the late 70's and early 80's he was still doing it.

Late in the summer or early fall, we went to Houston to my first new car showing. A number of the salesmen, Cecil, Henry, and I went down the night before. We ate out that night and then went back to the hotel we were staying. Cecil and some of the men sat around and played cards and had drinks until about midnight. Some of the salesmen had other ideas about activities they wanted to be involved in. They invited some ladies to come over they had gotten phone numbers for. It ended up turning into a party that went well into the night. I watched Cecil play cards as I couldn't afford to gamble, and watched the craziness of Henry and the others until I had enough of it and went to bed.

The next morning we had breakfast and attended the showing of the new models. Cecil had hoped to get at least one or two of the new models to drive back. It was still sort of a big deal for the new model showing and he always liked to drive one and show it around in advance if he could. He got his wish and a new model was taken back to the dealership. The front of the new models had a new design and stuck out in the centre like a big nose. After we got back and were standing around with other salesmen and employees we started comparing notes on what we thought of the new model. It had a mixed review as I guess anything would that had a fairly major change. I commented to some of the others it reminded me of a big nose or a ship's bell or something, and then I tapped it and went ding ding. Cecil overheard me and started to jump on me right then but instead invited me to immediately visit him in his office.

This was my second lecture. I was told I should never run down or criticize our product. Pontiac had been good to all of us and provided our means to make a living. If we ran the product down in front of others they wouldn't think much of it and a bad attitude would spread. We needed every salesman and every employee excited about the product and have them tell everyone they knew what a great model we had for the year to come. I was also instructed in the future to keep any comments or criticism about anything around the company to myself.

This lecture didn't do much for my attitude and I was beginning to again question what I was doing. I could see the only ones on the gravy train at the dealership were Cecil and Henry. I had hoped to make some good money and enjoy working. It wasn't happening to work out that way. I started to think then that I must find a way to make a good living. It kept coming back to the same thing, an education. I knew I had to go back to school and get a degree. I had to get into some sort of profession as it was going to be the only way to get ahead. I just didn't know what.

I had watched Cecil at a distance for years, going back to when I went down to get the car serviced. He always seemed to be busy; always doing some sort of a deal or something. He would sit on the showroom floor by a desk that had a phone. He would watch what was going on and visit with his friends. Half the time he would be on the phone—either he had called someone or they were calling him. If it were of a more private or secret nature he would go into his office. It was very intriguing and looked most impressive. He was commanding his world from his post. I never did know just what was going on half the time for years but it seemed he wasn't fond of me always being around.

Then one day he asked me what I thought about maybe being a dentist. I told him I had no desire to be one. He had already previously started suggesting that I think about going back to school. Some more time went by and then he asked me if I knew where Blauser's Pharmacy was. It was near where we lived and that is where he and Elizabeth traded. He had been talking to a friend and they told him that Blauser had made a lot of money out of his pharmacy. He asked me if I had every thought about becoming a pharmacist. I told him I hadn't. He said I should think about it and if I did become one, then later on, he would see about helping me get a store of my own. Needless to say, this was to me, the first glimmer of sunshine I had seen for awhile.

He said he would help if I went back to school. I went to talk to both my parents and grandparents about it as well. Dr. Joe had given us the lump sum before, which was now gone. He said he would help and if I would let him know how much I needed each semester for books and tuition he would give it to me. I knew when I went to see my parents it wouldn't be easy.

The situation at their house had not improved and we seldom went over to their house as a family. I would go on my own sometimes. They weren't drunk when we went to see them but if you stayed for a long time, you were looking for trouble. They wanted to see the kids and we took them by to visit but only once in a blue moon and then only stayed maybe an hour. Part of this was due to the fact that most of our spare time, both evenings and weekends, was spent at the Tindall's house. Cecile always wanted to be with her folks and I think Cecil may have even said something to her that scared her even more about my folks and their drinking. Later on at Christmastime we would go for only an hour or so to get the presents late morning and then to the Tindalls' until well into the evening. If I didn't agree to this, then we were in for a fight. I didn't like it and felt it was over-reacting and unfair. On the other hand, I didn't like my parents' behavior when they had been drinking. It did get out of hand more often than not. When I did talk to them about going back to school and asked for help, they said they would do what they could. As it worked out, they gave us some money each semester I was in school, as well as a present for us every now and then.

I still had to find out where I stood with my grades and the requirements. The good news was that the new requirements no longer required two years of German. Most of what I had would transfer—that is, once I overcame the condition I had previously identified. I needed at least 54 hours with a C average to transfer. This meant I would have to go back to San Antonio Junior College for at least one more semester. This was not all bad as we had a house to do something with, as well.

I went back to school and realized just how much I had forgotten in about a year. I was very rusty and at first had trouble getting back into the routine for class, homework and studying. I was more focused this time and felt I had definite goals. Previously, when I went to school and sometimes then, I would stop by my grandparents' house to visit and see how they were doing.

It was like starting over. The classrooms would bring back some of the memories of the first time around. I remembered how I was taking a test on that November day in 1963 when Kennedy was shot. They let school out right there and then. I happened to have the car that day and drove down to the dealership to see Cecile, and what was going on. I remember one man commented to another that J.F.K. had been shot, to which he replied, "Good, did they get that other son of a bitch, L.B.J., as well?" A third man overhead this and almost started a fight. Emotions were running high and not everyone loved the Kennedy family. Rumors were everywhere; more than one person involved, a private plane had flown across the border and so on. After seeing some of this I decided to go to my grandparents. I watched the whole story unfold on television including the shooting of Oswald. I visited with Golda on this and it was hard for her to believe it was happening. To this day I still think there is more to it than we know and I am sure some in the government were involved. I don't think L.B.J. was but I think he knew. I also think he knew that for the sake of the nation it would have to be covered up.

I was back in school and managed to pass my subjects with good enough grades to get me the magic C average and 54 plus hours. I was now ready to transfer to Austin and the University of Texas Pharmacy School, one of the top ten pharmacy schools in the country at that time.

CHAPTER 14

ON THE HOME FRONT

It was around 1964 that Cecil bought his first ranch at Bandera and shortly after, about 1965 or so, sold it and bought a larger one at D'Hanis, Texas, near Yancy. It was when we were at the Bandera place swimming one day, that we heard that Jim Reeves, the country singer, had been killed in a plane crash. He and Cecil had become friends and Cecil was in the process of looking for a ranch for him in the Bandera area, just a week or so before. He was invited by Mrs. Reeves to be a pallbearer at the funeral.

Over the years, Cecil was able to meet, and sometimes get to know, a lot of people that were well known and sometimes less well known. This was through the dealership, General Motors' promotions, other dealers, or just one introduction leading to another. At times it would lead to nothing; other times it may lead to a business adventure with them or getting to sell them (or their organization) a fleet of cars or trucks. A lot of times these people would go and no longer be around, just as fast as they came on the scene. It seemed as if Cecil had moved on to someone else and a new friendship almost overnight at times. He was a master at getting to know someone and then size them up as to what, if anything, they had to offer him, or how they might be useful to him. This trait, along with the ability to handle upset customers better than anyone I had ever seen, were surely two things that helped him to become so successful.

I tried to help do a few things for Cecil at Bandera. One time I tried to build a little wading pool on the concrete patio area by the big pool. The big pool was fed by the stream next to it and the water flowed through the pool. I knew nothing about construction but with some help from his Mexican ranch worker we built some frames for walls and put in a pipe for a drain. We then mixed concrete and filled the walls. After about a week, we removed the forms and painted the walls and bottom with swimming pool paint. It really looked pretty good and for the little kids it was great, being only about 18 inches deep.

The faults in our construction didn't show up until the first big rain when the creek came out of its banks. When we returned to the pool area, we found only a nice painted square on the patio area, everything was gone. We didn't try to attach the walls to the patio and we used no reinforcing steel in the walls. We didn't think we needed to worry about it since it was going to be only about 18 inches deep. We never considered the creek in full rage after a heavy rainstorm. So much for the little wading pool.

Another time was when Cecil decided he wanted to remove some tree stumps around the place as well as a concrete bridge that crossed the creek. His neighbor had been going through his place, right by the house area, across this bridge at the creek and then up the road and through a gate into his own place. They had some sort of a dispute about him having a right of way through Cecil's place and across the bridge, which went back to the previous owner. It got to the point that Cecil decided to take matters into his own hands to stop him once and for all.

He purchased some dynamite (60/40; 60% T.N.T. and 40% Nitro-glycerin). We had a wood dowel to use to form a hole in the end of one of the sticks, into which we inserted an electric blasting cap. You could then put several sticks together if needed. The electric wire would be run to a battery and when the wires were touched to it, the battery would set off the cap. The cap would set off the stick of dynamite and the whole thing would go boom. We did this with a few tree stumps and even put several sticks under a big oak tree next to the road. When we set them off, the tree lifted off like a rocket ship and went about 6 feet up in the air and then over.

When we got to the bridge we placed charges in several places under it. We knew that being a concrete bridge it would take a fair amount. We got everything in place and rolled the wire out as far as it would go—about 75 yards. We touched the wire to the battery; we saw smoke and the bridge went to pieces. Large chunks, small chunks and dust went everywhere. Then we heard the boom! Then it started raining pieces of rock and concrete all around us, from the bridge. We had used plenty of dynamite. There was no longer a bridge across the creek. A few other little stumps and things were blown off the side of the hill that was by the house but when the rock started raining down on the house, Elizabeth said enough was enough. Cecil had accomplished what he wanted and our blasting days were over.

I started to learn something about Cecil at Bandera but I never recognized it for what it was for a long time. One day he had several of his horses rounded up and put in the pens. He had started buying and racing some quarter horses as well as having some work horses at the place. We all went over to the pens to look at the horses. He had one go through into another pen and then he did something with another one and then something with another one again. Then he turned to me and asked me if I would get up on the fence and get on the back of one of the horses he had in what was like a run, with a gate at the end in front of the horse. He assured me it was fine, just sit on the horse. The Mexican had already put a saddle and bridle on the horse.

I climbed on the fence and got over the horse and eased down on it. Everything was fine. Then the gate was opened. The horse took about two steps forward and cleared the run. Then the horse started rearing up and throwing its head back. I grabbed on with both hands and started to lean forward so as not to go off the back. Just at that time the horse's head came back and hit me in the forehead. It almost knocked me off the horse and busted my skin open. The Mexican grabbed the bridle and pulled the horse down and held it. Cecil laughed and laughed. He told me he had just purchased that horse recently—a race horse, Tom's Cherry Ann. He knew the horse was high-spirited and not usually ridden except in training or racing. I didn't say anything but, as I was to learn, this would not be the last time I would be the butt of one of his actions.

I tried helping at D'Hanis, the second ranch he purchased, at first. I tried to drive the bulldozer and road maintainer. He was clearing a lot of land to put into new fields and fix up the dirt roads enough to be able to drive the car or a pickup truck over most of the place. One time he ran over a rock and punched a hole in the oil pan of the car. I climbed under the car and put a liberal amount of sealer around a large screw about the size of my little finger in diameter and half an inch long. I got it started in the hole and the screw took up the space as I turned it tight. We filled the car with oil and drove it home. Another time the bulldozer blew a hydraulic line that was used on the controls. I spent one whole day doing a temporary repair to the end of the line fitting. I got it going again and it was used for a couple of days until regular repairs could be made.

This was a change for me and I liked being of some help. Later after the swimming pool was in at the ranch, I would try to help keep it clean. Usually at the start of a season was the worst. It would get a lot of leaves and dirt in it over the winter and it took a lot of work to get it clean again. I learned over a period of time that the best thing for me to do was stay clear of Henry and his family as much as possible, when they were at the ranch. He always acted like it was a competition or he had to prove something. He would do the same grab-ass sort of stunts that he did in town. Early on we almost ended up in a fight at the ranch one day because of it. He always had to show he was boss and acted like it was his ranch. It got to the point in the years to come that I would avoid going if I knew he was there. He didn't know the word share or how to get along with someone.

We would try and make arrangements during deer season to go to the ranch when he was planning to be at the deer lease. We would then be able to hunt and fish on our own. If we wanted to sit in a deer blind and wait for the deer we could. Henry always liked to drive around and shoot from the truck. More often than not, sometimes during the weekend he would show up . . . it may be 11 PM on Saturday night. He would decide the hunting wasn't any good at the lease so he wanted to drive to the ranch to give it a try. He might stay up for several hours driving around that night seeing what was out on the road or the fields. If he thought it was a good buck he would shoot it. Sometimes it was a good buck but a lot of the time it was a doe that had a bush behind it. He would shoot and shoot at the deer in the lights. He would get his friend or wife to drive him around and around. Sometimes the poor animal would be gut shot and have its insides sticking out. He would hit them anywhere he could. He didn't want to take a chance on a trophy getting away. He would then tell the Mexican helper he had some food for him and would usually then drive him to the field to get him to pick it up and clean it. The next day I would try and sit in a blind. The next thing you would know, he would drive up and down the roads even where you were, just in case he might be able to shoot something. It was enough to put you off hunting—and it did.

Henry also started learning from Cecil about some of his traits. He would use people. Over the years I saw him with friends and family both, taking advantage of them. He would ask them to go with him hunting and then have them do all the carry this, clean that and wash this—and then turn on them by putting them down or play grab-ass stunts to show them he could still bully them into their place.

Even after Cecil purchased the new ranch (about 1200 acres at D'Hanis), they still had a hunting lease each year for a long time. It seems the deer in other areas were a lot larger and better trophies. Other game was also more plentiful including quail, doves and turkeys. I went a couple of times to a lease they had near Eagle Pass after I went back to college but that was about it. Eventually Henry got caught breaking the rules in the lease on what and how many he was allowed to kill, and the lease was cancelled and they were thrown off.

Craig Tindall Kopecky, my second son, was born on June 7, 1965. It was a surprise when I found out we were going to have another baby but then my folks assured us it was nice having two so close as this way they had someone to play with. Sam and Craig would be about the same distance apart in age as Joey and I were. I knew we had played a lot together when we were growing up.

I don't think it made me any more determined knowing we had another child on the way. I had already been reconsidering my situation and had decided to go back to school. We had put the house on the market in the hope that it would sell but I was unaware of the economy and what was going on. It seemed the economy was slow and houses were not selling. Cecil said he would keep the payments up and he was sure it would sell in time. It did after about six months. We started to rent it out but decided it may be harder to sell and get damaged. When it did sell, we got nothing. I only remember that, at the time, Cecil said take it as he had been handling everything with the realtor and felt it was time to get rid of it.

Sometime after we moved to Austin and I was back in school, Cecil purchased a place in Rockport, Texas at Key Allegro. It was a house built on the canal. You could keep a boat at the house and go out fishing into the bay or out into the Gulf of Mexico. It was awhile before we were invited or were able to go to the coast. In fact it was hard to go anywhere. I had started into school and was determined to make good grades and get through it as fast as I could. I went to school 12 months out of the year—both regular sessions and summer sessions.

Regardless if it was the coast or the ranch it was almost impossible to go. I had reading to do, papers to work on and tests to study for. I also had my part-time job that was necessary for both money and getting my intern hours by working in an accredited pharmacy. They always said just take your books or you can read in the car. The books got some miles on them but only by being driven around. It was impossible to do any serious study when everybody was trying to have a good time and the kids were all going in different directions. We did go a number of times to the coast but we still had some of the same problems. We would show up thinking it would be us and Cecil and Elizabeth. Then before you knew it, either the day before or later the day we got there, Henry and his family would show up.

It was just as well I was just as happy to fish in the canal behind the house as once Henry was on the scene, he would take over as captain of the boat and decide when and where it was going. But I could always count on company on the canal if the fish started to bite—he and his clan were elbow to elbow with me in a shot.

I had a couple more lessons at Rockport. One time we went out fishing in the bay for speckled trout. For the first time we picked a day they were active and it was fun. We had about a dozen good-sized ones when a game warden boat pulled up alongside us and wanted to check the catch. We visited and he checked our fish. Everything was fine. Then just as he started to leave he decided to see our fishing licenses. You didn't need them on private property but did out in the open. I tried showing him my hunting license and playing stupid, which he thought I was, but it didn't work. We all got tickets for no license. Elizabeth was upset more than the rest of us. Cecil said not to worry. He turned them over to a lawyer politician friend and they were lost.

Another time after I was back out of school, Cecil had me drive back a vehicle and tow the boat back at the end of the season. It was at night and as I was approaching the outer limits of a small town, an oncoming car had its bright lights on and I couldn't see. I flashed and flashed my lights but the driver wouldn't dim them. A few moments after the car went past, a highway patrol car pulled out with its red lights on. He was after me! He pulled me over. He asked me what was going on and I told him. He then asked how fast I was going. I said 55 I think. He said that's right. I'm going to give you a ticket. I asked why and he then asked if I saw the sign as I came to town. I told him no because I was concentrating on the car with the high beams on that I was flashing at. He said the sign was a speed limit sign of 55 but since I was pulling a boat I should only be doing 45. I protested but it didn't do any good. Cecil said he would have it taken care of. Then the next thing I knew was that I had a warrant out for my arrest. His friend did nothing—not even tell me he couldn't help and just pay the fine. I did this (paid the fine), after I wrote a letter to the judge protesting. I think the judge put the fine in the bank and the letter in the trash. I never asked for this kind of help from him again.

With Cecile and the kids wanting to spend what time away from Austin we could take, with her folks, it made it impossible to see my parents or grandparents—except on rare occasions. I had to admit it was more fun and exciting at the coast or even fishing at the ranch, with the comfort of a regular house than roughing it at my grandfather's place. But I actually liked my grandfather's place a lot better, with it having a variety of types of fishing you could do, a variety of fish you could catch, and closeness to nature that you could experience. That is all fine except that it is hard with two little kids and a wife that are having to use outdoor facilities and put up with a lack of running water, heating and cooking on a wood stove, and sleeping all in one big room with no heating. As far as going to my parents' house, well, things hadn't changed. They wanted to see the kids and wanted us to bring them over but we still had to be careful not to overstay our time limit of about an hour. It was towards the end of my university days that Dr. Joe decided to sell the ranch. He felt no one cared about it and it was just too hard for he and Golda to try to take care of it.

Craig and Sambo with Golda—
Christmas '65 at Lamont

Sam with Craig, and Golda with
turkey—Christmas '66

I'm sure my family knew we spent a lot of the spare time we had with the Tindalls and that when any holidays came around we spent the time at her folks. We made an appearance on Christmas Eve at my grandparents' house when all my family would get together to exchange gifts and have a Christmas dinner. Golda would buy lots of gifts for all of us and Paw would give the adults and older kids, money. Again he would usually make the check out to the wives. On Christmas morning we would go over to my parents house for an hour or so and then on to the Tindalls' for all of Christmas day and into the evening. This became our ritual.

CHAPTER 15

SHORT STORIES AND EVENTS

During my time at university a number of stories and events come to mind. Some bring back memories that maybe should just be forgotten; others tell a little about what was going on at the time; and some show the signs of the times.

Up to my teen years I spent every moment I could going to the ranch. It was a different world. The fishing, the hunting and just being outdoors exploring. The paths through the brush up the cliffs, always looking for a snake around every bend. Seeing all kinds of wildlife over the years—skunks, raccoons, opossums, squirrels, foxes, turkeys, doves, quail, armadillos, deer and a variety of snakes (diamondback, rattlesnake, copperhead, coral snake, cotton mouth and coach whip, just to name a few). Other types of birds were plentiful—red bird, blue jay, bobwhite, whippoorwill, owl, hawk and lots of buzzards. We also saw the odd bobcat but they were getting few and we had heard of the rare mountain lion but never saw any.

My brother Joe and I would go exploring along roads and through the brush to the fields where the deer blinds were built for the hunting season. Some of the deer blinds were on the ground and some were up in trees. We looked at them for what seemed like years, always wanting to know when we would be able to go hunting. We would wet our finger in our mouth and hold it up in the air to see which way the wind was coming from so as to see if our smell would give our position away to the deer in the direction they would be coming from. We would look on the ground for Indian arrowheads and look for gun shell cases. We looked for bones and deer antlers as we went in the brush. It seemed like each year we would find the remains of a dead deer that had been wounded by someone and had run into the brush to die. Sometimes you would find one that didn't clear a barbed wire fence and a leg would get tangled as it would go over. It would then hang with its leg in the air until someone found it, alive or dead.

My grandfather must have started teaching us to fish and shoot when we were no more than 3 or 4 years old. I can remember I had to lay the .22 rifle down on the table to steady it. If I placed the rifle stock against my shoulder I could just barely reach the trigger. I must have fired thousands of shots at cans, paper targets, rocks, branches and the odd bottle. [Bottles were a 'no, no' because of the broken glass]. We later graduated to shotguns and 'deer' rifles—3030, 250/3000, 243, 270, and so on. We became such good shots we picked out which part of a picture we would hit on a can, instead of which can, and we would place empty shell cases on a tree branch and shoot those.

One year I went to YMCA boys' camp at about 10 years old. They had a Junior Olympics with swimming, running, shooting and other activities. I entered the .22 rifle shooting and proceeded to take my turn at the target. It didn't seem too difficult but after I finished the camp judge came over and asked for me to wait. A couple of them were looking at the target and target area, and were in deep conversation. I couldn't for the life of me figure out what I had done. After several more minutes they came over and explained that when they first looked at my target they were sure I had one or two in the centre and the rest missed the entire target! I was shocked as I couldn't see how I was that far off. They then explained that upon examination of the area and padding behind the target, it appeared I had placed all my shots through the same holes in the middle and had a perfect score. I ended up winning the Blue Ribbon First Prize.

One time, later in life, I went hunting out at my father-in-law's lease near Eagle Pass, Texas. I was in a deer blind up in the air waiting for the deer to come in late in the day. As it became later and later, some turkeys moved into the area along with the female deer but there were still no bucks. It was getting towards dark and out in the far distance I could hear my brother-in-law driving down the road in his hunting truck. He never liked sitting still, preferring to run 'em down rather than sit and listen to nature. I decided rather than go back empty-handed, I would shoot a turkey tom. They were at about 100 yards and I had a 4-power scope on my 243 that worked very well.

I was raised not to shoot unless you could make a good clean shot and know what you were shooting at. I was also taught not to kill it unless you planned on eating it or had a good reason (snakes, and opossums and the like came in this category). Shooting a bird with a rifle does not leave much unless you shoot to take the head off. This works quite well if you get it right as the bird is killed outright and you have no waste. If you miss, well, you all have another day.

I took my time and found one turkey tom that liked to keep his head up in the air for several seconds looking around. I slowly squeezed the trigger and boom! Just about that time the truck came up behind me on the road to pick me up from the blind. I told them what I had done and we should go and check as I was sure we had a turkey to pluck. I then listened to a mouthful of 'oh sure' but after about 10 minutes, sure enough, I had a headless turkey to pluck. I was then told what a lucky shot it was and that it would never happen again. I then told him that the first one I did was the same way, years ago at my grandfather's ranch where I was taught 'how' to hunt. Henry didn't believe me but it didn't matter. I knew.

On one of the other trips to Eagle Pass after he first got the lease, Cecil invited the family to go along and stay at one of the motels in town as they had not yet set up a hunting camp with a caravan, except for one that would hold only about two people. The first morning at the motel I was to meet him in the cafe at 4:30. We sat at the counter and waited for the coffee to finish brewing. It was dead quiet in the place and you could have heard a pin drop. Only about half the lights were on in the place and the few employees were trying to get ready to open. A couple of other hunters came in and sat at the counter near us. A few minutes later two couples came in and sat at a table about 10 feet from us.

The waitress came back and poured us each a cup of coffee and then went to wait on the others. All of a sudden there was a loud fart that almost rattled the windows. Cecil jumped up and grabbed his coffee. He then proceeded at the top of his voice to tell me "Sam, I can't believe you did that. I am ashamed of you. You are not funny". He then walked down the counter to another area and sat down. Everybody in the place just looked at me. I finished my coffee and left. Cecil again thought he was funny after making me the butt of one of his jokes and having a laugh at my expense. I was to later suffer much worse in public in the years to come.

Not long after moving to Austin, during the first summer between summer sessions, we had an opportunity to go to Colorado Springs for the day. Elizabeth's sister Virginia and her husband Tony Defazio, along with their son, had come down to visit. For some reason Tony had to get back and he left Virginia to stay for awhile longer. Virginia had to return and a discussion was going on about how she was going to get back. We offered to drive her back as it was going to be easier for us to be gone for a few days than for Elizabeth. It was about a 16-hour drive if you took turns and drove straight through, which we did.

After we arrived we slept several hours and then drove up to the top of Pike's Peak. We also went to a Santa's Helpers Village. Sam and Craig got a kick out of the village. We drove by the Air Force Academy and saw the church and the school. We then had a bite to eat and got back on the highway to Texas. It was a quick trip and one of the only times I ever went to Colorado Springs. It was to help out Elizabeth because it appeared that Cecil wanted nothing to do with getting Virginia home. He just wanted them out of his place. It was a time that he showed how hard he could be if something was not going the way he wanted and he was demonstrating how difficult he could make everyday life.

During the years we lived in Austin each year we would go to the football games at the university. Cecil had previously been involved with the Lee High School boosters and helped talk Linus Baer into going to the University of Texas to play ball on a scholarship. He had also tried to get Warren McVea since he had a contact through his uncle that worked for him. This didn't work out because even after he took the entrance exams twice and consideration was given to him as a minority, being black, his scores were far below what was needed to get a scholarship at a Southwest Conference School. The University of Houston had no such restriction and Warren was able to get in and play ball there. This contact with the University of Texas coaching staff lasted for a number of years.

I was able to meet some of the coaches such as Darrell Royal, Willie Zapalac, Mike Campbell and Charlie Shira. During the season Cecil would have me go see Charlie Shira and he would take our student ticket cards and draw our tickets for us. When he drew them we always had good seats. I got to know coach Shira and his family and found him to be one of the best people I met during this time. After he went to Mississippi State as head coach and athletic director, we still would get a card from his family, even after

I was out of school and the family lived on Zornia. This continued until he died suddenly from a brain aneurysm that burst. His wife called us during the holiday season to let us know that he had died.

Through this association Cecil was able to lease a number of cars to the University of Texas. One year when the leases were up and the cars were returned, one of them was a '67 Pontiac G.T.O. We made a deal to trade our '64 Grand Prix for the car. This was the last trade we made until after I was out of school. Cecil took us a few times over the years, to meet some of the players and coaches in the dressing room. Sam and Craig seemed to enjoy it. They met Earl Campbell when he was playing for Texas, as well as a number of other top players. Coach Freddy Akers was an assistant when I first went to school in Austin and he later left for another job. According to Cecil, Freddy was having an affair with one of the other coach's wives and this caused problems. Darrell Royal got rid of him, only to have him come back and haunt him a few years later when Royal went to Athletic Director and Akers came back as head football coach.

As long as some sort of relationship existed and Cecil could get good tickets and sell some cars, they stayed friends. Then almost overnight it changed. Cecil would still get some tickets but not as good. He didn't associate with the coaches as he did and seldom went to the games. He was spending his time with new friends. Some were customers that had money and needed vehicles for their business. Some he had race horses in common with. Another was A. J. Foyt, the race car driver. They started running around together and did so for years.

Cecile and I were mainly trying to get by, day to day. Her folks were sending her a check each month for around $300. My side of the family helped with tuition, books and a few extra dollars from time to time. I worked part-time for both the money and my intern hours. A few months after we moved to Austin a house owned by a Mr. Lee Chlor was available to us to rent for $65 per month. The roof leaked and the first two years we lived there each time it rained we put out bowls and pots all over the house. The wallpaper was coming off the walls and to clean it up I put newspaper over the gaps and painted the walls. In the room that Sam and Craig stayed in, I covered the walls with wood paneling. It was during this time Tindall & Son Pontiac expanded and remodeled the dealership. The old wood paneling was put in a pickup truck and sent to us for the kids' room. The leftover panels I used in the garage to make a closed-off dark room. It was a large enough house for us and had a screened-in porch in the back and a good-sized yard for the kids.

Lee Chlor was a friend of Cecil's who went back to his childhood days in Cameron, Texas. I had been to Cameron a couple of times and met Cecil's parents. Cecil used to supply a car for his parents and would switch it out from time to time. Not long after I met them his father died and I was asked to be a pallbearer at his funeral. Also around this time, Cecil's younger brother, Darrell, died of Hodgkin's disease. He had two children, Hebert and Patricia. His widow was named Mary. I was also asked to be a pallbearer for his funeral. After this, Cecil introduced Lee to Mary. Mary was having a hard time with the death and was on the verge of having a breakdown. Lee tried to help Mary and they eventually got married. They moved not long after to Alaska. It was while they were in Alaska that we started renting Lee's house in Austin. It seems the move and the isolation were too much for Mary and she had a breakdown. She got worse as time went on and was having all kinds of strange thoughts that Lee was up to something. One day she went into the bathroom when he was on the toilet, took one of his rifles and shot him.

Cecil got a phone call that Mary had killed Lee, so he flew up to Alaska and brought the kids back to San Antonio. Darrell had asked Cecil to watch out for them and put Cecil in charge of their trust fund. After Mary was found insane she was locked up. Years later she was transferred to an institution in Austin.

Cecil found out the kids were eligible for a social security benefit that would help offset the cost of raising them. At first they lived with Cecil and Elizabeth, and later they lived with Henry. They didn't get along with Elizabeth and so they moved out. Patricia came and stayed with us, for a break, in Austin once. She lived with an aunt in Cameron for awhile and moved around to different family members. Hebert stayed with Henry. Patricia later got married and both she and her husband joined the army.

When they were still with Henry, Cecil would give some of the money to Edwynna, Henry's wife, to buy clothes for them. Later when we were back in San Antonio he would give Cecile money sometimes to get a few things for them as well. He only did this a few times as since we were so busted, his story was in danger of coming apart. It seems, according to Cecil, Elizabeth would get mad when money was spent on them that she thought was theirs. She said the money they got from Social Security was not enough as it was, and an extra thing like extra clothes was more than they could afford. Cecil's answer was to give money to someone else, let them buy the clothes and then say they had purchased the clothing.

Later, when Hebert was older, he almost got thrown out of Henry's house by Edwynna. Henry had taken Hebert across to Mexico to one of the houses of ill repute when they were at the hunting lease one time. Hebert came down with a case of gonorrhea and had to get treatment. Edwynna found out and was afraid his dirty clothes in the laundry would contaminate everything and they would all get gonorrhea—including her and the kids. She wanted him and all his belongings out of the house. Henry finally got her settled down and Hebert stayed.

Henry and Edwynna were high school sweethearts. While they were still in school Edwynna had become pregnant, and she and her family gave Henry and Cecil a lot of grief. They felt they should pay for the consequences of his actions. Cecil felt Henry shouldn't rush into marriage at such a young age. It was agreed that Edwynna would go away and have the baby and put it up for adoption. Henry and Edwynna were not to see each other after this and Henry would not have to marry her. It didn't work out this way as the power of love was so strong that Edwynna and Henry couldn't stay away from each other. They ended up going together again after the child was adopted out and they later got married.

All in all, the families had a lot going on in them. It seemed like no sooner would one episode close and then another would open. I can remember how Cecile and I would sometimes talk about how someday we would be able to afford a house that didn't have leaks and we would be able to spend more time doing things we enjoyed. All I had to do was get through school and go to work.

CHAPTER 16

ROUTINE AND NOT SO ROUTINE

When I started attending the University of Texas it was in the main school—taking some of my required general courses. Once I had some more of these courses and the pharmacy orientation course out of the way, I would be able to start my pharmacy courses. Unless you had your prerequisite courses and the orientation course passed, you could not start into pharmacy school courses. The orientation course was used as a weeding-out tool. It had to do with grades, attitudes, who you were, what you wanted and a whole range of values. If you were someone they didn't think they wanted to become a pharmacist, you didn't pass the course and you didn't go any further. I knew a few students that required an attitude adjustment and it took more than once before they passed the course.

It was during my second summer session in the first year I was attending school that I experienced a near miss. It was on August 6, 1966. We were well into the second session and I had been studying in the academic centre next door to the main building, known as the tower. I had an exam that was across campus and I was running late picking up my notes, my books, and getting on my way. I was thinking that if I didn't hurry I would be a few minutes late getting into class. As I had been studying just before I started packing up, I had heard a loud boom a time or two but ignored it. As I was starting to make my way toward the exit door I heard a loud boom again and the wall-size glass windows vibrated. As I crossed the room I heard the noise a couple more times. When I reached the door one of the security guards and teachers were telling everyone to get back, go sit down, and stay away from the windows. They had a report someone was shooting outside and they had no idea where they were.

I can remember thinking at first, what am I going to do about my test. The exams and schoolwork were always first on your mind. I decided to go and sit down back at one of the study desks and wait. I don't remember how long it lasted . . . I think about an hour and a half, or two hours. We heard more shooting and the loud boom noises. We saw a couple of uniformed cops run across the grounds, going from tree to tree, heading for the tower. All we could do was wait.

Later, we were told school was closed for the rest of the day and for all of us to go home. I decided to make my way across campus to where the test was to have been, to see if they left a note or if the professor was still around. This would also put me on a side of the campus that would be easier for Cecile to drive by and pick me up. Most of the time I would have Cecile drop me off for the day and I would phone her when I was ready for her to pick me up, if it was other than the regular time. This way I didn't have to worry about a parking place, and she would have the car and be able to go places during the day with the kids.

We had only very sketchy information on what had been going on. A few of the students had pocket radios and upstairs in the building was a TV but by the time information was passed around, you weren't sure about its validity as some of it was conflicting. As I made it across the main mall by the building and across campus, I came upon two different areas of blood. Someone had been severely hurt and I am sure with the large amount of blood in very large pools, they must have died. It was strange. The people had been removed and any emergency services were long gone. The areas were not closed off and of course, as yet, nothing was being cleaned up. I think it was such a shock and involved so many victims, it just overwhelmed the services.

The man in the tower was Charles Whitman—an ex-marine who had gone off his rocker. At least that is what they think. He had killed his wife and mother-in-law at the house, and then loaded a footlocker with guns, ammunition, supplies, petrol and other items. He put on workman's clothes and took the locker up into the tower as if he was a workman, and no one questioned it. As he got to the top he ran into some people and started shooting. After he cleared the area at the top, he set up and started shooting at people on the streets, people in shops, and students on campus. He killed 16 people and wounded 31.

Two Austin policemen made their way to the top of the tower. One went around the outside observation deck in one direction and one went around the other way. When one of them turned the corner and came upon Whitman, the shooting started and at the end of it Charles Whitman was dead. When he was autopsied, it was later released that he had some sort of growth in his brain. They didn't know if that had anything to do with his actions or not. He was the start of a number of mass murders around the country over the next number of years. I don't think they know why any of them do it.

Cecile came to pick me up and we went home. She wasn't worried as the school was a big place. I had a call later from my grandmother and I told her what had happened. She said maybe it was just as well I was running late or I would have been in the process of walking across campus when the shooting had started. Just another one of those 'what if's' in life.

Pharmacy school was a small school at the university. The entire pharmacy school had around 1,200 students spread over the 5 years of ranking. The group I was with, had only about 50 or 60 students in it. We were on target to graduate at mid-year instead of the traditional end of the second session in May. I was taking all the courses I could in summer school, to get some of the required courses out of the way in time to take my pharmacy courses. The adviser in the school would go over what you had and what you needed by when, in order to graduate. A lot of it was set by the pharmacy school and deviation was almost impossible. With a number of their courses being offered only once, at one time, each semester, you had to take it then or wait until another semester. It was for this reason the pharmacy students had a priority at registration. Once I was taking pharmacy courses I always had a priority. Each time during registration when I needed an outside course, the person providing the I.B.M. cards for each place in that course, had to provide me with a place. This way I would have all the courses I needed each semester when I needed them, without conflict. The pharmacy students were some of the few that could get what they wanted and be through registration in one morning.

But pharmacy school did make you pay for the privilege. Every semester you always started with an 8 o'clock pharmacy course. Your lecture courses were normally during the morning which left the afternoons open for laboratory work. I would usually have 3 laboratories a week but did have as many as 5. I would usually have a few hours free during the middle of the day. I found this to be a good time to study or work on my homework in one of the study booths at the academic centre.

As I got to know some of the other students I made friends with a few of them. One was James Pollock from San Antonio. He was a married student and was serious about school as well. He and a couple of his friends invited me to join their study group. If you had several students in a group you could get a private room for studying at the academic centre. This worked out if we had a semester project or were just helping each other with the courses we were taking. I also met another guy by the name of Jim Bowles. He was married and serious as well.

He belonged to a pharmaceutical fraternity, Kappa Psi. He wanted me to join and become a member. He told me that a number of the faculty liked to see the students take an interest in the professional fraternities and it wouldn't hurt my chances in trying to impress the faculty. I was not interested at first but as I watched and learned that they also helped each other with their courses, I became more interested. The professional fraternities would have projects and regular duties, as well as trying to help each other. They had only a couple of parties a semester, as their focus was not on being a social fraternity. For one of these parties I got them to hire the band that my little brother Charlie played in. They played the typical late 60's music. It was at a rented hall and everyone danced and drank a few beers. They were happy and Charlie was happy.

Each Christmas the fraternity would raise money to buy presents for the children with cerebral palsy that were kept in a state institution in Austin. It took some getting used to. We asked for an age of around 5 or 6 years old. We took all the presents to the institution and one of the guys dressed as Santa to give them out. The presents had labels, boy, girl, or either. As we went into the room all the people were jumping up and down hollering and clapping. They were from about 25 to 40 years old in age but they were all around 6-years-old in their minds. It was an experience but I'll promise you that no one ever enjoyed and liked their gifts more than that group did.

In another project we put together a handbook on over-the-counter drugs. It was done in conjunction with some of the professors that were to watch over us. It was broken into sections such as analgesics, antacids and so on. It gave a little background on how they might work, some of the things to look out for and what to consider. It would then list a number of the products on the market at that time. When the books were completed and published we had to sell them to raise money for the fraternity and other projects. It was one of the first handbooks ever done on this subject in this manner. We found they sold well in drugstores and to students that were in related health fields. One of the professors got the idea to make them available to other groups for fund-raising, where we would get only a very small cut of the revenue. This worked as well.

The fraternity house provided reduced rent on accommodation for members and a study area, as well as a TV room. Sometimes during the day I would walk the several blocks to the house and study there. They had a test and papers' room, like most fraternities. It was for members only. A lot of the professors never gave the same test twice and would give the old test back to the students. These would end up in the files of the fraternity. When you thought you were ready for a test you could get one of the old ones out and take it. You could then see if you were up to speed or not. This was one of the reasons I joined the fraternity about a year and a half before I graduated. Being a married student with kids and a bit older, got me out of a lot of the initiation stuff but not all of it. Once you were a member you were to always help each other whenever you could. This included later life as well. That is one reason they wanted the members to be committed and of good character. I would say the big majority of them were, during my time.

As I became more involved with my subjects and work at the school, I got to know some of my professors. One of them was a sponsor of the fraternity where he saw some of my photography work, which was my main pastime. I took, developed, and printed some of the events for the fraternity. He also saw where I had taken some photos with plus lenses for extreme close-ups. I had raised my grades and made the Dean's list in four of my last five semesters. I raised my grade point average to where, by the time I graduated, I was only one grade point below having raised my average to graduating with honors. I was really interested in many of my subjects and could have quite happily continued studying and gone on to graduate school. I hadn't really thought about it until this professor asked me if I had considered it. He was doing research on different types of plastics for use in the body. He would implant various types into rabbits and then document signs of rejection or allergic reaction. He was thinking my skills in photography would be an asset and be very useful if I did go to graduate school.

This subject was brought up but both Cecile and I agreed it was time to go to work and make some money. I had been watching the bulletin board at school where pharmacies around the state wrote in and offered job positions to graduating students. A lot of these jobs were not what I was looking for and even then at any one time, there would be only about 6 or 8 jobs posted. Cecile wanted to go back to San Antonio and be close to her parents. I considered staying in Austin but to get a job in a pharmacy back then was not easy. Too many pharmacists with the same idea. I visited with both my father and grandfather, and asked them if they knew of anyone.

They had a patient they had been treating and his son had a drugstore. They knew his son and were familiar with his store as well. He ran a large operation on the northwest side of town and he had a good reputation. Later, after they asked him about a job, he contacted them back and asked for me to contact him. Again it was who you know. He offered me a job and then told me he had already given a job to James Pollock as he knew him from the neighborhood. We would both be going to work at the same place. He would pay us a good wage until we passed our State Board exam and got our license, and then he would pay us $800 per month. This sounded like music compared to what we were used to living on.

The State Board exam was given twice a year and alternated between Austin and Houston, where the two main pharmacy schools were. This time, it was to be in Austin about 2 or 3 weeks after we graduated at mid-term in late January. All I had to do now was finish my courses and graduate. I had already completed my 1,000 hours of intern work in pharmacies.

CHAPTER 17

EDUCATION

The Pharmacy School at the University of Texas was known to be more inclined towards teaching the students from an academic point of view, than the other pharmacy schools in the state at that time. That is to say, we had a lot of theory, science, and mode of action. We did have some business courses and basic accounting but not nearly as much as was offered by the other pharmacy schools. We took, as a requirement, the equivalent course of first year medical school human physiology, as well as a number of other courses that were required for pre-med. The pharmacy school was proud of the number of professors it had, that had written textbooks and worked on other various projects in their careers. This went along well with the large number of professors in the main school science areas who had also done the same.

One day, when I was in class in the main school taking analytical chemistry from Dr. Ayers, one of the other students interrupted him as he was going over the answers to a pop test that he had given us. The student argued that the question in the book should be interpreted in another way as he was sure that was the way the author had intended. Dr. Ayers then politely asked him to please look at his book more carefully next time as he was sure he knew what the author had intended since he had been the one who wrote it!

It was not unusual to have the author of your textbook as your professor. This happened in a number of my other courses as well—several of them being pharmacy professors. One was a Dr. Davis who was also a medical doctor. He was getting up in age but still taught one of the best courses that had to do with drugs and their mode of action in the human body. He had been head of the Medical School in Arkansas at one time before coming to the pharmacy school at Texas.

Dr. Davis would talk at a moderate steady speed and give lots of facts. You had to concentrate to stay up with him while taking notes. Every now and then he would pause for a moment, and sometimes tell a story to try to help put his point across. One was on how to pronounce the work barbiturate. He preferred barb-i-tur-ate. He then told us the following story. The lion asked the bartender why he had indigestion. The bartender said to the lion it must have been the bar bitch you ate. "So, you see, there is a difference in how you pronounce it," Dr. Davis said.

Another time Dr. Davis was telling us about the effects of ethyl alcohol on the mind and the human body. He told us a story about a young man who years ago had won an Olympic medal running track doing hurdles. He was normally a shy sort of fellow. However, one day after a party, having a number of drinks, he wanted to impress a particular girl. He told her to watch him. The young man ran as fast as he could towards a very large hedge and then proceeded to try and hurdle it. He landed in the middle of the hedge and made a fool out of himself. The alcohol reduced his inhibition in direct proportion to his judgment. The alcohol was not a stimulant but a depressant and had depressed his good judgment, giving him false courage and false belief in his ability. He then said, "I know this is true, for I was there. I was the young man". He then pulled an Olympic medal out of his pocket and held it up for all to see.

Not all stories were so good. Another professor, a Dr. Hall who was teaching pharmacy management, marketing and other various business-related courses would also tell stories. We would listen intently in class to her stories and after awhile were wondering when she would start lecturing on the course. She never did. I found out these were the same stories she had been telling for years. She had her full professorship and full tenure. She couldn't be fired and had a job for life.

Dr. Hall was the only one teaching some of the business-related courses and you would have her 3 or 4 times over the years. I was once told that whatever grade you made in her first class, the first time you had her, would be the grade you would get in the rest of the courses you had under her. I made a B in the first one. I'm only sorry she didn't teach the course. The University of Houston Pharmacy School was known to push the business side of pharmacy and offered a number of courses on marketing, trends, competition, and other related subjects. They had a lot less emphasis on the scientific side. I can only assume that they felt in the real world, a strong business background would be of more use. I must agree with them if this is true, for most of us went into the neighborhood pharmacy after we were out of school. Dr. Hall didn't teach anything like the course description and nothing about the business side at all. Whatever a student learned was out of the outdated textbook we bought for the course. The tests she gave were usually of an essay nature and she would ask questions for you to describe or explain. This left it open for her to determine your grade. I did watch her when we were taking our final exams in the last course I had under her. The exam had a number of essay questions. I would watch as other students handed their tests in and left the room. She would glance at the pages turned in for about 30 seconds. She would then open her grade book and go down the list of names and then over to a grade. She would mark her paper and close the book. I answered all the questions on the test but the last half took me less than half the time. I still got my B, just as I had the several times before.

All in all, the professors I had at the University of Texas were good. I enjoyed their classes and felt I learned a lot. The one course that surprised me the most was physics. I had had a good high school physics teacher, a Mr. Cruse. He said if you understood and passed his course in high school, then you would have no trouble with first year physics at Texas. I took the course over a summer at Texas. I studied and worked hard at it, just like my other courses. I had learned that in order for me to get all of my work and studies done, I would sometimes have to get up in the middle of the night to study. Spending what little time I had with the kids and Cecile at the house meant I would sometimes spend the evening playing and watching TV. I would then go to bed at 10:30 PM and get up at 3 and then study until I was ready to get dressed for school. When I took physics I found it just as Mr. Cruse had said. I made such high grades on the test that the professor would not count my grade, as he had to curve the scores for the rest of the class. With the extra point questions I would sometimes make 110 on a test where the rest of the class may have a high score of only 70. The only thing that kept me from making an A both semesters was when in the second semester, I got messed up on the final exam with my slide rule (in the days before I had a calculator) and got the decimal point in the wrong place on several questions. I knew I could do the work so I found it frustrating to have made such silly mistakes and thus cost myself an A.

One of the professors told us they could never teach us everything if we stayed for many more years. What they hoped to do was teach us the basics, how to question things, and to know where to start to look for answers. We would be in for a lifetime of learning and it would be up to us to continue or fall behind. These were some of the truest words spoken to us at the university. Over the years it has always been a learning experience. Some of the learning has been by books and new skills—other times it has been by the school of hard knocks. I remember a quote I saw at the school that I never forgot. On the front of the Tower above the main entrance it has the words "Ye shall know the truth and the truth shall set you free." In the years to come I would find out just how true these words were to be to me.

Not all of the learning was in the classroom. I had to have a minimum of 1,000 hours working in accredited pharmacies for my internship before I could take the State Board exam. Some of the students would work for their hours during the summer, back home at their neighborhood pharmacy. Others, like me, had to try and get a job in Austin—which was not easy considering how many students were looking for part-time jobs.

The pharmacies that were willing to take on students for their internship, had to provide instruction and try to help bring the student up to a basic understanding in the everyday operation of the pharmacy. They had to have a minimum library of reference books and equipment on the premises, available for use. They had to be registered with the State Board for providing intern hours, and agree that the instruction would be both in the operation of the front of the store and in the prescription department. We were not allowed to "fill" prescriptions but could do most of the work under supervision. At the end of the internship we were to have a minimum of 600 hours out front and a minimum of 400 hours in the prescription department. Some of the rules had to be put in writing because, over the years, some of the storeowners would use the students only as a source of cheap labor. The only instruction for those students was on how to clean the floor and shelves, and maybe how to wait on customers at the checkout.

I saw an advertisement at the pharmacy school, as I remember, for part-time work at Ace Drug Mart. They had several stores around Austin and were in the process of preparing to open another one. I applied for a job at the one on S. Congress near where we lived. To my surprise I got a job and went to work. I worked in the back storeroom each day after school, with the nephew of one of the owners, a Mr. Donnelley. The large orders would come into the storeroom and we would check in the merchandise off the invoice for the store it was to go to, and mark the merchandise. We would then box it up and the deliveryman would take it to the store it was intended for. I did a little dusting and cleaning as well.

Not long after I started, they opened their new store in west Austin. They asked me if I would work at that store some of the time. I took the opportunity and worked there as well. The other owner, a Mr. Berry, worked at the west store most of the time when I was there. He tried to show me some of the basics on measuring and making ointments. He would show me how to look up refill orders for prescriptions, type labels, and get the medications off the shelves and put them next to the orders for the pharmacist. Along with the nephew, I also helped stock some of the shelves out front from the storeroom, and dusted the merchandise and swept the floor. I enjoyed going to the west store more than the S. Congress store—that is, until I had the pleasure of working with Mr. Donnelley. I found out very quickly that unless you were moving and doing something every moment, he would jump all over you. You needed to stay busy. He also let you know that you should always be dusting if you thought you had nothing else to do. He did not want you in the prescription department and had no intention of teaching you anything. He did like to yell at you and seemed to get pleasure from it.

As we got further into the football season the nephew wanted to go to more of the games. I wanted to go to the home games when I could but didn't care about the out-of-town games as it was impossible for us to normally go. We were scheduled on a roster as to who was to work when and where. One day the nephew came to me and wanted to trade Saturdays off. That was fine with me and we traded. I worked for him that Saturday and took the next one off. The next day I went to work was at the west store and to my surprise, Mr. Berry told me I was in trouble and Mr. Donnelley wanted to see me at the S. Congress store. He told me then that it was about me not showing up for work on Saturday, as well as something else. I told him I had traded with the nephew at his request. Mr. Berry then said to me "The little shit got you. He is always screwing somebody".

When I got to the S. Congress store and saw Mr Donnelley, he told me it was crap and that any changes to the roster were to be approved by the person who made the roster. He also accused me of taking money from the S. Congress store. I told him then, I wasn't there at that time and did not run the register. He told me then, it was out of the safe. I told him I knew nothing about it and I was not a thief. He didn't want to hear about any of it. It seems his nephew had already told him lots of tales. He gave me my last paycheck and fired me. The other employees and pharmacist all looked like sheep as I left.

I was shocked and angry. I had been taken advantage of by his nephew but even more aggravating, was being accused of stealing. I told Cecil what had happened and he contacted Mr. Donnelley and assured him I was no thief and that if he wanted to pursue this and accuse me, to get ready for a fight. Mr. Donnelley then said he had already dropped the idea that I was responsible for the missing money.

Ace Drug Mart was paying all the students $1.00 per hour and no overtime rate. The U.S. Government Department of Labor had a new minimum wage bill in place that said as long as a store did less than $250,000 in sales, and if it was a chain earning less than $1,000,000 in total sales, it was exempt from the minimum wage law. The minimum wage was $1.25 and had an overtime clause as well. Ace Drug Marts always claimed that the chain did less than $1,000,000 in total sales.

When I had worked with the nephew he had told me about how well his uncle's chain was doing and how much business some of the stores were doing. I estimated and added up the sales in my mind and came up with a number over $1,000,000. I didn't know for sure how accurate this was but decided to find out. I contacted the Department of Labor and filed a formal complaint on Ace Drug Mart for violating the minimum wage law.

Months later I got a letter in the mail and a check from Ace Drug Mart. It seems the Department of Labor audited their records and had found some violations. It said they had inadvertently paid the wrong rate to some employees and enclosed was a check to cover the difference up to the correct amount. It was a victory of sorts and did make me feel better. Years later when I was working at Charles Maund in Austin, Mr. Berry came in about a car. I wasn't sure how I would be received but when he saw me he told me that it cost Ace Drug Mart a lot of money. When it started, Donnelley told Berry he bet I was to blame . . . to which Berry had told him, "Don't get in a piss'n contest with a skunk". The Department of Labor went back in the records to when the new law came into effect and made them pay every employee that was owed money, plus a fine to the department. He said he and Mr. Donnelley had parted company years ago and anything that befell Donnelley he felt he had deserved. He had also been taken advantage of by Mr. Donnelley but it was all in the past.

It was later on that Mr. Bowles put in a word for me at Bray and Jordan Pharmacy for a part-time job so I could continue to get my hours for my internship. I got a job with this chain at their Twin Oaks Shopping Center store that was near where we lived. I continued to work at this store until I had all of my intern hours. I learned a lot at this store working with Bowles and learned about a piece of Austin's history.

It was about this time the U.S. Treasury had started a recall on silver certificates, as well as pulling silver coins out of circulation and replacing them with the clad coins—'Johnson Money'. It was called 'Johnson Money' as he was president and ordered the change, and the people felt both he and the money were phony. The price of silver had risen to between two and three dollars an ounce. A silver certificate was originally put in circulation with the understanding that it could be redeemed at the San Francisco Mint for one ounce of silver for each dollar. This was being done and then the silver was sold on the open market. To stop this, the government put a deadline on honoring the certificates. On silver coins, the amount of silver in them was more than face value of the coin. It was against the law to melt them down in the U.S. but not in Mexico or in Canada.

Each day at work, Bowles and I would take turns watching the cash register for silver coins and silver certificates. I was interested in collecting coins and had been building up a collection for a number of years. I would save what I could in the silver coins and the rest went into the pot. The silver certificates we both got went into the pot as well. About every couple of weeks either of us would take them to the coin shop on S. Congress and sell them for the silver merchants. It may not sound like much but some weeks we would make $10 or $20 extra that we would not have had otherwise.

The drugstore we worked in was very much a traditional store at that time. We had a tobacco section, cosmetics, gifts, over-the-counter drugs, rental equipment for the elderly, charge accounts, delivery service, and there was even a Western Union Telegram agent. The telegrams would come in and, depending on the urgency, would either be sent out with the deliveryman on the next set of deliveries or right away.

We were encouraged to wait on the customers and help them make their selection in cosmetics, vitamins and other merchandise. The cosmetics, fragrances and vitamins had stickers we saved on a card. When the card was filled we would turn it in to be paid a commission by the supplier. It was usually about 10% of the total but some items had a special $1.00 sticker that was nice to get.

Sometimes these ladies would come in that wore a lot of make-up and the older lady that worked there would say, "That's my regular customer". This was to let us know to stay away. They would buy lots of cosmetics, fragrances, and other toiletry items. She would sometimes fill almost half a card just off of one visit from her regular customers. These were some of 'Haddy's Girls'.

Other times we would get large orders of various products—douches, condoms, aspirin, mouthwash and the like. They would all be boxed up and charged, and then delivered by the old deliveryman that was working at the drug store. He would see the stack of several boxes and say, "must be time to go to Haddy's Place". As I found out over a period of time, 'Haddy's Place' was a converted motel at the edge of town near the end of S. Congress Avenue. It was the approved, protected place at the edge of town that was to be left alone. It had a long history, and a relationship with the local police department and various officials of the area. As long as this 'house' kept a low profile and stayed in its place, it was forgotten about.

The experience was necessary and the money I got was even more so. We got by and were even able to buy a sewing machine on time-payments. Cecile felt she could make some kids' clothes and do some sewing if she had a machine. She located one she liked and they agreed to sell it to us on credit. This was our first time-payment we got into on our own. I was able, over time, to buy a camera and some developing equipment with the extra money. Items at the student co-op were cheaper for the students and at the end of the semester we would get a rebate on what we spent. At the shopping center was a camera shop that would give us a break and that is where I purchased the dark room equipment.

I went to Austin to get an education. Little did I realize just what a well-rounded education was in store for me.

CHAPTER 18

Around the House

During the several years we lived in Austin, Cecile tried to spend some time with the boys while I was at school. She found it difficult to get housework done, take care of the kids and do other things such as shopping. Just not enough hours in the day.

When we moved to Austin, Craig had just turned 1-year-old, and Sam would have been just under 2 ½ years old. They were a lot of fun and both were happy kids. Happy kids by now, I should say for Sam. When he was little he had a lot of colic, and cried and yelled a lot. Craig at this stage would stumble around and growl a lot. He would put his head against yours and growl. Sam was always interested in what was going on and wanted to watch or help if he could.

Some days were more than a person could handle. It seems for whatever reason the boys liked finger painting. That was not so bad except the material they used was from the back of their diaper. You would then find the walls, floor, bed rails and anything else they could touch, covered in . . .; well you get the idea. On several occasions I found the kids locked in their room in a mess. Cecile couldn't face it and I think she felt it would help teach them a lesson if they had to stay in it. It would be my job to clean it up and straighten them out. This I did not think was a good idea.

The house had lots of leaks and drafts. In the winter when the wind blew, it would go straight through the house. You could fire up the gas heater, and the oven and stove, and not worry about carbon monoxide as the air was changed frequently by the draft. The house had a floor heater in the hallway that was between the bathroom and bedrooms off the kitchen. It was built down in the floor but everyone was afraid it would get the grate hot that was above it and the kids would get burned. When they were older and understood, I pulled the grate off and cleaned out all the dirt and toys, and fired it up. It heated the whole house. The grate did get hot but I'm not sure it would have hurt the kids.

The kids were always up to something and boys being boys, got into their share of mischief. I found out that one thing that scared them into paying attention was to hold them upside down above the toilet and tell them if they didn't behave I would flush them down it next time. It scared them. I was the one who was in charge of administering punishment. It seemed somehow to get started this way and it stayed this way over the years. I would get home from school—and in later years from work—and one of my first duties as I came in was to be informed of who had done what and who was in need of a spanking.

I guess it does go back to what you were used to. I usually gave the kids a good swat or three with my hand on their legs. Sometimes I found it useful to threaten them with a belt and then use the belt. With the belt you could hit the floor or the bed and make noise that scared them, as well as give them a couple of licks. I knew it hurt because I had been there before myself. At first I didn't think about it much . . . I was doing my duty.

As time went on, I hated it. I hated being the heavy all the time. I was the one who always hurt the kids. I wanted to be their friend. Sam and Craig over the years got more spankings than all the rest of the kids put together. I did finally learn and stopped. I still would and did, give a swat but it was then and there when it was needed and without being told I had to, and without scaring and hurting them. As I grew up and became older, I realized that some of the kids did not respond to this. In fact, later on it was better to restrict Sam than to hit him. You could hit him all you wanted and it wouldn't change a thing. You had to take something away or stop him from doing something, to get his attention. Craig would listen and with him I found you could usually talk to him to straighten him out.

Out of all the things I've done that I've ever regretted and felt sorry for, this would be by far at the top of my list . . . the way I hurt and scared my two sons.

Sometimes we would all go to the park and they would play on the swings and slides. Other times we would go to a little amusement park that had kids' rides. We couldn't do it very often because of the money. A few times we went to the park and flew kites. I liked taking pictures of the boys and usually did so at every opportunity.

I would try and make some home movies with the boys where they would act out little skits. Other times I would have them pose for still pictures. I enjoyed doing things with them and wanted to record these times in pictures.

We didn't know lots of other people and none with kids. The only people we knew with kids were the next-door neighbors. They were a nice Mexican family with two nice kids; a little boy and a little girl. We would sometimes have them come over and play with Sam and Craig in the back yard. They would play on the slide and go down into the little inflatable swimming pool. Cecile didn't like the boys going over to their house. I guess it was because she couldn't see what they were getting up to.

Kids from next door, in pool with Craig and Sam

I don't know for sure where it came from but later on, after Cecil and Elizabeth had been up, the kids stopped playing with the kids next door. For whatever reason, all of a sudden, they were off-limits. I stayed out of it but always wondered.

The boys would get tired of the same routine and wanted more of a challenge. I would spend what time I could with them. Sometimes it would only be watching TV and talking about the programs. They liked 'Lost in Space', 'Star Trek' and 'Yogi Bear', just to name a few. The idea came up that maybe they should be in a pre-school of some sort. Cecile had been doing some checking into this and found one not far from the house. They would go for a half-day in the morning to learn ABC's and numbers, and a few other basics. I think it helped and they seemed to enjoy it.

In 1968, in San Antonio the Hemisphere Fair was held in the downtown area. It was to be a celebration of the cultures of the hemisphere—plus some other countries sent exhibits as well. They had the rides for the kids and food booths but most of all they had displays of histories and cultures of the various countries that made up the hemisphere. Texas had a large display showing its history and the different backgrounds that made up its history, and this showed how it evolved into what it was today.

This was something you could not see in a day. They had a monorail that went around the grounds that would give you a good idea of the layout and where the exhibits were. Dr. Joe felt it was something that was well worth the time and effort to see. He felt so strongly about it in fact, that he purchased a family pass which was good for the duration of the Hemisphere fair, and had it available for each family to use. It was hard for us to get the time to go but we did go several times. I think I could have spent twice as long at it as I did. I shot a number of rolls of film and about an hour's worth of movie film which I later put on a large spool.

Cousin Ena came up from the coast with her kids one time and went when we were going. The kids enjoyed the company and as usual were more interested in the rides. They took some interest in the exhibits.

Another area did have restaurants that served some representative dishes from their country. Dad wanted to go at least once but couldn't walk and stand for the amount of time it would take. Arrangements were made and he went one time in a wheelchair. As I remember we met him and part of the family at the fair in the early evening. He wanted to go to the French restaurant. We managed to get in, only to find the only thing worse than the slow service was the over-priced food of mediocre quality. By the time he was ready to head to the car, it became obvious we would have never made it without the wheelchair. This was also due to the poor condition of his legs. He enjoyed what he did get to see and enjoyed eating out. I think that was still his all-time favorite thing to do. This outing did cause some stress with some members of the family but all in all we had a good time.

I never knew why Cecile didn't try and do more with the kids along the lines of basic education such as ABC's and numbers. Exposure to nature, museums and Hemisphere fair, were things they seemed to enjoy. I don't even know what she spent most of her time doing. We would watch TV together in the evenings and on weekends when we could. I remember one time when we were watching TV and they ran an advertisement for one of those music collections. It was one that had lots of artists and different songs all on one tape, and at the end they would list a lot of the singers before closing with "and many more". Cecile looked at me and said "I don't remember exactly who she is but she sure is on a lot of those tapes". I laughed and said you mean "Minnie Moore?" She said yes. Ever since, whenever I hear "many more" used on an advertisement, I can't help but think of this.

The boys still got into mischief from time to time but nothing really that bad. It was more along the lines that they hadn't picked up their room or the toys were all over the house and that sort of thing.

One day after we got the '67 G.T.O., I took it to school. I drove home that afternoon and started up the driveway. The driveway went alongside the house outside the kids' bedroom window. The driveway was blocked. From side to side it was about 3 feet deep in toys. All kinds of toys.

I stopped the car, turned it off and got out. I walked up to the pile of toys and looked around. No kids in sight. I walked around to the back door and went inside. I asked Cecile what was going on. She told me she had sent the boys to their room and told them they couldn't come out until they cleaned it up. She explained they had toys all over the room and in their beds, and she was tired of the mess.

When the door was opened to their room they were as proud as they could be. The mess was all cleaned up. I couldn't help but laugh. They had no place to put so many toys away in their room, so they came up with the idea to put them out the window. They had pushed out the screen in an effort to clean the room and then proceeded to push all the toys through it, out onto the driveway. I helped them get the toys off the driveway and back inside.

About the only people that every came up to Austin to see us were her folks. This was mainly during the football season. One time, Patricia Tindall, Cecile's cousin, came up and stayed with us for a short time. I took some photos of her and of the kids, while she stayed. I felt this was an error in my judgment as the green-eyed monster started to appear, and soon after this, Patricia was on her way. With all that had happened to Patricia over the last several years, I think she could have used a little attention and understanding.

We still went down to San Antonio for Christmas and would go over to my grandparents' house to see the family—usually on Christmas Eve. This was one of the few times of the year we would usually see a lot of them, especially all in one place.

We made it down to San Antonio when we could. My mother would have more to drink than she should at times and would then phone me up in the middle of the night to remind me of how sorry I was. This didn't help our relationship and made it even more difficult for me to take the kids by, so they could see them. My parents' only trip to Austin was when I graduated. The school had a little get-together one evening for the group of about 30 that graduated at the end of January in 1969. My parents stayed at a motel near the school. I am sorry to say they had too much to drink while they were there at the motel. We had taken the kids over so they could go swimming at the motel pool. The good news was they didn't do it out in public.

Dad had said he would give up drinking when Joey was in Vietnam. The entire family was afraid he wouldn't come back in one piece. Dad did give up for awhile and then slowed down some for awhile but after Joey got back it was all on again. Joey had been drafted and ended up as a mechanic in an armored division at Fort Knox for the balance of his training.

When he went to Vietnam, he was first sent to the DMZ with the Marine Corps. They needed tank mechanics so he spent some time there. He was later sent to Pleiku, to a depot that did repairs. While at this place he saw a lot of corruption, and misplaced parts and supplies.

They asked for volunteers for short-range reconnaissance and he volunteered. They had been under rocket attack at the base and he decided if he ever stood a chance of getting back; he was better off on his own. He was usually teamed up with someone else—one time, the guy was a cook who had volunteered.

Twice, Joe was put in for a medal, a Bronze Star, but was turned down because his official capacity was listed as a mechanic. They would go out and find the enemy, and then let the commander know at headquarters where they found them. It was twice when they were out, that they came across other U.S. troops that had been ambushed and pinned down. It was then that he and his team of one or two would then help break out the troops by being able to attack from the outside.

The longer Joe stayed in the army, the more he realized how much false information was being put out. At first he thought he might make a career of the military but by the time his tour of duty was over, all he wanted to do was catch the plane home and get out. He was not the same person when he returned home. He was more skeptical, had a shorter fuse and would get in a fight just as soon as not.

I wrote Joey a few times while he was in Vietnam but I am sure my letters sounded like I was from another planet. I was writing about school, football and all the things we had around us. He was shooting and being shot at in the jungle. When he was back at base he wanted to get rest and be left alone. My letters were not relevant to him or what was going on around him.

At the University you would see protests against the war on most days. It was usually around the Student Union Building on the main street. The protests were usually not very large and most people ignored them. I was so busy with school myself, that I hardly noticed them the whole time I was there. Maybe the protests got larger after January 1969 when I left.

During this period a ruling came out that each person that had a deferment from being classified I-A in the draft because of being a student or married with kids, had to be exposed to the draft for at least one semester. It had been ruled that this was only fair. When these changes started coming through I was contacted by the U.S. Air Force about joining under a special program. I could go in and be guaranteed a position as either a pilot or a navigator if I passed the test. They would then pay for the balance of my schooling and leave me in school until I graduated. It was a gamble and a few of the students went for the offer. With me having kids, it was a different situation so I took the gamble and waited for my classification to go to I-A.

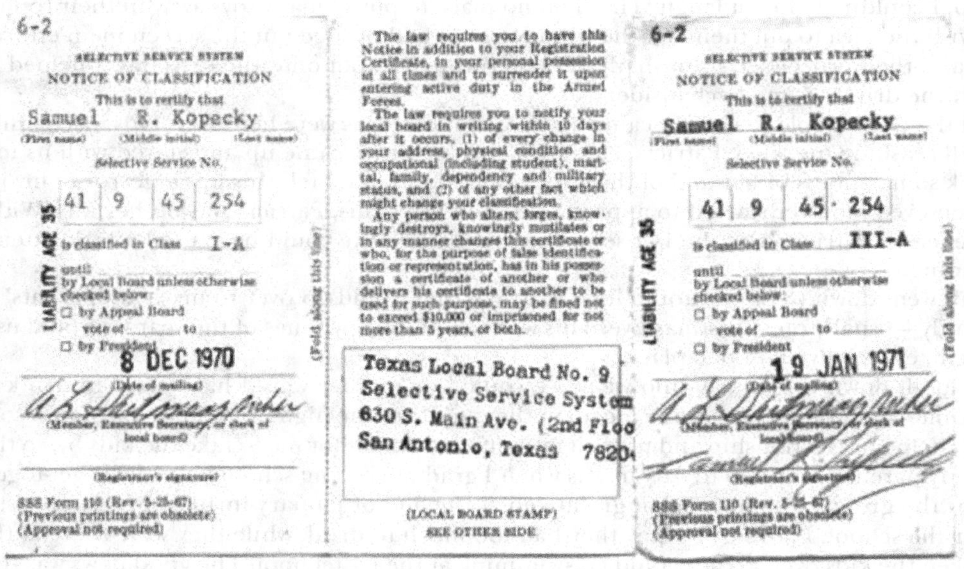

6-2
SELECTIVE SERVICE SYSTEM
NOTICE OF CLASSIFICATION
This is to certify that
Samuel R. Kopecky
(First name) (Middle initial) (Last name)
Selective Service No.
41 | 9 | 45 | 254
LIABILITY AGE 35
is classified in Class I-A
until
by Local Board unless otherwise checked below:
☐ by Appeal Board
vote of ______ to ______
☐ by President
8 DEC 1970
(Date of mailing)
(Member, Executive Secretary, or clerk of local board)
(Registrant's signature)
SSS Form 110 (Rev. 5-25-67)
(Previous printings are obsolete)
(Approval not required)
(Fold along this line)

The law requires you to have this Notice in addition to your Registration Certificate, in your personal possession at all times and to surrender it upon entering active duty in the Armed Forces.
The law requires you to notify your local board in writing within 10 days after it occurs, (1) of every change in your address, physical condition and occupational (including student), marital, family, dependency and military status, and (2) of any other fact which might change your classification.
Any person who alters, forges, knowingly destroys, knowingly mutilates or in any manner changes this certificate or who, for the purpose of false identification or representation, has in his possession a certificate of another or who delivers his certificate to another to be used for such purpose, may be fined not to exceed $10,000 or imprisoned for not more than 5 years, or both.

Texas Local Board No. 9
Selective Service System
630 S. Main Ave. (2nd Floo
San Antonio, Texas 7820
(LOCAL BOARD STAMP)
SEE OTHER SIDE

6-2
SELECTIVE SERVICE SYSTEM
NOTICE OF CLASSIFICATION
This is to certify that
Samuel R. Kopecky
(First name) (Middle initial) (Last name)
Selective Service No.
41 | 9 | 45 · 254
LIABILITY AGE 35
is classified in Class III-A
until
by Local Board unless otherwise checked below:
☐ by Appeal Board
vote of ______ to ______
☐ by President
19 JAN 1971
(Date of mailing)
(Member, Executive Secretary, or clerk of local board)
(Registrant's signature)
SSS Form 110 (Rev. 5-25-67)
(Previous printings are obsolete)
(Approval not required)
(Fold along this line)

My draft cards showing 1-A and 111-A

The day came and I was exposed to the draft for a short period of time. After it was over I was returned to III-A. I was lucky; I wasn't drafted as my number didn't come up. I was advised to hold on to my 1-A card in case any question ever came up about whether or not I had been reclassified for some period of time. This again came up after I graduated and was again classified I-A for a period of time until 19 January 1971. The cards also had the legal advice about burning, destroying and such, in order to make it easier for prosecution of protestors who burned their cards in public.

While we lived at the house on Linscombe Ave. we were given a little dog for the boys from the Holickman's out at Yancy. It was a cross between a beagle and a Chihuahua. I trained it not to bite the boys or me. I usually took care of it and fed it. The dog lived on the back porch and in the back yard. It was good about staying around the house and made lots of noise when a stranger came around.

Craig and Sam with Ace, in Austin

One day I noticed Ace was acting funny. I looked at him and found that in front of his back legs, below his spine but above his gut area, he had a hole. It looked as if someone had shot him with a .22. It had gone clean through him. I gave him antibiotics for a week and watched over him. He never looked back and recovered.

He stayed with us until he disappeared one day when we lived on Zornia. He never gave me a hard time or the kids. He liked to ride in the car when he could but always wanted to get under your feet. The only one he would try to bite and wouldn't have much to do with, was Cecile. I always felt there was something I didn't know.

CHAPTER 19

BACK TO SAN ANTONIO

As graduation approached and it became time to move again, we found ourselves making extra trips to San Antonio to look for a place to live. We knew we wanted to be on the north side in an area that would be convenient to Cecile's folks' house, and in the Northeast School District.

We wanted to live in a house but to find a house to rent in the area where we wanted to live was almost impossible. We considered buying a house but had no money. Cecil had already suggested I ask my parents or grandparents for some money. I was not sure how well this would go down with them as we hardly ever saw either one of them. We liked looking around at houses and found a new one under construction in an established neighborhood in the area we wanted to live. The builder was handling his own sales as well as building. This made it more straightforward to find out what he wanted for the house and what he was willing to do to make a deal.

He told us he would be ready to do the colors in the house in a few weeks and if we committed to buy it, then we could choose the colors of the paint, carpet and counter tops. The house would be ready for completion around the end of January 1969, which was about the right time for us. The house with a fenced-in backyard would be just a little over $20,000. With deposits and the down payment, we would need around $2,200 to $2,500.

I went to see my grandfather, Dr. Joe, as I knew my folks didn't have any money. My parents gave us a few hundred here and there but that was all they could afford to do. I was unsure what was going to happen but explained what our plans were and how much we needed. To my surprise, on the spot he agreed to help and said he would loan me the money for the down payment. About a week later I went back by his house to pick up a check and signed a piece of paper for the loan. He told me he should keep this on record for Internal Revenue and I could pay him back at some later date.

I think Cecil was surprised to see how readily Dr. Joe loaned me the money. In fact, I think he was surprised he did at all. We made our application for the mortgage and our approval came back in short time. We had very little credit but what we did have was good. A new college graduate with a professional job like I had, being a pharmacist, was almost a sure bet for approval. The only problem was that the weather had turned bad and the house would not be ready for weeks.

After some heated discussions with the builder, he finally agreed we could store our belongings in the garage of the house as the garage was already finished. He didn't want us to live in the house and "take possession" until after we closed at the mortgage company and the money had changed hands. If anything became a problem and we were living in the house, he would have to get a court order to get us out. It could be a real nightmare for him.

We moved back to San Antonio in January. Rudy Salies, a long-time general worker for Cecil at the company and the ranch, came up to Austin with a rented truck. The first time we moved we had a moving company, and it cost an arm and a leg. This time we didn't have the money. Between the car and the big truck, we made it all in one move. We put most of our belongings in the garage at North Star Drive and the rest we took to Cecil and Elizabeth's house on Riviera where we were going to live until the house was finished.

I started to work at University Drug Store for Moody Armstrong, shortly after our move. He wanted his new employees to get familiar with the routine and the store. The money he was going to start paying us didn't hurt either. I still needed to study for my State Board exam, which was only a few weeks away. Moody told us he would give us several days off for the exams as they would be given over a two-day period in Austin.

I noticed I had developed a little problem but didn't want to get problems started with my job. I was sure I had injured myself when we moved. I didn't notice it for about a week but I was getting sore in my left lower abdominal area. I had developed a left inguinal hernia. I purchased a hernia belt, which was used to give you additional support in the area of the hernia. I hoped this would buy me some time.

It was while we were living with Cecile's folks one day that we decided to see how the house was progressing and pick up a few items. We had a key only to the garage doors. We looked in the windows and saw a number of the items had been completed. We then went into the garage and to our surprise found a number of the boxes had been opened and someone had been through our belongings. We contacted the builder and told him enough was enough. The house should have been finished weeks before and now we were having our personal effects gone through and stolen. The best we could tell only a few small items had been taken. He agreed to change the lock on the doors that went into the garage and that he would be the only one with the new keys. I guess it was better late than never.

When I went to Austin to take the State Board exams, I went on my own and stayed in a motel. The exams were over a two-day period and were written, oral and practical, with the practical being at the pharmacy school in one of the laboratories. The written was over all of our various subjects. This included some of our pharmaceutical chemistry basics, drug interaction, law, and pharmacy calculations as they called it. We also had questions on matching trade names with generic names—which was not one of my strong suits at that time.

The oral part was short. We would go in a room with several members of the State Board and they would proceed to ask us questions about how we felt about issues, interpretation of the law in certain instances and what to do if a situation presented itself.

The practical part required us to fill several prescriptions in the lab in a required time. We were watched on our procedure, and any notes or calculations were checked on the back of the prescription. They even watched us to make sure we could type at a speed of at least 35 words per minute as was required. We were told it would take about 6 weeks before we knew if we had passed. You could not make lower than 60 on any one part of the exam and had to have an average of no lower than 70 to pass. The rumors also had it that if you didn't do well on the law section and if you "killed the baby" on the pharmacy calculations section, you automatically failed. The "kill the baby" was a problem given on the calculations section of the test each time. The problem was always slightly different but if you didn't do your conversion amounts correctly in calculating the correct dosage for the baby the prescription was supposed to be for, then you "killed the baby" and failed.

A lot of our training was aimed at knowing how the drugs worked, what was contraindicated and what the correct dosage was, just to name a few. We were the last line of defense between the doctor and the patient, before the patient took the medication that could cure him or kill him. We were not to make mistakes and were to catch the potential mistakes of others before they became a problem.

This is what we were trained and educated for. Each time we put the pills from the big bottle into the little bottle, we were to ask ourselves in our minds, what was it, what was it for, and did it go with the other medications the patient was taking? Did the dosage appear to be correct? If we were to compound the prescription, did the dosage and amounts make sense?

Then we were to triple check each step we did. Read the prescription and think about what it was and what it said. Get the medication off the shelf and put it with the prescription. Type the label—requiring reading the prescription again. Pick up the medication to count it out and then check to see if this was the correct medication off the shelf. Put the pills in the small bottle and attach the label. Read the label again and check to see if it was correct. Add any additional warning labels to the prescription bottle (such as drowsiness, no refills, etc). Return the medication to the shelf or place it out of the work area to the side, and again check it against the prescription as you placed the prescription bottle with the prescription for the person at the checkout. When you did any kind of calculations or had to measure ingredients, you again either double or triple checked each time. These steps became habits and it was the only way to overcome what could become monotonous and lead to mistakes.

Moody Armstrong was well known and respected in pharmacy circles. He had contacts on the State Board from being a member of a number of pharmaceutical associations and being active on a number of projects. About two weeks after we had returned from the exams and were working in our limited capacities in his store, he came to us and said he had some news. A friend of his on the State Board had phoned him and told him that both Jim and I had passed. This was a great relief. He also told us that since he knew we had passed he would pay us the full $800 per month from then on. I never knew what I made on the exams until many years later when I got a copy of my score, along with other papers, when I was moving to New Zealand. I had a final average score of 77. I was greatly disappointed but then the two things that came to mind were . . . no one ever asked what I made—only if I passed and had a license—and the other was that a number of students didn't pass the first time the exams were given. At least I had done that.

University Drug Store was a busy store and filled a lot of prescriptions. It was an older established full-line store of about 5,000 square feet. It had a large soda fountain area that served meals from breakfast to dinner. The gift and cosmetic area was run by Moody's wife. Moody oversaw the whole store but mainly watched over the prescription department and the over-the-counter drug section.

He was okay to work for and had approved a rotating shift for the pharmacists. We would start some days at 7 AM and had to open the store but got off at 3. The 3 PM shift would work until closing which was 10 PM or after the last delivery had been made. In the times of the flu, if you had to stay until 1 PM to get everything out, you did. I think the latest I stayed was about midnight. You rotated with this so that every third weekend you were off from mid-afternoon Friday until mid-afternoon Monday. Every third weekend you worked the entire weekend and the other weekend you worked only half of it.

When I worked for him I learned his ideas on pricing prescriptions. He worked out the basic cost of materials, then the medication, then the professional fee. He felt you should get a return on investment on the medication just like on over-the-counter products. He also felt you should get a professional fee for watching over what was going on and for the consultation that was often given to his customers. You then had a sliding scale—a large mark-up on the cheap end and almost only the fee on the expensive end. A lot of prescriptions were between $3 and $4 then. These may have a cost of $1.00. A prescription that was $20 would cost about $15. Another thing he did was not charge for the bottle. That is, if he had a prescription for a product that was rarely used, he would not charge the cost of the whole bottle to that prescription just to make sure he didn't lose money on it as a number of stores did.

That summer I worked for Moody was when we could take the long weekend and go to the coast. It was also the summer that my hernia got to the stage I could no longer ignore it and just hope it would go away. I had kept an eye on it as I was warned that if it became twisted, my bowel could block and the area could develop gangrene. I was sent to a surgeon, a Dr. Hill, by my father. He felt it should not be put off any longer and wanted to operate as soon as possible. I told Moody what the situation was and that if we scheduled it for a Thursday and it was a week that I was to have the weekend off, then it could be done with a minimum of disruption as I was sure I could start back to work the following week. He was not sure and felt I was optimistic but there was no choice.

I was admitted to the Nix Memorial Hospital and had the operation. It had all gone well and Dad had even brought a bottle of champagne up to my room under his coat. The next day around the middle of the day I was told that Sam had been admitted to the Santa Rosa Children's Hospital. They didn't know what was wrong with him but he was very sick. All of this had come on very suddenly. I no longer wanted to stay in the hospital for a couple more days. I wanted out and I wanted out now.

I told the nurse that I wanted to leave and she said I couldn't go until the doctor discharged me. I told her then if that was what she wanted, then she had better get on the phone and get in touch with him. I tried to get out of bed and could hardly get up. With the doctor being in the same building, he was in the room in a matter of minutes. He asked me to wait a few minutes while he examined me and looked at his work. He told me if I could stand the pain and stand up straight he would let me go. I got off the edge of the bed and tried to straighten up. It hurt. It was as if he had made me 2 inches shorter on that side. He assured me I wouldn't tear the stitches out. In fact he said if I did, he would do the operation again for free. I then proceeded to straighten up slowly. I managed to straighten up and take a few steps. Dr. Hill said "Okay, I'll discharge you and if you have any trouble call me".

Cecile and I went over to the hospital where Sam was. They had him in isolation and we had to wear masks and gowns when we went in to see him. They still didn't know what it was but he was getting better. The final diagnosis was toxic hepatitis of unknown origin. The doctors asked Cecile and her mother if there was anything Sam could have gotten into when they weren't looking. They always insisted that there was not. They also said when they looked around they couldn't see anything he had been in. The episode was dropped since he recovered with no apparent ill effects but I've always wondered what did happen to him when I was in the hospital. If someone was holding back information it could have been fatal if the situation hadn't changed and his condition improved.

I really wanted more money and Cecile wasn't overly happy with the shift work idea at University Drug. It seemed like I was always working and had very little time off. We wanted that new car we had never worked up to, so we ordered a new '70 G.T.O. before they came out. When the new cars arrived in the fall of '69, we had one of the first new G.T.O.s. We had a new house, a new car and some money left over after the bills. It would be years before I would be in this situation again.

I took on a part-time job working for a short time at the Pill Box Pharmacy. Gary Hyland, the nephew of the secretary of the State Board of Pharmacy, had a number of contracts with nursing homes for their drug orders. He had a new system where we would load locked cabinets with the medications for the patients for the different shifts and homes. I did this in the afternoon or early evenings for a short time with another pharmacist named George, but I didn't really like it.

I then heard that the discount store up the street, Gibson Pharmacy, was looking for a pharmacist. I went by and met a Herman Stoterd, the manager. He needed to replace a pharmacist that had left and wanted someone yesterday. The starting pay was $1,000 a month. I went to give Moody some notice but he didn't want any. He said I could go as soon as I was ready. I think it hurt his feelings. I hadn't been with him long and with time I am sure he would have paid me more and I know I would have learned a lot more from him on how to run a retail pharmacy. But I wanted to get ahead and didn't want to wait. I was about to broaden my education and didn't know it. I was about to enter the business side of pharmacy in a very different sort of way.

CHAPTER 20

MOVING AROUND

I was looking forward to going to work at Gibson's Pharmacy. I was looking forward to making $1,000 a month. I felt like I had made a big step forward as this increase was almost as much as the house payment. Herman introduced me to the one other pharmacist, a Mr. Pena. The store filled as many as 1,000 prescriptions a day, yet had only one pharmacist working full-time, with Herman helping when he was needed. University Drug on a busy day (when 3 pharmacists were on, with Moody helping when needed), would do about 600 in a day. It was once said a pharmacist on his own could do maybe 100 and with some help, do up to a maximum of 200 a day.

What they did at Gibson was very mechanical. Herman explained the only thing they had me there for was to put the labels on the bottles. That, legally, was the only thing his girls couldn't do. If a customer had questions and wanted advice, they were to be told to ask the doctor. Mr Pena one day showed me how you were supposed to do it. A lady asked if she could see the pharmacist. He raised his hands and yelled to her, "I am very busy. If you have questions ask your doctor. He is the one who wrote the prescription. I only fill them". He then put his head down and went back to work.

The half dozen or so girls that worked in the pharmacy would take the prescription from the customer and put it on the counter next to the last one placed down. The next girl typed the label and placed it with the prescription on her other side. The next girl would get the medication off the shelf and place it with the prescription. Sometimes they would count out the pills and put them in the little bottle and then leave them both with the prescription. They would usually price the prescription—that is, write the price down on the prescription. Most items had a chart attached that had the price already calculated for various amounts. The pharmacist would then look at the items that were in a pile with the label. He would then attach the label, go to the next pile and do the same. The girl would pick up the prescriptions and the drugs for the customer, and hand them back to the front counter girl to ring up. She would then return the unused medication back to the shelves.

This was very fast and with the minimum wage as it was, you could hire several girls for the price of one pharmacist. You had no consultation and a lot of the safety checks they tried to make a habit at school, all went out the window. The pharmacist had one chance to get it right on each prescription and if you took a full minute to read and verify everything, you ran behind. When it was real busy, the girls would make more than one row ready to put labels on. If a question came up on price you were to tell the customer "You know how cheap we are on your other medications. Just think of what they must charge elsewhere for this but if you want we will give you back your prescription and you can take it somewhere else". It was very rare for a customer to want it back and some were almost apologetic for questioning the price.

The truth of the matter was that the company had instructions to price the top 100 drugs below what the competition charged, regardless of whether it lost money. This was then followed by a formula for other items that made University Drug look like a discount store. What they gave away with one hand they took back with the other . . . in spades.

The next thing was what really hurt the independents. The law on unfair competition tried to help but made it possible for a chain like Gibson to buy in bulk from the manufacturer at great savings. Gibson could buy direct from say Ciba, a drug by the bottle of 500 for $50.00. This was available to any store with a direct account with good credit. Moody had such an account, and I did as well later on. The problem was that Gibson would then buy an entire batch number of the drug by the barrel for maybe $10,000. This was something an independent couldn't afford to do. This would bring the cost down to maybe $20.00 for

500. The barrel would be shipped to Gibson's warehouse in Louisiana where it would be repackaged into bottles of say 500. Each day we would phone an order to Louisiana for these top drugs and they would send them to us by bus. We would get them the next day. We paid a 3% fee to support the warehouse, as did all the other stores in the chain. The 500 tablets would cost the Gibson store $20.60, compared to the $50.00 the independent store would have to pay. That is why they could sometimes sell below what it cost the competition and still be making a profit! In the above example Gibson could sell 100 tablets of this for $9.95 and make $5.83 while the other stores were buying that amount for $10.00.

Another practice they had was when they opened a new store. I saw this when they opened a store in New Braunfels, Texas, not far from San Antonio. During the grand opening they sold a lot of items at cost and below cost, to help establish their image. The pharmacy prior to opening had price-shopped all the competition in the area and they priced all their prescriptions below the competition. They were to keep all their prices below the competition during the first year—even if it meant losing money. They were to try and run the competition out of business. After the first year they would go on to the regular pricing structure like the other stores.

I was somewhat nervous and didn't feel I fitted in real well with the others. The girls were all Mexican American, as was Mr. Pena. They all got on like a house on fire. One day when we weren't ultra busy, a lady asked to see a pharmacist. I decided to take a moment to see what her question was. I was with her maybe a maximum of 5 minutes. When I went down the counter, back to where I had left off, Herman was there filling prescriptions. Evidently one of the girls told him what I was doing so he came out to make sure we wouldn't get behind. He then took 5 minutes to tell me in no uncertain terms, how he never wanted to see me talking to a customer again. This embarrassed me in front of the others. He told me I was good at what I did but I needed to try to speed up and become faster like Mr. Pena. The girls seemed to help and do more for Mr. Pena but I figured in time everything would be okay.

Mr. Pena, as I told him one day, had the fastest hands in the west. When he was really moving he could fill a prescription, count out the pills and attach the label so quickly you could hardly see his hands. I don't think it took him 5 seconds on some. Then one day I detected something was going on. Herman had been on and off the phone, and the girls had been pulling prescription records and bringing them to him. Then a lady came in with a prescription and Herman went out to see her. He looked at the bottle and talked to her for a few minutes before she left.

I look back at it and almost wonder if they weren't trying to see if they could protect Mr. Pena. He had his initials on the label the girl had typed, as he was filling at that time. The prescription was for Lasix, a diuretic, for the pregnant woman. You could see she was pregnant. The girl and Mr Pena had read it as Lanoxin, a digitalis-type product for a heart patient. She was given the wrong drug and complained to her doctor that the medication didn't help her swelling and was making her sick. The doctor didn't write very clearly and had written only Lasix, with no strength like 40 mg which would have been a tip off. And on the directions he didn't help by putting only "take as directed". It is still the responsibility of the pharmacist and if the pharmacist has any doubt it is up to him to call the doctor.

The lady didn't seem to be hurt and it was doubtful it would have done any harm to the baby. Herman offered her free medication for the rest of her pregnancy and they would all see how things were after the baby was born. He should have stayed out of it to some degree and turned it over to the insurance company but in those days you could sometimes settle matters without lawyers and lots of money. I also found out this was not the first time Mr. Pena (fastest hands in the west), had been called up for filling a prescription wrongly. In fact he had a case pending at that time.

Business was not very busy and a couple of months or so later Herman called me in. He said he had orders from the chain to cut back on expenses and he was going to need to let one or two of the girls and one of the pharmacists go. He said that with Mr. Pena having been at the store longer and being much faster than me, he had no choice but to let me go. I was shocked even though I wasn't happy working at the store with the way they did things. I was also afraid that someday Mr. Pena would make a mistake and I would get the blame. With my final paycheck in my hand I went to the house.

I started calling a few of the people I knew . . . Jim Pollock, Gary Hyland and a few others. After a few days I got a call from Jim. He said he had been talking to Moody and he had heard that Harry Brusenhan at Laurel Heights Pharmacy was looking for another pharmacist. I went over to Laurel Heights Pharmacy on the edge of Olmos Park and the Laurel Heights area. I had an interview with the owner and gave him my references. The store had a soda fountain and was an old traditional-type store with doctor's office attached.

About a day later Harry called me and I had a job. This one was for $850 per month but I was glad to have a job. I would alternate with the other pharmacist that he had on duty and we would take turns opening at 6:30 AM and closing at 8 PM. We would have every other weekend off. His store was not as big or as busy as University Drug but was plenty for one pharmacist, and during the busy early afternoon it was good we were both on duty.

It was around this time that I had also taken on a relief job part time. It was at Lee's Prescription Shop in downtown San Antonio on the street level of the Medical Arts Building. Old man Lee told me his customers were mostly one-time people that would get their prescriptions filled on the way out. His few regular customers were people that worked in the downtown area. His policy on pricing was to get all he could on the ones he felt were one-time customers and be more moderate on his regulars. It was almost as if he would pull prices out of the air for each prescription. It was an experience but I was glad when my two weeks of relief work were over.

I was then able to work at Laurel Heights without the conflict of hours in the early afternoon. Harry Brusenhan was older than me by about 15 years and he had an older brother that had gone to school with my father. I think this may have helped me get the job as well. Dr. Brusenhan was a urologist and a couple of years later I had him look at Craig. Dr. Nau the pediatrician had always said that he thought Craig would grow out of a situation he was born with. The skin on the end of his penis was partly covering the opening. Each time he went to the toilet, he would have a small stream and it would go a good 10 feet. You could have entered him in a contest for who could pass urine the furthest and won a packet.

When Craig was in elementary school it started to become a real problem with the other boys starting to make fun of him. I told Cecile enough . . . to make an appointment to get him to a urologist and find out just what we had. Dr. Brusenhan felt it should not be serious and he could do it under a local at the office outpatient area. He would open the skin on the end and then possibly have to open the urethra more. The day he did the work we found out it was only a small piece of skin over the opening and nothing else needed to be done. We put some Neosporin ointment on the end for about a week and that was it. After all those years.

I had joined the Bexar County Pharmaceutical Association and had been a member of the Texas Pharmaceutical Association, as well as the American Pharmaceutical Association, since school. I had met a few of the others involved and had been asked to help with membership. I was not overly eager but decided to get involved with more pharmacists in case I needed to have more contacts. This was the sort of thing a number of the storeowners liked to see their pharmacist involved with.

It was not hard work at Laurel Heights Pharmacy. Only a couple of things concerned me. One was a patient that was an older man, a Rabbi that evidently had cancer. He went through injectable Demerol like it was water. By law, we were supposed to have a new written prescription in hand each time before we dispensed the drug. He came in late in the evening and wanted more, with no prescription in hand. I would have to get in touch with the doctor to make sure it was okay and then get the prescription the next day. I always felt I was sticking my neck out.

The other thing was more of an irritation for me. One of the doctors next door who rented from the drugstore, would come in once a month with boxes and boxes of samples. He would have us go through the samples and figure out what we could use and how much it was worth. He would then have us give him credit for it on his charge account. It shouldn't have irritated me. It was given to him for whatever he wanted to do with it and when Harry Brusenhan gave him credit, it was at about 50 cents on the dollar. They were both happy. This is, in fact, where I got the idea from to try to help Dad out a few years later.

I had been working for Laurel Heights only a few months when Cecil called me up one day and said he wanted to see me. He had been talking to Virgil Baer, the man he had at the company that handled selling insurance. He had given Virgil a job working out of the dealership when he talked him into getting his son, Linus Baer, to play football at the University of Texas. He was one of the top players the year he graduated. It seems that Virgil was friends with the lady that owned Zipp's Pharmacy in the Allena Village Shopping Center, where he got his prescriptions filled. This was not far from his house and not far from where Cecil and Elizabeth lived. Cecil had heard she wanted to sell and thought we had something to talk about.

CHAPTER 21

ZIPP'S PHARMACY

I was unfamiliar with Zipp's Pharmacy and had to ask Cecil to tell me where it was. He wanted to negotiate through Virgil at first as he felt if she knew it was H.C. Tindall of Tindall & Son Pontiac, she would hold out for a higher price. At this stage he mainly wanted to know if I was interested in having my own store. As one might expect, this was a silly question.

Only a couple of months went by when he told me that there had been several developments. One was that the pharmacist Mrs. Zipp had working at the store was going to quit (a Mr. Jackson), and the other old pharmacist that had been there since the start (a Mr Holcott), also said he was going to retire if she sold. Cecil thought it was a chance for me to work in the store and see what it was really like before the deal was final but I had yet to even set foot in the store.

I went over to meet Mrs. Zipp and find out what was going on. She wanted out. By law, the store could not stay open without a pharmacist on duty and she was tired of paying a fortune for a pharmacist, only to be taken advantage of by them. She and her husband had opened the store in the early 1950's when the shopping center opened. A few years after the opening, he died. Mr. Holcott worked for them at the time and had stayed on over the years. The story was that Mr. Zipp died of a bad liver as he had a drinking problem.

Mr Jackson (who was quitting) had originally been in a partnership in a store with Moody. He and his store, Hillcrest Pharmacy, were in trouble over bills and pharmacy law violations. His store was being run by the creditors and that is why he was filling in at Zipp's Pharmacy for some money. I think he was also trying to figure how to maybe get in on the store–until we came on the scene. Mr. Holcott had said for years he was going to leave Mrs Zipp if she didn't pay him more and give him more time off. She usually gave in but it was getting to the point he needed to retire. In the early years I think he also thought he might someday get the store. Mrs. Zipp said the last number of years had been real hard and he had not co-operated at all.

I wasn't wanting to move in yet and at best, only wanted to work at the store part-time. As soon as the two pharmacists got word about me, they turned in their notices almost overnight. This put me in a position of having to give short notice to Mr. Brusenhan at Laurel Heights Pharmacy to go to work at Zipp's.

Cecil had made the deal with her in principle, and on specific terms. I was going to work in the store and she was to introduce me to her customers and make a smooth changeover. She was to get a down payment with the balance being paid over 5 years. I would make monthly interest payments and an annual principal payment. I was to pay her the amount they had agreed on, plus the value of the inventory that was to be taken by Southwestern Drug Company's employees who provided this service. We were to split the bill for the inventory crew 50/50. I never had anything to do with the negotiations or the price agreed on, or the terms, and I never saw any figures or books!

I went to work in the store only a couple weeks before I was to take over. Cecil told me to build up the inventory. She wanted to run down the inventory. This way she would have small bills to settle with the suppliers and money in the bank. I would then have to stock the store and find money to pay the suppliers the next month. I tried to maintain a reasonable level of inventory but each day she would come over to me and ask why this or that had been ordered. You could see she was going from an unhappy person to a venomous angry person.

I had previously been instructed to ask my grandfather if he would help me buy the drugstore. I went over to talk to him about it before we had gone very far down this road. I was in for another big surprise.

He said no. He felt I wasn't ready to own a store, as I had not spent much time working in one as of yet. He felt I should have a number of years' experience before considering going into business for myself. I was hurt and a little angry. Cecil told me not to worry . . . he would take care of the down payment if needed, which was to be about $5,000.

The store was 3,000 square feet and originally had a couple of doctors' offices in the rear. They were now storerooms. The store also had a soda fountain with 5 employees, a cosmetic section, and a gift section with several women employed. You then had the pharmacy department and over-the-counter drug section with employees. The windows had a dark green plastic film on them to keep the sun out. This was to keep the electric bill down as the place had two air-conditioning units. The store was covered in grease from the cooking at the soda fountain, and tobacco smoke film from the patrons. They did meals from breakfast to early evening. The old linoleum floor was discolored and the yellow walls were dirty. The old shop fixtures around the walls and in the store had dark grey-blue shelving with a blond-colored wood trim. The only part of the store that looked modern was the prescription department that had been updated about 10 years or so before. The place needed a major clean and updating.

It was on May 1, 1970, that I took over. The night before, the inventory crew came in and over several hours, took inventory of the entire store. That afternoon the papers were drawn up and the lawyers met us at the drugstore. We signed the papers and the note. Cecil gave Mrs Zipp a check for the down payment—or said he had. The only thing I ever saw was the note with the final figures. It worked out that the amount was a little over $50,000 to be paid to her over the 5 year period, according to the terms set out.

I later learned she had been trying to sell for a long time and no one would have the store. It wasn't making any money and needed a lot of money spent on it. She had run it into the ground. That is why I never saw any figures on sales, expenses or the books. I am sure she would have been happy to have been paid a half-decent price paid out over a 5-year period, with interest and no down-payment–especially if she felt the note was secure. Cecil always assumed a drugstore was like a license to print money and Virgil told him they always had a lot of people in the store, even if they were drinking coffee and smoking cigarettes at the soda fountain.

Those people were employees, Mrs. Zipp's friends, and a number of the neighborhood gossips that would meet at the soda fountain each day to talk and drink coffee. If you prorated the square footage the fountain took up, for rent, and did the same with other expenses, the fountain lost a lot of money every day. If you only considered the wages and direct cost of food, if you were lucky some weeks you broke even. This ignored the aggravation with the staff and the ruined merchandise from the grease.

The women employees that worked the front area for Mrs. Zipp didn't want to work for me. Most of them left as soon as I took over—or had some reason why they didn't like the way I ran things and soon left. One of the exceptions was a Mrs. Marcie Ruffo that stayed with me up to the last couple of years I had the store. She must have been about 40 and her husband worked for the city power company. She had two children that were starting high school; a boy that played football and a girl that wanted to be a cheerleader.

When the dust and the exodus settled down, Marcie was a wealth of information on the neighborhood, customers, employees, and the history of the store and its previous employees. The two major problems I had at first were almost enough to make me go broke. It seems Holcott was lazy and did always want the store for his own. Marcie was protective of him but still let me know he had his ways of getting even with Mrs. Zipp. Over the years he never updated the prescriptions except for those that contained narcotics which he had to, by law, each time.

This was a problem with lots of old stores and the pharmacy board was coming down on them. I was determined to get this mess cleaned up before I was in trouble. Some of the prescriptions he had been refilling for 20 years and the people hadn't seen their doctors for at least 10 years. The price was also the same as it was 20 years ago! A number of the prescriptions were actually losing money. Some were being sold at around cost. He was still filling prescriptions for 50 cents. It had been shown for years that at $1.50 for water, you were only breaking even. When I started calling for renewals on the prescriptions it caused a bottleneck. A number of the doctors could find no record of the patients any longer. Others were angry and refused to give permission to refill the prescription until they saw the patient again. I had opened up a real problem. When I told the patient I could not refill their prescription and they would need to make an appointment with their doctor, they became angry with me. They never had this problem when it was Zipp's.

I knew I couldn't increase the price of the prescriptions overnight to a level that they needed to be, so I decided to do it over a couple of years. The only problem was some of the customers were taking 3,

4, or even half a dozen drugs at a time, and here I was, going up on all their prescriptions. I was the new kid trying to get rich overnight. If old man Holcott had still been working there when I took over the prescription department I think I would have beaten him to within an inch of his life. He was the type of pharmacist the State Board was trying to get rid of. He didn't know the laws—or didn't care. The first number of months the prescription department was in total chaos. Dozens of customers' prescriptions couldn't be filled while waiting on doctors to call back (to which most of them said no). If I was lucky they would say they would refill them one more time but to tell my customer to see them or it would be their last. Some people were taking antibiotics whenever they felt they needed them. Some were on tranquillizers with no supervision. Others were on thyroid pills, heart pills; you name it . . . with no supervision from a doctor for years.

This original fiasco cost me a lot of customers. I was too honest. Later George Shelton, my friend from the Pill Box Pharmacy, purchased Olmos Pharmacy and had the same major problems but he came out with his customers as a hero. He told me he had decided that if it had been going on for years a few more times wouldn't make any difference. He would then tell the customer a new law was or had just come into effect and that by the next time they needed their refill they would need a new prescription from their doctor so they should make an appointment. He then told them he was sorry for any inconvenience but he had to obey the new law. (When I was told no refill by the doctor, the customer didn't get any pills.)

As far as his old prices went, he only raised those he felt he could get away with. He too had an older employee that had stayed on to help and understood. She would tell him which ones he might be able to increase the price on. Those he lost on, he would try and make up on when they got a new prescription. The new wonders of medicine were like magic but they were expensive, was just one of his lines.

I was up to my neck in the prescription department and with the mess I had to concentrate on, I found I had to let the rest of the store run itself until I could get to it. A couple of the women behind the lunch counter both considered themselves to be the manager and had disagreements with each other all the time. The group of women was always fighting over something. I had one older white lady that considered herself to be the boss. I had a middle-aged Mexican American, Mary, who wanted to run the show. Two of the other girls were Mexican American and were related to the older one. When they had a problem, they would always threaten to walk out together if they didn't get their way.

I tried to work with them to the extent they had their own work schedule and ran their own department. They made up the menus, the specials, and set the prices. Once I had some time to spare I reviewed the department with Mary, as she had run the other woman off. I soon realized she only cared about how much she could get for the least amount of effort. She didn't care if the soda fountain lost money or not. I tried at arm's length to suggest some price changes (some up), and some ideas such as the lunch specials. They were doing lunch specials but it was what they wanted to cook and serve, not what the customers wanted. Some of the dishes that were popular, they didn't do often enough.

The attitude was shown at the end of a week as none of them would work on Saturday or Sunday. Mary would pack up items from the refrigerators to take home. She explained they were leftovers or items that hadn't been used and that by Monday they wouldn't be any good. This included meat that had been purchased for daily specials but they changed their minds and didn't use it after all. I soon became aware of the fact that I was subsidizing their food for home. A very real danger was that if you questioned them on any of these points, you were accused of discriminating against them or they had their feelings hurt and they were all going to walk out.

Their time sheets became such a problem I soon found it necessary to invest in a time clock with punch cards. I couldn't believe it. They would fill in each other's times, guess when they came in or went home, and sometimes filled in a couple of days at a time. With the new punch card set up, they were to punch their card only when they came in, had a break, or went home. The time clock did all the work and showed the time to the minute. It also had a column that showed the military time with the minutes converted to hundredths. This way an adding machine alternating between plus and minus on the numbers, checking in and out, would total up the hours worked to the decimal equivalent such as 6 hours and 45 minutes would be 6.75. You would then multiply the hours by the rate of pay and had their total pay down to the minute. It was more accurate than time sheets and the payroll went down when they weren't on time.

One day, after about the fourth time, I asked Mary why her daughter hadn't shown up for work again. (We would be short-handed during lunch again and this would cause problems). I was told it was her problem and not to worry about it. That was fine except she didn't care if the service was slow and customers walked out or said they wouldn't come back. This whole attitude got me to the point real quick, that my only real solution was to close the soda fountain and take it out. If I fired Mary or the others,

I was warned they would go to every government agency they could. They may not win but they would make my life miserable.

Moody always felt his soda fountain made the store look busy and people would pick up merchandise when they were in the store. This was maybe true if you had a good operation. I didn't. More and more of the older stores were getting out of the soda fountain business and putting in camera departments, gift merchandise, candy, or anything else they thought might work.

Originally I was told I would get $1,500 to $2,000 for the used soda fountain equipment. I talked to Behrens Drug Company out of Waco who serviced all of central Texas, as they had a department that would help design remodeling, and supply fixtures. They also offered a finance plan for the fixtures. I did some additional checking around and got some more ideas on what I could do. The man from Behrens was also good on coming up with ideas on how I could change the looks without a lot of money, in some areas.

Kopecky Pharmacy on Blanco Road, with doctor's office (rear right)

I had sent the old sign away that had been on top of the building which said 'Zipp's Pharmacy'. One of the big companies in town sent a crane out on a truck to lift it off and take it away. They salvaged what they could of the old material and made a new sign that looked more like the design on my prescription labels. The labels had a modern looking mortar and pestle followed by 'Kopecky Pharmacy'. The sign was in orange with green neon lights at night. The green neon was from the old sign and kept the cost down. The makeover of the sign was $1,200. A lot for me back then.

I knew we needed a cleanup, fix up, and changes. It was during this first year that I worked from early morning to late in the evening and sometimes into the night, to make this happen. I had very little money to spare and a lot of work to get done. I was determined to make this store work. It is what I felt we had been working toward the last several years—to have a store of our own.

I had it in my mind that it would be successful and provide for the family in the years to come. I was very unaware of and ill-prepared for, some of the tough times ahead. I needed a stronger business background, and less theory and idealism. With time, I came to realize just how big the mistakes were that I had made in the early days. With time, changes do occur and successful businesses have to see or anticipate these changes, and either change with the times or get left behind.

CHAPTER 22

GETTING GOING

Once I had decided what I needed to do and felt I had done my homework, I then started off by cleaning the store up. A lot of the work had to be done when we were closed as it was disruptive and could be dangerous with customers walking around and getting under your feet.

Cecile had a full time job taking care of the boys at home. A few years back we had decided not to have any more children until after I was out of school and working. We talked about it again, almost in passing, after I had gone to work at Laurel Heights Pharmacy. To my surprise, she told me she was again pregnant when all of this Zipp's business was going on. We both wanted a girl this time. With her being pregnant, it was best she concentrated on just the boys at home and stayed away from the remodeling. She wanted to help, so at first she did the payroll each week and would help write the checks for the bills on the 10th of the month.

Later that year, 9 October 1970, Laurie was born. I went down to the Nix Hospital and waited in the waiting room, as husbands did in those days. The boys stayed with Elizabeth, and Jim Pollock my friend came over to work my store for me that afternoon and evening as I waited. We were all pleased it was a girl. My grandfather went on and on about it. He had to tell again and again how it was the first girl in so many years and how few girls we had in the family at that time. He always wanted to see all the kids and from time to time over the years he would have my grandmother drive him over when she could to see all of us. Most of the time we would try and take them over to them. This was even less often after I was working and had my own store. At times he would go on and make such a fuss over Laurie we were almost afraid it might hurt Sam's and Craig's feelings.

Golda holding Laurie—December 1971

During the renovation period I had a fellow work for me that was one of those non-kin sorts of people. It was Charlie Veritis. Val Luckett back at the dealership was a first cousin of Cecil's. Cecil had introduced Val to a lady named Barbara Veritis, who he knew from somewhere. She was a widow whose her husband had been killed in Korea. Barbara had several children, one of which was Charlie. After a period of time they were married and Val adopted the kids, as I remember. So that is how they were non-related kin to the Tindall family. That summer I was asked if I had a job for Charlie as he was considering going into pharmacy. I said I did.

We weren't worried at that time about his intern hours, as much as him getting a feel for pharmacy and making some money. During the day I had him help me some in the store and do some things we felt we could get away with when customers were around. He helped get the film off the windows and did general clean up. (A couple of years later he worked for me again and got some of his intern hours with me then.)

When I closed the fountain I ran ads for people to come and give me prices for the used equipment. I found out then some of the freezers belonged to Tiny's Dairy, an ice cream company. They supplied the freezers as long as the fountain sold only their ice cream. Several of these surprises came up after Mrs. Zipp had left as she felt her transfer obligation was done about a week after the deal was signed. At the end I had one company that agreed to come on a Saturday and take the entire fountain area out and pay me $500 for it. This was a setback in the budget. However, a year later when I was talking to Parson's Pharmacy up the road, I learned that when he took his fountain out, he had paid $500 to have his (newer) one hauled to the dump.

Charlie helped clean up a greasy mess on the floor and walls when everything was gone. We had holes in the wall to fix and a big hole in the floor where a drain was. It was recommended that we cover the drain and seal over it, which we did. We also closed off the hole in the ceiling where the exhaust fan had been but left the outside cover in place. After we cleaned up the area we gave it a fresh coat of paint. When I had worked with the designer, we planned on covering the new wall areas with fixtures and shelves. About half the area was only waist-high solid wall, then a glass window went up to the ceiling. In this area we put in wall fixtures with shelves that came up just below the windows. The wall that had been a mess but with new paint looked okay, was covered by the new fixtures that had glass shelves and florescent lights in the top.

Blanco Rd store after the fountain was removed

I had shopped around some of the carpet and floor companies in the area and decided on one that I was a little nervous about. Mr. Wilton came into the store from time to time; that is how I knew him. He was to have a crew come in at night and lay down carpet as we moved the fixtures out of the way, one section at a time. The crew was to also put down new vinyl tiles in an area we were going to have fixed up with a couple of ice cream tables and chairs. It would have a couple of soda pop machines and snacks, as well as a fresh coffee machine we would operate ourselves for the customers.

The carpet was mixed color flecks with an overall look of burnt orange. It had orange, green, yellow and brown. I had wanted glue-down carpet but he assured me this would last longer and would not give me any trouble. It was also the only one I found at a price I felt I could afford, that still looked good. The first problem that presented itself was that his crew to lay the carpet consisted of one poor overweight man all on his own.

It took two nights with both Charlie and I helping him, to get the carpet down. Then, to top it off, on the last night he was about 3 feet by 20 feet short on carpet for the last section that was in the front of the store by the front doors. He had some carpet but the grain was the wrong way and when it was in the open it looked like a different variation of the same carpet. Mr Wilton had no more of the carpet, as it was discontinued stock. As a very poor compromise we tiled the entrance area into the store and used the carpet with the grain the wrong way. At one stage we moved the checkout area over this section of carpet but didn't find the layout satisfactory. We ended up having some of the carpet under fixtures and some exposed. If we had known this going in, we could have started at the front and the bad area would have been behind the counter in the back of the store by the prescription department.

The next major job after the new fixtures were in, was a false front that was put up above the old wall fixtures that had lights in it. This was to hide the air-conditioning duct and clean the area up. It looked like wood wall paneling on top of which we attached wood letters that we had made, that said 'Cosmetics, Drugs, Gifts', and so on. This also helped customers see what part of the store had which kind of merchandise. The prescription department already had letters above it from the remodel about 10 years before. Once this was up we noticed the lights had to be moved to the front of the wall fixtures behind the front edge, if the merchandise and area was to be illuminated. The old fixtures were set up to illuminate a plastic panel in the front with the light going out into the store. This took a couple of nights to move the lights.

After this was done we had to paint white, all the old shelves in the entire store on both the walls and the gondolas in the middle of the store. To make the wood grain appearance and color go together we found a contact vinyl paper that looked like wood grain that we then trimmed and attached to the wall trim and gondola trim. This took weeks, working after hours, night after night. We would remove the merchandise from a section and paint it after closing. I would then come in early the next morning before we opened, to restock the shelves in that section.

Cecil, at the dealership, needed more room so he had taken over to the adjoining property for more storage and parking space. It had a building that had been a donut shop and a large sign out front by the road that said donuts. When it closed down he had the sign changed to DRUGS and moved it to the parking lot outside my store. He took care of any details and it was installed with an electric timer. He was afraid the store didn't get enough exposure through being set back in the center. It was nice to have an additional sign out by the road and I hoped it would bring in the extra trade.

After several months of continuous work, several thousand dollars and a new payment book with two years' worth of coupons, the new version was up and going. The old store was dark, dirty, cluttered, and full of noise from the conversations and dishes banging. The new store was open with aisles I could look down, spacious, light, and had a soft quiet atmosphere with FM easy radio for background.

The new front area had more gift merchandise as well as general merchandise, sunglasses and such. The new area towards the back had an enlarged greeting card section as well as health care products to rent or buy, crutches, wheel chairs, and a full range of related products. I was now ready to concentrate more on the business side and try to get some of my other problems cleared up.

I had lost some customers early on because of my problems with the records. I then found out I was also losing some of my customers to Blanco Pharmacy around the corner, that had doctors' offices. The story was that the store and complex had been built by several doctors who had gone together and that the store was rented from them.

Several of my customers told me they had been to Dr. Zaccaria and he had called in their prescriptions to Blanco Pharmacy, or told them to pick them up on their way out as he had already sent them to Blanco Pharmacy. He'd had a falling out with Mrs. Zipp years ago when he rented the back offices from her. I wasn't sure what he was up to. The other doctor, Dr. Spector, also did some of this but not as openly as Zaccaria. Zaccaria and some other doctors around town, had reportedly gone into business together in a repackaging company. The company, Parkdale Pharmaceutical, would buy generic-made products like tetracycline and then repackage it under their label and brand name. Under Texas law at the time, if a doctor wrote a specific brand name then that is what you had to use. The wholesale going price for a name brand at the time was between $6 and $10 for a hundred capsules of tetracycline. Parkdale was something like $18 per hundred. This not only made the doctors a lot of money but also cost the patient a lot more as well. They had a whole range of products.

Cecil had already been on me to buy gifts for doctors and wanted me to call on them to introduce myself and see what I could do to get their business or get them to send me their patients. He saw nothing wrong with these tactics. I told him if it wasn't handled correctly it could do more harm than good. Besides a lot of my clients went to doctors in the downtown area or the new medical complexes, not to those in the neighborhood.

When I decided to call on the doctors I had a give-away product that held business cards in it, with my store name and number printed on the outside. I called in advance about dropping in and seeing the doctor for a few minutes. Most of the offices told me what time, on which days, the doctor would see people other than patients, so I could come and wait. I did this with a number of the doctors in the neighborhood. I introduced myself and told them how I had taken over Zipp's pharmacy and would be happy to help them or their patients' needs at anytime, and that if I could be of service to please let me know. I would then give them the little gift with the phone number and leave. I also did this with Dr. Zaccaria but found him to be belligerent. I then decided to ask him about what several of my customers had told me. This took him back and he denied having done any such thing. I then asked him what he thought about Parkdale Pharmaceutical. He claimed he didn't know what I was talking about. To this I explained that a lot of patients were being disadvantaged and if it continued I was sure someone might go to the newspapers about it. After this visit I never had any more trouble with Dr. Zaccaria or Parkdale Pharmaceutical, as the company dropped their prices to the same area in which other generic products were being sold. I don't know if my visit had any bearing on this or not but I do know that he knew I wasn't going to just roll over.

I still had a number of staff problems to work out, as it was not very easy to get good reliable help at a minimum wage level. I couldn't afford to pay much more than minimum wage and usually would give the employee a raise after a few months if they were working out. Both help for the checkouts and deliveryman position, had a regular turnover at first.

The other area was book-keeping. Cecile didn't have time and it seemed each payday it was done with an eleventh hour battle to have it ready. This was also true on getting the 10th of the month bills reconciled and paid on time. This left none of the actual bookwork done. The charge accounts that I had purchased with the store had a simpler solution that I took advantage of after only a couple of months, as the lady who did them on a part-time basis wanted more money.

I switched the system over to a computer system offered by the drug company. We had a multiple copy form, with a hard copy. Each customer had a plastic card that stayed in the store on a Rolodex. When they charged we would imprint the form, fill in the sale and have them sign it. If the card had a rubber band around it, they had bad credit and couldn't charge. Each week we sent in the hard copies for processing and at the end of the month we sent in the last batch with a card telling them to process for the end of the month. A few days later we had the hard copies back with the statements. They also supplied a printout of customers and their status each month. It cost on average about 50 cents a customer per month.

The hard part was a bookkeeper. Accountants were too expensive for a small operation and several of the bookkeeping services we tried were slow, inaccurate and charged more than they were worth. At last I heard of a company called CBS. Computer Bookkeeping Services. The man paid a franchise fee and would come by each month to pick up my work. I had to have the check stubs coded for him, so he knew what the checks were for. I also had a page I could list questions or items on and would give him copies of, say, a car purchase that needed to be set up as a delivery vehicle. I also gave him a copy of the daily sales sheet that listed sales, paid outs, charges, deposits, returned checks and so on. He would then take this away and the following month he would return with the material, plus a profit and loss sheet as well as a balance sheet, for the previous month. The bill was on the amount of work and number of entries, plus I would have him do the sales tax returns. It was on average about $100 per month. At the end of the year he would do the year-end taxes and personal taxes for about $150. It was a lot cheaper and faster than anything else around. I used him until I got out of the pharmacy business.

One thing was for sure . . . nothing stays the same. A professor at university in the business school said about business one day "You are going forward or you are going backwards in business, you never stay the same". It went along with the idea that the only thing constant, is change. I was starting to find this true back then and as time has gone on, I have decided they are most certainly true. Over the next several years I was to change and adjust to the changes going on around me, or go out of business. The time of major changes were just appearing on the horizon.

CHAPTER 23

CHANGES

Over the next couple of years everything changed—our competition, employees, and life at home. At first the business seemed to start to grow and the focus was on building the business and paying off Mrs. Zipp. We would talk about how we would no longer just get by but actually start to have some money once she was paid off. Then we could start to buy things and have more for ourselves.

At first the business grew and Cecile spent some time in the cosmetic and gift department. Cecile was still busy with the 3 kids and had a full-time job around the house. We had discussed her concentrating on these areas in the store and when the summer shows came up put on by the various drug companies, we would attend and do our major purchases for the Christmas season. The manufacturers would give additional merchandise for no additional charge, a reduced price, and sometimes offer what they called dating. This was buy now and pay later—usually pay in January after Christmas. You needed a good selection and a lot of stock if you were to take full advantage of the Christmas season. It was easy to overbuy and you always had to guess at what was going to sell. It wasn't until years later that I really learned how to cope with this, when one of the managers of the Winn's Store in the shopping center, explained their philosophy—especially on seasonal merchandise.

The seasonal merchandise was a big part of everybody's sales. You had Valentine's Day, Mother's Day (only second to Christmas in sales), Father's Day, the summer season, Halloween, Thanksgiving and Christmas. I really needed somebody in charge of buying, selling, displaying, and watching over this merchandise constantly. We had taken on several candy lines, which included King's, Pangburn's, Whitman's, and Russell Stover. We later cut back to only Russell Stover. We also brought in grey market fragrances and cosmetics, and started a costume jewellery and watch display. All of this took money to stock or we had to use dating and hope to sell enough before the bills came due.

The hard lesson to learn was that competition was getting tougher. People were driving a mile to save a couple of dollars and if you weren't careful you were stuck with unsold merchandise. This also started to happen in the vitamins, sunglasses, sun tan lotion and school supplies area. At the prices we had to buy at, it was impossible to match the chains' sales price and make any money. A few of the manufacturers (such as Parke Davis) stayed loyal to the independent. The best vitamin deal was a purchase of around $1,200 worth at one time. This applied to me, as well as the chain stores. This I could compete on. On pharmaceuticals, they had a winter antibiotic package with their range that covered a lot of the generic drugs you would get calls for. The package was about $5,000, with dating. Gwyn Pharmacy and I, would take turns on buying the package and splitting the merchandise. By doing this we could provide a major company's products at generic prices and compete with the chains.

It was years later that I learned from my friend at Winn's that their philosophy went like this, on seasonal products. If you had a shipment of Valentine's candy come in with a cost of $1,000, you would put it out at full retail at first. A couple of weeks later you would drop the price maybe 10%. Then maybe another 10% in a couple of weeks. A week before Valentines you would have it on sale for maybe 25% off. After Valentines it would be 50% off (about cost) for a week. Then you just kept cutting the price until it was all gone within a couple of weeks after the event. They kept track of the sales on a separate cash register key and after it was all sold, they would then total up the seasonal sale. They might have a cost of $1,000 and sales of $1,550. If they held out for 100% of retail the whole time, they would have $2,000 if they had sold all of the merchandise. But this didn't usually happen. It was through time and experience you knew how much to discount and when, with the aim of having all the merchandise gone by the week after the event, and as much sold as possible at the higher prices. No money tied up in dead stock, no storage problem, and you had the money to pay the bills and go on to the next promotion. This is part of what I didn't get at school. Common sense should have told me that if it isn't sold you haven't made anything.

Regular stock was also watched, for changes in trends. When a trend was starting to go out it was time to discount and clear the merchandise before you were left holding dead stock. Some items I had learned were traditional lost leaders and it was aimed at keeping women happy. Birth control pills were sold at cost; Kotex and Tampax were sold at cost. Feminine hygiene products were sold at a profit but at the lower end of the normal mark-up scale. Women felt they were being taken advantage of if you charged anything more than the competition for these items. It wasn't until many years later when I was in the car business I was told this philosophy in a much more memorable way. I was told not to ignore the woman when they come in about buying a car. Pay attention to what she wants . . . after all, she controls half the money and all the 'loving' in the household and will usually get her way. Women are a major force in buying.

It was in the fall of 1971, that I had another surprise. Cecile informed me she was again pregnant. This was not planned and was a surprise. It was the first time I ever saw her upset about being pregnant. She didn't know if she could stand the idea of going through everything all over again. Laurie was coming up on being 1-year-old and Cecile felt she was starting to be able to get out and get some freedom again. She wanted to know how I felt. I told her I was happy to have another kid but I also understood that it was her being the one having the baby, and being the one that would have to be at home day in and day out. I told her I could understand how she felt but it was up to her to decide if she wanted an abortion or not. I also told her whatever she decided I would go along with and support her. This was something she took a long time deciding.

It was during this season just before Christmas that my grandmother, Golda, came to see me at the store one day. She came over to get a few items and visit. We walked around the store and talked as she picked up a few things but I knew she had come for more than just that. She never said a word about it but I knew that day she had come to say good-bye. You could see it in her eyes. I could do nothing and neither could she. She just wanted to let me know. A few days later my grandfather found her one morning on the kitchen floor. She had a stroke during the night while doing the dishes after he had already gone to bed. She was taken to the hospital and put in intensive care, still in a coma. The family decided to still have Christmas at their house as they felt she would have wanted it that way for the little ones. That night Dr. Joe called us to the phone while we were at his house. She had come out of the coma for awhile and talked to several of us for a moment on the phone. We all told her to get well. Dad was upset and said it was not a good sign as many patients sometimes have one last rally like this before they go. Golda died on December 26, 1971, at an age of 80½ years old. She always seemed the same to me as long as I knew her. From when I was a little boy out at the ranch and she would take gum drops and put them on the thorn bushes and then tell us the fairies had come and left a gum drop tree for us—just so we could break the monotony . . . to when I was living with my grandparents and she and I would have our little chats after school over a cup of coffee and a few cookies. Golda always had time and always understood. Uncle Lloyd and Aunt Jeannie were the only two that came up from the coast to her funeral. They said she was one of the kindest people they ever knew and wanted to say good-bye.

Cecile and I had still not told anyone she was expecting. I know Golda would have liked another great grandchild. Scott was born on April 26, 1972.

The house we had on North Star was a 4 bedroom 2-bath house but all the rooms were small and after Scott was born, the house seemed even smaller. A real estate man once told me to buy all the house you can afford when you are young as you borrow hard dollars and you will pay back with soft inflated dollars. Prices will go up with inflation and houses won't get cheaper. We were in a time of inflation. Prices were moving fast and I had heard that we could already sell our house for about $25,000—almost $5,000 more than we paid for it. We toyed with the idea of selling and getting a bigger house, and even looked around at houses in the area.

One house we really liked, the people were asking something like $49,000 for it and I wanted to offer something like $45,000. The realtor refused to take my offer to the people. The deal was a bit more complicated because they wanted a smaller house in the area and it was a trade deal and this is how I saw the figures. During this time I met another realtor at the firm, who gave me an idea. He told me how his son had no money, like us, and wanted a bigger house. What his son did was to find a vacant lot in the area he wanted to live, then he bought the lot and built the house he wanted on it. He borrowed the money for the lot on a signature loan so the lot would appear to be clear. He would then up the value of his lot so it would cover the down payment he needed for the mortgage. All he needed to do was be able to make the monthly payments.

I figured we had equity in the house we had and if I scraped around I might find some more money. We looked around and found a lot on Zornia in Castle Hills. The man had two lots next to each other but I couldn't afford them both—in fact, I could only afford the cheaper and larger one. Mr. Sam Katz owned Katz Shoe Stores in San Antonio as well as a lot of property. He hadn't seen the lots in years but offered to finance me with the understanding I could pay it off with no penalty, in a short time when I was ready to build. The lot needed work and was next door to a Mobil service station at the time. I could see how it had good trees and a good building site in the front with the possibility of being able to screen the house off from the business area with some sort of row of trees or shrubs. I bought the lot for around $5,000 which was considered a very cheap price for a lot in Castle Hills. The price was one Mr Katz had set years before and the lot hadn't sold because of the service station next door.

Cecile and I then spent time looking at different builders' houses in different areas and comparing their prices. We had narrowed it down to a couple of builders that we had heard were good. They seemed to do good work and provide a lot for what they charged. One of the builders was Jimmy Schoal of Olmos Home Builders. He also owned Olmos Lumber Company, Olmos Flooring Company, and the string of Lone Star Ice Houses around San Antonio. When I first contacted him about building a house on our lot, he wasn't interested. He said he could sell his houses on his own lots about as fast as he could build them. He didn't need to get slowed down with a custom job. His foreman overheard his conversation and wanted to know where the lot was. He explained to Jimmy it was near their area. They had started out as a small custom builder and maybe they shouldn't forget where they came from.

When Mr. Schoal called me back, he asked if I had seen any of his houses that I liked. I told him we had seen several but wanted to consider a few changes. He said to come by his office to see his foreman. He would pull out plans they had already built that might be like we wanted. After pulling out a number of plans, we found one that, with only a few changes, would do quite well. These were making the downstairs area sunken, having open arched walls, a half wall with a rail upstairs (looking down), a half bath in the entryway, and putting two sinks in the bathrooms.

He said it would cost us $150 for his designer to redo the plans and after that he could give us a firm price. Since he had built the house not very long ago he felt he could give a very accurate price. We agreed to this and hoped it would be near what we thought we could afford. After several weeks we got a price for the house of around $48,000 for the house only. This would have no fence and only a tar seal driveway to the garage. The sewage connection fee was for us to pay, as well as other incidentals, and of course the lot would be up to us to pay off and provide a clear title to, as well as a letter of credit from the mortgage company that was good for 6 months. He would take care of the interim financing and would guarantee the price for 6 months, as well as try and have it completed in that time period.

We would have to clear the debt on the lot, find more money, and get a mortgage. I had a customer, Mr. John Steele, which was in the personal loan department at the National Bank of Commerce where I had the drugstore accounts. He said he would loan me the money to clear the lot on a signature loan, knowing that when our house sold we could pay him off. Until then, he would charge me only the interest every 90 days. We then approached the mortgage company, Farm and Home Savings. My parents had their mortgage with them as well. They had a small company office in San Antonio. I went to see the manager with the plans, specifications, and a letter from the builder with the set price for 6 months.

With the newly adjusted price of the lot, the figure we needed to borrow was at our upper limit—plus we needed to come up with a couple of thousand dollars at closing. I felt confident we could somehow manage and agreed to the terms. We had to give up front, a 1% loan origination fee ($430) to the mortgage company. They would then give a letter of credit, good for 6 months, to the builder and lock in our interest rate at 7% for the same period. We were ready to build our dream home.

By the way . . . the lady with the $49,000 house. Later on, when we sold our house, we got our $25,000. If the lady had taken our offer she would have been $2000 better off. I had figured our house at $25,000 when doing my figures—the offer being our house and $20,000. When she sold, she sold with no trade and got only $43,000.

CHAPTER 24

THE NEW HOUSE

During this time I worked all I could as I felt we could not afford a relief pharmacist very often. I would drive by the house under construction every evening and sometimes in the morning, to see if the workers were on the job and to see how it was coming along.

A number of the other pharmacies would get a relief pharmacist in at least once a week and sometimes over a weekend, so they could have time off. The rate at first was $5.00 per hour and soon went to around $7.00 per hour. At this time the minimum wage was around $1.40 per hour, so you see it was an expense that was considerable. We drew $1,000 a month out of the store to live on and if we were short I would draw additional money. We tried to keep this to a minimum as that was about all the store could afford. It was hard to find a good relief pharmacist and one of them I had to let go because I knew he was helping himself to the cash register and trying to cover it up.

I went without any relief help for a long time at the start and again later on when we couldn't afford to have the help. I did have a man who was a captain in the army that worked relief for me on and off for a number of years, and an old man that would fill in for me in case of an emergency. He was originally a veterinarian and later became a pharmacist, so everyone called him Doc.

He was a nice man but age had taken its toll on him. He was slow and hard of hearing. What we would do when I had to get him in, was have my best girl who helped in the pharmacy department, work with him. He had a little microphone in a suction cup that he would attach to the phone. When a doctor phoned in a prescription he would record the conversation so he could play it back for the information. This way both he and the girl could verify all the instructions. His only other problem was he had a wooden leg and he couldn't stand up for a long time. It showed his age when he told me the story about his leg. When he was young he lived in the country. As he got older all the boys wore a gun. His mother didn't want him to wear a gun, as she was afraid it would lead to trouble. What he would do is hide his gun and put it on after he left the house. One day when he came home he took his gun off to hide it under the mattress on his bed. The next day when he went to get it out to take with him, he accidentally discharged the gun and the bullet hit him in his lower leg. He almost bled to death and then he had an infection. The only thing they could do was amputate his lower leg. The gun did get him into trouble but not as they expected.

The economy had been strong during the Vietnam War but so had inflation. Prices were going up and up. This was a perfect time for the discount chains to come in. In the matter of only a couple of years we had a Globe discount store and pharmacy on San Pedro and a SuperX discount pharmacy on West Avenue, not far from me. The Globe store would lose money on prescriptions and used the department to draw in customers. They hurt me not only in the prescription department but in general merchandise as well. SuperX was closer but at first had less impact as Globe had already done the major damage. The supermarket H.E.B. at the other end of the shopping centre I was in, expanded their over-the-counter drug section and cut prices. My customers purchased more and more at the supermarket just out of convenience from being in the store between one to several times a week. Several years later they also opened a prescription department to draw more people in.

The neighborhood was getting older and the new complexes that were being built were for low-income housing. More and more I was filling welfare prescriptions. The state fixed the price and would only pay for 3 prescriptions per person per month. The people had very little money and if you extended them credit it was always difficult for them to pay you back.

A couple of the old customers I had were Beck and Duderstadt. These two men were in partnership in a foundation company. They repaired foundations on houses, buildings, and did new foundations for bridges, overpasses and even part of the airport runway. I had explained to them how I had a lot of low area in the back of my yard on Zornia. They told me they had a job in the area where they were excavating and could divert their trucks by to dump the dirt in the back until the level was better. They then had one of their men come over with a machine to level the dirt out. They charged me a total of $50 for the man. They were glad to have a place to dump fill and I needed it. This was one of the good things that happened when we built.

As with any new house being built, a few things always seem to go wrong. At first everything was fine. Then Mr Schoal told us he decided to have the ground tested before he did the plan for the foundation. It came back okay and he then had an engineer design the foundation. But he didn't like the way he had done the pier and beam foundation and decided to beef it up, as he didn't want to skimp on what he felt was such an important area. However, we had a very large and old oak tree that we thought would be just out back from the house. When they surveyed the site the tree was several feet inside the house. We couldn't go any closer to the street, as the set back by law was 110 feet. If we moved the house behind the tree and saved it, then the driveways would cost more and we would be even further off the road. He even tried to see if he could come up with an idea to build the house around the tree and modify the plans. All too expensive. At the end we had to bulldoze the tree and burn it. I had taken some pictures of it when it was down, as the tree was huge.

When we noticed that the bay window area we had added in the breakfast room was not being bricked on the outside, I phoned Mr Schoal to find out why. The foundation company didn't catch the change and didn't pour a ledge for the bricks. It couldn't be done now. He would try and make it up. A few weeks later when they were working on the second storey I found they were flooring-in under the eaves. I had access doors to the area but no flooring, as we couldn't afford it. The foreman told me Mr Schoal felt bad about the brick around the window so he decided to floor in all the areas under the eaves for free to make up for it.

As they came across different stages of construction they would sometimes get an idea and call us to offer a change before it was too late. We were always warned that if you change something the price goes up. With this in mind we tried to leave things alone. However, sometimes we found the changes didn't cost a lot. They started to do the wood ply for the roof and realized if we would go to the next thickness up, we could have our first re-roof done on top of the old one without having to remove it. The total cost was only about $150 more.

Another time they called us about a new product. The bathrooms downstairs had a phony marble counter top and the kitchen was Formica. The company had a new Corning product out that looked like marble but didn't burn or cut. It was at a special introductory price but would have been several hundred dollars more and we just couldn't afford it.

When they went to do the half bathroom they found they had a marble sink in the shape of a shell they didn't use from another job. He offered us this sink at no extra charge. Cecile didn't like the change much but considering he was doing it for free we went along. He actually got rid of something he already had and didn't have to buy one for our house, if you want to be cynical. The other little items we went over on were the hardware and lighting allowances. But the one that almost caused a war was the paint. Cecile wanted to do a number of the rooms in different colors. She wanted to do the upstairs kids' rooms in an off-white cream color. She picked out the various colors of paint and the carpet, and we picked out the vinyl floors and wallpaper.

One day, after work, we went by the house. They had finished painting the upstairs. We almost fell over. It was a bright pale yellow. The outside color around the front didn't look right either. I again called Mr. Schoal. He told me he would check into the problem and call me back. Later he called me and told me the colors were correct. That is, they were the ones we picked out off the paint chart. He even made sure they had been mixed correctly. He told me the outside paint was not a big problem as he had another house he could use it on. The inside color he had no use for. He offered and suggested we use his standard colors. The beige and brown on the outside and a white color inside. It was not his or his crew's fault so as a compromise, if I paid him $150 for the new paint needed, he would pay his crew for painting the areas over again.

I told Cecile what I had found out and she went through the roof. She absolutely insisted the colors were wrong and that they were not what she picked out. She wanted him to do it again and was not paying another dime. She talked to Mr. Schoal and Mr. Schoal called me. He wanted me to know that the same result could be expected if the colors weren't changed. He would take no responsibility and the problem could be all mine on my own. I then told Cecile if she wanted to get the house finished we should just go with standard colors. After we were in, she could always change them if she wanted. After several days she agreed to go back to the standard colors but she wasn't going to pay for their mistakes.

Mr. Schoal and I agreed to keep it between us. I would get a check to him for the $150 and he would get the pale yellow paint to me at the drugstore. I put the paint in storage and he got his check. It was several months later that Cecile came across the check for the paint. She got mad all over again. This time it was directed at me for paying him the money and doing a deal behind her back. All I could say was that I was trying to get the job done and keep the peace. It just wasn't working out that way.

As the time drew near to completion, the prices for tar seal had gone up dramatically. To do a concrete drive to the garage and around the front yard was more than we felt we could afford. The prices for the basics were locked in and were guaranteed by our contract. I knew after we had Mr. Schoal give us another price to switch to concrete it was still too much. He then suggested we cut 6 inches off the width. The cost difference was a big help but still a lot of money. After worrying about it, I finally decided it was short-sighted not to spend the extra on something that would be permanent and last for years. After all this was the last house we planned to buy.

The completion was around February 1973 as I remember. What I remember most vividly was the last several months leading up to the closing. I had an idea of what we had spent and what we needed. It was more than we had and more than I could draw out of the store and be able to pay my bills. I had a whole-of-life insurance policy I had taken out when we were first married that was worth some money if I cashed it in. I had also taken out two life insurance investment policies on Sam and Craig when I was going to school in Austin. It was a new company and they had a stock option or something attached to the policy. The company had changed hands but the two policies could still be cashed in for money. These added up but we were still several thousand short.

I had, years back, started collecting coins and money. I had purchased folders and had almost complete sets of Lincoln pennies, Jefferson nickels, Mercury dimes, Roosevelt dimes and Washington quarters (except for some of the very key coins). I still had some of the keys such as the '50 D nickel (worth about $12 at that time). I also had some very worn semi-key quarters, a 1909 vdb penny, and numerous silver coins, dollars, half-dollars, quarters and dimes. I also had proof sets and mint sets I had purchased. I also had a lot of special coins given to me by my parents and a whole box of coins given to me by my grandmother. They were commemorative Texas coins, coins of her father's going back to the civil war, nickels and pennies, and gold coins from Mexico. I also had lots of coins from my grandfather's trip overseas from Japan, Russia, and China. All in all, I had a box two feet long, one foot wide and almost one foot deep, full of coins, folders, jars of silver coins, and paper money with special seals and types.

My father had a patient who at that time owned Riverside Coin Shop in downtown San Antonio. I didn't want to sell these but I also knew we needed money for closing on the house. I got wholesale prices and I don't think all that great a deal but when it was all over, it was a little over $2,000. Between the coins, the insurance money and what I could draw from the store, we would be able to just have enough for closing. The proceeds from the sale of North Star would only be enough to clear the note at the bank for the lot.

Just when you see the light at the end of the tunnel, you need to check—it may be another train coming. The agreements we had were for 6 months. The interest rates had started to rise with inflation and had gone to 7 ½%, with talk of 8% not far away. The house was running a little behind as we had a lot of rain and the driveways were not in. We would need an extension. I went to Farm and Home Savings and saw our loan manager again. Our best estimate was from 10 to 30 days depending on the weather. After much discussion he came back to me and told me they wanted to work with their customers but they were also at the mercy of the markets. They could extend the guarantee for a maximum of 30 days and hold the interest rate. After that they would have to go up.

We had the house for sale on North Star for months with no success. We didn't want to sell too soon and have to get out with no place to go. We also didn't want to try and pay for two houses. As the time was near and our realtor was doing nothing, I felt it was time to consider a change. Our contract was up. I talked to several realtors including one who was a customer. I talked to her and she assured me she could sell it very quickly, as they all do. I told her if she really had prospects it wouldn't be a problem to give her a 30-day listing. This we did and she sold it in a couple of weeks. I then introduced her to my neighbors who wanted to sell and she sold their house to some of her other prospects. Although we didn't get as much as we wanted, it was a big relief not to be faced with paying for two houses.

Mr Schoal wanted us in the house, and to get his money. He was able to finish and get us in before the deadline. It didn't go smoothly. He had to keep the temporary power hooked up for about another week after we moved in, as the city couldn't get a new line and transformer in until then. We went to the title company and paid the money we gave them a check on our personal account after stopping by the bank to make a transfer to it from our savings account and from the drugstore. They called us within a couple of hours of closing to tell us our check was no good. I had to then get with John Steele at the bank to get it all straightened out. If they had told me they needed a cashier's check I would have brought one with me. This was not my last dealing with the title company. In fact it was only the start of my dealings with them and in finding out how useless they really were.

When the day was over, I remember standing out in front on the drive with all the lights turned on, praying the temporary power wouldn't blow and taking a photo of our new home. At last.

CHAPTER 25

THE OFFICE

While I had been busy watching over the new house and with the competition getting tougher in the drugstore business, the boys started school. I had not spent very much time with them and at times I would go for days with never seeing them awake. I would leave before they were up and get home after they went to bed.

It was during this time that Sam was getting into trouble at school. He wasn't getting into fights like I did all the time but he just couldn't sit still and was disruptive. One of the teachers suggested to Cecile that she should take him to the doctor, as she was sure he was hyperactive—or whatever name is now 'PC' for this. To my surprise Dr. Nau seemed to be very willing to put him on Ritalin. I was not convinced and opposed this course of action. They tried him on coffee, caffeine and some Ritalin for a short time. I felt it made him worse. I don't think Sam knew what to make of it and I finally put my foot down on the Ritalin and said no. The teacher made arrangements to get him into the Northeast-testing center. For most of a week Cecile took him over each morning for testing. The results showed that he was way ahead of his class in ability on most levels—even up to age 12 in some areas. He was just bored. School was not a challenge and it was not interesting so he tried to amuse himself in his own way.

I don't know why they didn't put him up a grade. I can only guess they felt he didn't know enough of the basics yet. I left the everyday operating of the house and the kids up to Cecile. Sam still had to be guided but seemed to get along better. He was always a handful and always wanted a lot of attention. I would usually warn him once or twice and that was it. I would then come down on him. I would try to explain what I expected, and would tell him what I wanted and would stick to it. Over the next several years he would do like most kids do as they get older, he would test the limits. I wouldn't tolerate much and he would get his swats. On the other hand he and Cecile would get into yelling matches and then she would want me to do something about it. This eventually came to a head several years down the track.

I had become more convinced over the next year that more changes would need to be made. Before we built the house we had a run-in with her father. This was in about the fall of 1971. We had decided the '70 G.T.O. was not big enough and we should consider a larger car. I went down to the dealership a couple of times to see them about a car. Cecil was not around much and Henry didn't seem to care. I asked them to give me a price on a couple of different cars so I could talk it over with Cecile. Cecil kept ignoring the issue and Henry hinted it would be too expensive. We both finally got tired of it and decided to go out on our own. We ended up going to Tom Benson Chevrolet on San Pedro and picked out a new Impala coupe. We did our deal and agreed to pick it up the next day after it was serviced. Someone at the dealership, who knew who we were, saw us and phoned Cecil.

Cecil came unglued. He was so mad he could hardly talk. He told us that as long as he owned a dealership his daughter was going to drive what he sold, Pontiac. He had talked to them at Benson's and they agreed to cancel the deal. We purchased a new '72 Grand Prix. He felt we couldn't afford it and that is why he tried to put us off buying. At least that was his story. I guess I should have asked him why he didn't just give his daughter one if he felt that strongly about her driving a Pontiac and us not being able to afford it. But then that would have just started another fight.

I don't know if this and building the house on our own, had any influence on him or not. I know he felt we were living outside our means and a few times when I did take off to go with them on a weekend trip he would offer to pay expenses. I was glad he did, as I was the first to agree we didn't have a lot to spare and needed to make more.

I think it was all of this, along with the inflation fears, that really got me to thinking about the future. I was afraid that in the long-run, the drugstore would go out of business in this neighborhood. I started thinking about finding a new location. Should I try and move my existing business in the area or should I just open another store in another area. I wasn't sure so I started another project of looking around to see what seemed to make for a more secure future.

In the family, things were not getting any better. After Golda died, Dr. Joe was lost. I don't think a man could have loved anyone more than he did Golda. He was heartbroken. Aunt Mary, Uncle Gene and the kids moved in with Dr. Joe to help take care of him. After we moved into our new house I went and picked him up and brought him over to see it. He asked if we had to have a map to find our way around. He found it a very big house yet I doubt it was any larger than Lamont. He continued to do an office practice as he had, with Aunt Mary or Uncle Gene driving him back and forth to work. We saw him less and less. We didn't go over and see them as much as we should have, and after my aunt and uncle moved in we went over even less.

It wasn't until years later I found out Dr. Joe would call up Cecile and ask her to bring the kids by so he could see them. She would usually indicate she would try and drop by. He would then go and sit on the front porch until after dark waiting for them to come. They never came. I would like to think it was a misunderstanding in communications but Cecile never told me about it and never told me she had taken them over there visiting to see him either. I think she felt she had more to do, and the easy way out was to say she would and then do what she wanted. It was years later that my Aunt Mary told me about it and how it had happened over and over again.

The situation on Wyndale had become worse with my parents. Their drinking was getting more out of hand and my mother's health was becoming affected. She was starting to have trouble with her liver and her memory. Over the last few years I would help them buy a car when they wanted one for themselves or for one of the other kids. They bought Tom a couple, and one for Beulah Ann—a Firebird. Charlie was busy doing his own thing and wanted to study music. I tried to talk to Dad a few times and even started to threaten him with getting another doctor involved to have him put into care.

He had started to dry out a couple of times but never got very far. Mom had even less luck and was becoming seriously ill. I told Cecile I felt I had to try and help out by doing something. We had talked about him moving into the offices behind me. I still felt that his going to work with my grandfather was part of the problem. I even talked to my grandfather about it. Gradually Dr. Joe came around to the idea and felt it may be almost like a last chance for him as he would like to see him straighten out, while he was still alive.

One of the women in the office downtown, Annie Lou Aaron, had gone to work for my grandfather when she was very young. Dr. Joe thought he would give her a chance but figured she would be married and gone in a few years. She knew my father while he was still in school and she was working for Dr. Joe when Dad joined the practice. She always liked Dad and agreed she would come to the new office with him. She could act as receptionist, bookkeeper and caretaker. She knew the problems and wanted to help.

I cleared out the office area and painted it a cream color—sort of a bright pale yellow. I carpeted the rooms and had a reception desk built. I then had a couple of my delivery guys go downtown and move his office furniture and equipment to the new location. Annie Lou had organized what could go, on that end. We got his records, some furniture, some reception furniture, examining room equipment and a few other basics. Dad was better but he didn't always show up.

Mom got so bad one time that she went to Hitchcock to live with her folks for awhile. Her sisters, Bobbie and Jeannie, helped take care of her and Dad would call them all the time and send stuff to her. She went on about how she wanted a divorce and told them all sorts of stories that made no sense. I don't think they ever knew what was really going on.

I got to the point that I would check each day to see if he was at work or had stayed at home. One day he answered the phone and I knew he had been drinking. I went over and found him still in bed with a bottle of vodka. I took it away and poured it and everything else I could find, down the sink. I then told him if I was going to have to watch over him, he was going to have to be closer. He was broke and in debt. He and Mom agreed they needed to sell the house and move into an apartment near the drugstore. This way they could clear all their debts.

I had told Cecile what needed to be done. She must have told her parents because Cecil wanted to talk to me. He didn't want me getting into debt or a situation that would cause problems. I told him what the plans were and he said he wanted to look at the house with a few friends in the construction business. I had already had a couple of people I knew, start to give me some estimates on repairs. Cecil came back to me and had a proposition. He felt it was too difficult for me to try and sell their house, fixed up or not.

For me to borrow the money might not even be possible. He offered to buy the house from my parents on an 'as is' basis. He would then worry about fixing it up and selling it. He had come up with a price that he felt was fair. I told my parents the plan and how much his offer was. They felt it was quick and easy and took the offer. They moved just that quickly to the apartments near the drugstore.

Cecil, with his builder friends, took the best part of a year to fix the house up and sell it. He told me it had a lot more to be done to it than he had realized and it cost a lot more than he planned for. He had paid my parents something to the tune of about $30,000. He then claimed to have spent so much he didn't make hardly anything on it when it sold for something like $57,000. I took him at his word back then but knowing him now as I do today, I would like to have seen the checks, the bills and all the invoices.

The good news was that Dad was close and I could watch him. It wasn't the last time I had a problem—in fact far from it. One time when he got started again, I found out that he had his old neighborhood liquor store charging and delivering to him. I went to see them in person and told them I was delivering their last check. Next time the bill would not be paid. We had some words but at the end of it they understood that if they allowed him to charge again, they were giving it away.

I don't know why it had to be this way at first because after he settled in, we had probably the best relationship we ever had. He even told me once that for the first time in years he enjoyed the idea of going to work each day. Annie Lou watched out for him, and did everything she could to get him patients and get the money in for him. I would sell him his office supplies at cost plus 10% and his rent was something like $300 per month, which included the utilities. I would take samples in trade towards his office bill, as well as his personal bill.

He got a routine going and at different times of the day he would come out of his office into the prescription department or into the store itself. Sometimes we would visit about the day, and other times about drugs and side effects or what might be best for a patient of his. It was during this time I got to know how good he really was. He enjoyed reading some of the magazines and would go and take them from the magazine section and then put them back. He liked *'Time'*, *'People'* and *'News Week'*.

I sent him patients when I could and sometimes they were only a cold or the flu but he needed the patients. I did get a few of the harder cases for him—like Fannie, who had been run around by the other doctors in the area (like Zaccaria). She was told she was a pill head and that is why she always had headaches. Dad saw her twice and sent her to a neurologist. They took a tumor the size of a baseball out of her head. She died in less than two years but her mother always told us how grateful she was to find out what was really wrong with her. She wasn't a pill head.

Another one was Joseph Grosenbacher. He was a self-confessed con man and hustler. He had a problem of being addicted to Talwin, as I found were several of my customers. He would always try and give you something and then con you out of it along with something to go with it. Dad was trying to help him with his array of ailments. He was to be sent back to prison for fraud. He told both Dad and his wife they would kill him if he were ever sent back, for having given evidence for the state. They found him hung in his cell. It was said to be suicide but Dad and his wife never believed it. It just wasn't him.

At first Annie Lou went without her pay being on time and once Dad got going she still watched out for him. It was towards the beginning of this that I looked up one day and saw Dr. Joe coming into the store. I don't think he was ever in the store more than 2 or 3 times. I think he always stayed in touch through Annie Lou, on what was going on but on this day he wanted to see for himself. He had a look around and then told me he thought it was modest but okay and hoped it would work. I think he felt it was not as good as he had always wanted for his son, my Dad, but then again if it got him going, well it might just be alright after all.

CHAPTER 26

A New Store

After I had done more research on the area I was in, I had decided the only possibility was to maybe locate a store in a new shopping center going in at the major intersection down from Churchill High School. I contacted the management and found out the price of a new space. You got a dirt floor with four walls and a roof. Everything inside was unfinished. You had to also add your own air-conditioning and heating as well. The price was then 30 cents a square foot per month plus a percentage of your sales on a sliding scale. I did some quick calculations and knew it was out of my range.

I hadn't given up but was thinking I would need to consider a new store in a new area. When it was up and going, depending on what the old one was doing, I could then either keep them both or just move to the new one. I started looking in a new area that was growing fast, off Perrin-Bietel road in the Northeast part of the city. I found several vacant lots that were zoned commercial or retail. I contacted the owners and found one man who owned two of the lots, and another man who was a developer with a larger one.

The large one of 64 acres was interesting as it was near a school just off the main road. It was much more than I needed but then if you sold off the rest, you may end up clear on what you kept. One of the others was on the corner of Perrin-Bietel and the owner wanted $12,000 for it. Another one was in the neighborhood and next door to a small strip center with a 'Stop and Go' and a couple of shops. This one was $5,000 and the owner would throw in his plans for a strip center. He was a lawyer who had obtained the land from a client, instead of money, for his fee. He then had the zoning changed to B retail and as he was short on money, wanted a deal soon.

I knew Cecil was always interested in a deal so I went over the idea with him—to get a property and build a new store for the future. If it was a small strip center, the rent from the others may pay for it and you would end up being rent free and own the center. We went and looked at all three properties. He felt as I did, that they were all a good price but the big one was just too much. It was later sold and that is where the main San Antonio post office stands today. The one on the corner was again more than he felt we should consider. It sold two weeks later to another person who, in turn, sold it several months later to 'Circle K' for $25,000. The last property he liked best because it was cheap and had plans.

He called Linus Baer who was now a loan officer at Alamo National Bank. I had previously taken the proposal to NBC where John Steele was and had been turned down. Linus looked at the idea and wanted to know if Cecil would be in on it as well. I said he would be but not like a legal partner. He told us he would go along with the idea on the store. Some feelings must have been hurt and interest rates dropped. NBC came back to Cecil and they agreed to finance the interim and permanent mortgage on the strip center. Cecil wrote a check for the $5,000 to get the property and the plans.

I then found a builder for the center. The bank insisted that the architect who had drawn the plans would oversee each step as it was approved, for payout to the builder. The work was done by the builder and I, and the architect drew a check. The terms were for 10 years on the mortgage and the only completed part was the drugstore. The rest had a concrete floor, glass front, a back wall, and a roof over the area, with another wall on the end of the building. The parking lot would be paved. I would also have to pay a fee for a new power transformer to be installed in the corner of the parking lot for the power supply to the center. All up the center would be $63,000 and I would have a new payment book.

New shopping strip center on El Sendero, San Antonio, with new Kopecky Pharmacy

The loan from Alamo National Bank would be for a new store in the new center. It was for the carpet, fixtures, equipment and some stock. Cecil had told me to take merchandise from the old store and use as much as I could from there to keep the cost down. I had started buying merchandise with the idea of having two locations, so by the time we opened most of it was taken from the old store. I think the loan was about $20,000.

New pharmacy with flags up at opening

The new store on El Sendero was a plan for the future. I had planned on Cecile working with me in the old store as she was tired of being at home and wanted out. She wanted her own project without me involved as she felt I always had to put my ideas in. She wanted something of her own. She agreed the new store could give her more freedom. We still needed employees and a pharmacist.

Inside new pharmacy on El Sendero

Over the last couple of years of Cecile being at home with the kids, she became more restless. She felt she wanted more freedom and attention. When she hit her 30th birthday, she had a crisis. This was

April 1973. She felt she was overweight and unattractive. She went to Dr. Carter, her doctor, and he gave her some diet pills—amphetamines. I warned her about the side-effects as I was none too fond of them. I had seen people become paranoid and suspicious.

It was over this period of time that Sam fell out of the tree at Cecil and Elizabeth's, and broke his arm. Cecil took charge at the hospital emergency room and started calling his doctor friends, wanting the best. It was nice that he cared. Sam's arm was broken in such a way that they didn't want to put pins in it at his age but instead wanted to try to keep it in place in a cast. They put him under a general anesthetic and set his arm using an x-ray machine to guide them. Then for the next six weeks he had an x-ray done on his arm each week, to make sure it hadn't moved or they would need to start over. The insurance company (through the pharmaceutical association), at first refused to pay the entire bill as they felt it was exorbitant. After numerous letters and explanations, along with the association's support, I got the bill paid.

At a much later date after we were living at Zornia, I was using a chainsaw to trim some of the dead limbs out of the trees. I was working early one Saturday afternoon I had taken off, when the chainsaw went through the tree limb very rapidly after it had been stuck in one spot for about 5 seconds. It went through so fast it hit me on my left foot before I even knew what had happened. It felt like a quick hot bee sting. I looked down and saw my shoe was cut open with my foot cut. It was a very deep cut from the top. I knew I was in trouble.

I turned the saw off, climbed down from the tree and went to the back porch where I called for the kids and Cecile to come. I asked her to bring a towel. I removed my shoe and sock (what was left of them), and saw I had blood going everywhere with a massive cut that exposed cut bone. I placed the towel under my foot and started to stand when blood shot up as high as I was. I then wrapped the towel around my foot, and made my way across the vinyl and marble floor to the front door and out to the car. I got in the back seat and held the towel as Cecile drove me to the emergency room at the hospital.

After my first examination when the bleeding had all but stopped, the doctors decided they needed a specialist to put the pieces back together. Since I had nothing to eat since early that morning and had not taken any pain killers, they were able to send me to the operating room within a few hours. I was supposed to be out in a few hours but it was 10 PM before they sent me downstairs as they had a hard time getting me out from under the anesthetic.

On Sunday the doctor came by to see how I was and I explained I needed to go home as I needed to go to work on Monday. He told me he wanted the foot elevated to help keep the swelling down. He had put things together the best he could but I had cut bones, tendons and muscles. After I showed him I could stand on it, he put a walking heal on the cast and sent me home. I went to work on Monday.

It took a couple of months before the cast came off. I was unable to move much of my foot at first and I had difficulty with standing on it. It took over a year for it to get to the point where it no longer bothered me and I was able to move a couple of my toes only about 20%. I was lucky I didn't cut half my foot off.

Charlie Veretis had returned to work for me one summer to finish getting his intern hours. At that time I had already been thinking about another store. He wanted to return to San Antonio and eventually have his own store. I talked to him about the possibility of first going to work for me in the new store and maybe later becoming a partner. I told him he would have to work a lot of hours at first to get it off the ground and live on just a base pharmacist salary. He was married now and wanted to talk it over with his wife, who was a nurse. After some negotiation we agreed on a set salary and that I would get a second delivery car for the new store which he would be able to use to get to and from work. He also insisted on an afternoon off during the week each week, on Thursday, so he could spend the time with his wife. This made it necessary for me to get my relief pharmacist in each week to work the old store and I would then go to the new store so he could have the time off.

At the start, and later after he had been working for a short while, he wanted to buy into the store. I told him it didn't make sense to come in now while the store was losing money—besides, it would be even harder to set a price for his share when we didn't even know what we had. He would need to trust me. I would try to be fair and give him some credit for the extra hours he had worked. This was a sore spot for him, his wife and his family. His brother even came and talked to me once about selling Charlie part of the store now. I explained it could take from one to three years for the store to just break even. Why would they want to put money in something they might lose it in? I should have been more worried about me as it turned out and taken the money. I sure as the devil needed it.

The situation with my folks settled down for a short time. They were living at the apartment and getting by. Charlie, my brother, lived with them from time to time, as did Tom. Mom even asked me one time to give Tom a job, as she was sure he had straightened out. He would go on deliveries for hours at a time, which should take only an hour at the most. I don't know how much he got away with but one day I saw him out of the corner of my eye, going out the side door through the doctor's office. I just knew he was up to no good. I ran out and caught him in the parking lot. He had gone into the office and into the safe, and taken a bottle of pure crystalline cocaine I had. We had a fight in the parking lot, after which I sent him on his way and told him not to return. After this, he then threatened the kids and me. I told him then that from then on, I would shoot him on sight if I ever saw him near the house or the kids. Tom at this point was about as bad as he had ever been.

Cecile was getting more involved in wanting to lose weight and would sometimes turn the stereo on in the house and dance for exercise. Henry had been a member of Trim and Swim Gym for years and talked her into joining. She would then go and work out several days a week. She started acting strange and every time I turned around she was accusing me of flirting or being interested in one of the girl employees.

It got so bad that the only thing I knew of that I could do was to let her do all the hiring of any girls. I would run the ad and set up a time for interviews, and Cecile would then interview each applicant and decide who was to be hired. She even became so worried about the short skirts that were the fashion at the time that she had a rule on how short they could be. When she saw an employee that she was sure was out of order, she would get a ruler and check the length of her skirt.

A problem that was starting to cause me even more trouble was that Cecile didn't like any of the girls working or helping me in the pharmacy department. I had already taken over the bookwork and had taken over doing the payroll each week, as she didn't have time. I would bring home the bills for the 10th of the month and stay up late at night, either at the kitchen table or in the upstairs playroom. If I was going to do more at home, other than work, then I needed to finish more work at the store. I needed the girls to do as much for me as they could so I would be free to do other jobs—regardless of whether it included talking to customers or doing a payroll.

Several of the employees became very upset with this and quit. Others needed the job and hung in, and tried to ignore how Cecile behaved. At times when we would be without a deliveryman, I would have to call Cecile to come and deliver the packages to the customers—sometimes on her own and sometimes with the kids. When the employees saw the car coming down the street and turn the corner they would all call out as if it was a raid. They would all try to get to an area they felt was safe ground and start doing anything they felt was acceptable. After she left they would go back to continue working on whatever job needed to be done.

It got to the point she was so paranoid that I took her pills away from her and flushed them down the toilet. We had a major disagreement and she cried as she watched the pills go down. She went back to the doctor and he switched her pills to Tenuate Dospan. She took them from time to time but always felt they weren't as good.

I was not the only one concerned. She had evidently talked to her parents and they didn't know if they should believe her or not. I assured Cecil when he asked me, that nothing was going on. He had been concerned about Cecile as he felt she was not keeping house as she should and each time he came over, the half bath was always dirty. He pointed this out to her but it only made her mad. We did try and get a housekeeper a couple of times but they didn't work out. Cecil became even more concerned when about a year or so later she started to wear short skirts and outfits. Some were so short that they came with matching panties, as you knew they would show sooner or later because they were so short. He all but banned her from coming to the dealership in these, as he was too embarrassed. He got mad at me and chewed me out for not having more influence over her in forbidding her to wear such outfits. I had no control over her and she did what she wanted. He didn't know the half of it.

It seemed like everything was going wrong. The sales at the old store on Blanco Road were falling. Each season was worse. The situation with Cecile was almost a constant war. She was unhappy and wanted to go out more. She wanted to go dancing, which we started doing, 3 and 4 times a week. It was at the discotheques. They sometimes didn't even get going properly until 9 or 10 at night. We started putting this on a credit card, as we couldn't afford it.

Cecil was more into the horses now and owned a lot of them on his own or in partnership. He had also made a lot of new friends such as James Keefer and Joe King. Joe King was younger and took us dancing a few times with him. He spent money like it was water. Cecil introduced them to my Dad, as they needed a doctor from time to time.

Mom became very ill and was put in the hospital downtown. She was now under Dr. William Gordon's care. He was the son of Dr. Marie Gordon who my grandfather had helped. Her husband was in the Foreign Service and when they were in Panama many years ago, he left her. My grandfather had met her and helped with his contacts to get her into and through medical school, and thus she became a doctor. The Gordons had been long-time friends of the family and wanted to help.

I went after work and when I could, over several weeks, to see Mom while she was in the hospital. She looked very bad, with her liver failing and causing multiple problems. I feel that during our visiting we found a mutual understanding again and developed an almost calm between us.

In the early hours of the morning of August 29th, 1975, Dad called me at home to tell me Mom had died. She was only 52 years old. We had told all the doctors that Mom could not handle Talwin for pain, as it would make her wild. For severe pain Dilaudid was one that she usually used. During the night for pain, one of the nurses injected her with Talwin from orders by Dr. William Gordon. She died of heart failure according to the autopsy. She had many problems from the drinking but her death was brought on by being wild with panic from the Talwin. Dad and I went over the report together. He had decided we couldn't do anything but raise hell and that wouldn't change things. Besides he felt she had suffered enough and he didn't think she had much quality of life left as it was. It was hard for all of us but more so for him. In spite of what she may have thought at times, he still loved only her. Over the next several months it was evident just how much he missed her—and much more than I would have predicted.

CHAPTER 27

CRUNCH TIME

It was like a three ring circus with the new store and Charlie, the old store and Dad, and then Cecile. Dad was truly upset with my mother's death and the loneliness. He started drinking again. Both Annie Lou and I tried to give him some time and tried to understand. I tried to talk to him a couple of times without being threatening and was ignored. Annie Lou tried too, as well. I finally felt enough was enough and had another one of those confrontations. I doubt it did much good and I sometimes think he may have decided on his own it was time to get back to work.

It wasn't overnight and you could tell his heart wasn't in it at times but he was trying. He tried to get more interested in work again and during the week he did better. It was when Monday came you weren't sure if he was going to make it or not. I saw him during the week and I am sure that was enough of me for him but I now wonder if we shouldn't have tried to see him at least on some of the weekends. I know Cecile had other plans and if we weren't dancing, she wanted to go to the ranch and see her folks.

I had about all of Henry I could stand, and the idea of him and his family at the ranch was not my idea of fun. Cecil would usually take off with the kids and if I wanted them with me, it only spoiled their fun. There was many a day I would go to the dirty clothes, as did the kids, and we would find our cleanest dirty shirt and put it on for that day. I found it restful and constructive to stay home on my own, and get the housework and laundry done. Between this and doing some cooking at times, Henry would always have to tell me I would make someone a good wife someday. They would return on Sunday night and another week was upon us again.

One week was much like the last and over the years I had become accustomed to eating cold food when I got home at night. It was difficult for Cecile to cook and feed all the kids at a decent time and then do something for me several hours later. We decided if she would just serve it up and put it on top of the stove, I would eat it when I got home. When I first took over Zipp's, it was open 7 days a week from 7 to 9 PM.with half days on Sunday. I soon cut the hours back to 8 to 8 P.M., with a 6 PM close on Saturday and closed on Sunday. I was soon followed by some of the other stores in the area.

I wanted a way for my customers to be able to get in touch with me in case of an emergency. I found that I could have another phone put in at the house as it was in the same exchange as the store and it would just be like a long extension cord. I could then have an answering machine at the house and could monitor after-hours and weekend calls. The phone company charged by the mile and it cost about $30 per month for the extra phone. I could answer the store phone at home. Over the years I never had a true emergency but only a few regular customers who had become sick on the weekend and wanted to get their prescriptions filled with me. A few other calls were for refills they forgot during normal hours because they were busy. It was a service that I guess wasn't really wanted.

Charlie Veretis seemed to be interested in the store and came up with a couple of ideas on selling some of the candy and making a few of the customers happy. I sometimes think if his wife had understood better, she wouldn't have always been on him for more time off, more money, or part of the store. It was like a broken record. I gave him a raise, even though it was not a lot, but it was more than I could afford. They just couldn't understand that each month the store lost money and I would have to find some to pay the bills. This was a 'rob Peter to pay Paul' situation that only got worse with time. I would pay the help, the taxes, the utilities, the insurance, the bank, and then the suppliers (slower and slower) and last of all, us.

At the end of the first year the store was almost doing enough business to break even. We had started with doing maybe a dozen prescriptions a week and maybe $10 a day in sales. We were now doing maybe 20 prescriptions a day and sometimes $200 in sales. It takes time and advertising—and that all takes money.

I had found a company that did gift merchandise along with a catalogue. They were out of Tennessee and the merchandise was mainly from Taiwan, China, India, and so on. The catalogue was about 24 pages long and the merchandise would be from $1 to maybe $150—with a lot of merchandise in the $5 to $25 range. Cecile and I would order the merchandise into the old store and set it up by catalogue number in the storeroom. We would then order the catalogues—about 3,000 for the old store and 2,000 for the new store. I would then pay the delivery boys overtime to put the catalogues on the doorknob of the houses with a rubber band.

I found sometimes that the guys would throw them away and they would then be looking for another job. Other times it was almost impossible to get anyone and this is when Sam and Craig would be driven around by Cecile in the early days, and they would take them to the door of the houses. The sales were good but as with most such things the supplier would sell out of the good merchandise and we would all have the other stuff left over that we had to close out. It made money and gave us a lot of exposure. After a few years it started to become old hat and a lot of the merchandise was showing up in the discount stores. Things were still changing.

Another program was a flyer that looked like a two-sheet newspaper. The company claimed if you did it their way, the advertising campaign would cost you nothing. Now, the way this worked was that you purchased several thousand dollars worth of merchandise and they would then supply the flyer, which you had to get out. The merchandise was anything and everything—sardines, citronella candles, garden tools, seeds and bars of soap, just to name a few. Some items were sold at cost, some below cost, and some you made money on. After the sale you were to put all the merchandise in a stack by the front door and keep cutting the price until it was all gone within about a week or two. This was to be done about every 3 months. It was true if you put all these sales into one pot, the money came in to pay that bill and that was it. No money for the bills of the store, the girls, or me—just the advertising promotion. We did this a couple of times, mainly to get exposure for the new store. It was once said people drive in to a store and not out. If you can get them in once you have a much better chance to get them to come back, as they know where you are. If you get them in twice you might make them a regular customer.

After our first year with the new store I felt optimistic. Then the Veretis family gave me an ultimatum . . . to sell him part of the store, pay him a lot more money, or he was going to quit. I tried to talk to them on a price and even showed them the books. I never got them to make an offer. I tried. I think they started to worry it might not make a lot of money and that if he did get into it as a partner, he would get to make up part of the loss and have more hours and more worry. I told him I could not pay him a lot more in a salary and if another $50 a month or so would help, I would do that if he would stay on. He seemed to settle down and then a couple of months later he told me he had another job and I had a week to find someone else.

In a pharmacy you are supposed to have a pharmacist on duty at all times when the store is open. This is the law. If I got turned in for running a store with no pharmacist on duty, I could lose my license for the new store, as well as my pharmacist's license. I was unable to get another pharmacist that quickly and it wasn't the time of year to get one out of school. I was able to get some part-time relief pharmacist in who I paid by the hour but this was costing me a fortune. I did this for about two months while I asked around to see if anyone was interested in buying a store.

I was going to have to make a decision. I had, over the last year and a half, rented out some of the space in the center. Once to a Baptist church for a kindergarten sort-of-thing and another time, part of the space, to a Century 21 realtor franchise. This had enabled me to finish the rest of the center with walls, flooring, ceiling, and heating and cooling. I paid for part of it, out of the rent that came in—just so I would get it finished and have tenants in the space.

Now, should I close the new store (and the future), and strip and sell it—or should I close the old store and strip it. The old store was making about $18,000 a year at that time and the new one nothing. I had run up bills with my suppliers to the tune of about $25,000 dollars and all up, had bills for the new store of almost $50,000. I wanted to keep the new store but with it not making any money, I could see no way of paying the debts off. I had to close the new store and sell what I could. I closed the new store and moved all the merchandise back to the old store. I then started running ads to sell the fixtures.

Over the last couple of years as Cecile became more and more independent, I would have the kids come down to the store either after school or during the summer when they were older. At first it was just Sam and Craig and they would help by cleaning and stocking the soda pop machine. I would pay them for their work, with the understanding that half of what they made would go into a savings account and the other half they could spend. I did this with them on and off over a period of time. The savings accounts were at NBC as when this was started, that was the bank we were with. That way when the delivery boy took the deposit to the bank he could also take theirs for the savings account.

Over the period I had the drug stores, I was broken into a number of times. Only once at the new store where they knocked a hole in the wall with a sledge hammer but set off the alarm once inside. The old store was broken into 3 or 4 times and they usually came in through the air-conditioning duct on the roof. Again once they were in, they would set off the alarm as I had learned early on to have motion devices in the store.

It was bad enough with the damage and the small amount of stolen merchandise but the one that took the cake was when it involved the police. I was called out one night by the security company as the alarm was a silent one. They had also called the police. When I arrived the police were outside waiting with the security company. They were already inside as the security company had a key. The burglars had come in through the roof but ran away as the cars drove up. I was talking to them in the prescription department and looking around for drugs that may have been taken.

All the narcotics and amphetamines were in locked cabinets or in the safe. I went one way around the counter and checked the cabinets and then came back. When I came back I noticed a bottle of 500 Valium tablets was gone. I kept the fast-moving products up on the shelf in front of the work area and had one open bottle and a full bottle behind it. They were both in place the first time but on my return the full bottle was gone. Three or four policeman had been in the area since I had walked through. I went over to the officer in charge and told him what I knew. I told him I wouldn't even worry that much about the $35.00 bottle, as much as it was a controlled substance and I had to account for all the tablets.

This started a barrage of interviews with various people in the police department. They finally asked me to take a lie detector test and assured me the officer they had in question had agreed to it as well. I passed with flying colors. He refused to take the test and resigned from the police force. That was the end of it.

One day when I was trying to get off work early, we got busy. I felt I couldn't go and by the time I was able to head home several hours had passed. Cecile had left the house about 30 minutes before I got home to go to the school to get the kids. I drove in the driveway and just after I did, she pulled in. When we went to the house, the door was open. We looked inside and found we had been burgled. The TV sets were gone, the stereo, the gun I had, the cameras, jewellery, and even a bunch of our clothes had been taken from the closet with the hangers. The good news was they didn't take the dirty clothes so we still had a lot to wear.

As we found out later, it was done by professionals. The police didn't tell us at first but there had a number of these in the area in a short time. The burglars would case a house and find the routine. They would then decide when to hit and several would break in and stack items by the front door. In the bedroom they would empty the contents of the drawers and put items on the bed along with clothes. They would then pull the four corners of the bedding up and tie it off. All of this would be by the front door. The other person would then drive the van up to the door, and they would all load the van and be gone in minutes.

I always kept receipts so when the insurance company asked, we had them. We had a very detailed list we could back up. The bad news was the insurance we had been sold was not replacement. They depreciated all the items—TV sets, clothes, everything. We were thousands of dollars out of pocket. You should get replacement insurance.

These were just a few of the other things going on in our lives as all the rest was still going on around us. This several year period was not boring. It was a time that tried you and just about got me down. I didn't know the best was yet to come.

CHAPTER 28

AN ACCIDENT

I had no real choice. I had to close the new store. At least with the old one, it was making some money. I was overstocked as we had built up the inventory in the new store having purchased packages for quantity and price breaks. As I reduced the inventory, I paid down what I owed the drug companies. As I sold the new store's fixtures I paid off even more debts.

This all took time and I finally had it down to three drug companies I owed most of the money to—with Southwest Drug being the main one. They also got the most business. In a little over a year I had reduced the debt from almost $50,000 down to about $26,000. The hard part was that a lot of the easy money was gone. The fixtures and extra inventory had been sold.

The Century 21 office wanted more space and moved into what had been the drugstore space. As I remember, it was about 2,000 square feet. The space in the middle was 1,000 square feet and at the end it was 1,600 square feet. We moved part of the fixtures that were left into the middle, as the realtor was in the end space. The payment was about $830 a month, plus taxes and insurance. The realtor agreed to pay 30 cents a square foot, which was $600 per month. This took some of the pressure off but not all of it.

Cecile didn't want to work in the drugstore and wanted to get a job. She started looking around and found one in the area with a bookkeeping company. They would do something like my bookkeeper did, except the person in her position would sell new accounts, pick up the work and drop off the statement each month. A person in the office did the entry work and the information was sent to California for processing. She would get paid on new sales and a part of the ongoing account. She was also able to get bonuses and extras.

She did well in sales and started to make some money. They soon wanted her to act as sales manager and take over getting new people in, just like she had been hired. She did well again and before long they wanted her to take over the office when the manager left. She would go all over town and would not always be able to pick up the kids after school. At times I would have to get them and sometimes I would need to send the deliveryman to bring them back to the store.

The younger ones were in Orange Goose School, a day care which, at times, the boys had been in as well. The children had to be picked up on time or you were charged $1 per minute for each minute you were late. This happened several times and on other occasions I had to leave the store to go and get them at the last moment.

When you figured the expense of day care, petrol for the car, and the wear and tear on the car, plus other expenses, the actual profit was not a lot. I had tried to get her to stay at home with the kids until they were in school. I felt they needed their mother and that the environment for them at home with her would be better for them. She insisted on getting out and away from the kids. She said she needed the company of adults, and wanted to get out and feel she had accomplished something as she felt life was passing her by. The job was not primarily about making money to help pay the bills.

The fact was, that at first, with the cost of day care, it cost us more for her to go to work than to stay at home. She had taken care of paying the bills at home and for years I had left it up to her. If she needed extra money she would ask for it. One evening on the way home I stopped in at the Shamrock Service Station to buy some gas. I got the gas and gave the man my credit card. A few moments later he told me my card was on the list of bad cards and he was to cut it up and send it in. I would have to pay for the gas. I usually didn't carry much money on me on a day-to-day basis and after scraping in my pockets I had just enough. When I got home I asked what was going on. I had given her some extra money a couple of times over the last couple of months. She explained that their bill came in about the middle of the month and she didn't have time to pay bills more than once a month so they could wait until the following month. It seems that a time or two she had also overlooked the bill in the stack as well. Shamrock had a solution; they cancelled our credit card.

Cecil's friend, Joe King, started to hang around in San Antonio more, as did his friend, James Keefer. Joe King came in the store several times, saw Dad for prescriptions and explained he had some people working for him back in Louisiana. He wanted to get some diet pills for himself, and a few other things, and take them back with him. As Dad had seen him, he said he would prescribe some items for him. He would ask me from time to time, to send him his prescriptions and some of the other merchandise, and he would pay me when he was in town. I did this a few times and everything was fine.

One day Mr. King came to me and asked me to keep a package for him in the safe. He would collect it in a day or two but needed a safe place to keep it. I put the package in the safe and a couple of days later he picked it up. He used the pay phone in the front of the store several times a day when he was in the area. Cecil asked me if Joe King had asked me to do him any favors. I told him about the package. I told him I had assumed it was money from the way he acted and how it felt. He then told me that Keefer was a horse trainer of sorts and King was his helper. However, their main job was gambling. They would fix horse races sometimes; which he claimed he didn't like and why he eventually got out of the horse race business. They were also in the numbers business and they were in San Antonio to see if it was possible to open up a new market. Joe King was supposed to be connected with a group out of Louisiana that was involved in gambling and girls. Cecil claimed he had asked around and the federal authorities and local police were already aware that someone was trying to move in the area, and they were on the lookout for them. He then said for me to not get involved and to stay away from them. My main contact with them after this was either filling prescriptions when they were in town or mailing them to him in Louisiana, which happened only a few times.

As Dad seemed to be getting back on his feet, two of my brothers, Charlie and Tom had been living with him on and off. At this time Tom was staying with him and came and went, just as his behavior went back and forth. After I had run Tom off, a friend of mine up the road with a furniture store, said Tom had come by looking for a job. I warned him what a con man Tom was, not to trust him and not to hire him. He still hired him and months later he told me Tom had taken off. When he left he owed him money that he had advanced him, and for used furniture that he had sold him. He said I was right and Tom got him. I felt nervous about Tom being around Dad as I felt he would try and get him to write prescriptions for things he shouldn't have—or just steal the prescription pads and write them himself as he was a good forger. Dad insisted he was helping around the apartment.

One morning, early, at the drugstore, I got a phone call. It was a doctor at the emergency room out at the Methodist Hospital. He said they had Dad there and he had a head injury. It was very bad and they had decided that if they didn't operate he would die. They also said that because of the nature and location of it, they would most likely kill him if they did operate. They needed to know what to do now as time was also a factor. I told them to at least give him a chance and to operate. I found out, according to Tom, that he had heard a noise in the early hours. He later went into Dad's room and found him on the floor next to the table by the bed. He thought Dad had fallen and hit his head after he had gotten up to use the bathroom. Tom said he then phoned for an ambulance.

Paw was shaken. He didn't know what to think. He was afraid Tom might have hit Dad for refusing to give him money or drugs. He had tried to help Tom on and off for years. He reviewed a lot of Tom's history and wondered if this problem might have been avoided if Tom had been a better shot. Later, he was sorry for having said this. Some of Tom's history makes you wonder how he ever made it. When his trouble first started, Dr. Joe offered and paid for him to go to T.M.I., Texas Military Institute, a private school. That was short-lived. Tom had tried to commit suicide once a few years before. He was in the kitchen at the house on Wyndale when he took the 3030 deer rifle and shot himself. The bullet went through his side, and hit his liver and spleen. They had to remove his spleen and he recovered. Also years before when he was little, he had fallen out of a tree when we lived on Harrison and the side of his face was torn open when he hit the cyclone fence. Back when I still lived on Wyndale, I also had some people come to the door looking for our parents. Mom and Dad had gone out to eat. I went up the street to where a car had hit a motor scooter. Tom had been riding on the back of it. His leg was torn open and the broken bone was sticking out so he was taken to the hospital and given morphine for his pain. He recovered from this as well. I always wondered if this introduction to pain relief might have contributed to his willingness to take drugs.

Tom stayed at the hospital waiting for word on how Dad was. We contacted other members of the family as we could and Aunt Mary did as well. Dad came out of surgery alive but in a coma. They had no idea on how long he would be in it or what condition he might be in. They did know if he lived, he would have a long hard road to recovery. Even then, they didn't know how well he might recover. Days went by . . . and then weeks. All up, he was in a coma for about a month. Even then, he could only make sounds but seemed to understand what you said. It was decided to transfer him to the Audie Murphy Hospital as he was a veteran and the private insurance might not keep covering things. His bill in the hospital was $23,000, which was mostly paid by his insurance. Beulah Ann had been contacted overseas. She decided to come back to see what she could do.

While this was going on and everything was up in the air, Cecile told me she wanted to talk to me. She told me she wanted me to know that even though we had room in our house, she did not want my Dad to come and stay with us. She also said that if I did try and do anything like this for even a short time, she would move out. She did not want to take care of him and she didn't think it would be good for the kids to have him around. I asked her what she would do if it were her family. She said she would do it for them as it would be her parents. She never said but I always had a strong feeling that she had been guided and told to bring this up and settle it before anything got started. It wasn't like her to just jump out with something like this—even though she felt that way.

When Beulah Ann came over, we had a chance to catch up for the first time in years. I tried to spend as much time with her as I could but I was in one of those situations where Cecile didn't want to come along but she also didn't want me to go. Beulah Ann offered to take care of Dad. This put a lot of pressure on her and Tommy. When Beulah Ann did have children she had a very difficult time. She would have to stay in bed most of the time to try and get as close to full term as she could. She took care of Dad for years, and took him to therapy and got him back to where he could get dressed and eat on his own. He could talk and move around. I always felt he understood a lot more than he could express. It was going to be a long difficult road for him, as well as Beulah Ann and her family. He would have never recovered as he did without her help over the years.

Beulah Ann had to stay and take care of him when he was well enough to come home from the hospital. He always missed Mom and I was told he would pick up the phone at times, as if to make a call. When asked whom he was calling he would say he was calling Mom in Hitchcock. He would then have to be reminded she was dead. He would then say "Oh, yes" and nod his head.

Beulah Ann had to make arrangements about what to do with his belongings. Some had been in storage but as time had gone on, it was evident he would never be on his own again. Various furnishings were split up amongst her and my brothers. I really didn't have any use for any at the time and when they had moved out of Wyndale I had gone back and found a lot of photos on the ground. I had picked these up for later distribution and that is about all I had wanted. When my grandmother and mother died I was offered some items then. My Aunt Mary and Mom had decided I should have Golda's set of Dresden china that I had eaten off all the time I lived there. So I took it. When Mom had died, I was given a set of dark blue and gold French Limoges china. That is all I had of them. And Cecile had been given some pieces of jewellery by my mother before she died.

It was hard to make the decision to close Dad's office. Annie Lou didn't want to but also knew that it was all over. She closed things up as best she could. The office was cleared out except for the reception desk. Annie Lou found a job doing bookkeeping at a lumber company. We were all very sad.

It is a strange feeling when you lose your grandparents and parents. It is someone you have known all your life and see every day at first. Someone you love and trust. These are the people that, in the back of your mind, you always have, to fall back on. They sometimes help with money, sometimes with advice, sometimes by just being there. Then you lose them and they are gone. It is a very lonely feeling.

CHAPTER 29

THE NEW BUSINESS

Cecile worked for the bookkeeping company and learned the basics of the business. She spent more and more time with clients, and enjoyed the freedom and feeling that she could do as she wished. I felt bad for the kids and felt that their complaints about the daycare were somewhat justified. I couldn't totally change it. I did put a TV set in the back room where the doctor's office had been. After school I would have them down at the store. I did this as well during the summer and sometimes on Saturdays. It was like a prison to them at times—yet I would still rather they were with me where I could watch over them and try to give them some things to do.

I would try to get them to help in the store where they could. I would also let them have a soda pop, crackers, sandwiches, and candy from the store. They would need to ask, and I would try and control it.

Along the way, Cecile had heard of a company that offered a franchise for the bookkeeping service. You would sign up with them for a fee, and they would supply the materials and the computer processing. She wanted a business of her own. She went to talk to Cecil and after some discussion he agreed to back her. The franchise fee as I remember was $5,000. She would open her office in the middle of the strip center, as 1,000 square feet was plenty.

She was used to working with businessmen and had become quite good at this. It is just one of the things she had learned while with the other company. She did some travelling and had to fly to Dallas to meet with the main person in charge of the franchises. This would be one of the main people she would need to work and deal with. She conducted her business, closed her deal and had her new franchise.

At this time, we still had a fair amount of the new store fixtures and the large wood section that had been above the prescription department with the name on it. I hauled this back to the house on Zornia and purchased pre-made letters. We made a new sign that said Professional Business Systems, her new company. I then installed this on the front of the center above the space. It was then a matter of getting phones turned on and setting up the fixtures around the room for partitioning off space. Some additional furniture, office equipment and supplies had to be purchased but it was kept to a minimum.

Very quickly, she decided that if she was going to spend her time out selling and calling on clients, she needed someone in the office to answer the phone and do the processing. She found a lady to do this and hired her. Her business was now ready to go. She let some of her old clients know where she was and they came over to her. Some of the others told their friends and they came as well. It was now a matter of selling new clients.

She spent a lot of time every day out of the office. I had hoped this would make money and be a way to help us out of our situation. She still wanted to go out at night almost as much as ever. With her being her own boss I had also hoped this would mean she would be able to spend more time with the kids. It just didn't work out that way.

After getting up and going it wasn't long before the expenses ate up what little reserves she had. Even with her not paying any rent, she still had utilities, telephone, processing fees, gasoline, car expenses and the girl working for her. It then became another expense for me. Every month or so, when she was short of money, I would write a check on the drugstore to try and help her out. She was putting in a lot of time and I was sure it would pay off in the long run.

Dr. Joe died February 23, 1977, at the age of 90. Aunt Mary told me they found him dead in bed one morning when they went to check on why he hadn't come down. They think it was a stroke. I found this very sad, yet I knew he would be much happier being with Golda again. I think at times he wished he were already with her. It was a large funeral, and a lot of the doctors and old friends came. None of the Rayner side of the family came or sent anything that I know of. They had hard feelings toward Dr. Joe and still acted as if they blamed Dad and his side of the family for Beulah's death at such an early age.

In accordance with his wishes, the house on Lamont was sold. It sold for something like $176,000. A dentist purchased it and had plans to enlarge and expand the buildings. Dr. Joe had felt that, over the years, Dad had got more than Aunt Mary did as he was always helping Dad out. He had also requested the estate be divided up with a larger share going to her. I was so busy with problems at home during this time I was unaware of what all was going on. Beulah Ann got with Aunt Mary and worked out various issues. She took Dad's share to administer it for his needs.

On the 26th of March, 1977, my other grandfather, F. H. Rayner died in Hitchcock at the age of 76. I was sorry the relations with the families had become strained and we had not seen a lot of any of them over the last number of years. They had come up a few times after I got the drugstore. Dad and I would try and send them samples of medicine they needed or I would send it to them at my cost. They had told me they didn't want things for free. Dad would help when he could and would give them free advice and samples.

Cecil offered us his demonstrator motor home to go down to the coast. He figured we could go down for the funeral, stay the night, and get back. He also knew it would be a lot easier on Dad in his condition. The worst of the oil crunch was over and he had added motor homes to his business. Cecile, the kids, Dad, Beulah Ann, and I all went down. We parked at Aunt Jennie's house the night we arrived and went to the funeral with them the next day. After the funeral some of the cousins and Aunt Bobbie came over to see us. The next day we went to leave and just as Cecile turned onto the highway and got in the middle lane, the motor home died. We later learned the wiring harness was pinched in the adjustable steering column and when she went to adjust it, the harness was pinched and shorted out.

We called Cecil and he had Mr. Kline get in contact with Gilmore Pontiac in Houston that also sold this brand of motor home. They made a deal to send a wrecker to pull the motor home to Houston and also send a car to us to drive back to San Antonio. The dealership purchased the new car as a dealer trade for stock. By the time this was all over and we drove back to San Antonio, it was in the middle of the night.

The oil crisis of the early 70's was a major blow for us. Business in general was bad and for Cecil it was a disaster. No one wanted large cars and it was almost impossible to get rid of them. At one point the factory was selling their executive cars and an almost new Pontiac Grandville Convertible was sold for $1,500. Cecil was able to get this car and we bought it from him for Cecile to drive. It was a gas hog and got about 8 miles to a gallon. My drugstore business suffered as well and inflation got worse.

Cecil had years before, dropped Mercedes Benz as they were too much trouble and demanded too many standards to comply with. A new Japanese car company was trying to get into the United States and he needed a small car. He took on Subaru but they had a lot of problems with just starting to set up. Not enough parts, not enough help with problems, and a lack of quality. I had purchased one for the drugstore and had problems with the brakes and with it not wanting to start. As soon as the crunch was over he dropped the line.

The government came in with wage and price controls to try and stop the inflation. We had to post a list of the top 100 prescription drugs on an official poster by the pharmacy department. Other prices were frozen. It was a little late for us as our expenses had gone through the roof at the store and at home.

Utilities at home when we first moved in were around $70 per month, with the air-conditioning running all the time and the lights going. When they started going up we went to $125 and then to $150 almost overnight. Later when we tried to conserve, we were still looking at bills of $175 to $200. The price of gasoline was high but the lack of it was even worse.

When we first moved in at Zornia we had a Mobil Service Station next door. In a short time we saw them digging up the ground and putting in new tanks. The new tanks were filled with gasoline. Not long after this the station closed. It was converted into offices later, after it was sold after the crunch.

My neighbor at work (and a customer) had the Exxon station up the street. He told me they filled his tanks each night but he was only allowed to sell what he was told. If I ever needed gasoline just let him know and give him the keys when I closed. He would come over and get the vehicles during the night and fill them up and take them back. I only had to do this a few times. One of the transport drivers that knew my friends Beck and Duderstadt told them that one of the other drivers had been driving for one of the refineries and how each night, he would take a load of gasoline way out in the desert and dump it. It was always amazing how once they had the price up, you had all the gasoline and other energy you wanted . . . just like that.

When we purchased the lot on Zornia I had never gone over every inch of it. Later I found a pipe that was almost completely buried. It was a storm water drain from the intersection in the parking lot of the Mobil, which picked up the water from the station's parking lot. This then dumped onto our property in a flow that fed to the storm water system behind the house. When I contacted Mobil, they didn't want to know about it or me.

I had contracted with a company to put up a fence around the backyard. This would be a privacy fence on the end by the house, and on the side where the shops and station were. The rest would be a cyclone fence. As they started to put in the posts and set up for the fence, a policeman came by and said we couldn't put a fence at the end of the house across to where the businesses were. If we did, we would be blocking an easement.

I had a diagram of the property when I first went to purchase it, with the dimensions, and it had no mention of an easement. When we closed at the title company they also did not show or mention an easement. I called a lawyer (who one of my delivery boys used for tickets) that was in the area. I had heard he was a straight talker. I explained to his office assistant Jill, what had happened. Dan Rutherford, the lawyer, called me back and told me to build the fence as it would be cheaper to defend a case than to try to take them to court. The next day the builder put up the end fence and the police came to give us a summons to appear in court.

This dragged out for a number of months and when they had a hearing in the City of Castle Hills, they found in favor of the City of Castle Hills which had a record of the easement. I had even considered trying to work with the city on the basis of a new drain that would be underground, if they would pay for it. They wanted me to pay for most of it and I said no. We appealed it to the county court. When it came up at the county court, they threw out the case and dismissed it. The easement didn't count because it was not registered in the county courthouse. All of this sort of stuff on a property has to be registered in the county courthouse. That is where it is checked for.

I became friends with Dan Rutherford and used him a number of times in the years to come. He knew I didn't have a lot of money and consequently either didn't charge me or charged me only a modest amount. In return I testified for him several times at trials about drug interaction and potentiation of some drugs. This is when the effect of one with another adds up to more than would be expected. A sort of a 1 plus 1 equals 3. Today you hear about how someone was taking something and he didn't know better so he drank or took something else, and consequently had unexpected results. This was something new in some of the court cases then.

We did lay a small pipe about 6 inches in diameter under the ground from the Mobil pipe to the city system in the rear before we sealed off the large pipe and buried it all. One of my delivery boys and I did the work in the evening to get it done so we could tidy up the backyard. Beck had told me to do this so any water that built up in the system could have a way to drain out or I would end up with a swamp. I spent about $500 with the lawyer and was lucky that was all it cost. He had a dislike for City Hall at Castle Hills and seemed to almost enjoy beating them. He also lived in Castle Hills in a new area near Cecil. I also learned that a title policy is almost worthless except for certain instances—yet all the mortgage companies insist you have them. The title company didn't want to know me, or about the easement, or the court case, or the cost. All they could say at the end was that is what we told you—they had no easement.

CHAPTER 30

PUNISHMENT

I ran the store's inventory down to the point that it actually hurt business. I wasn't missing that many sales but the problem was, that the shelves looked empty—as if I was going out of business. I was still trying to pay the drug companies off and was on a cash basis with Southwestern Drug. It made it harder to do business and I felt they were doing me more damage, and thus themselves, by not allowing me the 30 days credit. The salesman I knew for years told me that they had a new set of managers and the head office in Dallas had told them to get tough with overdue accounts.

They wanted me to borrow money from Cecil or have him pay the debt for me. They wanted me to go to the bank to get the money. I asked them what bank would loan me the money when I was trying to pay off normal purchases I was behind in paying, due to my mistake with the new store. I reminded them how much I had already paid off and that each month I was paying something towards the balance. Some months it was $250, sometimes $500, but I was paying and it was better than nothing.

The boys had started playing football and getting involved in sports. I was glad they were getting to do things as I felt they were both good athletes. I even managed to get away once and film part of their games. It was still difficult to get away as you could imagine, with being broke.

I didn't have a lot of time to spend with the kids and what little I did was usually cooking out back, or trying to get them to help me with the yard. I passed and kicked the ball to them some—but not as often as I would have liked. I had always taken care of the yard and cut the grass. Even when we moved into the new house I was the one who planted the conifers for the hedge and would water the grass after dark with one hand, while I drank a beer with the other. I spent a lot of time cleaning up the old vacant lot-type of mess in the back and all around the grounds.

When I was outside working or cooking I would sometimes have Scott bring me a beer. He got to the point he could open it and if I wasn't careful, he would drink half of it before he got it to me. He wanted to help and when I worked on the lawn mower, more than once, he would watch and hand me a tool when I asked him for it.

I don't think Scott had his first hair cut until he was about 2 years old. Cecile didn't want to have it cut, as if she wanted him to stay her baby and not grow up.

I had started to have doubts about Cecile and what she was doing. No matter how much she worked, she never made any money and always asked me for more. I started to drive myself crazy with my imagination at times. Other times I was worrying myself almost sick about the money I owed and how I was going to pay it back.

We had just managed to keep the bills up to date at home. We were still charging and the balances kept going up. I didn't understand how we kept spending so much. We were at the point all we could do was make the minimum payment and hope we had enough of those to go around. It was cut so close that many a time we would drive down to the mortgage company's office on the last day we could make the house payment without a late charge and make the payment then.

Tom had gone off the rails and was back on the street. I had a call from the San Antonio Police Department about him and they wanted to have a talk with me. He had made a deal with the police to give them information on some drug operations in exchange for not prosecuting him. However, part of the deal they insisted on was to have him committed to an institution as a ward of the state for treatment. They needed me to sign the papers as he had told them I was the closest next of kin they would be able to get in contact with. I drove downtown and the policeman in street clothes met me outside in the street. He showed me his badge and identification, and pulled out the papers. We placed them on the hood of the car and I signed them, standing in the street. I hoped it would help. I had told them that Tom had been in such a mess I was sure he would end up killing somebody or being killed himself if he continued as he was. At least with him being locked up this way, he had a chance.

Late one afternoon when I was at home from work after closing on a Saturday I started picking up the kitchen and having a few beers as I started to plan for dinner. The older boys and Laurie were in the back yard playing. It was always a challenge to figure out what to fix, as usually the cupboards didn't have much in them unless it was the day the shopping had been done. About an hour went by when I heard this blood-curdling scream and crying out back.

I ran to the back door and Laurie was just approaching the patio with blood all in her hair and pouring down her face. At first it was hard to tell how bad she was hurt. She had a cut in her scalp and a bump on her head. I put some ice in a kitchen towel and had her try to hold it on the spot, as I went to ask the boys what had happened so as to get a better idea about her injury.

At first they just stood in front of me and wouldn't answer. Then Sam told me they had thrown a rock up in the air and when it came down it hit Laurie in the head. The way they told the story and the way Craig went along just didn't fit. I was sure this was not the complete truth. The more I questioned them, the more the story started to shift and the angrier I became. I was worried about how much Laurie might actually be hurt and was about at the end of my rope with everything that was going on in my life.

I gave the boys short quick slaps to the side of their face with my open hand and told them they were not telling the truth and I knew it. I then grabbed them and put them on the ground on the grass so as to keep them from trying to run away. I questioned them again and told them each time they didn't tell the truth they would get a slap. I did this several times and the side of their faces showed some redness and a few marks from my open fingers. They then told me that Sam had become angry with Laurie because she wouldn't play the way he wanted her to, so he picked up a rock and threw it at her, hitting her in the head with it. He then had Craig agree to go along with his story as he felt he would get in less trouble.

I then tried to explain how dangerous this was and how important it was for me to know how she actually became hurt. By not knowing, I might think the injury was less serious than it was and she might not get the treatment she needed. They didn't want to see Laurie hurt bad and didn't want to see something happen to her. They got several swats for what they had done and several more for not telling the truth.

The bleeding seemed to have just about stopped and the bump was fairly large but not getting any larger. They were all crying by this time and Cecile came in. She had just arrived home. As I tried to explain the series of events she started yelling and going on about the kids. The next thing I knew she had gone in the next room and phoned Cecil, and he came over to see what was going on. He saw the kids and all he could see or talk about was how Sam and Craig had marks on the side of their face. He didn't want to know what the story was and said he was going to take the boys to his house for now.

By the time Monday had come you could hardly see any mark at all on the boys. I had thought about what had happened. I had taken out my frustration from everything going on in my life on them. I was ready to step into my usual standard roll of being the one to discipline and administer punishment to the kids. Now I felt ashamed about what I had done.

I decided from then on, Cecile could administer justice unless it was something directed straight at me. We had a talk on this subject and had gone over how Sam had just about become uncontrollable now that he was 13 years old. I reminded her of how they would have yelling matches, and he would cuss and call her names. This is the point at which she would usually call me in to do something. I said, "It is over. I am staying out of all of it from now on. If he comes over and yells and calls me names or does something to me directly then I will do what it takes to straighten him out but that is it, I am staying out of the rest of it".

In the meantime Cecil had been busy. According to him, and I am sure he did, he had contacted the Castle Hills Police Department and talked to one of the people in the department he knew. He told them I had abused the kids that weekend and that you could still just make out the marks. He didn't want to press charges this time but wanted to put this somehow on record so if he decided he wanted to, he could have me prosecuted at a later date. He phoned me at the drugstore–to not just tell me but to threaten me with this. I told him I was sorry for what had happened and I had already talked it over with Cecile. We agreed she would do the disciplining of the kids. What I did wasn't right but I felt Cecil had gone over the top by what he had done and it upset me greatly.

From this point on, I never did swat the kids. I stayed out of it. I would hear them yelling and cussing and calling names. I would walk out of the room or turn the TV up. It was turned over to Cecile and that is where it stayed. For the first time since we had kids I didn't have to be the one to swat them and I was glad. I should have done it sooner.

Cecil and Elizabeth had been having some rough times over the years but most of the time it was kept to themselves. One of the few times I saw anything was when we were living with them upon our return to San Antonio. They had been out at some function one night, and when they returned they were yelling at each other and calling out names. They had been drinking and before it was over they were pushing each other in the hallway and bouncing off the walls. The next day Elizabeth had bruises on her arms.

Cecile and I got out of bed and went out to the hallway where Cecil told us to stay out of it and get in our room. This went on for about an hour and the basis of it was jealousy. She had said something to him about how he was carrying on and he then started accusing her. It became known to me later that Cecil was a jealous person. In the past he would call Elizabeth all the time and try to know her every move. He always wanted to know where she was, who she was with, and what she had been doing. He actually wanted her to stay home where he felt he could keep an eye on her.

He always wanted to show Elizabeth off, like a prize, on his arm. When I first met her back in about 1961, she was very slim and wore a size 8 dress. As she became older she put on weight and like we all do, showed her age some. We had always gotten on well and then about the time I got my store, she changed towards me. It wasn't until years later that I found out Cecil had told her a bunch of stuff he wanted to say to her and then said I was the one who said it. It had to do with her putting on weight and I had supposedly told him it was because she made no effort on her eating, and if she would make an effort to see the doctor he could give her various things that would help her, she wouldn't look so old and fat.

Elizabeth did go to Dr. Carter at one point when she was going through the change of life and she was put on to hormone replacement therapy. I must admit when Elizabeth was going through this time in her life it was hard to be around her.

Later, she went to my grandfather, Dr. Joe. They got along very well with each other and they both liked each other a lot. He didn't think everyone should look like a 20-year-old. He was interested in her weight but in relation to her age and her health. I sometimes think she wanted to have someone to talk to as much as anything else. He never told me what they talked about or what he thought. It had always been clear to me that he had little use for Cecil and his opinion didn't change.

Cecil got to the point he acted like he didn't want to be seen with Elizabeth in public. He always felt she could have done more to make herself look like she did 18 years ago. It is a hard cold fact that we all get older and when we do, we look older. One of my textbooks had a set of drawings of a man and a woman with body shapes that are typical at various ages. It starts at about 2 years old then shows 12, 20, 50, and 80, or something to that effect. If you think about it, why do we insist a 50-year-old look like a 20-year-old? It is part of the natural process for our looks and shapes to change as we go through life and become older. We can try and take care of ourselves but why try and be something we are not. Some of us have a tendency to be tall, others heavy, and some of us stay slim. We are what we are.

I confronted Cecile on a number of occasions about what she had been up to. She assured me she was not meeting someone else and even became quite angry. Her attitude toward the family and me had changed but she would not tell me anything and she would not talk to me. She still insisted on going out, and going to 'Trim and Swim' sometimes in the evening. At least she was now wearing pantsuits and not the ultra miniskirts but make no mistake about it, she still did as she pleased.

CHAPTER 31

ENDING'S NEAR

Business was slowing down at the drugstore. I had tried various ideas—including changing the mark-up on the front end drug merchandise to 25% instead of the usual 33%. I would use a bright red price sticker and round all the prices to 3, 5, 7, and 9 on the end. According to the discount idea, prices that ended with these numbers gave a feeling of being discounted more. So a price would be maybe $3.97 instead of $4.00; or it could be $4.09 instead of $4.10. At any rate I passed on more price savings when we purchased deals, to try to win back more of our front end drug business. It didn't appear to help as people would only pick up an item if they were in the store as long as the price wasn't sky high but they wouldn't make a special trip to get it from me.

The advertising flyers had helped in the past but most of the people seemed to only come in for the specials and we didn't see them again until the next flyer. Over the years I had added a system that would keep a patient profile on each customer that had prescriptions filled with me. They could come in without their refill number and we could find their prescription for them. We kept a list of their allergies and drugs they were on. We would fill out insurance forms at no charge and we could give them a total of how much they had spent on medication each year with us.

It only happened a few times but the patient profiles saved a couple of my patients from ending up in the hospital or even worse, dead. They were on a number of medications, usually heart patients, and their regular doctor would be out of town and someone else would be covering for them. They would get sick or hurt and the doctor covering would prescribe something for them over the phone. A few of the doctors wouldn't ask if they were on anything and that is when the potential problem would come up.

One patient that had been on the fragile side called into a doctor on duty, and told him that he had trouble with his arm and elbow. He was on a lot of heart medication including Coumadin. The doctor called in and ordered butazolidine for him. When I told him what the patient was on he almost came through the phone. "Why didn't he tell me he was on Coumadin?" Another time a doctor called in Norflex with Darvon for a patient who had hurt some of his back muscles. When I pointed out that in the literature there was a warning from both companies that they should not be used together, he jumped down my throat. I told him it was fine with me but if anything happened, he would be wide open for a lawsuit with no defense. He changed his painkiller.

All of these services, along with charge accounts, delivery service and even after hour emergency service, didn't mean anything to most of the public. All they wanted to know about was price, price, price. The neighborhood drugstore was fast becoming a thing of the past—just like the soda fountains (the predecessors of 'fast food') had been the place to go and get something to eat, and see and be seen, which were now long gone. The public wanted the super discount store that sold garden supplies, clothes and drugs, all at a discount price. They would have to pay on the spot and wait in line for their prescription. If they wanted an insurance form filled out, it was extra—or in some cases they wouldn't do it at all. The receipt given at the time of purchase was the only record provided. If they had any questions, well you know, "Ask your doctor, he wrote it. I only fill them". I had a good customer that was on a lot of medication and he switched to SuperX. He came by and showed me that he spent about $1,200 a year with me. At SuperX it would cost him only about $930. He lost the services and would have to do all of his own insurance work but he could save $270 a year. I told him some of what I knew about their buying power and tried to ask him to consider the service I offered and if it might not be worth that extra $22.50 per month. I also pointed out that his insurance paid him back 80% after his first $100, which meant it cost him only about $54 a year more to stay with me but he felt he could put his $54 to use in a better way and moved his business.

It seemed more and more people did this—even the ones that spent a lot less. The ones I held on to were the loyal customers who felt the difference wasn't enough for the amount of service lost. I wasn't sure I had enough customers that felt that way. I had a number of really good accounts, including one from a trust fund at Bexar County Bank. The trust officer had all of an old lady's needs go through me and each month the bank paid the bill. She lived in an old house on Blanco Rd. that was set on about 20 acres. Towards the end she was on a special cancer drug that was $20 a vial and she had about 10 of them on hand at any one time. When she died the nurse sent all the unused medication back to me.

I told the drug manufacturers of my returns. Most of the companies would not normally take back items under these circumstances and by law I couldn't sell them again. I didn't know for sure how they had been taken care of, for one thing. Parke Davis was the company that had manufactured the expensive medication. They told me to ship it back to them and they would give me credit for it. The care of the lady had been under a nurse and they were sure it was okay and would donate it to a charity clinic. I called the trust fund manager at the bank and explained I would be sending the final bill and that I was able to get some credit for some of the returned medication. He thanked me but explained it wasn't necessary. He was happy with my service and felt we had provided for her at a reasonable rate. He then told me he would have expected no less as he knew I was Dr. Joe's grandson and he was one of his patients. That is how I had obtained the account in the first place. I still wonder how many discount stores would have done this and if anyone does it today.

[As a side note. She must have been the last in a line because after her death the property was put up for sale and a developer purchased it. As I remember the house was removed from the property before it was developed. With its size and location I would imagine it went for a lot of money.]

This was only part of my problems as I had to cut back my staff to the bones. I would have to let some of my employees go—and these included some that had been with me for a long time. I couldn't help but think about some of those that had come and gone over the years.

I still had my deliverymen, one of them being David Schultz. He had come to me after I ran an ad and his mother called me. She explained he had a hearing problem and was now wearing hearing aids. She didn't tell me he was big and strong and had a behavior problem. It wasn't until late in his childhood they were able to do something about his hearing. Consequently he spoke with a thick accent and he didn't always understand everything said to him. He still used sign language and read lips. He had been teased a lot as a boy and always felt people were making fun of him.

I decided to give him a try as I had taken on a few problem kids in the past with mixed results. It took a few times to teach him how I wanted things done and early on we had a shouting match in the back when he thought the girls were making fun of him. I assured him they all liked him and wanted to help him just as I did. He became one of the most dependable and trusted employees I had. He did his job like clockwork and figured out ways to help and make things run faster and smoother. He didn't know his own strength and if you asked him to help move a refrigerator he might just pick it up and move it if you didn't show him how to use a dolly.

I had two other delivery boys over the years that had come to me with problems. One was Jerry Martinez who moved out from his mother and wanted to get on his own. He was angry that she wanted to marry another man after his father died. He worked for me several years and got past his anger before deciding he wanted to be something. He joined the Navy and a couple of years later, called me from a station near Alaska and told me how he had been on various ships and was now a radar man at a far outpost. He thanked me for giving him a chance that allowed him to decide what he wanted and said how it had kept him out of trouble by having a job and a place to go each day, where he felt he did something.

Another one, Tim McGinnis, was a boy who had been in prison at a very early age. His grandmother came and asked me to give him a job and a chance. This was early on when I had first taken the store over. He had been convicted of stealing a car. I later found out he was working for a gang that stole to order and he had stolen about 100 cars. He was only about 14 at the time when he started but was older when arrested and given a choice of several years in juvenile and no record, or 1 year in prison with a record. He took prison and it was now a couple of years later. He was now about 19.

He was a problem at first and never tried to do anything extra. He finally became dependable and was working very well. He wanted to get a used car so he could get to and from work more easily after he had been working for me about 2 years. He picked out a used Ford Thunderbird at Cecil's used car lot. The loan through GMAC was first turned down because of his record and lack of credit. He asked me to co-sign the note for him and I wanted to help him, so I talked it over with Cecile. Cecile felt this would maybe also make him feel obligated to us, even though he had said he planned on staying with us. I co-signed the note for him.

About six months went by until one day he didn't show up for work. He ran off to California. It seems the car broke down when he got to California and he had pushed it off a cliff. GMAC had contacted Cecil as the car note was overdue and the police in California had contacted him as the lien holder and he was the recourse dealer. They now planned on contacting me about paying off the car. I had always figured if it was taken back I would only be looking at the difference of between what it was sold for versus what was owed on it. I never dreamed he would pull something like this. Cecil gave me a long lecture about this and how stupid I was. I must agree it was not the smartest thing I had done. I was sure he had gone straight and would never do anything that would hurt me. How wrong I was. Cecil said to leave it with him and he would see if he could get the insurance to pay out since he didn't think they could prove Tim had anything to do with it being over a cliff. After all, how did they know it wasn't stolen? He must have gotten them to see things his way as neither he nor I ever paid the car off.

Marcie Ruffo had quit a couple of years before. She had become tired of the problems with Cecile and the length of the skirts, and who was in the prescription department with Sam. She knew my fuse was getting short with all of the problems and sometimes I would snap at the employees if they weren't doing their job as they were instructed to. She had also gotten to the point she would forget what she was doing and would sometimes forget she had set a phone order down to do something, and then remember several hours later. It was little things like this. I also had wondered if she was day dreaming about a rep that used to call on us from a company in Waco. I had suspected for years that she was seeing him on the side and then when he was transferred, she changed. I didn't care what she did on her time but she almost acted as if she had a broken heart. I was fortunate as when I ran an ad for help, a lady by the name of Ester Petri applied with experience in drugstore work. She stepped into Marcie's place almost overnight.

Gertrude Nicholson had started work behind the soda fountain just before we closed it. She was a waitress but acted more like a clerk. I needed some additional part-time help at the time and told her I would give her a try. She worked both full-time and part-time for me over the years. She had a rough life and had been 'Queen for a Day' once on the TV show. Her husband was a drunk and he had fallen from an oilrig and broken both of his legs. She won a bunch of appliances on the show and that was her big break.

When she was working for me her son was arrested for murder. It seems he and a friend of his went out for some drinks and ran into a couple of guys and got to talking to them. Before they knew it the place was closing so they were asked by these guys to come to their place and have a drink or some breakfast. They went there and then realized their new friends were gay, and a fight started. This is where, from here on, the story has two versions.

One was that during the fight someone pulled a knife and one of the gay guys got stabbed and it killed him. The police weren't sure who did the stabbing. According to Gertrude's son they were both okay when they left. He thinks they had a lover's quarrel after they left and one gay guy stabbed the other. However, the next day when he heard about a guy being killed he didn't know what to do. In the meantime his friend turned himself in and said he had nothing to do with the killing. He turned state's evidence and said Gertrude's son did the stabbing.

Gertrude and her son's wife borrowed on everything they had. She wanted the best and went to Fred Saman. He said he wanted $10,000 up front to take this case. After they gave him the money he turned it over to a junior partner and they never saw him again. The lawyer told them with what his friend had done to him, he was in a very bad position. The lawyer then assured them if he pleaded guilty, he could get a reduced sentence. They took the $10,000 worth of advice and the judge gave him 25 to life. A very expensive guilty plea.

I had tried to give her moral support and when she had some trouble with tenants on some vacant land I offered her advice. She was upset because she was going to have to repossess her lot and sell it again. I reminded her that when we set it up and sold it the first time, she got a down payment and then a number of payments. The person had put in a water well and now it was hers all over again. She would have some minor legal expenses but what they had paid her she could keep. I guess she told her son how I tried to help her (she was now about 60), because while he was in prison he made me a leather wallet with my name on it and sent it to me to say thanks.

These were some of the employees and some of them were still working for me. It was almost like a second family; after all, some of us had been around each other 5 days a week for about 7 years. I had been watching my sales versus my purchases and some departments were kept separate. This included the tobacco department. I noticed that our tobacco sales were about the same but our purchases had gone up and were almost as much as our sales. I decided to inventory the tobacco–not just in dollar amounts but by brand as well. Sure enough, we were having some stolen. About two to four cartons a week. I wasn't sure how long it had been going on but I knew someone was taking cigarettes and even which brands.

I then started checking the sales and the inventory after each shift and identified which shift they were disappearing on. Was this an employee or just when someone took the opportunity? I was sorry to find out it was an employee. I caught them and confronted them. They made it easy and admitted to what they had done. They took orders from friends and then sold them the stolen cigarettes for extra money. Gertrude Nicholson knew what a hard time we were having and knew we couldn't afford to give her a raise. She was having a hard time making ends meet so she decided to sell the cigarettes for the extra she needed. She had hoped to be able to stop before she ever got caught.

I told her I was sorry too. I wouldn't prosecute her but she would have to take her final pay and not come back. I also told her not to apply for unemployment as I would protest the claim and tell why she had been fired. She didn't apply for it that I know of. Cecile and Cecil wanted to know why I didn't have her arrested. I said I could only guess she had taken maybe $1,000 worth of tobacco and she couldn't pay it back. I also could see no good coming out of trying to send a 60-year-old woman to jail. In some ways I felt maybe it was my fault for not being able to pay her more after all the years she had been with me.

The last few years had been very hard for me. Nothing was working in my life for me, on any front. The store was a big problem and the continual financial battle was hard for me to come to grips with. It seemed no matter how hard I worked and tried to make a success of it, it just didn't happen. I knew with all the hours I put in, I was not seeing as much of the family as I would have liked to. With not being able to provide things for the family at home, it just created more worry and tension for me.

I knew Cecile was unhappy and had gone through various stages the last few years. She had to have her freedom and space. She wanted more, and wanted to go places and do things. She wanted to live more like her folks and her brother, and not have all the money worries. I tried to do what I could and maybe I shouldn't have let her get away with as much as I did. But then, I don't think I could have stopped her anyway. I tried to give her money all the time for her business—to the point where it just compounded the problems I already had. I just felt that at any time, her business would start to make money and this would help our situation.

I didn't know what to think about the drugstore. At times I felt like the only choice was to keep doing what I was doing for several more years and hope to get all the bills paid off. After all, the store was still in the black—it just wasn't making much. I knew that Cecile wanted no part of the drugstore and she had already expressed to me that she wanted nothing to do with it ever again. I was just about at the end of my rope and I wasn't sure what to do next.

The next piece of news I received was devastating but at least I found out I wasn't going crazy and imagining things. Cecile admitted to me she had been seeing someone but it was over. They had talked about getting divorces but didn't want to upset the families. They were not going to see each other anymore and it was over. It was the boys' football coach. She had been meeting him during the day and sometimes in the evenings. When they felt they could meet they would but it was now over. I told her it would only work if she stopped seeing him and tried to put things back together at home. If the third party continued to be a factor it would only confuse the issues and make things worse, and there would be no hope of working things out. I wanted to try. I wanted to make things work for me and for the kids. I didn't want to be away from them and I didn't want the family to break up.

CHAPTER 32

IT CLOSES

Over the years a lot of things had happened while I had the drugstore. I had almost lived in the place. Opening and closing, day in and day out. I had not taken any vacations as we couldn't afford it. I couldn't afford to get off for an afternoon. I was tired and worn down. I was wondering what it was all about and if it had been worth it. It was supposed to have been the start of a new future for the family—a source of income that would allow us to live in a manner we expected. It was to get better in the years to come and allow us to send our kids to school, and help them out when needed. It just wasn't working out this way.

I was fortunate as I had never been held up. I had been broken into but that was not threatening. I had called the police several times when I had phony prescriptions presented for drugs and I knew they were forgeries. One set of people was even arrested by the police, although they never prosecuted them and let them go. Another time I had a black man stumble in the front doors saying he had been shot. I told him to lie down on the vinyl floor in the entry. I got him some towels and he told me he was afraid his girlfriend was coming after him to shoot him again. She was mad as she suspected him of cheating on her. She had had enough and took a .22 caliber pistol they had and started shooting at him, hitting him a couple of times in the upper leg. I guess she wanted to try and put him out of business. She didn't show up at the store, and the police and ambulance came and that was the end of it.

The store did have a lot of memories but they were becoming increasingly bad. I had worked after hours into the night to get the place cleaned up and fixed up. I had a discount photo shop built almost at my front door in the parking lot and there was nothing that could be done about it. Discounters had come into the area and taken a lot of business. I had concerns about the ethics of some of the doctors in the neighborhood. I had seen my father's office come and go during a time in which I had seen promise, and shared a time with him I would never forget. I had a greater respect for him and knew what a top-rate doctor he really was.

Southwestern Drug Company started putting even more pressure on me and their area salesman told me the company planned on filing a lawsuit on me if I didn't pay them in full soon. I told him to tell them if they started that, they would be the loser and would most likely end up without a dime. They must have called Cecil because he called me and wanted us to come over after work to discuss it.

Cecile and I went into the front dining room with Cecil at his house to discuss the options and Elizabeth took care of the kids in the other room. He wanted to know how we felt and what we wanted to do. He asked Cecile if she wanted to continue with the drugstore. She didn't hesitate as she told him no. He asked me how I felt and I told him I had mixed emotions. I didn't like the idea of giving up and walking away from it after all this time and effort.

He wanted to know what it would take to make it into a better store and not just pay off the debts. I told him I owed about $23,000 all up but if the store was restocked, debts paid off, refurbished again, I could see it being maybe $50,000. He then said to me that he already knew how Cecile felt about going through it all again and asked how I felt. I told him I had a hard time trying to figure out what the point of it was. If I did take the money from him and worked like hell, I couldn't see how it would ever make any money that amounted to anything. Times had changed with discounters and competition, and the changes you could already see coming in such as third party pay—be it insurance companies or the government—weren't looking good for the small independent pharmacy either. I said no. I couldn't see beating a dead horse and with Cecile not wanting any part of it, I could not see any reason to go deeper in debt and continue with insane hours for no money.

I didn't know what I could do if I got out of the drugstore other than work for someone as a pharmacist. I really didn't want to work day in and day out, locked up in a drugstore again. It was almost like getting out of prison. I had considered trying to go to work for a pharmaceutical company. I might be able to get a job with a good company as a medical rep. Eli Lilly normally only hired pharmacists, and several other top companies preferred someone with a strong drug background since they would be mainly calling on doctors. It was something I could ask around about and apply for, after I was out of the store.

We decided I would try and sell the store if I could. If it looked like Southwestern was going ahead with their plans then maybe I should declare bankruptcy and get out. I was to talk to Dan Rutherford in the meantime, and find out some of the things to do and not to do. This was upsetting for me but I didn't see how I had much choice. I had been trying to sell the drugstore by having the drug companies aware that I would sell if they had a buyer come along. I had talked to one pharmacist who had taken up real estate but he was only interested in our house. It seems we were one of the few new houses with 5 bedrooms as well as den, playroom, and other extras, on a big lot in Castle Hills. He claimed to have had a doctor at that time that would have purchased our house for around $100,000 to $120,000. It would have been more than enough to clear the debts. We only owed about $43,000 on it but I knew we would never be able to get a house like this again and I didn't want to upset the kids by having them move—and possibly even have to change schools and friends.

A couple of months went by with no success. During this time, after talking to Dan Rutherford and Cecil, we made several arrangements—one of which had to do with the strip center on El Sendero where Cecile's office was. Cecil had put up the $5,000 going in but the mortgage and papers were in mine and Cecile's names. Right after we purchased the vacant lot, I had a developer call me and he offered me double what we had paid for it, as well as offer a good lease if I rented space in his new building. Maybe I should have taken it but I didn't. I had managed to finish all the space in the building so the center could now be rented to anyone—with floor, ceilings, heat and air-conditioning all in place. Cecil told me he had checked around and it was not a good time to try and sell the center.

The Century 21 office was paying $600 per month, Cecile in the middle was paying nothing, and the end space was vacant but should rent for about $480 per month. The center had about 2 years paid off the 10-year mortgage but with the depreciation and other tax write-offs, it would actually pay for itself without a big tax liability. As it was, it was only about $350 a month short of paying its expenses and mortgage, with only Century 21 paying rent. It was a good proposition for Cecil to take it over for free. The idea was it would all be transferred into his name for any money that I owed him for the center and the drugstore, if someone should ask. He would then hold on to it "for Cecile and the kids" later on. I guess I should have asked him "how about me?", when he told me that. I gathered up the papers and everything to do with the center and took them to his office—including a rent check for $600 from the realtor. I signed all the papers and it was his.

Dan Rutherford explained to me that I must pay any and all taxes if I could because the government was one of the only ones that can come after you even if you are bankrupt. He had things set in place and told me whenever I was ready he would only need about 24 hours notice. I had asked around but could find no one interested in buying the store as a going concern. There was just too much competition in the area. I continued to pay down the debts with the drug companies but it was getting increasingly more difficult. I felt time was running out.

I had very little luck and had just about given up when Rudy at Gwyn Pharmacy called me one day. He told me he was not interested in the store but as we were in the same neighborhood he was interested in my customers. He would buy my prescription department inventory at cost and pay for my good charge accounts at face value. He wanted my prescription files and thus my customers. I needed somewhere for them to go without difficulty and who else would be able to buy prescription drugs by law, if not another pharmacy. I wouldn't get any premium for the business but I would get a good price for merchandise that couldn't be sold to the public, and market value for the accounts. I talked to Rutherford and he told me how to handle it if I wanted to go down this route.

I had nothing to think over so I talked to Rudy and he wanted to complete the deal as soon as possible, as I did. He would need a few days to make arrangements and suggested he and one of his men, along with me and one of mine, take the prescription department inventory and load up the files and drugs for him on Thanksgiving Day. Once he had this, I was out of business. I told the few employees I had left at the eleventh hour, that we would be closing down at Thanksgiving. I gave them their final paychecks and told them good-bye. David helped with the inventory and the loading of the files, and in the matter of hours on Thanksgiving Day 1977, it was all over. I had the check made out to Dan Rutherford as Trustee, and took the check, the keys, various records and checkbook to his office the next day, and turned it over to him.

He filed a Chapter 13 Bankruptcy petition for me on the drugstore. I declared business but not personal bankruptcy, as it had only to do with debts of the drugstore. It was amazing to me that this went on for about 9 months before it went to court and had its final hearing. During this time a court-appointed trustee took his time in trying to sell what was left. The store was broken into about 3 weeks after it closed and several thousand dollars worth of camera equipment, watches, film, tobacco, and such, were stolen. Other merchandise such as the candy was just left to turn stale and old, as he took his time running ads and then eventually had an auction with what little was left.

I had always figured it would be close to breaking out even but with the poor way in which this was done, as well as some of the good merchandise having been stolen; it didn't work out that way. The check I had turned over was for about $11,000. The store account was down to about $1,000 but all the taxes had been paid. I never knew how much they ended up getting but I was told that the court was paid, Dan Rutherford got his, the court-appointed trustee got his, and Alamo National Bank that I still owed some money to, got theirs. The only ones that didn't get paid were the drug companies, of which most was owed to Southwestern Drug. In a funny sort of way I thought it was fitting that they took the biggest lick as they were the ones who pushed for it.

I was in one way relieved it was over and yet I was very depressed and sad. I had failed and this was something I never wanted to do. It was hard for me to accept that I had. I was surprised that at home I had no understanding or sympathy. For Cecile it was just another day at the office and she acted as if nothing had happened. I was hurt, embarrassed, depressed, and felt like a failure after having tried everything I knew of, with no positive results. I felt alone as she carried on with her bookkeeping business and ignored me totally in what to me, was a time of need.

Cecil had offered me a job with him until I figured out if I could get a job with a pharmaceutical company. I went to work for him in the body shop at first as he felt they needed a hand and I might be able to figure out why it wasn't making any money. He started me off on a salary of $1,000 per month before taxes. I was still in a state of shock and didn't even think about it.

It became apparent to Cecile very quickly that we couldn't get by on $1,000 per month. It would hardly cover the house, utilities, vehicle cost, insurance and some food, much less anything else. Elizabeth came over a couple of times early on and brought sacks of groceries to help out. I was glad she did and I think it came from her back to Cecil, to raise the salary to a more realistic level. He called me into the office and told me that maybe he'd better pay me a little more if I was to get by, and he raised my salary to $1,500 per month before taxes. With this, we would be able to get by as long as we stayed within our means and paid off our bills making minimum payments.

It was now up to me to learn the body shop trade and what was going on, while I tried to apply for other jobs. Several jobs came up at first and I applied with no results. One was with Hoffman La Roche as a medical rep in the new medical complex area but they wanted someone with sales experience. Another was with Texas Pharmaceutical but again they wanted experience—and the starting pay was only $800 a month plus a car and that wouldn't have worked.

It was now December and most places were waiting until after Christmas and the New Year before any changes would be made. It was time for me to make the best of it and try again later. My life at home still needed to be straightened out and I needed to overcome my feeling of being a complete failure as well.

CHAPTER 33

BACK TO THE DEALERSHIP

I found it strange going back to work at the dealership at first. Some of the people I had known were still there. Val Luckett was now the office manager and Wilroy Ristow, Cecil's nephew, was now assistant service department manager. Elizabeth Cornelius was still in the office and had always been a friend to me. She later told how Cecil had come to her when Sam was born and wanted her to go out and buy a bassinet for him. She said that it was the way in which he did it that made her decide to buy the best, most expensive one she could find. He almost fell over when she gave him the bill.

The body shop was across the street and behind the used car lot. It was in its own little world. I didn't care much for the body shop manager when I arrived but about a month after I came he took a job at another dealership and left. The new manager was totally different. He showed me how to estimate a wreck and use what is called a crash guide to get prices for parts, paint, and labor. The only hard part was estimating the amount of time to straighten or repair a panel instead of replacing it. This came to me fairly easy and after about two months I was writing up estimates for jobs.

If the insurance company or customer had any questions about the amount of work that needed to be done or the price, then they would talk to the manager. He would then review the estimate and sometimes would try to get used or exchange parts to get the price down to an acceptable level.

We also had warranty work and transportation damage work to do. This had to be scheduled along with the big jobs that made the money. Another young man was working there as an assistant manager and was a lot of help. He knew the body and paint men well. He was able to fill me in on what was going on with the different men.

The body men would be paid on a commission basis for jobs. They would turn in their weekly time slips on Thursday each week for pay on Friday. Some of the men would charge more time than they had completed on jobs and this would cause problems. Some were bringing in personal work and would take part of their time to do it on the premises. They felt it was their time as they were on commission. The problem was the dealership's space was then not generating income for that department.

The paint shop had actually been sub-leased out to the painter. The painter was paid by the ticket on the job and the men and supplies were his problem. It sounded good but again he would do everything that he felt made him the most money than what might need to be done. He would also try and skimp on materials and get you to raise his allowance when he could. All in all, the department was every man for himself.

The new body shop manager knew his business and started to try and clean up the mess. The body shop had also been known to do cash jobs where the money never made it to the dealership as a ticket was never made out for the job. He was going to have an uphill battle but he was determined to make it work. I told Cecil what I had seen and what I knew. He didn't want to go into it and as I had told him the new manager was working towards getting it in order, he was ready to drop the issue.

Each year the dealership would have some sort of a Christmas party. The employees would take up a collection for a gift for Cecil and they would present it to him at the party. At the party he would have the managers give out checks to the employees, a Christmas bonus. It was usually $50 for employees and something more for managers. Over the years I had seen the employees become more resentful about pitching in for a present. At the party they would have a food table, and a table set up with beer and drinks. It would usually last about 2 hours, start to finish.

As the year closed and the dealership closed on New Year's Eve, I noticed a number of the employees in the service department waiting room. As I walked over from the body shop area to the main building, several of the employees called for me to come over. After I turned in the papers to the office I went back to the service department area. A number of the service department employees, the service writers, the manager, the cashiers and a few from the front, had all come to the back to have a drink with each other. I talked to Val for awhile and learned about some of his background and how he had been working for Cecil a long time. I talked to some of the others and found that most of them didn't mind working with me, as they didn't think of me as the son-in-law of the owner since I didn't act like it.

I got to know the service manager who was arrogant and abrasive. Cecil liked him as he had a good warranty claim rate and kept angry customers off him. The service cashiers and warranty claim girls were friendly. That is, until Cecil showed up. They then gradually moved to the other side of the room or decided it was time to go. I had never seen him like this before. He would go over and put his arm around them and pat them on their backside or try to take a little squeeze. It was embarrassing at first but then I realized the rest of them were used to him acting like this.

I had several beers and was about ready to go when Cecil came over to Val and I, and started talking to us. Then, the next thing I knew, he mixed me a drink and said there was no hurry as Cecile and I were going with he and Elizabeth to the country club's New Year's Eve party. We talked about the dealership and what I had learned, and then he put another drink in my hand. We visited some more. Then to my surprise it was about 4:30 in the afternoon. I needed to go and was not in very good shape to do it. Cecil started laughing and thought it was funny. This was just one more time when I had let my guard down and he got me.

I managed to drive home and told Cecile what had happened. She was angry as she was looking forward to going to the country club. I told her I would be ready to go on time but she should drive. Cecil called about that time and was having a big laugh when Cecile got mad at him for almost spoiling her evening. We went to the party and had a good time but it was the only New Year's Eve I ever started out drunk and sobered up as the evening went on. I drank coffee the whole evening as the idea of another drink almost made me sick.

After we returned to work after the first of the year I applied for a couple of more jobs. I had to get time off for the interviews. This was usually only a few hours. I had a good interview with one company and a few weeks later they called me back and asked me to take a series of test. One I could take home that was several hundred questions on things like would you like to go swimming or would you rather build a boat. It was a wide variety but aimed at personality. The next test I would take would be at the manager's house. It would take half a day and each test would have a time limit. It was math, science, general knowledge, and some of it was like an I.Q. test.

The manager for Mead Johnson told me it was down to me and a couple of other candidates. The job would start out with training and I would get a salary of $1,200 per month plus a car. I would have a salary review after 6 months and then annually. The pay plan also had bonuses for targets during the year as well as annually. The other benefits were like the other major companies—medical insurance and moving allowances. If they transferred you they would give you something like 3 months to sell your home. If it didn't sell they would get three appraisals and average them and pay you that for the house. When you moved they would pay for you to stay in a motel for awhile until you found a place and then they would pay you an extra month's salary for incidental expenses. These were the types of benefits with companies like Mead Johnson, Ciba, Hoffman La Roche and Eli Lilly.

A couple of more weeks went by and then the manager called me. It had come down to one other man and me. The other man was currently working for another drug company and had a good reputation. He had experience and knew both doctors and pharmacists in the area. Both he and the head office felt they had to go with him but if they had another opening come up, they would let me know. I was let down but then he told me that a lot of the companies give this battery of test that I had taken and as I had passed with flying colors in every way, if I had to take them again I should not worry about them as I would do well.

It was maybe a few weeks later that I saw an ad in the paper where Eli Lilly was looking for a rep. I contacted them and they had me send them my resume. A little later on I received a phone call and they wanted to interview me. I went to their offices in the Central Park building a few days later with my stomach and heart in my throat. This was the chance I had hoped for—a top company. In fact, at the time, one of the best to work for in the pharmaceutical industry. I went to my interview and felt it went well. I told them of my background and even what the Mead Johnson manager had told me. The manager really sat up then. He then told me that if everything worked out he was sure the job was mine. I was by far the best qualified that had applied. The only thing he wanted me to do first was to check with Cecile and talk over a move. The opening was in El Paso, Texas. If we wouldn't move then there was no need to continue any further.

I had mixed emotions at first but knew this was a chance of a lifetime. I knew I would have to start at the bottom but then a lot of the top drug companies' reps were making anywhere from $40,000 to $60,000 a year after just a few years. It was our chance all over again to accomplish something for our future. I could hardly wait for her to get home to talk to her about it. When she came home I told her I as good as had the job. All I had to do was let them know if we were willing to move to El Paso, Texas. She immediately, and without hesitation, said no. I tried to tell her what an opportunity it was and that I might never get a chance like it again. I tried for about an hour but all I did was make her mad and say no even more emphatically.

I was knocked to my knees. I couldn't believe after what I had already been turned down for, that now that I had a chance with a top company I was going to have to tell them no. I was sick. I knew Cecile wanted to be near her folks and she had just started the business but I felt it was a real chance for our future. I didn't want to make the kids move either but I felt in the long run, the benefits would outweigh the loss. It wasn't to be. I called the manager back at Eli Lilly and apologized; as I hadn't realized that moving would be such a big problem. I asked him to please keep me in mind if anything else came up and he said he would. I never heard from Eli Lilly again.

Back at the dealership Cecil decided it was time for me to move out of the body shop. It was under control now although he and the service manager butted heads from time to time. Cecil asked me how I felt about going down to the motor home department. He had taken on motor homes but found out it took a certain type of salesman as the customers were different and it was like selling a house on wheels. It took a lot of time and you needed to know about everything from stoves, to generators, to showers, and refrigerators. After that, you needed to know about how they were constructed and what kind of motor they had. You needed someone who could help teach the customer how to use all the appliances and do basic maintenance.

He had one old man that worked at the department but most of the rest of the salesmen didn't want to mess with them as they took up too much time—and even then you weren't sure it was going to lead to a sale. The motor home market was turning slow again and he really wanted to clear them out. He still had about 25 new ones. They ranged in price from $16,000 to $40,000 new. He also had several used ones that were around the $10,000 price range.

I was more interested in getting back into sales, both for experience and the money. He decided that what he would do is keep me on the salary as a guarantee and if the commission was higher he would pay me that. He had sort of the same arrangement with 'Pop', the old man who was down there that he paid $1,000 a month. We were to take care of the lot and the motor homes that were on it. We were to keep them clean inside and out. If they had a dead battery it was up to us to charge it and if a repair could be done by us on one of the homes, we were to take care of it.

We spent part of each day correcting problems on the used and the new homes. Pop would check the ad for the weekend paper each week and we would take turns on waiting on people that came in. This was all down in the old used car lot and office that I had worked in years before. I took my lunch most days and I would watch the lot as I ate my sandwiches.

The real joy was the Executive motor home demonstrator. It was supposed to be Cecil's but in reality Henry used it most of the time. He would take it for a weekend or on a trip to go hunting. He took it with the family once on a trip to Colorado to go hunting. He no sooner got there and was so homesick that he turned around and drove all the way back—about 14 hours each way.

Henry would then drop it off at the lot and we had the privilege of emptying the tanks and cleaning it all up inside and out, ready for the next time. Such was my start in the motor home department.

CHAPTER 34

BACK TO NEW CARS

I could see I had a couple of real problems and I didn't have answers. If I were to get a job with a good drug company I would most likely have to move to a place that was low on the ladder of places people wanted to be. If I tried for a better city such as San Antonio, I would be up against reps with experience. I didn't like my chances. I wasn't sure how it was going to work out with me at the dealership but so far I had been far away from Henry, so that was working out. If I stayed at the dealership, how was I ever going to make any money and be anything? The only ones that made money were managers and salesman. As this was the only opportunity I had at present, I felt I needed to do well in the motor home department.

I got the knack of selling motor homes as it was a cross between selling houses and cars. You had to spend the time with the customer and make sure he was happy with the one you were trying to sell him. He had to feel comfortable with the equipment and ability to do some of the maintenance. He had to really want that motor home before you ever went too far into price.

We had our own sheets made out that we attached to the window. It listed a lot of the major equipment and then had a suggested retail price. This way the customer had an idea if he was looking at a $25,000 home or a $40,000 home. I found that if they weren't rushed and you sold them on the home itself, the sale would usually follow. As Pop was the manager, he got all the motor home department mail. He showed me that some of the manufacturers like Itasca would run sales promotions which gave us a chance to make a little extra. One time they had gifts. I won a Seiko watch from them that I had for years. The best ones were when they needed to move certain models. It would be maybe a 24-foot side berth model. When you sold it and your name went in as the salesman they would send you a check for $350 from the factory.

I don't know if the main office knew about this or not as it was direct from, and paid for, by the factory. Some of the other promotions I found out about later were offered to the dealership and the dealership usually kept them. I know this happened with one that Executive ran and they offered a rebate from $1,000 to $2,000 on models, and the dealership kept it. This is a decision that owners usually make. They don't feel extra money should go to staff—it should go to them.

I met some good customers and converted them to doing business with us. The best opportunity for this sort of thing was usually at a motor home show—one time was at the Coliseum and another time at the Central Park Mall parking lot. If you had a show and had say a dozen or more brands, then the people would come to compare. It was at Central Park that I met Mr. Speers. In the years to come he bought a motor home and about a dozen trucks from Cecil–either GMC or Chevrolet.

In the matter of about 3 months we had sold the motor homes down to a total of about 10, both new and used. Pop was not a lot of use but at least with two of us there, one could always leave for something. Next thing I knew Cecil had decided that Pop could go back to used cars with no guarantee and I could run the motor homes on my own. We were now into daylight savings time and he wanted me to stay open until 8 PM like the rest of the sales. Previously we closed at 6 PM but were open 6 days a week with no time off. I had hoped to be able to spend more time with the kids but this was not working out that way. In fact it got worse.

When I ended up on my own at the lot he finally agreed I would have a late night on Thursday, as this was the traditional late night. I would work until 6 PM on the other days. As we got into spring, and later summer, an old habit returned. I would think I was going to spend time with the kids and then Cecil would take them instead. They would go to the ranch. This was something he had done to me for years when I was in the drugstore. It was almost as if he was trying to keep me from seeing the kids. Time and again he would take them just as I thought I was going to spend some time with them.

Now it was even more of a kick in the teeth. I was to work all day Saturday on my own at the motor home department while he and the kids, with the rest of the family, went to the ranch. "I needed to work" and "he was counting on me" is what I was told. I had always assumed, like a fool, that he would understand the importance of me spending time with my kids and thus allow me some time off from time to time to be with them. It didn't happen. It was as if he was trying to take my place. I then had to decide if I would drive out on Saturday night or Sunday, or just stay home and do housework and laundry.

I did a little of all of the above. Sometimes Cecile would stay in town and just let the kids go. When she was busy with tax time she would be out a lot. I even tried to help her that year with her clients' returns. She would offer to do their personal returns for an extra fee at the end of the year. I helped some at home and when it seemed she always needed something from the office, I offered to help there. The problem was that someone needed to stay with the kids. I did what I could but ended up staying at home with the kids most of the time in the evening. Sometimes she wouldn't get home until late. It wasn't until later this became clear to me why.

She still wanted to go out dancing and just get away from everything. I had tried to talk to her on a number of occasions about the lack of relationship we were having and I didn't feel she was making any effort. All she could say was she didn't want to talk about it and she was doing the best she could and to just give her time. I couldn't help but feel like she was seeing someone by the way she acted and treated me. I couldn't reconcile the amount of time she was spending out in the day and occasionally in the evening. I asked her a couple of times and when I did, she blew up and reminded me that she had told me it was over, and to just get off her back and give her time.

Her folks had some problems on and off around this time. Her father even came over to talk to her about if he had a girlfriend and wanted to take her somewhere with her, if it would it bother her. She said no. She would still love him and Elizabeth just the same. She didn't want to be in the middle—she wanted to be friends with them both. Cecil even moved out from time to time and lived in an apartment.

One evening he called and wanted to know if we would go with he and Sue to a place and have a few drinks. Cecile agreed and we told the kids we would be back soon. We left and went to a neighborhood-type bar that had a dance floor and band. We visited a little and then Cecil wanted to dance and show off. This was one of the first times I had ever met Sue. He told us to get up and dance as well. We danced and sat down. A little later he wanted to dance some more so he grabbed Cecile and told me to dance with Sue. As we went around the dance floor and Sue and I were in front of the band, Cecil came by and pushed his hip against us as hard as he could and gave us a little push. We weren't ready for this and lost our balance and fell over into the band. He came over to help us up and apologized to the band, saying I had too much to drink and he would take care of it—but I was as sober as a judge. It was as if he wanted to make a point of showing he could do what he wanted to both Sue and I.

It was strange to go out with him and a girlfriend, and have his daughter there when he was still married to her mother. Once before, they had talked divorce and she even started to get a lawyer but didn't know who to get. At that time, a year or so before, we had suggested Dan Rutherford. He talked to her and explained if he took the case it was his job to represent her and do everything in his power to make sure she got her share. Years before, when her parents died they had a farm near Seguin. Her share was enough to get Cecil started in his first used car lot. That is what started him on his way to Ledlow Pontiac (as used car manager), and then Ledlow-Tindall Pontiac. And, of course, next was Tindall Pontiac.

Dan was sure that he had hidden accounts and assets Elizabeth didn't even know about. The next thing Cecil knew was he was served with a whole bunch of summonses and requests for records. He told Elizabeth (and us) that this was silly and it would only break him, and no one would have anything except the lawyers. He persuaded her to switch to a lawyer friend of his at another firm and assured her she would be well represented. But after the switch, the divorce was off again, on again, for a couple of years.

We went out with him a couple of more times but each time something would happen. One time he didn't like the way a guy looked in the bathroom so he hit him in the face with the fist that had a big ring on it. The guy was all bloody and never knew what happened. All Cecil wanted to do then was leave then. He slipped some money in the guy's pocket and said it was for his shirt and that he had thought he was somebody else.

By summer I had managed to sell the motor homes down to only a handful. Cecil wanted to rent the lot to another dealer, Orsinger Buick, across the street. He decided to move the few that were left to the back of the used car lot that was across the street from the main store, and to the body shop lot that was behind the used car lot. I moved to the main building and was to continue selling the motor homes and to also start selling new cars. I was glad to stay in sales as I had filled in one time as the service dispatcher while I was still in the body shop and I was afraid I might be sent back to the service department.

I worked with Mr. M. E. Klein who had been with Cecil for years. He wanted to show me how to order cars and take care of the new car inventory. They also had me learn from Virgil Baer how to spec out trucks and order them. It was different at that time as you had to watch the axle and spring weights with the amount of equipment, and they had a number of does and don'ts. They were forever having orders sent back to them, as the specs were wrong.

I came to know Klein a few years before when I was out at the ranch during deer season. It was one of those evenings when Henry decided to show up and he had Klein and Hebert Tindall with him. He wanted to go and drive around, and put out more corn for the deer for the next day. If he saw anything worth shooting he would do that as well. It seems that Klein's wife was out of town and Henry had talked him into going. Klein enjoyed his drink and had too much by the time he got to the ranch. We all got in the Jeep and Klein was in the back seat next to Hebert. As we drove around, Hebert and Klein dropped corn out the back. As we started to go up a hill, Henry had to give it some gas and the Jeep surged and went over a bump. Klein popped out the back like a cork out of a bottle. He landed on his head that was partly bald and the ground scraped the skin off of it. We took him back to the house, washed it off and cleaned it up with alcohol. He couldn't feel it as he had already filled up with alcohol. I told him to get an old product by Roche called Tashan Cream, if he could find it, at a drugstore. They went back that night, as they were worried about him. He got some cream the next day and he claimed by Wednesday when his wife got to see him that she couldn't see where he had scraped his head.

I knew Virgil from over the years, and he and his family had traded with me when I had the drugstore. He taught me about the ordering and about some of the locally-installed options for the Suburbans. This included electric windows and door locks. He also taught me the inventory control and what kind of availability there was on different models.

It was just as well because soon after this I waited on a customer who told me he represented a buyer. He would negotiate and find out what we were willing to do and he would let his client know if we were reasonable or not. I was curious about how much he wanted out of this deal. He wanted to order a Suburban. They were hard to get and they could sell all they could get for $1,000-plus over invoice. I talked to him and found out what he wanted, including electric windows and locks. I then told him on an order basis that the best I could do was $1,000 over dealer invoice plus the options that were installed locally. He said he was sure this would be okay but wanted me to wait a few minutes as he discussed it with his client.

When he came back he said it was okay and to give him the order. I explained they were hard to get and we would do our best to get it as soon as possible but it would be at least 8 to 10 weeks. I would give him a copy of the order but we would need to send it in to the factory. I then asked what he wanted out of this, as there was not much I could do since the deal was on a minimum basis. He said he was sorry that I didn't seem to understand. He didn't want anything as his employer paid him for this kind of work. He didn't mind paying the going rate but he didn't want to be taken advantage of. He then told me his employer was in pilot training at the air force base. He was in the Saudi Arabian air force and was a prince, a son of the brother of the king. He was from the largest and richest district. He would take the order and turn it over to a representative of General Motors he was to see in New York next week at a function his father was putting on. We had our doubts but gave him the order.

About 10 days later we had a strange number for a Suburban show up on our allocation sheets for production. Then to our surprise the vehicle showed up in less than 30 days from when we gave him the order. He did know somebody. I had the electric windows and locks installed and made sure the vehicle was all ready for him. I called them to come and pick it up. I reminded him we would need a check for the balance and gave him his final figure. When they came to get the vehicle the man told me the prince had employed him when the oil company let him go. He had been the negotiator between the Arabs and the oil companies. They had trusted him and didn't want to lose him so they employed him in this way. He then asked me if I would do one more thing. I asked what. His employer wanted me to go to Saudi Arabia with the vehicle, as it was a present for his father. He wanted me to show him how everything worked on it and he would pay all my expenses.

I asked Cecil what he thought. He didn't think I was serious at first but I assured him I was. He then assured me it was not a good idea and not to go. I have always wondered what it would have been like if I had gone.

I was being taught a lot and found out why. Both Klein and Virgil needed some help from time to time and Henry didn't want any part of it. He would come in and tell them to order some more trucks with certain equipment and in some of the colors he picked out, or just said to get a variety. On the cars it was mainly Trans Am's he watched over and would always say to get some more. I don't think he understood how the allocation process worked. He wanted more of the good and didn't want any of the slow models. The factory wanted you to take some of the slow and sell it as well. If you played ball with them, then when they had any extra good stuff you would get your share. Otherwise it was on an earned basis.

Henry would do the new car advertising and would come up with gimmicks. One time, he went to the service department and had them take everything off a truck that was not required by law. The hood, the doors and so it went, until he had a real stripped down vehicle. It was legal to sell and what he would do is run an ad at the low price, having taken credit off for the doors and such. The truck would be on the showroom floor and we would watch the people as they came in to look at it. Some would laugh and say I knew it was a have but I had to see what it was. Some would say typical car dealer and storm out. Once in a while you would get one that wanted to hit somebody. He did finally stop it after it started to do more harm than good.

The other thing I learned was that as long as Henry could have his cars and trucks worked on and fixed up his way, he was happy. He would have the big tires and roll bars with lights on his trucks, and the cars would have CB radios and radar detectors. What he didn't like were unhappy customers. If he had a couple of unhappy customers come up front looking for him in the morning he would check out for the rest of the day and go home. He just couldn't face the problems and do something about them. He only knew how to run. The salesmen would see a really mad customer heading for reception, asking for him, and they would say "that will send him to the house for the rest of the day". A few minutes later, to the house Henry would go.

CHAPTER 35

It's Over

I had become more and more suspicious about Cecile but was afraid to ask. I started trying to check up on her. I called the doctor's office and told the lady I was working on my taxes and insurance, and was trying to match up my checks with the charges but was having trouble. She was kind enough to read off the appointments and what they were for. This included an infection and a check up for her birth control pills. This was interesting, as we had agreed when Scott was born that I would have a vasectomy, and did so, as she didn't want to continue taking the pill.

My heart sank, as I knew she was not telling the truth. She was seeing someone. I didn't want to confront her until I had more proof so I started to check on the charges and any kind of receipt I could get my hands on. A lot of them didn't make any sense. She was buying various items but I didn't remember seeing them. She had purchased on lay-by, a picture of a lion's head or something, according to the receipt. I started adding up the petrol on the charges for the gasoline tax that could be taken as a deduction. I started to notice a license plate number started coming up all the time and it wasn't ours. The more I looked, the more I became upset.

I finally decided to confront her again. She blew up and told me I didn't know what I was talking about. She even told me the doctor's office must have pulled the wrong file. At first she said that if I didn't drop it she would want a divorce anyway, as she couldn't live like this. Was I imagining things or not? She told me that the upcoming weekend was Father's Day, and she and the kids were going to the ranch to be with Cecil. She told me after work she didn't want me to show up and to stay home. She wanted the time to herself to think.

When she returned that Sunday it was already dark. She wanted to put the kids to bed and wanted some sleep as well. She didn't want to talk and as I started to push her, she admitted she had been seeing the man again but said it was only a few times, it wasn't recently, and she would talk about it tomorrow. I sat up that night for several more hours having several more drinks. I felt for the first time, almost like wanting to commit suicide. I was still depressed about the drugstore and I was again speechless when she finally admitted she had been seeing him again.

The next day we started to talk and she admitted then that she thought she wanted a divorce. Looking back at it years later, I think my pushing at that time had pushed what was going on out in the open before she was ready. I called in sick for the day and we spent most of the day going over a lot of ground.

She admitted that, shortly after they had called it off, she was so lonesome for him she had contacted him and got him to start meeting her again. This staying away from each other only lasted for a short time, as she was to have said good-bye and they were to not see each other. We never had a chance as she never even gave it a try. She admitted that one of the real reasons for not wanting to move to El Paso was because she didn't want to move away from him. He was supposed to be seeing about getting a divorce . . . but she was supposedly not seeing him.

She assured me again that they were unable to see each other a lot in person but they talked on the phone and she had been working a lot of the times when she said she had. She said there were a few times he had lent her his car and that is why his plate number was on some of the gas receipts. This didn't make any sense to me at all. It was as if she was holding back.

She wanted a divorce but she wanted to see what happened with him. They had been seeing each other but only a little. They talked on the phone a lot. He would loan her his car sometimes. It was as if some of the pieces were missing.

That evening Cecil called and wanted to know what was going on. I think the kids had told him there had been some yelling going on. The next thing I knew, Cecil was over at the house. He wanted to talk to Cecile by himself for a moment and they went into the kitchen. It was almost as if they were arguing at the end.

He then called me over. He told Cecile to tell me the truth. She admitted she had been seeing Walter and that they had tried to stop at first but she called him as she said, and they had been seeing each other ever since. Cecil knew about it almost from the start as Cecile had been going to him for money as well. She hadn't worked very much and it was the only way to keep the business going. Cecil then claimed he had hoped she would get past it and everything would return to normal.

I was flabbergasted. At first I couldn't believe he knew all the way back to when they first started seeing each other. I was having such a hard time with the store and I was giving her money to keep things going, and he never said a word to me. I felt like a fool . . . the odd man out. I was always told blood was thicker than water–now I had seen it.

He told her to tell me the rest and she said she didn't know what he was talking about. They started yelling at each other and she kept denying there was anything else. He then said if he told me to drive to a certain area, an apartment complex, there would be a green Continental with his license plate number. She started to bluff all the way until we got the car keys and started to leave.

She then admitted he had moved out some time ago and had an apartment. She had bought a number of items for the apartment over a long period. She had spent a lot of time at the apartment with him. When they would go on her calls to pick up work, they would take his car and charge the gas to us as it was for her business and it would keep the suspicion down with the gas bill staying up. She had forgotten about the license plate number. They had talked about divorces but she was, and had been, waiting on him to see what he ended up with. Once they knew how badly he was hurt by his wife then they would know how much to try and get from me!

We all talked some more but most of it was out. I wasn't sure I even knew who I was talking to. I didn't think I knew her. I wasn't sure what was true and what wasn't true, that she had told me. Cecil left to allow us to talk some more. She admitted she had met him at times after work at the park. She would sometimes take the younger kids with her and let them run around as she visited with him. She wanted to talk to him some more as they had not totally decided on what they were doing and what they wanted. I again asked her to reconsider and to stop seeing him as she had never given our marriage a chance by continuing to see him. I was sure if she tried and didn't see him, we could work something out—if for nothing else, for the kids.

The next couple of days went by and it was hell. I would try and go to work but my mind was always wondering what she was doing and wondering what she would decide. I was trying to decide what to do, going through all the 'what if's?' in my mind. I didn't want to think about it being over. It had always been her in my mind and it was always her that I was going to be with. I couldn't imagine it any other way.

At first in the evenings we would try to get through the meals and get the kids settled to watch TV. I would then want to know what was going on and she would usually say nothing and that she didn't want to talk. Then after several days of this she told me she and Walter had talked. They wanted me to move out and she wanted a divorce. This again started another round of arguing at first. Elizabeth had become aware of what was going on and she even came over one time during these arguments. She was mad at Cecile and one time told her she wouldn't speak to her and that she wouldn't ever allow Walter in her house.

Cecile assured me that this is what she wanted and that she didn't want to give it another chance—she only wanted Walter. They would be stretched financially by his wife and the settlement he would have to make with her keeping their house. If I did as they asked without a big fight, they were willing to allow me to take my personal effects and some of the items we had extras of (plates, cups, glasses and such). They wanted the house, her car, and, of course, her business. They would also pay for the divorce. In effect they wanted me to move out of my house, give them everything and in return they wouldn't ask for child support. I told her I would do them one better. I would do what they asked, as well as take all the charge account bills and debtswith the exception of the 'Trim and Swim' membership. She was to destroy all of her credit cards and not use any of the accounts. In return I would ask them not to sell the house or move until after the kids were out of school. I also wanted them not to try and come between my kids and me. I wanted equal visitation rights to the kids. This was every other weekend and alternating holidays.

She had wanted me to move out right away. I told them to go to hell. I would sleep in the other room and start looking for a place to move to. I would move as soon as I found a place that was suitable and affordable. I also asked her what the plans were for money during the period they weren't married.

Walter was going to give her an allowance and Cecil had told her if she got in a jam he would help. This was mainly only under the condition that Walter didn't move in until after the divorce was over and they were married. Cecil didn't want things to look bad for the kids.

She asked me not to tell the kids what she had done. I asked her if she wanted to tell them. She felt Sam and Craig were old enough and she wanted to tell them we were getting a divorce but that was it. She would take care of Scott and Laurie in time. I told her again that as long as they didn't try and come between the kids and me, everything would be fine. If they ever abused them, I would come after both of them. Other than that I didn't care what they did and I had no desire to run her down in front of the kids for some sort of revenge.

The question then came up about Sam. She wasn't sure he would want to stay. I had told her from the start I would take all four kids. I didn't think she really wanted them as she was always wanting to put them off in a day care center. After going over the situation she finally agreed that after awhile when the older ones had given it a chance, if they still didn't want to stay then they could come live with me. When the younger ones got older and were about 12 or so, if they didn't want to stay, they could have the same option. I assured her that I would not allow them to go back and forth just because they didn't like something. It had to be because they wanted to move out and live with me. She assured me she would go along with this and not cause problems if they decided to move out later.

She talked to Walter again and he agreed. We were to go to Dan Rutherford as soon as possible and get things underway. Rutherford explained that this was unusual for a settlement and I explained that it was as if she was getting paid in advance. I was giving up my equity in everything I owned. I would have my clothes, the bills, my credit, and a job. I also reminded him it was her affair and her desire to get rid of me, not the other way around. If the kids needed help I would be there for them–just as her family would be. He said he would shop around for a judge that might listen and he would let us know how he did.

On July 7, 1978, our 16th wedding anniversary, I moved out of the house on Zornia. I had found an apartment near Churchill High School. I took one that was furnished as I had no furniture, in the section that allowed kids, in case Sam moved in. It was across from the swimming pool and I thought it would give them something to do when they came over. I didn't know they were going to spend a lot of time at Walter's and that it had a swimming pool. I got set up and realized just how little I had. I had taken only bits and pieces of broken sets of dishes, flatware, and some household items. Cecile was going to help me at first and then refused to. I was afraid if I took some items it would only lead to a fight. I decided to err on the cautious side. She had suggested I leave the china my mother and grandmother left me, as it would be safer with her until later. We had agreed she would keep the movies and the pictures but I could get them at any time to make copies of. This proved to be easier said than done when I tried at a later date.

When I went through the things at the house finding the items to take, I went under the eaves to go through the boxes in storage. I accidentally came across a box that contained letters, cards, and notes that Cecile and Walter had written. Most were written by Cecile. They went back to the start of their relationship. It hit me hard then, how she had lived almost a double life and how much she really cared for him. It only reinforced the feeling of betrayal that I had. The thought about the truth will set you free came to mind . . . in a way it did just that. I started to realize just how things really had been and I stopped looking back. I didn't go on searching much after that. In fact I probably left a lot of my things behind. I guess I always figured she would give them to me later when she came across them. It doesn't work that way. You need to take what is yours at the time or kiss it good-bye.

I soon found I needed to go shopping and bought from Radio Shack a combination record player, radio and cassette player with speakers. I also bought a TV and a stereo TV stand with glass shelves from Sears. I was glad I had kept my credit up or I wouldn't have been able to get anything. I purchased, sheets, towels, bedding, and over time, purchased a pair of twin single beds for the kids to stay. I was starting over.

It was good I was on my own at first. I had to still go to work and get myself together. I wasn't ready to be around people all the time. I needed the evenings off. It wasn't long though before and Sam and Cecile were having arguments all the time. It got to the point I think that Cecile was afraid Sam was going to scare Walter off. She was afraid he was going to make their life a living hell. He told her he didn't want to stay and wanted to live with me. I guess it was about a month or so later when she called and wanted to know if I would take Sam to live with me. I told her I would but I wanted to talk to him so he understood what it would be like.

I told him I wanted him to come and live with me but it wouldn't be a situation where he could come and go back and forth between us, just because he didn't like something. I also told him I expected him to behave, to help, and co-operate with me. I would try and help him with his homework, and try to do things with him when I could. We could try and get along. He said he wanted to come and so he did.

This would be the beginning of Sam and me getting to know each other all over again. I am only sorry I wasn't able to make better use of it in the years to come—yet I still feel we developed a certain bond that we wouldn't have had if it weren't for that time we lived together.

Craig asked about coming and I told him to give it time. I also needed him to stay with the little ones for now as they needed him. In time if he still felt he wanted out, he could come then. I always felt Craig made a sacrifice for his brother and sister at that time. It was unfair for me to ask but it was something that needed to be done. However, in a way, it was a sacrifice for me as well. I don't think Cecile ever realized just how much the rest of the family had to sacrifice just so she and Walter could have their way.

CHAPTER 36

BACK TO WORK

I had no sooner moved out that Cecil and Henry both came to me at work and told me they thought I was making a mistake. I should try to get my equity out of at least the house. I told them I was giving up all my rights to everything as part of the deal—the house, the business, the property in Minnesota, and anything else.

After this, the terms of our agreement came up several more times. Dan Rutherford had found a judge who would consider our request. Our divorce was moving faster than Walter's and Cecile would be single before he was. It was as if she was getting nervous that he might change his mind about marrying her. She denied Cecil had put her up to it but she wanted me to agree to pay a token child support just in case something happened and she needed it. I told her she should have learned by now that my word was good. If she ended up needing help with the kids, I would either take them over or see to it that they got what they needed, and not to worry about them. If she had worries about her own future that was her problem as she already had everything I had worth taking. I would not change any of the terms and I expected her to stay with them. I also told her I felt that if I opened the door by having a token child support payment, it would only be a matter of time before she would ask for more.

I had always felt that if I agreed to start over with nothing, then anything I gave them in the way of child support was paying them twice and made it easier for them to spend money on themselves. I couldn't stand the idea of supplementing their standard of living after I had agreed to make it easy for them to live in the house on Zornia. It was for the kids' sake I had done it and it would be for the kids that I would give any extra and thus it would go directly to them. It was more than the house I gave up . . . it was my life up to that time, my savings, my coin collection . . . that had meant more to me than money. I had given up something that was given to me by my grandmother that contained coins from her father, my great-grandfather, and coins that had been presents from my parents. A lot of this was about principles and sacrifice; it wasn't just about money for me.

Again, the day we went to the courthouse, on the steps on the way in, Cecile asked me to pay a token child support. I told her no, as she already had all my reasons. I also assured her that if she started anything funny I would do as I had previously told her and her father. I had told all of them along the way when they wanted to change the rules, that if they continued down this road and forced me to, I would fight for custody of the kids. They said, "you won't win". I said, "I know". But when I got through with telling everything I knew and it was all over the papers, the lot of them would have a hard time walking around town. Nobody, not even Walt, would want to know her—or any of them. I knew this fear of exposure was worse than anything for them and they would then leave it alone.

They had told me it was not necessary for me to appear at the divorce hearing in person as Cecile was the person who had filed and I had already signed the papers. But I wanted to make sure nothing happened at the last minute. I wanted to make sure that if anything did happen, I would be there to protest if necessary. As it was, everything went smoothly until the judge asked Cecile if she was sure she was happy with the terms of the settlement. She hesitated and I believe that if I wasn't there she might have answered differently. She answered yes. He said very well then and proceeded to finalize the divorce. I don't remember the exact amount of time anymore but I think it is 60 days after this decree in court that the divorce actually becomes final. Both parties, from my understanding, have this time to file for an appeal if something is wrong. Also the court reviews it during this time and re-opens it if something is not right in law or procedure. With this in mind, I knew I still had some time to go.

It was a very strange day for me when I left the courthouse. I think for most people that get a divorce there are times that you can look back and remember the good times, the fun, and the happiness during the years. It is this that makes it hard. I had also told Elizabeth not to stick to what she had said about never allowing Walter over. It would be important for the kids to see their grandmother and have things as normal as possible. I told her that I understood. Besides I also knew that with time, blood would again prove to be thicker than water. I found it hard at first to put it behind me. It wasn't that I was going back, even if I could have. I was on my own and found it strange after so many years of being with someone. I was starting over and I had nothing to go by. It was a new day.

You don't realize how much you consult or consider how someone else might react to something you buy or even do, until you are on your own again. I realized how it no longer mattered and I no longer needed to ask. It only had to matter to me. I no longer had to let someone know if I was going to stop on the way home for a few minutes and have a beer.

It was funny in a way. The few times I really enjoyed having a beer with someone was when my Dad and I would have one across the street from the drugstore at the little neighborhood bar, Dos Diablos. It wasn't often but you wouldn't have known it from the reaction I would get. Now that I didn't have to ask, it was no longer an option for me. After I went to work at the dealership at the main store I found out that from time to time after work, some of the employees would go across to a little bar and have a drink with each other before they went home. It was usually a few of the salesman and M. E. Klein. Sometimes Cecil would show up. This was usually the case if a few of the office girls ended up coming along.

Cecil had been asking me why I wasn't dating anybody. I told him I didn't feel like it and he couldn't understand it. Sometimes I would go over with one of the other salesmen, Earl Floyd, and Klein. We would have a drink, and talk, and then go. Cecil showed up one time when a few of the office girls did. They would usually be out and on their way by 6:30. He started buying drinks for the small group of us that were at the table. The next thing I knew he had about three of them in front of me. I ended up drinking them and wished I hadn't. I watched as the others drank theirs. He was getting a real kick out of getting those in the group smashed. The light started to come on to me then. He wasn't doing it to be nice—he was doing it to exercise power over us. He wanted to show how he could get us drunk and then make fools out of us or do whatever else he wanted. From that time on, I only drank what I wanted and left the rest. I would tell him no more and he would continue to buy at first but after a few times of me walking out and leaving a row of drinks on the table, he stopped.

It took some adjusting for me and I found I didn't sleep real well at first. I would usually try and go to bed early, as I had nothing to do. The problem with this was I woke up early, sometimes 4 A.M., I would get up and go grocery shopping in the middle of the night or in the early morning at the 24-hour grocery store that was only a few blocks away. The only problem with this was if I wanted to buy some beer and it was between midnight and 10 AM they couldn't sell it. This was not a big problem but one that was pointed out to me at the checkout one time.

I had known a girl on a business basis when I had the drugstore. She had been a customer and had gone through a divorce several years before. She appeared to be somewhat down at first but got past it and got a job with a company putting displays in stores for carpet. It sounds funny but the samples were on the rack, and the people could contact them for a free measure and quote—which is what she did. If they made a purchase from the lead obtained in my store then I would get a commission for the job. She put a display in but I never got any commission from it and after about 6 months the company closed and they took the displays back, and she was out of a job.

I would see her from time to time when she would come in the store and sometimes we would visit for a few minutes. I decided to try and get in contact with her to see what she was doing. I managed to contact her and started visiting her from time to time. She told me after awhile that she enjoyed having me as a friend, as friends were hard to find. She felt I was always kind to her when she was a customer and going through a rough time. She then admitted she had a regular boy friend she was involved with but that he was a married man. She didn't plan it that way but that is how it worked out. She didn't want to talk about her relationship with him unless she brought it up–otherwise she didn't want the subject to come up. She wanted us to be friends and when we would go out to eat or do anything that cost money, she always wanted to pay her share, just like friends.

It was nice to have someone to talk to and visit with. I didn't care much for her idea at first but then after awhile I did see the advantage that neither of us had to worry about how far we were going to go with each other in the relationship. It helped keep things simple between us. Lynda Bergman and I became what I would consider very good friends. We would both talk to each other about our problems and most of the time ignored any advice the other one gave. It was a help to just get it off one's chest sometimes.

I dated or should say, went out with a few other girls here and there. Cecil and Sue had become almost a full time story by now and Sue even put me in contact with a couple of girls she knew. I wasn't really worried about it and was in fact enjoying my freedom. Sam had moved in with me and we were trying to figure out the ground rules. I would sometimes fix dinner and sometimes he would. Sometimes Elizabeth would want him to come over, and sometimes Cecil would call up and want to take him with him. Sometimes it was the ranch and at other times he wanted him to just stay over so I could go out because it was the weekend coming up and none of us liked the idea of him being home alone.

It wasn't too long after this—I don't remember exactly when—that Lynda called me and asked me if I would like to meet a cousin of hers who was divorced. She thought we might get along and have some fun. I agreed and as I remember she gave me her phone number and I called her. I went over to her apartment to pick her up and take her out to eat, and this was my first date with Sharon Ferguson.

I was getting along with most of the people at work with my one full-time exception, Henry. He hadn't changed over the years and if anything, was worse. He played the boss and had to have a couple of people around him he could use. At this time it was his cousin, Hebert, and a salesman, Mario Mendiola. He would also sometimes try and use Earl Floyd and Don Thompson. A few years before, Cecil had made a good move by picking up a GMC truck franchise to go with Pontiac. It seems the truck franchises were picked up by a lot of Pontiac franchises during the crunch time when they needed different product to sell.

There was a time when the price of pickup trucks—for the amount of equipment and being a new vehicle—was much cheaper than a car. The public saw this and purchased pickups for second vehicles. Another factor was the so-called heavy half. That is, if a pickup had a load rating of 6,200 pounds, then it was a heavy half and could run on regular fuel with no catalytic converter. It was hard to believe that about 10 years before, the factory had to force trucks on dealers. In order for dealers to get cars at both Chevrolet and Ford, they had to take a certain number of trucks. Today they were as well-equipped as a luxury car and you could get velour upholstery, electric windows, air conditioning, power steering, stereo systems; you name it and you could get it. The public was buying them at record levels.

It worked out that the 1978 model year was the last year for the heavy half and regular fuel. The pickup that ran on regular was so popular you could hardly keep any in stock. Henry even started buying them from small town dealers at prices above invoice just to get enough to meet the demand. The mistakes came out of the woodwork and they even sold. We got one truck in that was yellow with a green interior and another one that was green with a red interior. These were not your standard color combinations, regardless of Christmastime.

The new big boom was the converted van. Again 10 years before, a van was something you sold to tradesmen for work vehicles. Now they had special paint, large side viewing windows, sinks, fold-down beds, tables, built in refrigerators, TV, dual air-conditioning, and almost any other extra you could think of. Again they were hard to get. When we did get them, Henry would ship out several at a time to the conversion companies and have them converted into new special luxury coaches.

It was during this time he began dealing a lot with the GMC storage yard near the factory. Here they would store vehicles for various reasons until they were able to sell them to dealers. Some were normal vehicles but the dealers had gone over their floor plan limits and the vehicles couldn't be shipped to them. Some were orders that were cancelled but it was too late to stop production, some were factory mistakes, and some were extra production where they would build the vehicles and use them as a sweetener for those who took some of the problem ones off their hands.

Almost every week Henry would talk to the girl that had the inventory sheets at the yard, on the phone. He would try and make deals with her to get vehicles the dealership needed. It was during this time that Henry developed a relationship with this girl on the telephone. It was a relationship that almost got him into a lot of trouble but I doubt Edwynna would have ever divorced Henry because she always knew what side her bread was buttered on . . . and she always liked her butter.

CHAPTER 37

WHAT TO DO

I worked a lot with Klein every day. Some days we would go and straighten out the cars in the storage lot. Some days we would order cars. They did very few dealer trades at the dealership—something I was surprised to learn later, was very common among other dealers; even the very large ones.

It became increasingly more of my duty to order trucks and get with the salesmen to make sure their orders were correct. I became the so-called truck manager. I was gradually getting myself back in shape and was able to wait on customers to try and make a sale. I was even able to get to work on time when I was due in at 8 AM In previous times, it was always up to me to take the boys to school and drop them off at Eisenhower Junior High. By the time they were up and Cecile had their stuff ready for them, we were usually running late. When I would get in at 8:15 or so, Cecil would always complain. I found it ironic that he would complain to me about this, as I would then be at the dealership for the rest of the day. Other salesmen would check in at 8 o'clock but would check out at 8:10 and go to breakfast for the next half-hour and nothing was said as they were at work on time.

It did pay me one time for staying at work even though I didn't get there on time. A man got out of a taxi with a briefcase and a suitcase. He was unshaven and a bit untidy. He wanted to see the new hot sports car Pontiac had. I told him he must mean the Trans Am Firebird. I went outside on the lot and he picked one out in about 20 minutes. He wanted to know if he bought it, whether we could have it ready that afternoon. I assured him we could and so we went inside to make a deal. After about 10 minutes we had a good deal on paper and I told him I would need to get the manager to approve it. I also needed to know how he planned on paying for it. He said he would pay cash. I went to the office and found Klein to sign it, as it was way too early for Henry to be at work. I went back in the sales office and told the man we had a deal. He said good and opened his briefcase and started counting out the money. His briefcase was full of nothing but money. He had just returned from the mid-east after working there for the last several years. He had just flown in that morning. He wanted to buy a car, then go to his house to get cleaned up and take a nap. He would then return for his car that afternoon. Klein and I teased all the rest of the salesman that came back from their $200 breakfast that morning. That is what it cost them in commission by not being there for the sale that morning. It was the way to start the day and it made me feel good.

Another time, several months later, I was standing by my sales office door opening when a young man rode up on a motorcycle. The salesmen in the area all scattered like a covey of quail. They wanted no part of wasting their time on a young kid riding a motorcycle. What was he going to do? Trade it in? I decided not to adopt such a negative attitude and go over and find out what he wanted. Who knows, he may have only wanted to use the men's room? He was actually a nice young man. He liked riding motorcycles more than driving cars.

He wanted to look at a couple of vehicles and then decide what he wanted to do. After going back and forth between a couple of cars he decided he would buy one for his mother and one for himself. He purchased a Trans Am for himself and a Grand Prix for his mother. He planned on paying cash and was not trading in his pride and joy, his motorcycle. He owned a couple of Mexican food restaurants and was doing well. I know he was doing well enough to pay for two cars. I really enjoyed getting those two cars ready and watching the other salesmen's faces when my customers picked up their cars. Over the years, both then and later on, I can't tell you how many times salesman have been guilty of sight qualifying and then have it blow up on them. I actually got to the point as time went on, of wondering if the next most unlikely person wasn't going to be my next sale.

Not all of these kinds of encounters were happy. One time I waited on an older man, around his late 40's. He looked a bit untidy and unshaven. I waited on him and he was pleasant enough. He traded in a firebird for a Trans Am. It wasn't an easy deal and it got to the point that Henry was ready to turn the deal down over $50, after I had worked him for about an hour and a half. At the end of it, the man did come up with the extra and we made a deal. The car was on the showroom floor and the others watched as we went back and forth negotiating.

The deal was made and the car was moved outside in front of the showroom. We got drafting instructions from his banker and he drove off in his new car. Several hours later he called and wanted to know what was going on. He said there was a scrape down one side of his car and we must have done it, as he hadn't. He came down to the store so we could see what he was talking about. We assured him it wasn't like that when he left in it. This is when things turned nasty. He called his banker and wanted him to turn down the bank draft for the car. I could just see my commission going out the window and a damaged car coming back.

This is where the owners need to get involved and also know the ins and outs of what can and cannot be done. The fact of the matter was that when he drove off, it was his car. When the bank officer gave drafting instructions over the phone he made a verbal contract that was binding. So if he had a problem, the buyer first needed to realize that this is the way it was going to be and a solution would have to be found by some other means.

After a lot of talking and going back and forth, a friend of his that had been with him, admitted that the customer had a few drinks and he may have scraped it as he was getting in his driveway. He was very upset about having a "wrecked car" when it was only a few hours old. The good news was that the damage was minor and it could be fixed to where you wouldn't even know it. We made arrangements to get it in and out of the body shop in a couple of days. He came back, paid his bill, and left. I never heard from him again.

These were the bright spots in my days. The rest had a certain amount of aggravation that usually stemmed from Henry and his grab-ass games. As time had gone on, Henry was talked into getting this girl from the GMC yard to come down to San Antonio for the weekend. She was to fly in on Saturday morning and go back on Sunday evening. She was to stay at a motel and Henry was to make arrangements to take her out to eat and spend some time with her at the motel.

By Saturday morning he was a nervous wreck. He was having more than second thoughts about what he had gotten himself into. Mario and a couple of the others had helped push him along but he was also showing off on the phone and playing to an audience half the time when he was talking to her. He finally got Hebert and Mario to pick her up at the airport and take her to the motel. They were to say he was real busy but would see her later. When later came, he just couldn't do it. He finally gave Mario some money and told him and Hebert to take her out dancing, out to eat, whatever she wanted to do and make some excuse for him. This did nothing for their relationship.

There was one girl along the way that was crazy for Henry. She was so crazy, he couldn't get rid of her. I don't know the entire story but I do know it got so bad she even started calling Edwynna and told her she was going to take Henry away from her. Edwynna let Henry know in no uncertain terms that if he didn't get this straightened out; he was going to have the most expensive divorce he could dream of. Again I don't think she blamed Henry. Anybody that was that nutty, you couldn't believe what they said. Besides, if you had to be that nutty to like Henry, where did that leave her?

One thing for sure. Henry never was the man Cecil was in that respect. Cecil devoted his life to that cause, as I was to find out as time went on. I was still a bit unaware on how things really were. The more I was around the dealership and all the goings-on, the broader my education became.

Some of the other used car dealers and wholesalers I got to know at this time were laws unto themselves. As time went on, Cecil had me start looking at the used vehicles to see if I could learn how to appraise them. I was fortunate that it came to me quite quickly and it was almost a knack for me. I think the first time he started to take notice of this was when they had me looking at a used pickup truck that was being traded in. I looked at it and noticed not only the condition and what needed to be spent on it but also the fact that it was a model that had that little extra the buying public really went for. I told him and a Mr. Dove what I thought about the truck and put a figure on it I thought it was worth. It was then that Cecil at first looked at me like I was way off the mark. Then Mr. Dove spoke up and said to him "that boy knows his stuff, he can appraise vehicles". From then on I started appraising trade-ins. We shopped some of them to other dealers but mainly we stayed with what we traded for.

One of these wholesalers that came in from time to time was named Bud. That's right, Bud Treadwell from days gone by. The wholesalers would buy cars from dealers and sell to another dealer. They would find vehicles somebody was looking for and try to get it for them. They told me that Bud was taking a lot of pills and one day when he was driving down the street, he saw a car that was of a type he was looking for. He pulled up to it at a red light and jumped out of the car. He ran around the car and patted his hands on the fenders and hood as he ran around it and yelled "I've got to have it; I've got to have it!" He then pulled a roll of money out of his pocket and started to talk to the guy. It was his brother driving the car; he had already bought it.

It was unfortunate but later I heard Bud had gotten so bad that he started thinking all sorts of things and getting paranoid. He came after his brother with a gun and was acting crazy. It ended up that his brother had to shoot him and kill him.

Another wholesaler, Booger, came in one day to the main showroom and walked over to a special edition Trans Am. These were hard to get and usually sold for full window sticker price. He wanted to know what he could buy the car for. Henry told him he didn't want to insult him by pricing it to him as it would be too high. He insisted again. Again he told him he really didn't want to cause any hard feelings and refused to price it to him again. Booger was a real character and would put his money where his mouth was. He said, "I tell you what I'm going to do. I'm going to put a $100 bill on the hood of this car for you to price it to me one time. If it's too high, I'll walk out and you keep the $100. If not, the car is mine". Henry said okay. Booger put the money on the hood. Henry gave him a price. Booger said "You're right, it's too high". He then turned around and walked out, leaving the money behind.

Some of the characters were the salesman that had been around for some time. One was a Mr. Charlie Clark. He had worked out in California on some of the real fast yards. I think he was also a frustrated actor. Unfortunately his downfall was he loved to drink, and it was hard to keep him sober and coming to work. He was about mid-50's and had long grey hair, with some black in it. He always wore a suit and tie. One day when he was on a roll and had sold several cars already, he said for us to watch him. He wanted to show off.

He had waited on a young couple and started to sell them a car. After they had been negotiating for a period of time, the couple wouldn't budge on their offer and they started to get up and walk out. As they started to cross the showroom he ran after them and after talking for a moment, he fell to his knees and started begging them and telling how his kids had nothing to eat in the house. Then he started having tears roll down his cheeks as he started to cry. The couple decided to buy the car. They said the extra was worth it just for the performance they got to see.

They told me how in the days gone by the offices use to be bugged—before it was against the law. At one time it was in a phony telephone on the desk, another time it was behind a wall tapestry picture on the wall. They were wired to a station in the meeting room. They would tell the customer to talk it over, and then go and listen in at the other end. Sometimes they learned what it would take to make a deal; sometimes they would learn they were just too far apart. At least then they knew what needed to be done for better or worse.

I actually started to enjoy work and liked the car business. If one did a good job in sales he would make good money. It was funny, Henry would run sales contest from time to time with extra money up for grabs. One time he changed the pay scale from the 25% of the profit up to 50% with a sliding scale if you sold over 50 cars during this period. It also had bonuses. The top salesman worked really hard and sold 63 cars in 30 days. Henry actually threw the man's paycheck at him and said that would be the last time he ever did that. He resented paying the man as much as he did. Henry hadn't done his homework and gave too much away so he took it out on him. Bill Van was upset. He told me that if he hadn't been with the company so long he would have quit. He told me Henry should have thought about how much he made the company if that was his share and he should have wished for a dozen more just like him. You know, Bill Van was right too.

CHAPTER 38

GETTING ON WITH IT

It was becoming obvious to me that my chance of getting some other job at that time was slim. I enjoyed the car business and even admitted it to myself. With Sam living with me I needed to have a stable job with a steady income. I still had the problem of Henry. I knew that it was only a matter of time before I would have to leave. I didn't think, no matter how hard I tried, I would be able to get used to how he treated me. It was now more than his games. He would now do insults as well, in front of others, and try and show how he was the boss. More than once I would have walked out if I had had a place to go. One of the things that helped was on more than one occasion after such an episode, some of the other employees would come over and tell me not to worry about, it was just Henry and to ignore it.

I had started seeing Sharon on a regular basis and we were spending a lot of time with each other. She was divorced with two kids, Bryan and Tammy. Her ex-husband worked for IBM as a repairman and lived in Corpus Christi but his parents lived in San Antonio. In fact I later found out it was near to where Cecil bought a house after he and Elizabeth broke up.

Sharon was a schoolteacher and taught elementary students in bilingual programs. She was fluent in Spanish and had always been the one to look out for the down and out. Her old beat up car had been in an accident and was junk on four wheels. Her father was a Methodist minister who had retired from the army and lived in Comfort, Texas, just a few miles north of Boerne. He came down to the car yard with Sharon one day and helped her buy a new car from me.

Cecil had seen her on several occasions and we had even gone to a few places together. I was unsure about a lot of things in our relationship and was in no hurry to make any decisions about how far I wanted to go with it. Sam tried to get along with the two younger kids but they got on his nerves at times. They got on mine as well. Sharon tried to be nice to Sam at first and we all got along, although it took some effort on all of our parts.

I would try to get Craig, Scott, and Laurie every other weekend. Right at first, it was almost as if it was a game. I told Cecile one time at the beginning, I was going to take them out to eat and just spend some time with them as she wanted to know what my plans were with them. I went and picked them up and it looked like the clothes she had them put on were the oldest and most worn out they owned. They had holes in them and didn't fit properly. I ended up taking them to a place and buying them a change of clothes. Later I relayed a message to them and then again on the phone, told her not to play games. If that was the best they could do on taking care of the kids and couldn't afford clothes for them, then I would take the kids over and get them the clothes they needed. She didn't pull that again but it was only the start of a continual battle that would last for years to come.

I would phone each week to talk to them and see how they were and what was going on. More often than not she would tell me they were asleep even though it was early, or they were not at home and she would tell them I had called. I would mail them a greeting card for things like Valentine's Day, Easter, and of course birthdays, as well as some of the other holidays, for years. To this day I don't know if they ever got them or the message that I had called.

On a number of occasions I would call about my turn being the weekend coming up, to make arrangements about getting the kids and I would be told they had a church camp that weekend or they had plans to do something with the kids. It might be going skiing or something that they did not usually get to do. I would tell her then that I was quite happy to let them go and get them the following weekend. About half the time, especially at first, the next week would come and she would again have plans or just say it was their weekend and that was it. We were to alternate holidays, which meant I would get them one

Christmas and she the next and so on. This also did not seem to work as they usually had some sort of plans. I did get them on some of the holidays but it was by no means every other time.

The kids could see how silly she was acting for themselves at times. One time when I took them to the Kendall County Fair with Sam, we saw a little cactus pot plant. We all got a laugh when we saw it and it expressed our feelings and frustration on how she was trying to make things difficult for us. At first we decided not to buy it as a gift for her but as the day went on, we decided to get it for her. It might make her laugh and get a message across at the same time on how we felt about her antics. The pot plant gift was a statue of an old cowboy with whiskers and looking a bit rough standing up, with his hands holding his pants out in front of him at waist level. This made for a large round opening for the dirt and the plant to fit in as if it were down in the front of his pants. Out of this stuck up a single cactus in the shape of a cucumber with a little flower on the end of it. When the kids took it in the house and gave it to Cecile they were to tell her this was for her from Dad.

It was evident she and Walt had no sense of humor or appreciation for the carefully selected gift. They started all this stuff about how I would never be able to see the kids again if I act this way and do this sort of thing with and in front of them . . . and on and on and on and on. I then had an opportunity to talk to Walter. I told him if it made him feel better I would apologize, providing they quit playing all their silly games. The agreement was to share the kids and not cause problems with or for them and all they were doing was making things difficult. I then pointed out to him that I really no longer gave a damn what they did and I would have thought they would have liked to have some time together on their own. I also thought he would like a break from taking care of somebody else's kids. He actually would listen and try to make some sort of sense out of things. It was Cecile that was getting all high and mighty. After this, things did improve and we had fewer problems with the arrangement. Although they did still get the kids more as they could take the kids on more special things to do and outings. I didn't see why the kids should be penalized and not allowed to go skiing or something just because it was my weekend.

Cecile had told me once before the divorce came through and they were married (which was about 30 days after it was final), that Walter was concerned that I might try and pull a knife on him or something. I told her I didn't know where he got such an idea. First, I had never been a person to use a knife. Next I had no intention of going after him. If I had, it would be more likely I would shoot him from a distance and he would never know it was coming. Lastly, I had already been contacted by Joe King back when he heard about what had happened and he wanted to know if I would like for him to send some of his friends by to have a firm conversation with Walter and perhaps help change his mind about this whole affair. He felt like he owed me a favor and if there was anything he could do for me, to just let him know. I told him, and both Cecil and Elizabeth later on, that I had no intention of making trouble or causing problems for them. If, after all was said and done, she still didn't want to stay with me, then it made no sense to try and force her into something she didn't want. It wouldn't work. It was like I told her when I left, when I admitted it was over, it was over for me.

I guess that is why to this day I have never been able to understand why Cecile always tried to cause problems with me and the kids, or just even give me a hard time. Later, I don't remember just how, it came up about me getting the china that was mine from my grandmother and mother. She then refused to give it back and insisted on keeping it. She said she was afraid I would give it to someone else and she was keeping it safe for Laurie as it should be hers. This actually turned into a big rift for awhile with all the kids volunteering to get the china out of the house so I could pick it up. I told them it would only cause more problems. I was happy for Laurie to have it. I was worried they might break it as I learned they used it on a number of occasions when they had people over. I doubt to this day she knows it shouldn't go in the dishwasher. I am sorry that when Laurie looks at it, it won't bring back happier memories. For me, I miss seeing it and having it remind me of the years I spent living with my grandparents—a very special time for me and something she tried to destroy by taking the china. But it is something in my memory that she can never destroy.

Both Sam and Craig went to school with two of Walter's boys who were about their age. From them, they learned a lot of what had gone on. Partly because of this, it was not possible to keep it from them about what had actually gone on between Cecile and Walter. Cecile had said she didn't want to tell the two younger ones until they were older. From what I can tell over the years, she continually lied about it whenever it came up and only made it worse. I used to wonder if this was possibly the reason why she tried to take things out on me. I quit wondering after awhile. I could no longer see any point. Who cares why? I only wanted her to not give me a hard time.

Sam started to settle down and devote more of his time to homework and school. We started to get along most of the time and did some things together. One day when I was driving down a street back toward the neighborhood where my parents had lived, I saw a white '67 GTO in the front yard of a house with a sign in the window saying 'for sale $500'. I stopped and looked at it and drove it around the block. It had only 57,000 miles on it and the interior looked new except for the driver side. It had need of some body work and you could see where it had been worked on before. I decided I wanted to buy it and fix it up. It could be a car for Sam and I to have some fun with.

The next day I went to the bank and drew out the money and had a friend from work drive me over to pick it up. I paid the man and took the papers and the car. He had purchased it new from Tindall Pontiac and was the original owner. He drove it to work and back 5 days a week, which was in downtown San Antonio. He rarely drove it much more than that. As I was to soon learn, he didn't believe in changing the oil very often, as he didn't drive it a lot. I drove it to work the next day and started to see about some basic work. Wilroy Ristow was now service manager as the other man had quit. He wanted more money for the job and Cecil refused, so he left. It was interesting after he left as they found a whole stack of warranty claims worth thousands of dollars in his bottom desk drawer. The customers were happy, the work was done, the dealership didn't know they weren't paid for the work and rejected by the factory as they had never been sent in. It did keep his work and factory ratios up.

Wilroy gave me some tips and I had them look it over, mainly the front-end suspension and steering gear. A few of these items just needed adjustment. One strange thing it did was after it was warmed up and you went to start it, it would hardly turn over until it cooled down. Wilroy thought it might be the starter motor getting 'heat soak' as they had some trouble with that at times. I drove the car another couple of days and that weekend Sam and I went for a little run up the road that went out of town from where we lived. We decided to see how well it accelerated from a dead stop and a couple of times in a row we accelerated from 0 to about 90 very quickly. Then all of a sudden the motor just stopped. I coasted to a stop and turned the key. Nothing. You could smell sort of a hot oil-type smell.

We ended up walking a few miles back to the apartment and calling a tow truck. I had it towed to the dealership. On Monday I found the motor appeared to be frozen but with great force it could be turned over with a bar through the pulley. It appeared to need major motor work. I couldn't afford the price they would charge for a motor overhaul so I started asking around. Don Thompson told me of a friend of his that, as a hobby, worked on hot rod motors and was a highway patrolman by day. In fact Don had been a highway patrolman and at one time Henry was also going to quit the auto business and join. Cecil put a stop to that. The $1,000 a month pay wouldn't go very far with Henry.

I ended up getting with his friend and had the GTO towed to a storage shed he had. Sam and I went out to his place on several nights as he took the motor out and eventually to pieces. I paid him a flat fee of about $400 for the labor and paid for all the machine shop work and parts separately. This took several months from start to finish as he only worked on it part-time at night. To our surprise we found the oil in the bottom of the motor was like tar. He must have only changed the oil every couple of years and the rest of the time just added to it. The oil pump was unable to draw enough oil to the main crankshaft bearings and as they heated up they became tight and would try and stop it from turning. That is what had happened when it locked up. It spun the bearings out of the holder on the crankshaft side and scored the crankshaft. The bearings were burnt and as flat as a piece of paper. They looked like an old beer can that had been run over and left outside for a year.

The good news was the engine block was not hurt. I purchased a rebuilt crankshaft and new bearings. We checked other items and found the wear was almost nil. We sent the block and heads to a shop where they boiled them out clean and redid the heads. I decided to buy various other new parts and a heavy-duty oil pump as well as the optional full race cam that was offered by Pontiac. I got most of the parts through work with my employee discount. All up, the bill for parts and machine shop was about $600. When it was finally back together, it ran better than new. I found out it had the 400 cubic inch motor and when we put it back together he showed me how to 'crush' the bearings going in. That way even though the motor was new, you could turn the motor over with your hands when the heads were still off. It reduced the friction that much.

Sam and I would take the car out for a short drive a few times and we were both impressed. I told him I would then make arrangements to get the needed bodywork and interior work done. The interior only needed an armrest covered and a seam redone in the driver's seat. The body would need more. Plus it would need some moldings replaced and the front bumper was damaged. With this in mind, I went to see the body shop manager I had worked with. I talked to him and with his permission talked to one of the body men named George who worked some on his own. He gave me a price to do the bodywork, and it was up to me to get the moldings and a bumper. To my surprise again, I found an exchange bumper for

$65.00. Most of the moldings I was still able to get through parts; the exception being a couple around the grill area in the front.

The paint man, Arturo, agreed to paint it for me after the bodywork was done—providing I would wait until he was not busy and then he would give me a special price. As I was in no hurry this was fine with me. Besides I needed to find the missing moldings and my best bet was to phone around to junk yards. I was able to locate the moldings and even an original GTO clock for the dash after about a week of calling around. Sam and I went to the junkyard and got the moldings and the clock.

I didn't know it then but it would be about 4 months before I would drive it again. Everything went well at first. The bodywork was done after it sat for about 2 weeks. Then he needed to redo one spot as the paint man said it wasn't good enough. This took another week. Then it sat and it sat. The paint man was in no hurry.

Then Cecil heard the car was over in the body shop and wanted to know what was going on. Was it going through the 'books' as he didn't want any cash jobs? I told him it was now waiting for paint. The guys were just trying to help me out and it would sit until they had nothing to do. It wasn't like a cash job that was costing him and yes, it did have a ticket on it. He was still a little touchy. It seems that Edwynna's sister, Pam Ferris, had wrecked her car and it had been in the body shop but she didn't have any money. She had been working but not lately, as her job was mainly as a 'lady of the night'. She had tried to make a deal with the guys in the body shop and when the manager found out what she was doing, he sent her to Henry. They were all upset about her wanting to trade some body work for bodywork.

I did finally get my car back and I must admit that when it was finished it was like new. You couldn't see where they had done the bodywork and the paintwork was as good as, or better than, that of the factory. The only thing left was for me and Sam to give it a good clean up on the inside and do something about the inside of the trunk to make it look like new, which we did in time with 'trunk paint'. I had planned on teaching Sam to drive in the car and eventually maybe even let him have it. I knew after we got it back this was unlikely. I loved him too much to let him have it. The car had about 400-horse power, going by the ratings, and was absolute power and speed. The only problem was the brakes in those days were all drum brakes. After you stopped from 60 to 0, you couldn't do it again right away. When they got hot, and that was very easily done, they faded away to nothing. You had no brakes!

CHAPTER 39

ANOTHER DEALERSHIP

Sam had done very well that year in school. He made straight A's in all his subjects every six weeks. At the end of the school year he was nominated to join the National Honors Society. I asked him why he had done so well. He told me he wanted to try and see if he could do it. Now that he knew he could that was enough for him. He didn't want to spend and devote that much time to his studies again as he felt he was missing out on too much. I told him as long as he kept his grades up and did well, I didn't mind if he didn't make straight A's all the time.

He had gone out for some sports and wanted to play football but the coach had a bad attitude and first of all, felt Sam was too small. The sports had become a major force at this school level and from here through high school it only got worse. The idea of sportsmanship and everyone getting a chance just didn't happen. It was win, win, win. That was all that counted. The coaches were at the point of being past the mark with the way they would yell and treat the kids. Sam did have a run-in with one of these guys but after a couple of phone calls, including one from Cecil and some of his contacts, it was all straightened out. I have always felt that all the high schools have allowed sports and winning to get way out of proportion, and if they teach anything now it is negative in how to act and behave. Who cares if the year before or 5 years ago, they lost a game; we no longer remember now. But we live with the attitude and the behavior of these men around us every day for the rest of our lives.

I was sitting on a chair on the showroom floor watching for a customer to come in when Cecil came over and told me he wanted to talk to me. He said let's check out and go up the street to get some coffee. I had no idea of what he wanted. The day before Henry had put me down again in front of some of the others but that was nothing new and I hadn't said anymore about it to anyone. When we got to the coffee shop we sat to the side away from most of the rest of the people. It was very rare for me to go to coffee with him and I had no idea of what he was up to. He then told me that he was looking at a deal but before he went any further he wanted to know how I felt and if I was interested in staying on and working for him. He was looking at buying another dealership up in Boerne that needed a lot of work. If he got it, he would need someone to put in it that could run it and get it going. It would require a lot of work and eventually new facilities would be built and the dealership would move into them.

He then told me he wouldn't be able to pay me much until it was up and going and making money but I would be building an asset for my kids in the future. Henry was going to get the dealership in San Antonio that they were in together. If he went forward with this deal, Henry would own no part of this one and it would be for my kids if they wanted it in the future. I would also need to get an insurance license and help with a number of details if he went forward and the deal went through.

I thought to myself that he must know I am not overly happy working with Henry or he wouldn't have said what he did. I told myself this was an opportunity. I had no idea how it might work out in the long run but if I could do something like this and possibly build up a business the kids could come in to as their own in the future, it had to be worth a try. I knew a good dealership made a lot of money although he was very careful to never let me see the books. I knew how he and Henry both spent money and the company still made money and paid all its bills. I told him I was interested and yes, that if he did get the deal I would do whatever it took. He then told me to not say a word to anyone until it was final. He didn't say how long it would be until he knew; I don't think he knew. I did get the feeling we were only talking weeks until we knew.

The next couple of weeks seem to take forever to go by. Every day I would wonder if anything would come out of it. 'What if . . . ?' went through my mind a thousand times. The one thing I did know was that I wanted out and away from Henry. I wasn't sure if Henry knew anything about it—he never said a word or mentioned it to me. Cecil said very little to me and as I watched him come and go, I never knew if he was going on business about this or just out to meet someone in the afternoon.

J.M. Tindall, Cecil's brother, was still friendly towards me but spent less time around the dealership. He had been a customer of mine in the drugstore days. He had contracted some sort of disease in one of his eyes and in the matter of about 2 weeks he lost one of his eyes. When I had first gone back to work at the dealership he was still very active in card games, horses, and various other affairs. One day as I was leaving to go home he asked me to come in his office for a minute. He had been a card dealer professionally at one time in his life and would play cards or deal for a game from time to time. He was to go to a game that night but had bad feelings about it and was afraid he was being set up. He reached in his pocket and took out a large roll of money. He separated off about $3,000 and gave it to me. He said for me to hold on to it until the next day for him. If he was set up, he didn't want to lose all he had on him.

I had always gotten on well with J.M. and he used to always ask me how his favorite niece, Cecile, was. He always paid his bill at the store without problems, and would pay the one for his wife and daughter. I got the impression he didn't live at home half the time. I found out that part of the problem at this time with all the coming and goings, had to do with J.M. being in trouble. He had wanted to go in on the bookmaking and started to but at the last minute backed out when he heard the cops were watching. It seems some of this had caused some hard feelings. On top of this, he and Mr. Dove (who had a wrecker yard as well as a used vehicle business), also ran some horses together. During their various business deals along the way, they had taken in trade a farm tractor which they sold on to another person. It turned out the farm tractor was stolen and the police were in the process of deciding who they were going to charge with theft. The story was a long convoluted one about how they got it in a game or something, and went on from there. The cops were going around and around as if they were playing pin the tail on the donkey. The only problem was they wanted to make J.M. and Mr. Dove, the donkeys.

I never did hear for certain on how this came out. I do know that they never served any time in jail. If they got off, or made a deal, or paid a fine and pleaded guilty to a lesser charge, I don't know. I knew Cecil's other brother, Finley, as well and I went and saw him in the hospital in Austin when I later lived there. He died of cancer. Cecil's brothers were all as different as they could be. J.M. was the one I had more dealings with by far. He was quite a character and yet very loyal to those around him.

The day did finally come and Cecil came to see me. He had made a deal. He wanted me to get with the representative from M.I.C. Insurance, a division of General Motors, and get started on my insurance license. They told me of a crash course school that had classes 5 days a week. I would go all day, study at night, and then about a week later I could take the State Board. If I passed I would have my agency license and be an agent for automobile, life, health and accident insurance with M.I.C. being the primary company I would represent. This would allow the dealership in Boerne, once we took it over, to sell insurance of various types—including accident and health—on the finance contracts.

Bob Chapman was Cecil's finance man at the dealership, as well as handling his personal books on the side. He was to teach me how to sell this type of insurance to customers. He was very good at it. He and Cecil had a deal where he would be paid a base salary plus a little extra for the personal work. He would also get a small percentage of the A&H insurance that he sold. Bob did so well that Cecil got to the point he didn't like paying him so much and actually got him to lower his percentage of the take. This would eventually get up to a respectable level again and cause a rift which would eventually see Bob Chapman leave and go to another dealership. I guess it was with this in mind, Cecil told me the A&H and automobile insurance was all his and the dealership's. I could have whatever I made on the mechanical breakdown insurance. This would later amount to about $2,000 a year for me, whereas the A&H in San Antonio would be about $10,000 a month.

That is why he wanted it for himself. You had to be careful on how this was paid because according to the insurance laws, only an agent could take a commission. He was not an agent and usually the dealership took it as rent or some other form of a roundabout way. Some of the dealers actually got their licenses just to avoid any problems. I went through the course and took the exam, passing it the first time I took it. This was not always done; in fact a number of people took it 2 or 3 times before they passed.

While I was doing this, a problem had come up with the deal Cecil had made. It seems he had been taking to Mr. Eperson in Boerne on a more-or-less one-on-one basis and when he was near a deal, had his wife and a friend of theirs witness the agreement. Some had said Mr. Eperson was not mentally competent. He would have temper tantrums and appeared to have some lapses of memory. With this a consideration, Cecil had some witnesses. He had done almost the whole deal on the QT. The factory wanted Eperson out as he hadn't done anything with the franchises—Chevrolet and Oldsmobile—for years. He had almost no facilities and sold only a few cars each month. The best I could tell, Cecil had let Eperson go first on setting a price and it was around $250,000.

Cecil went back with a simple contract and a cashier's check made out to him for $100,000. Eperson was to get $100,000 up front and a salary of $30,000 a year for 5 years, even if he didn't show up for work. Someone told Eperson this was not a good deal and he wanted to back out. Eperson had no facilities and on the day Cecil was to take over, the parts would be inventoried and paid for at book value. Several wholesalers were to make offers on his handful of used cars and he could take the offers, or leave them and sell the cars himself. The new cars would be switched over to us. Now none of this was acceptable to Eperson. Tom Benson of Tom Benson Chevrolet had made some offers in the past and was now back after him. He told Eperson he would have paid him a lot more and would have given him $500,000 up front. I don't know if he was just trying to stir him up. The opinion was Cecil had "stolen" the franchises at $250,000.

Cecil set up a meeting at Eperson's lawyer's office in Boerne. He explained to Eperson that he had made his deal, signed it, taken the cashier's check and even had his wife and a friend of theirs witness it. If they had felt it was a bad deal and he shouldn't do it or if they felt he didn't know what he was doing, then they should have stopped him. They didn't. If he didn't proceed with the deal as agreed, Cecil said he would sue him for the franchises plus expenses and damages. He then asked Eperson's lawyer to tell them what chance he had on winning.

Eperson's lawyer explained that under the circumstance, Cecil had a very high probability he would win. If they tried to back out now it would only prolong things and cost them a lot of money. At the end of it, they would end up with most likely nothing. The Epersons were angry but after talking it over agreed to go forward with the deal as it was.

It seems Cecil had heard before, how Eperson would make a deal and then change his mind for various reasons. In the past no one had ever got him to sign anything and take any money. This was one of the reasons he tried to have a simple contract and a cashier's check to wave under his nose. He couldn't see him turning down $100,000 when it was in front of him for the taking.

This set the tone and the atmosphere for Eperson and I to work together. Eperson's son had worked on and off at the dealership in various departments. I was to learn his son was a dope addict and spent half his time out selling dope. He and his friends were bad news. They weren't supposed to be at or around the dealership when we took over but I could see this being a problem for us in the future.

Eperson had a part-time bookkeeper, one mechanic, and a body and paint man, with his son being his helper. This was the staff. All together, he had about 20 new vehicles all up, and none of his used cars were worth keeping. The rented space was next to an auto parts (which is where they got most of theirs from), and the showroom was large enough for, at the most, 2 cars. It had one toilet facility and two offices. We had no heating and no air-conditioning. This was going to be a challenge.

We were supposed to take over toward the end of summer, around August as I remember. I had a lot of preparing to do and arrangements to make.

I told Sam what was going on once I knew the deal was going forward. I told him we could stay in the apartment where we lived and he could continue to go to school where he was. If he wanted we could move to Boerne and live closer to where I would work and he could go to school up there. He didn't think about it very long before he told me he wanted to move and go to school up there. I was a little surprised at first. Then I realized how he hadn't been very happy where he was and it was going to be a new start for him. We were both going to start anew.

CHAPTER 40

WE MOVE TO BOERNE

Over the past several years Cecil had developed a friendship with A. J. Foyt. Sam and I had even gone to Bryan, Texas, to see some of his races at the racetrack there. Cecil had been invited by him to attend the Indianapolis 500 auto race and had gone for several years in a row. He was given a pit pass and on one occasion was photographed as a member of his crew along with the others.

Sam and Sam Jr at races in Bryan, Texas

Foyt's mother had become ill with cancer and A.J. wanted to buy her something to make her more comfortable when they went on trips. He called Cecil and made a deal for one of the Executive Motor Homes we had in stock. This was one of the top of the line models with everything on it. He wanted to surprise his folks so he wanted it delivered to his race car garage in Houston. Cecil didn't want to take any chances and wanted someone to show them where everything was. I was the one who was nominated. I drove it over and delivered it to him at the garage. I met his Dad and showed him a few of the items he had questions on. After that Mr. Foyt Sr. drove me to the airport and dropped me off. I purchased a ticket for the next flight back to San Antonio and flew back that same afternoon.

A.J. and Cecil had become such good friends that he transported his racecar in which he had won the Indianapolis 500 and allowed him to display it on the showroom floor for a promotion. The dealership ran radio and TV ads and had a lot of people come in to see the car. I don't know that we sold any more cars because of it but we got a lot of people to come and find out where we were.

That same summer I had made another trip to Houston with the kids, and Sharon and her kids. We took them to Astroworld and they spent the day on rides.

We spent more time with the kids and they played with each other when I would get them on the weekends. Before we headed back to San Antonio I drove down to hospital in Hitchcock which was about 40 or 50 miles away. My grandmother, Nana, had become very ill and had been admitted to hospital. I went in and visited with her for a short time as she was not doing very well and was weak. It was not long after this that she died—on the 4th of July, 1979. I made arrangements to drive down for the funeral and drove back to San Antonio the next day. I stayed the night with Aunt Jeannie and Uncle Lloyd.

During the summer I saw more of Sharon and her kids. The next thing I knew everyone was asking me why I didn't marry her. Even Cecil told me he thought it was a good idea if we got married. It would be good for Sam, he said. Everyone wanted me to marry her but me. I didn't feel I was ready. For one thing, I wasn't in love with her but I had decided that maybe it was just me. Maybe it was me having cold feet and it would be good for Sam. I had already decided that being in love with someone was not necessary for marriage or for living with them. I finally decided maybe I should give in, and Sharon and I talked about getting married. She didn't hesitate and told me her father could marry us at his place up in Comfort, as he was a minister.

In August 1980, her father at the little church in Comfort married us. After the ceremony we went to her parents' house and they had a little reception for us with her family. I met her sister who lived in Houston and was married to an environmental petroleum engineer. I asked what that was. He was the one they called if they had an oil spill or other such problems. Her parents were nice and they seemed to try really hard to make it a nice day.

With this entire event happening over a period of weeks, a number of issues came up. Sharon's lease was coming up for renewal on her place and it made no sense to renew it. So they moved in with Sam and I, and we put most of their belongings into storage. She now needed to decide if she was going to teach again that fall in San Antonio and commute back and forth, or find another job. We also needed to find another place to live and it was already decided to move to Boerne.

We decided to look at some new houses being built in Boerne on a back street, as we had heard they were not very expensive. A little three bedroom house was about $65,000 and had very little but it was still almost more than we could afford. I wasn't even sure I would be able to get it with my past history of financial problems over the last couple of years. We decided though, to give it a try. With the special finance package they offered I would have just enough for the down payment.

Sometimes when the kids came up to stay we would go down to the creek near the house and play. Laurie and Scott would get so wet sometimes we would have to go back to the house and put their clothes in the dryer in order to have them dry in time to go home.

Laurie and Scott—wet after playing in the creek

I found out Cecil wanted me in Boerne and wanted me to be part of the community. He told me it would be good for me to have a high profile in the community, as it would do the dealership a lot of good. He had already made some friends in the community and when Sharon and I decided to get married and move to Boerne, he was all for it. He made some inquires about a teaching position and they told her to apply as they needed someone in the bilingual program. She got the job. This was good for us. She would be working in Boerne as well. The pay was higher in Boerne and she decided to take the pay on a 12-month payout, as she wasn't any good on budgeting but if she knew how much to expect each month she could manage.

The apartment complex I was in had agreed to rent the apartment to us on a month by month basis if it was going to be for only a few months. We held our breath and waited to hear from the mortgage company, Lomas and Nettleton. To our relief the application came back approved. The house was scheduled to be ready around the end of summer, by the start of school. The house was ready on time and we moved out of the small apartment into the new house.

I had started work at the store in Boerne and continued to drive the Pontiac Grand Prix demo as it was too late in the model year to put another vehicle in service. I almost wasn't sure where to start with the store. It had no systems, no organization, and no structure. Alvin Brandt, and soon another mechanic Max Voigt, would show up at work and do their job. Alvin would schedule work in, do his own ticket and charge it out. He would collect the money from the customer or say they were okay and let them charge the work. The body man and his son worked on a couple of vehicles that they said they had scheduled in for work. If I needed a vehicle cleaned up I would either do it myself, or try to schedule the body man and or his son to do it. They didn't like it at all. As time went on, I found out they really only liked doing what they wanted when they wanted.

I was it up front and it was up to me to do paper work, wait on customers, and try and clean up the place. All the factory bulletins were all over the counters and floors. Just stuck any place they fell. That was about the best way to describe the place. Over from next door was a little building all on its own. It had been a barbershop and was now part-storeroom and part-office storage.

The factory bulletins and campaigns, as they were known, were important, as were product recalls. The list was of vehicles believed to be in your area. It was the responsibility of the dealership to try and get the vehicle in to get it modified. Some of the modifications seemed minor but some were major and could be life-threatening. If an accident resulted from it and you could show no proof a good effort had been made to contact the owner, then you could be up for a lawsuit. The factory paid for the modifications and for us it was an easy source of income for the dealership.

I told Cecil I couldn't do everything and we needed to hire some help if we were going to get anything done. He didn't want to increase his payroll. He finally said it was okay to try and find a part-time girl that could do book work. I started to ask around and I was told to contact a lady named Patsy who was from a long-time Boerne family. She had done bookwork before, at the Ford store. I interviewed her for a job and we got along well. She knew basically what we needed, and Cecil had his accountants lay out some of the basics and we were off. General Motors had their way of doing things and the books were all standardized. She was a wealth of knowledge and knew everyone in town. With her you found out who had money and who didn't, who to let charge and who not to.

With all the paper shuffling going on, Cecil and I had to go to Houston and go to the Zone Office for Chevrolet and Oldsmobile. It was to sign the official transfer and approval of the franchise over to him. He had come up with all kinds of ideas for names like Foremost Chevrolet & Oldsmobile. At the end he was told to keep it simple and just call it Cecil Tindall Chevrolet and Oldsmobile, and that is what it was. Chevrolet was our managing division–meaning they were the ones we had to work through for approval of anything that the factory had a say on, and Oldsmobile would follow. We went to both divisions to do our duty calls and went back the same day.

I was told then; it would be Chevrolet I would have to work with for the approval of the plans for the new dealership building and premises. They were the ones who wanted changes and had helped back Cecil on the buyout, as he had promised to both divisions that he would be in new facilities in a year. He was now actively looking for land out on the Interstate Highway. In about a 3 or 4 week period he had narrowed it down to two pieces. He showed me the one he preferred that was about 60-odd acres and near the county line but still in Kendall County. He felt the extra land could be subdivided up and sold off.

In the meantime I found out that it would be a big advantage if I was a Notary Public for doing title transfers, and made arrangements to become one. I was also now officially the Vice-President and General Manager of the dealership, and Cecil was President and owner. It was up to me to get everything up to speed as soon as possible. The service department had a lot of work but was charging only about $10 an hour. In San Antonio it was about $30 an hour. I found out when I read the manual and talked to the rep we could either have them set a price by doing an audit and giving us points for various things such as equipment (this is what Pewee Eperson had done), or they would pay the same price as the public if we had signs made saying what our rate was. The rate around Boerne was about $24 an hour so we had signs made and started charging the going rate. This made a big difference as most of the work was warranty work and this is what the factory would now pay. All of our charges were by the factory manual. This now meant a customer knew how much the labor would be on a job. If it said it was 2.5 hours by the manual then it was $60.00 for the labor (2.5 hours times $24 per hour).

Cecil made a deal on the property he wanted, with the deal pending on his getting approval from the Texas Motor Vehicle Commission. He was already a dealer but in the rules if you moved a dealership from its present location, and after the move it was within 25 miles of another dealership of the same franchise, they could protest. This didn't affect those that were already in the limit. It worked out that Ancera Winton Chevrolet in San Antonio on Bandera road near the loop was going to be just in the area after the move. In principle on the phone, the factory and everyone else had already given permission and it was now down to what Ernesto Ancera was going to do.

Cecil had already started talking to him and we were to go with him in his private plane to a new car showing in Fort Worth. We flew up to the meeting with him in his twin engine plane. I looked at the vehicles and did what I needed to as Cecil spent his time visiting and taking to Ernesto and various factory people. By the time we returned to San Antonio, Ernesto had agreed it didn't bother him about the move and he would not protest. He also told Cecil that he would do dealer trades with us on the same basis as everyone else. He stocked about 500 vehicles and on any normal stock would let another dealer have them for $150 over invoice. If he needed one from us he would pay the same. I thought to myself this was not a deal as he wouldn't take another vehicle in trade—he just sold it to you outright at a profit. Still the main objective was accomplished.

The little dealership was a full-time job just trying to run it on a day-to-day basis. I had Eperson's customers coming in with all sorts of problems and complaints. He had made various promises and never delivered. It was anything and everything; from switching out to another type of radio, to a paint job, as the customer didn't think the factory had done a very good job. Cecil made it clear from the start that if the factory wouldn't pay to take care of it, then it was between the customer and Mr. Eperson.

These customers we would turn to Mr. Eperson when he was around and he would usually either try to leave or just stand there and smile like he hadn't heard a word.

After about two months he still had half the yard taken up with his old used cars. Cecil gave him an ultimatum to get rid of them or he would charge him rent and have them hauled off. Whenever Eperson would start to get mad he wouldn't say a word. He would stomp his feet and kick the walls, and storm out of the place. It got to the point that it was like having a loose cannon show up. Finally Mrs. Eperson talked to Cecil and they agreed he didn't need to come to work and he would still get his $30,000 a year. That is what was paid annually each year to him anyway. After this we didn't see him at the dealership again.

We did have some trouble with vandalism on the vehicles and someone had come in and taken some tools, spare tires, and parts. We all knew it was most likely Pewee's son but couldn't prove it. We changed some locks and dropped it.

CHAPTER 41

ANOTHER DIVORCE

One day Cecil was up at the store in Boerne visiting me when a young man came in looking for a job as a salesman. He was dressed like most of the folks in town—cowboy hat, boots, blue jeans, and a western shirt. He told us, as we visited, that he had sold vehicles before for the Chrysler store up the street. We asked Patsy what she knew of Joe Sill and she said he was okay. He was a Boerne boy and had been married once before but was now with his second wife. He was honest and a lot of people in town knew him. That was a big thing for Cecil—to be well known in the small town. We hired him as our new salesman.

Joe understood the workings of the small dealership better than Cecil did. He understood that in a small place you had to do a lot more than just sell. He helped keep the new vehicles in the storage lot clean and made sure they would start. When we sold a vehicle he would clean it and make sure it was ready to go. If he could do a little something like polishing a door, changing a light bulb, or drop a customer off up the street, he would do it if it made them happy. With his experience as a salesman he already understood the car business and was able to step in and start selling right away.

With Joe around each day now, it allowed me to turn my attention to what was going to be needed at the new dealership in terms of facilities, as well as devoting more time to other various problems that were popping up at work. For one thing, the body man and his son were becoming increasingly difficult. They were "sick" a lot and wanted a raise. Everyone wanted one and we did give them some small ones to keep them on. As time went, on I became more aware that the body shop had been doing small cash jobs on the side for a long time. They didn't like seeing this come to an end as they had become quite used to charging the materials to Eperson, using his facilities, and then pocketing the money for the work.

When I started demanding tickets for each job, purchase orders or copies for each charge at the auto parts to be put with each ticket, they became very uncooperative. After I got them a small raise they still complained they didn't have enough work to make any money. I told them as I did the rest, that if they stayed with us, when we moved to our new facilities within the year, everything would get better. I hoped it would for all our sakes.

The sales picked up and we actually started selling from about 12 to 20 new vehicles a month. We sold no used, or maybe only one every now and then. Cecil didn't want to tie up money in used vehicles and each one we traded for was wholesaled to Henry at the other store, unless it was something he didn't want. He took all the good merchandise at what we traded for it at and sometimes it was a very good price. The rest we usually had to shop around before we made the deal and had a place for it to go. This included Harvey Harper, who, a number of years before had a falling out with Cecil and was now on his own. It seems he was having his girlfriend's car fixed up through the used car lot and the bills were charged to other vehicles in stock. We also sold to other wholesalers we had dealt with.

This cut our profit considerably. The new vehicle was about 30% to 40% of the profit on a sale. If a new vehicle stock number 100 sold and made $600 all up and you took a trade—in, number 100A, it would sell and make another $600 to $1000. If you took another trade 100B and it sold, being older it might make $500. When the factory looked at your sales they looked at what they called the washout on a vehicle. A new vehicle might washout for an average of $1,500 to $2,000. We only had the first go of the new vehicle, $600 to $1,000 on the top merchandise. This was only about half of what we should be getting on a washout, as we did no used vehicles.

It was frustrating as we had calls all the time for good used vehicles and we just had to miss the sale. At that time I couldn't understand why Cecil didn't keep the vehicles but instead insisted on selling them to Henry—not even for top price or market value, just to him, unless he didn't want it. I would learn why in time.

I made several trips to Houston and worked with Chevrolet on the plans for the new dealership. They had guidelines for what they wanted. They had each store rated with what they called planning potential. They might say a store should sell 50 vehicles a month today and in 5 years time be selling 75 vehicles a month. With these numbers they then had guidelines on how many square feet your showroom should be; how many square feet of parts department; how many stalls in the service department and body shop. It was then up to me to work within the recommended ranges and various layouts, to find what we felt would work best for us.

Some of the plans had the service department waiting room in the front with the showroom. Others had it down the hallway next to the service department off the service drive. We worked out which we considered best for us and left it expandable to a second floor in the parts department. Other areas such as offices and a changing room for the mechanics were all gone over, one room at a time. The plans were then approved and furnished by Chevrolet for bids.

Tindall Starts Construction

Sam Kopecky—Vice Pres. and Gen. Mgr. of Tindall Chev./Olds of Boerne checks out new construction.

If you have been driving on I-10 south of Boerne, you have surely seen the activity and new construction that has just begun.

This new addition to Boerne is the Tindall Chevrolet and Oldsmobile Co., a established firm in the automobile business.

This complex should be completed by mid-February 1981 and according to Vice Pres. and General Mgr. Sam Kopecky, this new location will give total and complete service to their customers.

The new building will contain 12,000 sq. ft., of which 1,300 sq. ft. will be showroom space. There will be service waiting rooms with a covered service drive in on the South side of the building.

The building will house a complete parts department, with 10 mechanical stalls and 4 body stalls.

On the outside, 62,000 sq. ft. of paved parking and display area will be built.

The Used Car Dept. will have a display area, which is a new feature. Heretofore, the used cars have been wholesaled out, so having this new area will be an added benefit.

The Tindall Co. will handle Oldsmobile cars and Chevrolet cars and trucks.

The Grand Opening activities will be announced at a later date.

Newspaper cutting for new Boerne dealership

This was back to Cecil for prices and financing. He didn't want the factory to finance as everyone told us it was like another partner every time you turned around so he then made arrangements and hired a builder. The building company specialized in these types of buildings, which were more structure with partition walls than anything else.

By about mid-October 1980 we were ready to break ground. We had the local newspaper go out to the site and take a picture of me and run a story. We had made arrangements for permits, septic system, drilling a water well, electricity, telephone, and getting natural gas from the main pipeline that ran in front of the building. Other arrangements were made for a contractor to stack the topsoil to one side away from where the building and storage lot would be. He would take this in trade for some of the asphalt paving he would do around the dealership later.

I was busy from early morning, opening the store until late each day. Some days we would close at 6 PM but if we were busy we would stay with the customer. Cecil had already said that when we were in the new building in spring, we would start staying open until 8 PM. I still had to find time to order vehicles, process the warranty claims, do the transfer and registration on vehicles, and sign the checks for bills and payroll. I had to watch the bank balance and if we started to have a cash flow problem, I had to let Cecil know we needed more money before we were past due. Some things you didn't want to do. One was not pay your bill on time with the factory or be caught out of trust when they did a floor check on the vehicles on the lot. Sometimes when we knew we had a couple of sales going and it was a matter of getting the used cars sold and the money in, Cecil would have me wait for the money. Several times GMAC came for the floor check and they would want a check for the vehicles that were off the lot before they left. I would have to run him down and get the check run up to me for the bank from the other store right away. It was nerve-racking as well, at times.

For some reason Sharon decided it would be nice if we started taking turns cooking dinner. I told her this was not going to work during the week and I didn't mind cooking on weekends when I was home. It just didn't make sense for everyone to wait until I got home to start cooking dinner just because it was supposed to be my night. I never knew for sure what time I would be home. It might be 10 minutes after 6 or it might be 7 or 7:30. A lot of times it was 6:30 and if I started then it would be 7:30 to 8:00, and that was too late for the kids to have to wait.

The next thing I knew, she drew up a duty roster on who was going to do what and when. I had started putting in a yard with grass and had purchased a lawn mower to cut it. She then told me she wanted Bryan to cut the grass and get paid for it. I told her fine but the only problem was that he never cut it. It started to turn into continual conflict. Sam was accused of picking on her kids so he would stay in his room and hard feelings started to develop between everyone.

She changed religions several times from that summer until mid-autumn. I thought she was just trying to see what some of them were like because she had met someone who was a friend that belonged to the various ones. It was more than that to her and she was very serious about finding the right one. The next thing I knew she started wanting to fight over every small thing that came up. She even started getting violent at times and so to stop her and protect myself, I would get a hold of her and hold her down on the floor so she couldn't kick and hit. It was as if she was a different person. She was spending more time after school with some of her friends and I didn't know if this was a problem or not.

We talked about it several times and both agreed that if we couldn't work it out we might as well go our own ways. Neither of us wanted to fight all the time. Her ex-husband caused enough turmoil when he would call about picking up the kids for the weekend and then wouldn't show or even so much as phone. He would get with some of his friends and start drinking and smoking grass and just forget about picking them up. They would sit on the sofa by the door with their bags for hours, waiting. The longer they waited, the madder she got. She was a real feminist inside and when we would get into our arguments I would use this to really get her going.

I won a trip through Chevrolet at the dealership to go to Hawaii. It was a 4-night 5-day trip. Cecil said we could take the trip and go. It was just before Thanksgiving—in fact we would get back the day before. This would be the first vacation I had gone on since I was a kid. We both felt it might be a chance to relax, enjoy, and just forget about everything.

We would fly to Honolulu and then transfer and fly to Maui. We would stay at the new Hyatt Regency that had just opened. They had activities for us to do and sightseeing trips as well, if we wanted to go. Each evening we would eat at one of the main restaurants in the hotel. Everything was to be paid for by Chevrolet.

We arrived and made our transfer to Maui and got to the hotel. We arrived late in the afternoon, almost early evening, and were to go to a reception. We were shown to our room. It had a small living room area with a balcony that looked out over the swimming pools to the ocean. It had a queen-size bed and large private bathroom. This was the highlight of our trip. From here on, things went downhill.

That evening we went and she said she didn't feel good and was tired. The next day we went on a tour that morning but cancelled the one in the afternoon. She said she just didn't feel like it. We took a shuttle bus that was in front of the hotel, to the little town near us and bought T-shirts and things for the kids. She didn't enjoy the restaurant and wanted to argue. The next day she said she felt sick and wanted to stay in the room. By later that day all she wanted to do was fight. We walked around the area on the beach and on the last night went to a going-away type of party. I found it interesting, meeting some of the other people from other dealerships. One evening we even met the trouble-shooter for the hotel as some of the Chevrolet people were getting out of hand at another table and he came to calm things down. His job was to go to the new hotels and get the bugs out for the chain.

We arrived back just in time for Thanksgiving and were to go to her folks in Comfort for it. It was as if she changed again in a 24-hour period and was like her old self when we were at her folks' house.

She only complained once—about me wanting to watch the Dallas Cowboys on TV with her father and brother-in-law.

She told me she wanted to go to a marriage counselor and wanted me to go too. At first I resisted and told her no. But then after we talked about it some more, I told her to find one, go first and see how it was and then I would go. She spent more time with some of her teacher friends and at times I wasn't sure what she was up to. I put it off to old suspicions and old feelings. She still wanted to argue and demand what was going to be done around the place.

As Christmas approached she told me how many of her young students didn't have anything and she wanted to get them something for Christmas. We agreed it would be nice but we couldn't afford a lot. She said she only wanted to get them each a little something—a coloring book, crayons, a cheap doll, nuts, just something small. We set a limit and purchased about $100 worth of gifts in total. She then made plans to get this to each of her students. She acted as if it made a big difference in how she felt and for that alone I thought it might be worth it.

She would do okay for several days and then it was as if someone else showed up the next day. She gave Sam an increasingly hard time. I was afraid this was going to cause problems between he and I, and I was determined not to let this happen. We had traded for a used Trans Am that needed a lot of work—mainly looks. It had a lot of miles on it so the value was low. I asked him how he felt about getting that for a car to fix up as Cecil had already given him a car but he was not very happy with it. We made the trade and he had a project. I think this also caused problems with her.

For Christmas we were to go over to Cecil's place a few days before Christmas. Sam could see him then, and the rest of the family over the holidays. Sharon could make arrangements for her kids over the holidays. Everything around the house had been very up and down, and very unpredictable.

One time Earl Floyd, who worked at the store in San Antonio as the new car manager and Henry's helper, called me from the jail in Boerne. They had stopped him for DWI. I went over to get him from the sheriff as he kept on insulting the sheriff and making things worse. I took him back to the house and caught all kinds of hell. I just wanted to get him out of jail and out of town. I had Sam drive his car and I drove him back to town. He had broken up with his wife and was heartbroken. That is why he had gotten drunk and decided to come and see me as he knew I might lend him an ear. He insisted on going to his ex-wife's house. She took him and the car keys, and Sam and I went back home only to find more abuse waiting for me. Sharon told me how her friends had told her how they thought I ought to do this or that, and how this counselor had told her he was sure it was all my fault and wanted to see me.

The next day or so I went in to the bathroom to shave. When I opened the cabinet I notice she had some pills; Elavil. The bottle looked old. I asked her what was going on. After several minutes she admitted she had a nervous breakdown in the past due to her husband and had seen a psychiatrist. She would still take some of the pills from time to time. I wasn't sure how much of this I wanted to know about or if I was ready to take on the responsibility of taking care of her.

Christmastime came and we went over to Cecil's place for the day. We took a few gifts and Sam, Bryan and Tammy came along as well. Henry and Edwynna were there with their kids, and Sue's son was at the house as well. Everybody was in different rooms visiting and watching television. I went over to the kitchen area and was talking to Edwynna as they were getting all the food ready. Sharon came over and I said something to her about getting a plate and helping or some such. She hauled off and slapped me as hard as she could, right then and there on the spot, out of the clear blue sky. I didn't understand. Edwynna standing right by me didn't understand. Sharon then said she wanted to go to her ex-in-laws around the corner with the kids and be dropped off.

I told the kids to get their stuff, and Sharon and the kids loaded up. We went only a few blocks and she went to the door and told them she wanted to stay with them with the kids. She said she wanted me to move out and that she wanted a divorce. I had already decided that after this, I was ready to quit as well. I didn't know how deep her problems were and didn't want to find out. I felt Sam and my kids were my first priority and I wasn't going to allow this to cause problems for them or me.

I went back to Cecil's and ate. I took Sam and told him we were going to move as it was over. I would find a place to rent and we were getting out. Sue's son said he would help us move when we knew. Cecil said he had some old furniture he didn't use anymore—a sofa, a chair, a dinette, and a coffee table. He used to have it in his apartment before he got the house. I wondered how long he had an apartment.

In a way Sam was going to miss Bryan and Tammy, and having other kids around but neither one of us wanted to live in continual fighting and turmoil.

CHAPTER 42

WE MOVE IN

After Cecil and Elizabeth had split up and became divorced, Cecil and Sue started living together. They had been going together for several years. Elizabeth, from what I was told, had agreed to $3,000 a month for the rest of her life, plus health insurance and a new car each year. She was to get the house and contents on Riviera, all her diamonds, the ranch house and a few acres around it, which included the tank area. She was to give up any interest in the property on Potranco Road. Cecil was to get the rest of the ranch, the dealership was his, no cash lump sum upfront was to be paid to Elizabeth, all the race horses were his and she was to sign off on anything else he might have. They all seemed happy so I guess that is all that counts.

I had a much less complicated settlement with Sharon. I found a place with much less trouble than I anticipated. Joe Sill asked around for me and found that an old lady had moved out of her house and her family wanted to rent the house to someone. I had us a place in less than a week. We moved all our personal stuff and the GTO to the house. I then asked Sharon after she moved back into the house, to call her parents and have them come down so we could talk to them. I wanted them to advise her as I felt she needed the help. I told them we didn't have much and it was really only the house. Sharon wanted to stay in the house but I had put up the down payment. I told her father I would take $1,500 for the equity in the house and she could have a year to pay it with no interest. Or, I would do it the other way and pay her the $1,500 and take the house. He said they would help her and if she couldn't pay the money in a year they would pay me for her. She kept the house.

We agreed to go to the same lawyer in Boerne together as we had made our agreement and had no children, it was straightforward. She paid half the bill and I paid half the bill. In a matter of about 60 days it was over and I was again single.

Sam spent a lot of his spare time working on his car. He wanted to get it painted as the old paint was oxidized silver. He picked out a metallic red and helped the body and paint man prep the car. After it was painted we ordered a new Trans Am Firebird decal for the hood. It was about $100. I found out how to put one on and Sam and I put the new decal on his car. He had already put new tires on the car and done some of the maintenance. He paid for part of the work and Cecil gave him some of what he needed, like the new tires. Sam was working part-time at the dealership when he was not playing football.

Sam had gone out for football at Boerne and was doing very well. He worked out with weights and with his fire and determination, it was hard for even the larger kids to handle him. He had a place on specialty teams and started playing offence and defense. Boerne had been a 3A school but was trying to go to 4A. The school was getting larger in population as the area grew but many were not sure and were thinking it was better to stay at the top in 3A instead of the bottom in 4A.

I was able to see Sam's games when he played in Boerne on Friday nights and if the game was not far away, I could drive over to like Gonzales and see the game. Cecil refused to let me off early and allow me to go to the games that were far away. This was also true with the games Craig played in. He was going to Churchill High School, a 4A school that had one of the top teams in the state. He played a lot and toward the end played all the time. I was only able to see, I think, 2 of his games because I couldn't get away from work. It was starting to dawn on me just how selfish Cecil could be.

Each day during the day and after work, I would pop out to the construction site and see how the new building was coming along. The time to stop a potential problem was before, instead of after, it was done. One such problem came up right at first. After work one day, Joe and I went out to the site. As we looked around and checked the plans we noted that no provision had been made for cables, phone and electric, to go from the main building to the future used car lot building.

They were to pour the foundation in the shop area on Monday and no workmen were around. Joe and I went and purchased plastic pipe and ran it like a conduit from where the power boxes and phone boxes were to be, down to the ground. We then put the plastic pipe in the trench across the floor and out the other side of the building. This way the next time they had equipment out for digging, they could take the pipe the rest of the way to the area of the used car lot. Now all power and phone lines would be underground just as it was on the other side of the building. Transport trucks and birds would not be a problem, and extra expense would now be avoided that would have come up at a later date.

Small things came up as the facilities went up but overall the construction went well and by February we were ready to move. We wanted into the new building as soon as possible, even if some things had to be done after we were in. In the old building it was cold. We had one electric heater and I would sit in my office with my coat and extra clothes on, trying to keep warm as I did paper work. I would clean the bathrooms and the building sometimes, just to keep moving and to become warm.

It was just as miserable trying to wash or clean a vehicle for delivery. The water was like ice and you were half frozen by the time you had washed it. The heater in the shop that was natural gas hung from the ceiling in the corner and was old. Alvin told us it was dangerous and didn't like using it. One day we had a try at lighting it and getting it going. It seems that it would have some sort of gas buildup when it would try and cut on before it would ignite. When it did it one time it went boom and the blast blew a couple of the windows out in the shop that were next to it. I could see why he felt the way he did.

I had started to build a relationship with the factory reps; Clarence Love with Chevrolet and Jack Heiser with Oldsmobile. Jack's son went to school with Craig and played on the football team with Craig. Cecil always wanted nothing but the best-selling models and never wanted to take any of the slow ones and help the guys out. I knew if I was going to work with them and get what merchandise I needed, it was time to try and get along with them and stop trying to push them around. I started taking the odd Chevette from Clarence and the Omega from Jack. All they wanted was a little help every now and then. In return they always remembered me when they had extra models of good merchandise.

I got along with both reps and was able to get the extra Corvette, the extra truck, Suburban, Oldsmobile cutlass or 98. I didn't always tell Cecil as he had me running the store and I would sometimes use a vehicle like the Chevette for a price leader in an ad, to try to get people in. It got to the point that the reps would come to see me and try to avoid Cecil unless they had to see the owner for something. They would get tired of him trying to bully them around.

A new subdivision ('Fair Oaks') off the interstate had opened and more affluent people were moving in. KENS TV in San Antonio had made a deal for a news presenter to come to work for them. He was originally from San Antonio and as I found out later, had gone to school at Robert E. Lee with Cecile. He was Chris Marou and part of his deal was for the station to furnish him with a new Corvette. They wanted to get it from the local dealer, so service would not be an issue. With Clarence's help we were able to get one with no trouble.

The only trouble we had was with the car. It unfortunately had a short in the electrics and kept on blowing fuses and the tail lamps didn't always work. Alvin had tried and couldn't figure it out. We had him leave it over the weekend, and Sam and I went down to the service department, got the manual out and started taking the car apart. I had remembered that back when I bought the '60 Chevrolet it had a short that was caused by a screw under the doorsill plate that had cut into the wiring harness. I was sure if we could follow the right wiring we would find something similar. After about an hour and a half we found a similar sort of problem, fixed the short and put the car together.

We didn't do as much together as I would have liked. Cecil started trying to get Sam to come and see him and Sue, or go with him somewhere. He said it was to allow me to be able to get out and have some time on my own but as I look back at it, I think it had more to do with trying to keep some sort of control over Sam. The only time I had off was Saturday night and Sunday, and not always then.

Sam and I would sometime take turns again on fixing dinner. We had a couple of disagreements about his housekeeping-skills, or lack of. We finally agreed his bathroom and his bedroom were his problem but the rest of the house was mine and to be kept clean. If he put his books down, or his shoes, they were liable to be picked up and thrown into his room. We had words with each other at times but overall we got along . . . at least as well as most parents do with a teenage son.

When the big day came to move out onto the highway, we had some help from people like Rudy who had been at the other company a long time. In just one day, with a few pickup trucks and one rented truck, we moved everything to the new place. Cecil and I had already gone to a used office furniture place in San Antonio and purchased desks, chairs, tables, and various other pieces. All we had to do was let them know when to deliver it.

A few items had to be fixed or finished (like some of the paving) after we moved in but most was done. We had the phones switched over and after only one war with the phone company, they were on and working. We ended up using an old established well drilling company in Boerne and the old man at this firm used a stick to divine where to drill. It worked as far as I was concerned, as we had a good well and the storage tank was set up with the idea that the fire department could use the well and the storage tank in case of a fire.

Cecil Tindall Chevrolet & Oldsmobile—new facilities open on Interstate Highway at Boerne

Joe was with us, as were Alvin and Max. The body man and his son were on thin ice as they had been directing jobs to their shop that was now almost across the highway from where we were. They still complained and always wanted something—one being a spray booth with ventilation. The OSHA department actually said we should have it and we were on a collision course. It just happened that at the dealership in San Antonio, one had been taken apart that had been used by a company before Cecil took the building over. It needed some work and a new fan motor.

I made arrangements to have it taken apart and put back together after it was at Boerne. It would just fit inside one of the stalls in the body shop. This cost $1,000. The electrician came out and put a new motor in and checked all the switches and lights. It had to be done in such a way the paint vapor would not blow the place up. This cost another $500. After it was all done we had a ventilated paint booth that was as good as a new one.

We also picked up some used equipment for the service department, such as the scopes for engine tune-ups and emissions. We had already found all the special tools from the factory and put them back in their boxes and moved them from the old store. It was now a matter of getting some of the other departments going.

Cecil had already talked to his parts' manager's son in San Antonio about taking over the parts department in Boerne. He had worked at the store in town so knew what they had and how to run one. It was good for us that he decided to take the job to get the parts going. We also needed a mechanic service manager.

Cecil didn't want a regular service manager as he felt there was not enough work to keep him busy. Instead he wanted someone that would do two jobs. We could get the service manager from the Chrysler store that had been a mechanic and did the warranty claims. He didn't want to do mechanic work anymore. Cecil got him to agree to be service manager, do warranty claims, and help with the mechanical work, all for a flat salary.

He was promising a brighter future to all of us if we would just help get it all started and work for a small base salary for now. As I remember he got the parts man for $1,000 a month and the service manager at first for $1,000 but had to go to about $1,300 to keep him after awhile as he was doing 3 jobs and could hardly pay his bills at home.

Cecil told me he had hired a retired man for a salesman to help out as he could only make a limited amount as he was on Social Security. As long as he could have a car to drive and a few extra dollars he would be happy.

Patsy was still on board and offered to open at 7:00 AM in the service department as she was always up early. I still worked until we locked up at night so this was a help to me. So, ready or not, we were in our new dealership building ready to go to work.

Out on the Interstate at night with no other lights around, the dealership would light up the night sky and all the surrounding area. You could see it coming up for miles as you drove towards it. I felt like it was a light shining for our future.

CHAPTER 43

DOING SOME BUSINESS

Business started to pick up after the move and people started coming in; not just to look at new vehicles but for service as well. Some were from Boerne as before but now we started getting those from the new subdivisions like 'Fair Oaks' as well. Some were professional people; some were sales reps with major companies. We had done what they called courtesy deliveries before but very few. This is where a major fleet leasing company sends a car to you for clean up and pre-delivery check over. You take care of this and the registration, and they pay you a flat fee for doing it for them.

This could be a new vehicle for a drug company rep that lived in your area. Some dealers didn't like doing this and didn't like doing any of the service on the vehicles after delivery. They felt they had missed out on a sale. We needed business and the money—besides we didn't have any way to sell to the national companies. It sometimes worked out as you hoped. I did one such delivery after I gave a man a quote for it when he came in. We took care of him and his company car. A few months later he priced a new car with us for his wife and then he came back and purchased it from us. He told us we were a couple of hundred dollars more than Gunn Oldsmobile on an equivalent model but we had always taken care of him and we would be close to where he lived and that had to be worth the difference. It was a shame more people didn't think and act as he did but it was nice to get one like him from time to time. It helped the attitude and made you feel like you were doing something right.

The body and paint man, Ruben, had a call for doing a paint job on a customer's car. I wasn't sure we should do it but he assured me he could do a good job and make money on it. I decided to try it. With the new booth, our ability to put out quality paintwork had increased greatly. He had done some warranty paint work and it came out okay.

The job ran behind schedule and the customer was unhappy with a couple of the panels. At first Ruben refused to do anything but polish it some more. I became involved when the customer became extremely angry. I had Ruben do some of the work over and finally made the man happy. Cecil was pushing for us to start going to commission on the service mechanics and the body shop. I didn't think we were ready for it yet and the men we had were good workers but were all older. They were interested in a steady income and salary not commission.

The day finally came when Ruben didn't show up for work one more time, as this had become a habit. I told him after he came back—and his son, who also pulled this from time to time—that I couldn't tolerate this anymore. If they were to be off I needed to know why and give permission. If they were sick, I wanted a doctor's note from now on. It wasn't long before the day came when the son didn't show for work so I fired him. His father said if I did that he would quit, so I told him it was up to him. He didn't show the next day so I fired him, assuming he hadn't quit. Sure enough they filed for unemployment. This was something they had been trying to work around to for a long time. I knew this and had kept notes on what had transpired along the way. When I sent my reply back to the unemployment office they were turned down.

I knew them well enough to know they would try something else. Sure enough, about a month later, the inspectors from OSHA showed up about our facilities. This was one reason I wanted the paint booth. After he went around he came up with only a few items like we should have a fire extinguisher on the show room floor, and better signs above extinguishers, and other small items. We also had a request about reviewing the wages we had paid them. I took care of this and it went nowhere as well. They didn't get their pound of flesh.

It was a shame because they could do good work when they wanted. They were just never satisfied and when they were unhappy they became petty and did all sorts of things from poor work, to slow work, to no work. Now we had to find someone else. It wasn't long and before we knew it, a young man came and applied for the job. He could do minor bodywork and paint work. He had references and seemed to be okay. He looked a little rough and I was a bit nervous about him at first but we needed the job filled so I gave him a chance.

Meantime up front, Joe was not very happy. He still tried to help with the lot work and various other odds and ends. The part-time man only wanted to work the prime hours and didn't want to help. He wanted to grab the good prospects and this started to cut into Joe's sales a bit. Like all of us he needed more money as well.

I don't think Cecil held a grudge about what had happened before we moved. Cecil was as guilty as he was. What had happened was that one day, two young guys came in and Joe knew one of them. He was the son of the coach at Boerne. As it was they were in business together doing road painting. They also painted parking lots and that sort of thing for parking places. They weren't living in Boerne but another town north of there.

The coach's son's friend had brought Joe the business and told him they needed a couple of company cars. One would take a Toranado and one could have a Cutlass. We worked the deal out and by mid-Saturday afternoon had all the paper work done and agreed on. The other man then wrote a check for the two cars. I didn't like putting cars out like this unless I knew the people or was able to see if the check was good at the bank. We decided to call Cecil back, as we stayed in touch with him when we did our deals each day. He always wanted to know how busy we were and how many we had sold. When we talked to him he spoke to Joe about who they were. They decided they should be okay as the coach's son was a good fellow, so we took the check and told them good-bye as they drove off.

As luck would have it, a couple of days later the check came back. It wasn't worth the paper it was written on. This started a string of lies and phone calls to banks. The partner assured us a transfer hadn't gone through. Then he had money coming in. Then his family would advance him money. Then the bank was going to loan it to him. They could only be charged with theft by bailiff and it took 30 days before you could get started on that.

The more we got into it and the police became involved, it came out that the friend was a con man and had a record but it seems the coach's son didn't know this. The cars were registered and had miles on them. The coach came in and offered to buy the car himself. We made a deal with him to make that part of the original deal good and wouldn't try and have his son charged if he co-operated, which he did. Before it was over I was called as a witness in front of the grand jury, after which they had orders put out for the other man's arrest for fraud. As I remember at the eleventh hour, his family came to the rescue and came up with the money for that car. It was nerve-racking and a hard way to make a sale,

None of us every dreamed it would come to something like this. Cecil would take a chance if he felt we would come out ahead at the end. One Mexican worker who knew Joe, had bad credit and wanted to buy another work truck. It was a used truck we had just traded for. Joe told Cecil he could make a big profit on the deal but GMAC wanted a big down-payment as the man had poor credit. The guy promised to pay the down-payment in payments to us on the side, if he could have the truck. This was a no, no. Cecil agreed and sure enough after about 2 months the guy stopped paying. Joe had to start running the guy down and each week had to go after him. By the time 6 months went by we had our down payment and GMAC was looking for the man and the truck.

One day GMAC showed up and wanted to see the file on the deal. It just happened we didn't have any note in the folder about the down-payment on the side and it showed only the final deal. They wanted to see if anything was funny about the deal as they had repossessed the truck and wanted to see if they could charge the loss back to us for having done something wrong like taking a down-payment in payments on the side. It was only by good luck we didn't have any reference in the file.

Joe introduced Cecil to a lot of people in Boerne. It opened a lot of doors for him. Cecil wanted to make a big impression in the community and when they had the junior livestock show and auction, he really wanted to make a big splash. One man he met, Mr Lynch, had Clajon Oil & Gas Company. Two of his kids had livestock in the auction; well, chickens that is. The Dad wanted the price driven up on the chickens and wanted the boy's to bring a higher price than the girl's. Cecil purchased several animals where he was sure it would pay off in the long haul and then sold them back at market price. He was then obligated to pay the difference. This didn't help with chickens that were now dead.

When the bidding came around the girl's chicken went for something like $1,000. When the boy's came up the bidding was fast and before you knew it the chicken went for $1,500 to Cecil. He was sure the Dad was going to take the bid off of him and didn't. So now he was sure he would pay him back, or had he asked a number of friends to bid his kids' chickens up? I told Cecil he could have Sue make some of the most expensive chicken and dumplings we ever ate but he didn't see much humor in it.

Over the time Joe worked for us he helped Cecil when he could. But he started feeling like he was being used and not rewarded for his help or loyalty. Joe told me one day how he had been a rodeo cowboy for awhile. He actually had a belt buckle he wore that said "All Around Cowboy—Chickasaw Rodeo". He said he got so tired and broke that one time when his old '55 Chevrolet quit running one more time, he had no money to get it fixed and it wasn't worth anything. He said he took the title and signed it and put a note with it and left it with the car. It said whoever found it could have it—it was nothing but trouble for him.

He had found out his first wife was cheating on him and started drinking a lot after he felt he had lost her. One day he saw the truck driver she was going with so he went over and pulled him out of his truck. The man had a pistol which Joe proceeded to take away and whip him with it. He admitted he was a little crazy and was taken to jail for beating the guy up.

For a while he was lost and one day when sitting on a bench at the Kendall County Fair, half drunk, he tied a corn cob on to a string. He would toss the corn cob out into the walkway where people were going by and pull it back in and do it all over again. After awhile a couple stopped and asked what he was doing, he said he looked up at them and said "I'm trollin' for pigs". It wasn't long after that the sheriff came over and tapped him on the back. He said he didn't know who it was but it made him mad so he stood up and turned around and hit the guy as hard as he could. That is when he realized it was the sheriff. He knew Joe, so Joe was lucky, it only cost him one night in jail. It was after this he decided to get straight and go on with his life. He had decided his ex had already ruined part of his life but why let her destroy the rest of it. I knew just where he was coming from too.

I tried to get him to stay, as I was sure it would get better for him but he had an offer to go to work back at the Chrysler store where he had worked before and he had just had enough. It was a real loss for us at the time. I heard later he had come back and worked there again a couple of times after I had left.

Business was picking up and the one part-time salesman wasn't enough. It worked out that Steve Rameriz, who had been a service writer and then a salesman at the San Antonio store, was looking for a change. He had a brother that had some drug history and he was looking for a job as a porter and wanted to do car detail work as well. Steve assured me he would watch over him and he would make a good employee. We still needed a person for this position so we decided to take a chance and hire him, as well as Steve.

When Steve moved in one of the offices he fixed it up as if it was his home. He had a few photos and put in a couple of pot plants. He put knick knacks around the office on his bookshelves. He had put bookshelves in his office and a lamp. He brought his own adding machine to use as well. He was a company man and was like Joe, in that he would help check cars in that came on the transports and do other odd jobs that would help as well. He had his brother working and in a routine of cleaning the offices, doing the storage lot vehicles and a number of other tasks.

With the workload increasing in the office Patsy felt they needed more help, at least part time. Gloria applied for the job. She told me she had gone to school with my older brother Joe but I never could place her. She was hired and was working out well. The big problem was Cecil. He would come up and try and put the make on Gloria and in the past I'm sure, Patsy. He started acting like he wanted an excuse to fire Patsy. I am sure it stemmed back to him making a pass at her and she told him where he could put it. He didn't like that.

Each time he came up he would complain about something about her and yet she wasn't doing anything any different. I was afraid it was only a matter of time.

CHAPTER 44

THE SPECIAL DEAL

Patsy did her job and when Cecil had his accountants come in and do a check, as well as give her some pointers on what to do, they told her she was doing a good job. Chevrolet had given us a business management award. It was made out to me but part was due to the fact she always had the work in on time and done correctly. Still the day came when she came to me and told me she was going to quit. I knew not to stop her and to let her go. Now I wanted to know what Cecil was going to do.

His plan was to have Sue come down and do some of the work. We had originally set the place up with a mid-sized office in the front by the showroom, which was mine. The next office, across from the general office, was larger with a bathroom and shower. This was his office. Sue was to work in that office and do the books.

A number of changes came up when we moved. We now had to get online with the factory for claims, reports, and ordering cars. It would speed things up and each night when I locked up I had to make sure the machine was in the receive mode for information to be picked up and received during the night.

From the time we took over during the previous year until we got on the highway we lost about $30,000. The first full month we were open on the highway we made about $36,000. We still had a lot of work to do but from here on there was no looking back. The factory had promised that once we were in our new facilities they would make sure we would get our share and then some, of the top vehicles to sell. We needed to increase our inventory but didn't want to bury ourselves in debt. Interest rates were still high and the factory was subsidizing dealers' interest rates to keep them ordering vehicles for stock.

After a lot of discussion Cecil agreed that he wanted to keep only about 100 vehicles in stock—total. This was both Chevrolet cars and trucks, as well as Oldsmobile. This was going to be a feat in itself as this required me to keep extensive records on what sold, what was on the ground, in the pipe line, and what needed to be added in terms of new orders. As they said, you can't sell from an empty basket but it was hard to keep just the right mix in the basket. This was a weekly task and required me to put in extra time to be ready on time with the right mix for each week's new orders.

Cecil would send us business up from San Antonio. It was usually people he knew that wanted an Oldsmobile, or wanted a truck, and they didn't have the right one in stock down there. It became increasingly more obvious they didn't have any inventory control or watched what they had or what they needed to replace. It was also obvious they were unaware of trends in equipment and color combinations. A few of the salesmen started calling me on a regular basis for trucks.

The car situation was very touchy. At the end of the previous model run it seems Earl Floyd got carried away and ordered something to the tune of about 150 to 200 Grand Prix's. They had to get extra space to store them and had to run all kinds of sales to try and get rid of them before the interest ate them alive. Henry wasn't watching the store and my contact was limited to our used car situation that Cecil still insisted on "giving" to San Antonio.

We had a break that came up around the start of summer 1981, as I remember. The people high up in Chevrolet at General Motors had made a big mistake. They had a fleet deal with the government of Argentina. They had over a thousand trucks and Blazers in storage yards for them and the deal had fallen over. Now they needed to get rid of these; most of which had been sitting for a long time with strange equipment and some storage damage.

I got a call and was to check with Cecil to see if he wanted any of the trucks and Blazers. They were Silverado level with carpet and well-appointed inside; as well as another lower level with air conditioning, power steering, power brakes, and other equipment, but they all were manual transmission with 6 cylinder motors. I don't think we had sold but 2 or 3 standard transmissions with 6 cylinder motors in 8 months. They had a couple of equipment levels and various two-tone paint combinations. They would make a special price to us for the vehicles and they would all have full warranty. For those that had transportation or storage damage, they would also pay to have this fixed at standard rates.

Cecil was mildly interested at first, as was I, since we didn't know what kind of price they were talking about. I let the factory know we were interested but wanted to know more about the price. They gave me more of the specifications and started to tell us the price, which included very large discounts. At first we talked about maybe 24 trucks and 12 Blazers. They told us it would be a minimum of about 50 trucks and 12 Blazers. I figured up the price on a new vehicle and told Cecil it was like getting the trucks and Blazers $1,500 to $3,000 below normal cost, depending on what the final deal was.

We both felt you couldn't go wrong with this deal with that kind of a price drop. We got back to the factory and told them we wanted 100 trucks and 50 Blazers. They said most had now been spoken for but would see what they could do. They wanted to know who carried our vehicles while in stock, which was GMAC. They must have given a good report because before the day was over we were assured we would get around 100 trucks and about 24 Blazers. They would start shipping in the next few days.

Steve checking in some of our special trucks

As the vehicles came in we noted the damage. Those with minor damage we sent to the paint shop right away. Those that needed more work and time were put to the side. We wanted as many ready to go as soon as possible. We found out Ancera Winton Chevrolet in San Antonio was the only other dealer in the area that went for the special deal. We were either going to make some really good money or look like fools. We wanted to hit the papers first, if possible, with special prices.

We had about 40 vehicles ready to go in about 10 days and ran our first ad. We priced them down to test the market. The people came out of nowhere. We had priced them too cheap at first. We were making about $1,000 on the trucks and about $1,500 on the Blazers. We raised the price and still the Blazers sold. We ended up getting about $2,500 profit on the Blazers and still sold out in about 30 days.

We made a real dent in the trucks and sold all the easy ones very quickly. We then had an assortment of about 30 trucks left to sell. Some had more damage (about half a dozen of them), and it would take the best part of a month to get them ready. It would be maybe damage on the hood and roof but this would require painting two large areas to make it look right.

Some of the employees wanted to see about buying the special vehicles as well. Cecil made it clear they would have to pay the same price as the public. I could understand he felt it was our chance to make some real money by taking the risk and giving it away was not the thing to do but by the same token, these people worked for us and had done a lot to get us on the highway so maybe they were owed some consideration. At the end, the only one that purchased one was me, for Sam.

Sam had gone through the Trans Am and sold it, then went into a Camaro Z28 on which the insurance was sky-high. We decided it would be nice to have a truck. He got one of the Silverado types with two-tone paint and short wheel base, then we added a nice radio and he purchased a graphics equalizer. It was a nice vehicle but not as fast as the Camaro.

I had been to meetings for Cecil and worked Saturdays until we closed. I had worked evenings and even gone down on Sunday to finish up paper work. I had asked about getting off a couple of times on Saturday and he told me it was important to keep working and if it was work-related that might help the dealership, he would consider it then. This did irritate me some as he and Henry worked when they wanted and took off on Saturday when they felt like it, which was more often than not.

I had been dating a girl for a number of months that I had met back after the first of the year. Her name was Linda and she worked at USAA. This is a large insurance company which mainly caters to military and retired military. They had a purchase plan for vehicles through them and they also had to buy insurance replacements for vehicles that had been totaled. Her position was now a group or section leader that dealt with various types of claims but she had worked for the company a number of years and knew a lot of the other people.

Each year they had a picnic during the summer at Raymond Russell Park, which was down the interstate from us back towards San Antonio. She wanted me to go to the employees' picnic and said she would introduce me to some of the people who might be able to help in terms of vehicles. I told Cecil about it and asked for that Saturday afternoon off. I gave him about 3 or 4 weeks' notice and assured him this was genuine and might be an opening for us. He said he would let me know closer to the time. When the day came he told me no. Henry had decided he wanted to do something so he had gone, and he planned on taking off later that day to do something as well. This did not help my attitude. Not just the time off. It was the fact it was only an afternoon and even then I had planned to spend it trying to drum up business for him and he couldn't be bothered about it, much less about me.

I got to thinking about the past number of years. Wilroy had worked himself into such a state as the service manager that he ended up in hospital with a bleeding ulcer. All Cecil wanted to know was if he was going to be able to come back and when. If not, who would take his place? A nephew didn't carry much weight. A cousin, Val Luckett hadn't done very well either. He was still his business manager but didn't make enough to amount to anything and had worked for him for years and years. The more I ran various people through my mind, the only ones I could see he cared about were himself and Henry.

Everyday employees, even though they may be loyal and work for him a long time, didn't get any consideration either. Elizabeth Cornelius was an example as well as his ex-part's manager who had retired, Victor Kott. He seemed to have had some hard feelings when he left. I knew of two different salesmen that had sued him over promises but I had always ignored the smoke. I was wondering if maybe I wasn't just another fool he was using. Uncle Gene had come and gone a couple of times. He always felt Cecil didn't deliver on his promises. Was this just Uncle Gene?

J.M. didn't seem like he wanted to do anything but be a salesman, and he and Cecil had always had a strange relationship. During the past year at Christmastime, his son Tommy was coming back from school and was going to go to the Christmas party for the dealership. He was speeding that evening after dark and coming down what had been in the country until recently, near the turnoff for his neighborhood. The city had put in traffic lights in the area while he had been gone. As he approached the intersection the light turned and a car pulled out. He couldn't stop and he swerved to miss it and hit a telephone pole. He never knew what happened. After that, J.M just wasn't the same. His family was everything to him.

We won some more contests and won prize points as well. I was able to get a few extra items with them and the MIC insurance was now worth about $2,000 a year at the rate it was going. I was doing more finance for the dealership and was making the dealership several thousand dollars a month without trying but my heart wasn't exactly in it, with the way things were going.

We had some others come to work in Boerne. Mr Pope came from the San Antonio store as a mechanic. He had worked for years at Smith Chevrolet. He was mainly a rear end specialist but did a lot of general work. Another high-flying mechanic who had a lot of his own special tools, worked in San Antonio and made a lot of money. He was interested in the job at Boerne as a manager but wanted a minimum of about $4,000 a month to run the shop. Cecil liked to have choked when he heard this.

Hebert Tindall had gone off to school and had his degree now. He had come back to San Antonio and was working at the store in San Antonio with Steve. They ran around together from time to time. One time they had gone somewhere together and when they were driving back they smoked some grass. As they went down the highway Steve told Hebert, "look there is a bridge coming up". Hebert said, "I know". After that they hit the bridge and both ended up in the hospital. The car was a total loss. It was lucky they weren't hurt bad. Steve asked him later why he hit the bridge as he told him it was coming up. To this Hebert responded, "yes I know but I thought you were driving". Hebert had moved into our area and was now working as a salesman with us at the dealership.

I took care of all of Cecil's special customers. Part of the reason was that this way, he didn't have to pay commission to the salesmen. I took care of his Lone Star Beer distributor, Mr Burkett, the cement company and their trucks, as well as the Stolhandskis, his favorite lawyers. I had picked up a few in the area myself, including old man Richter of Richter's Bakery, the road manager of Moe Bandy and Joe Stampley—all names of 'has beens' now I'm sure. The poor road manager had a noise in his car that sounded like it was tearing apart. After many an hour we found it. The rear seatbelt bolt was the wrong length and when weight was in the back, the body came down far enough to rub against it when you drove up and down small hills and dips. He was so happy to get it fixed he gave me some cassette tapes of the singers' music.

Cecil had been worried that Mr. Burkett might come over and find out that I drank Budweiser, so he always wanted me to keep a six pack of Lone Star in the fridge just in case. We were originally also a medium-size truck dealer for Chevrolet. We didn't stock any but when Lone Star needed one, we got it from A. J. Foyt Chevrolet in Houston and painted it the colors he wanted, just to make him happy.

Sam was working part-time at the dealership and it turned into a war with him at times. I think it was just his age. He didn't show up when he should or he complained that the jobs he got were "shit jobs", as he put it. It was hard to find jobs he could do when he wasn't trained. One day he started yelling at me again in front of the other employees. I told him that was it. I took him with me to the parts' storage area and locked the door after we went in. I started to take my coat and tie off and he asked me what I was doing. I told him he didn't seem to understand anything but violence and we were going to settle it once and for all. If I won he was going to do it my way, if not, we would do it his.

I told him to take first hit and after that there were no rules. He knew I was mad and was serious about what I said. He started to cry. He didn't want things to come to this. We ended up having a talk and after this I don't think we ever had another major confrontation. I don't know what would have happened if he had hit me. I guess we will never know. I am glad he didn't and things turned out like they did for us. I think it brought us closer.

I wasn't overly happy but then I wasn't worried. Things were starting to look brighter and I felt that in maybe a year or so, some changes for me might be made. It was just taking one day at a time. Cecil would put me down some at times when he was up at Boerne and I had to put up with Henry at times on the phone but most of the time I was on my own and just worked with the other employees.

The time of year came for our annual review with the factory on a number of areas. One was ownership and structure of the company which I was unaware of in terms of number of shares and par value etc. and unsure as how to answer the questions on the form, I called Val Luckett. I knew he must do it all the time for the San Antonio store. He told me we should have a box with the information and a seal inside it. I told him I didn't have it so he was going to have Cecil look in his office for it.

Cecil had a look around and found it in his office and said he would have it sent up to me. He didn't know why he had it and that it should be up in Boerne. While he was looking he found the papers from the strip centre with the check from the real estate company for $600. He had forgotten about it and it had been put to one side. He was going to have Val see if they could still collect on a check that was several years old. They couldn't but the company sent him another check for it as they had always wondered what had happened to it.

When I received the box in Boerne and opened it so I could fill in the ownership papers for the factory, I almost fell out of my chair. I couldn't believe what I had in front of me. I knew why he had it in San Antonio and if he had remembered he would have never sent it up to me. That $600 check had him side-tracked and he forgot why he was holding onto the box. There it was on the corporation papers with number of shares and all. Oh, I was vice-president and general manager with ownership of shares at zero. It was the other name that owned 25% of the shares in the company—it was Henry Tindall. Cecil had lied to me from the start.

How long he had been lying to me and just what my position was I no longer knew for sure. I had a lot of thinking to do. I knew one thing for sure; I would never bust my butt and build up a company for Henry and his family. This one was supposed to be for my kids.

I went over everything in my mind, over and over. The times Cecil had made me out a fool in public, the time he pushed Sue and I into the band. He wanted to use me just like he did everyone else. He used other family—Wilroy, Val, Hebert, and his brothers over the years. He treated Elizabeth badly and cheated on her; it was no better with Sue. I was only one more for him to use to get what he wanted. He never paid anyone any more than he had to—the cheaper the better. And how about all of those broken promises to others I had heard about. Was it just smoke? I didn't think so. He was a user and I needed to admit it to myself. I didn't know then, not only how true all of this was, but just how far he would go with it. It made me sick in the years to come when I saw . . . and it was too late to do anything about it.

My immediate reaction was to tell him I knew and what I was thinking about him and all his lies but I didn't need to cut my throat so I decided the best thing for me to do was keep my mouth shut, take some time and think it over. I couldn't stay; I knew that—not with a liar and a user. I would be damned if I would work myself to death to build something for he and Henry. This wasn't the way the special deal for my kids and the future was supposed to be. I would need to find another job and get away from him. But where? How would I find another job?

CHAPTER 45

A New Job

The start of school for the next school year was just around the corner. Sam went out for football and become somewhat disgusted at times with the other kids. They wouldn't put in a full effort. This really came out as the season went on. One time after a game where the others had let the team down, he was so mad in practice that he wanted to take the other kids on one at a time all by himself. The coach eventually let him do it and many a kid wished they hadn't made him mad. I wanted him to play as long as he enjoyed it and wanted to. Then he told me one time he was going to quit. I told him he had committed to the team for that season and they were counting on him but if he wanted to quit after that season it was okay with me and I wouldn't say a word. This was some of the sort of stuff I wanted him to get out of sports—not that they had to win every game or else.

I still went to the games when I could and Cecil still wouldn't let me off so I could go to them all. This really didn't sit well with me now. One game I went to you could see how they always used two guys to try and stop Sam. He became disgusted one time and was taken off the field for a few minutes. He went over to the cups of water and knocked a bunch of them off on the ground and pushed the water boy. This was the kind of stuff I didn't want to see Sam do. He later apologized for it and I don't think he ever did it again. He was a lot better kid than that.

He still had his fights. One time I had a call that he had been in a fight at the 'Stop & Go' store where he was getting gas outside by the pumps. Two guys started giving him a hard time so he tore into both of them. They were complaining about it. I told them I could understand how they felt but it was fair—two of them and only one of him made it about even. Unfortunately he would get into some trouble in the years to come, as Cecil would always get him out of it and think nothing of it. I didn't want to encourage Sam but when he was picked on I felt he should be able to defend himself. Cecil was a bully and in the past I had seen him pick fights just to hurt somebody. I didn't want Sam to be like that.

Cecil, Sue and Gary (Sue's son), moved to 'Fair Oaks' and bought a house. They were always wanting Sam to come over or go out to eat with them. If he wasn't doing this, he wanted to go over to his girlfriend's house. He was gone more than I was. I had mixed emotions and wanted to spend more time with him but I didn't want to stop him from doing things either. He was keeping his grades up and I couldn't complain about that. I didn't want to tell him what I knew about the store as I still didn't know what I could do about it.

I had done so well with the factory they had made us part of an experimental service program. They had given me a special stamp with a code—I think it was code 90. When I used this we would get paid for warranty claims that were unusual and that you would not normally get paid on without prior factory approval. We still had to keep the old parts and if they checked the claim it still had to stand up but this way we could just do it, get paid, and get the customer on his way with no waiting.

I had one very good customer—a lady who had a horse ranch and had purchased several trucks from us. One day, their new truck just quit when they were pulling a trailer with horses near their ranch. I had the truck towed in and we found the transmission case had a flaw and it had fallen apart, had collapsed inside the transmission and ruined it. The whole thing was junk, inside and out. We needed a complete new transmission; something you normally didn't do. I used the code and ordered a transmission by special airfreight. The factory had to take one from the assembly line which cost them a unit in production. It was flown to San Antonio where we picked it up and then installed it in the truck. In a matter of about 3 days we had them on the road from start to finish. The service rep called and couldn't believe what I had done. He was instructed to see the old unit. When he saw it he agreed and everyone was happy except the factory. They had lost a unit of production and had a bill of about $1,300 to pay to us.

I decided that I would take a big chance and in passing, mention to the two factory reps, Clarence Love and Jack Heiser, that I was interested in making a move. I had done very well with them and felt we were friends. Clarence told me he was near retirement and we visited. He told me he had heard that Brown Chevrolet in Devine was possibly looking for someone. I didn't know what I wanted but I knew Brown knew Cecil and would tell him if I contacted him. Should I or shouldn't I contact him. Would it be just another place with more of the same? I decided I would think about it.

I mentioned it to Jack Heiser when he came by. We visited and he told me how every time he saw Cecil at one of the football games (where his son and Craig were playing for Churchill), Cecil would holler at Craig in the stands and show-off. It would get embarrassing for him and I knew just what he was saying too. Cecil would then go on about how he wanted this and that, and expected him to deliver. Jack told me he only went to see his son and get away from all of that, and Cecil just didn't understand that all that crap didn't cut it with him. I thought to myself, how I had only seen about 1 or 2 of Craig's games as I could never get away. Cecil did—at my expense, was how I felt about it. As Jack went on, he told me he could only tell me of something he had heard and if it came up he had nothing to do with it as he could get in trouble.

He understood how I felt and we were friends. He told me to contact Charles Maund Oldsmobile-Cadillac in Austin as they might be looking for someone—but to talk to Doug Maund. After a day or so I got up the nerve to phone him. I talked to him on the phone for a minute and told him who I was, and that I had been referred by Jack who had heard a rumor. We visited for a couple of more minutes and he asked me to send him a resume. He then wanted to know about my coming up for an interview. I told him to just let me know when and I would make arrangements.

A few days after I sent my resume I had a call and they wanted me to come up for an interview after Thanksgiving, about the first week of December. I knew I would have to tell Sam what was going on. I talked to him and told him that when we were off on Thanksgiving, I wanted us to drive to Austin and find where this place was and have a look at it. It was at 8400 Research Blvd., off the interstate highway.

We drove up and found the place. We both almost fell over; it was huge. A big store with a showroom that looked like a palace. We drove over to the 'Nighthawk' restaurant and had a Thanksgiving dinner and talked. He understood how I felt. I told him not to worry about this until I knew if I had a job or not. If I got it and decided to take it we could go over our options then. He was sure he could stay for his last part of high school with a friend if he needed and didn't want to move. I said we would go over our options after we knew if I had the job.

Charles Maund Oldsmobile-Cadillac on Research Blvd. in Austin

The first week of December came and I was to go to Austin. I told Cecil I had an appointment with a dentist or something and would need most of the day off, from late morning until late afternoon depending on how it went. I drove to Austin late that morning and met with Doug. We talked over what I had done and some of my background. Heiser must have already spoken to him because by the time about 30 minutes had gone by he started telling me the pay plan and what they had to offer, and wanted to know if I could start after the first of the year.

I told him I would need to give my present employer some notice and didn't know how long it might take for him to get a replacement. He said for me to stay in touch but he wanted me to be up in Austin by no later than the first of February 1982. We shook hands and I told him I would let him know as soon as I could. I met George Peters, the current Oldsmobile sales manager, with whom I was supposed to work, and told him I would be in touch with him as Doug had said it may be easier to get in contact with him.

I left and drove back to Boerne as fast as I could. I had figured if it went well I could make a round trip in about four and a half hours. Now I had something to think about and I didn't even know myself just how good the job would, or could be, at first. They wanted to see how I worked out before they made too many promises. They told me the starting pay was $2,000 a month. I would have a demo, health insurance scheme (and they paid half), as well as a retirement savings' scheme where they did matching funds up to a limit. They also had goals for us to meet during the year with bonuses attached. They expected us to make about half the bonuses as they were to be a challenge but not totally out of reach. As a manager I would also have profit-sharing in the company's profit but that was about all that was said.

I was still on the same pay I had been on with Cecil since I went to work for him back at the end of 1977; $1,500 a month. One time, about the time Sharon and I got married I started to ask him about something one day and he jumped to the conclusion that I was fixing to ask for a raise. He jumped in as if to head me off at the pass and told me "when things got better" he would look at my pay then but now was not the time. We needed to get the new place up and going first. I had no plans of trying to play one against the other. I wanted to tell him in person that I was leaving him and give him a chance to get a replacement in. I was sure this way I could make the transition smooth by showing the new person the ropes.

With Sue working there, Cecil came up to the store several times a week; even if it was only for a short time. I felt that he would be up in the next day or two and I would tell him then. It would also give me some time to think about how to tell him. When he came up I told him I needed to talk to him for a few minutes. I told him I had found another job and would be leaving him to go to work at another dealership in Austin. The first thing he wanted to know was how much they were paying me. I told him $2,000 a month with a few other extras.

He wanted me to know that it wouldn't last and that they would most likely fire me after a few months. He then reminded me he had told me that they would review my pay after the new store was up on its feet. He wanted to argue at first and I tried to tell him I wanted to give him time to find a replacement. I didn't want to leave on bad terms because of the kids. He would still be their grandfather and we would all need to have contact with each other. I didn't want to get into everything about why I was leaving or how I felt about a lot of things he had done. I just wanted to keep it simple and let him think it was for more money and maybe just felt I should make a change.

He told me he had some business he needed to take care of; we would talk about it later and not to make any commitments until then. The next day he came to Boerne and wanted to go to lunch away from the dealership. He and Sue and I went to lunch at a café-restaurant sort of a place. He told me that he felt they could pay me $2,000 a month starting right away. He wanted me to stay and said it was in my best interests as well as Sam's and that I wouldn't be able to hold on to the job in Austin and would be on the street before I knew what happened, if I took it. It was a big store and I wasn't ready for anything like that. Then he wanted to know about Sam. I told him he would live with a friend until he finished school, and then come and live with me in Austin. He said that wouldn't be necessary as he could live with them at 'Fair Oaks' if it came to that.

I refused to give in at lunch and I could see he was getting mad. He didn't want to show it at first but you could tell. After trying several times to undermine my self-confidence he decided it was time to go back to work. He then told me to think it over before it was too late. We went back to work and he went back to San Antonio.

Days went by and it was as if he had resolved the issue of me leaving. He did nothing about finding a replacement. I didn't want to tell him I had until the first of February so I had told him I had to go in January and let it go at that. I decided to leave him alone for awhile and see what happened. I would get on with my arrangements of finding a place to live in Austin and planning to move in the meantime.

Back around November, Mr. Lynch of Clajon Oil & Gas came to see me and wanted to buy a car for his daughter, Susan, for a graduation present. He purchased an Oldsmobile Cutlass with a T-Top and all the extras for her. I got to visit with him some and he asked me what plans Sam had about college and wanted to know if he would play football. He was a big supporter of Texas A&M and felt that as good an athlete as Sam was, they would surely have a place for him. Sam was small and this was the first thing coaches saw and wouldn't give him a second look. He said for me to talk to Sam. If he might be interested in Texas A&M he would see if he couldn't get them to take a look at him.

The Boerne football team was not on the top of the coaches' scouting list for college players. Some schools were interested in some of the kids. They would usually look at highlights of game footage to see if they were interested. I asked Sam what he thought about it as I didn't know if it was anything or not. He told me he had no interest in Texas A&M under any circumstances. It was a shame in some ways but I wanted it to be his decision. We had talked about him going to college in general terms and his first step was to take the entrance test and see how he scored.

After I knew I was moving to Austin and we talked about it, I told him he could always live with me, at least at first, and go to school there at the University of Texas. It was big and it was hard but it was a good school and he could get a good education if he went there. He thought it sounded like something he might want to do but didn't know. Between girlfriends and family he wasn't sure about a move. He had been going on and off with Denise Traeger.

I knew Denise and had met her on a number of occasions. I liked her, as she seemed to have her head on and appeared to be a good kid. I felt she and Sam had too many arguments and told both of them this. At times I felt it was so bad and being Sam's fault, I told both of them she should quit seeing him and find someone else. I knew at times Cecil was always telling Sam to see more girls, be with more girls, and would also give Sam a hard time about Denise. This didn't help. I really didn't want to cause problems and felt it was their relationship and they would need to work it out. I liked her and if they could quit fighting all the time, I was quite happy to see them as a couple.

Again, I figured that in time some of these issues would sort themselves out. I just wanted him to know I wanted him in Austin with me. I still needed to make a decision about Linda. She had two kids that were young and I had spent a limited amount of time around them. I think she didn't want them to get attached to someone in case it didn't work out. I liked her but was in no way wanting to marry her at that time. In fact I needed to decide if I thought I ever would want to marry her. She had offered to move to Austin. She could get a transfer to the USAA office in Austin and they could live there as well. I told her I needed to see first of all, if the job was going to work out or not. Cecil might be right and I could be on the street in a few months.

I knew I needed to make some decisions. If I let her move to Austin I needed to make a commitment. If the job was working out, which I hoped to know in a few months, I would need to tell her by then. I would need to know my own mind and how I felt about our relationship by then but in some ways I already felt I knew.

As the Christmas party at the dealership in Boerne approached, the word got around that I was leaving. Hebert came to me and told me he wanted my job and asked what I thought his chances were, of Cecil giving it to him. He had a degree in business and had been around the car business. He could have made a good general manager but I knew Cecil would never even let him have a chance at it.

Cecil always looked at Hebert as if he was thick. He wasn't and had the ability. They had used him in service and in sales in San Antonio, before he came up to Boerne. They never gave him much of a chance at using his own initiative as Henry always wanted to use him as a playmate and pulled him off jobs so he would have somebody to go with him. I told Hebert I would do what I could and put a word in for him but he knew Cecil as well as I did so I just didn't know. I didn't want to hurt his feelings and tell him as I liked him too much to do that.

CHAPTER 46

ON TO AUSTIN

The dealership had been broken into not long after we moved into the new building out on the highway. They didn't take much; there wasn't much to take. We had iron bars put on some of the windows to make it more difficult but didn't have any more trouble until about the time I told people I was leaving. We had a couple of new vehicles stolen and MIC had come out to look over the place and ask us questions to see if they could get any leads or ideas.

A number of the employees came up to me at the Christmas party and asked me not to go and seemed to be genuinely upset that I was going. I had tried to be friends with the employees and get along with them. I wanted to help then when I could and wanted them to know I wouldn't ask them to do anything I wouldn't do. I didn't want to be a bully and push them into working for me by threats. I liked to have a clean atmosphere where we all got along and helped each other.

Cecil did his standard $50 bonus to the employees and I guess he felt he had already done his dash with me by telling me I could go up to $2,000 a month. That was it for Christmas. I never did get any kind of bonus when I worked for him. I never even got so much as "you're doing a good job"—even though we won some contests and moved up in the service rankings to a respectable level. In sales with Oldsmobile, we had gone from off the chart of the top 45 in the Houston Zone to about 30th and were still moving up. The names of some of the other dealerships around our standing level were good stores but none of this made any difference to Cecil.

Between Christmas and New Year when Cecil was up at the store in Boerne, I asked him what he had done about a replacement. He became angry and after we spoke for a few moments I knew he had done nothing. It was as if it was all going to go away and I was going to stay as I was told to and now I was stirring the problem up again. I knew I needed to get a move on. He basically told me not to worry about it and he would take care of it.

After the first of the year he still hadn't answered me or given me a time frame. I asked again. He became angry and told me if I was going to leave I could quit driving his demo and turn it in. "And by the way, that furniture I loaned you, you can bring it back and not take it with you" was his next remark. I had no intention of taking anything that was his. I decided then I might as well give him a push. I told him I should be gone by the 10th. I hoped this would put some fire under him as all he had done for about a month was try to stall me and get me to stay, by destroying my self-confidence and bullying me.

The next number of days went fast. I found a place to live in Austin—a duplex out on Research Blvd., a number of miles away from the dealership. I liked the place. It was hard to find a place and nothing was cheap. I made arrangements for a U-Haul rent truck for my furniture as I had bought a king-size bed and a few other pieces. I had my own washer and dryer, as well as the furniture in Sam's room. We took Cecil's furniture to the dealership where we were told to take it and put it in the parts' storage area. I turned in my demo and started driving my GTO. Sam was to drive it up to Austin and I think it was Gary who was going to drive Sam's truck. I would drive the rent truck and we would make the move in one trip.

I had turned everything in and was basically told I could go, as Cecil didn't need anyone to help show anyone the ropes. It was only in the last few days that I found out to my surprise that the new general manager was to be Gene Colbert, my uncle. I didn't know why he had taken the job. I could only guess he was made an offer and he felt it was worth a try. I was glad for him in some ways and yet sorry, as I knew nothing would ever come of it for him from Cecil. He didn't even want me to take the time to show Gene what I knew and what I had done. So very unceremoniously I left the dealership in Boerne with mixed emotions.

I was excited about the new job and scared to death. I had been in touch with George Peters and even made a couple of dealer trades with him. He told me after I got settled in, to come and see him and they would get me started. I knew I had a few days to unpack and get my feet on the ground.

The move went well and by the end of the day I was in my new place surrounded by boxes. The weather was turning cold and I had a little fireplace in my duplex, as well as the central heating and air-conditioning. I spent my first couple of days getting set up and popping out to get only a few things I needed. It started to snow and it was the first time I had seen any snow in a long time. That winter in Boerne it got down to the lowest it ever had. It went down to right at 0° F, the coldest I could ever remember and now it was snowing.

A couple of days went by and the weather improved. I decided it was good enough to venture out in and drove down to the dealership even though snow was still piled up along the road and in the parking lots. I went in and asked for George Peters. He came out and we went to his office. We visited and he got me my standard papers to fill out for the office and told me they would take a $20 deposit out of my first pay for the lock box key. He then gave me some keys to the building and started going over some of the procedures for the dealership. He guided me into picking out a demo, a Cutlass 2 door, and said he would get it into service and have it ready for me the next day. We spent a little more time and he then suggested I take the rest of the day off and finish whatever I needed to do.

Over the next number of weeks it was a matter of getting my feet on the ground, learning who was who, and what to do and not do at the dealership. As far as it went on the home front, several twists came to be that were unforeseen. I went down to San Antonio on a couple of weekends to see Linda, and she came up to see me on a couple. I could see things weren't going to be. I felt like I needed to make a move. I told her I thought we should stop seeing each other for awhile and I wanted some time on my own. She didn't like this and we still talked on the phone some but I knew it was over and we should break up. It wasn't going anywhere.

Out of the clear blue sky I received a phone call from Sharon, my ex-wife. She had a cousin in Austin and was going to come up and see her, and she wanted to come and see me about something as well. I had seen her a few times on and off while I was still in Boerne and found her getting even more unpredictable. She would be with one guy one minute and then another the next, and then change to yet another religion. She came and told me she was getting married and wanted to give me one more chance before she did. I tried to be polite but she got mad when I told her I wasn't interested. She then called me after she got back to Boerne to ask me one more time. That was the last time I ever spoke to or saw her. I later got a check in the mail for the divorce settlement.

I had started to settle in now and had decided to purchase some furniture—a dining room set-up and some living room furniture. I had finally worked my way out of debt and was now ready to start over again. This time the payments would be for something for me. I had started into a routine that on Tuesday afternoons, my afternoon off, I would come home and clean the place, and do my laundry. I would do any shopping and by the early evening as a reward to myself, I would go to one of the country bars in the area. One was 'Dallas' and the other one was the 'San Antonio Rose'. They both had a happy hour with reduced prices on drinks and free food. The crowds sometimes were better at one place than the other as at times, the really young ones would come and take a place over. This was not good as a lot of them were looking for a fight more than anything else.

As a rule I would get something to eat and have a few beers. I would watch the big screen entertainment on the walls and those on the dance floor. The big screens would sometimes have old movies on and most of the time, sports. The music was always country and western. 'Dallas' had a kitchen and you could order a hamburger and fries, so a lot of the time I went there. I would talk to some of the others some of the time and very rarely asked someone to dance. I had a bad experience before I left San Antonio when one time I asked a girl to dance and halfway through it she stopped and looked at me and said, "You've got to be kidding" and walked off. I knew I was not Fred Astaire but I didn't know I was that bad. Nevertheless, I still danced once every now and then. Sometimes you would see where a guy just wouldn't take no for an answer. Once a couple of girls had a guy that kept coming up and pulling on them, trying to get them to dance. They wanted no part of him and after about 10 minutes I had enough. I went over and told him in no uncertain terms it was time for him to shove off. I sat with the girls for about 15 minutes and then left, as everything seemed to be under control. I usually didn't do this sort of thing as I didn't need or want any trouble.

I would usually stay to about 10:00 PM. If I was having a good time and sometimes it was only just to have a break, think about things and listen to the music, I would stay to about 12:00. This was a routine

I had started to get into and was happy with it. I was getting used to living on my own and decided it had both its good points and its bad.

Once every now and then, Sam would talk about coming up to see me. I would try and get the kids to come up for weekends. What I would have to do if I were to be with them all the time, was go down after work on Saturday and pick them up. They would spend the night and we would have some time on Sunday and then I would have to drive them back. It had been in my work schedule that I worked on Friday nights until we closed at 8:00 or 9:00 PM in the summer. It would be awfully late for me to go after the kids on Friday night after work as I wouldn't even get to San Antonio until 9:30 or 10:30 PM. It just wasn't going to work.

Sam called me one time and wanted to know what my plans were for going out as he and a friend named Scott, might come up. I told him I would go to 'Dallas' for awhile and he could find me there. If I left the place it would be that I decided to go home and they could find me there. We left it at that and I was going to keep a watch out for him during the evening.

I went to 'Dallas' and the crowed seemed to just be starting. I had sat down at the rail by the dance floor near the bar and had a beer. I decided to get up and get another one. It was still a bit early for Sam to show if he was coming. As I got to the bar and was waiting to be served, a girl came up and wanted to get a couple of drinks. Because she seemed to be frustrated as she dug for her change, I offered to get her drinks for her as she told me that she and a friend had come out for the evening. She also told me that these would probably be their last drinks. She then invited me to come back with her to where her friend was sitting by the dance floor at the rail to meet her. I had no plans and decided it would be nice to have someone to talk to for awhile, as I waited for Sam and Scott to show.

Pam (Fowles) Duncan when I first met her

The girls name was Becky and she introduced me to a girl named Pam. Pam seemed to be a little distant at first but after we started to visit she became more talkative. We visited and as I remember we even danced. The next thing I knew I saw Sam and Scott coming across from the other side of the room. When he got over to where I was, I introduced him to Pam. She didn't believe me at first that he was my son. I hadn't really thought about it. I got the boys a couple of drinks and after a little while they decided they were going to try and see what some of the other places were like. Becky was making noises about going and I didn't know what to do so I told Pam that if she wanted to stay longer I would be happy to take her home. I didn't know what was going to happen. She agreed and stayed.

Later we left and I drove her home. We sat outside for awhile and talked some more. She was staying with friends. She was from some place called New Zealand. As the evening had gone on, the more we visited the more I liked her and really wanted to get to know her. It was the first time in a long time that I had met someone and just liked them, like that. She wrote her phone number down on a paper napkin that I had in the glove box with her lipstick, as we couldn't find anything else to write with.

The next day when I got the paper napkin out. It had become hot in the car being parked in the sun. The lipstick was hard to read and had melted some. I started to panic some and was thinking what if I can't figure out her number. I wasn't sure I could find her house again. It was late that night and I had only been to it once in a town I wasn't familiar with. I started writing down variations of the phone number on what I thought it might be. I started calling these variations of the phone number and asking for Pam. I was lucky and on about the third try I got her. I was relieved. I visited with her a few minutes but the main thing I wanted to know was if–and (if she would) when—would she see me again? She told me yes and I made plans to go by and pick her up that evening. This was the start of my relationship with what was to be my third wife.

We found we both liked a lot of the same things and enjoyed each other's company. We started spending a lot of time together and this didn't go down really well with the people she was staying with. It seemed that Mr. Burris was not very fond of car salesmen and painted us all with the same brush. He was sure I had no other plans other than to take advantage of her and have my own wicked way with her. He had a few talks with her and would have been very happy if she would stop seeing me. As he told her "Nothing good ever comes from meeting people in bars". For whatever reason she didn't listen to him and continued to see me. It didn't take long and before I knew it I was wanting to spend every spare minute with her.

Sometimes she would just come over to my place and we would fix dinner, watch TV and visit. One time when she was there alone, the phone rang and when she answered it, a woman's voice asked for me. She thought it must have been Linda as the next thing she knew they hung up. A few days later I got a letter in the mail from Linda. The summary of it was she was mad. She felt I had deceived her and the real reason I didn't want to see her now was that I was seeing someone else. She never wanted to see or hear from me again. I was sorry she felt this way but when I had decided to stop seeing her it was what I felt was the best for us. I knew I didn't love her and didn't want to marry her. It was only by chance that Pam had just come into my life. I decided maybe it was for the best for Linda. This way she could be mad at me and maybe that would make it easier for her.

In a way I was sorry it had ended this way between Linda and I but I also felt a relief that it was one piece of unfinished business that was now taken care of, even if it had been by accident.

CHAPTER 47

GETTING DOWN TO WORK

Work went well for me and before I knew it, George and I had made our first bonus for the year; $3,000. The Maunds were happy with my work and told me we would have a base pay rise to $2,500 per month. It was not all roses as there are always some problems. The main focus of our problem, and would be for a long time, was Bryan Pascoe, the used car manager.

The joke around the dealership was that Bryan was an illegitimate son of Charles Maund. As the story went—which was all fiction but sometimes you had to wonder—was that Charles had been away on business many years before and had an encounter . . . Bryan being the result who looked him up years later. Charles being responsible, took him in as a car man and tried to teach him the used car business and provide a future for him. That is why, no matter how incompetent Bryan seemed to be, Charles always understood and Bryan never got into any trouble and was always paid way more than he was worth. This seemed to hold for years until a surprise came to be, years later.

The story that did happen as I was to learn over a period of time, went like this. Charles Maund had a used car manager who had been with him a long time. He had been known to drink a little too much at times but even worse, was his habit of going after women—even if they were married. It seems he became involved with one of the salesmen's wives and when the salesman learned of it, after they had some words, he returned to the used car lot office with a gun. He then proceeded to shoot and kill the used car manager before turning the gun on himself.

The young man who was good at making impressions on one and all at that time was Bryan Pascoe. He was moved up to used car manager. Under the old system, the used car manager was on a different pay plan. He was paid a percentage of the used car department's profits. The plan went back to the late 50's and the percentage had remained at a level that was now too high for a dealership of this size. Bryan didn't care if he took trades from the new car department as his focus was only on his department. If he had 5 used Oldsmobiles and that is all he wanted, then he would give us a very low price for the trade. If he got it, he could make a lot of money; if he didn't, he didn't care as he already had a good stock on the lot. This could cost us deals in the new car department and often did. This is of course was overlooking the fact that Bryan also didn't know a good vehicle if it jumped up and bit him in the ass.

Bryan had no limit on his number of vehicles or a monetary limit. Mr Charles Maund always said it was better than money in the bank. Where else could he put $8,000 in something and sell it in say 30 days, and make $1,500. He said the trade-ins should all be traded for at wholesale market value if need be, to make a new car deal. The used vehicle could then be sold retail or wholesaled off, if he had too many. Bryan was encouraged to "steal" the trade, as the new car salesman was paid on a unit basis—so much for each car sold, regardless of the amount of profit. The used car department salesmen were paid on how much profit they made and they were to make all they could but they had a cap of $175 commission per unit sold.

This way if the car was traded for cheaply on the new car side, the new car salesman would still get his $45. The used car salesman could make a gross profit of $1,500 on the trade-in but was capped at $175 commission on the sale. The dealership then keeping most of the profit. This worked fairly well except for two things.

Firstly, Bryan, along with the times, had increased the volume and the profit per vehicle and his percentage now meant that some months his pay could be as high as $10,000. It was known that on really big months his pay would be much more. This was far more than the Maunds had ever planned but Charles was a man of his word and he stuck to it, as it was the agreement and the deal he originally made. This encouraged Bryan to keep as much of the profit in the used car department as he could. Over a year's time, Bryan would usually make upwards of $150,000 a year.

Secondly, with Bryan not profiting from the dealership and the new car department doing well, he had no incentive to co-operate with us to make a car deal and sell a new car. In fact it was in his interest to "steal" as many trades as he could. If he didn't like the car or want it, then the price he gave us was so low he made sure we didn't get it. This is where we had problems selling new cars and needed a cure.

George had come up through the ranks as a salesman at the dealership and there was some bad blood between he and Bryan. It also seemed that Charles didn't like George a lot for some reason but Doug did, so he was made new Oldsmobile manager. When, at one of the manager's meetings, it came up about how we could make more deals, it was mentioned that we had a problem with the prices we were getting on the appraisals of the trade-ins. At first it was the usual reaction that we always say that. Then after some talking it over we seemed to hit on a plan but had opposition from Bryan.

This plan was given notice only after the previous General (and Cadillac) Manager, Bill McLean, retired. He had been with Mr. Maund for many years and was the only other person to own any of the dealership other than the family. They were looking at his replacement when they started to think about Dale McConnell. He had been a salesman with him in Cadillac but had quit and was now an independent used car operator who was mainly doing wholesale. He had become disgusted with Bryan and his appraisals to the point he felt it was costing him too many deals and thus income, so he left. He had expressed this to me when I first came to the dealership, which was about the time he quit.

I had become acquainted with one of the older Cadillac salesmen named Gene Webb. He was a hard worker and a company man. He was helping out by doing the ordering and helped keep track of the Cadillac inventory. I suggested they consider him for the job of Cadillac sales manager if they wanted to promote from within but the Maunds seemed to really have a thing about Dale and he was younger, being about mid-30's. They negotiated a pay plan with Dale and he became the new Cadillac Manager and General Manager. I later learned his income was more than Bryan's was on a yearly basis.

When Dale came back as manager, George and I felt we had a real chance for changes. Dale was still a bit careful but did join us in presenting the plan to Mr. Maund. The idea was finally heard and put into place. The idea was simple. Bryan would appraise the cars. If we needed more for the car to make a deal we would get back with Bryan and if he gave us enough to make a deal, fine. If not, then he was to turn it over to George or me, and we could shop the trade-in to try and get enough for the vehicle. If we made a deal, then the trade-in was ours to wholesale to whoever gave us enough to make a deal. This was something I had done in Boerne when needed. It was now up to me to make sure the people I contacted would honor the deal and buy the vehicle from me at the agreed price. George knew a few dealers in Austin and would try them as well.

I knew that some of the used car dealers in San Antonio were always interested in good vehicles. I talked to Harvey Harper, Denny Stephens in Mineral Wells (who had worked for Cecil in the past), and several others. They all felt they could work with me and all agreed to give it a try. We now had a way to try and get market value to make a deal once Bryan no longer wanted the trade-in.

I should have known this was not going to be easy. Bryan tried every way to make the deal go away. He would turn the car back to us and we would make a trade. My man would drive up to Austin to pick the car up on say Tuesday, only to find that Bryan had sold the car to one of his wholesalers on Monday. This happened a number of times but my people stuck with me, knowing he was playing a game.

Another thing that happened was that I would appraise cars when I was the manager on duty in the evening or after he left on Saturday, or if he was off the lot—which was often. I had earned this responsibility after the Maunds saw I had the ability to appraise vehicles the way they wanted them appraised. What Bryan would do, is stick the vehicle to the side and sometimes either wholesale or retail them at a loss, and then say I had appraised them too high. He was told to inform me at once if he had such a trade-in come in to him. I was then to see if I could wholesale the vehicle. He tried me a number of times on this at first, only to find that I was able to wholesale the vehicle for the amount.

I worked with the salesmen from all three sales departments—Oldsmobile, Cadillac and used cars—when I was the manager on duty. I learned after awhile that the used car salesmen were not all happy with Bryan. At first I put this down to the standard complaining salesman do at all dealerships. They then started telling me of how he would charge his girlfriend's car repairs to used cars and how various wholesalers who had purchased good merchandise gave him gifts from time to time. The suggestion that money was sometimes the gift also came up. All of this was interesting and may have explained why he was so protective of his patch but no evidence could be produced.

I worked as acting used car manager when Bryan would go off on vacation. I stayed and worked most of the day in the used car office—only doing what I had to on car orders in the Oldsmobile sales office. I found a number of suspicious charges to used vehicles and found the systems very loose and open for possible abuse. I had no proof so to go and run off at the mouth to Dale or the Maunds was a sure-fire way to get into trouble. With this in mind I decided to keep quiet and just watch for now.

As in all dealerships, you have to learn the ropes. When I first got my demo it was nice and clean but of course became dirty. The dealership had a number of porters but they all had their jobs to do. One day during my lunch hour I went over behind the used car lot and used their facilities for washing cars. I was told not to do that again and to get someone else to. Easier said than done but in a few months the dealership put in a full size automatic car wash so all I had to do was drive through it.

On another occasion when I was appraising a used car, as I pulled out on the road in front of the building, it just quit. I coasted off the edge of the road and opened the hood. I wanted to see if I could see why it quit, for several reasons, and wanted to warn people it was broken down. A few minutes went by when one of the men from inside the building said Charles had sent him out to tell me to leave the car alone. He wanted me to get the used car mechanic to look at it and worry about moving it.

It was with a few of these experiences that I learned I was to stop doing everything as I had always had to in the past. I was hired to manage, to point and tell. He didn't want us spending our time on things others should do. It took some getting used to.

It was a large place of 11 acres. At any one time I would have about 300 Oldsmobiles on the ground and Dale would have about 150 Cadillacs. Bryan usually had about 125 to 150 use cars. The service department, parts department, body shop, and parking areas took up a large amount of the space. I think all up there were about 175 employees. I had 16 salesmen, Cadillac about 8, and used cars about 8.

The amount of time to get a vehicle in stock from paper to the dealership was about 45 days. We were to try and keep about 90 days of inventory available between what was on the ground and what was on its way. Many a time if we didn't have the vehicle in stock we might have it due in within days. If this were not an option we would trade for a vehicle from other dealers. We mainly traded in an area from Houston to San Antonio, and as far north and south. Some weeks we would do none, or one or two. Other weeks we might do 4 or 5. As George and I worked out a better system and I spent more time on it, we reduced the number of trades we needed to make and sold more out of stock or from those due in any day.

The Maunds wanted to make as much money as they could out of their operation. They were fortunate in that over the years Charles had paid everything off and owed no one any money. With this extra capital available they would try things for themselves. They saw that doing interior and exterior protective coatings was a big business. They bought the product in bulk and our new car department did it and the dealership self-insured the guarantee. For a number of years vinyl tops were popular. They hired 3 full-time employees to install vinyl tops in our body shop. The new car managers would then tell them which cars in stock to put vinyl tops on, body side moldings, and pin stripes. This increased our profit at the dealership.

These were the basics I did on a regular basis—the other thing being that each week George and I would work over and decide what newspaper ad would be run. As time went on, this became my responsibility and the budget was $50,000 a month for newspaper advertising. The Maunds did not like other forms of advertising, such as radio and TV, and so we were instructed to stay in the newspaper. This was one of the things where they were set in their ways. I felt we were missing out on exposure and wasting money by spending so much just in the paper. However, it was their money and they were the boss.

CHAPTER 48

Continuing Education

In the back of the main building of the dealership behind the showroom on the right hand end, was an apartment. This was past the offices of Dale McConnell and Charles Maund, down a short hallway. The apartment had a large living room area and a dining room. To the side was a desk and sofa in case Mr Maund wanted to work in there. Across from this was a kitchen and at the end of the room was a hallway that led to a back door that went to the outside. Off the hallway was a bedroom and bathroom.

The floor was wood parquet covered by a very large Persian rug. The furniture was expensive and on the table in the living area was a Remington sculpture. Various original oil paintings were around the room on the walls. I was told the rug alone was worth over $100,000. Built into a cabinet was a large TV with cable. This was an area that was only available to the Maunds—although it was okay for Dale McConnell, at the end of a day, to go in and get a drink sometimes before he went home.

On the days when Mr. Maund planned on being at the dealership for lunch he would have Ella Lee cook for him in the apartment. Ella Lee had worked for him for years and originally helped bring up the kids at the house. When they became older and she was no longer needed for this, Charles gave her a job at the dealership. She would cook lunch for him and do some of the cleaning in the main building. One of the salesmen used to joke when she would vacuum his office. He would say, "Isn't it funny how time flies, another month gone already". She was just one of several black people that he had on the plantation plan. They had worked for him for years and rather than let them go when they were no longer needed, he would find a place for them and keep them on.

As I got to know Mr. Maund and Ella Lee, I was invited to lunch in the back. He would usually have Bryan Pascoe, Dale McConnell and an Oldsmobile sales manager. If he had a guest, such as factory reps, he would usually drop one of the managers. Over a period of time I became a regular for lunch in the back. It was at these lunch time meetings we would talk about problems, various things to do or not do, tell stories about what had happened in the past, and suggestions were made that were aimed at us for guidance in what he would like done.

He felt the meetings were good as it was a break from out front and he didn't want us disturbed when we were with him at lunch. It gave us a chance to exchange ideas. It gave him a chance to ask us questions and point out mistakes he didn't want repeated. He would also give us his philosophy on how he wanted us to run his business. He told me to give a customer anything we owed him or promised him and if we didn't owe him anything not to worry about it. He would stand behind us. We were to sort out problems and find solutions that made sense. Sometimes it might be a misunderstanding; sometimes the customer might be trying us on but if it made sense to give away something, then to do it . . . after all, we were spending a lot of money to get people in each month; we didn't need to try and make enemies.

An example of just such a problem, as well as the difference in the way in which George and I would handle it, came up with a couple of customers. They took delivery on their new vehicles and returned later to complain they found a scratch on the bumper of their new car. They were sure it was not there when they picked the car out but didn't check the car over at time of delivery and were sure we must have done it. George told the man he owned the car when he left in it and there was no way to know when or where it had happened. Therefore it was his problem and to hit the road. The customer left unhappy and said he would tell all his friends.

I had a similar case and felt the man was genuine in his belief even if it was erroneous. I pointed out some of the same arguments but offered a solution that was different. We would go out and pick out a demonstrator of the same model and I would have the bumpers switched. The customer agreed and went home happy. The demonstrator was always sold with a few nicks and dings as a rule and the people expected it. So for the price of an hour's labor in the shop, we saved a customer. Over the years I don't think I gave away a total of $1,000. And not once did Mr. Maund ever question so much as one of the transactions.

It was only after several years that he told me the basic story of his background, at lunch one day. It seems his parents died when he was very young and an aunt and uncle in east Texas raised him. When he was a young lad he would go down to the farmers' market where produce was brought in to be sold. He got a job grading tomatoes and put the rejects to the side. The farmers could take a small amount for the rejects or take them with them back home. He would buy the rejects from the farmers and stay after closing. In the early evening, a Jewish produce merchant from the town would come and buy the rejects from him. He said he made more off the sale of the rejects than he did from his hourly wage as a grader. When the company offered him a promotion to oversee some of this area he refused, as he would have lost out on the seconds and would have made less money.

He then told us a story about how he would go into a shop that was selling avocados for $1.00 each. He would look at them each day and wonder what they were like for he had never eaten one as $1 was a lot of money. He knew nothing about them but in spite of this, he figured that if they were charging that much they had to be good. So he got a dollar out and bought one. He took it outside to eat it and it was hard and green. He said it was awful. He knew then they really had a deal going for them if they could get $1.00 a piece for those things. Later in life when he learned what to look for and how to eat them with some lemon juice on them, they became one of his favorite foods and we would have them often at lunchtime.

Later, as he grew older, he worked at the ship docks when World War II broke out. He made good money and saved some up. After the war, cars were scarce at first. You had to have a ration coupon during and right after the war, in order to buy a car. He got to know a guy in Port Arthur, Texas, and started selling cars with him. They went into business together for a period of time and built the business up. They had a falling out and Charles wanted out and into a dealership of his own.

He spoke to the factory reps and they told him Mr. Goud who had Cadillac and Oldsmobile in Victoria, San Antonio, and Austin, Texas, might be willing to sell the store in Austin. Charles was interested in a franchise that was to be offered in Corpus Christi but they told him he wouldn't have enough money for that operation. He was instead, advised to consider the one in Austin even though he didn't like the idea of Austin much as it was a sleepy little town, and the action and development was in Corpus.

But the factory let him know that if he wanted a franchise with only as much money as he had, he only had a shot at the one in Austin. He purchased the store and after it was set up and changed over, he had enough money in the bank for about 3 weeks. He said none of the bankers wanted to know him or help him and he never forgot it. He struggled at first and did almost everything himself—including going out and making repossessions. He told himself that if he could ever get the store paid off, he was going to stay out of debt.

He put all the money back into the store to pay it off and he and his family lived very modestly. He started financing his own car deals that were good, so he could make the money himself. As time went on he grew larger and went into business with others in other dealerships, property, and apartment complexes. He said his one rule he had stuck to was to get out of, and stay out of, debt, as much as possible. When he moved from the downtown area of Austin to Research Blvd., he paid cash for the land and all of the facilities at the new place.

This advantage kept growing over the years and he would pay for all of his cars as they came in, so as not to pay interest on the inventory. When General Motors offered reduced interest rates to dealers to get them to keep their inventory up during times of high interest, he and several other dealers asked what their incentive was. General Motors said none. They felt this was unfair and took GM to court. He and the other dealers won the case and the settlement was that as long as they paid cash for their cars, they would get an extra 1.4% discount off the price of the cars. This doesn't sound like much but multiply 1.4% times 300 Oldsmobiles at $10,000 and 150 Cadillacs at $20,000 per month and this makes the dealership about $84,000 a month more or about $1,000,000 a year, just from that.

Charles Maund was known in many circles and his honesty was respected in them all. He was known to have a passion at times for gambling and would bet on football games. He played cards a lot—often for very high stakes. He kept this separate from the dealership and his private life was kept separate as well.

He would walk down to the Oldsmobile end of the building sometimes just to see what was going on and ask how many had been sold. If he was out at his ranch on Saturday he would always call in before closing to find out how many each department had sold.

After I had settled in at the dealership, he and Doug told me that there were two things they really wanted to do. One was to outsell Covert Buick in town, our major competition, and the other was to sell as many Oldsmobiles as possible to get our market penetration up. They knew it was only a matter of time before the factory would put in another Oldsmobile dealer but the longer they could keep it to themselves the more money we would all make. The more we sold and the higher the penetration, the better. The service department rating was important and needed to move up in the zone standings and they were working on this as well.

In time, they added a new waiting room to the service department and changed the service manager to Tiny Krespa. They gave him a lot of what he asked for and almost from then on, we had very few service complaints that ever came up to the front for us to take care of.

The salesmen were also a part of the new factory rating system and they were to be graded on product knowledge, sales presentation, and other basic understanding of things such as the warranty. Oldsmobile had a checklist that each salesman was to go over with each customer at time of delivery. The factory would follow up with a mailout to the customer asking them questions about how well the salesman had done. We were then scored on these responses. This was an area that I was given as part of my job to make sure the salesmen did their part and kept our scores up.

The hard one was market penetration. We had a lot of pump-ins that were a problem. This is when a fleet customer sends a lot of cars into an area such as Austin—either by courtesy delivery or delivered straight to the rental lots such as Hertz or Avis. Other sales that were minor but also counted against us, were when another dealer sold a car in our area; like Gunn Oldsmobile of San Antonio or Classic Oldsmobile in Round Rock, Texas.

We sold a lot of cars out of our area so they actually ended up counting against us, increasing Oldsmobile's market share in these other areas. We would then be expected to have as high a market share but the only sales that counted were those in the Austin area. Even Mr. Maund knew we were in a losing battle but he wanted us to do what we could. He knew the fleet business was not something he wanted, even if he could get it. We would be selling the cars at dead cost plus $25. We would tie up the shop, the clean-up area, and the office, all for just numbers. In fact it would probably cost us money.

Nevertheless we were to explore some new areas such as leasing, and specialty vehicles like conversions, which were Doug's idea. He came across a company that would take a Toranado, cut the top off and make a convertible out of it. This would increase the price of the car by about $10,000. This did not turn out to be a successful venture. We also started using a company that would take the Calais small car and add spoilers, air foils and such, and made them more like a sports car (for about $1,000). This did work to the degree that we made a little more money on them, and sold about an extra half dozen or so cars a month.

In the Houston Zone for Oldsmobile, the dealership was usually in the area of the top three. One year we outsold Cavender Oldsmobile in San Antonio and Ed Hollis, the then-manager, called us up to congratulate us on a fine year. It was the first time Charles Maund had outsold them that we knew of. Ed Hollis at Cavender and David Moffit at Gunn Oldsmobile in San Antonio, were some of our competition in some ways but were also some of the best to work with on trades, or if you ever needed any help. The unwritten rule was to never trade for a car on a deal from them and then turn around and send it back to that town. This worked both ways. Charles Maund Oldsmobile was about the 21st largest selling Oldsmobile dealership in the United States and was the largest-selling dual line Oldsmobile-Cadillac dealership in the country. It was a continuing educational experience working for them in many ways.

CHAPTER 49

PAM RETURNS TO NEW ZEALAND

It seemed the games Cecile wanted to play never ended. Sharon had wanted to meet Cecile as she felt their mother might like to have some sort of feel for the person her kids were spending time around. I told Sharon this wouldn't happen and it didn't. We had previously agreed on a procedure that Cecile preferred. No one was to come to the door but instead I would honk the horn in the driveway to let them know I was there to pick the kids up. I always picked them up and if Sharon was going to pick them up, I let Cecile know of the change in advance.

After Pam and I had been going together for some time she offered to go to San Antonio and pick the kids up. This way if she went down on Friday afternoon, she could be back by the time I got off work. This would allow me to spend more time with the kids. This was shot down at first. Cecile didn't want to meet Pam but she didn't want just anybody driving her kids. I assured her she had not only a New Zealand driver's license but also an International license, as well as a Texas driver's license. But it still took some time before this was allowed.

This was just one of the games she started out of the clear blue sky. She had previously pulled the stunt of holding onto the pictures, movie film, and the china. I still called each week to talk to the kids as the dealership had an 800 line for long-distance that we could use during off-hours for personal use. I still got through to the kids only about half the time and never knew if the message was passed on. I still had continual problems such as plans having been made for a church camp on my weekend or they were to go somewhere with them. I could not see what could be accomplished by causing a fight so I continued to go along and get them when I could–even though it was far from even.

Sam came up to see me several times at first, fairly frequently. One time when he got there he told me the truck had started making funny noises. I went out and had him start the motor. Sure enough it sounded like a rod was about to let go. I let him take the GTO back for the week and I had one of the Chevrolet dealers haul it in for repairs. They did a motor job on it during the week under the warranty and Sam picked it up the next weekend. It was not long after this that he sold the truck, put the money in the bank and was waiting for another vehicle to come along that he liked.

Sue at the dealership in Boerne had started calling me several times a week with questions. It seems Cecil had turned more and more over to her, for her to do. This included ordering cars, some trucks, doing a preference list, and how to handle all sorts of related problems. I felt sorry for her and tried to do what I could. Cecil should have taken me up on my offer to help before I left, instead of ignoring me. I don't know if someone said something or not but one day after I got off the phone, the Maunds asked me if that was Boerne calling me all the time. I told them that they needed some help and had a few questions, and I was just trying to help them out some. They let me know they didn't want it to turn into a full-time job holding their hand.

It was around this time I decided to sell the GTO. I just didn't want to have to worry about what might happen with it. I talked to Harvey Harper and he agreed to put it on his lot and charge me a commission if he sold it. None of us knew what it would bring. It took only about 3 weeks and he called me up and told me he had a buyer for the car. He needed to charge me for another spare tire as someone had stolen it out of the trunk. This was a shame because I had found the last set of Uniroyal Tiger Paw tires like the original equipment that came on it back in 1967. I told him it was okay to do the deal and he said next time up he would bring me the money as the man had paid him cash. He brought me $2,100 for the car. I think I must have recouped almost all I had put in the car.

I decided I needed to replace the car. In the business they used to say you always need a getaway car as you never knew when you might need one. I also thought Pam needed one she could use when she needed a car. She was sharing a car at the Burris's house with the others but this didn't always work out. Especially if she wanted to come and see me on her own.

Bryan started to trade for a 1976 Oldsmobile Cutlass Calais coupe with a large 454 V8 motor in it. The car was baby blue with a white interior and bucket seats. It had all the power equipment, automatic transmission, and air conditioning. It had a water leak that had ruined the carpet, and it needed some other minor repairs as well as some maintenance and paintwork. The miles were low but Bryan just didn't like the car. I asked him if we traded for it, if I could buy it. He said he would think about it but was sure he would sell it to me.

He added, as I remember, about $500 to the price we traded for it for, and I bought it for $800. I then sent it out to a couple of the shops for tires, interior work, and paint work, and had the used car mechanic fix the leak and do some of the maintenance. I then had a bill of about $1,000. Bryan said I had spent too much, which I had, except I planned on keeping the car and letting Pam use it.

I then contacted Pam, showed her the car and told her it was hers to hold on to and use. She was happy as she now had her own way to get around. She could go places to do things, or come and see me and not have to worry about getting the car back for someone else to use.

This made me happy as well. This was now late spring of 1982 and Pam had just turned 29 in May. She had been planning on going to work in Canada for the New Zealand government at the High Commission but the girl that was leaving decided to stay on and the opening then fell through. Before Pam had left New Zealand, she and her husband had split up and she had filed for divorce. She wanted to get away from everything and had planned on going to Canada for awhile where she had met some people previously. She was then going on to England and Europe with some friends. This didn't work out partly due to the lack of funds.

First of all, it takes about two years to get a divorce in New Zealand. She didn't want to stay and part of her agreement was that her ex was to send her lawyer her share of the equity in their house so she could continue her trip. He didn't do this and was holding back on selling the house or borrowing the money for her share. He was trying to force her to come back, which she didn't want to do. She then heard of the job at the High Commission and upon application all but had the job. However, she needed to leave the country of Canada and then apply to return with a work permit. She could do this through the Canadian Consulate office in Dallas but Christmastime was coming up. Her friends in Austin told her to come and stay with them while she waited until after the first of the year to apply through Dallas. Unfortunately it was after this she found out the job had fallen through.

The Burris family put her up and wanted her to stay. They wrote letters and got her visitor's visa extended but she was now at the end of her time and it appeared she could get no further extensions. Besides, she had run out of money and needed to return to New Zealand as she had no Green Card and could not work legally in the States.

I was not happy with the idea of her returning to New Zealand. She was sure that after a few things were taken care of she could get another visa and get back into the States but what then? I really didn't know what to do. All we could do at this stage was to agree to stay in touch. She gave me her phone number and mailing address in Palmerston North and asked me if I had taken my vacation that year. I said no, so she asked if I would like to come to New Zealand and see the place. I told her I would see how it went and I would try to make the trip but I only would be able to get a week off. It would take a day to fly out and a day to fly back; this left 5 days to see something.

The same problems with Bryan persisted but with our plan in place we were usually able to overcome his low appraisals. Sometimes he would bid a car low, simply because he was either unfamiliar with them or had limited experience in selling them. This happened when we were trying to trade for a Pontiac Trans Am that was a special model which came in a gold color paint scheme with the 400 T/A motor and the extras like T-tops. The car needed some work but was a good model and the car was sound. He priced the car ridiculously low as he didn't like Trans Ams. After he turned the car back to us I got on the phone to Harvey, and to Cecil and Sam. I wanted to know first, if they were interested in it and next, if Sam might want the car as he still had his money in the bank. Bryan ended up letting us have the car for something like $3,500. After Sam spent some money on it and fixed it up, Harvey offered him $5,000 for it. It was a good buy for Sam.

Sam Jr. with Sam Sr. and the gold Trans Am

When Sam and the other kids first came up to Austin with me after I moved there, we would sometimes go around the town and I would show them some of the sights where I went to school and where we used to live. I would point out places such as the 'Tower' at the University of Texas where the shootings had taken place, as well as Barton Springs and some of the parks where I would take them for some time to play and take some pictures of them. It was very difficult to do much when all I really had was Saturday night and part of Sunday, as I also had to be the one to go after them.

Sam, Laurie, Scott and Craig in front of Littlefield Fountain and University of Texas 'Tower' at Austin in 1982

When Pam left and went back to New Zealand I found myself very lost. I spent a lot of time writing to her and running my phone bill up to ridiculous levels talking to her. It was over this time period we both came to the same conclusion. We wanted to continue the relationship to see how it would turn out. We decided that I would come out and meet her family and some of her friends, and see a little of the country.

She would then come back with me to the States and live with me—and not Leo and Mary Burris. She would come back on a tourist visa and we would go through separate immigration lines. If we could not get renewals on her visa, after a while we could always get married. If it didn't work out we could always get divorced—it wouldn't be the first for either of us. We had found out to get into the country being engaged or married without papers would be a nightmare. The easiest way was to get in, and then get married, and then do the paper work for immigration and then apply for a 'Green Card'.

Pam didn't want to upset her folks or the Burris family. She wanted to talk to her folks and get their blessing, and then hope to get the Burris family to understand and go along with our living together, as well. We even went so far as to get her mother to write a note to the Burris's saying it was okay and to please understand that we were only being sensible. We wouldn't know how they would react until we returned and saw them.

It was a big step for me as I was going to be responsible for her and would have to support her as well. It would be some time before she could get a 'Green Card' and be able to go to work if she decided to. I knew I wanted her there with me but would still have a little attack of cold feet. I did have some fear it might not work out but then again, I didn't like the idea of not trying at all. The separation reinforced for me, the fact I didn't want to be without her and I had to try. I wanted us to be together.

CHAPTER 50

QUICK TRIP TO NEW ZEALAND

I made arrangements to go on my trip to New Zealand, returning on Labor Day weekend when I could have the Monday off as it was a holiday, which would give me an extra day off. I arrived at Auckland airport at about 6 o'clock in the morning. As I came out of immigration and customs I saw Pam with her folks, waiting for me. She asked what I would have done if she hadn't shown up. I told her I guess I would have made arrangements to stay in the area and see what I could during the week before I went back to the States. There wasn't much else I could have done.

We met Paddy and Guy Ronaldson for breakfast—Pam's mother's first cousin. We then went to Thames and stayed at Thornton Bay in a little bach they had. We then proceeded to Palmerston North, seeing what we could along the way. I met family and friends, and one evening we all went out to dinner together. I remember the Chisholms, as well as her Aunt Joan and Uncle Kit. There were a number of others as well, such as their close friends and some of the people they worked with. I felt like I was most welcome but did wonder if I wasn't maybe being subjected to review for possible approval.

Typical dirt road through the bush on the Coromandel Peninsula

We also made a quick trip over to Pam's friends' farm. Pat and Rob Orr showed us around and we stayed the night. Rob showed me his project on bio-gas as he had great plans to develop a plant that could be built on a farm, which would convert waste into methane gas to be collected, stored, and then used in various farm equipment. The leftovers could then also be sprayed onto the farm as fertilizer, completing the recycling of by-products. It was most interesting and he asked me to try and get him a few items, including some accounting software, upon my return to the States.

Rob with his gas plant and spray truck

No sooner did I seem to get there than it was time for Pam and I to go. She decided, being practical, that she had a number of items that would come in handy upon our return. These included household items and things such as kitchen utensils. She put these in one of her suitcases to bring back with us. If immigration had taken a look, I think we would have had more explaining to do than we would have wanted to but we didn't really think about it at the time.

Pam did get worried something might go wrong as we flew back and by the time we got to Los Angeles airport she had just about made herself sick. As we stood in different immigration lines she told one of the people she felt sick. They took her off to the side and put her through immigration. I don't know if this helped speed things up for her or not but she was through and in the country.

We checked into our hotel near the airport it was about 5:30 PM. We then decided to catch a shuttle bus to Disneyland a few miles away. Little did we know that by the time we would get there, the closing fireworks display would be going off. We had time to get a hotdog and ride only about 3 rides before we had to catch the last shuttle bus back. I told her the way I figured it; we had a bus ride and a $50 hotdog, as that was about all we got out of it for the price.

The next morning we got started and were ready to get underway when we decided to look at the tickets again. We then noticed we had looked on the wrong line the previous day for the time and the way I saw it, if we ran to the window of our hotel real quick, we could see our plane taking off out the window in the distance. We had missed our plane on a holiday weekend! Would I be able to get back to get to work on time? We didn't know.

We decided to go to the airport and see about getting another flight. We were lucky as we were able to get on another one and we got into Austin only a few hours late. We had called the Burris family, as they were to pick us up at the airport. It was at this time that Pam knew she would need to talk to them soon about moving in with me. Pam decided to wait a couple of days until things settled down before talking to Leo and Mary Burris.

When she did try and talk to them they became very upset. Pam gave them the letter from her mother in hopes that it might help. It didn't. They almost told her to never see them again but didn't. Leo had told her once that if she ever showed up with a Black he would shoot him. I wasn't black and that is the only thing that saved me from being shot by him. As it all came out, they were more worried about what the neighbors might say more than anything else. It took some time before they got over it and Pam could see them again. Leo never did like me and after this he could just barely stay civil.

As we started living together in the duplex we enjoyed doing more things together. For the first time since I couldn't remember when, I wasn't worried about the bills and money. I still had some payments but my income had increased to the point that they were not a worry. The job was going well and I don't think I could have asked for much more. I was starting to get my life back under control and felt with time, things would work out. I would even be in a position to help the kids if they needed it.

I got a call that fall that Sam had been in an accident. It seems he was driving a car from the dealership, a Chevrolet Citation, and was returning from Denise's house back to Boerne. The roads were wet and he was most likely driving too fast. He went into a curve and lost control and slid sideways across into the other lane. A large full size Ford hit him broadside and tore the car into two pieces. One half went off the highway in one direction and the other half went off in the other. I gathered he was unconscious at first and had been knocked around with the floor gearshift cutting into his back. He had been taken to the hospital in San Antonio but would be okay. With all the other family there and with him going to be released in 24 hours, they all said I shouldn't come down, as there was no need. They also wanted my insurance information as I had him listed as a dependent on my medical cover at the dealership.

Everyone was co-operative when he was in the hospital but after he was out I found it very difficult to get information the insurance company wanted. It took me numerous times before Cecile gave me the information I needed and some copies that the hospital had given her. Sometime later I got a refund of a small amount from the insurance company. I decided to keep it as it would have been okay for me to be out of pocket, and I would have been if I hadn't persisted in my efforts for the copies to be sent to me. I just couldn't be bothered in seeing how or if it should be divided up.

This was an early signal of unhappy times to come for Sam. It seems he had started into a series of getting stopped and charged with DWI. He lost his license for awhile as I remember and had to do community service. He also got into some real trouble about hitting another boy with his car. My understanding was that the other boy and his friends had started to pick a fight with Sam and his friends inside a roller rink. They followed them outside to the parking lot as Sam and his friends started to get in the car and leave. They started acting like they were going to hit the car and various other acts of jumping in and out at them. Sam took off and swerved as if to miss or hit one of them, just as the boy jumped. It seems the car hit him. According to Sam he didn't know he had hit him until the police came looking for him. I don't know exactly what happened after this because Cecil took it over with his lawyer friends and after some time and effort, the whole thing was dropped.

I have always wondered if there wasn't some sort of payout, most likely from the insurance company . . . especially if this is what the other boy was after—getting some money out of it. This raised my suspicions that maybe it wasn't such a good idea for Sam to be living with Cecil. Maybe he would have been in as much trouble if he was with me but I have always doubted it.

When the time came for Sam to make some decisions about college I was told his scores on the entrance test were not high enough for him to get into the University of Texas in Austin without taking some remedial courses in a couple of subjects. This only meant that he would have to take a course for a semester in say math, until he had a basic knowledge level to go on with. I found it hard to understand how he hadn't scored well enough but this was not a problem. Sam told me how Cecil had told him he wouldn't be able to make it in Austin and he should stay with him and go to school down there. I tried to assure him it would be okay and he could live with me and I could help him. He also didn't want to leave Denise and his friends. I told him it was up to him if he decided to stay. I mainly wanted him to just go to university.

As he proceeded through school we talked a number of times about what he might want to do. One was marine biology. Cecil told him there was no future or money in it. Another time he told me he was interested in computers. Cecil told him that wasn't anything, punching holes in cards. A couple of other ideas came and went. To look around today and see how they beg for people in marine biology for all kinds of research in various industries, food, drug, and just basic research. Computers . . . well not much should need to be said with everyone wanting people at all levels, programming, networks, web pages, you name it.

As time went on, it became more obvious why Cecil wanted him to stay. He wanted to control Sam. He had Sam work part-time while going to school, which was fine. But when Sam dropped out he made no real effort to get him to go back to school. He gave him jobs and guided him into filling the positions in which he needed help. Cecil wanted a long-term replacement for the dealership and Sam didn't need a degree for that. He made him Service Manager and Sam did an excellent job for him. He did warranty claims and got the dealership up in its standings. He did all you could ask and more, in the years to come. Cecil still paid him peanuts. At one point he told me he was being paid $2,000 a month. The job was worth twice that much in a dealership that size. And what about the future for my kids, his grandchildren? He never gave Sam any cut of the dealership as promised. I didn't think he would treat one of his favorite grandchildren this way and take advantage of them. But he did, time and time again.

Craig did well in school and wanted to go with his friend to Baylor University. His friend was offered a full football scholarship, Craig wasn't. But he did tell Craig that if he would come and go out for football, he was sure that not only would he get a spot on the team but very possibly a scholarship. This was a year later than Sam, as Craig was a year younger. Craig told Cecile and Walter what he wanted to do and got the papers for Baylor. They said they didn't want to give the information to the school about their financial position in order for him to be considered for any kind of scholarship. He was disappointed as they also said they couldn't afford for him to go to Baylor as well. They then turned around and told him they would think about it and to give them the papers. It was only at the 11th hour that he found out they didn't send the papers in, as they didn't want to give the information to the school after all. They wanted him to stay at home and go to school at the University of Texas in San Antonio so that he could also work for them for extra money and a car. He had worked for them in the past for money and when he got his car, they picked it out for him and gave it to him, along with the payment book. I always felt he should have had some say since he was the one having to pay for it.

Scott and Laurie did as they were told and spent a lot of time with them at church and various church-sponsored events. It seems Walt had been involved with the Baptist church before, and when he and Cecile got married she turned religious. In fact she became one of the "born agains" and wanted all of the kids to be as well. She brainwashed them to the point it was trying to poison them against me. I was evil because I drank beer and smoked cigarettes. Laurie would play tapes of songs that had to do with anti-abortion. Her mother now saw everything as black and white and believed that is how they should see it as well. I still to this day, cannot understand why she didn't live what she preached and act Christian in many ways. It was all as if it were a bad interpretation of a bad dream.

We tried to visit with the kids and take them to do things from time to time. It was hard to watch, as they would develop closed minds on many subjects. I could only hope that with time their eyes would open and they would start to see grey and other colors as well.

I felt like we needed more room and we considered looking at new houses. We looked at some and were surprised at the prices as they had gone up in a growing area. We left it for a month or so and started looking again. The same houses had gone up several thousand dollars in that very short time. We didn't like the idea but couldn't do much about it so we started looking with more determination.

The next thing that came up was a problem. We got a renewal on Pam's visa but the next one was going to be a problem as we would need to go to San Antonio. I talked to Sam about going by a place and get a form for Pam. It wasn't that simple as their hours were almost impossible to get in to see anyone. Cecil said he knew someone at the U.S. Marshal's office and that they might be able to help. After some difficulty we were able to get the form through his friend and an extension again for Pam's visa. What to do next time we weren't sure about–we would cross that bridge when we came to it.

CHAPTER 51

THIRD TIME LUCKY

Doug had decided to go on a hunting trip to Africa and was gone for several weeks. George and I ran our end of the dealership and all went well while he was gone. I didn't think anything of it and a few days after Doug was back, he came in and told us that Charlie had said what a good job we had done while he was gone. Charlie then gave us an envelope and told us it was a little something for having done a good job for him while Doug was gone. We opened up our envelopes and each had a check for $5,000. Needless to say I was speechless. I had been told that Charlie was a good man and would treat his help accordingly. I sure couldn't argue with this now.

George filled me in over a period of time with some of the other things he felt I should know about Charlie. I don't know how much truth was in it but I didn't see any sense in rocking the boat. He told me all the prices in the paper should be devisable by 3 for luck. So we would run a car at $8996.00 not $8995.00. Charlie hated red cars and not to stock any as a lot of dealers felt a red car was bad luck. He also told me of some unwritten rules; which were mainly to try to avoid possible problems. I knew from my past experiences that if you fired a Black, or Mexican American, the first thing you had to prove was you weren't discriminating when you did it. Charlie had both Black and Mexican American, as well as female employees.

But he did not have any of these in the sales department. He was afraid of problems if you had to let one of them go. We were not to hire any of the above. He already felt they had enough trouble with the salesmen always chasing the operator or the girls in the office, so to add them to the sales force was only looking for trouble. When they had made their minds up on some things it was no use in fighting the system as you were only looking for trouble. One day we had a woman come in looking for a job in sales and she filled out an application. We told her we didn't have any openings at the time. Doug came in and wanted to know what the hell we were doing. We told him, as he knew we had to take the application and had told her we had no openings. She did have a lot of experience and looked real good on paper. He took the application and later came back to tell us that he had spoken to some of her previous employers off the record. She could sell but was trouble. Anytime anything went wrong and they called her in on something, the first thing she did was start to yell discrimination. In fact she was currently in negotiation with a previous employer. I know all women weren't like this but this didn't advance the cause for us any.

I was sorry it was like this as Steve Ramirez had come up looking for a job in sales a couple of years later. He told me that after I left, his brother got home one night and had been drinking. His brother got into some sort of dispute with someone and ended up in a fight, and he pulled a knife and stabbed and killed the other guy. Steve's brother claimed self-defense and called Steve to get him out of jail. Steve needed to post a bail bond and needed about $1,000. He didn't have enough money but on Saturday, a man had picked up a vehicle that had been in the body shop and gave the money to Steve. Steve used this money for his brother.

When Cecil found out what happened he became very angry. He allowed Steve to keep working until he had enough pay coming to cover his debt to the company and then fired him. Cecil claimed Steve tried to hide it and was going to steal the money. I don't see how he would have figured he could have gotten away with it but I wasn't there. He told Steve he was going to tell everyone he was a thief. Steve was hoping to get a job where someone knew him and would take him on. I told him we had no openings but knew if I told the Maunds the truth about him, he wouldn't get the job anyway. If I didn't tell them and they found out, it would be my neck. It was a shame because I think Steve was okay. I told him he could put me down for a reference if he wanted but I never heard any more after that.

I did find out that the new man in the body shop was the one responsible for the stolen vehicles. He knew Eperson's son and along with a couple of others had worked out a deal. They would let him know what they wanted and as he worked on the vehicles he would get the keys off the keyboard in the office during the day and return at night with the keys. In a matter of hours, the vehicles were in Mexico and sold but MIC Insurance figured it out and had him arrested.

I doubt it would have made any difference in his case but when you don't pay employees enough, and you don't treat them right, then you are looking for trouble. They always said locks only keep honest people honest. It's also said that if a number of the population are tempted and they think they can get away with it, they will try. True, some people always want more, no matter what, and those you can't do much but to watch out for them.

It seems Cecil had been taken advantage of to the tune of about $100,000 in the early days by a bookkeeper who had a girlfriend. It almost busted him. After that he always insisted on an outside auditor. It was a shame his friend Harvey didn't take this tip from Cecil. While I lived in Austin I heard that his bookkeeper had floored all his cars (borrowed money on them and used them for collateral) and by the time Harvey found out he was almost bust and was very deep in debt.

Charlie used not only outside auditors but had a rule that any new employee had a credit check done on them. If they had bad credit and it showed them in debt, he felt it only gave them a reason to steal and thus no job. He also sent out questionnaires to car buyers on both new and old salesmen. He would ask them to verify the figures on the deal for the amount of money, trade-in allowed, and so on. A salesman had been know to get more than one top sheet signed and when it went to the manager it might not be the same as the one the customer had signed.

We had one salesman who sold a lot of cars but he was a bully. He would actually threaten other salesman, saying that the person who came in was his customer and to turn them over to him. He pulled all sorts of tricks. He would even get the customer to pull the trade out of the deal as if they were going to keep it. He would put the amount of cash in to make up the difference. He would then take the trade-in and sell it himself on the side. Boyd Pearson had half the sales force in turmoil. He had a couple of his friends from Houston come over and go to work for us as well; Clarence Cleveland and Eddie Powell.

The switchboard operator's father died and left her some money. She was a nice person but nothing special. As soon as Boyd heard about this he was always hanging around her. He would get her to direct the new car calls to him and she would call him to the desk when someone came in who wanted to see a salesman. It got so bad I finally had to tell him to clean up his act or I would fire him. When I went to Doug and told him what I wanted to do he hesitated at first, until I told him how his disruption of the entire force was actually costing us sales. Not long after this I had to let Boyd go. He stayed after the operator, Shirley, and they did get married. He then proceeded to build her a house and helped her spend her money.

It was unfortunate but later on we had to fire Clarence. His sales had fallen off really badly and he was caught doing a deal on the side with a trade-in. He said he was only buying it for someone he knew but that was still outside the rules. Eddie stayed around for years, and came and went several times.

Pam and I went to Eddie's wedding later on. As I got to know him I found that although he was a very nice person and a super salesman, he had two bad habits. One was gambling to the point he had a real problem with it and the other was a very low pain threshold. Whenever he had the slightest pain he would have to get strong painkillers or the pain would make him climb the walls.

He was one of those people you meet and you just can't help but like them. He had the ability to make friends with customers in the matter of minutes and would joke with them when he could. On a real good day he was fun to watch. One time a customer asked for me to come in when Eddie had just sold him a car. He told me he had never enjoyed buying a car so much in his life and wanted to give Eddie a little something extra. He took a $50 bill from his pocket and gave it to him. This may give you an idea of how good he was.

George and I had worked out an improved system on not just ordering the cars but also keeping track of their equipment and how well they sold. We had a large notebook and a section might be Oldsmobile 88 Sedan. In that section we might have three equipment levels for that model, from light in equipment to medium. Then we would have a record of what color inside and out was ordered. The next section might be Oldsmobile Brougham Sedan which would have equipment from a medium level to very loaded. Again we did the same on the colors. When the car was sent to production we noted the date on the sheet next to it, the same with the day it came in, and the day it was sold. We would then calculate how many days it had been in stock. From this we knew which colors were selling and what equipment mix was working.

This took a lot of time until one day the dealership told us we were going to go computerized and this would be part of the package.

They decided that George (a Rice University graduate and Vietnam vet), was to go off to school to learn the computer system, and how to make reports and all the rest. He was to teach me when he came back. George had a couple of daughters who worked at the dealership and his wife worked at IBM. He had a side hobby and business of guns. He bought and sold guns, and knew all about them. He also had his own reloading equipment to load his own bullets and at one stage hired Pam for a short time (before she got her Resident Alien status) to reload bullets—until she got too bored to continue. This was down the road from the dealership near the radio shop we used. There was a time when Delco radio of General Motors was not competitive on their prices and all the dealers were getting their radios put in by independent companies for a lot less money. We did it as well to stay competitive.

George had one fault and that was women. He had been known to have a girlfriend here and there along the way. Sometimes he would spend some time on the phone talking to them. I never found it a problem and didn't feel it interfered with his work. At times I had to do more of the paperwork but didn't mind as I was happy staying busy. I could still feel there was an underlying conflict between he and Bryan. Bryan was a real cocky sort of person and was most likely the only used car manager that wore $500 suits and $10,000 Rolex watches. He and George just didn't get along.

After I had been there a year and as we were starting our new year, we had a meeting in January to set our goals for the year. Doug had come up with several short-term sales goals with bonuses and a yearly figure for us to try and achieve. We were to sell 3,000 Oldsmobiles for the year. If we did, we would get a year-end bonus of $30,000 each. This looked like a mountain as you had slow months in the winter to overcome and of course you had to get enough good merchandise at the right time as well. Nevertheless the goals had been set and it was up to us to try and reach them.

We were also allowed, with prior permission, to have sales contests. We tried to make them as fair as possible and provide an opportunity for the salesmen to make some extra money as well. Unfortunately those at the bottom said it was not fair as all the extra money was high up the sales ladder. Those at the top said the lower guys got too much at the lower levels. In time, this complaining from people like Boyd did nothing but get everybody upset and the sales contests were dropped. Then nobody got any extra; they all got the samenone.

The new car sales pay plan was something George and Doug had come up with. The new car department was geared for volume and the pay was on a per unit basis. The pay was $45 on small cars (all those smaller than Cutlass), $55 on mid-size (Cutlass & 88's), and $70 on large cars (98's and Toranados). On top of this each week, we would count how many cars had been delivered between Monday morning and Friday closing. For 4 deliveries a salesman would get $100; for 5–$125; for 6–$180; 7–$210; 8–$320 and so on. It took this, with the base pay, for the guys to make a living. At times we had 16 salesmen in Oldsmobile and a lot of the time from 12 to 14. If we sold around 250 in a month, those at the bottom made hardly enough to get by on and those at the top made good money. We would sell a car at $50 to $100 over invoice all the time. If we needed to, we would sell them for invoice. With this in mind, Charlie said any salesman that couldn't sell at least 10 units a month was either lazy or couldn't sell anything, and needed to go.

The salesmen did get paid on some of the extras as well. They were paid on extended warranties they sold, interior and exterior seal protection, and if they got the person to finance with us through GMAC. Also each Monday morning in the sales meeting, we would let the guys reach into a wooden box for each finance deal they had that previous week. The box was full of paper money. Lots of $1 and $2 bills, with a number of $5, $10, and $20 bills mixed in as well, and one $50 bill. It helped to have a lot of luck for some guys would reach in 4 times and get only $4, while others may get $45 or $50, and sometimes the $50 bill would come out.

The top salesmen in each department made from $50,000 to about $75,000 per year. They also had a demonstrator to drive, medical insurance, and shared in the retirement fund if they went into it. Most did the 2%. You had to be at the dealership 2 years before you could join, and then the dealership would match you one for one on what you put in up to 2% of your income, the limit. The vesting was 10 years, set up so that if you left the company say at the end of three years, you got your money back and 30% of what was put in on your behalf, as well as 30% of what your share of the money was that the plan made. The balance was then split up to those that were still in the fund. If it was after 10 years, you got 100% of your entire amount in your account.

It wasn't until after my first year I fully saw how the managers' payment on company profits were done. It was only the managers that were in on this—to help get all the departments to work for the company as a whole (with the exception being the used car department). It was, as Charles Maund said, the so-called line 51 of the statement used for General Motors . . . before taxes and other various expenses that many other dealers would take off before paying bonuses or pay, based on profits. The company made about 3 million dollars that year, nett before tax, and George and I got paid one-half percent of the amount, which was $15,000 each for the year. George told me that if we needed the money we could draw against it as the year went on, as long as we stayed below what we were owed. He said it was best to draw a couple of times a year as this gave you more to live off and let the Maunds know that the base was not enough on its own. I wasn't sure about this but as time went on, it worked out I needed to make draws several times a year to stay even.

At the end of my first year in Austin I was happy. I had been told at work that I was doing a good job several times, both by word and with money . . . something I was not used to. I liked the Maunds—even if Doug was a bit of a problem at times as he was still growing up and learning how to run the store. He would get something in his mind and as we used to say, "don't confuse him with the facts, he has already made up his mind". I figured it would all be okay in time and didn't worry about it. I made something to the tune of about $55,000 that year, which was a far cry from my $18,000 working for Cecil—and not so much as a thank you from him. And best of all I had met Pam.

Everything was going fine with us, with only the exception of immigration and extensions on visas. We had started to look at houses seriously and were always enjoying our time with each other. We spent some time with the kids and I wanted them to like her but didn't want to push her on them. Up to about this time she never knew how much money I made. She knew I had a good job and enjoyed it but that was about it.

As they say, all good times must come to an end. Well it wasn't that bad but it got to the point it looked like it was going to be impossible to get another renewal on her visa. It was going to be a major battle. We both looked at each other and decided why wait any longer. Why not just get married and then fight immigration for her new status. If it didn't work out between us, as we said before, we could always get a divorce. We weren't really that whimsical about it but we did decide we really had no reason not to get married. She told me, so as to make it easy on me to remember, she wanted to get married on Valentine's Day, the 14th of February 1983. We made arrangements to be married by the Justice of the Peace who had an office by 'Dallas', where we had met. Eddie (our intended witness) was to meet us there but didn't get there on time, as we didn't tell him what it was for. After we were married we went out to eat with Eddie and Clarence that evening before going home. The next day I went to work and that was about the extent of the celebration but we were happy as we had each other.

CHAPTER 52

IMMIGRATION

During the year the dealership was entered into various sales contests and programs the factory offered each year. At different times it would be a trip or prize points for winning at various levels. We did well and won lots of prize points. Some people didn't like them as the number of points required for an item was like paying a high price for the merchandise and we had to report the value of the points on our income tax. Nevertheless we enjoyed picking out items from the catalogues and waiting for the merchandise to show up. We got everything you can imagine—clothes, towels, bedding, small appliances, radio-tape players, glasses, a wine cart, you name it.

After we were married it was necessary for us to go to San Antonio to the immigration office. You could not get them on the phone and you had to appear in person. The doors opened at 8 AMand as soon as they felt they had enough people in to process for the day, they locked the doors. This may be at 8:30 AM so I made arrangements at the dealership to take off all day on a Tuesday so as to miss only one morning's work and George came in early to cover for me. Pam and I went down and waited in line.

When we first got into the building it was sign-posted and we were moved like cattle down the hall to a large office that had various windows with lines in front of them again. After standing in line for a few minutes I wasn't sure we were in the correct line and went to the front to see what I could, and try to ask. I was told to get to the back of the line and wait. They refused to talk to me at all. This was the attitude we experienced all the way through. When we got to the front of the line, we were told we were in the wrong line and needed to go to the back of the line several windows over.

We finally got some papers and started filling them out. We also needed a picture of Pam that had to be taken by the man set up in the hallway with his camera. As we got up to the front of this line and were ready to have her picture taken, the photographer suddenly hung a sign over his camera that said "Out to Lunch"—he would be back in an hour. We and all the rest of the people stood and waited for him to return just so he could take the required picture for Interpol to check her police record.

We finally got to a situation where we were to be interviewed both separately and then together. They wanted to know, how did we meet, how long did we know each other, was this a marriage of convenience, and a number of other questions like what was her favorite color, when was her birthday and so on. They wanted to see if our stories were the same and just how well we knew each other. We had taken a number of documents and her passport with us.

After it was over we had other items we needed to get and send to them—such as a letter from my employer about my employment, and a statement from me that I would be financially responsible for her while she was in the States and that if she was to be sent back I would pay for her ticket. We were instructed she was not to work or leave the country during this time as this would make her application null and void, and she would have to start over again. We were to wait several months while they ran checks on her to see if she had a criminal record and if her background checked out.

It was amazing to us how uncooperative and rude the staff were, although I realized that a lot of the people trying to get in were from a number of countries such as the mid-east, Mexico, and various other central and South American countries, and that a number of them didn't speak any English. This may have made it hard for the officers but it was as if they wanted to make it so difficult that they would run all the people back to where they came from. I know I was ashamed of the way they acted and treated us. Yet in spite of all of this, a number of undesirables still get into the country each year so I doubt their approach is working very well.

Pam and I decided to buy a house, or should say have one built. Conan Homes was actually a customer of Don McLean, the previous general manager, and we figured after looking around that his work was okay. He was also building a less expensive group of houses out near Buda, Texas. We picked out several floor plans we liked and had them take out the parts we liked the most and put them into the plans for our new house. It was going to run a little more than those do in the neighborhood but that didn't bother us and by being one of the first in the neighborhood we had a large selection of lots to choose from. We chose a site that had lots of trees.

We told them we wanted to save as many of the trees as possible and even marked the ones to save, around the house. Pam and I went out to the building site several times a week. As usual with us having our own set of plans that were different, some problems did come up. One was when the roof trusses over our open plan lounge area were put up back to front but they corrected this with very little trouble.

The one problem they did create and we never were happy with, was the drainage. The lot sloped down from front to back. The front door was at ground level almost and the back patio was about 2 ½ feet off of the ground. They didn't want the expense of extra fill or cement when they did the foundation, so when we first moved in we had a danger of the storm water from the road and front yard coming in the front door. We had a neighbor make a stone entry that raised the front porch a few inches and we put in a mound of dirt from one side of the property to the other, across the front. It was only about a 6-inch high mound that was almost invisible when covered with grass but it diverted the water from the road to around the sides of the house in heavy rain.

We had a privacy fence put up on all the sides of the property except where the driveway went into the carport. We had a large oak tree in the driveway by the carport we had the builders leave. It was possible to get around the tree and get in and out of the carport but it took several goes to do it. We had the carport built in such a way we could have converted it into a playroom very easily at a later date but wanted to save the money going in. We did have a number of extras built in from the start but these were mainly items that couldn't be added later very easily. We had security lighting around the outside of the house, with switches in the area by the back door and by the master bedroom headboard area so they could be turned on without getting out of bed. We also had a new style fan-forced fire place and an extra large bathtub in the master bathroom. We had sliding doors off the living area onto the back patio, as well as from the master bedroom. When we first moved in you could see deer in the backyard from bed and one day Pam saw a bobcat.

Back when we first started to go out to Buda after we had picked out the lot, we took the kids to see where the house would be built. Scott heard some noise under a tree in the leaves and I went to check it out. It was a rattlesnake. I killed the snake and we put it by the next door neighbors' driveway near the garage area so their workmen would see it and know snakes were around. We were later told by the neighbors they saw it but didn't know if someone was trying to cast a spell on them or something. I assured them this was not the case.

Scott holding the rattlesnake killed on the lot in Buda, Texas

We saved some money in a few areas like having a carport instead of a garage, as well as leaving the wallpaper out of the kitchen and bathroom areas. Pam assured me she could hang wallpaper and as long as they did the sheet rock to a stage that was ready for paper, it would be easy. We also did some projects after we moved in, like converting the entry closet into a bar behind the bi-fold doors, and a built-in planter that divided the walkway to the kids' bedrooms from the living area. We also purchased a wall section of furniture that was a combination of bookshelves and space for the TV and stereo. It was nice wood but to make it go with the house the whole thing needed several coats of pain. This was another hidden talent of Pam's. I actually had someone who enjoyed projects and doing everything from painting to yard work. This was very different from my past experiences where I was always on my own. We had put a lot of our ideas in the house and we found it to be comfortable even though it was only 1,400 square feet.

Craig, Scott, Pam and Laurie in front of the new house under construction in Buda

When the house was almost ready for us to move in, we notified my landlord that I would be moving out as I was near the end of my lease. He said he would rent the place on a month-to-month basis on the understanding the place could be shown to others for rent or sale. He had decided to sell the duplex and wanted to know if we were interested. He had mentioned it before but wanted $110,000 for the complex. It was not a bad price—it was just more than we felt we could afford if the other side wasn't rented out. I wasn't very fond of the idea of worrying about renters although we thought it would be fun to have a full 3 bedroom 2 bath set-up with all the works, next door, for family and friends. But in the hard light of day we gave the idea up very quickly as the new house was only going to be around $79,000.

When the time came for us to move it worked out that only Pam and I were available to do it. I rented a moving truck with a lift on the back and after we closed on the house, we took all day and until the middle of the night to get everything moved from the duplex to the house. Pam helped me move the washer, dryer, and the refrigerator and king-size bed, as well as all of the other stuff. It was amazing how much I had purchased since I moved to Austin—something that was made possible only because of the income I received from Charlie. In the early hours of the morning we went to sleep on the mattress that was on the floor, for a few hours. I then had to get up and get ready to go to work after returning the truck that needed to be turned in. I was so stiff and sore I could hardly move. It was as if someone had beaten us. I told Pam I couldn't remember being so stiff and sore since the days of spring training for football. By the time I got home from work that night Pam had most of the place in shape. After a few days she had it all but done. It was time for those projects and buying some of the other things we needed, like window treatments, so we could close out the world at night.

Before we had left the duplex we decided the Oldsmobile Cutlass was not going to be a lot of use to us for projects at the new house. We decided to sell it and get a little Ford Courier pickup truck. Pam cleaned the car up and we put it in the parking lot of the grocery store near where we lived with our number in the window. It took a couple of weeks and after a couple of calls Pam had an older lady who was very interested in the car. She and her family came out to look at the car and test drive it. They liked the car very much but she had trouble pushing in the button on the top of the gearshift lever for the automatic transmission. She could only do it when she used both hands. We were asking about $2,600 for the car and this didn't seem to be a problem as much as the gearshift. After several days she called back and offered Pam $2,400 cash and figured she would just have to use both hands. I told Pam I should have her on the sales force if it wasn't such a 'no no'.

The little truck I purchased was okay and seemed to run alright. It was to get things for the yard such as grass and plants. It wasn't going to be much for Pam, just something to drive but she didn't seem to worry and could always take my car if she needed to. The truck had a 4-speed transmission and no air-conditioning, which was going to make it very hot in the summer time but I also figured we would keep it only as long as we needed it and would then get her something else that would be a bit nicer later on. The little Ford Courier truck was clean but was a funny sort of a light green color. It did have some paint stripes and mag wheels so that should have made it alright. We would joke back in those days about dressing up a vehicle by putting on a vinyl top and pin stripes to sell them but it really did dress them up and they sold.

Night picture of Buda house after snowfall

Unfortunately during this time Pam's sister, Chris, back in New Zealand was not doing very well with her MS. It appeared she was becoming very sick and might not live. We talked to her mother and decided she should book a flight back to New Zealand as soon as her papers had cleared. She couldn't do much until then as immigration wasn't about to make exceptions and even Pam's Mom didn't want to see us start over with immigration. Not long after her papers came and Pam had booked her flight, her sister died. It wasn't by much and her mother told her not to worry or rush. She would rather have her come after the funeral to help her then. We decided we would send her home and she could decide how long to stay after she saw how things were.

It was a very unhappy time for Pam and she had to put to rest a number of ghosts. It was going to be up to her to help her Mom and Dad and her sister's young children, and try to get things back on an even keel. I wasn't sure how long it was going to be either but felt as long as she was going to be coming back I would be alright and would get past being alone. I told her I would write often and try to keep the phone bill under control.

CHAPTER 53

STARTING TO LIVE IN BUDA

While Pam was gone to New Zealand to help her family, Craig told me he had decided to go to school up in Austin and live with me. I told him, as I had told Sam, he could live with me for the first year and I would help where I could. He would have enough getting into a new routine at university, without sharing a place and staying with other people he hadn't known before. After that, if he wanted, he could move out into another place to live and I would consider sharing the expenses with other members of the family.

I did warn him that I didn't think his mother would like this idea at all and he had better make sure this was what he wanted to do before he told her. I also told him I wouldn't be surprised if he was able to leave with only his clothes. He assured me I was wrong but when the time came they were upset. They told him to leave his car with them, even though he had made the payments, and to leave some of the other items he had in his room. At the end he had his clothes and not much more.

He moved in at the end of summer when school started and I told him he could use the little truck we had for now. He was not very happy with the vehicle but it was all we had—and better than nothing. I told him to watch the water, oil and gas, and if anything seemed out of the usual to let me know. Craig was a good kid but not very mechanically-inclined. He had a girlfriend from high school who had decided to go to school at Baylor in Waco where he had wanted to go. After his mother and Walt had pulled the rug out from under him at the 11th hour and refused to provide the information requested by Baylor for him, he seemed unhappy as all his friends were off to somewhere else and thus he didn't want to stay at home and go to UTSA. Cecile and Walt, along with Cecil, wanted him to major in business—I think they had plans for him to work for them in some capacity. At times they would revert back to the attitude they had previously when I still lived at home, when they felt Sam was the more active and brighter one, while Craig was bigger, stronger, and steadier. When the kids were little, Cecil would always ask people to guess which one was oldest and then go on about how big Craig was. I got tired of this and I am sure the kids did as well. I had told Craig to study what he wanted as I just wanted him to be happy and graduate in a field he wanted to.

I would help with some of Craig's school expenses and told him I would give him an allowance out of which he would need to buy his gas and pay for his long-distance phone calls. At first he called Waco a lot and the phone bill was much larger than I felt it needed to be. I felt he could write a few letters as I had to do in the past and as I still had to do with Pam. I knew if he had to pay for his calls out of his allowance (this did not include the calls to his mother), it would slow him down. I wanted to help him but also felt he needed to be responsible. I wanted to help with his other school expenses but felt the others should help as well. I never knew why they (or he) didn't ask me in time to try and help with him going to Baylor. I don't know how much I could or would have done, as they never asked.

Back at work, we were in a little contest for a weekend away that Oldsmobile was to pay for. George said if we won the contest Pam and I could take it. He had asked us if it was okay for him and his wife to take a cruise we were in a contest to win as he felt they needed to spend some time with each other, as things had been a bit shaky at home. The trip for the weekend away as it worked out was to be about the time Pam was talking about coming back.

We decided to try and organize her return for that weekend so we could get a couple of days away from everything. Craig had moved in while she was gone and this would be another adjustment for all of us now that she was coming back. We wouldn't know if we won the trip until about a week before but it looked good. It was only to stay at a nearby lake resort but with free accommodation, free food and drinks, and somebody else to do the work, it sounded good.

The next trick was to try and get her back with connecting flights. Usually you had to stay overnight in Los Angeles as the connections were very tight, trying to get the last flights out heading east. If you ran with your bags you might be able to catch one to Texas to one of the main centers. I told her to ring me and let me know and I would drive over and pick her up. I told her to try for San Antonio, Houston, or last of all, Dallas. As it worked out she was able to just catch a flight to Houston and as it would be in about 1 AM, I would have enough time to drive over after work and pick her up. We could spend the night in Houston and drive to the lake resort the next day for the weekend.

Everything went fine and I picked her up that night and we headed out the next day. We drove to the resort and got there about early afternoon and I went to get the key and check in. We drove to what was like private apartment set-ups and found our unit. We unlocked the door and started to carry our bags in when we thought we heard voices. We went around the corner to the living room area and there was a couple that were just finishing putting themselves back together. I held our key up and said there must be some mistake.

We talked to each other for a minute and found out they were from a dealership in the Dallas area and we must have been double-booked by mistake in the s e unit. I said I would call the office and see what was going on. The resort said they had instructions to put two couples in each unit. I told him we were unaware of any such instructions and after I visited with the other couple, they told me they were unaware of any such stipulation or they wouldn't have been exploring the living room. I got a hold of Jack Heiser and told him Pam and I were leaving. She had just got back into the country after being away and we wanted time alone, and should have been told we were to share a unit. I gave him a hard time, as I knew our plans were shot for the weekend.

The other couple had been looking forward to getting a weekend on their own as well. We told them to stay as we only had maybe an hour or so to drive to get home and they might as well have the place to themselves and not ruin their weekend too. We both said, any other time it would be okay to share a unit with another couple but not when we had looked forward to being with each other after such a long time apart.

As we drove back to Austin we decided why not just go and check-in to a hotel and stay on our own anyway? We didn't really know where to go so as we saw a Hilton off to the side, decided to go there. We checked in and we went to our room in the back of the complex. It was old and the room had a mildew sort of smell. I told Pam no. We would get a different room, as this was not acceptable. We were told that was all they had left, the old wing, as they had a convention staying at the hotel. We decided to leave and go elsewhere.

We drove to, as I remember, a Marriott and checked in. It had a nice clean room and we decided to stay and go downstairs to the restaurant and have a meal. We were able to spend our evening catching up and the next day after breakfast we were ready to return home. It wasn't our planned weekend but at least we got away from everybody for awhile.

Pam had always liked all the kids and had found Craig easy to get along with. But when Craig returned it was the start of a strange relationship. He would go home to San Antonio on the weekends a lot and see his mother. The first few days when he was back with us he would hardly say a word and acted as if something was bothering him, yet he wouldn't say when asked. But by the end of the week he was usually talkative and friendly again. He would spend time talking with us and sometimes after work he would go with us to a place like 'Dallas' and have a beer.

He would then go away and return on Sunday night and it would be as if we were strangers again. It was like this almost the whole time he lived with us. Pam was very worried about it and I asked him several times if something was bothering him and he would never say. A couple of things had come out but I don't think that is what was bothering him. He told me one time his mother had said to him "Don't you think they might want to live on their own and have a family?" To this he replied "Didn't you say Dad had a vasectomy?" It seems the roots of this problem may have been some more game-playing by his mother but I don't know how much.

I felt he should still have some limits set on him and he should have to pay for some of his things out of his allowance. His allowance wasn't much but I figured he could help me out around the place some for pocket money or get a part-time job. I didn't want him to get one at first as I wanted to make sure it wouldn't hurt him with his studies. His mother eventually decided to let him have his car back. It was just as well as the little truck had broken down a couple of times and I don't think it was in good-enough shape to have lots of miles put on it on a regular basis.

Craig did get a part-time job at an ice cream parlor for awhile. He made pocket money and seemed to be happy enough. He was still adjusting to school and living with us as well but I felt like he never did settle in with us for some reason. He would help some but would rather go outside and work out with weights and get all the neighborhood girls looking at him.

One night when I came home after work when it was dark, I came through the carport and went inside. Craig told me Pam was across the street at Diane's house. Pam and Diane had become friends and spent a fair amount of time visiting with each other. I called and was going to go over when I looked out on the carport after I had turned the lights on and saw a large rattlesnake under the weight bench in front of the storeroom door. I called Craig to get my handgun, a .357 magnum, and also called back to get the girls to bring over a hoe as I couldn't get into our storeroom.

I told Craig not to shoot in the carport, as the bullet would go all over the place. I wanted the gun only if it got out into the yard. The girls brought me the hoe and gave it to me. I reached slowly with the hoe underneath the bench and placed the hoe above the rattlesnake's head. I then slammed down the hoe as hard as I could behind its head and pushed back and forth. The girls said, "Don't let go" and I told them "What do you think I am, an idiot?" I then proceeded to cut the head almost off and killed the snake.

Craig later on made a few friends and with one he knew, started to make plans for several of them to go together to share an apartment. He presented the idea to me and to those in San Antonio. He had some resistance and evidently some suggestions were made. Craig and his friends made a few adjustments in their plans and budget, and had another try. It sounded okay to me and I told him I would pay him my share if the others would do the same. Unfortunately those in San Antonio refused to go along and pay any share, and the deal fell over.

I think this was another step in their getting him to return to San Antonio. He went back to live at home and worked for them. He went to school at U.T.S.A. and seemed to resign himself to this. The good that came out of this was that he got his degree, and also met someone that turned out to end up being his wife and a big influence on his life.

At one point after he was married and had graduated, he didn't seem to be very happy in the business world, working for family and others as he had. The idea came up about him wanting to maybe go back to school and go into medicine. I remember how some members of the family said he would never make it and that it was a waste of time and money. I am glad he tried or he would have never known for his own sake—and we would have been without a top-notch doctor in the family. But this is later on and another story.

Pam and I were sorry when he decided to move out. We both felt like we had failed in some way as it hadn't worked out as we wanted and felt it should have. I felt we had tried and had done what we could. Pam told me she never knew until then, how hard it was to live with someone when they wouldn't talk and tell you what was bothering them. I guess she had become too used to me. I usually said too much and let it out in a hurry and then had to pick up the pieces but no one had any doubt about what was on my mind. I didn't carry it around with me and let it keep on being a problem. Once it was done it was over but now we both had to decide to put it behind us, knowing we would still always try to stay in touch and be friends.

Pam and I had the topsoil in and the grass sown during the first spring and summer. As we had most of the work done we needed the truck for, I got Pam her next vehicle, a Chevrolet Camaro Berlinetta. We were trading for the car and again Bryan didn't like it much as it was a charcoal-colored sports car. The Camaro was Chevrolet's answer to the Firebird by Pontiac. It was a nice clean car and Pam enjoyed driving it. She liked to go to San Antonio and pick up the kids, which she was finally allowed to do. I think Scott and Laurie didn't mind their step Mom picking them up in a sports car at that time either. It seemed for awhile they all got along and enjoyed coming up. Pam told me sometimes they would go walking through the neighborhood before it was built up and they could see the vacant land with the cactus and bluebonnets in all of its wild state.

CHAPTER 54

VISITORS AND SIGHTSEEING

While we lived in Buda we had some of Pam's family and friends come and stay with us from time to time. I also had my father come and stay with us for awhile as well. This was during a time when Beulah and Tommy were being transferred and were in the process of moving. It was easier for him to come and stay with us during the move and then fly him to where they were to live after they settled in.

I had stayed in touch only to a limited degree with them over the last few years. The same excuses we all use, just busy. I had seen Dad once before this, back when I was with Sharon. One weekend Sharon, Sam, and I drove to Del Rio to see them. It was a quick trip. Tommy took Sam and I out to the air force base and showed him the flight suits and let him put some of the stuff on. We then went outside to one of the training jets and he let Sam sit inside in the pilot's seat. I visited with Dad and was surprised at how well he had recovered. Beulah Ann had put in a lot of time and effort to get him back into some sort of shape. He could now use a walker, bathe and dress himself, and of course feed himself. He was hard to understand as his voice box was messed up and he had to make a real effort to talk. He seemed to understand things very well and what he seemed to have forgotten was more recent things rather than those in the past. He told me he wasn't allowed to drink but Beulah Ann did allow him to have a beer or wine once in awhile. She had become tired of worrying about him smoking both health-wise and possibly falling asleep and starting a fire. So one day she came in after shopping and gave him a carton of cigarettes and told him that was it—he could smoke them all at once or over a long period of time but once they were gone that was it.

I think it was actually good for him that he had quit. It hadn't hurt his sense of humor. As we sat having breakfast he couldn't find the butter and after a few minutes I asked him what he was looking for. This was after him telling me the stories of what all Beulah Ann had cut out of his life. He said it didn't matter, as it was probably something else she decided to cut out as well. He then told me it was the butter he was looking for. He was saved as it was just overlooked that morning and we got him some for his toast.

When this came up about his staying with us for awhile I wasn't sure how it would work out. But Pam seemed happy enough to give it a try and we told Beulah Ann to go ahead and make plans. Dad was able to take care of himself as long as you gave him enough time. He always enjoyed reading, and watching TV. He enjoyed staying in the air-conditioning and visiting. He liked Pam and liked talking to her. Pam told me she would try and fix him something he liked for breakfast and some days they would spend most of the morning visiting.

Dad was not a big eater and if you could get him to have a good breakfast you had done well. He would eat a little something for lunch but not much. Dinner in the evening was hit and miss. If it was something he liked and hadn't had for awhile you had a chance. We did take him out to eat a couple of times, as this was something he always enjoyed.

He got to know Diane as she came over to see Pam. She was kind and friendly, and would sit and talk to Dad and pay him some attention. One evening she came over for dinner to eat with Dad and us, as her husband was working—playing in a band. Dad wanted her to wait on him all the time, and they were laughing and having a good time. When she went to get him his dessert, she went to use the aerosol whipped cream on it for him and accidentally sprayed some of it and it landed on his bald head. She reached over with her finger and wiped it off and licked her finger again and proceeded to clean him up. He laughed and laughed. After that evening all he could do was talk about her, and want to know where Diane was and if she was coming over.

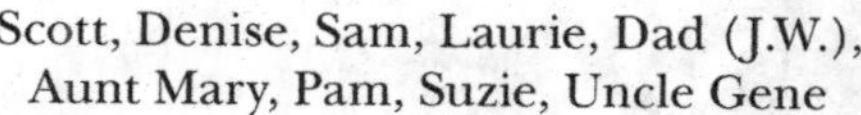

Scott, Denise, Sam, Laurie, Dad (J.W.), Aunt Mary, Pam, Suzie, Uncle Gene

Brother Charlie with Dad in Buda

One weekend we drove Dad down to San Antonio so he could see his sister, my Aunt Mary, and some of her family. While we were down there he was able to see Sam and Denise, as well as the other kids. The stay went much better than I feared. I had been afraid it would be too much trouble for Pam and it would be a big burden. It did take time and it wasn't always easy but Pam told me she really did enjoy it and was glad she had a chance to meet and get to know my Dad some. It was actually a bit strange without him there after he first left, as we had become used to having him around and Pam especially, missed him.

We had a travelling Kiwi come through one time for a night or so. It was a friend of a friend of Pam's. She was told if she was passing through our area of the country to give us a call and stay with us. It seems a number of young people would travel this way. They would catch a bus and head out and stay with friends or whom they could along the way, to save some money and still see the world. It was a call out of the blue and she was gone as fast as she came.

We did have some of Pam's family come and stay. Her Aunt Joan and Uncle Kit came and stayed with us for awhile. They would help her some with landscaping the gardens, as did some of our other guests from New Zealand. The kids seemed to have some trouble understanding how these people would come and do garden work for us while they were there with us on holiday. This was also true of Pam's parents helping Pam at times as well but they all loved to stay busy and wanted to help us out.

The one that was a surprise for us both was Len. He was the father of her friend Pat who had the farm with Rob where we had stayed. His wife had died some time back and they all felt it would be good if he got away for a holiday. He just wouldn't go, as he didn't want to go on his own. Pat called Pam and asked if it would be okay if he came over and stayed with us for awhile as that way she might get him to go. Pam knew him some and said okay but when she asked for how long, was told "a few weeks". We were both afraid this might be a problem but felt we must give it a try.

As it turned out it was no problem at all. Len enjoyed and liked doing everything. He would help Pam with the yard outside for part of the day and then go shopping later in the afternoon. He liked looking at the stores and all the sights he could see. It was all like a big new world for him. He would buy some of the food and pay for some of the drinks. We would go several times a week after work, to happy hour at places like 'Dallas'. He loved to watch the people dance and would listen to the music. He couldn't get over the big screen TV and all the entertainment. One night when we went they had door prizes and his ticket won two concert tickets and a limousine for the night to see 'The Boss', Bruce Springsteen. He gave the tickets and all to us. Before we left we had people coming up to us and offering $100 for just the tickets.

One day at work Eddie and I were talking about him, and Eddie came up with the idea of taking him to lunch one day and surprising him. We would take him to another place called 'Sugars' that he had been to; a high-class businessmen's sort of place. They had a good steak lunch at a reasonable price and during the day most men came in dressed in suits.

We made arrangements and one day we took him to lunch with us. It was sort of dark when you first went in, from being so bright outside. We went over and sat down, and the room had mirrors around on some walls and a dance floor off to the other side. Len sat there and watched the girls in the mirror, dancing. We ordered a few drinks and lunch and started visiting with each other. About that time one of the girls came over from behind Len to tell him hello. He almost fell off of his chair as he exclaimed,

"Christ, they're real!" He had been looking in the mirror and figured it was another giant screen TV or something, for entertainment; he hadn't realized the entertainment was live.

Another time we decided to take him to Mexico. We would drive down to Laredo and stay on that side of the border on Saturday night. It was about a 3-hour drive from Austin. We would go out to eat that night at one of the top restaurants and then go shopping the next day and show him some of the diversity the place had to offer before we headed back.

Pam, Diane and Len at the U.S.—Mexico border

He got to know Diane from her coming over and seeing Pam. When we were talking about going to Mexico we decided to invite her as well, as her husband, Chuck, had plans to play with his band. We told her she could stay in a room with Pam, and I would share a room with Len. She decided to go on the trip as well. Once we were down there she decided that Len was okay and as the room was set up with twin beds, she didn't mind sharing the room with him so that Pam and I could spend some rare time off together.

We showed him around the town and the vast assortment of merchandise that was available–from cheap handmade items for $1.00 to ornate jewellery and things that ran well into the thousands. It was a country of extremes. From rich to poor, from plain to ornate. It hadn't changed from when I was a kid and I doubt it has changed much since we went.

Diane buying a handmade doll from Mexican street vendors

Pam in 'Marty's', Nuevo Laredo, surrounded by merchandise

As time went on, Pam and I developed an almost automatic tourist route–depending on how long someone had to stay and what their interests were. We knew areas and restaurants in Austin and San Antonio, as well as further afield in Nuevo Laredo in Mexico. We joked about how maybe we should take Kiwis on tour for a fee and make some extra money on the side.

Cowboys getting their boots shone outside 'Marty's'—a store with items from a few dollars to thousands

I think the first visitor we had was Barry Ries from Canada. This was back when I lived on my own in the duplex. He had talked to Pam about coming down to Austin to see her and some of the sights. She had met him when she and her ex-husband were in Ottawa for a year while he was going to Carlton University on a scholarship. It was a little strange at first as Pam and I had only known each other a few months at the time but it worked out. We both enjoyed showing people around and taking them places. We took him to some of our favorite places like 'Dallas' and the 'San Antonio Rose', as well as the 'River Walk' in San Antonio. It was summer and it was hot. I remember how he remarked that during that time of the year it took nothing to be a weatherman. It was all the same day after day, hot clear and sunny, hot clear and sunny . . .

CHAPTER 55

TRIPS AND COMPANY

If Barry Ries was the first visitor we had over the years, I guess you could say the last ones to come over and stay with us later on, after several trips, were Pam's parents. They would try to come when they could and Pam would try to go home each year for awhile if she could. It was always a pleasure and a lot of fun to have them come and stay. It was fun to share with them, the places we went to and the things we did so they would know what it was like for Pam after they were back home.

Over the years we saw parts of Texas, went to Mexico, and saw sights in our area, New Orleans, the hill country, the coast, and San Antonio just to name a few. We visited some of my family and made some new friends. We would sometimes just go out to eat and go shopping. But we always had a good time and enjoyed it, and always hated to see it come to an end.

Early on we would take them to happy hour at some of our favorite places. One time we met an unexpected guest, Kizzy, and had our pictures taken with her.

Kizzy, Sam, Peg, Pam and Alan

Kizzy and Sam

After Pam had returned from New Zealand and our getaway weekend had not gone as planned, we decided to see about taking some time off and going somewhere on our own. Pam had got to know a travel agent and they talked about going to Mexico. At first Pam was thinking about Mexico City but she was assured that with 13 million other people, this was not what she wanted; to spend time alone together. The travel agent suggested we take a couple of days and go to Xtapa, a small village with a new resort, and then go to spend a few days in Acapulco. Pam wasn't sure about going to a tourist city at first but agreed we would give it a try, leaving the travel agent to book us where she had recommended.

We first flew to Mexico and went to Xtapa and stayed at a place that was a new hotel built on the beach of the Pacific Ocean. It sloped down the side of the hill and each room had its own private view of the sea and the beach. It was a quiet place—the sort of place you go to just to relax and take it easy and do nothing. The food was okay and the fresh coffee (with chicory) you could smell in the morning was like no other. Pam said it was the first time she'd had coffee that tasted as good as it smelled.

The area was a new tourist area that the Mexican government was just starting to open up. The service was okay but once you got to Acapulco you could see there was no comparison, as Acapulco was a 24-hour city dedicated to tourists, and their wants and needs.

Xtapa hotel on hillside sloping down to beach

View of Pacific Ocean and beach from hotel room

We were booked in at the Hyatt Excelcius on the beach at Acapulco Bay. We were both not sure about what we were in for but were now ready to do a little more than just sit around and watch the water.

Acapulco Bay with the Hyatt Excelcius (closest in picture)

We were happy to find that our room was large and had everything you could want. Down in the hotel were several top restaurants and information was available about tours of the area or even day trips to Taxaco, a world-famous mineral and jewellery production center.

As we started to settle in at the hotel, we found our way around and booked into one of the restaurants for the evening. It had an 'Old World' flavor. My menu had prices where Pam's did not. It was a most enjoyable meal with service that was second to none. At the end of the evening when they brought the bill to me, they took her a little box that had chocolates to keep her busy as I took care of the necessary business.

We decided to book on the day trip to Taxaco which meant we would leave at 6 and return about 8 PM that evening. We were one of 4 couples who would go in a Chevrolet Suburban with a guide. It was a long drive over the Sierra Madre (and two other) Mountain chains, almost to the top. The little town had been settled and founded back in the 1500 to 1600 time-frame, in an area that was rich with very pure silver and lots of gold. The craftsmanship of the jewelers was world class yet most of the places sold the jewellery for only the market price of the stones and gold. That was one of the main reasons why people made this long trip to this little town.

We were taken care of for morning snacks and a mid-day lunch. Once we got to Taxaco we would have only about 3 hours to look around and do our shopping before we would have to leave to make the long trip back.

Taxaco church with gold leaf-covered altars. Built by one of town's founders (and mine owners) it had handmade floors, fitted without nails

We found some small pieces of jewellery for Pam but decided not to go outside of our budget and get anything too expensive. Later we wished we had not been quite so careful as we should have purchased some of the bargains when we had the chance.

We enjoyed the trip to Mexico, even though we didn't have enough time to do all the sights or do anything such as fishing or para-sailing. Little did we know at that time, we would soon be returning and have even more fun. As it worked out, Pam's parents had planned a trip to come over and see us later on during the year. Pam told them what a good time we had and wanted to know if they would like to go when they came. They agreed and Pam took care of the details.

This time we decided to add fishing and para-sailing. Alan had always wanted to go deep-sea fishing and out off Acapulco you could fish for sailfish. When we returned to Mexico with her folks we were also in for a surprise as well.

When we went to check in we were asked to please wait. After a few moments the concierge escorted us to the elevator and he gave each of us a key for the elevator, which we would need in order to get off on our floor. As the doors opened we were met by a couple of young ladies who were holding tan-colored rolled up items on a plate which they offered to us. Alan was first and said no, thank you. As they presented them to the rest of us, we took them as they were fresh wash cloths and towels to refresh yourself with before continuing. We later asked Alan why he turned them down and he told us then that he thought they were tacos or something and he wasn't hungry.

The girls had their own desk and reception area on that floor just outside the elevators. This was the Regency Club floor. It seems that since we had been there recently we had been automatically upgraded to this floor. We had our own area for free drinks and snacks and anything we wanted. All we had to do was ask the girls and they would take care of it. Our rooms were very large with marble floors and walls, and we each had our own private balcony that looked out over the bay.

It is hard to say which part of the trip was our favorite as we loved it all. We enjoyed the sightseeing and going to the Acapulco Princess Hotel which Howard Hughes had built and died in. We enjoyed seeing the cliff divers (from the Elvis movie) who would time their dives to hit the water below, as the waves went up and over the rocks. We enjoyed the restaurants—especially the ones when we had the Maruichi bands come over and play at our table. It was the time of the year for Pam's birthday and for a surprise I went and asked the maitre'd, if he could get the band to do a little something special. To our surprise later on, he had not only about a 12-piece Mariachi band come over to play for us but a procession of them led by a girl carrying a huge candelabra (for Pam to blow out all the candles) and leading a donkey, across the restaurant to our table. We could see why this hotel's basement restaurant had an international reputation amongst the world's 10 best restaurants.

Pam, Alan and Peg at the Acapulco Princess Hotel built by Howard Hughes

Some of the Mariachi band that played for us at 'La Cascada' restaurant at Acapulco's Hyatt Excelcius Hotel

Alan and I took one day for ourselves and went fishing. We had been down on the beach when we saw some of the locals promoting a fishing boat. I talked to them and they told me they were getting enough people together to go out the next morning. As I spoke to them I explained we didn't want to just be a couple of more guys fishing on the boat. I wanted to rent the boat for the day so just Alan and I would be on it. They had game fish limits and if the boat was able to catch its limit and you hadn't got one, well that was just bad luck. We made a deal for about $350 (U.S.) as I remember, and I gave them a $50 bill for a deposit. They were to pick us up on the beach the next morning, and they wanted us to bring some ice as it was hard for them to get it. At first Alan was a little concerned that might be the last we would see of the $50 bill. Normally I would agree with him but this time I felt they were on the level and would be back as they wanted more.

Sure enough the next morning we were on the beach with the ice and ready to go. A smaller boat came to the shore to pick us up and take us out to the 'Bacus'. It was a good-sized boat with cabin and two diesel motors. We had a full crew on hand and as I requested, it was just the two of us for the fishing. I wanted to make sure Alan got his and told him to take first turn and I would be in charge of taking the pictures and drinking the beer. As the morning went on we had a few little fish hit here and there. Then Alan got a good strike and after a good battle had a sailfish about 8 foot plus. No sooner did he get that one on and he had another on the line. When he got that one on board it was closer to 10 feet. We let the guys have the meat and made arrangements to have the fish mounted and shipped to New Zealand. As they were not sure where or what New Zealand was, the arrangements were to be made through me in Austin, and the payments in U.S. dollars. It took some time and some ingenuity on Alan's part but it was mounted and shipped all the way to him in New Zealand.

Alan, with one of the two ten-foot sailfish he caught off Acapulco Bay in Mexico

After we got back in we still had time for some more adventure. We had seen the people para-sailing off of the beach by the hotel. They would hook you up and pull you behind the speedboat up and down the bay. You would get almost as high as the hotel and when you came down you landed standing up on the beach where you started. If you did come down over the water you had a life jacket on. If it was over land you had the parachute but needed to hope it was on the beach where you were supposed to land. We both went up a couple of times to take pictures and make sure we had some for our records of the day.

Sam taking off (behind boat) over Acapulco Bay

That evening we had another good time in the hotel's seaside restaurant. We enjoyed ourselves and prepared for our trip to Taxaco the next day. This time we would be going on a tour bus. They did warn you that when you got to checkpoints on the highway and the soldiers came on to the bus to check peoples' papers, not to make jokes as they were serious. The areas out from the city had some trouble with bandits and some tourists had been held up. It was a long trip and as luck would have it, the air-conditioning broke down on the bus. You couldn't open the windows and it got very stuffy inside. We had forgotten to tell her folks that at night when you were on the highway and people wanted to pass, they would turn off their lights so they could try and see if someone was coming. They would then pass in the dark. They never said what happened if both directions had their lights off at the same time but we did see a lot of crosses next to the highway.

After our return, Peg couldn't understand why anybody would want to make that trip twice—over 3 mountain ranges—in such a short time. It was because we wanted them to see what Taxaco had to offer, as we had seen it. This time we did get a few items for Pam and her mother and it was still amazing to see the variety and size of the jewellery. Then you still had other decorative items as well–such as huge, solid silver, model sailing ships, large jewel-encrusted gold and silver crucifixes, and marble, onyx and rosewood chess sets with solid silver and gold pieces.

Sam, Pam, Alan and Peg in Acapulco, Mexico

We had other trips and adventures together. Some were short and just in the area—like going to the Rodeo in San Antonio, or going to 'Night in Old San Antonio' during Fiesta Week. We spent one New Year's Eve in New Orleans where we went out to eat at was supposed to be a top restaurant. They were having a bad night and before it was over, the maître'd in trying to flambé desserts, set one of the tablecloths on fire. Some of our trips together were as much fun because things didn't go as they should, as much as having fun because everything was perfect and couldn't have been any better.

Sam, Pam, Alan and Peg boarding the Natchez in New Orleans

Over a period of time I was able to get to know my in-laws some and they were able to see what Pam was living with and talking about. I must say that I don't think I could have ever found or been able to get any better in-laws than I had—even if I had put an order in for them. They were not only fun but also generous and understanding. They always wanted to help and were never a burden; something I don't think either one of them ever could be.

CHAPTER 56

TIMES CHANGE

As the next year progressed our sales picked up. It seems that Austin was in a boom and the economy had taken off. We were enjoying crisp sales as the year went on and the factory had already planned on several sales promotions that offered either rebates or reduced interest rates to new car buyers. At the end of some of the promotions we were down to maybe 65 to 80 cars in stock, as opposed to the usual 300 or so Oldsmobiles we tried to keep on the ground at any one time.

It was obvious that one problem was getting enough good merchandise and keeping a steady stream of it coming, or keeping it in stock. Our ability to keep the merchandise turning over did help as the factory allocated production on what they called an 'earn and turn' formula. The more you turned, the more you earned. This sometimes did catch you out if you weren't careful. During one period we were selling a lot of the '88 coupe models. A lot of people wanted a good-size car that was in the moderate price range and yet still had a sporty sort of look. It was more to the luxury side and larger than the Cutlass Supreme models. The Cutlass had been the number one selling nameplate in the U.S. for about 10 years running but was now starting to slow down. We were called one week by Heiser and told we had earned production of something to the tune of about 70 of the 88 coupes for one week, as we had been the number one-selling dealer in the country for that model. We liked the car but 70 of them in one go, for a week's earn, was more than we needed by a long shot. We were able, after some discussion, to get the factory to put a portion of the production into the sedan models instead.

This was towards the end of the large car, rear wheel drive model. Everyone is afraid of change and some felt people were trying to buy some of the last of the models before they were replaced with a smaller front wheel drive model. This also held true with the '98 models as well. Oldsmobile and Buick had a model lineup that used the basic underbody from both smaller and larger size cars in the General Motors line. The '88 model used the same under frame as the Chevrolet Caprice and Pontiac Bonneville whereas the '98 used the larger frame of the Cadillac Sedan Deville. Oldsmobile was now priced at only about $25 above a comparably-equipped Chevrolet and hundreds of dollars less than a comparable Cadillac. In the dealer network of GM, you had the BOP group, (Buick, Oldsmobile, Pontiac), and then Chevrolet and Cadillac. Many felt that over the years the BOP group had been given numerous advantages that were now truly threatening the line on both—but opposite—ends of the scale. At a number of the dealer meetings, the topic of discussion was what the factory was going to do about it. The factory said that when the next couple of generations of new cars came out that were now on the drawing board, things would change. Little did we know how true this was going to be at that time.

As we came to the end of the model year, we were calling the factory each week trying to get cars. The Maunds did get one thing they wanted—the ability to demonstrate that the factory was unable to supply us with all the merchandise we could use. So how would they supply a new store in the area as well?

We finished out the year knowing that we would not reach our yearly sales target. Part of it was the fact we were just not able to get enough merchandise when we needed it. Most of the other dealers were in this situation as well and it was just the way it was. As the year had gone on, we were not given any more short sales goals with bonuses as we were already putting the cars out as fast as they came in and there wasn't much point. It was not unusual to have 2 or 3 transport trucks come in during a day and have all but 1 or 2 of the vehicles on them already spoken for. It was a very busy time.

With the year over and the final numbers in, it was evident we had missed our goal by only several hundred cars when Charlie came to us and told us what we had missed our goal by. He also told us that he felt we had done an exceptional job and had done everything in our power but fell short only because we were unable to get the merchandise we needed which was out of our control. He then continued that he normally wouldn't do this but under the circumstances, he felt we should not be penalized and should also share in what had been an outstanding year. He then handed us each an envelope. We were each paid an additional $20,000 for the year and the effort.

It was these sorts of gestures, both in word and pay, that made you happy and feel appreciated. It made it much easier to get up and go to work or stay late when you had to. It made it possible for us to be able to afford the holidays and allow Pam to go home and see her family. We had resolved ourselves to the long hours and working 6 days a week. (On Monday I worked from 8 until we closed at either 8 or 9 PM—and usually worked about 60 hours a week.) It was this sort of appreciation that made it possible to bear. We only had a week for our holiday, so we had to make the most of it. As Charlie had said one time "It doesn't cost any more to go first class, you just can't stay as long, that's all". This was sort of how we looked at it. We only had a week, so why not enjoy it the best we could—and this was how we were able to pay for it.

I wanted to help the kids when I could or when they needed it but I also didn't want everyone to know completely just how well I was doing. I knew it would only cause problems with Cecile and the family. My base income was still $2,500 a month and the rest was either by bonus or company profits—both of which could come and go. As we did get further into the next year, for whatever reason, Charlie came to us and raised our base pay to $3,000 a month. They had also slowed down on the sales bonus and it was almost as if Doug couldn't be bothered messing with it.

During spring we had a hailstorm come through the area like one would see only once in a lifetime. It was strange. At the dealership, which was 11 acres, we had damage on one end of the lot that looked as if someone had taken a large hammer and had beaten the cars for hours. The hail must have been the size of softballs. At the other end, you couldn't find any damage. Most of the cars we had in stock were damaged. We needed to get the insurance company out and make a settlement or reach some sort of agreement and also needed to get in some new merchandise that wasn't damaged. The first fear was that we were going to have a period of time in which we would be "out of business" and not able to sell. This would cause lots of problems as the sales force only got paid when they were selling.

Charlie jumped in and in conjunction with his service department manager, body shop manager, and his lawyer, had an agreement with the insurance company. As you can imagine, you could see the options from wanting the insurance company to buy all the damaged cars and make it their problem, to the insurance company wanting to pay for only patch jobs on the vehicles. The used vehicles were in this trap, as that is all the insurance company wanted to do. But what do you do with a new vehicle. What would the public go for and more importantly, would they buy a new vehicle which had a lot of damage, or even some damage?

A lot of the new vehicles now had aluminum hoods and the damage to these was major. It was finally agreed the insurance company would pay for replacing the hoods and deck lids on cars that had major damage. They would also pay for most of the moldings that were replaceable around the windows and various places. They would pay for repairs to tops of fenders and rear panels. This was also true of the roofs as well. It was then going to be a matter of agreeing on the estimates of how much. Each car had to be individually inspected and an estimate prepared and cost-out done. It took a team of adjusters sent in by the insurance company to write them up, with our employees coming behind and negotiating on any they felt were not reasonable, over the best part of 10 days.

After this was done and Charlie had agreed to the settlement, the insurance company then gave him a check for the damage. It was now time for us to all get to work and start a sales campaign. We had marked all the stock cards with the amount of damage and put all the cars in one area and kept them together. We then started running our ads and gave people choices. They could have the car repaired and buy it, or we would fix maybe part of the damage and negotiate a lower price, or they could buy the car 'as is' for a lower price.

We had one guy phone in and wanted to buy the one with the lowest price and the most damage. He was a salesman who went out in the oil fields and each year he would put on about 70,000 miles, and the cars would get a lot of minor body damage. When he went to trade them in, he always took a large decrease in value. We had a 4 door Cutlass sedan that had well over $5,000 worth of damage. The only thing he wanted fixed was a new windshield put in and then took it as it was with a large discount.

We had each customer that bought one of these cars, sign a statement that they had been told of the damage and that they bought the car on that basis with a consideration already given in the negotiated price. Some of the vehicles looked good when they had a new hood and trunk put on and the other dents removed. Especially if it was a model where you could put a full vinyl top on it to cover up the top. We even learned that with some of the dents, you could take dry ice and use it on the area, and they would pop out good enough to where you left alone what little was left.

It took about 3 months with some heavy pushing at first to get them all gone. None of us wanted them staying around too long as they would only get harder to sell. When we were down to the last few it seemed harder to get them sold than it did the first 50 at the start. For the first time since I was there, we were trying to make money and not just sell vehicles on the new car side. With us negotiating how much to discount the damaged cars, we made money on the damaged vehicles. In fact when it was all over with, because of the amount Charlie was able to get out of the insurance company, the dealership made something well over $100,000 more profit than usual for that number of vehicles. It was the old story, when you are given lemons, make lemonade and that is what we had done. Some knew Charlie by his nickname, "Lucky", and maybe this is one of the reasons why he had earned such a name.

George had been busy with a particular spark in his life and was devoting his attention and more time on the phone in this direction. I had picked up a little more on some of the work but it wasn't a problem and we were getting along. He and his wife had taken the cruise trip but it didn't seem to make much difference. George had to stay on a strict diet. According to him he had been exposed to Agent Orange or something in Vietnam and had problems with his digestive system. This allowed me to eat more often in the back with Charlie and the others. I got to meet a number of the heads of GM in various departments and even the poor guy that was to head the new Saturn project when it was starting up. He later died of a heart attack before it was up and going.

One day when I came to work, the place was abuzz. It seems that the night before, George and Bryan had become embroiled in an argument and almost got in a fight. At the end, George had locked the office door with Bryan on the other side or something. I never did understand all the details but gather that Bryan must have gone to Charlie about it. Charlie was still was not overly found of George for some reason but was letting Doug try and run the place so when Doug wanted to make him Oldsmobile sales manager, he let him. Now Charlie was unhappy and planned on getting to the bottom of what was going on.

That day at lunch Charlie asked me a question and wanted me to give him a straight answer, as he put it. He wanted to know if George had been spending a lot of time with a girlfriend and not taking care of his duties. I told him that I understood he did have a girlfriend or was seeing someone. And yes, he was spending some time on the phone talking to her. I had picked up some work at times but I didn't feel it was a problem. I felt a lot more had been said but that is all he wanted from me.

Later, he came in the office and told me they had decided to let George go. I couldn't believe it. I felt that whatever had happened, Bryan must have put some story on them. I also knew that if Charlie wanted him out it was over and all I could do was keep my mouth shut. He then told me he wanted me to work from "can to can't" as we would say, and he would make it right later on and to trust him on it. I told him I would and he walked out of the room. I then let Pam know what was going on and that I would be working all the hours until they found someone else.

I was surprised and shocked. George had some funny ways at times but he was okay to work with and would try to be fair most of the time. I knew there was nothing I could do and as he and Doug were friends, if that didn't stop it, well, I guess nothing could.

Bryan danced around as if he had a victory under his belt. Still nothing was said and no more details were given. It was now up to me to just keep working and wait. I didn't want to work all the time with not even one afternoon off, forever, but I also didn't want them to hire some idiot that was just going to make my life more difficult. It was now time to just hurry up and wait.

CHAPTER 57

HANK COMES ON BOARD

It seemed like only a few weeks had gone by when one day I got a call from Dale McConnell to come down to his office. Doug was down there with a man sitting down across from Dale. He was dressed in a suit and had that sort of smooth look that reminded me a little of a snake. It was just a little something about him, a false sort of feeling, that made me feel uneasy. They then introduced me to him. He was Hank Harmon who would be the new Oldsmobile sales manager.

They then qualified what they said and it came across to me that things like titles were important to him. I was surprised that, since I was the one that was going to have to work with the guy every day and see more of him than I would my wife, they didn't have me in on the final interviews with prospective replacements for George. Dale and Doug had evidently made this their decision and that was it. It may have been just as well as I wouldn't have hired the guy. There was just something about him.

Doug had been working with Charlie on taking over more of the responsibility in running the dealership. The idea was that Doug would soon be the man running the place. The problem was that he was not ready yet and had developed some bad habits. It seems that he enjoyed using that funny stuff in his nose on weekends and from time to time, and it was affecting his moods and behavior.

Calvin was Doug's own porter. He was supposed to be the one for the new car department and from time to time he would move some cars and go on a dealer trade. However, most of his time was spent going on errands for Doug and his wife, Janice, or looking after their kids. One time Doug had Calvin fly over to Houston to get a pair of shoes that he wanted for a party. Calvin was gay and a real gossip who also liked to show off so it was some of these sorts of things that other employees knew about, that didn't help Doug's image as they felt he was overly extravagant.

I was told that back when he was in college he spent more time playing cards and setting up card games than he did in class. He did very well at it and when he was on a run at times, he would just keep buying new clothes and putting them on while letting the dirty ones pile up. When he met Janice, she sent them out to a laundry and had his place cleaned up. He had something like 50 new shirts that had only been worn once.

He later seemed to have found himself in some trouble over having set somebody up with a card game and then had it knocked over and the funds taken. The people involved were not very happy and it wasn't until his Dad got involved with a large amount of money, that the problem of people looking for him went away. At least that was the story.

Janice was from a banking, ranching, family at Fredricksburg and her father had the bank there. She got Doug straightened out to some degree, and later on got him together with his Dad in the dealership as they were at a stage they weren't talking to each other a lot. They had the usual conflicts of who was running the place . . . and "I thought you told me I was taking over" sort of stuff.

It was sort of in this area when I came in. Doug and George were friends when George was a salesman and they both liked guns as a hobby. When he made George sales manager after the other one left, Charlie didn't like it but stayed out of it as Doug was running the place.

Later on they had a write-up in the *'Austin American Statesman'* about how at the Austin Country Club, a car dealer and his son had been in an altercation and a knife had been pulled. From what we had heard, Doug and Charlie had been drinking and they got into an argument about the dealership and how things were being run. It turned nasty and one of them pulled a knife on the other. It was all settled down and they were asked to leave. There was some talk about banning them but that didn't happen.

When Doug had turned 21, as the story went, Charlie had given him a million dollars in a bank account so as to make him officially a millionaire. But no matter what transpired, they seemed to spend a lot of time disagreeing with each other and this time might be the last. Things were strained around the place for about a month and then one day we heard they had made up and Charlie had promised that no matter what, that from then on, he would stay out of running the place as such and would let Doug make the decisions. It seems that Hank was the result of his and Dale's work.

Doug had taken on a project of building a big new house in Austin in one of the exclusive areas of town. The house itself was going to cost $1 million. He also wanted his Dad to sell his own place and move into the new area but Charlie said he was happy with where he was. He didn't want a lot of attention drawn to him. When the house was finished there was a write-up in the newspaper showing how his and his wife's closets had clothes racks that rotated around, like in a dry cleaner. It also showed how he had rows and rows of clothes and shoes. This was something he liked spending money on and he liked to show it off. This was something that his Dad had told him was not a good idea.

As time went on, the Saturday morning managers' meetings became worthless. At first we would talk over problems or bring up questions we had on deals or employees. We would talk about the competition, sales campaigns, ideas for promotions, and topics that needed to be brought up on Monday mornings to the sales force. Over a period of about a year it got to the point I didn't even want to say anything for fear of being cussed at. It seems that half the time Doug would show up and be bent out of shape over something. One time Hank brought up the subject of having a sale of a particular type (not knowing that it had been talked over in the past and that Doug hated them) only to have Doug give him a 5 minute cussing out and calling him not only stupid and such, but also names; questioning how he could be so ignorant. It was this type of abuse that none of us wanted to subject ourselves to.

Another time after business had started to slow down a little, Doug came in and saw a letter from Oldsmobile about a contest. He grabbed it up and snapped what is this. When we told him it was a contest for sales managers put on by Oldsmobile he remarked we should be thankful they funded it or we wouldn't be in it. He then threw it on the desk and walked out. The contest was for some tickets to the Super Bowl and a short trip. The funny thing was we won it. Well, sort of.

It seems that Doug watched the results as we went along in the contest, with interest, as he wanted the tickets. When we were close to the end he had the Houston office make sure they had him listed as the sales manager. We won the trip and he got the tickets. I hadn't heard a word on this until one day Hank told me. I couldn't believe it so he picked up the phone and called the Houston office and he had the guy tell me who won it and who got the tickets. I didn't mind that Doug wanted the tickets and wanted to go. If he would have even just said to us to please try and win them for him it would have been okay. Instead with the way he had done it, it reminded me of my old days and I felt as if something had been taken from me. This was even a turn in personality for Doug. Was Calvin telling the truth about Doug's nose's activity?

Hank hated cigarette smoke and didn't want me smoking in the office. I cut back at times but it was more of the fact how he acted that made me want to smoke more. He wasn't any good at paper work and after picking up behind him all the time, I decided it was easier to do most of it myself and did all the ordering, inventory control, advertising, and watched over any promotional money we needed to collect on demos or rebates.

There was another area that I got myself into more by accident. They had hired a man and then later another guy to be our lease manager. It was a joke. They didn't know how to figure a lease. In fact at first, it was only George and I that were allowed to do the calculations so we wouldn't have a problem. There was one time when I was gone for the weekend getaway that we had our first problem. Our Finance Manager, Jim Arnold, didn't understand how they were calculated and when the guy wanted to switch vehicles and make some changes, he didn't think it mattered, as the price difference was only about a hundred dollars. The residual value in the book was very different and he wrote up a loss for the company. Doug wanted to know what happened and after I figured out my figures had been changed by Arnold and the vehicles switched, it all came unglued. At first Arnold tried to deny it and when he was in the corner he got his back up but Doug knew he was responsible for the changes. Doug lit into him and cussed him out. He made Arnold feel about 2 inches tall.

Our guys who were to specialize in leases knew even less. Whenever mail came into the dealership the office manager would separate it and go through it. He would then bring the Oldsmobile information to us. If it had to do with leasing I turned it over to Mr Gray and David Smith. I would glance at it but figured it was their job to be familiar with all the information. Later when Doug and Dale decided that they weren't working out and made them salesmen, a large portion of the paper work was then put back on me.

It was going to be the managers and F & I figuring the leases. The dealership had a company, Charles Maund Leasing, that owned the vehicles as such, and the deals were put through it. I then had a stack of information and bulletins that had been given to the guys by me that had come in through Oldsmobile. They evidently had never read it. I couldn't believe what I had read. If I was reading it right, the company was eligible for rebates on the cars that had been leased providing they met certain requirements on model type, motor type, and equipment level.

I then spent about two weeks going through all the deals that had gone through the Lease Company that were Oldsmobiles. I filled out the forms and told our Office Manager, Jerry Rushing, what I was doing. I told him I didn't think the other guys had every applied for the money. We waited to see if the claims would go through and all but about 2 or 3 did. After we took care of some paper work on those, they were paid as well. The total in rebates for the company came to over $100,000!

I got a passing sort of a thank you from Doug and it was mentioned to the others. I actually felt they should have said a little more as I had recovered money for them they didn't even know they had coming because of the idiots they had running the leasing. I then figured they must have felt it was just part of my job picking up after others.

It had been the duty of the new car sales manager to appraise vehicles for trade-in when the used car manager was not around—either during the day or when they were the manager on duty. George and I had worked out the procedure to use because of Bryan and it was running fairly smoothly. That is, until Hank came on board. He hired a few of the salesmen he had previously working for him at Capitol Chevrolet and they seemed capable enough but as I got to know them, they would joke about Hank in front of me. It seems they always knew that Hank didn't know how to appraise a car. If it had some sort of fancy wheels and a few stripes on it, he would usually appraise the car too high so they preferred to take them to him.

Bryan started making noises about Hank's appraisals and Hank didn't have any connections to get rid of the merchandise. It was up to Bryan to get out of Hank's mistakes. He finally made enough noise that both Dale and Charlie at lunch, told me not to let Hank appraise vehicles. They told me that whenever one of the men needed an appraisal they wanted me to take care of it. I felt it was sort of funny in some ways and in other ways I felt it was a bit of a compliment, as it was something they only wanted me to do and not him.

Hank liked visiting and acting like he was important and in charge. He would, on occasion, go into the sales office with a salesman and try to help close a deal. He would spend a lot of time sitting around with the salesmen and visiting with them. I felt this was okay as I felt he needed to do something. He wasn't capable of doing 90% of the paperwork or ordering, and he couldn't appraise a car.

It was a number of months down the track when I started to notice a couple of things about Hank. He would spend some time on the telephone and act a bit secretive about it. It seems he had one of those same weaknesses that George had. He liked the ladies and would have a girlfriend from time to time. In fact he would sometimes make out like he had to do something and actually go out drinking at some of the bars. Sometimes it was with his old salesmen friends and other times he would meet some of his acquaintances. Either way he didn't want home to know all about it.

Right after Hank went to work at the dealership a couple of changes were made in our pay plan. They first told me they were giving me an increase in my base pay to $3,500 a month. They also told me that with the next year, we would be going to 1% on the company profits instead of the ½ % we were on. We were still going to have sales bonuses but this proved to be a lot less often. I felt these changes were to accommodate Hank when they hired him, to provide a larger base pay.

CHAPTER 58

TIME TO MOVE

As I got to know Hank a little better I learned that one of his really big preoccupations was time off. He told me that when he worked at Capitol Chevrolet he made $50,000 a year and had various benefits. He didn't do a lot other than oversee the sales department and appraise the cars sometimes for trade-in. He had something like several weekends off each month and wanted to see if we couldn't work out some sort of deal where we took turns on getting more time off. As I began to think about it, I realized he was looking at the base pay package as his pay, with the chance of maybe a little more but what he was really concerned about was getting time off.

I tried to explain to him that the Maunds expected us to work probably more than we should but paid us accordingly and expected for it to stay that way. If he wanted to try and make changes it would be very difficult and he should take a slow approach. He then told me he had figured out already that they shouldn't object for he and I to take turns on weekends off. I assured him that this was out of the question. He had also figured out that if that was the case, then it shouldn't be a problem if between the 4 managers (including Bryan and Dale), all took turns and had one weekend off a month. I told him I still didn't think this would work either.

He also explained how he felt the salesmen should have more time off and that his guys were used to having more time off and wanted something done about it. Over a period of time he came up with an elaborate schedule for when the guys had the day off—and made it up a month in advance. In the days gone by, the guys were expected to work and if they needed a day off we took it on an individual case basis. This idea was brought up with Doug and he didn't like it. At first he started to shoot it down but something came up and he dropped it. Hank decided that since he wasn't told explicitly no, he would put the plan in for the salesmen.

A few times Doug felt it looked like we were short-handed and wanted to know where all the salesman were, and one time he was looking for one of them to turn a deal over to when he found out it was his day off. He didn't like it but acted as if he remembered something about it but couldn't quite remember it all. He dropped it but told us not to let this get out of hand; or else.

In the meantime, Hank had absolutely no results with his plan of the managers getting time off, on any basis. I did understand how he felt. I had worked my 60 hour weeks, month after month, and at times felt I was getting dull and worn down. A few days away from the place would have helped. Even the odd trip to a meeting was a help and usually you could pick up something from the others about what was going on or what they were doing about sales. It was just one of those things Doug had made up his mind on and all you were going to do by bringing it up again and again was make him mad.

From time to time Hank would call in sick—or I should say his wife would call in for him. Sometimes it was on a Monday and other times it was just here and there. After a day or two, he would be back at work and that was it. Later on after he had been there over a year or so, he told me one day that he wasn't really sick the other day when he didn't come in—he had been on a job interview. In fact he had been on job interviews several times. He said he didn't mind working for the Maunds but not getting enough time off was something he couldn't live with forever and he was looking for a change.

I told him I could understand how he felt and wished him luck. I was now in a bit of a situation. I was as happy as could be, that he was planning on leaving. Should I tell the Maunds or would this just stir things up. What if they let him stay after I said something? I would have a hard time working with him then. Would they think I wasn't very loyal to my fellow worker if I turned him in? Would they feel I wasn't loyal to them if I didn't tell them? I decided that he must be serious or he wouldn't have told me about it and he wouldn't have gone on an interview. He wasn't stealing and I was watching over his work anyway. It would be a problem that would be self-correcting and so I decided to sit back and watch, and keep my mouth shut.

By the time we were into 1986, business had started to slow down. The economy in our part of the world was slowing down and unemployment was on the rise. Oil prices had fallen to well below $20 a barrel and companies were going broke left and right. This had a roll-on effect to the support companies. The valley had problems since the Mexican currency had fallen in value to unbelievable levels. The Peso had been 12 ½ to 1 U.S. dollar for a long time. In a matter of a year it would go from several hundred to 1000 to one. The valley had 26 % unemployment. Mexico and the Mexicans couldn't afford to buy anything in the States.

Other changes were coming as companies complained about Japan dumping computer chips in the U.S. market and this was costing market share for producers. This also held true for Japan and their car industry. They had one advantage that they had built up themselves over a period of time. They now built a quality product and took care of their customers. The American public would now pay not just window sticker price for cars like the Honda but would wait for months to get one and then pay over sticker price. The market was changing and the factory was wanting to know what to do.

Business in general always seems to go in cycles. Sometimes the good times are long and sometimes short but business always seems to go up and down with time. We had been in boom times and at one point Austin was the fastest-growing city in the U.S. Real estate, which we had seen ourselves, had been sky rocketing.

We lived in Buda for over a year and the only problem was the distance to work. I was more often than not, late for Monday morning sales meetings. The traffic had become so heavy that if I were as much as 5 minutes late getting out of the house, I wouldn't make the meeting on time. The miles were stacking up on my demos and we always sold them before they had 6,000 miles so the customer could get an extension for a full factory warranty. I was getting a car it seemed like, every 6 weeks. We never lost money on any of them and I was always aware of what was going on with them.

Pam and I enjoyed looking at houses and getting ideas. Sometimes we would stop in one of the new neighborhoods and go looking at the houses. Our neighborhood had been built up overnight. We were the most expensive house in the area. A lot of the people that had moved in didn't like taking care of their places and they had the old car in the front yard. We were both afraid we were living in what was going to be a slum in another 10 years.

One day when we were out just looking at houses we spoke to a realtor and she told us she had somebody that wanted into our area. She had kids and it was the school district she was trying to get in for them. She wanted to know if we wanted to sell our house. I told her I would be interested at the right price but I also wasn't worried about selling. She told me she wanted to list it and see if she could sell it. Both Pam and I had some hesitation as we were not sure we wanted to make a move. We had just finished getting our new house close to how we wanted it and were now ready to enjoy it.

We told her we would give her only a 30 day listing so she could see if this person wanted the house or not. We told her we wanted top price or we wouldn't sell. She explained to us the lady was going to be limited by the amount she could get on a FHA loan. She calculated out that the lady with her deposit could only pay $102,000. This would give us about $30,000 before expenses and we had lived there only a little over a year. We decided to give it a try.

The lady agreed to the deal and now had to get the official approval from the Mortgage Company. If it all went ahead we would need to move in about 30 to 45 days. We decided to put Pam onto a full-time job of house hunting. We had put ourselves in a bind. The market was still very active at this time, as we were reminded when Pam went looking. She looked in all areas of Austin that were known as good areas and out to the lake areas as well. One day she found a house by Lake Travis that she knew was just what we wanted; it was a Monday. By Tuesday, and my afternoon off, it was too late. The realtor had signed up some other people the night before.

We were disappointed but kept on looking. We found one house that had been a model home for Randy Morine. He had sold out his company to another builder and the houses he had in inventory needed to be sold or the other company was going to take them over at a lower price than he felt he could get. It was sort of one of those situations where he was better of getting half a loaf instead of no bread at all for his houses in inventory.

It was on the south side of town and near where the new expressway leg was going to be. It had a vacant lot and street next to the property which we were afraid was going to be an apartment complex or something. The house itself was all brick with a large yard that was landscaped and had a sprinkler system. They agreed to put in a privacy fence, change out the bathtub in the master bathroom to a larger one and put in a spa in the back off the patio. This was over a period of time and at the end even talked about a finance subsidy for a lower interest rate. But we were afraid it was going to be too much money and still on the south side of Austin, next to an unknown property.

As time had gone on, word had spread around the sales department that we were looking for a house. I found out that Dale had purchased a new house in a new area and was going to sell his house. It had been rented out at one stage but was vacant now. It was in a good area and not far from work. Dale and Doug both encouraged me to take a look at it.

Pam and I decided to go and have a look. They told us it needed a little work but he had added a swimming pool and a privacy fence. It was a house, as you say, that "has a lot of potential". It needed a lot of work. It was still back in the 70's and showed it. It had gold shag carpet, pumpkin counter tops, avocado green, and the standard yellow of the day. The house needed painting, and the drainage needed work as it smelled wet under the house. The house was on a pier foundation and you could walk under the house but the water was also going under it as well.

Before it was over we had an engineer make a report on the foundation and the structure, and it all came back fine. We just had a lot of work to do. Pam and I both had reservations but felt it could be fixed up and if we did a lot of the work we could come out on it. It was less money than we had been looking at but even then, the payments were more than we should have been considering. It would be up to us to get financing and time was running out as our buyer had finally obtained her financing approval and moving day was not far in the future.

After some negotiating with Dale we decided to buy the house. It would make it simpler for us as he was also willing to rent the place to us and we could move in right away. As soon as our financing was approved and we could close, it would then be switched to a purchase and it would become ours.

I think this had something to do with it when I look back at it. We should have never rushed into the deal as it was. It became a financial burden later on. We spent all the money from the first house and a lot more, fixing it up and redecorating it. The house was, in some ways, better than a new one. We had fixed the problems the house had, as well as redecorating it. In fact we had a carpenter, named Dayne, work for us almost full time for several months.

When we moved this time, we had some help from Sam as well. The kids joked that it seemed like we always found a place to move into that was uphill. The house was on the side of a hill and had large trees around it. It was in town yet had privacy and a country feel to it. I reminded them that Kopecky was "the man who lives on the side of a hill". So the place must have been for us.

Pam spent many an hour cleaning and fixing the place up. She had Dayne lined out on what she wanted him to do and that was a lot. He replaced the counter tops in the bathrooms and kitchen, a new skylight, and a new outside deck set-up with built-in cabinets and planters just to name a few. Pam painted and papered the house from one end to the other.

The new challenge for her this time was to redo the tile on the swimming pool area that came loose and match the new tile counter tops on the deck. For her to match the pattern on the pool, she had to do each small piece, one at a time, and clean and refit them by hand. When it was done, it looked as if it came out of the box. It was perfect.

This took well over a year of hard work and during this time we had visitors and Pam took a trip home to see her folks. It was again a very lonely time while she was gone but painting kept me busy and helped the time pass. I think they say painting is good therapy and about this time I needed some therapy as things were not always going smooth, especially at work.

CHAPTER 59

WORKING AT IT

Doug always seemed to be snapping at somebody about something. The best thing I could do was stay away and keep my work up. Oldsmobile had been changing out some of their models with varying success. The larger cars, the 88 and 98, had been replaced with smaller front wheel drive models and they were doing well. Oldsmobile had also come out with a Ciera several years before but it was now doing well and it had taken off. Some of the leftover lines like the Firenza were small but going nowhere. We tried to help Heiser out by having and selling a few but they were not popular.

One surprise was how fast the sales of the popular Cutlass Supreme had died. The four door was always slow and the Ciera had taken over in this area by great guns. The coupe that had been so popular just stopped selling. The other coupe models were slow as well; it was a sign that times were changing. The large Toranado didn't sell well for us but the new one that was smaller and sleeker held promise. That is until we found out it was an electrical nightmare.

We had people telling us they never knew if the car was going to start or just stop running when they drove down the street. The factory had problems and no answers. Before it was over with, I knew of two that the factory had to buy back from the customers under the new "Lemon Law" that the state had put in place. We had decided not to push the sales on the vehicle and wait for the factory to sort out its problems. I found it interesting that during this time, the kids told me that Cecil had sold one of these to his daughter. It reminded me of how out of touch he usually was with what was really going on.

I had picked up on the changes in sales and what the people wanted. I would visit with the salesmen from time to time and always asked them to let me know if they were getting calls for cars equipped in some way in which we were not doing it. I watched the numbers and time of turnover and noted that some models would sell loaded much better than plain, while others were the opposite. It also made a big difference in what color they were ordered. It was a continual learning experience.

We were now selling a lot of 98 models, mainly the Brougham models. We were also selling a lot of the Ciera models. As long as the numbers balanced out to a 90-day supply, I kept adjusting the amount we ordered. We had been in balance with few exceptions and the only problem was running out of good merchandise when the factory couldn't supply. During one spring, Heiser told me they were going to have about 4 building periods of very high numbers because they were going to close the plant for repairs and maintenance. It was the plant where we got most of our 98's from. It meant we were going to have to either stay in our numbers and not take the extra now and run out of cars during the summer, or load up and put excess inventory on the ground for several months.

It just happened that day when the call came, Doug was not in. Heiser needed to know something then. I decided to go to Charlie and explained the situation to him. He wanted to know what I was thinking. I told him it was one of the best-selling models for us, as well as a number of other dealers at the present time. If we did load up, we would be able to trade them off for anything else we might need. We also wouldn't run out and have a poor sales period during the summer—usually one of our better times.

He told me to go ahead and do it and he would make sure they were covered in the office when it came time to pay for them. He also told me not to tell Doug what I was doing and to tell the factory it was me. This way he felt, we could have some leverage on favors with them. I think looking back at it now; he didn't want Doug to think he had been interfering with the operation. Over the next number of months we had 98's parked and stored all over the place. The inventory sheet that Doug was given each week never reflected this large number of 98's.

Over the summer we were one of the few dealerships that didn't run out of the model and were able to trade for anything else we needed by offering other dealers a 98. We made a lot of extra money that summer by not running out when others did. It took Charlie's money to afford the inventory, and our plan to think past the 90-day limit and take the chance.

This was not the only time I did this. Over the years I must have taken well over 1,000 extra cars that Doug never wanted. The factory would say for us to take them now or do without, and Doug would tell us to pass and not load up. I knew on good merchandise that we would be sorry and would then be trying to sell from an empty basket. He never knew how much money I made him over the years by using my head and taking the inventory we needed. It was a gamble but I knew what was selling and how fast it was going out.

This also held true on equipment levels and colors of vehicles. He would have a friend wanting a Ciera with a leather interior and just knew we would have to order or trade for one. We knew they sold and had a number of them in stock. The only time I started to get scared was when we had a most beautiful metallic red that had a gold flake in it and it was offered on the 98 line. I ordered one, and another, and another. They were selling as fast as they came in. I started carrying 3 or 4 of them and they were usually parked out in the back. Charlie did walk the lot from time to time to see if the inventory needed to be moved up front. He came in one day and wanted to know about the red cars out back and if they sold. I told him that I had ordered them and they had been selling extremely well. He bit down on his cigar as he did from time to time and told me it was a pretty red but not to get too many of them and to keep an eye on how they did. That was it.

Doug was worried that the cars had too much equipment on them and that is why sales had fallen off. The only problem with this idea was we carried an inventory that was staggered in equipment levels and ordered accordingly to how they sold. The low end equipped ones were the ones that weren't selling, not the loaded. He would see where we would have a car with reclining seats on both sides and gauges instead of idiot lights, and start to say see, this car is $150 higher than it needed to be. We also had the car without—and the one that had the extras usually sold first. People wanted these and the other dealers didn't have them as they were living in the past as well.

The competition from the import market was tremendous. They offered plain and cheap but also offered the gauges and leather, and this is what the people wanted. The people also wanted a car that was reliable and a salesman that knew his product—and not just someone who was a fast talker and trying to make a dollar off of them. Oldsmobile came out with a program to educate the salesmen and get them to learn how to do a presentation of the product. They were also going to have to learn a step-by-step delivery process to make sure all the points the factory wanted covered with the new car buyer, were done at time of delivery. At first Doug was not interested in the program until he found out it would reflect on the review of the dealership and how it was performing. This was another way for the factory to get another dealer into Austin.

I had been to a lot of meetings over the years and had always been able to pick up something from each one I had gone to. I felt this program was going to offer some positive things but would meet a lot of resistance. For whatever reason it fell on me to be in charge. I would spend time with the salesmen getting them familiar with the information so when they had to take a test they would at least pass. The reports that came in from customers about their sales and delivery experience were sent back to the dealers. We then were given them and would show each salesman. Some items, such as did they get a full tank of gas at time of delivery? should have always been yes and it was up to the salesman to point it out to the customer. We were to get our standings up to or above the zone average. With some time, this is what we did. When the salesmen knew they would have one of these report cards come back from the customer, it did make a difference.

The other part was a contest where one of the salesmen who scored at the top would be able to go to an area meeting, then zone, and so on, to national. It would be partly, written questions on the product and then a sales presentation of a vehicle to strangers who were actors and would ask questions. The finalist would go on a trip to a national competition with their sales manager. We would get prize points at each level and at the end the manager would get to go on a trip with his wife and get more prize points. The salesman got points and the trip but if he won, he won a new car from Oldsmobile. For two years running I worked on this with a salesman, Chester Odom. Some of the others didn't like him—including Hank and Doug.

Chester would always ask why. He always wanted everything explained to him and it was something that would get on your nerves from time to time. He was also the only one that would put in the hours of learning and practice to try and make it work. It was his hard work that got us to the finals each year.

Unfortunately he finished second. Doug gave him no help or encouragement. Some of the other dealers furnished video equipment so the salesman could practice and learn from it. They also paid cash bonuses to them as they got higher in the competition. Some even paid an extra wage for the time off of the floor it took to learn and prepare for the competition. Doug wanted none of it and felt if Chester did it, it was his choice. Chester later told me that the thing that hurt was the fact that Doug (nor any of the rest) had never come to him and told him well done for going all the way to the nationals and representing their dealership. He knew they didn't really like him but this is what hurt. He was right; it wouldn't have been much to say well done to someone who worked as hard as he did to try and bring some good recognition to the dealership.

Pam and I enjoyed the trips and had fun. One was to San Francisco and it gave us a chance to see the area and went on a wine tour to Napa Valley with llunch at Domaine Chandon (as in Moet & Chandon). We walked all over the place from Fisherman's Wharf, to Telegraph hill, through Chinatown, and back to Union Square and the St. Francis Hotel where we stayed. The other trip was for us to fly to Reno, Nevada, and then take a limousine to Lake Tahoe and stay at Harrahs' Hotel and Casino. Again we saw the area and the lake, as well as the shows and the casino. We had set our limit before we went and enjoyed playing the quarter machines with 'lunch' money GM gave us. When we felt we were cold we would just stop. One evening I was lucky and hit the jackpot. It was 1,000 quarters. They gave me $250 for them so I wouldn't have to walk funny. We put it up and enjoyed the rest of our trip and came home with more than we left with.

We had become friends with a few of the salesman and spent some time with them. It was mainly Roger Rogers and Gene Webb. Roger was an ex-marine (and Viet Nam vet) who lived out near the lake. Gene was a Cadillac salesman who had been a friend of Dale and Doug's. He had helped figure out how to do a swimming pool at Dale's old house. We didn't spend all of our time with them but some.

When Pam had most of the house about done we had both realized we were in a different situation. We were no longer getting the extra sales bonus money offered and it was getting tight. I was having to draw on my year-end money as a matter of need. She wanted to do something and had a Green Card now. She went on a few interviews and told me of a job that was interior design and decorating. The company was a national one out of Atlanta. You could have your own business and work with others. It was multi-level marketing but this company had, and made, their own merchandise. You could have everything from pictures, to rugs, to furniture . . . to you name it and they had it. She was excited but didn't like the idea of sales. I told her that is what we all do every day. We are always selling ourselves, our ideas. That was also where you could make the most money, in sales. You weren't being held back but you did have to produce or get nothing. I told her not to let it put her off and if it were something she wanted to do, then I would help any way I could.

I think by now we were starting to look out for ways to either make more money or cut our expenses. It was looking like we were going to go into one of those down cycles for awhile and I wasn't sure how long it would last. I did know that it wasn't as it was when I had first gone to work at Maunds. Business was slower and we were not getting offered the opportunities for the sales bonuses like we had been. Since Hank had come it was different. Some of the guys told me they had seen him from time to time talking to Dale and Doug down in Dale's office and he spent a fair amount of time around them on my afternoon off. Some of them felt he was putting me together and setting me up. I told them I was sure they were wrong and besides, I told myself inside, they were smarter than that; after all they told me to be the one appraising the cars and doing the paperwork.

Hank got along with Bryan but didn't like him a lot. At one stage after I had worked as acting used car manager when Bryan was on holiday, he asked me what I thought about being used car manager. I told him I wouldn't mind but you would never get Bryan out of the place. He expressed some concern about business being a bit slower and I knew he had no luck in finding another job, as he was still with us. I think he was looking down the road but I felt his worry was out of place. Business was not that bad and I was sure the Maunds wouldn't let good employees go just like that.

CHAPTER 60

OTHER OPTIONS

People have never ceased to amaze me. I came to work one morning and as the day got underway, the place became abuzz once again. It seems that out of the clear blue sky, Bryan had decided to quit. In fact he went in that morning and told them he was leaving at noon that day. He had another job at a BMW store in San Antonio as I remember.

Well, I felt if they wanted to make some changes, now would be the time to do it. I had put in a couple of stints in the used car department and felt they could see I was capable of doing the job. I was thinking about what Bryan had done and couldn't get over it. I knew Dale and Charlie had been on him some about his inventory and doing something about some of the cars he had in stock. Bryan didn't have to write down his cars as such and would take his problem children and put them off to one side. I think Charlie knew he was building up a number of pieces of bad merchandise that were going to cause a loss. Bryan didn't like selling anything at a loss as those hurt his pay check, and all these went across Charlie's desk and he usually wanted to know why.

Bryan wasn't any kind of a used car manager that I could see. He needed to stay on top of his inventory almost more than we did. Our new car was still the same price month after month for the model year. His changed value each month and if you weren't careful, you could have one that could have gone out for a small profit, turn into a big loss if it just sat and sat. I wondered if Bryan knew his time was up and before they could make a large adjustment in his pay, he was ready to get his check and run because that is what he did.

We started to run it as usual when they decided to put Dale in charge of used cars for awhile. They were going to turn their attention to a department that had been neglected. They started looking for a used car manager as Dale tried to clean up the stock. It was after he was in the department for awhile that I think they realized how many cars Bryan had just stuck to one side and let them go, as he didn't want a loss to affect his pay. They found a used car manager and put him in place. He was a very different sort of guy. They had also changed the pay plan as they now had a chance to start anew.

I was a little surprised they didn't think about me for used cars, if Hank was right about being worried about somebody being let go. But I had heard that Charlie had said once a new car man is not a used car man. I think what he was saying was you just can't make one out of the other. I had started in used cars and did have the ability to do the job as I had done when Bryan was on vacation. Nevertheless, I figured maybe Hank was just worrying more than he should since they hired a new man just like that.

Charlie was very upset about Bryan leaving and was even mad. He felt he had done a lot for him and was not treated very fairly in return—either by such short notice or by his leaving a number of losers stuck to the side, instead of doing his job as they came up one at a time. This wasn't the only disappointment for them on that end of the building. Dale had hired a Buster Naylor, a preacher of sorts, and they had fed him deals and helped him. They later caught him stealing trade-ins and selling them on the side. That was the end of him.

Another was a fellow by the name of Crampton. He had become flavor of the month and was also given house deals to help him out. They later found out he had a record and spent some time in jail for fraud and forgery. He seemed okay and they didn't want to let him go. It wasn't until later on when he got married and he invited a number of us to it, his problem came out. Pam was afraid very few would go to his wedding and wanted us to go. We did and he was so thrilled he wanted us to ride with he and his wife in a limousine up and down 6th street as they went to some of the bars and nightlife after the ceremony.

It was during this time we found out both he and his wife, as part of their celebration, were using that stuff in their nose. He started acting even more stupid and in one place knocked a number of glasses off a table with his walking stick that he carried with him when he wore his tux. One of the others paid for the damage and we left. We were finally able to get back to our car and away from him. We didn't want to be associated with him in case of trouble. This is what we always tell our kids isn't it? . . . to stay away from trouble or you will get dragged in as well.

They must have passed the stories around at work, and even Dale and Doug were nervous that he was an accident waiting for a place to happen. If he was caught with this stuff in his possession they could confiscate the vehicle. Before you knew it, he was gone. He should have left that stuff alone and just done his job.

These others that were favorites from time to time, cut into Gene Webb's share of house deals. It was the company's way of paying a little extra to those that helped. Gene always helped with inventory, dealer trades, and even ordering the cars. It did take time–and time off the floor selling. Gene had made the same mistake a number of us did in the boom times. He purchased a new house; a nice house but more than he could afford in normal times. When business slowed down he was desperately trying to make his payments. They knew he was having trouble at work as he was not making the money he had. He was still helping but wasn't getting the extra deals he needed. At one point I suggested that maybe they should consider making him like an assistant manager and pay him say $1,000 a month for all the extras he did. That did not go down well and I was lucky I wasn't shot at dawn the following day.

At one point he was broke and short of making one of his payments. He came to me and asked if he could borrow $500. It was something he didn't want to do and something I didn't want to get started as my previous experience along this line had always been a disaster but I talked to Pam about it and she felt we should try and help. I told her we may never see it again and that she needed to be prepared for this. She felt it was something she hoped someone would do for us if we needed it and told me to go ahead. Then Pam wanted to help them even more. She wanted to show Sharon Webb what she was doing and see if she was interested in going in with her. If she was, then she would loan her enough of her stuff to help her out and even front her some of the set-up fee until she made some sales.

A month or so went by and one day Gene came in and gave me the $500 he had borrowed from me. I didn't have to ask him for it and I was glad to see he didn't need reminding. He was still in trouble and making a draw against his pay each time he had enough to cover another bill. In the meantime, Sharon had started to work with Pam on and off. No matter how hard Pam tried to help her though, she wouldn't follow through and would let things fall over. It was a lesson to us that we are still learning. Some people no matter how hard you try to help them; it just doesn't matter until they are ready to help themselves. Sharon had no commitment to do the job like the others, although she helped at times. She didn't have her own money in it like the others and didn't have the drive to make it work, even though she had the ability.

Pam and I considered refinancing the house when interest rates had dropped to a much lower level. We went through all the paper work and as it had only been in the last couple of years since we bought the house, we knew most of the steps. The company only guaranteed the new rate for something like 45 days. We had put up our deposit for the refinance and stayed in touch with them. As it was getting closer to the deadline it was clear they were not going to make it as they were not getting everything in on time, like the survey. This meant we would have to take a higher rate than we thought we were going to get, as the rates were on the rise again.

I decided to see what I could do and found out exactly what they were running behind on. I ordered the survey myself and made arrangements with the insurance company to provide proof of cover on the last day we had to close. When they started to tell us we just weren't going to be able to get it done in time, I told them I had already taken care of things, and the survey and insurance were taken care of. At first the lady said I couldn't do that but couldn't tell me why as there was no reason.

Pam and I went to the Title Company and signed all the papers and she told us everything was fine. However, the next day the company that was handling the brokerage said the deal was off and we hadn't made it as the insurance company had not provided proof of cover in time. As I ran this down, I found out the insurance company agent's office had sent the form directly to the Brokerage Company and not the Title Company as per usual. This company denied ever receiving it.

What this meant was that we would have to take the deal at a higher rate. I told Pam I bet the company didn't lock the money in at the lower rate and that is why they were trying to force us into a new rate. They didn't have the money available as they told us they did. New mortgages and such are registered at the courthouse and reported in the court reporter. We subscribed to the service for car registrations but it also had this information. I looked up a number of these and contacted the people who had put a mortgage through this company. A number of them had the same experience and were forced to either pay more or take a higher rate. I was thinking they were dishonest.

Pam and I talked it over and as I had given them an earful on the phone we decided she would go over to their office and talk to the manager and see what she could learn. She would tell him how important it was for us to get the lower rate and wring her hands and do all that sort of stuff. She went over and got a chance to see the manager. As she visited with him in the office he pulled out the file and went through a number of the items and explained how they had not received any notice in time from the insurance company. They were still claiming they hadn't received it. Pam watched and as he went through the folder she saw a packet from an express company in the file. She was sure it was our notice and they were not telling the truth. I could only wish I had been there as I would have taken it from him and opened it up. But I wasn't and all we could do was talk it over.

We ended up going to a lawyer and he contacted the company. No one wanted to know about it and they all said it would cost a lot more than it was worth to pursue. This company was getting people in on false pretences as they quoted a lower rate for less money than the competition but when it came time to provide the goods they either wanted more money or a higher rate as they were unable to close on time, over and over again. We were finally offered either the higher rate or our money back. We decided to leave it as we still were considering some sort of lawsuit at the time. We just hated to see them getting away with it.

Pam was learning how to work with Trans Designs and the lady that had her join and helped train her was Barbara Smith. The company provided a lot of aids and help in training in a number of areas. They did sales training but it was in conjunction with teaching product knowledge and how to put a plan together for a client. We had decided that it was no good for Pam to try and do the job if she didn't have the materials she needed to do it properly. With this in mind, she purchased the larger sales promotion kit. It had more samples and storyboards that gave you a better chance of making an impression as well as providing the client with a clearer and more professional decorating plan.

Pam went to the training and worked with her materials at home to get familiar with them. It does no good to finally get a chance to show a client what you have to offer and then spend half your time digging around through your bag trying to find something to show them. If anything it makes them lose confidence in you and that you know what you are doing.

Pam liked the business of decorating and enjoyed working with all the various aspects from fabrics, to floor coverings, to artwork. After she had her feet on the ground she started trying to make some sales calls. At first it was to some of the people we knew but with time, through referrals and working with some of the people she had met when we did up our house. As she gained confidence and started making sales she really enjoyed it. It wasn't just the money. It was the thrill and sense of having accomplished something when you made a sale and somebody started on a plan to decorate their home. I told her then she was hooked on sales. A lot of people in sales enjoy this part of it as much as the money. It did make you feel good when it was working. She would, as we all did, have to learn to overcome the slumps or valleys she would have in sales as well.

It was with this new adventure we hoped that Pam would be able to make the extra money we needed to get some of the financial worry off us. We knew it wouldn't be overnight as it was going to be like building up a new business and it could very easily take a year or more before any steady stream of income would come in. This didn't put us off and we both figured it could develop into a business that could be very profitable. Some of the others that were in it did make a lot of money; it was now up to us to make it work.

CHAPTER 61

PROBLEMS

It was during this period that several obvious problems were staring us in the face. One was what had been going on at work and how the income had slowed down. This of course created problems that led to us to looking at cutting back on expenses, as well as Pam going to work. The stress and strain at work was starting to show up at home as the finances became tighter.

It wasn't as bad as it had been years before but we were now having to watch what we did and not able to save as we had done in our own way. We had in the past, put some away in our IRA accounts and in the plan at work. We also had Pam take some money with her one time when she went to New Zealand and along with some she already had there, purchase a piece of property. Again later, as we were doing our remodel on Mountain Ridge, Pam made a trip home and took some money with her again to invest. Interest rates were very high in the U.S. but overseas they were even higher. The exchange rate was at the point she almost doubled the money she took over and on deposit with her lawyer friend, John Armstrong, she was getting over 20% interest on her investment.

Back when the previous general manager retired, he had said he wanted to get out while he could still enjoy life and had his health. I didn't think that much about it at the time but it came clear to me as time went on what he was talking about. Pam and I had talked about a lot of things in general terms over a long period of time. The obvious question had been talked about a lot of times—in fact, over and over again. We were at a stage we were enjoying life, doing things, buying things, having a house we wanted, and working ourselves to the point we needed to ask what it was all for.

We both realized that it would be impossible to keep up this sort of pace forever. If no changes were made over a period of time, then you would either kill yourself trying to do it or have to quit. I had told Pam originally I guessed I could last about 10 years or so. I figured I would watch it and see how it went but knew there was a day coming when I would not be able to continue all the long hours and put up with the stress. The stress was harder to put up with than the hours. The situation with Hank, and Doug going off and yelling all the time, was hard to put up with and would get on your nerves.

It had been with this long-term general plan in mind that we said "some day" as we all do. Our someday, was that we might go and live in New Zealand for awhile and allow Pam to be near her folks, family, and friends for a change. For the foreseeable future we would live near mine as we both felt it was important for me to be near the kids for now—especially the younger ones, Laurie and Scott. I told Pam I really didn't want to think about going until Scott was at least 18, and out of school and on his way. If he was settled in some sort of college and it was working out and he didn't need me as such, then as far as the family went, I wouldn't say no to going. It would then come down to a matter of work and finances. It would be one of those things I felt we would know when the time was right and it would then just be a matter of selling up and going.

That was something we had both agreed on from the start and was never a problem. The other thing was more of a problem. It was should we or shouldn't we have a family? First of all, since I had a vasectomy right after Scott was born, it would take an operation and we had no idea of how much it would cost or if it would even work. I didn't know if it would be easy or very difficult. This was something we would take a step at a time and was somewhat out of our control. The larger problem, as such, was should we? I already had 4 children and so of course from my standpoint, was not worried about having any more. This, of course, would be a selfish attitude on my part if that were all that was to be considered. It wasn't.

Pam had decided she wanted to try to have a family . . . but it didn't have to be tomorrow. Although she knew she did want one, she didn't want to do this just to say she did. She had already decided she didn't want one with her previous husband—mainly because she wasn't sure it wasn't going to end in divorce and she didn't want that for any kid who might be involved. It was the fact that she felt she wanted a family with me. She felt we could both contribute to the upbringing of the child and both had something to offer. She knew how much I loved all my kids–and in fact, loved kids in general. She knew I had always felt cheated by not having them with me or being able to spend the time with them I had wanted to. It was not from that point of view that I was holding back.

Pam was afraid that she was not getting any younger and as she got older it would be more difficult for her to have children as well. The fear of problems and abnormalities with age were also a worry and a consideration. As far as she was concerned she wanted us to check it out and get started and 'try',sooner rather than later.

I was unsure. I was unsure how much of a problem it would cause for the other kids and felt the older they were the better the chance was that they would understand. I didn't want to make any more problems than I already had. The kids at times didn't act like they cared a lot as it was. This was mainly true of Scott, the youngest. The others would visit and even when they acted a little strange didn't seem to be mad or upset. Laurie would even talk about the stars and subjects I didn't think she talked about at home. The two younger ones had been given a very heavy dose of 'born again' doctrine and at times you could see a sort of disapproving air about them towards us.

Scott was as if he was mad and wouldn't say why. I tried to talk to him and get him to talk to me. I pushed him real hard one time about a subject and he asked what I wanted him to say. I told him to just tell me what he was thinking or how he felt about it . . . that is what I wanted to know—not a standard answer that he was supposed to say. He didn't say a word. I never was able to get him to communicate with me. As time went on it got worse, and later he would go for years and never even contact me.

I can't say to this day it was any one thing. I just wasn't ready to go down that road and didn't want to face all the possible problems it might cause. In some ways it may have been me being selfish as I wanted the time we had together for us. I knew this would change as soon as we had a family and I guess I wasn't ready to give that up yet as well. This led to a sore point and Pam did bring it up a number of times. Although she accepted that it might not be physically possible, she did not want to wait forever to try; and the best I could do was tell her it would be later and possibly when that "some day" came and we moved, and made a major change. I just didn't know. She had a hard time finding this a satisfactory answer. If there was ever one thing we argued about at that time, it was this. And it was my fault.

If I had that crystal ball we all need from time to time, this would have been a time it would have come in handy. If I could have known how much happiness our little one would bring later on, well, I would have done it sooner. But I was right; it did cut into our time together. It always does and is just a part of it. You have to give something up but what you get back—at least in my case—makes up for it.

Pam had learned a lot about decorating and remodeling when we redid the house. It also gave her some contacts at the companies we used and they did give her some referrals. She had also met Dayne who did our carpentry work for us. He would prove to be of help in the future as well. He was always of help and did that little extra.

We decided it would be more practical for awhile to have a pickup truck and the opportunity came up for me to get a late model Chevrolet Silverado for Pam that had all the equipment on it. She kept the truck until later when it was more practical to put her back in a car.

Chevrolet pickup truck Pam had while remodeling

When we were in the middle of remodeling the place it worked out that Beulah Ann and Tommy were on the move again. We were happy to have Dad come and stay with us once again. We were able to take him out to eat at some new places as we were now in town. We were not far from one place that played jazz and did a New Orleans style menu. We took him there as he really enjoyed it. One time when we went the younger kids went with us. I remember Laurie couldn't get over how much he liked the music and didn't want to go home.

During this time, my brother Joe came down from the Dallas area to see Dad as they were on their way to San Antonio to see his wife's family. They showed up on Friday before the weekend, just as Dayne was finishing up. He watched them for about 5 minutes as the kids ran wild and chased the cats we had been given by Diane—who ran down the stairs in an attempt to hide. He took some of the lattice and nailed it across the opening, saying he would fix the holes on Monday as until then, he felt we would need all the help we could get.

He was right. This was the first time I had seen Joe in many years. His wife, Janie, acted as if it was a holiday, and the kids did as they wanted. She expected to be waited on as well. Pam didn't complain, and cooked and cleaned and watched the kids. The kids did have some consideration. One night the light went on in our bathroom and it woke us up. We asked the little girl what was going on. She said she needed a band-aid and was getting one from the cabinet. We told her there were some in the bathroom where her Mom and Dad were. She said she knew that but she didn't want to wake them up.

One of the kids was hitting a glass on top of the glass end tables. Pam heard it all the way in the kitchen and came out to see what was going on. Janie just sat there and ignored it. So, full of adrenaline, Pam lifted the table (full of records), and put it out on the side deck and locked the door. She told Dad who was sitting by the other glass end table, that if he didn't protect his, it was going next. After they left, it took both Pam and I together, to lift the heavy table up off the side deck and move it back to its place.

Pam finally decided that in order to make some money and have others to work with, she needed to do the part of the business she had at first said she didn't want to do. That was to recruit and train other people. She had started in a funny sort of way with Sharon Webb. She could see how having somebody else to work with could at times make it easier and more cost effective. If they took a booth at the home show they could split the expense of the booth and the time to man it. They would have a 'giveaway' to register for and thus people to follow up for their service. They would have both the ones they had talked to and the ones in the draw who would be shared out to those that were in the group. They could give each other ideas and help when they had a problem. It was partly the idea that two heads are better than one.

Pam ran some ads in the paper and interviewed people at the house. She did pick up a few good people this way. One thing I learned about it was how many people were out there looking for a way to make some extra money. I was really starting to wonder if things weren't maybe a little worse than we had suspected.

Very few salesmen knew of our long-term plans. The Webbs, along with Eddie Powell and Roger Rogers were about it. We didn't want the word to get around we were even thinking of leaving 'some day' as this might be misinterpreted. We had no plans to leave for years at best but employers get nervous if they think you are even thinking about leaving. Some of this was told in error to people like the Webbs, as Pam felt she could trust them and was talking in confidence to Sharon one day. When I found out, I told Pam to not let this become public knowledge. I was afraid that Gene might even say something to Dale or Doug at some point in time. He had a bit of a mean streak in him I had seen and if he felt he should get even with you over something, this is the sort of thing he might do.

With sales having fallen off at work, Doug felt we needed fewer salesmen. We had several that were not producing—a couple of which Hank had follow him from Capitol Chevrolet. One of the guys was laid back and smoked a pipe. He was never in a hurry. His father had died and he was in the process of getting a divorce—it was just more than the guy could handle at the time. His sales were off and one day when he was out by the door on the showroom floor, a lady came in and asked him for Doug. He took his usual slow way to go to the operator to see about letting him know someone was there to see him. He also evidently didn't communicate very well with the lady and left her feeling out of place. She complained to Doug about him and he wanted to know who it was. He also wanted to see me in his office.

When I went to his office he told me of the complaint and ate me out. I tried to explain the guy wasn't himself between the divorce and his father having died just a few days before. He told me he didn't care. He had decided that he and another salesman, Bill Hibdon, needed to go. Bill Hibdon was an older salesman and was honest and dependable.

He would sell about 10 to 15 units a month and stay out of the way. That was about all you could say about him. Doug didn't care and felt those towards the bottom needed to go. I was told to fire them that day and get their demonstrators and lock box keys from them. As this was about 2 weeks before Christmas it made me feel bad—but it did Doug a lot of damage. A lot of the other employees, both in the office and in the sales force, decided he was a cold heartless person. He lost a lot of respect and loyalty from his employees if that is how he could treat these people just a couple of weeks before Christmas.

He was to again demonstrate his lack of understanding of the need for keeping his employees loyal and supportive in the not-too-distant future. Doug was as opposite as he could be from Charlie. It was as if he had learned nothing from him.

He later decided that with business slowing down, the office didn't need as many girls in it. He proceeded to let a couple of them go and told Jerry to reshuffle the work around to the girls that were left. They knew we weren't making the money we had but were disappointed he didn't try and keep them on, even part-time.

Not long after this, a man came in from the service department to the Cadillac end of the building. He was one of those flash sort of guys and wanted to see Dale or Doug. I wasn't there at the start but Calvin told us how the guy got them started into betting on flipping a coin. He gave Calvin something like a $100 for helping him call the coin while it was in the air. He lost several times to Doug and then they started raising the stakes. It was raised to the point he bet his and Dale's Rolex watches that were both worth about $10,000. He flipped the coin and let Doug call heads or tails but Doug lost the bet and the man left a big winner.

Charlie took Doug to the back and tried to explain to him this was not good public relations, having just let go some of the employees because business was off and they weren't making a lot of money. Yet he could lose that kind of money on the flip of a coin in front of them. It just wasn't good business. The other obvious thing he tried to explain was never try to beat a man at his own game. A lot of guys that were good with a coin could feel it when they went to catch it and could turn it as they put it down. Again, if he was going to be that silly, he was going to lose and he should try and not do it in front of the employees. It didn't help his image.

This sort of behavior did make you nervous as you didn't know what to think. No one knew who was going to be next. All I wanted to do was keep my mouth shut and my head down. It seemed like the best option for now.

CHAPTER 62

CHARACTER

One thing that always amazed me, with Doug and Dale both, was what a poor judge of character they seemed to be. It was one of those things people either have or don't have. I felt like it was one thing I had and had learned to develop it more than some of the others.

This is when you go to interview a person or even meet them in a situation and in a matter of minutes you have a feeling about them as to whether they are phony or not. This was true of customers, employees, and acquaintances. I didn't always worry about what my impression was—especially if it was not my responsibility. If I didn't think it was really my business then I usually didn't worry about it. This later proved to be a major problem for me.

When George and I were working the sales force we hired mainly experienced salesman. They already knew how to sell and it was more a matter of working with them in some way to put a deal together. They would get a commitment on paper, as they were told to do and then they would bring it to us. We would work with them from there and try to make a deal. The salesman would take the position of the good guy trying to help the customer get a deal he wanted from the management. It was only on rare occasions we really had to go in to close a deal.

When the sales force was changed with time to more of Hank's old crew, it did change. We had retired military, school teachers, and various other previous occupations he had taken on board and tried to train. This is not bad in itself but it does require spending more time watching over them and each deal they try to make. We would sometimes get involved in one of their deals only to find out they had not really sold them on a car yet and were thus not ready to make a deal at any price. Other times they wouldn't get the customer committed on paper. They would just come in and give a figure to us in the air that they were thinking about.

There are a lot of steps in the sales process before you ever got to price. Some of those that had no experience—and those that were sure they knew it all—would sometimes skip some of these steps. This was a sure-fire way of stacking the cards against yourself and missing a sale. I had been to a lot of sales seminars and training over the years. They all had a lot of things in common. You had to sell yourself first, then your product, and then the price.

When I worked with a new salesman, the first thing I wanted them to do was become familiar with the product; then how we ordered cars; and last, how we wanted a deal worked. They were to get to know their customer and make friends with them. As they did this, they needed to find out what they wanted and any other information; such as had they been shopping at other dealers, what were they looking at, what was their budget, and so on. They could then show them what we had to offer in the equipment and price range they were looking at. Then if he got an offer on paper they had something we could all work from to try to make a deal.

It was irritating—even with Hank—when you would have a customer leave and then find out they had wanted a car just like that but wanted a reclining seat, or they only wanted power door locks and none of the rest. I would then remind them we ordered our inventory so as to stagger the equipment and price. We had most combinations in stock or coming. If we didn't, we would trade for it from another dealer or even order it especially for them from the factory. The usual response was, "Oh, I didn't know that".

For whatever reason, it took a long time for Hank to get it into his head that he needed the salesman to have a written, signed commitment on paper before we could try and work a deal. We had a work sheet and it was always to be used. It didn't have to have all the spaces filled in but if they had even the stock number and say something like "Will trade today for $10,000 drive-out price". Then we had a commitment.

The best thing was to do that and get a check for even a $100, as a deposit. The customer had then made the commitment in his mind that he was buying a car and that car was his we were talking about. Without this, many a time, a guy would look at your counter offer and just say "I'll think about it" and walk out.

This was the area Hank was supposed to be spending most of his time in as he wasn't doing anything else. I didn't think much of his ability as he wasn't getting the salesmen to do their job properly first. Without the salesman doing his job first, you didn't have much chance of closing a deal that wasn't there to begin with.

Not all the salesmen that Hank hired had no experience. Some were the younger flashy type. It was funny because this was the type that Hank, Doug, Dale, and even Bryan were likely to be taken in by—examples being Buster Naylor, the preacher; Tony Crampton who had committed fraud; Brady, a high roller; and Tony Moncrieff.

Brady worked for us on the Oldsmobile sales end. He was very aggressive and could be a good salesman when he wanted but he spent as much time working the management as he did the customer, and would actually bully people like Hank into pushing the trade for more for a deal. He did it in such a way that everybody thought he was great. He would complain about the appraisals and tell you how much he knew. He would always threaten to walk out and go to work at another store. He wanted to be in management and was trying to find a way to get into it. He did finally quit one day and went to work as a used car manager or something at a Pontiac store. I wasn't sorry to see him go but others were.

The best was Tony Moncrieff. He was in used cars and worked for Bryan. He was loud and had an attitude. I had suspected he was either not all at home or was using something from time to time. He sold a lot of used cars and he would bully some of the other salesman out of the way at times. It was unfortunate that he and I had a run in. It was not all his fault or mine.

It was one Saturday morning after the sales managers' meeting and I sat at the computer putting in the balance of the week's sales. Hank was on the phone and talking to either his wife or girlfriend as usual. Bryan had taken off right after the meeting to go somewhere on personal business. This had become a habit and was getting to be a real problem, covering and doing his job for him all the time.

Tony came in and walked over to me and with his appraisal book, started hitting me on the shoulder. I told him to stop and was finishing up on my last entry when I turned to look at him. He started hitting me again, bounced back like a fighter and acted as if he was going to hit me. I jumped up, grabbed him and pushed him by the wall. I told him to stop and to cut it out. Just as I said it, he hit me and split my lip with the ring he had on. The others jumped in and grabbed us.

I had to go to the emergency room at a clinic about 6 blocks away where the doctor put some stitches in. After that I went home, changed clothes and went back to work. I told them what had happened but didn't go into the fact I was irritated about being the one that was constantly covering and doing somebody else's job. It was me they had to come to, not Hank, as he wasn't capable. Bryan, who made a hell of a lot more, was always gone and it was up to me to cover for him. I didn't get into any of this but knew it didn't help my attitude.

I still was not sure why Tony was acting as he was and why he felt he had to haul off and hit me as he did. They told me they fired Tony and told him to get out. They really didn't want any trouble at the dealership and I didn't either, so no plans were made to call the cops and on the insurance form we just put down it was an accident. I felt for some reason this wasn't going to be the end of it.

Later on, starting the next week, Bryan was complaining about them having fired Tony. His wife had come down and asked for him to come back as they needed the job and the money. Bryan kept on complaining about it and talked to Doug. Doug came to me and told me how much Bryan wanted Tony back. He said he wouldn't let him come back unless he apologized to me in front of everyone at the sales meeting and if it was okay with me.

This was a 'no win' situation. I still didn't know why Tony had acted as he had and yet if I didn't say everything was okay, well, then it would be me the bad guy. I told Doug it was okay if they wanted him back but not to make him apologize in front of everybody as this could only cause humiliation and bad feelings. Tony did stop by the office and saw me for a minute and we shook hands, and that was the end of it. For now. But I still found it interesting how Doug and Bryan had both handled the situation, and how they treated me and didn't consider Tony a problem.

It was sometime a few months or so later, that over at used cars Tony and Bryan had been picking on one of the other salesmen. It seems Tony had a run-in with him and threatened to take him outside and beat him up. Bryan had told a joke about a Jew and the guy was Jewish. He claimed it was more than bad taste and the way Bryan and Tony had treated him was discrimination. He quit, and went and filed a complaint against them and the company for discrimination.

Not long after this I came to work one morning and Henry was cleaning up part of the showroom floor and some explaining was going on. It seems that the night before, Tony was on duty at the used car lot. He had been having some trouble with his wife—going back a-ways—and they had been having some fights. She had even moved out of the house. That night she drove down to the lot with her boyfriend in the car, to tell Tony she was leaving or something. Tony lost his temper again and started hitting the car windows as they had put them up and locked the doors.

Henry, Charlie's number one porter for a long time, was doing lock-up when he heard all the noise going on. As he got to an area he could see what was going on. Tony broke the windows out with his fist and tried to grab them inside the car. They took off. Henry came over and knew who Tony was. He took him inside the main building through the showroom to the men's room so he could clean his hands up. He wrapped them up for him and told him he should go to the emergency room.

The story came out the next day when Henry had to clean the blood up. I wasn't told what was said on the other end of the building but Tony was fired again. He had them in trouble with a discrimination suit and now he had become violent again—and this time to the point he would have really hurt somebody if he hadn't hurt himself first and allowed them to get away.

When it was over, no one said anything to me. No one said that maybe they had made a mistake; maybe the man was dangerous and they weren't such a good judge of character. I know for me, it was just one more time of reinforcing what I already knew—they were no hell in judging people.

This was but a few of those they had made mistakes on in misplacing their trust. I made mistakes but they led to disappointment rather than surprise. Eddie was our favorite at the company. I watched him and felt he was basically honest—at least at the dealership. I had not found anything that he had done to the company. He was having hard financial times, and came and went a couple of times. One of the last times, Doug let him go. It wasn't something he had done at the company but rather something Doug had been told on the side.

Eddie had a bad gambling problem and as the story goes, he had used Doug's name a couple of times with some of the bookies. Doug didn't want there to be any misunderstandings—any bets he made he would place himself. Doug was sure Eddie was using his name for bets and that it was going to lead to trouble. If he did end up way over his head, then it would lead to stealing and who knows what. I couldn't disagree with Doug and if it was true that Eddie was using his name, well it was looking for trouble.

A couple of times Eddie had told me that he had talked to Charlie when he was walking around the showroom floor and Charlie seemed very pleased with me and my work. He also told me a couple of time that he felt Hank was up to something and was spending time with Doug and Dale buttering them up. This didn't overly worry me at first but later on Rodger Rogers another salesman I tried to help from time to time, told me the same thing. Maybe I should have taken notice.

It was one day after Doug had been on another of his rampages most of the week that Dale asked to see me in his office. He asked me why I hadn't been participating in the managers' meetings on Saturday. I told him if he really wanted to know, that between us, it was because of the way Doug would attack us, and yell and call us names. I didn't need that and I figured the best thing to do was keep out of the way. He also asked me something to the effect of how and what I was doing. I told him I was doing all of the paper work and then went over a number of the things I was doing such as appraising cars, the advertising, inventory control, and so on. I told him I had left it up to Hank to watch over the sales force as he needed to do something for his money. I also told him that if he had a problem with me or any part of my job and how I was doing it, to please let me know and I would be glad to do whatever was needed to correct it. He assured me that everything I was doing was fine and he had no problems—it was just he wanted to know why I had become so quiet in the managers' meetings. I was to later wonder if there wasn't more to it.

Eddie came by the house one day after he had been on the downside for awhile. He drove up in a broken down Ford Maverick that was putting out lots of smoke from the oil it was burning. I teased him and told him he shouldn't park it out in front as it would give me a bad image in front of the neighbors. He was down that day and we both talked about how the last number of years in Austin had changed things for us. He told me (in his joking voice), "Austin has been good to me. Ten years ago I was single, drove a nice car, and had $10,000 in the bank. Today I'm married, broke, no job, and driving that smoke-belching pile of junk. Yep, Austin has been good to me".

Things had changed for all of us over the last few years. Pam and I had decided the only way to get our finances under control was to come back down to earth and sell the house. The sooner we had a lower overhead, the sooner we would be able to go forward again. We then started looking at realtors to put our house on the market. Yes, Austin had been good for me and we weren't going to lose that now.

CHAPTER 63

IT GETS TOUGHER

After the remodeling was finally finished and Pam was underway with Trans Designs, we decided to have a 4th of July party at the house. We wanted to treat the salesmen and their partners to a few drinks, some food, and to let them see what we had done with the place, as well as show off Pam's ability to decorate. I felt it was time to try and maybe have some sort of bond with the salesmen and hopefully lift their spirits. We started early that morning and were to finish up about 10 PM that night. This was to allow people to come and go when it was convenient for them. It worked out well and even Dale and his family came and saw their old house and what we had done with it. In years past when we lived at Buda, we had gone to Willie Nelson's 'picnic' on the 4th of July.

They were hot and dusty but you did get to see a lot of entertainment. We had gone to one with Diane and another neighbor. Since then over the last year or so, Diane and her husband Chuck had broken up. It was a shame but they still spoke to each other. She still worked as a dental hygienist and he worked as a jeweler by day and played in a band at night. He called me one night when Pam had gone back to New Zealand to see her folks. He was at a club called 'Alley Oops' on 6th street and he wanted me to come down as they were going to have a surprise guest that night. It was to be Willie Nelson and Ray Charles, as I later found out, making a video. I didn't get away that night as I was doing some painting.

Diane became involved with a veterinarian and they decided to move to Chicago after her divorce had come through. They didn't want to take the two cats she had so that is how we ended up with them at our Mountain Ridge house. It was a shame to see her go as she was a character, and one of the few people Pam really enjoyed spending time with.

One time they took Laurie with them to Barton Springs to swim and go sun bathing. They have an enclosed area for women to sunbathe topless, as well as the open area showers. Laurie seemed to be embarrassed by this so they tried to see if they couldn't get her over being so self-conscious by both showering out in the open area.

Diane didn't have any problem with shyness, as Pam told me. One night when we had gone to 6th street to see all the party goings-on during Halloween, they decided they had to go to the toilet. They had to wait in a long line to get into the building, then the bathroom door, and then the stall. When Diane got inside the ladies' area she saw no one was using the sink. She asked if anyone was using it and got no answer so she said "I am sorry girls but I've got to go". She proceeded to hitch her dress up and went over and used the sink. This was all some of the rest needed for encouragement, as after that, the line (which Pam stayed in) moved twice as fast with a number of women using the sink as well. Diane had spent too many years as the only female travelling with her husband and his other musician friends, to suffer from false modesty.

Pam said Diane was a child of nature. She liked the outdoors and when she grew up on her Dad's farm, she had to help. She loved to go horseback riding and would do so in the nude sometimes to work on her tan simultaneously. She got herself stranded outside in the barn one time when some friends came over to see her Dad, and she was still in the barn in the nude. She told Pam that she had to help plow the fields at times and when she would do this, she would sunbathe so as not to be the only girl without a tan at school. She didn't want the white areas from the bathing suit so at times she would drive the tractor in the nude and at times would even kneel on the seat to keep her bottom up, so as to again avoid white areas from where she had been sitting. She was most surely not shy and when she had a nature call, had no problem in going in the bush off the side of the road. It was no wonder that when an unused sink seemed to her to be going to waste, it was put to another practical use that would help out the situation.

Pam had made some new friends and worked with some in Trans Designs but none took the place of Diane, after she moved. We decorated the house when we had it on the market and had several open homes. The original lady we had selling the house, had come up with a figure of around $200,000, maybe even $210,000. We told her to go for it, although I told Pam it was more than I had figured it was worth. It wasn't long before we had the feeling that maybe she was either overly optimistic or didn't know what she was doing. The problem was that we were the only house on the block that had been fixed up. The others were similar in size but were still in need of repair and redecorating. So people, on the surface, couldn't understand why our house was $200,000 and the one next door was $155,000. At any rate as time went on we did lower our price and when we went to $185,000 I felt sure we were in a reasonable area and only needed to wait. That is what we did and concentrated on my work and Pam's business.

Doug had his old house on the market for over a year and hadn't had a serious buyer for it. It wasn't selling and it seems the realtors told him it was all the old dark colors in it. It needed a face-lift. Dale had evidently told him about what Pam had done to his old house and they both knew she was decorating. He asked if she might be interested and she went to talk to him. They went over some of what he wanted—to spend as little as he could and do more of a vinyl top and pin stripes so he could sell it.

She went over and looked at the house and made a list of what she felt needed to be done. Two areas that were of major concern were the master bathroom (with all its gold-plated faucets) as it had no shower, and the living room area where he had a wood beam ceiling put in after the house was built. Along with the dark wood floor it made the room look as if it had only a 6-foot high ceiling and it felt like a cave. The rest of the house needed some repair work and neutralizing the color as they had all the rooms painted and carpeted in different strong colors.

Pam gave Doug an estimate of about $10,000. At first he hesitated but then told her to go on and do the job. She had plans for replacing some of the broken tile in the kitchen with some that had designs and to replace some of the rest to give it a face-lift. She could buy replacement light-colored panels for all the appliances except for the refrigerator which was to stay. It was painted in a make-shift paint booth at the house and it looked as if it was done in the factory. The plan was to get rid of the harvest gold and avocado green. The house was carpeted in a neutral light color and to lighten up the cave, she had the walls spray painted a light color as they were originally done in a brown grass wallpaper. Other repairs to some of the wood eaves and such were to be done by Dayne.

It was unfortunate, and a lesson, when Dayne came to Pam and told her some of his work was taking more time than he had estimated and he would have to charge her more. It was as if he was saying I want more or I will leave. I guess he felt Doug could afford it, so why not. Pam had originally not figured anything much in for herself as she felt this would give her an opening into another area of referrals which would be worth more than making something on the job. She went to Doug to let him know how things were going, and that the work with Dayne was going to be more–something like $500. Doug came unglued. It was as if somebody was holding a gun on him or was trying to cheat him out of something. He got great delight from coming down to the office I was in to tell me how he wouldn't hold still for it and how he explained to Pam that if she was going to be in business she was going to have to learn that this was not acceptable—at least not with him.

Pam had made a mistake by trying to do the job too cheap where she couldn't afford to cover any overruns herself. She had figured that Doug would understand as she was doing him a job at a bargain rate but all he wanted to remember was something about $10,000 and it was as if that was in stone. He didn't want to know about any more. As it was, Pam wanted to give him some options as she went along, like maybe adding in a shower in the master bath. After this, any changes were out of the question—especially if they involved more money. The best she could hope for now was to finish the job as soon as possible and hope he was happy with it.

Pam would have preferred to do some of the things differently but Doug didn't want to know about it. As the job progressed she got to know his next door neighbor, Doris. She told Pam when the job was finished that Doug should have given her a big bonus as she had done miracles to the house with only $10,000 to spend on it. Doris felt Pam had given Doug his money's worth and more. As she got to know Pam, she purchased some of the fine art that Trans Designs offered, for her ranch house. In a way Pam was getting something out of the job—it was Doris.

When Pam finished and was ready to get with Doug, he couldn't even be bothered to look at it. He paid her what had been agreed on and acted like an unhappy client. He had no appreciation for what had been done for the price. Pam had spent many an hour helping at the house as well. It does show that sometimes friends, and I am sure relatives, are harder than the general public. This is especially true when you try and do something for them for nothing. As time went on, I never heard him say anything about the job Pam did, to anyone. The house remained on the market and still wasn't selling.

He had made his mind up that the house was worth so much and that was it. He didn't want to know. Sounded familiar to me. He later rented the house out I was told and he eventually did sell the house at a reduced price well over a year later. It was as if he blamed Pam for it not selling and as if the money he spent with her was wasted. Yet I myself knew what a massive improvement had been made to it. It still had those obstacles he didn't want to fix and I am sure that, along with a falling real estate market, had more to do with it not selling than anything else did.

Pam now had a small group of women working with her. They were getting together and doing things like an open house, and sending out invitations to prospective clients and existing clients to come and see. They would also pool all their merchandise that was used as samples and have a sale to turn over their samples. This also helped replace those with scratches and marks. Pam was also working with the leaders in Trans Designs and when they were told Rick Rush the artist was coming to Austin for the launch of the Texas Sesquicentennial commemorative limited edition art piece, she was to help organize it. They had a reception for him and Gene got a Cadillac from work and we had an older driver we used, act as chauffeur for him.

Pam was moving up and going to various training sessions, meetings, and eventually the national convention in Atlanta. This gave her a chance to see the factory where some of their product was made and the main head quarters for the company. It gave her a boost as she learned they were expanding into more furniture and other items which meant you could decorate the entire inside of a space from floor to walls and almost everything in-between.

It was just as well, as work for me was not getting any better and we had noticed that the real estate market was actually falling in price for the first time since I could remember when. We were having to take a hard look at our price and had decided we needed a realtor who knew what they were doing. We had tried with our current one and were not even getting any offers. We had done a lot of what she asked and it still made no difference.

When it was time for renewal of her contract we decided to talk to other realtors, as we needed results. The facts as we learned them at that time were not pleasant. During the previous year the prices had been falling—not just a little bit, a lot. The economy had become so bad in Austin, we were over 13% unemployment and the people in the unemployment lines were white collar workers who had never been out of work in their lives and were used to making over $100,000 a year. It was a lot of these people that could no longer get jobs who had to sell their houses—and a lot couldn't. This led to repossessions and auction sales on the court house steps. The prices were getting so ridiculous at these sales that the banks were starting to hold back and keep the houses until the market recovered some. A lot of people had their houses sold out from under them at prices that only covered about half or two thirds of their mortgage.

The oil price slump for Texas was a disaster, as well as for some of the other oil states. The industry had a large share of the production from small companies and they were all going bust, and this meant their suppliers and support companies were going bust as well. The only ones that were going to be left at the end were the large companies and OPEC. Washington didn't want to know about it but before it will ever be over with, we will hate the day when the large companies and OPEC were allowed to take over the oil production and control it. The problem with Japan and its micro chip dumping was still being ignored as well, and this was causing problems in Austin's huge I.T. industry as the home of 'Texas Instruments', 'Motorola' and 'I.B.M.', amongst others.

The last straw was when the government pulled the plug on the "Star Wars" program. Hundreds of families had been moved to Austin and a facility had been built there as part of the plan for research. These people were all top, high dollar people—and now they were standing in the unemployment line. They were cut loose just like that. With the economy in a state of disaster the real estate market took a nosedive and everything was just snowballing. It was no wonder we were not selling a lot of cars. A lot of people were just trying to hold on to their houses. A lot couldn't and this had driven the prices down on the court house steps, which affected all of us.

CHAPTER 64

It's Finally Sold

After we had returned from New Zealand and Leo Burris finally overcame the shock of us living together, he decided to at least speak to Pam again. It was a shame, as Pam wanted to stay friends with them as they had been such help when she needed it after leaving her ex-husband. As such things go, not long after this, Leo had a heart attack one night and died. It was upsetting and Mary was not herself after this. Pam, along with Dayne, helped fix her place up after some of Leo's insurance money came in. Mary wanted to stay in the house which hadn't had any repairs for years, so Pam organized and oversaw the necessary tradesmen to do this work for her.

It was during this time when Mary was interested in decorating, that she decided she also wanted to help Pam with her business. It was a funny in a way because Mary, along with her son, had been looking at a development out at Lake Travis and thinking about buying a unit or two in the complex. She introduced Pam to some of the people involved and they told her they were interested in having somebody that could help all their buyers decorate the units. They would even like to be able to sell the units furnished where people could either have a choice of several packages in different price ranges, or customize them. They asked Pam about putting something together and giving them a presentation.

I looked over the information on the complex and with Pam, we put together a plan with options on several packages. We even went and researched what it would cost for appliances and items right down to a toaster, for the units. This was going on while we were still in the house on Mountain Ridge. We learned that they would take existing homes in trade, on units in the complex. We figured that if Pam got the okay and was made the official decorator for the project, then it would be a big advantage for us to live on the premises of the complex. If they took our house in trade it would eliminate one of our problems as well. We could even fix our unit up with one of the packages so people could see what it really looked like.

Pam did her presentation and the group was left speechless. She offered more than they hoped and said it was the best presentation they had seen by far. As far as they were concerned Pam had the job and it was only a matter of a few details and final approval from the parent group. We even went out to the project again and they took us out on the company boat so we could see the islands they were making and the surrounding area. It was going to be really something and the first stage was about half up at the time we went on tour.

Then we waited, and then we waited. It seems the parent group wanted to reconsider the project. The economy had slowed down and they had not pre-sold as many condominium units prior to the start of construction as they had originally planned. They were now at a critical point as construction was well underway. Should they continue even with the sales below the projected level or stop? If they stopped they could face a big loss now. The other idea was that government money was available for projects that were to be long-term care facilities for the elderly. With some changes in the plans they could make a facility for the elderly. It would still be attractive for investors and money was available for such projects. The area didn't have anything like this one as it would be—in effect—a country club for the elderly. We learned about the change in plans when it was announced to those that had put up a deposit on units in the project, like Mary Burris. She took her deposit back and we watched Pam's plan disappear from our grasp that would have had her business running in style.

Pam and I knew we now had to make a hard decision. The realtors and one in particular, had more or less given us a picture of what had happened in the market in the last year. When the pieces were put together, what we could make of it was we were over a year out of sync. The house about 12 to 18 months previously might have sold for $185,000 but with the market falling more and more each month, this was now way off what the market would bear. We shouldn't have listened to the first realtor and when we had no results at her high price in a week or two, we should have dropped it then. We should have stayed on top of what was going on ourselves instead of leaving it up to the so-called professionals.

We were now looking at something in the area of $160,000 . . . maybe. I told the realtor I never understood why we weren't presented with an offer. If we had been, we might have negotiated to a sale price but we had nothing. The only advice she could offer was that maybe the previous one had too little experience to encourage offers or was afraid to present them if she felt they were low. The only other explanation was that so many good places were going to auction at bargain prices, why bother to pay market. This would also be one of the problems for us now as well. The only good news was a lot of the lenders were now holding on to the houses as the prices had just fallen too low.

Pam and I knew we didn't want to continue on trying to hold on to the house at all costs. The sooner we were out from under the expense, the sooner we could start trying to save up again. If we didn't sell soon, we might not have an option and we would be forced to hold on until the market recovered. We felt it was just a cycle but how long until the recovery—a year, two, three, four, we didn't know. We just knew we didn't want to have to struggle that long. We agreed to put the house on the market with the new realtor for about $160,000. After all the time and money we had spent on it, it just about killed us to do so.

A few weeks went by and the realtor called us and said she had some people she wanted to show the house to. A few days later she told us she had an offer. It was something like $150,000. I told her that was just too low. We negotiated back and forth several times and on the last time we finally took it at about $156,000. I told her I didn't want to have to pay to get rid of the house; she assured me I wouldn't. Maybe we were too scared to keep trying, or maybe we listened and believed the doom and gloom too much. Whatever it was, we knew we were selling at a price that was much lower than it should be but we would now get this problem off our back.

Pam tried to sell some of the custom decorating to the people who purchased the house. We had included the bedspread that matched the curtains in the master bedroom but at first these buyers didn't want to know about anything else, so we packed up and made plans to move to a condominium complex Pam had found that was in the area. That way we could keep the same phone number that we used for her business. It was a nice place that was a split-level. We were just above the ground floor and the next floor up was the mezzanine bedroom that looked down below to the living area. It was more than I wanted to spend on rent but it was still about half of what we had been spending. This place had a pool and a social meeting area. We lived in an adult complex as such but the kids could see us on weekends.

I was not going to have to worry about doing lawns or cleaning the pool. The cats were going to have to get used to the place and we had a small patio off the living area. I was hoping it would be big enough to bar-b-q on. With two bedrooms and two bathrooms, a living area that adjoined the dining area and kitchen, it was just big enough for the two of us. At least we would be able to concentrate on business, save some money and get started again.

When the day came to settle and move, I was not very happy. It worked out with the pro-rated taxes, real estate commission, interest on the house loan to the day of closing and so on, I owed them $500. It was salt in the wound to have to pay them $500 to take the house as well. I wrote the check and expressed my feeling to the realtor as I told her that this was what she had assured me was not going to happen, and then we left.

I was lucky that I was able to get some help from the kids again. Sam even drove up after he finished each day and then drove back each night after we finished. It took us about two days to make the move into the apartment and we had the house all ready for the people to move into. The people were Susie Bush and C.B. As time went on we got to know them quite well, I was always a little unsure of C.B. Maybe I shouldn't have been but he was another person who only went by his initials—and the other one had taken some watching over the years.

After they moved in, they called Pam. They didn't realize just how much the decorating items that Pam had in the place had helped, until they were gone. They wanted to know if she was still interested in selling some of them. They had purchased the sofa and chairs we had in the living area, as they needed them and felt the ones we had went perfectly with the place. This was a chance for Pam to not only sell them some of what we already had but maybe get her started into a decorating plan as well.

Pam realized after her meeting with Susie that it was C.B. who controlled the money–even though it was Susie's money. Susie was allowed to purchase some of the items and Pam gave her a good price. Pam decided that after talking to Susie that she might be a better prospect to join her and sell decorating, rather than have her as a client. She told her how it worked and even showed her the catalogues. The only problem was she now knew how much the items were marked up and from here on it would be hard to get much more than that—especially with C.B. looking over her shoulder all the time.

As we got to know them some, we found out Susie had a little girl from a previous marriage, who lived with them. C.B. was at first a friend and was on the board of a small town bank. The banking industry had gone through some changes in Texas the last few years and I remembered it was possible for a group with some backing to get their own little bank going nowadays. Susie's mother was involved with the bank and that is how Susie got to know C.B. He was helping take care of the family affairs, especially the finances—and later Susie, when she got her divorce.

C.B. had been involved with some other investments, including both of them having gone into some oil well investments together. He was on the board at the bank and would oversee the loan approvals. I remember back in those days, some people were getting into trouble by being part of several companies and getting into a plan that was questionable. The developer would borrow money to buy land for a development. The builder would build the development at inflated prices. The development would go bust as the amount borrowed was too high, and the bank would take it over and sell it at a loss. The problem was that the people involved at the different levels were the same people, and usually one was on a bank board to get the loan approved even though the numbers didn't make sense. This way, the group made their money on the land and the building of the development. After that, they were gone and left the bank holding the bag. I had picked up, after being around C.B. a lot further down the road, that he was being asked some questions about loans he had approved and other companies he might have had some involvement in. But this was later—for now he was running Susie's life and was overprotective. He always wanted to know where she was and he would even go with her when she went to pick up the kid from school, as if he was afraid to let her out of his sight.

It was a great relief to have the house sale behind us—even if it was irritating to have lost all the money we had put into the place. I kept on telling myself it was a lesson learned and we would make it back with time. We were not going to get above our raisin' again, as they put it. Word got around at work that I had sold my house and moved into an apartment. I didn't say much about it to anyone really as I felt it wasn't their business, and I was a little sheepish about the whole thing since I felt it might show we couldn't really afford it (in a recession) and had made a mistake.

The used car manager they had hired to replace Bryan had become sick a few months before with ulcers. He was better now and was working again but you could tell the boys were up to something. They acted as if they were afraid he would get sick again and that they would be stuck at an inconvenient time without his services. They weren't saying anything to me about it, as such, but I felt like they were looking around in case they needed or decided to make a change.

I had gone off that year to the new car showing at Ft. Worth, in the company's jet, with several of the salesmen. It was a break from Hank for me. Charlie loved to fly and had a plane for a long time. He always had a twin-engine plane, as soon as he could afford it. He felt they were safer as he had lost an engine in the past. When he went to wanting a jet he found that a Citation was one of the few twin engine jets that, by law, required only one pilot to fly it. He had his own pilot, Ron Benson, who was on the payroll and flew with him everywhere he went. When we went on a trip, the pilot flew the plane and he would let one of us sit in the front with him to watch the instruments and tell him when we reached speed on takeoff and it was time to, as they say, rotate.

Sam Kopecky with some Oldsmobile salesmen, preparing to fly to new car showing in company jet

I knew Ron Benson from his coming down to the dealership to see Charlie when, sometimes, he would have lunch with us. He didn't have a monster salary but the deal was that if Charlie wasn't using him, then Ron could fly for somebody else and get paid by the hour by them. Of course the other person had to either have, or rent, a plane for Ron to fly. Ron got to go a lot of places with Charlie who paid for all expenses when they were on trips.

Charlie liked fishing and had some ranches he would fly to, and on occasion he would go to Las Vegas to play cards, or some of the popular resorts to see a person about some business. Charlie had apartments, ranches, and other holdings. He was involved in a number of other dealerships and most recently had been buying land and building the facilities for new dealerships–becoming the landlord. He had done this with a man out of Tennessee on a couple of Honda dealerships. One was in Austin that they had just completed in the last year and they were looking for another location in San Antonio. He told us one day at lunch, that if a person could buy some land on any part of 1604 on the north side of town, they couldn't go wrong in the next few years. My understanding was he did buy and build another store, a Honda Accura dealership.

Pam also got to know Ron and his wife, Jan Benson. Jan was a funny sort of woman—small, blonde, blue eyed . . . a former 'Miss Tennessee' who acted as if she had just gone out for head cheer leader. It was unfortunate that she had a little girl from a previous marriage with cerebral palsy. They did have a sense of humor as she told us that one day when Ron was asking about this and that, and why things hadn't been done, she told him she couldn't do everything. He then wanted to know about dinner and plans for later on. She told him she could only be good in one room, so to make up his mind about which room he wanted her to be good in . . . the kitchen or the bedroom. Well, he did most of the cooking from then on and seemed to enjoy it.

I know the finances were getting to him as well. Jan had become a client of Pam's and had ordered some items. When they came in she had almost a fit, saying they were the wrong things, the wrong color, and she wanted her money back. Pam had already run around town helping her out with ideas on how to do things and save money. Ron even came to me and wanted to know what we were going to do about it. Pam and I had agreed in the past that making enemies was not in our interest. We gave her the money back and picked up the items but Pam noticed then that Jan had done some of their ideas on the cheap instead of ordering the things through her. Pam also reminded me of how Jan had been so slow paying the deposit to her for the order. I wonder if it wasn't a smoke screen because they couldn't afford what they had committed to and changed their mind—or if Jan had made a mistake by not first obtaining permission from Ron and he was making her send it back. It was just a real overreaction in the way they sprang into such an aggressive stand right from the start.

It was another lesson for us but I put it in a more general customer category. Some customers are like this, regardless of what the product is. They change their mind, or decide they can't afford it, or can do it or get it cheaper themselves. The way they then justify the change is to make it your fault and attack—especially if they think they might be liable for something and might end up losing a deposit or part of the purchase price. They can't be honest with themselves, much less you, and don't want to take responsibility for the consequences of their own actions.

Now that we were in the apartment complex I had decided I would help Pam more if I could. I was happy to try and help with the paperwork and try to teach her how to do some of it. Pam did not like that part of the business but it was part of it. The other thing that Barbara Smith had asked Pam about, was maybe having me give some talks to the girls about sales. It was to be more of an overview and things in general. I agreed to do this and did give a talk once. After the talk I decided I didn't feel it went very well, as it was hard for me to get what I was trying to say across to a group in a short period of time. I went back to work as I had told Hank I needed to go somewhere for an hour or so. I think I was gone more like an hour and a half and in a funny way I felt guilty about taking this time off—something that had never bothered Hank.

CHAPTER 65

LET GO

The situation at work was not getting any better. Sales were off and we were down to selling about 130 to 150 Oldsmobiles in a month, where we had been doing around 250 previously. Other stores were in the same boat since we held about the same position in the zone as previously. The new models were starting to come in now for the year and the new Cutlass for the 88-model year was going to have a major change. The first ones in were spec'd out by the factory and it looked as if they were considering going to an order system similar to what the Japanese did with the Chevrolet LUV truck. You ordered the vehicle, the color and which package of equipment you wanted—package 1, 2, or 3, and that was it.

I remember when the first one came in. The shape reminded me of the new 2-door coupe models in the other lines, and it had black wall tires. It was a very different approach to what had previously been the image for the car. I wasn't impressed at first and was thinking we would need to have a rethink perhaps, on the way we equipped and sold that model. Some of the other models had taken off and the idea of a 'touring car' suspension, large black-wall tires, alloy wheels, leather-wrapped steering wheel and so on, had worked for some of the other models.

When we were on Mountain Ridge I had sold the little Ford truck and we decided the Berlinetta was not very good for hauling large items for Pam so I ended up buying a red Chevrolet Silverado pickup for Pam. It had all the equipment, electric windows, dual fuel tanks, V8 motor, the works. The only thing was that after awhile it was obvious she was better off with a good-sized car; between getting the kids and carrying samples in a secure manner. This led me to the next vehicle. A few years before I had an Oldsmobile 98 demo that was white with a red interior. It was a loaded car and an older lady had purchased it. She returned to buy another one and so we traded for my previous demo. I asked the used car department about it and they put $500 on the price before I purchased it for Pam. It was a nice car and served her needs quite well, although she still missed her sports car at times.

We were happy with the 98, and the model that everybody was afraid of when they came out, was selling very well. The public didn't want the old large monster—as it had been previously believed. I think this one, and a few of the other models, were prime examples on how the public taste had changed over the last few years. It was very important to keep up with, and identify, these changes, as soon as possible. This is how we had stayed on top—by adjusting our inventory to what people were demanding, and not just restocking what had always worked in the past. In a way you could see the foreign car influence as these models reminded you much more of them than the previous Oldsmobile models ever did.

Word was out that the city and highway department were thinking of double-decking Hwy 183, Research Blvd., which was out in front of the dealership. If this did happen it would most likely make it very difficult for people to come and see us about a car. Charlie had purchased some other property in the past that was further out Burnett road. He was in the process of making a deal with the city to donate some land off this piece for them to put part of a new expressway on. He was willing to do it with the understanding that he would have an exit/entrance set up for his property which would be zoned for an automobile dealership. He was always trying to plan ahead.

He told us one day at lunch how one of the big dealers in Dallas was in trouble. They had owned the land in downtown Dallas and after much negotiation had decided to sell it to a big company and build a new place on the main highway system. They got something like 50 million for the land when they sold; they were sparing no expense on the new place and had spent millions on the new setup. It had marble floors, crystal chandeliers and everything. Then the old guy in the middle of all this died of a heart attack. Now they had a mess with the estate and the finances were all out of whack.

He then told me, "I guess you already know. The Pontiac store you used to be at in San Antonio was sold to Evans Pontiac. They really didn't have anything to sell but they got 3 million dollars for it". I could have fallen over. This was the first I knew of it. Cecil and Henry had made a nice little sum and now they were all up in Boerne. I could only think "Poor Sam", at the time.

I was nominated to go to a meeting in Houston that was to be a group of the top dealers in the area for Oldsmobile. The factory had gone through changes and the old Houston Zone office was no more. We were now part of a new group out of Dallas. Jack Heiser was even forced to move from San Antonio to Lansing, Michigan. The meeting was to be on what we could do to improve the situation by working with each other more. The price of oil was now so low that the economy in Houston was almost destroyed. Charlie and Doug didn't want to go but felt we should be represented and see what everyone else was up to. They told me to get a ticket to fly over and back and to just get a taxi at the airport to get to and from the meeting, as that was the easiest way to do it.

I flew into Houston and the place was very quiet. Out on the curb, the cabs were all in a row and just sitting. I took the one at the front and told the guy I needed to go to a meeting at the hotel in the 'Galaria'. As we visited he told me how bad it had become. When oil was higher and gasoline was $1.00 a gallon he couldn't keep his tank filled up and was run all over the place. Now that the price was down, he would fill up on Monday and have the same gas in the tank the following week. The fare was $20 to the hotel. When I went to pay him he asked if I would do something for him. I asked what it was and he told me to please call him from a payphone and ask for him when I was ready to leave. He would stay at the hotel, at no charge, even if it was all day, just to get the fare back to the airport. If I would do this, it would most likely be the most fare he would have in the whole week. If I didn't, he may not have another fare for the rest of the week.

When the meeting was over, I did as he asked. Sure enough, he pulled up from the back row of taxis and took me to the airport. It showed how desperate it was getting when you could get a cab to sit outside a hotel for half a day at no charge, just to get a $20 fare back to the airport. Maybe we should take some sort of warning from this as well. I knew I was glad we were out of the house and in the apartment.

When I returned to the dealership Doug asked me how it went. I started to tell him what it was all about and before I could get halfway through what had been brought up at the meeting and what the dealers wanted to do, he interrupted and said it sounded like the same old stuff. He then walked out and that was it. I guess I shouldn't have been surprised. He had already made his mind up. I knew if I had just paid a guy, and paid for his trip to a meeting, I would want to know all about it and what his thinking was on it before I dropped it. But then this was Doug.

Hank was still doing as usual and had asked me what I thought they might do about the used car manager whose health was not good again. I told him I didn't have any idea. He then asked what I thought of maybe going to used cars, and started bringing up some of these ideas again, as he had in the past. I thought to myself that he was acting as if he thought he was general manager—and I would have been happier if he just concentrated on doing his job and took over some of the paper work from me, so I could spend time sitting around on the showroom floor and visiting with the salesmen as he did.

I felt something had to change and the dealership needed a new direction but how this was going to come about I didn't know. You weren't going to get new ideas in the managers' meetings to kick around. That forum had been destroyed. Doug didn't want to know about what others were up to; he had shown that after my return from Houston. They were not interested in changing the advertising from the newspaper only, as that was how it was done. They did try a little radio once but unfortunately it was one of those package deals on FM and a couple of stations, for about 30 days. When they didn't knock the doors off the hinges coming in, it was all over. They really needed to formulate a plan that was image, sales, and name recognition, that would be over a period of time, say a year. It would need to bring together all forms—radio, TV, newspaper and maybe direct mail. To even bring up such ideas you were taking your life in your hands; much less get around to formulating an actual campaign.

I guess in some ways I was waiting for Hank to come back and tell me one day that he had found that job and that would have made my life happier right there. I was also thinking that we would not be able to go back to the good old days until the economy turned around. You couldn't have massive car sales when people were out of work and worried about keeping their houses. Maybe with time we might be able to train the sales force, or at least part of it, like Oldsmobile was getting at but I felt we had a lot of resistance to overcome from both the salesmen and Doug, before this would ever get off the ground. The idea was that with the improved methods, you would sell a higher number of those you did get into your store and since there were not as many buyers around, this was something we could benefit from to get our sales up.

As the sales fell, the weekly bonus plan became increasingly hard for the guys to make it. At one stage back when sales were still good, Doug had raised the numbers needed for the bonuses as he felt they were too easy to reach and that we were just giving money away. Well, now it was slow and the subject came up about lowering the numbers needed. He reminded us that it was written in chalk on the black board and was not a permanent part of the pay plan. If they didn't like it, they could always leave. We admitted that with less business, we needed fewer salesmen and if we had fewer, then they could split the pie, so to speak, into bigger pieces for those that were left. This was his answer. I was sorry we couldn't do more to try and hold onto the best salesmen as they were the backbone of the dealership. If we didn't sell, nothing happened. I didn't want to think about having to start from scratch in building a new sales force up either. It could cost you a lot of sales when you had inexperienced salesmen.

Hank came to me towards the end of a week and told me he had made arrangements with the powers that be, to have the weekend off. I don't remember what he said it was for because it didn't really matter to me. I remember I was busy with all the standard stuff as usual and that was all that mattered. That weekend was a lot like the others and was disappointing in sales. Before Hank left, Doug came by the office and told him to enjoy it, since he didn't know when the next time would be that he would let him off. I didn't think anything about it at the time as it was something that you got used to hearing from Doug.

When Monday came and the meeting was over with, Doug called me and asked me to come to his office. When I went in, he asked me to close the door. I had a feeling something was going on but didn't know what. He told me that "they" had been talking it over at the dealership and with business being off as bad as it was, they were going to have to let one of the managers go. He said they knew I had sold my house and had less responsibilities than some of the others, and that even though I did a good job, he felt that if he pitched in, they could order the cars and take care of the inventory without me. It was not easy but after considering things, they had decided to let me go. I was then told they would pay me through the end of the month (October 1987) but as soon as I had shown Hank any of the paper work he needed to know about and I had cleaned my desk out, I could go.

I was numb. I couldn't even talk. I wasn't mad at the time. I was just shocked. I remember talking to Pam on the phone and telling her, and she couldn't believe it either. I went down to Charlie's office and told him in person how much I had enjoyed working for him and thanked him for everything he had done for me over the years. It was the only time I can remember that he couldn't look me in the eye when I spoke to him. He didn't want to talk but told me I could hold onto the demo until I had something sorted out, as he knew I would take care of it. He also told me that his friend might have a place for me in Tennessee but was leery of hiring people that had to move a long way as they would get homesick and want to move back. He told me he would give me a reference and I told him good bye and left his office.

Peggy Hillman, who took care of my pay and oversaw a lot of the office, was also upset as were a number of the others in the office that had heard. No one could believe it. As I told some of them good bye they had tears in their eyes. Peggy told me she would get me a reference written up as Charlie had offered me one and I could get it later. I then left and went to the apartment.

I just couldn't believe it. What happened? Why? Did the word get back to them about our "some day" plans? Had Gene Webb told them? Were Eddie and Rodger right–had Hank been doing a job on me behind my back? I was sure Doug and Dale were smarter than that—or were they? I just went in circles again and again.

In fact I never knew for sure for years—not until July 2000. I decided that maybe I might get to the bottom of it now if I talked to Dale and asked him. So with this in mind, I called him one day at the dealership. I was thinking that enough time had gone by now and that he might tell me. I had heard that Hank had come and gone a couple of times since then. After we visited and he told me what had happened to some of the others over the years. He told me Hank had started spending a lot of time around he and Doug, and had convinced them that he could do everything—and in fact that he was the only one who could close deals and train the sales force. They believed him and decided to keep him without interviewing us both, and going over what we each really had to offer, and what each of us could really do.

He told me that they were sorry later they had kept him on, as he always wanted time off. He had left them a couple of times but they let him come back as they never had any reason not to. That is, until the last time that he worked for them. They finally figured out after all those years, those sick days were days that he just wanted off. He had let it slip one time when he was talking about his kids and mentioned that they were home from school. They then asked him why—if they were sick?—as it was a school day. He told them that they always let the kids have a day off about once every 6 weeks as they felt it was good for them. The light then came on for them as they then realized that this is what he had been doing to them.

He was at that time (July 2000), working for another dealership and when after all those years, Dale had a run in with Jim Arnold about doing his job differently in F & I, he left. And when he did, he went to work for Hank. Dale told me that Bryan had gone from dealer to dealer over the years and the problem was he became 'born again'. He would tell the dealers he worked for that they were the devil. He had called Dale about a year before and told him he was out of the car business for good. He was up north in a school learning how to be a minister and was going to work for God.

I was sorry to hear that Jerry Rushing had a pain in his chest, pulled off the road and died of a heart attack. Peggy Hillman, just a few months before, had also died. And Gene Webb had gone broke and lost his house after all but kept on working for the company. He had back pains and chest pains as well. He went for a stress test and on the way home had a heart attack and totaled the car. He was dead from the heart attack by the time they got him to the hospital.

As far as Dale went, he said he was doing well. He had a triple by-pass 3 years before but was fully recovered now. In his own sort of way he let me know that yes, it looked as if they had made an error in judgment.

And as for me, I guess I finally got the story on what had happened. Just something I should have known better on. I should have heeded the warnings. It was something I had never been good at—office politics. It is something we all need to watch out for. Even if you don't want to play, you need to watch out and protect yourself from others. If you don't, you may end up like I did . . . in one hell of a mess. Because of when it happened it hit me hard, and took me a long time to adjust and get over it. It also put Pam and I in a situation where we had to again make some choices—not all of which we wanted to make at that time. One thing seemed to be almost for sure . . . if I had of been able to stay, would I have had my turn on by-pass surgery or a heart attack?

CHAPTER 66

DECISION TIME

For about the first week I operated in almost a daze. I just couldn't understand how this could have happened. I knew I needed a job as Pam had just reached the point when her business was breaking even and making only a little money. This was actually good when you considered what a short time it had been operating and how soft the economy was. The first thing I decided to do was apply for unemployment. I had never done this before in my life but I was afraid it wasn't going to be easy to find a job and any income would help.

I went down to the office that was in our area to apply and found they were very busy. There was a wide range of people and we were all being moved to various areas, in groups. We filled out an application to give them a list of previous employment and amount of earnings. They also wanted to know why you were let go. If it was any sort of misconduct, then you were not eligible for any benefit. They would send a copy of your application to your previous employer so he could protest any payment if he felt he had grounds. They then wanted you to give them more information on what kind of job you had done and what you were looking for. After a couple of hours, they told the group about what you had to do each week and what you had to report to them each week. You would then get your check each week in the mail. We would be eligible for 26 weeks' benefit up to the amount we were eligible for by their formula. I was in the top bracket and would get about $600 a month. This was only beer and gas money. Needless to say I needed a job.

Each day I would check the papers and with Pam's help, we redid my resume. I applied for all sorts of jobs and most I never heard back from. Those I did were the standard form letter, "Thanks but no thanks". I went to a couple of dealerships that were looking for salesmen and/or managers. They didn't want to know me as they first of all figured they couldn't afford me, or were not sure about me. Why did they let him go was always going to be hard to overcome. If he was any good, why didn't they keep him? These were questions I had to ask myself as well. It would sound like sour grapes if I went on about how Doug was, or any of that, as I had chosen to just do my job and not spend all my time ass-kissing.

It wasn't getting easier and in the back of my mind I was hoping they might realize what a mistake they had made after Hank was on his own, and would give me a ring. I also knew he could be clever and it might be a long time. I started looking at any job that looked like I might be able to make some money and wouldn't be demoralizing. I knew I would need to be willing to take almost anything because about a week after I was let go, we had the stock market crash of October 1987. I knew that this would make a lot of businesses and people very nervous, and about the last thing they would want to do is put more employees on.

I read one ad which was one of those that were vague and promised lots of money. I had nothing to lose so I contacted them and they asked me to come by for an interview. I was to see a David Gibson. When I got to the building it was 'Mid-Western Oil and Gas'. It was in a new building—which there were a lot of in Austin—and most of it was empty. Mr. Gibson interviewed me and he explained they were a small company that did developmental oil well drilling. They mainly worked in known areas and would put packages together for people who wanted to invest in oil wells. They were working in a couple of areas at that time and needed more people to sell their investment packages. He also introduced me to one of the geologists who worked for them and after we visited, we figured out he had gone to high school with my sister in San Antonio. They offered training and helped prepare you to take the state board test for brokers, as you would need a license with the Securities Exchange Commission to sell this sort of investment.

It was a commission-only job and they paid all expenses and provided leads and prospects. I told Pam I would keep on looking for a job but since it was in the area, it might be worth giving it a try as $600 a month wasn't going to cover much. She agreed and I told Mr. Gibson I would give it a try.

At first, all he wanted me to do was study the booklets on this part of the law and be prepared to take the next set of boards that would be given in about a week. I would need to make the application and pay the fee. If I passed and went to work for them, they would give me back the application fee.

During this period, we had a call one night from Pam's folks. It was to be a surprise for us and they wanted to test the waters on how things looked for us around Christmastime. They were thinking about making another trip to Texas to visit us. We hadn't told them yet about what was going on as we still didn't have a lot of the answers ourselves. Pam broke the news to them and they were as surprised as we were. They had met Hank on previous trips and they also knew how hard I had worked for the Maunds at my job. They just couldn't believe it either. After some thinking it over, they wanted to know if it would still be okay for them to come over. They said it wouldn't be necessary to do as much as we had in the past as they were happy to just come over and see us. With this, we told them to come on.

I passed the test; in fact I scored 100% on it. I was told this at work before I went over to pick up the written notice. The lady that gave it to me at the board office was the same one who gave the test. She said she knew I hadn't cheated as on that day as there were only 3 of us taking it and she sat with us the whole time. But she wanted me to know that it was very rare for someone to score 100%—which did make me feel good, as this was the first piece of good news I had been given for some time.

I went to work in an office with two other guys. One was a retired colonel from the army, and the other, a graduate from Texas A&M with a geology degree, who was having a hard time finding a job. They had both made sales and with their help, I was sort of fast—tracked to the point where I was ready. The company gave you a script to use but you could modify it and use your own words. They had a procedure to follow and wanted all the legal parts adhered to. They showed me that with the leads they gave you, if you made 100 phone calls a day (this included anybody that answered the phone), you would talk to about 30 people and of these, about 10 would want you to send them more information. Of the ten you sent out, about 3 would talk to you again and consider buying either then or in the future. If it worked out as it should, you would have at least 1 of the 3 buy now. When you sent information out, it was by federal express and you would then contact them back in 1 or 2 days. If they invested then, we would have federal express pick up the package with the check inside.

After I got started I talked to unemployment and they told me as long as I wasn't making money outside the guidelines it was okay. As soon as I was over any limit I would need to let them know and go off unemployment. This lasted until about the first of the year, as I remember. I had learned that they were right, on qualifying hard on the phone or you were wasting your time. A lot of the leads were people who had invested in the stock market and such. Some had just lost a lot of money with the October crash. Others were looking for other types of investments.

I was starting to learn a whole new type of sales. I had never thought people you had never met, would send you a check for thousands of dollars after several phone calls and a package in the mail. But it was working, as I could see the others in the office doing it. At first, I worked from about 9 until 5 or 6 PM and also went in on some Saturday mornings. The next thing I learned was to work smarter not harder. I noted that most of the people I had that were interested were owners, and some retired people, and they were available at work between 10 and noon. Then after lunch, say about 1 or 2 PM until about 4 PM., after which they were gone for the day. I also made sure I had a set time to call people back that was good for them and would then note when this was and make sure that was when I called them. With this in mind, I did as much as I could during these times on the phone and spent the other times getting organized or even trying new ideas.

A lot of this did come down to having yourself prepared mentally and doing a lot of those things you hear about. Talk with a smile, be friendly, and so on. If I got some bad calls and was upset by a prospect calling out names and giving me a hard time, I would take a break and regroup. This 10 minutes away from the desk and clearing my mind was a key in going back in and getting on the phone again in a positive way. If I didn't have the right attitude I was wasting my time and the prospects I called.

I was called by Jan at the dealership a couple of times as they were having trouble with car orders and with the computerized part of our program that did the reports I had run all the time. I told her a few things on the phone that helped but decided it would be easier and faster to just go down and show her. I went to the dealership, dressed as I did at the oil company, in a shirt with blue jeans and cowboy boots. They were not used to seeing me like that as they had always seen me in a suit. When asked how I was doing I told them fine and when Hank came by, I told him I was my own boss at the oil company and took off when I wanted. I helped Jan, as what they had done was dump a large portion of the paperwork on her. Neither Hank nor Doug were doing it. Doug saw me in the office and later wanted to know what I was doing in there. He told them he didn't want me in there again. He was funny—he wanted them to pay someone else to struggle instead of having a free 1-hour visit from me. I wasn't vengeful—even though maybe I should have been.

I heard that later on, they hired an advertising agency which charged them plenty, as well. Some of the guys were letting me know what was going on. It seems Hank was still asking for time off. The used car manager got sick again and during this episode they hired a guy from San Antonio, Don Thompson, to run used cars. I couldn't believe it. I had worked with him at the Pontiac store when he started selling new cars after he left the Texas Highway Patrol. He always liked the girls and put himself at number one. I had heard he had gone to Boerne and worked for Cecil as some sort of manager but they had a falling out when he drove a diesel demo until it was out of warranty and then turned it in. That should have made them a nice loss. He had left and gone to Riata Cadillac, and had now come to Austin. I was wondering if he would take advantage of them at every opportunity as he would in the old days, or if he would turn over a new leaf. Only time would tell.

I was still hoping that I might get my old job back if something would just happen and they saw the light. I felt like they were already having to spend more to replace me than they planned and one of the guys told me that at one stage, he had heard that Dale said how maybe they had made a mistake. I didn't know if this was true or if this was something he was saying to make me feel better.

During the previous couple of months we had become friends of Susie and C.B. and had spent some time with them, going out to eat with them several times. C.B. was showing some interest in me and I was trying to figure out what he was up to. If he could put me in touch with someone for a good job it would be okay with me but later on, I decided that he was trying to see if I had any 'money' and was worth getting to know. He had told me he knew some people in the oil well investment business and at one time, started to say if I was interested he could put in a word for me at that outfit. I wasn't interested at that time in switching horses for the heck of it, so I let it lay. He liked playing cards for money, especially 21. He told us about Las Vegas and how he could get our hotel rooms for free if we wanted to go with them sometime. Pam liked Susie and tried to work with her but the more we got to know them, the stranger C.B. became at times, always wanting to control Susie, and where she was and what she was doing.

Pam's parents came not long before Christmas. We told them we had made some plans for their holiday and one was for us to go to Las Vegas for a few days as C.B. was going to work it out so the rooms didn't cost us. This would be over the New Year and we could see it in at Vegas. So plans were made and we got our tickets in advance for our flight. We spent time with some of the people they had met before on earlier trips and planned a Christmas at the condo.

On the day after Christmas, Boxing Day, we were sitting at the table having breakfast and reading the papers. We were talking about our plans for the day when Alan started to stand up at the end of the table. When he did, he started to fall over and went pale—as if he was going to faint. We got hold of him and helped him back down but decided something was wrong. He wasn't complaining about chest pains but was confused so we took him to the bed in the room where he was staying. As this was going on, a call was put in to our doctor (who was off duty) and spoke to one of his associates who suggested we get Alan to the hospital and at least have him checked over. He would meet us there and it was also suggested he go in an ambulance. So the call was put in and we told them it wasn't necessary to have the sirens on when gave them the address.

We all got ready in a matter of minutes and by the time the ambulance came, Alan was saying he didn't need it and didn't want to go. But we told him it wasn't an option and it was better to be safe and find out what was wrong. With this, we loaded up and went to the Catholic hospital we were told to go to.

It was obvious that something had gone wrong and we sat and waited as they started to examine him. Pam was worried, as was Peg. It was so sudden and such a shock. As we sat there Pam and I talked about it. We knew he had a heart problem and had been taking medication for years. Each time they went on a trip they always took medical insurance out because they were afraid something might happen when they were on a trip. This time was no exception and Peg found the details in her purse.

Pam started to cry a little at times, realizing that she could lose him just that quick. She had already had a number of her relatives pass away while she lived in Texas with me and didn't want this to happen with her parents as well. I told her as we sat in the hospital that maybe our "some day" was here. Perhaps we should consider making that move now.

I told her that we should think about it real hard. Here I was in a situation where I didn't have a good job. We were living in an apartment and could be out with notice in a matter of months. True we didn't have much money. In fact by the time we cashed in everything and paid everybody off, we would be lucky to have $10,000. But if we stayed, we couldn't tell how long it would be before I made any real money and my best bet would be to see if Charlie could get me that job in Tennessee. But we didn't really want to leave Austin and if we packed up to make a move that far away from the kids, it might as well be to start over in New Zealand.

None of us knew how long her folks had left and we had always wanted to spend some time with them before something did happen. Maybe this was a wakeup call to us and we shouldn't just ignore it. If we did move and it didn't work out, we could always come back and start over again. We wouldn't be giving up a lot now—like a good-paying job—although it was a shame to close her business down just as it was just starting to take off and make some money.

Pam told me she knew from her own past that it was very hard to move to another country and adjust. In fact, she knew she had felt like going home at times. It would take about 2 years from what she had felt, to adjust, if you were going to give it a fair chance. I told her I was willing to give it 2 years and if it was unbearable after that then so be it—but no, I didn't expect it to be the same or perfect or be smooth sailing. And no, I wouldn't give it up in a matter of months, or a year, if it didn't work out at first.

We agreed, as we sat there in the hospital . . . as they were running tests and trying to find out what was wrong with her Dad. We had some serious thinking to do. I knew I didn't want her to be away and never spend any more time with her Dad, and then have him pass away while she was living far away with me. I also knew I was somewhat worried about our future if we stayed and while I knew I didn't want to leave the kids now, I also knew that a phone call or letter from afar was the same—be it from Austin or halfway around the world. If it worked out, we could take trips back and forth from time to time. If it didn't work out, we could always move back. Pam said previously to me, that if she didn't have her folks, then she wouldn't have any strong reasons not to move back to the states later on. So, I knew it wasn't a matter of never, if that is what we decided.

It was now time for us to see first of all, what was wrong with her Dad and hope that we still had time to spend with him and her family. There was no longer any time left to put off such a decision. It was now time for us to make our choice.

CHAPTER 67

SURGERY AND RECOVERY

The doctors let us know they were sure he was out of immediate danger but wanted to find out for sure what had happened. They were thinking he had a small stroke and wanted to find out why. With him being on Coumadin, the blood thinner, they needed to get this out of his system before going any further. This would take the best part of a week. It made no sense to take him out of the hospital after a few days and then put him in again for several days before they ran this diagnostic test so it was decided to leave him in the hospital over New Year and they would start the test after the first of the year. We teased Alan that we would go to Las Vegas without him and gamble all the money away. He said we could go without him rather than cancel our trip but we assured him it wouldn't be the same and so with this in mind, we all stayed with him for New Year.

Our doctor was back and explained that Alan and Peg needed to make up their mind on what they were going to do if the test showed he needed an operation. The test had some risk and expense and unless he was willing to act on the results, there was no need in continuing. They told him that as they had a 90-year-old man they had done by-pass surgery on so he could take care of his wife, Alan was not too old by any means. The doctors also told him that the operation would most likely give him more years of useful life so Pam's folks decided to proceed with the test.

Now that it was after the first of the year, Peg had given the insurance information to the hospital office and they were checking it out. Peg also made contact with the insurance company from our apartment right at first, so they would be notified. For some reason after the initial okay from the insurance company, it seemed they were starting to back out. We couldn't understand why and didn't want to alarm Alan so it was decided not to tell him while he was in the hospital until it was cleared up. They admitted he had a policy with them and we were sure it must be some sort of mistake in the paper work. I told Pam to tell Peg not to worry as we would do what we could as well.

After the test results came back we found out what was wrong and we were all surprised. Alan had a hole in his heart the size of a U.S. 25-cent piece. He had been a 'blue baby' from birth and it was never picked up. He had worked harder all his life to compensate for this as he didn't get as much oxygen in his blood as easily as the rest of us. This had caused his heart to enlarge to the point that he now had a problem with a grossly-enlarged heart. It was from this hole area, that clots had started to be thrown off and that is why he had a stroke. None of the doctors in New Zealand had picked this up—including the cardiologist he was under. They all assumed some of his irregular heartbeat was from when he was electrocuted and burned when working for the city power company years before. The doctors said the operation would be to close the hole and do any other repairs that were needed. It would most likely add 10 years of quality life to his life span but it would not reverse his enlarged heart problem (and resulting eventual congestive heart failure) which would maybe at best stay the same.

We couldn't understand how he could go all his life without a doctor picking up this problem. He was in the New Zealand Army from the start of World War II and had served in Africa and on into Italy. He told me he never had a health problem as best he could remember. He told me he had a run-in with one of the officers when he was in the upfront engineering corps that would help build bridges and that sort of thing. The guy told him he would get even with him and had him transferred to a group that was clearing mines. That was a nerve-racking job. It was enough to make you want to be back with the other group of guys. About the only story he told me was how one time when they were building a bridge and they had lights on at night that were connected to a generator, they came under fire. He was one of the men who had to run to the generator to hold down the kill switch to turn it off and kill the lights. The generator would slow down and the lights would dim and the shooting would make the guy nervous so he would run back from the generator. It would start to pick up speed again and the lights would come back up to full brightness. It took the poor guy several attempts before he finally turned the generator off, and the lights. Alan was never injured during his tour during the war; it was something he felt very lucky about.

His electrocution injury happened when he was working for the power company in Palmerston North when the kids were young. He was working on a power supply at a substation and through some miscommunication, the power was turned back on before he was ready and while he was still working on the supply. The power hit him and the short turned the lights off over a large section of the town. He had severe burns all over his body. He still refused to lie down when he was in shock and ended up walking into the hospital under his own power.

The injury was so extensive they didn't think he was going to live. His ears were as good as burnt off and the skin over a lot of his body was destroyed. Time and time again they tried new methods of skin transplants on him and used him as a test subject. A number of the nurses couldn't stand to look at him, much less nurse him, and so it was up to Peg (a nurse) to take care of him. If it hadn't been for her hard work and many hours of taking care of him, he would have surely died. Even after he was out of the hospital it took years for him to get back to anywhere near how he was before the accident. He would sometimes show me some of the scars from the transplants and make jokes about it. It always amazed me how he could be so jovial and philosophical, and hold no bitterness.

His medical file was many inches thick and the doctors always assumed that any problems he had were a result of his being electrocuted. They would always jump to this as a reason for his problems and look no further. It was a trap that they had fallen into and now it had finally come to light what his problem was, halfway around the world. Unfortunately the damage had been done and was not reversible.

Alan was in almost perfect health, other than his heart condition. That made him an excellent candidate for surgery. He was in the operating room for what seemed like a very long time. When the doctors came out they said everything was fine. In fact he didn't even need any bypasses or anything else at all. He had done well and was now in the recovery room. He had tubes going in and out all over the place and was covered in the antiseptic they paint you with, as well as some blood. After he didn't start to wake up on time as expected, they asked Peg since she had a familiar voice, to go and speak to him to wake him up. She had done this sort of thing too many times before when she had to take care of him in the past but did it anyway. It was hard for her to see him this way but she managed to rouse him. Pam went in to see him and help Peg as well. It was a shock for her to see him this way but may have, in a funny sort of way, reinforced the seriousness of the situation. It also reinforced our decision that we needed to make arrangements to try and make the move to New Zealand.

Peg had called back to New Zealand to let family and friends know what had happened. She also contacted Pam's brother, Peter, and as she told him on the phone about what was going on, I was surprised to see how much she played down the seriousness of his father's condition. She said she didn't want to upset or alarm him. I was to learn as time went on, that it wasn't possible to upset or alarm him. At this point we told Peg to do as she wanted but that she shouldn't protect Peter in case something did happen.

I had met Peter and his wife during the time I went to New Zealand. He was in the Navy and his wife was much larger than the average person, as I remembered. She had numerous children from various partners and ran the family. Peter just went along with things. In fact when we were there on our last night we all went out to eat at a restaurant. He sat across from me with his wife next to him. He said something to me that she didn't like and she hauled off and swung her arm around and hit him in the chest so hard she almost knocked him off the chair. It caught him by surprise but he didn't say a thing. I told him he was a better man than me–I don't think I would have been able to react in the same cool manner he had.

Each day we would take Peg to the hospital to spend time with Alan and later each evening we would visit and watch videos back at the apartment. We had discussed with Peg what we were going to do and she had some suggestions on how to go about immigration. She helped make some contacts and got the ball rolling, as under normal circumstances, it could take a year to get the okay from immigration. We found out we had numerous forms to fill out and were to supply them to the New Zealand embassy in Washington D.C., which in time, would contact us about coming up there for an interview—after which a decision would be made about my immigration status.

We still hadn't told Alan about the insurance company's reluctance to pay out on his claim and when Peg talked to the hospital office they told her not to worry, saying that if he needed the operation then he should have it. The other could wait and be taken care of later. This did help as she was afraid, to some extent, that what she had heard about the hospitals in the States might be true–no money and you were on the street. She knew they had some money at home but it would take time to get it out of investments. She came up with the idea of using her American Express Card and for the only time in my life, they came in handy as they pre-approved the entire (open heart surgery) hospital bill being put on her credit card.

The insurance company had backed out saying it was because this was a "pre-existing condition". The policy she had, didn't disclose any pre-existing conditions and if she had known this, the premium would have been about $50 higher for the trip. She knew it would take time to find out what had happened and it wouldn't be until after she was home. Pam did contact her New Zealand lawyer friend, John Armstrong, and he wrote some letters and made some calls. The hospital bill was about $24,000 U.S., and the other fees and bills were several thousand more. By the time it was over it would cost them about $46,000 NZD—a very large portion out of their retirement savings.

When it was time for Alan to come home we let him know what was going on as the situation was now fairly clear. We told him that his main priority was to get better so he could go home. That would be about 12 weeks if everything went well. He would need to do breathing exercises by blowing into a graduated tube. At first he could hardly move the ball and he complained how much his chest hurt but by the end, he could push it to the end repeatedly and never felt a thing. It wasn't overnight but again he did as he was told and after he got past his post-operative blues, was positive and made a speedy recovery.

We were encouraged to buy a number of items in the States and take them with us when we moved, as the savings were significant. This included clothes, shoes, boots, and other items. We knew the electricity was 220 and not 110 volts so a number of items wouldn't work if we took them. The T.V. standard was also different so the only thing our new T.V., stereo, V.C.R. set up was good for was videotapes, radio, and CD's. That was true only if I could get it to run on a transformer. I started on a campaign and after several months located a transformer of about 15 amps—about one standard house circuit in size. It was from a company in Houston that made them for oilrigs. It cost me about $100. During this time I found out from Japan, that all of their electronic equipment was 9 or 12 volt D.C. inside (after it went through a converter), so if the transformer could supply enough power at 110 volts, then it would run. I contacted several outfits about the T.V. and no one knew for sure if it would work on the transformer. Later we found it did for the tapes, with only a slight flicker which was because of the difference in the number of cycles per second in the power standards.

Her folks tried to help and suggest what might come in handy, while they stayed with us. We still went out to eat but spent more time shopping for things we might need. We also went to some sales where stores had gone bankrupt and the inventory was being closed out. The economy was still hurting.

It gave us the longest time together we had ever had. It gave us a chance to get to know each other more than any other time. They assured us they would try and help us in any way they could and we could live with them at first. We had talked about going on a tour of New Zealand during the first year after we moved. We spoke of going camping and even purchased a family-size tent. Alan suggested that if we did build a house later on and wanted some circuits of 110 volts for our items we were bringing out, then we should take some 110-volt fixtures with us. We went to the store one day and purchased a breaker box, breaker switches, wall power outlets, and so on. It was starting to become a full-time job just thinking about what we might need to buy and take before we packed.

A lot needed to be done and yet with all this going on, Pam and I still needed to do our everyday jobs. She still needed to make some money with Trans Designs and decide what to do with her customers when she went to leave. I needed to keep on selling and make some money at the oil company as the more we got into our plans to move, the more money we wished we had. It was hard for me to forget what happened to me at the dealership and I would find myself still thinking about it from time to time. I just didn't think what happened to me was fair.

As more time passed the more I became irritated about it. How could Doug think a couple of weeks pay was fair compensation when a person in my position was being let go after 6 years of service. I had done nothing wrong. I had even overlooked how he had acted and treated me at times. This continued to eat on me. I had heard some time after the first of the year that Hank had left over a dispute or something and they were trying a guy that had been working on the Cadillac end as a salesman. I had met him before and knew he was a jerk. I had a flash of wondering if . . . but I knew Pam and I had now made our commitment and circumstances had changed for us once again.

I had mentioned to Pam before, that I was thinking of writing a letter to Charlie to let him know some of what had happened and how Doug had treated us from time to time. She didn't say I should or shouldn't but suggested that maybe I work on it with Sharon Webb as she was a good typist and would be able to type it out in short order. I knew that if I did this, I would never have a chance of going back. I also knew realistically that with me moving to New Zealand, I was most likely never going back anyway. I didn't want to be (or come across like) an idiot of some sort but felt it was something about the unfairness of it all that I wanted to get off my chest and point out to them. Maybe inside I was hoping that they would at least admit it to themselves if nothing else, that they had been unfair to me.

In the daytime I was spending my time at the oil company and making sure I covered my phone call periods I had worked out. It was starting to pick up at work and they had added on more sales staff. The good part of this, with increased sales, was the wells were being sold out and getting drilled. The excitement was going through the office as each new well started to come in. This led to my clients becoming more enthusiastic and they started buying as well. I was starting to make money again.

Pam had gone together with a number of girls in her group and had rented an office space in a nice new building in the area right off the expressway. It was an impressive-looking place and helped with their credibility. They painted the office and decorated it with Trans Designs products. It looked real sharp and you couldn't help but feel it was a real place when you went in the office. They all used it as a place to meet their clients or prospective people they wanted to bring into the group. It was now going to be another item that would have to be taken over by the girls or closed, and Pam's name on the sublease needed to be changed.

Pam had made friends with a number of the girls but more so with Jan Crider. They all understood why Pam was going to move back to New Zealand but it didn't help. Pam was the glue that held them together and it looked as if they would all go their separate ways. Pam was afraid that if they were not in a situation where they could help each other they would all fall by the wayside. One exception was Jan Crider. She would most likely go her way but this was more so because she needed money now and couldn't wait. Jan took a regular job to support herself and her (student) husband. Pam decided to finish up her current orders and start turning over her clients to different girls she thought they would get along with. This was not easy and it became evident how many clients she already had. She had developed a business.

We had an objective to accomplish and each day we took another step towards completing it. Alan was better and we were making preparations for the move. But before this was to be over with we still had a number of things we had decided to do together. It was during this time we all found out life still had some surprises in store for us.

CHAPTER 68

PREPARATIONS AND WORK

After I had started to work at the oil company I knew we needed two vehicles. I was still using the demo but didn't want to abuse the kindness that Charlie had shown. I told Pam that a second vehicle would come in handy from time to time and if we purchased an older one in good condition, it shouldn't cost a lot. I started looking around some and remembered that Rodger had left the dealership and was working at the Chevrolet store up the road, so I contacted him and asked him to watch out for a vehicle for me.

The first time he called me they had traded for a Chevrolet Monte Carlo that was about a 1976 model. It was okay but was large in size and Pam didn't like that. It wasn't long after that, he called me about a Ford Courier pickup with a camper shell on it. They had just traded for it and the manager told him if he could sell it right away as is, he would make a good price. We went down to the store that evening and ended up buying the little truck. It was clean and in a price range I could pay cash for it. It didn't have air-conditioning but we felt it would do for now as a second vehicle.

I ended up turning the demo in at the dealership and picked up my reference from Peggy. I didn't go back after this (except for the time to help out Jan), until the next year. I went back after the New Year to get my check from the retirement fund as Peggy had explained that it was best to close the account after year's end and since it was so close, it was best to wait. The check came in handy as now Pam and I could pay off those credit cards and charge accounts we still owed money on.

Hank came back to his job and they took him back after he had been gone for only a couple of weeks. They did realize now that you couldn't put a person in the position stone-cold. They also found out the other guy wanted a lot of time off as well. Hank was lucky that he could come back just like that. I visited with him some and he told me he had looked at oil well investments before but didn't do anything as he was not sure he understood how they worked. I then took a few minutes and explained the difference in developmental drilling and exploration—wild catting.

They were not doing exploration at this point and we were doing well so Hank wanted me to get some of the information to him. I got some together and dropped it off to him. I stayed in touch and found that he had talked to a couple of the other guys at the dealership and his mother-in-law. They were interested as well and wanted me to stop by and explain the investment to them as well.

Each time I let Hank know how easy it was for me to come and go as I pleased, and that if I wanted to take a few days off, all I had to do was tell them. This was true. I had started selling and was one of the top salesmen at the company. In fact, whenever the sales manager was out, I was one of only three guys who helped the other salesmen in closing their prospective clients on the investment. I got 'salesman of the month' a couple of times and earned a percentage on several wells. The bonus plan was set up so that the top salesman on a well, would get a small portion of one of the company shares. It would take something like 10 of these portions to make up an amount equal to one full share like I was selling. I liked the idea. It was an extra and if they worked, I would get an income from the wells I was selling, for a long time.

The projections we used were based on different prices for oil and for different rates of production. This way an investor was able to get an idea of what he would get for one share of a well at different prices or different production levels. The price of oil was still low and the production levels on these wells were not very high. The idea was that they were in a known area where a well would produce for 20 to 30 years. If the well produced 20 or 30 barrels a day at $15 per barrel, you still would get something like a 12% return on your money.

The way the industry worked was that the landowner who had land and oil the company wanted, would work out a lease on a percentage basis. In this company's case, they would give the owner 25%

of the production and the company would take 75% of the production but pay 100% of all costs. That meant that if a well produced and sold say $1,000 a month worth of oil, the landowner would get $250. The company would then pay all expenses out of the $750. The money left after expenses was then split up and paid to the investors on their share of the well.

There was a point at which you would have a loss if expenses were too high, or production and/or price was too low. However, at 20 barrels a day and $15 per barrel on 30 days, you would have income of $6,750 for the company. Expenses were usually several hundred for the electricity for the pump, and foreman that oversaw a number of wells. You also had well maintenance as the pumps needed work and cleaning, and the pipes and tubes would get clogged up and also need cleaning or replacing. As it went on, these expenses could get up there at times and you still had office and administrative expenses to pay.

The second part of the plan was to pool several wells together and use steam under pressure to drive more oil out when production fell off in later years. It was on the basis that you would take a group of wells and those on the outside you would put pressure in, to drive the oil to the well in the center. This would require some additional cost and equipment in the future. It would also require the owners' percentages to be recalculated, as you would flood say 4 wells to get the oil out of the 5th one in the center. Most didn't worry about this as they felt if the first went okay then they would worry about this later.

The liability was to be limited to the amount invested in the well and some clients were more interested in the tax write-off. The government was still allowing writing off more than the investment, to encourage investment in oil. The wealthy clients either wanted a write-off or a real good well. They didn't want a small producer. Those in the higher brackets would not lose as much since they could write-off something like two times the amount against their income.

The wells started to come in and the geologist would run an initial production test. This would be to get a maximum rating in a 24-hour period. This would then be the official rating for that well, registered with the state. If the state set production at 60% for the month, then you could only produce and sell 60% of this registered amount for that well. The railroad commission had this power going back to many years before. In recent times the production was set at 100% each month.

It was something a lot of us didn't know for a long time but were soon to learn. When the initial production is checked on a new well it is usually higher than it will normally be able to produce. So if it "comes in" at 50 barrels a day, it will actually, after maybe 30 days, be able to produce only say something like 30 barrels a day. This depends on a lot of factors and type of formation the oil is in and so on. It was much later, I am sorry to say, that I found out those in the Bigfoot field area would fall off to only 4 or 5 barrels a day. They would run for 30 years or more at a very low level.

As the wells came in and the i.p. (initial production) figures came in at 64 and 80 barrels a day, the wells were starting to sell out in a matter of a week or 10 days. Hank jumped in and invested and even got his mother-in-law to come down to invest in one with me. He called a friend of his in Houston and had me call him. He and his boss each purchased a unit. Chester Odom and a retired Colonel friend of Hank's, a salesman at the company, purchased a unit. It was a small oil rush for me.

The only other thing we were getting calls for was a wild cat wells. I had a couple of investors and so did the other guys, who wanted to invest or gamble in one that might be big. They wanted to either lose all the money or hit one that might make you rich. The company had been looking for one that just might do that and had finally come up with one—and a lease—after a year of negotiating with the landowner.

I had gone down to Bigfoot as it was just south of San Antonio and I wanted to see the place, the wells and the equipment. I wanted to be able to take some photos and mail them to my investors who lived all over the state, so they could see something too. I also, in the early days, wanted to make sure the company was doing what they said. One way was for me to go to where they were supposed to be and check it out for myself. The company started encouraging us to take prospective investors down to the wells after I had started taking pictures and mailing them to my investors.

A Burns oil well pump at Big Foot

It was later on and not long before we were to leave for New Zealand, that the wild cat well south of Austin was to be sold. The plan was to drill three wells in the package for the investors and hope that one might hit. It was about a mile from a well that was a legend as it had produced over a million barrels. People for years had tried to hit another well like it in the area and had either hit small wells or nothing at all. Our geologist, along with some others, had used some sort of magnetic field mapping of the area and figured they had a better than even chance of hitting it big.

It was to be sold to all investors on the basis that it would either most likely hit it big or be a dry well. We were also to tell them that going by past history in the area, there was a high chance they would lose all their money. We had a new plan and a new idea and that is what the gamble was based on. Right or wrong, Pam and I were interested in this one—but not a full share. After much talking and going back over the pros and cons, we decided to take a chance. We talked to Susie and C.B. as they were familiar with this sort of thing and even had a couple of well shares in Colorado. They were also not sure but decided that at the price of half a share it was worth a gamble. We went together and purchased a share in the Hoffman project.

Oil drilling rig being set up at the Hoffman project

It was now up to the company to sell enough shares to close the investment and get to drilling. This would take a little more time as each investor knew they had a high chance of coming out with nothing. I sold several shares in the project but most of my clients would rather have a small steady return than an 'all or nothing' situation. I later drove down to the project with a couple of the kids and took some photos of it. I wanted to have at least that to remember my money by.

That was one of the things I had to do. I needed to tell the kids that we had decided to move to New Zealand. I wanted to tell them as soon as I could but also wanted to make sure I did it in such a way that they would understand. I don't remember exactly how I did it now other than telling them, and explaining why it was going to be now and not later. I wanted them to understand that it was because of Alan's health we were going now. They needed to understand that sometimes in a relationship you had to be willing to give and do something for the other one, even when it wasn't something you wanted to do—at least not then. It was trying to be fair to Pam and her needs, as much as anything else. She had tried for me in the past and now it was my turn.

I could tell the kids weren't overly happy about the idea of us moving but seemed to understand. Scott seemed to have more trouble with this than the rest but it was hard to tell as he was already not speaking to me most of the time and never would say how he felt. I wanted to spend as much time as I could with them before I left. However, they seemed to be happy to just carry on as usual.

Sam had dropped out of school and was working at the dealership in Boerne for Cecil now. I didn't like this and wanted him to get his degree. I told him to go back and get a degree in anything, as it was important to have that piece of paper. I felt as if I was a voice on my own and knew inside that he most likely would never go back. Cecil was happy as he had his boy to do things at the dealership at slave labor prices, and yet knew he would work hard and remain honest.

Craig was to get married in mid-February to Elizabeth Lasher. He had met her when he was in school in San Antonio. She and her family were very supportive of Craig and her Dad genuinely wanted to help Craig any way he could. They were to live with her folks at first at their lake house. I was sure they were going to be good for him and I was glad he was going to be happy. Peg and Alan wanted to stay until after his wedding and we made plans to go to the wedding.

We also made plans to take Peg and Alan down to Galveston and show them where I was born and had spent part of my early childhood. We would also go and visit some of my relatives who lived in Galveston and Hitchcock. I wanted to say goodbye to some of those in my family before we went overseas, as I didn't know how long it would be before I would get back. I also wanted Pam and her folks to know a little more about where I had come from.

We all knew it might be some time before we would be able to go touring around and see more of Texas for some time so with this in mind, we planned several short trips after Alan was able to travel. It is a strange feeling when you know you are going to be moving and it might be a long time before you every get to come back to where you have lived all your life. It was okay with me to say goodbye to some parts but I knew I would miss the kids and my favorite parts of Texas.

CHAPTER 69

OUTINGS

When the time came for us to go to Craig's wedding we were all a little apprehensive. We were told it would be at the Baptist church in San Antonio and the reception would be at the country club near Boerne. The Lashers were not in favor of serving alcohol at the reception and our understanding was there was not to be any. We were hoping that way, with so many split families coming together, any unpleasantness that might be felt would be kept under control.

At the start everything was amicable and it was good to see some parts of the family I had not seen for awhile. Craig and Elizabeth were happy and everyone at the reception was visiting with them and with each other. It was towards the start of the reception that Cecil went to the bar and wanted to see about drinks. Some inquiries had been made and some had been sold on an individual basis. We went over and were getting some ourselves and visiting with those in the area. During this time the Lashers changed their minds and offered drinks—for which they would pick up the tab.

We visited some with Elizabeth Tindall, Sue Tindall, as she was by now, and some with Cecil. Cecil was in one of his moods and was teasing the bridesmaids and other girlfriends of the family, to the point it was getting hard to ignore the gestures and sexual overtones he was making on a continual basis. It got to the point that Sue was embarrassed and although she wanted to say something, knew better as it would only make him worse.

We wanted to stay and enjoy the event as we wished every happiness for Craig and Elizabeth. We planned on staying until the traditional parts had been done and it was appropriate to go as we also knew that under the circumstances, it would be best we did not overstay our welcome and would let Cecile, Walt, Elizabeth Tindall, and the Lashers, enjoy their day.

We started to make our move that it was time for us to go and were just letting Craig and Elizabeth know we needed to get going. Cecile and Walt were off to one side with the Lashers and others when Cecil started to come over to where Pam and I were standing. I could see he had been drinking but didn't think much of it as first as we had avoided any confrontations all evening. As he got to about 3 feet from us he asked Pam in a loud voice if she was proud of herself for ruining the kids' lives by taking their father so far away from them. He had an angry look that I had seen before when he would sometimes drink and turn mean. I told him to hold on—that if anybody had ruined anything it was he and his daughter. About that time he started in on Pam and I again, and I started to remind him of what his daughter had done to the family, the kids, and me. At this point he grabbed me and started to hit me so I grabbed his wrist and clothes by his neck. At this point Peg, Pam's Mom, tried to step in and Craig and others grabbed us and tried to get things under control.

They tried to get Cecil to stop and not spoil the day for the kids. At first Cecil wanted to continue yelling and by this time Pam was crying and everything was going to hell. Peg got him to agree to let go and to stop. So with this I let him go and as I did Cecil hit me again with his fist. It was good that he was able to hit me from only about 6 inches away as his fist with his ring, only made a small cut and red spot on the side of my face. We all then split up and one of the kids got my car for us as I remember, and we made plans to leave. We talked to Uncle Gene and Aunt Mary as we were going and agreed to meet at 'La Louisianne' to eat.

At first I couldn't get over how Cecil had behaved. However, the more I thought about it, the more I realized how typical it was for him to act this way over the years. He would always twist things and make it someone else's fault. He always tried to manipulate people by whatever means he could, including intimidating them or bullying them. When he felt he might, or would, be shown as being in the wrong, he would turn to violence and resort to hitting until he got his way. I knew he had it in him but I didn't think he would stoop to such a low as to hit me when it had been mutually agreed to stop and let go. I was wrong. It showed me again why I had left and why I no longer had any respect for the man that I would have done anything for, at one point in my life. I was sorry for what he had done for the kids' sake, for the wedding, and for showing them the kind of person their grandfather really was.

It seemed like it only took a few minutes to get to the restaurant and we were lucky to get a table. We went there because it had always been Dad's favorite place, and Gene and Mary knew this as well. I told them that this would be my treat but some of them were so upset they could hardly eat. To our surprise Gregory, the waiter, that had waited on Dad and us for so many times in the past, was still there and remembered us. He asked about Mom and Dad and he was sorry to hear of how they were. Gregory was working but must have been 80 years old. It was because of him that we had a good seat and still tried to enjoy the evening.

A couple of weeks later, we made our trip to Galveston to see the relatives. It was a short trip and we stayed with Uncle Lloyd and Aunt Jeannie. We went out to eat in the evening and one day they drove us around Galveston Island, showing Pam and her folks where I lived many years ago, and where my grandparents' house was that my uncle Freddy still lived in at the time. We had a chance to see at a distance, the old medical school the family had so much contact with over the years, and the area of town that had been in the process of being revitalized when the finances collapsed and brought the project to a halt.

We even tried our hand at fishing off a pier at the wrong time of year and again off of the jetties. We didn't do any good but Pam and Peg had a chance to get in the water up to just past their knees. They couldn't get over how warm the water was in early spring. It was the first time they had come in contact with the Gulf Stream. It is the warm water that comes from the equator that keeps the water warm in spring, hot in summer, and feeds the storms in summer and autumn.

We visited with Aunt Bobbie, one of my mother's sisters, and when she walked up she had a six pack of beer in one hand. So I asked her if she wasn't planning on staying very long. It was this sort of humor that made some of the times with this part of the family fun. Uncle Freddy drove off the island (unheard-of for him) to the house in Hitchcock to see us as we had missed him when we went by during the day. When we had sat around with him and visited with Pam's folks, he had them entertained and laughing so hard they started to cry. It was an opportunity for me to relive and share times in my past with those that were with me—a chance I knew I might never have again.

One of the shorter trips we made was back down to the Bigfoot oil field with her parents, as they wanted to see an oil well up close for themselves. It was interesting to see the equipment, storage tanks, and pumps working. We walked around and you could smell the oil in the air from where it had spilled on the ground. It was a contrast to see this in the middle of land with cactus and scrub brush and nothing else around except for the wild flowers that were starting to come out.

Before it was time for her parents to go back, we had word from the New Zealand Embassy in Washington D.C. that we needed to come and see them for our interview. We already knew that we were going to move—we just weren't sure when. We also knew that it would be impossible to take the two cats with us that Diane gave us, so Pam decided to call her in Chicago first to see if she wanted them back before we made any other plans for them. Diane wanted the cats back, so arrangements were made for them to fly with us to Chicago on our way to Washington D.C. When we had a short stopover at Chicago we saw Diane for a few minutes and turned the cats back over to her. We were then on our way.

After we landed in Washington D.C. we went to get our bags and discovered they had been lost. The airline didn't know anything about them it seemed. They were not sure if they were lost, on a later flight, or if we would ever see them again. This was the first time this had ever happened to me and Pam reminded me this was why you should always have a carryon bag with your emergency items in it just in case this happens to you. We told the airline which hotel we would be at and took a cab to go and check in.

This was not a very good start for our quick visit to the nation's capitol. We gave up fairly quickly on getting our bags that evening and decided to go out to eat. After we ate we decided to see some of the city that night. We did what had worked out for us before in New Orleans. We called for a taxi but asked for one where the driver knew the city so as he could give us a tour. The taxi drove us around and by the end of the evening we could at least say we had seen the Lincoln Memorial, the White House, Arlington National Cemetery, and all of the other places you hear about. I think the surprising thing to me, although I had heard that, was how close all the places were to each other. Pam and I said it would be nice to take a holiday and go to see the places—like the Smithsonian Museum—properly. The taxi driver knew his town as he told us it would take at least a week to just see the museum. He also pointed out the civil unrest and where different problems had come up before. We drove by the Watergate Hotel and I remember thinking how unimpressive the place was, for having played such a major role in the history of the country.

Late that night after we had returned to the hotel, our bags showed up. At least we had them for the next day. That morning we had a taxi take us to the embassy and as we waited inside we looked at some of the artwork on the walls in the waiting room. Pam pointed out to me who the famous artist was from her country and what the significance was of the Maori in their country. This, in the years ahead, I would become acquainted with more than I could have possibly dreamed of at that time.

The forms we had filled out previously for the New Zealand government enabled them to check with various agencies to see if I was a wanted criminal or had any kind of history or background that might make me be considered as an undesirable. Nothing had evidently come up and they were not holding any of my past associations against me. At the interview he asked how long we had know each other and what our plans where. I remember thinking to myself that if he seriously was thinking this had been a marriage of convenience to get into New Zealand, then this had been taken to the extreme as we had already been married about 6 years. As the interview went on he asked about my income and what I had done in the past, and how much we had saved and planned on taking with us. When I told him how we didn't have very much but had managed to pay all of our debts, he was not impressed. In fact, he made reference to the fact that for someone that had made such good money the last few years, I sure hadn't saved any. I responded to him the only way I knew how . . . I told him no, we hadn't saved much but we sure had a good time.

When the interview was over after about an hour, we were ready to catch our plane and head back home. I told Pam how silly the way the various countries did this sort of business was as they already had everything on us from the forms and learned nothing by having us go to an interview for an hour. It irritated me at the time to spend money for airfare and a hotel just so they could see me for one hour. If they had found something on my background then no matter what I said I would be out. And if I was clean as I was, then how did they think seeing me for one hour would change it? I wished I could have sent them the bill as we needed the money.

We were now to wait until we received official written notice on what they had decided. We were all sure it would be okay and we continued to make plans. The best guess was that we would hear in about 30 days. We still had a lot to do as we needed to decide on a shipping company and what we were going to take. It would run about $1 per pound for us to ship items. We had already mailed some that we wanted to make sure reached there before we did. We had also decided to give most of the furniture and appliances, as well as the other T.V. and stereo, to the kids. Pam and I had also decided to give the little truck to Scott and Laurie as they were getting old enough to drive but had no vehicle. I even made arrangements for Sam to take the papers and the fee to the dealership to have it transferred to them.

We told the kids what our plans were and at the time Craig and Elizabeth were the only ones getting married. I asked them to share out the furniture and stuff with his brothers and sister as they needed it and when it might help. Scott did get one of the T.V.s and stereos as I remember. Sam and Denise were starting to live together and this relationship was still up in the air. I told Laurie and Scott they would get the truck at the last minute and I was sure this would cause problems in the house so be prepared for it. We knew we couldn't do much but wanted to give them what we could.

Scott, Sam, Laurie and Craig—Christmastime at Mountain Ridge Circle in Austin

Most of our outings were now over with and it was time for her folks to go home. They were going to start to get ready for us to arrive and they had the insurance company to still clear up which had refused to pay any of the heart surgery bill. Neither of us lacked for something to do and we still had to decide on how we were going to make that last move when everything had been shipped and we still needed a place to live until we left too. Our solution ended up being a surprise for us in more ways than one.

CHAPTER 70

FINISHING UP

We had considered staying with friends but felt this could strain friendships when living in someone else's house every day. This was by far, not an ideal solution. Mary Burris had become even stranger since her husband's death and was spending a lot of time out at night, seeing a few different men. The house was always a mess and with Mark, her son, it wasn't any better. I had told Pam it was the only place I knew where you had to pick something up before you could put something down.

I had started trying to see about maybe renting a furnished apartment but this still required you to have a certain amount of your own stuff to use. I was thinking of maybe even an old-type tourist court like we had gone to once when we were kids. As I remembered we only took our food and clothes. I didn't know of any in Austin but was thinking of checking around. It shouldn't be for a long time—maybe something between 3 and 6 weeks we were guessing.

As Pam checked into moving companies it became apparent they were all crooks. It was hard to get a straight answer much less a price. We finally decided on a recommended firm that had been around for a long time in Austin and the older man seemed okay. They were connected with Global for international moves and he explained that we could pack or they could. It became a matter of them helping only on some items, as the extra help was expensive. The boxes would be placed in a container they would build and it would be nailed up, after which, it would be placed in a shipping container for shipping. He told us it would go to California and then by ship to New Zealand. We told him we wanted it sent to the port of Napier as it was near Pam's friends that had the farm. If it came in before we got there, or even after, Rob would take his big truck and carry it to his farm for storage. Arrangements were made and when it was actually done and weighed, we had to pay in full before shipment, a little over $2,000 U.S. plus the insurance, a couple of hundred dollars more.

During this time we still saw Susie and C.B. from time to time. They offered for us to come and stay with them. We could stay in the front bedroom when we were down to living out of a couple of suitcases. We hesitated at first but had not come up with anything else and it was an easy out for us—or so we thought—so we agreed. It can be hard to live with relatives or close friends for even a long weekend, much less a number of weeks. To try this with friends that you didn't know really well was almost a disaster.

At first we got along and we tried to do what they wanted. C.B. seemed to want to go out to eat about every other night so we agreed. When it came time to cook at the house, either he wanted to cook or wanted Susie to cook what he wanted. The only problem was, it was usually something relatively expensive and pre-packaged from the 'Skaggs Albertsons' Deli or the neighborhood 'Simon David' store. We would bring home our own beer and wine and stuff but also didn't want to get into their way.

We picked up and cleaned our own room but after a few days C.B. started acting funny and evidently had been giving Susie a hard time. It was only after Pam spent some time with her, she found out several things. C.B. was a bully and was telling her what to do about everything, especially when it came to her money. It seems he also wanted her to clean and vacuum the house from top to bottom several times a week, as well as a number of other items on his wish list. This is how his previous wife had done things and he could see no reason why she couldn't do the same. He also told her he was thinking that we should buy <u>all</u> the food as they had given us a place to stay. Pam and I were under the impression we had been asked as guests, and were already putting some money in towards the food, and were planning on getting them a gift when we left.

CB was threatened by Susie's relationship with Pam who assured her everything would be okay and that she would even try and help with all the housework, and we started giving them more money right away for food. I remember only going shopping with them one time at Albertsons and he was busy getting everything that was the most expensive. He paid a premium for items that were packaged up or had come in from faraway places that were supposed to be the best. Again we made a contribution. This made the little boy happy for now and we learned how to tip toe around them at the house. We also learned we didn't want to be at the house anymore than we had to. We were right; it just doesn't work in these sorts of cases.

We had already agreed to leave a small amount of money in the checking account to make sure all the checks had cleared and we put Susie on the signature line in case she needed to take care of things for us. We were still hoping the Hoffman Wells might come in as they still were being sold and had not started drilling yet. If they worked out, it would be convenient for us to have our share of the monthly check go into our checking account. We were now down to the final days and were waiting on the drilling to begin.

When we moved out of the apartment, the kids came up to help and they loaded all the stuff in a U-Haul truck to take back to San Antonio. We fixed the apartment up and cleaned it so well the lady told us she never had such a clean place before when someone left. She was able to rent it out right away and we got our deposit back in full in a couple of weeks.

We saw Mary Burris a few more times and decided to have our mail forwarded to her address as the situation with Susie and C.B. had gotten to the point we didn't want to add any extra work of any kind on them at all. Pam had made arrangements to have some of her artwork put with a lady who had a shop, in the hopes some of it might sell. We had purchased several of the Texas Commemorative pieces done by Rick Rush and decided to give one to each of the kids. We liked the artwork itself and were hoping that with time, it might even turn into being worth something for them. We were both finishing up and getting to the point we were ready to go.

Jan Crider with her husband Steve Scearce, decided to give us a going away party. Jan had some help from the girls that worked with Pam and some from Sharon Webb. They had it at Jan and Steve's house for us and had invited a lot of people. It was nice they had gone to so much trouble for us. Gene Webb, that evening, had more to drink than he should have and when we started to go, he started to cry. He had appreciated what we had tried to do for him and again, I couldn't see how he could have had anything to do with my situation at Maunds. I had previously given the letter I had written, to Peggy, to give to Charlie. I had also given her a copy and Gene had one. This was in case someone started saying things were in the letter that I hadn't written. From what Gene told me, after Charlie asked Doug some things about the contents of the letter but it was never brought up again or anything said about it, to the best of his knowledge. Maybe it had been a waste of time but it was done and that was that.

We had considered shipping a vehicle over to New Zealand and I estimated it would cost about $2,000 U.S. or so. This was right before the deadline stopping importation of left-hand drive vehicles, as the rules were changing. The best we could find out from family and friends was that it would be a gamble, as none of them really knew all the ins and outs. They also had a wide variety of opinions on what to bring in. Even up to the point (when we were living with C.B.) that we still were looking. He told us his son had a Pontiac Trans Am Anniversary Edition that had the silver leather and all the extras which needed some work and he would sell it cheap. We went out to a place where it was stored and to say it needed some work was an understatement. It would have been a lifetime project. Again we had placed ourselves in a situation where C.B. was rubbing his hands together and we were trying to think of a nice way to tell him we weren't interested. At the end of all this we decided to send nothing.

We offered the Oldsmobile 98 to a few people but they were thinking it was too much money for it. We tried for only about 10 days and after one of the last guys that looked at it backed out, we decided to wholesale it. I took it to a friend, Mike Driscoll, who we sold cars to at the dealership, and he gave me a draft for the car. We gave him the car and took the draft to GMAC where we still had a balance on the vehicle. At first the people at the counter didn't want to do it this way so I asked to see one of the managers. He was a man that I had known ever since my days in San Antonio. He had been moved to Austin and we would run into him from time to time when we would go to Dallas and the San Antonio Rose. I also had dealings with him when I was at the dealership. He came over and I explained the situation to him and he agreed it wasn't how they would usually do things but there was no reason why they couldn't take the draft and get the money from Driskoll's bank when they gave them the title, and then send on to me the balance that was over the amount we owed on the car. I was glad he helped as it made it so much easier and faster, and we had the check from them in a matter of days. This then, left Pam and I driving the little Ford truck.

We were as good as through working and I was mainly going in to see how the drilling was going, as they had started drilling the wells on the Hoffman project. We were still drilling a well down at Bigfoot but were drilling the last one at about this time. Some disappointment was starting to develop as each of these wells' production started falling off to an alarming level. They were now putting out on the order of about 4 barrels a day. Some of the first wells drilled had problems with what they called paraffin build-up in the tube lines that would become blocked. This would necessitate a cleaning out of the tubes and a repair bill. Another one of the wells' pumps had a major breakdown and a large repair bill, as the company had used reconditioned equipment to keep the cost down on the project. The company later agreed this bill would be paid out of its share and not charged to the investors. As time went on, some of the wells were showing a loss at the end of a month instead of a profit. The company said they would not bill the owners for a share of the cost as they felt that the negative balance would be cleared in the next month or two to come. I was concerned, as this was not how I had intended for the project to work out for those of who had invested with me. The only one I must admit that I didn't feel sorry for was Hank and it kept coming to mind how he had encouraged his mother-in-law to join in and invest.

The first Hoffman well came in and it had shown signs of oil but not what they were looking for. They started to ask for completion money and some was sent in but others reminded the company that the deal was to bring in a top-producing well or none at all. Some were afraid it would be nothing but another Bigfoot-type of producer and eventually the company decided to back off and not go to production on the well, as it looked like it would only be a poor producer at best. They then started drilling the second well and about halfway down to the planned depth, they had encouragement from the samples they took from the well drillings. But after about a week they again decided they were not in the right place—they had oil but only a little, and were not sure it was worth trying to develop into a producing well either. They then talked to a couple of other geologists and showed them what they had learned on the first two wells, as we still had one more to go.

C.B. and Susie were as nervous as we were. I had picked up after being around them more, that "their" money was Susie's and it was from her divorce. C.B. didn't have much as he was paying his ex-wife off. I had even picked up on the fact that C.B. wanted Susie to try to get more money; he wasn't being able to live in the style he was accustomed to. This was one of the reasons he had such an interest in us at first. They had gone in on the well with us as a gamble—sort of like going after 'Lotto' when you have nothing else to try. We had set our limit on what we were willing to lose but it appeared he had more of an attitude of desperation and you could see him getting almost bitter after the first two wells came up dry. The company told us that after they reviewed the data from the first two wells they had decided to move the location for drilling the third well. It had something to do with being on the same side, or other side, of a creek bed and where they felt a fault line might be with the oil.

They gave it a try and the reports came in each day as to what depth they were at, and if anything had shown up. As they approached the agreed depth they were to drill to, they had to decide if it looked like they might do some good by going deeper. This went back and forth for about two days and then they finally decided to go for one more day. At the end of the last day we all waited to hear from the drilling site. When the call came in, it was as we feared. Nothing. Another dry well. It was over and we might as well go. It was a letdown and a disappointment. It seemed like for us, everything wasn't working out lately. The job, the Lake Travis project, the insurance company not paying on her Dad's claim, and now this. It was a gamble and we knew it. But we also knew that if it had worked, we would have been able to come back from time to time to see the kids. Now we were back at square one again.

We made arrangements for Sam and Denise to pick us up at the house on Zornia after I dropped the truck off with Laurie and Scott. When I started to go that day, I knew inside it might well be the last time I would ever see them. Everything was coming to an end. I rode back to Austin in the back of Sam's truck as we drank a few beers and tried to visit. Denise and Pam were in the truck and drove us to Susie and C.B.'s house. They stayed and visited for awhile and then had to go. It was hard to let them go and it was getting to be very unreal for me. I was afraid I might never see any of them again.

The next day we had Susie take us to the airport and it was time for Pam and I to head out. We had planned on staying over a few days in Fiji on the way, so we could have time to adjust ourselves before we started living with her parents. Pam had said most of her goodbyes but I felt it was going to be Susie who was going to really miss Pam, as she was one of the few friends Susie really had. I can remember how sad Susie looked. I think she knew she had her hands full with C.B. and wasn't sure she wanted it.

As for us. Well as I said before, what was done was done. We were both ready to go, yet sad. We had both had some great times while we lived in Austin and in a lot of ways, neither one of us wanted to say good bye and leave it behind but we also knew it wasn't the same place where we had met about 7 years before. It was just one of those times in your life when you knew you were closing a chapter and starting to open a new one. We had been on top of the world for awhile and like I told the man at the embassy, we sure had a good time. Now it was out of our control and we knew that is why we had to move on. In a way, it was sort of exciting starting over and not knowing what was ahead for us. It was easier in some ways as we only had to worry about each other—and besides, that is also what made it possible to leave Austin behind, we had each other. It was now up to us to see if we were ready to leave the fast life behind and enjoy that "lifestyle living" you hear about. Austin had been good to us . . . I only wished we were taking more money with us.

CHAPTER 71

On our Way

We had one more stop to make before we headed out of the United States. Beulah Ann and her family, along with Dad, were now living in California. They were at Edwards Air Force Base, out in the desert. I had checked with them about staying for a few days and seeing them and Dad before we were off overseas. Tommy had done very well and had been promoted over the years to the point he was in charge of a portion of weapons development. He had flown all of the B-1 bombers except for 2 that had previously crashed. He was in the middle of a switchover at the base and would be busy but we were still welcome to come.

We arrived in Los Angeles and rented a car for our drive to the base. We found the landscape interesting as it was so different from what we had seen before. When we got to the base it was like a little oasis. We told them at the gate who we were and where we wanted to go, and were given directions to their house. We found the place and it was interesting to see the planes continually flying around overhead. They had made arrangements for us to take over their room and they would stay with the kids in the kids' rooms. This was not convenient for them and I am sure they were glad we weren't staying for 6 weeks.

Dad had his room and own TV. I found him in good spirits but felt he had gone downhill some since we had last seen him. We visited with him and as we found Beulah Ann up to her eyeballs with so much going on, we took over trying to help clean up Dad as he was now having some accidents. Beulah Ann showed me some of the crafts she was doing and also showed me some of the toy company things she was involved with. This was on top of trying to do things for Tommy and take care of the kids and Dad.

The house was not air-conditioned but instead had a water cooler. I found the heat a different kind of hot, as the air was very dry. That is why the water cooler system worked so well–it was the evaporation. It was strange how fast water would evaporate. We found that they needed to use their Ford vehicle for driving the General and as it was dirty; Pam and I offered to clean it for them. As we did, I couldn't get over how fast the water would dry as you tried to clean it. When we did the inside and found the gum, the candy wrappers, toys, paper, trash, the long lost sock, and you name it, from their kids; it brought back memories of when my kids were little. It had been a long time since I had come across so much lost treasure hidden in a vehicle.

Tommy had told us that he wanted to take us and show us around while we were there. He was so busy it was almost impossible until one evening he asked if we wanted to go. It was now or never as it was almost time for us to leave. He took us and showed us the hangers with all kinds of planes, rows and rows of planes; all sizes and types. We saw a B-52 and a cruise missile. Off in the distance was a hanger almost on its own. He said he couldn't take us there as it was top secret. Years later we learned it was the B-2 Stealth Bomber they were working on at the time. He then asked if we wanted to see a B-1 up close. We did, so he took us to an area where we had to empty our pockets so nothing might fall out near the planes. The openings for the engines were so big you could have walked in them except they were too high up on the plane. He then had us climb a ladder and go up inside. We were able to get up into the pilot seat and look around at all the instruments. The area for the men was actually very small. All the space was used for the machinery, instruments, and whatever the plane needed. Later when Pam told a pilot relative of hers about it, he told her he would have given his right arm to have been able to do that. It was an experience we would never forget.

Tommy, Beulah Ann, Tommy II and Sean Hughston

Tommy gave us a tour and told us about the various planes. Before we knew it, time had passed and it was time for us to go. Beulah Ann fixed us some tacos as she figured it might be some time before we would have them again. She was right. We told Dad good bye and promised we would try and write. He seemed in good spirits, yet sad. It was something I couldn't put my finger on. I didn't know it at the time but this would be the last time I would see him alive. I was glad we had taken the time to stop and see him those few days and was grateful that Beulah Ann and Tommy let us stay with them as it wasn't easy for them. It was an imposition.

We drove back to Los Angeles and turned our car in. We had a flight that was leaving that night and we would be on our way. All we had to do was kill a few hours in the airport and we would be gone.

We had heard virtually nothing about the government of Fiji having been overthrown just a couple of weeks before our planned visit. I can only assume that if it had been an extremely dangerous situation we would have been so advised. We arrived at the airport and made arrangements to get a taxi to take us to the place we had booked in at. We were in Suva and didn't realize that we should have purchased things we may have wanted to take to our room then.

The drive was about an hour through the countryside to an area that had various resorts built on or near the beach. The driver tried to get us to look at some of the other places to stay at as we approached where we were to stay. We looked at one that was very large but very old and depressing. I was sure I had found where all of those old motels and tourist courts had gone that were around back in my childhood. I think the driver was trying to get us to stay with some of his friends and would have most likely received a commission. We assured him we wanted to go to where we had booked.

The place was nice but not fancy. It had a number of the Fijian women working around the place sweeping the floors. It was an open-air type of architecture and in the main building it had a dining area with an area for performing. To the side was a circular bar that was positioned so it could serve both the dining area as well as the swimming pool that was on the opposite side. Past the swimming pool was a large lawn area with palm and coconut trees. This was the area that went down to the beach and had the small bure-type of accommodation.

We were taken to our bure ('little house') which was about 75 yards from the pool and about 50 yards from the beach. It had a porch on the side and a sitting area as you went in the door. The room was large with a double bed and a dressing area. At the end of the bed by the dressing area was a small refrigerator. The room to the side was the bathroom with toilet and open area shower. It wasn't fancy but clean and private. I knew we would be alright as we had a refrigerator in our room; I just didn't know that the stores were back in Suva, an hour each way from where we were.

We were both a bit lost and at first it was hard for us to sit still. We tried down by the water at the beach and wrote a few cards. We went to the bar and had a drink. We made plans to eat at the place we were staying at that evening and they told us they would be having a Bar-BQ that night outside by the bar. That was fine with us and Pam looked around at the menu on the wall. She started figuring out real fast they made a lot of curries and it was most likely how they used up the leftovers from the day before.

We learned that if you went in the water by the beach, which was only about 1 to 3 feet deep, you had to watch for water snakes that were poisonous. That put me off on wanting to walk around in the seaweed and rocks. They also told us not to go out to the reef where the water was breaking to go swimming, as the deep water there was where the sharks were. Nice place. It wasn't so bad for us as we were more likely to walk on the beach or read and have a drink. With the swimming pool we had a place to cool off. That is if we needed to. It was late May and at that time of the year you had cool nights and warm days. You didn't need to cool off.

We went for an early morning walk on the beach as we woke up before they opened for breakfast. Our clocks were still on Texas time. It was nice to walk on the beach in the early morning and we would cross little streams that came down from the hills through the bush to the beach. The small tidal pools were left in the volcanic rock and we would check them for small fish and shells. It was as if we had the area to ourselves with not a person in sight. We returned to the place for breakfast and then went back to our room. Some of the native Fijian women came by, selling fresh fruit and this reminded us we wanted to buy some items to keep in our refrigerator so we went back to the desk to see about getting a ride to town.

This is when we learned that the nearest town was back in Suva. We hired a taxi and made our trip back to town. We found the main shopping area and purchased a few snacks, some wine, and Fijian Beer. The market area reminded me of Mexico and after we looked around for a short time we went back to the hotel. We started picking up on the fact that the native or indigenous Fijians were black and reminded me of Blacks. Some looked as if they may have some Australian Aborigine in their past history. These were the people cleaning the floors, selling door-to-door and on the streets, and were usually not so well off. The other group of Fijians were of Indian origin who had been brought out by the British in the century or so before, to work in the plantations. They were now the shop owners, taxi drivers, tour guides and those that were better off. We saw only a few white people in the work force and this was back at the hotel which was owned by an Australian couple.

The unrest in the population had resulted from the obvious. The original Fijian people, the Blacks, were at a disadvantage. The Indian Fijian people were running and owning everything. In some ways it was as if they had tried to put in place their class system they had in India. The people wanted the government to address some of these issues but had little success. The new government was still mainly Fijian Indian but had a new constitution and the people hoped it would make more progress towards helping the indigenous Fijians.

Pam was in hope of getting lots of nice seafood but soon learned this was not offered. We went up the road one night and ate at the restaurant in the Hyatt Regency. The place and the food were okay but didn't have the character that the place had where we were staying. It was very different from our place indeed. The last night we ate again at our hotel as it was the night for their performance.

The food was okay but the performance was most interesting with the dancing, and the women coming over and trying to get you up to dance. They didn't want the guests not being a part of the evening. You couldn't help but feel that the Black Fijians were being taken advantage of. It was okay for us to sit around with nothing to do but we wondered how others got along. They didn't have any tours of the area set up as such, and no crafts or art was displayed from the local population. It just didn't seem like they were organized.

When we went to leave and I was checking out, I noticed the man at the desk had quoted and charged us a price that was higher than their standard rate. I learned in years to come, that he was adding on the travel agents' commission where normally it was paid out of the standard rate. They were not very professional in that respect as we were to also learn in the years to come but then the industry is full of such people. We took our taxi ride back to the airport and were soon on the last leg of our journey.

We arrived at the airport in New Zealand on my 43rd birthday. We had to clear customs and immigration and once we were past this we found Pam's parents waiting. They were ready to take us to a motel near their cousins, Paddy and Guy Ronaldson in Papatoetoe, Auckland. We were going to see them and Alan was going to get some work done on his car.

When we were at the service station we saw a small TV that was on sale for about $400 NZD. It was a color TV with radio and alarm clock. It could be used in many ways and with us on our way to Thames, we figured it would come in handy at the bach. In fact it came in handy many a time. But it was taking some time getting use to the prices and to the expressions or slang people used.

That evening, we were to go out to eat and we all went to a restaurant in the area. We were all dressed nicely and I was dressed in a sport coat, new boots, and new blue jeans. When we got to the door and started to ask for a table, we were told we couldn't come in and eat there as I was wearing blue jeans. I couldn't believe it. I knew I had some adjusting to do having just come from Texas but found this hard to believe as these were as good as new. I had just left a place where very well-to-do people go out to eat all the time in blue jeans. At first we started to argue but could see we were not going to get anywhere so we left and ate at another place that was less worried about what we wore.

It was about this time Pam's mother made a confession to us. Just before we had arrived she had heard from the shipping company. They had our goods in Auckland at the port and wanted more money to get it off the wharf. None of us knew why it was in Auckland but they threatened to sell the stuff in a matter of days if they didn't receive about $1,000NZ. She wasn't sure what to do, so she paid them the money as she was afraid we would lose what little we had left. It was then necessary to make arrangements for the goods to be sent down to Napier where they were supposed to have gone. We needed them near Pat and Rob so we could store them for now. This was just the beginning of many written letters and phone calls to try to find out what was going on. This was our welcome to New Zealand, our new home.

CHAPTER 72

NEW ZEALAND AND BACK

The next day we left and headed out for Thames. We were going to stay a few days at the bach Pam's parents had at Thornton Bay, and show me the piece of land Pam had purchased a few years before. During this time the government had changed their departments around on how they handled things such as road repair and improvements. The previous department had widened the highway where our land was and had cut out the old drive that went up the side of the hill to where a shack had been. The power company was moving power lines from poles on the beach to up on the land so when Alan found out about this he contacted them. He explained how we had plans to build a house on this land and if the lines were underground it would be much nicer. After some correspondence he got them to put a transformer to one side that looked like a good place for it and they agreed to put the power underground.

Originally Pam purchased one lot. On another trip later she learned that the owner of the three adjoining lots wanted to sell them. She negotiated a good deal and purchased the other lots. The reasoning was that the extra land would give us privacy and if we didn't need it, we could sell them off. After the access was modified it looked like we might need two lots in order to get up the side of the steep hill and have enough room for a drive. After I climbed over the lots, I was sure that it really had only one good building area toward the center. It was sort of a large flat area with the hill toward the rear going up steeply. It also had slopes going up at each side and it looked like a small spring was off to one side. I wasn't worried about the place at this time and was sure we had enough to work with.

The lot was in a little bay between Rocky Point and Windy Point. It was just across the highway from the beach. It was a rocky beach but had some sand and lots of interesting large boulders. I could just see us fishing off of them at some time in the future. There were only a couple of small weekend sort of shacks at the end of the bay by Windy Point at that time and a house up high at the other end. All the rest was covered in thick bush. When I climbed over the sections I was surprised by how thick the bush was and found a variety of large ferns and types of palms. It had a couple of groves of Ponga tree ferns and several springs with small ponds. The lots overall were very steep and after I went over the land I was sure that the one flat area would most likely be the only building site. I couldn't understand how they had figured it was 4 lots originally, with only one area to build on. This would become clear with time.

We had a chance to meet the neighbors where Peg and Alan's bach was, and Alan made arrangements for us to receive our mail through a retired mechanic friend of his, Don Forbes. He had a machine shop and mechanical background but was now retired. During the Second World War he was a conscientious objector, so served in the medical corps. He was Baptist and we were warned he didn't like drinking, so as not to insult him. Alan also introduced us to another couple, Dot and Les who lived next door to the Forbes. Les, a retired commercial fisherman, made his own home brew beer and was kind enough to offer me some from time to time, to make sure it hadn't gone off and the quality was kept up.

We now planned on heading down to Peg and Alan's house in Palmerston North so we could regroup, and start to look around and learn about what they had to offer in building houses on our land. We had some ideas from the States and wanted to start to research what sort of cost we were looking at. We were considering doing as much of the work ourselves as we could. We also still had our plans to go camping and had offered to first go and stay with Pat and Rob for awhile, to help them. We needed to go to see them first and make our trip to Napier to retrieve our goods before we were stuck with another bill. We weren't lacking for things to do.

Pam went to the bank and to the finance group that she and her mother had put her investment with previously. The interest and some principal could be paid each month into a checking account and we could get a draw if we needed it. I was sure we would work something out before we spent it all but when she went to the bank about credit cards we found that my past credit history meant nothing. They agreed to give Pam a credit card with a couple of thousand-dollar limit as she had a bank account with them both now and in the past. More adjusting for me to get used to.

I was trying to keep a positive frame of mind and give our move a chance but I was upset about the moving company and felt we had been taken advantage of. We learned with time that this was not uncommon and was experienced by many people that moved to New Zealand. The wharves and moving industries were a law unto themselves.

When I questioned back in Texas by phone, why our goods were sent to Auckland instead of Napier, our moving company said they were told that Napier was not a deep-water port. This, as we already knew, was not the truth as it was a major New Zealand deep-water port. We asked them why we were not told of any changes, and the only answer I could get was it wouldn't have made any difference.

After both Pam and I contacted various agencies, consumer groups, the U.S. Department of Commerce and so on, we found out that none took responsibility. The U.S. said they couldn't as it had gone by truck to Houston and then by ship, so it was up to Texas. Texas said it wasn't their jurisdiction and so said New Zealand. We fell through the cracks once more and at the end of all of this, Global sent us a check for a few hundred dollars as a partial refund for the additional expenses in getting the goods to Napier. The shipping industry had learned where the jurisdiction started and ended, and how to use it to their advantage. I was sure I had found where the pirates of old had gone . . . to the shipping industry.

This was but the first of many surprises—situations where we were being taken advantage of by those who were not honest and made a living by such means. I soon learned that New Zealand did not have many consumer protection laws and the public was at the mercy of the dishonest. We had a lot of learning to do and this was just the start. As Dorothy said, "No Toto, this doesn't look like Kansas anymore".

We went over to Pat and Rob's with the idea of going to Napier to collect our belongings and then repay them by staying with them for awhile to help them around the farm. Pat had always told Pam how Rob could use a hand from time to time and I told Pam before we left, I would look forward to getting outside and helping, just to do something different. We would also stop in the town on the way and see her lawyer friend and a few others she had known before she left. This is also where Pat's Dad, Len, lived and we planned on catching up with him as well.

When we went to the Port in Napier, after several phone calls, we learned we could handle the clearing of the items through customs and MAF. MAF was the Ministry of Agriculture and Fisheries and was responsible for protecting the country from insects, diseases, and other unwanted items from entering the country. The inspection would cost about $50 and at first the person on the phone was not sure if we would have to pay duty or not. The administrative office in Napier was our first stop to pick up the needed forms and then we were off to the docks.

We had a list of all the items and the man at the docks also had a list that had come in with the shipment. They had the box moved over to where we were and they decided we needed to open it as they wanted to inspect a few items (such as baskets) for insects, and a bike that Alan had purchased new when he was in the states. When he was recovering from surgery he would watch the TV infomercials and advertisements which amazed him. All you had to do was call on a toll-free number and give them your credit card details and it would be delivered to your door. He wanted to call on numerous items and was asked to control himself. That is, until this bike came on that you could fold up and carry, or adjust to many sizes. He just couldn't leave it alone and despite many a logical argument from Peg, his heart was still set on it. We told him to order it and we would ship it with our goods.

The man doing the inspections was friendly enough and after he checked these couple of items, didn't see any reason to look anymore so told us to repack and go. As luck would have it, we had the baskets and bike about a third of the way in the back of the box so we had some repacking to do before we were ready to go. The man with the forklift was kind enough to put the box on the back of the truck and we were ready to return to the farm.

This gave Pam plenty to do as we planned on unpacking the big container box and storing the small boxes and various goods in the shearers' cottage. Pat and Rob said they didn't have shearing gangs come and stay on the farm anymore, so it would be okay. During all the unpacking Pam found only one item damaged. It was where a forklift had gone through the bottom of the box and into a box of goods that had my cowboy hat in it. The hat had a piece taken out of the rim and that was the only item hurt. This was not enough to claim on. I was glad in a way, as we had heard of others who had big claims on damage and were only paid out after long and difficult negotiations.

I started spending my time each day with Rob. I followed him around as he visited with me and felt that any day he was going to have me start helping with some jobs that needed to be done. I found it interesting how on some days that were cold and wet he would do little jobs outside. On another day when the sun was out, he would do small jobs in the garage, or do paper work. After several days Pam tried to suggest through Pat—and I myself tried to hint—that I was able to do various jobs if he would just tell me what he wanted done.

He started to show me how he wanted a pile of used lumber sorted and stacked but rather than show me a few and go, I had to watch as he continued until the job was done. He then decided to clean the garage one day and I was able to help move some of the boxes outside—but only after he was sure it was okay to move them. I was then going to sweep the floor when he decided he wanted the broom and took the job over until it was done. I told Pam I couldn't handle being treated like an idiot and was capable of doing much more. I wanted to help but was not prepared to waste time day in and day out just watching.

We would visit in the evening at the end of the day and would have a few beers. We would help wash up the dishes several times a day. Morning, lunch and in the evening, we had dishes to wash. It was like they were breeding in the sink when our backs were turned. It became an ongoing joke about the numerous dishes we washed every day. Rob would talk about his various projects and plans that centered on the gas plant. He acted oblivious to what was going on around him at the farm and after he displayed some anger and becoming upset over things like a young child, I told Pam I thought he needed some professional help. I didn't want to upset her friends and wanted to remain friends with them but felt we needed to go.

I was upset that it hadn't worked out, as Pam and I both genuinely wanted to help Pat and Rob. For whatever reason he just wouldn't turn things over to others and let them do a job for him—even something small that might take time or that he just never seemed to get around to. But we were determined not to let this ruin our plans or our relationship with them and returned to Palmerston North to stay with her folks.

We had our day trips out and looked at some of the houses that were show homes by builders who worked nationwide. We picked up the odd item from time to time when it was on sale at a good price—like a clothesline. We decided that if I drew a house like we wanted, as we had done before, then maybe we could get a price for either the shell or the whole thing. It was becoming more evident that we would need to do a lot ourselves as we didn't have near enough money to build one completely. If we could get a shell built, then we could live in it and do the rest ourselves over a period of time.

I started spending evenings trying to draw various views of plans of what we had worked out over time that we wanted. We took a trip back up to Auckland to a home show for ideas and another trip with her folks back to Thames to talk to some builders and to stop at one company's factory to see about a shell price. Most were not interested as they didn't want to work with something they didn't already have plans for. One did put us straight on some obstacles we may have with the council and between that and estimated cost, it looked unlikely we would be building anytime soon.

At the bottom of the hill at Thornton Bay was a large older place that had been put on the market. It was across from the beach and had previously been a guesthouse. After Pam and I had mentioned it, her folks said why don't we look at it. So we did. We didn't know what we had in mind but looking had always been free. It had numerous small bedrooms and the lady claimed it had been profitable in the past. The large area upstairs was grand and it had a screened-in porch that went around on one side and across the front. It was a real mixture but it gave us something to think about and we weren't afraid to kick ideas around. We could see it with kids going across to the beach. It was a natural for families to stay at and while it would be at the lower end of the accommodation market, it might be fun.

We returned to Palmerston North with a lot to think about and as we were in no hurry, didn't feel we needed to make a decision then. If we were more than just interested then we needed to check it out more. Someone told Pam that she should go to the council and see what they had to say about the place. This was all new to me and I was more of a spectator as I didn't know what they were talking about.

We no sooner had returned to Palmerston North than one morning we had a phone call and Peg said it was for me. It was Beulah Ann who called to let me know that Dad had just died. They were planning on taking him back to San Antonio and having the funeral there, where he would be buried in Sunset Memorial Cemetery with Mom. The family had extra plots there as he had purchased 5 of them, years before. This was the same cemetery that my grandparents were also buried in.

She wanted to know if we planned on coming so they would know about how long to put off the funeral. This was something we had not planned for, of course. We had just come out and it was now just July 28, 1988—only about 2 months since we left. The expense for airfare alone would be about $1,500 each, and food and accommodation extra. We could try and stay with family or friends but didn't know how this might work out. Pam told me to go and said she would stay home to help with the expense. She didn't want to stay behind but we already knew we hadn't brought enough money. She felt it was something that I needed to do and it was something she had always wished she had done—gone home for family funerals when she could have.

I told her I didn't know how long I needed to go for, as Beulah Ann had already said something about helping with the funeral. I didn't understand this as I knew Dad had had life insurance, plus some other benefits. I told Pam I may need to stay and help, or I may be able to go—I wouldn't know until I was there. We also agreed I would go to Austin and see if I could find anything out on the shipping company. I would also go and see Mary Burris as we had not heard from her. I also wanted to see Susie as I had received a note that she had paid herself for looking after a couple of small items that came in. Pam had also decided that her artwork that hadn't sold might as well come to New Zealand now too, so I was to pick it up and bring it back.

I let Beulah Ann know that I would be coming back for the funeral. In short order Pam contacted Air New Zealand and explained the situation. They offered a compassionate fare and I could go that night or the next. I needed to get my residency permit updated so I could get in again when I came back. The lady was good about it and gave me a permit that was unlimited on how many trips I could make in and out. As her folks let several people know what had happened, I received a few requests for car parts to bring back. Before I knew it, I was packed and ready to go.

I had made plans to try and catch a flight myself by running at Los Angeles Airport and hoping to catch a late flight to San Antonio. I had talked to Sam and he agreed to pick me up—just let him know when I would be getting in. I told Pam I would be in touch with her and for her to continue on with what she needed to do. She had managed to obtain a New Zealand credit card for me and I still had those in the States. We agreed that I would need to use what little money was in the account we left in Austin and I might as well close the account. With this, I flew out of Palmerston North for Auckland to catch my late night flight back to the states. I don't think I had ever seen so many arrangements made in less than 48 hours. I always found I had a lonesome feeling inside whenever I knew I was going to be away from Pam for a while, and this was no exception. She told me later she had cried all the way back home from taking me to the airport—and often in the weeks to come.

CHAPTER 73

TRIP BACK TO TEXAS

On my flight back to the States the plane was less than half full. I was near the station where the stewardesses prepared food and drink and I had the whole row all to myself. As we flew in the middle of the night, I was able to use all the seats and get some sleep. With the time difference, the plane arrives in late afternoon in Los Angeles. I knew if I was going to be able to get a flight to San Antonio I would need to run. As soon as I cleared customs and immigration I ran to the counters for domestic tickets and the first one told me that the only flight that had not left yet was Delta for Dallas. Once I reached Dallas I would be able to catch a flight to San Antonio.

I ran to the Delta check-in and purchased my ticket. I checked my bags in and they told me they didn't think they would make the flight but would follow. I got to the gate and boarded the plane. The plane was again only about half full and after I sat down they announced there would be a delay. We sat for about 30 minutes before we left for Dallas. We arrived that night in Dallas and I was able to get on one of the last flights to San Antonio. I called Sam from Dallas and told him my plane would be in around midnight.

When we left the terminal and went outside to the parking lot, the hot humid air almost knocked me down. It was still 90-plus degrees and very humid. This was one thing I hadn't missed about Texas. We went to the duplex where he lived with Denise. They had started living together. She was working for the phone company doing shift work and Sam still worked for Cecil.

We made arrangements the next day to see Dad at the funeral home, and see some of the relatives. Uncle Gene, who had his own little used car lot, offered to let me use one of the cars that was on his lot. This was a help and I was able to spend more time with the family and not be a problem for others to drive me around.

From the coast, Aunt Jeannie and uncle Lloyd, along with aunt Bobbie and cousin Ena with her kids, came up for the funeral. The evening before the funeral and the night after the funeral, we had agreed to go out to eat together at the 'Red Barn Steak House'. We all sat at one big table and were able to visit. Beulah Ann and family were there, my other brothers and some of the family, those from the coast, Sam and Denise, and Craig and Elizabeth. The charges for the evening were put on one big bill and each time we had a large shortfall. Both times Sam and I put in way over what we had spent. I told him it was funny as at the present time, we were the two that could least afford it and were having to carry some of those that wouldn't pay their own way. I told him this was a lesson in life that not only shows up in the general population but in your own family as well.

The afternoon after the funeral we all went to Uncle Gene and Aunt Mary's house. This gave us a chance to see each other and tell stories. We had plenty of beer and snacks, and as the afternoon went on we were able to not only catch up with each other but send Dad off in style with many a toast and good story. I questioned Beulah Ann about Dad's state of affairs as I knew he had several life policies and that the premiums were taken care of with premium waivers. I told her to talk to Gene as he had sold Dad a number of the policies over the years. She told me that Joe was the executor of the estate but she would most likely handle it for him. We all agreed to this and for her to let us know about the funeral expenses, and that we would pay for it out of our share if that was okay. We later had an estimate from Beulah Ann and paid her our share until things were final. We later found that he had not only enough to pay for his funeral but each of us 5 children received something like 10 to 15 thousand from the insurance companies. It later came in at a very handy time for us back in New Zealand when we were desperate for funds.

It was during this time I was able to visit with Charlie and Beulah Ann, and found out what had happened to Dad. Charlie had already passed his state boards in Texas for becoming a doctor. In fact he came and stayed with me in Austin when he took his test, at the time when we were remodeling the house and Pam was overseas. From what I understood, Dad had some problems and had been put in the base hospital. They were running tests and using a bronchoscope on him, when the inside of his lungs were scratched and started to bleed. He had taken large doses of aspirin for years and I don't think the hospital staff were aware of this and had also given him some blood thinners. At any rate, the bleeding continued and he basically drowned in his own blood. Charlie had told me that he had been in contact with Beulah Ann about Dad several times, as she had expressed some concern about him. He told me that his quality of life had become worse and suggested it might have been for the best. Dad never was one for wanting his patient to hang in and suffer at all costs and I'm sure he didn't want to suffer or become a total problem for Beulah Ann or himself. Charlie and I both felt that the situation could have been avoided and again one of our family had suffered at the hands of those in the profession we had all so upheld.

I didn't want to take advantage of Uncle Gene as I knew he needed his car back. I talked to Sam and he told me that at first, Cecil was thinking about letting me use a car but for whatever reason changed his mind. I told him I needed to make one trip to Austin to take care of a few things and would be gone most likely for one or two nights. I would do what I could over the phone first and then make the trip if I could use his truck. He had a Toyota truck and Denise had a Datsun or Nissan Z sport car.

He said that would be fine and I started making my phone calls, and writing down the amount of time and giving the kids the money for them. I was both phoning and writing Pam. She told me she planned on going back to Thames and checking out the place with the council. I had also contacted the government office in Austin about the mortgage company. We had left it alone, as at the time we were told it would be too expensive and with us contacting people about them, might start to expose us to slandering the company or some such. We no longer cared and wanted to at least see if the government consumer department was interested. I had taken copies of our letters and such with me and they told me to come by their office and drop them off.

I had a chance to visit with the kids and went shopping at the store with them several times. I didn't want them to be out of pocket with me staying with them, and had decided to buy food and supplies to help out. I was sorry that Laurie and Scott didn't get to come to the funeral and the activities after. I wanted them to see that in our family we were sad when people died but we also celebrated their memory. I wanted them to meet some of their other relatives and see some of the other side of their family. I was told they were at a church camp or such and wouldn't be able to come. I was able to see them after this and before I went back to New Zealand—mainly at Sam's place.

When I had made my plans and was ready to go to Austin, I took Sam's truck. I had most everything planned and would spend one night at Mary Burris's house and one night at Rodger Roger's house. I went by Susie's (and our former) house to explain what had happened, and that as I would need to close our account, I might as well take everything with me and close it now. They were very cool and I left. I went to the bank, closed the account and took out what little money was left. They told me that only one check had not cleared for $15 that was written 4 months before. I told them I was sorry but could not wait any longer for them to get around to depositing the check after 4 months.

I went by the state capitol and government offices, and spoke to them about both the moving company and the mortgage company. They took the information but basically didn't care. I was not surprised later when nothing became of it. By late that afternoon I had met up with Mary Burris and she wanted me to go with her to a place she went to all the time that had snacks and drinks, and the crowd was about 40's through 60's in age. As the evening went on, it was apparent she was having a good time and planned on staying until closing—much later than I wanted to. I went back to her house and slept on the sofa that made into a bed in the front room. She came in sometime, much later on.

I talked to her the next day and explained what was going on. I also made sure it was okay to have the mail forwarded to her place and she could send on anything that needed to be. She was still not the same Mary we had known years before and after this I left. I don't think we ever heard from Mary after this. It was as if she disappeared. She never sent any of our mail and I can only guess it is still on the kitchen table buried under a stack of mail from the previous weeks.

I went by the shop where Pam had left her pictures and explained to the lady what was going on. She gave them back to me and I left. I spent that evening with Rodger and felt like a stranger. I told Pam later, it was as if I hadn't seen these people for years instead of just 2 months. How soon we are forgotten.

I returned to San Antonio and spent some time packaging up the pictures for the return trip. I visited with the kids and stayed about another week as I waited to see if anything was going to come out of my trip to Austin and the government departments. I felt I had accomplished very little and if it was a matter of staying longer I didn't mind but if it was going to be a waste of time I might as well go.

Pam told me that she had learned in the meantime that the old place by the beach had let their 'Existing Use Rights' go and the council didn't think that they would be able to get them back as they would now not meet many of the guesthouse licensing standards today. She was much less enthusiastic as she had seen it as a way to make some money from home for her, and maybe us, if I didn't have a job. She then told me that the realtor she had spoken to told her of another place up the coast at Te Puru.

It was a large place that did have Existing Use Rights but was unfinished and up for sale. It was in financial difficulty and a person who didn't mind doing a lot of work might be able to make a good deal on the place. She had some preliminary numbers and ideas but wanted to see how I felt. I told her that it still wouldn't hurt to look and to check into it. With it not being finished, it might be possible for us to buy it and do it ourselves. She was going to see what she could learn by the time I came back which would be soon, as we had decided there was no reason for me to stay any longer.

I contacted the travel agent and she said for me to just call the airline direct as I could do just as good a deal since I had my return ticket for New Zealand already. I found out when I could get my flight booked on Air New Zealand and then I made arrangements to get to Los Angeles. I still needed a way to get to the airport as my plane was to leave around midday. At first Sam was going to drop me off, and then he told me that he decided he wanted to stay with me at the airport until I left so he told Cecil he wouldn't be in until after I was gone. He told me he had told Cecil that it was too bad if he didn't like it but he didn't know when he would be able to see his Dad again, and with that in mind planned on staying with me until I was gone. This did make me feel much better and I was glad to see that Sam and I still had that close a relationship and that at least ours hadn't disappeared in the 2 months, like some of the others.

I checked in with my extra baggage of pictures and explained how I had just come back for my Dad's funeral. The people at American were nice and didn't charge me excess but told me they didn't know how it would go at Air New Zealand. When I got to Los Angeles and checked in, I again told them of my situation and they too put it through at no extra charge. It wasn't until I reached Auckland and was switching to a domestic flight on Air New Zealand for Palmerston North, that the man gave me a hard time and was going to charge me excess baggage, when it was starting to cause such a disruption that he decided it was more trouble than it was worth and let me go on at no extra charge. I told Pam that was one of the few things on the whole trip that turned out to be free, and one that surprised me.

I was glad to be back and I told Pam that in a funny sort of way it showed me just how quickly things change and people forget. We had been gone but a short time and all these good friends that were going to write or see us some day had almost no use for me when I showed back up. It was strange. It also showed that if I was thinking I had a place to go back to with friends, I was wrong, and I might as well get that out of my mind and just settle down.

In the meantime, Pam had learned a lot about the place in Te Puru. She had seen it start to go up years before, when they would go up to her folk's place. It was a large white building on the side of a hill. She had seen an ad for it in the Harcourt's real estate magazine but felt it was far more money than we could afford but she now knew the vendor's situation was desperate and if we purchased just the main area with the building, the price would be less. Her folks had talked it over with her and had agreed to help if they could and for us to find out more if we were interested.

The main thing we needed to do was to go back up to Thames and find out more, as well as have a closer look at the place. I was no sooner back than we were off again, back to Thames. It was good in some ways as it gave us something to do. We still hadn't given up on building but felt it was way off in the future. If this could be worked out, then we might have something in the long run.

I had just one other thing to do before we returned. Pam and her Mom had made me an appointment with a urologist who was supposed to be very good. I had my checkup and explained how the other urologist (a friend of my Dad) had done the vasectomy by removing a piece of the tube on each side and tying the ends off. [I had also just checked on this while I was back in Texas.] It had now been 16 years since that was done and this urologist told me it would only be a guess on odds, if it would work, as it had been a very long time. But since I was in good health, he could see no reason not to try and told us the estimated cost would be $2,000. We agreed for him to make arrangements for the operation in the private hospital and to let us know when it would be. This later worked out for us to return to Palmerston in early November, only some 8 or so weeks later.

We were now off to Thames. I had no idea of just how busy Pam had been. In a way I was glad she had taken care of making arrangements so we could get on with it. I had no reason not to at this point in time and had always told her that we would try at some point in the future. But for now it was up to us to find out what we were possibly getting ourselves into.

I thought to myself, with it being a place on the side of a hill again, maybe it was for us. Maybe this was again a place for a Kopecky.

CHAPTER 74

OBSERVATIONS

After I had seen New Zealand for the first time, I remember how I couldn't get over how the countryside was so green and the vegetation so lush. Around each corner was a picture and with very little effort I could find things to take photos of, all the time. The hills, the mountains, the sea, the beach, the bush, the sky, the sunsets, the sheep, the views, and on and on. It was even interesting to see the houses and buildings. The big city glass skyscrapers were much the same but not the older buildings, corner dairies and houses.

I had not travelled far and wide and had only seen a few places on my trips with the car companies in the years past. I had been to Vancouver, Canada; Maui, Hawaii; San Francisco and Los Angeles; Lake Tahoe; Colorado; Mexico; and various parts of the other states, as well as all over Texas. They were different, and Maui was the closest in resemblance to New Zealand. I found the country a real mix—much more so than many other places. Here you had cities and towns, yet not far away countryside with bush, and a skip away the beach. The mountains and lakes, with recreation for people, were also popular. The people were different—both good and bad—and the customs and the way they talked, made it unique.

It was a mixture of new and old. The houses all painted different colors along the beach, and the corner dairy that was solid red with 'Coke' painted on it, or blue with 'TipTop' ice cream painted on it. It was going into a shop at 10 AM or 3 PM and not a soul in sight. Then, when you asked to be waited on they became indignant as it was their tea break. Of course this was not known to us outsiders. And as long as we are talking about tea, I was forever trying to figure out what they were talking about. "Oh, do come by for tea this evening". I didn't know if we were going to eat it or drink it, as they used "tea" for what I called dinner as well.

"Good as gold." Now that is a favorite expression used a lot and I learned that many that use it on a regular basis, are those that bear keeping an eye on. What you are assured is as good as gold, will most likely will turn into something brown and sticky. Other expressions or terms that had various meanings are bugger and dag. They should not be used by the unfamiliar as they may get you into trouble.

As we all do, you turn blind to what is around you when it becomes familiar. When I first came, I couldn't get over how Thames had such a wonderful setting under the hills and by the water. It seemed like a location with tremendous potential yet the locals only complained about the sea and worried about the dairy farmers.

I found the metal roads—which I knew as dirt or gravel—most interesting, as they would wind their way through the bush and hills. I was assured the land around the peninsula was marginal farmland at best and many people that lived on the life-style blocks were hippies who had never left after the 1970's. These people were environmentally friendly, as they put it, and would grow their own vegetables and sometimes small cash crops. Some of the others on the peninsula would find extremely difficult places to grow their large cash crops, as they did not want the authorities to know how/where they made their living.

I soon learned that you could divide the population of the area up into several main groups. You had the farmers, the greens and/or hippies, the town merchants who had roots going back several generations, and the new people that had shown up like us. The economy was geared for the farmer and the town had become very dependent on them for business. Then banks, as we were told, had taken a beating on various business ventures in the 1980's and after the crash of 1987 didn't want to know about anything but farms. If it didn't have tits and could be milked, then the bank had no time for you. They had been burnt badly by getting involved in some speculative investments and their answer was to not get involved in anything again. It was a very backward approach and both Pam and I couldn't get over how useless the banks were; both then and in the years to come.

I guess one of the first things we noticed was how the merchants in the town would try and take advantage of you, if you let them. The prices were already very high and took some getting used to but when they were sure they had you, they would just smile and laugh. It was very much on the basis of being an outsider, as we had not grown up in the community for generations as others had. We joked about it—that maybe in 20 years they would accept us. Unfortunately this was more truth than fiction as I didn't realize at first how much my American accent stuck out. If the local community thought I was a tourist then it was okay. If they knew I lived there, they could sometimes be indignant. Many were sure all Americans were rich and they would show no mercy. With time I learned there was still a deep-rooted prejudice against Americans that came from several sources. One was the Second World War when the American soldiers came to New Zealand on R & R and spent all their time defending the country by getting all the women pregnant. The old saying that what was wrong with the American soldiers was, that they were "overpaid, oversexed, and over here". Long before Pearl Harbor, all the New Zealand men were off overseas in battle getting killed. New Zealand and its other allies who were part of the British Commonwealth, had been in the war since the start with England. A quarter of this country's population took part while the United States sat on the sidelines until December 1941, after many Commonwealth soldiers had already been killed. Then the states wanted to brag how they won the war—this didn't help. New Zealand had been in every war overseas with the United States (like Korea and Vietnam), as well as a number the United States was never in. We forget how at times in the early days of World War II, that Joseph Kennedy was supporting Adolph Hitler and his causes. Not all of the rest of the world forgot.

Pam observed, and I concurred, that Americans by and large, do not know where New Zealand even is or that it is not part of Australia. Australians are like Yankees from the States and New Zealanders are more like Southerners. We both agreed on this but it seems most of the Americans that come out to New Zealand are Northerners.

With this in mind, another area that didn't help was the attitude of Americans who came over on vacation. The reason you hear so much about the rude American tourist stereotype is because lots are like that. I myself soon started to learn to hide from them so as not to be associated with them. It was always the same—it isn't like this back home; back home we do it this way; ours is much better, faster, bigger; and so on. Then you would get them trying to barter the price down and waving around their money as if everything had a price. No wonder so many people didn't like Americans.

The last type of behavior along with the bragging of how America was better than any place in the world, would get old real quick. It was the attitude that Americans were better than anybody else was, and a bully sort of behavior would come out. This style would turn people against Americans and jealousy would come out at times. Everyone knew the Americans had been very successful and most had more than many could ever dream of. The people still didn't like having their noses being rubbed in it, and so jealousy and resentment would surface rather than a feeling of being friends and wishing them well.

I experienced discrimination several times over the years because I was an American. Other times you could tell there was a dislike and the body language said it all. I didn't like how I was treated but I knew I was being painted with the same brush as all Americans. After I lived in New Zealand a number of years and watched the American tourist, I couldn't much blame the New Zealanders and wanted to join them myself at times. A lot of Americans need to take a good hard look at themselves in the mirror and see how the rest of the world sees them—although I doubt this will ever happen.

The country is relatively clean, and violence in crime is less common than in the States. The issue of gangs, drugs, and crime are still there in the country but not as bad but one big difference is the penalty imposed on a person that commits a crime. It can be of a fairly serious nature, and even on a repeat basis, and most of the time the criminal gets some sort of probation and community service. It is a joke to say the criminals are punished. Even on very severe crime the penalties are minor compared to the rest of the world. If ever the world wanted to know what a society would be like with only minor penalties for crimes, then all they need to do is study New Zealand.

When I first came to New Zealand I saw very few indigenous Maori people. I expected to see more of them as I was use to seeing a lot of Mexican Americans around all the time in Texas. As I got to know more about their background, I began to feel their situation was a cross between those of the Mexican Americans and the Blacks—but still different. They had the issues of discrimination, lack of education, lack of money, and worst of all, lack of motivation. I was sure that the government must have by now, had some sort of programs in place that were designed to help them. They needed to be able to get an education or training, and then of course a job afterwards, if they were to get out of poverty. I was sure that whatever was available wouldn't be perfect but would be a start.

I did learn over time that a lot of these issues had already been addressed in varying degrees but that a lot of the Maori didn't do anything about it. I wasn't sure if they didn't care because they were getting too much on welfare, or what it was. I still don't know but I suspect that a number of them figure that when the Waitangi Claims are paid out they will get a big fat check and everything will be okay. Too many feel that, from what they have been told–it is owed to them, so why work. They don't seem to understand that if they want to take control of their own lives then they need to do something about it themselves and not wait for others to do it for them.

It reminded me of my friend, Milton McKnight, who was a Black in the States. He went through various government programs where schools were required to give so many seats to Blacks (regardless of their entrance test scores), so they could get an education. He took the opportunity and others like it—including twice where he got a good job when companies needed to fill a quota for Blacks. He told me how others in his neighborhood wouldn't do the programs and gave him every excuse from his being used, to being an Uncle Tom. After it was all said and done, he had an education and a good job that paid a lot more than he ever dreamed he would make, so who was the fool? He took his opportunity and the chances offered but how do you motivate others to go and do it for themselves and stop waiting on others to do it for them?

Pam had given me some background on the country's history and the Maori people. She explained to me how race problems were not an issue when she grew up and discrimination was minor compared to the states. It was only in the last 15 years or so that things had started to change and an air of unrest had come about. This bothered her because she always liked the Maori people she knew, and didn't understand what was going on at first. It was only after some time and learning more about their history and what had happened to them, that her eyes became opened. She found out that the relationship was not as rosy as she had believed when growing up and many an injustice had been done to them over the years. We both knew that some changes were coming and felt they deserved more than what they had. It was time for a reasonable settlement to be made with the Maori people.

Pam and I couldn't help but wonder if part of the problem for a lot of the Maori people was that they had lost their land with all its history, and therefore their sense of who they were. They no longer had a deep pride in who they were and what their ancestors stood for, as many seemed to have lost this along the way during the colonization process. If they were proud of their past, would this give them the motivation to make a future for themselves and their kids? From what little I have learned about the Maori people as a whole, they have an interesting history and a lot to be proud of. They have a lot to offer the country–that is if they decide to share it. It seems a certain portion of the Maori community always use the excuse something is "tapu" (sacred/prohibited) and thus, a secret. I hope they don't wait too long until they have nothing to pass on but the history of the street gangs, for heritage, as with the Blacks in Chicago.

Even after living a number of years in New Zealand, I still can't get over how much potential the country has to offer—yet it just can't seem to get it together . . . or maybe they are starting to get it together but they just can't quite pick it up yet. The country is a jewel in the Pacific and offers an unsurpassed place to live, with a lot of infrastructure already in place. How many other places in the Pacific can offer what this country can? Could they maybe not be the Ireland or Switzerland of the Pacific? Or some place that offers quality living to those who will pay for it? The government and the people need to make a plan and decide where they want to go and what they want to become. They need to stop their brain drain by getting the jobs and good pay here so they don't have to go overseas. I still remember what I was told that was so true; the only thing that is constant is change. The sooner this is acknowledged, along with the fact that all we can do is control and aim it and get on with the job, the better off the whole country will be.

CHAPTER 75

THE FINAL OPERATION

When we returned to Thames we lived in the coastal bach that belonged to Pam's folks. I had the idea I would need a job and started looking at the newspaper. We started negotiating with the realtor and tried to find out from either he or the owner, a Mr. Carter, some of the particulars on the property for sale at Te Puru. A lot of the time we would ask something or even try to find out if he would consider various options in regard to the property, only to receive no response or one that would be a long time in coming.

I had landed one job early on with a car dealer in Thames. This was mostly by accident. During a Market Day in Thames we were looking at the items up and down the main street that were for sale. Alan spotted a Nissan Van for sale that was very unusual as it was a Japanese import. It had the interior finished out with seating for 9, and had air-conditioning, which was very rare at this time. Alan urged us to consider buying it as he was afraid it wouldn't last long. We went back to the bach, discussed it and decided to make an offer. Pam's folks had been letting us use their little Chevette and told us we could trade it in if it helped.

After spending most of an afternoon going back and forth with the dealer who claimed he was selling it on behalf of an individual, a deal was made and we purchased the vehicle. Alan looked shocked when he found out we really had traded his Chevette away. Peg was to make arrangements at the investment company back in Palmerston North, to transfer the balance of the money we needed for the purchase, from our invested savings to our bank checking account. It was during this time we got to know Lester Yates when he raised the idea of my going to work for him, after I 'negotiated' this vehicle deal with him.

A week or so later I went to see him and he told me he had plans to enlarge, and would take me on as a salesman. It was different in New Zealand as the labor laws required him to pay me a minimum rate as a salesman, regardless of what or how much I sold. This gave him what he considered the necessity of always providing the other salesmen and me with something to do. This broke down into washing the cars every few days, cleaning the lot, the office, and being available not only during open hours 5 ½ days a week but also on call after hours and on Sunday.

I started off trying to help and knew I would need to learn the ropes. It became apparent he was worried that one of us might catch a customer and sell them something and he would then have to pay us a commission too. He did more to run off potential buyers than I could believe and after several weeks of washing cars it came to a head one Saturday.

He wanted us to look like salesmen but do the work of porters. He didn't want to pay us commission and I told him that if I was going to work for him I wanted to sell and make some money. One Saturday I went to work and by about 9:30 AM a lady came in driving a van that had kids in it, and he asked me to please take it and clean it up, and do a good job inside and out. I decided I would go along with this as I wanted to know what was going on. He had me kept busy doing the clean up as he visited with her and waited on anyone that came on the lot.

After I finished I found out it was his sister-in-law and her vehicle. I guess it must have reminded me of years gone by and I couldn't take it. I told him that I was sorry but I could no longer work for him under these conditions. I had understood I was to be a salesman and that is what I wanted to do and make some money. I had no intention on working for low wages and being his personal porter. With that I gave up the job and left.

That afternoon Pam and I purchased a couple of quart size bottles of tap beer from the pub and took the rest of the day off and went to the beach. It was like getting out of jail. I felt free again. I told Pam I would find another job but I would not be humiliated and treated like an idiot. I had already forgotten more about the car business than this clown had ever known. I later found out that one of his favorite tricks he would pull over the years was to take a vehicle out to a buyer's house and then stay until they finally agreed to buy it. He was known to stay until 2 AMand the people would buy just to get rid of him. This was his level of expertise.

I had heard that the Mitsubishi Store might be looking for a salesman so the next week I went by to meet one of the owners and gave him my resume. A few days later I had a job—this time as a salesman who only had to help out a little. Paul Sutherland was the new owner and he was buying the old owner, Colin Judd, out. It was a shame as the family was an old Thames family and this was one of the last businesses the family had in town. It was a necessity for Colin to sell, as he no longer wanted to run the business and spent most of his time just celebrating the end of each day. He was a nice enough man and left the running of the business up to Paul.

Paul was out of Auckland and had worked at some of the stores up there. It seemed that another man was involved with the transaction and had put the money up as he would come down and check on the operation. It became apparent real quick that it was run on a shoestring and was always in a desperate need of money.

I was to work with one other salesman, a Bill Costello, who was a semi-retired dairy farmer. He knew a lot of the local people and most of the farmers. Paul was to help us with the deals, and each month he would set goals, bonuses and bonus cars. He was to help get us vehicles we needed when we had a buyer for one but this very seldom seem to work out. If he traded around for one, it was usually for one of his own deals but nevertheless, it was a big improvement on what I had been in and I started making good money almost right away.

It was a very simple thing I had learned before. It took a little time as it required waiting on people, and getting their name and number and what they wanted. Then I would follow up and call them when I got a vehicle that might work for them. By just following up, I made sales because no one else did. I would also try to put the people in a vehicle that would work for them, and then sell it to them instead of trying to put them in this week's special. Sales picked up and before I knew it, Paul was starting to complain about how much I was making. It felt good.

We continued to negotiate on the property at Te Puru with very little success. It reached a point that we were both disgusted at the lack of communication. This is when we decided to take a more drastic approach so as to get the purchase either on or off. We told the realtor to make arrangements with our solicitor in Thames, to have a day set aside for us to all to get together in a conference to try and see if we could work a deal out. Up to this point we were unable to get a response or a straight answer to our questions. We were still under the impression that the Carters needed to sell from a financial point of view, yet we could not seem to get any dialogue going.

After a couple of weeks when we finally managed to contact Mr. Carter ourselves down in Wellington, a conference was set up. It seems that, according to him, he had not received half of our messages or questions. The realtor was putting most of these through Carter's solicitor, Peter Roscoe. As time went on we found out that Roscoe was stalling us to instead see if he could put a group together to buy the property out from under us, and that was why he wasn't passing the messages on.

When the day of the meeting came we met with our lawyer, Jim Poulgrain, in Thames, who the realtor had come up with to represent us. The realtor, Maurice Leonard, came, and Mr and Mrs. Carter came—but to our surprise brought Mr. Roscoe along with them. It became evident that the Carters were in more serious financial trouble than we knew. They had about 5 loans on the place and were only a few weeks away from foreclosure. The property was in three parts, as they saw it. The main property with the building also had a front lot being subdivided off, but the title had not yet been applied for as the surveying had not been done for the paper work to be completed. The large 60 acre block to the rear of the main property up the hill, had a separate title but no legal access as this was still in the process of being obtained from the local Maori people, whose land it presently went through.

These various obstacles had put off the local buyers and most felt it was too much time and money involved to be worth the trouble, especially as the main building itself was still unfinished. I have no doubt now that Mr. Roscoe had originally intended to let the property go into foreclosure and a bankruptcy auction, at which time he and his people planned to pick it up for a song.

As we got into negotiations, we told them all we were prepared to discuss buying the whole group of properties or just the main portion. We went over the various properties and they were still not forthcoming on all they knew about each piece. It was a real 'buyer beware' situation. Previously, we had walked on the front section down by the old building that the Carters had used to live in as they built the main building. Next to this was a grave. It was old and had a white picket fence around it and a tree. When we asked the realtor, we were told it was an old Maori grave which was not a problem—as long as we respected it and let the relatives come up from time to time, we would have no trouble. Pam also went to the council after this and talked to a Mr Alan Jefferies who told her not to worry as the grave, "was of no historical significance" and that as the Maori could bury their people where they wanted in the past, that is why it was there.

We reached a point where we finally decided to make an offer for the whole group of properties and worry later about the various issues since Mr. Carter had assured us that he would help on getting us the access to the farm up back and so on. But they did not like our offer and felt it would be unacceptable to the various mortgage holders as it did not cover all that was owed on the place. Our lawyer urged them to check with the various companies and see what they were willing to take, as the properties would not bring what was owed on them under any circumstances. Roscoe agreed to check into this and discuss our offer further with the Carters over lunch. We would all meet back at the meeting room after lunch and see where we were.

After lunch we returned to the meeting room and waited for the Carters and Roscoe to return. After about a 30-minute wait, a phone call came in for Mr. Poulgrain. It was Roscoe, who told him that he had been in contact with another group of buyers and they were also going to make an offer. It made me mad after working so hard and long to get this meeting to try to negotiate a deal with the owners, only to have this side show thrown at us in the middle of it. Pam and I were footing the bill for this meeting with the lawyer and meeting room, and now they were changing the rules to our party. It was made clear that Roscoe had taken a real smart-ass sort of approach. I was to later learn that this was his true nature and was well known by other lawyers as being "that slimy sh—".

After discussing the various points of the properties, we agreed to concentrate on the main property (with the building) only. We were also told that it would most likely be part of the deal that they we would need to allow access to the farm, through our front properties, if we did buy the main property. We then changed our offer to an amount that included only the two front properties, as they had not been subdivided as yet.

Roscoe again got smart on the phone with Mr. Poulgrain and had him relay a message to us that our offer was unacceptable. Mr. Poulgrain then went over the offer with us again and we raised it some, even though Mr. Poulgrain suggested that it might not be necessary since the mortgage companies were the ones with the real say. With this unconditional offer, we also spelled out some of the various terms—including the shed in front—and what was to stay and what was to go. This offer was to then be faxed over to their office and they were given a deadline of 5:00 PM. I told Mr. Poulgrain that Pam and I were both very angry about how we were being treated and that this offer was only good until then, after which time it would be withdrawn. It was a cash offer, which he verified by picking up the phone and calling Pam's lawyer friend, John Armstrong. We would sit in the waiting room until that time and then leave.

Pam had made an arrangement for the money, with John Armstrong, through the company he represented at his lawyer's office. We were to put the property up as collateral, as well as her parents' house in Palmerston North that was mortgage-free. After the deal was closed and values could be formally established, he would then release her parents' property as soon as he could. Most of all of these agreements with him had been made over the phone with trust. It was the only time that we experienced such trust and help from any kind of financial institution—then or since.

As we sat in the waiting room, we went over and over the offer. I told Pam that even if we missed out, I was glad it was going to be over. We had actually about another $30,000 we could have offered but under the circumstances, didn't. If anything, Roscoe with his attitude cost his clients or the mortgage companies this much as he had made us so mad we refused to go any higher. At about 4:30 PM Poulgrain came to us and wanted to know if we would go any higher. I assured him we wouldn't. He then came back and called us in. He told us that they had agreed to take our offer. The two front properties would be cleared of debt and the various companies that were still owed money would transfer their liens to the farm block behind.

In the years to come we would look back at this and go 'what if'? We were to find out the locals were right—it was too much time and money. It was one of those things you sometimes do that when you put the numbers in black and white, they don't work. It has to be something you want to do. It is that lifestyle sort of thing. We could see this place being a lot more than just a bed and breakfast, and in time it could be an attraction in its own right.

We didn't know it then but over that weekend, Roscoe still continued to try and get his group together to knock us out. He felt if he had a better offer by Monday then he could wiggle out of things. This was his normal way of doing business. His offer was higher than ours for the whole place but it was dependent on some in the group selling their properties first and since no one knew how long that might take, his deal fell over.

The next week we went up to Te Puru and saw the Carters. We wanted to make sure we all understood the contract and what was to be left, and that they were to be out by Labor Weekend in October. This was when we were to move in.

It became apparent that Carter was so busy trying to work deals with Roscoe that he hadn't read the contract. Mrs. Carter just signed it and of course Roscoe didn't point anything out, as he didn't care. On our last offer we had put that the out buildings were ours and the list of contents were to stay. I wanted control on getting rid of the sheds to get any scrap value. I was afraid if I left it up to them, it might be a year before they got out. I had agreed to keep the water going to the farm and maintain the pump to the farm for 3 months. I had also agreed to allow access to the farm via easements with normal terms and they would not have to pay us for the access. I was talked out of asking to be paid for access as some felt I was being too hard—yet how many places do you know where you get access through a property and not have to pay for it? In the years to come this would be one of the points that would haunt us again and again.

When we visited, they started talking about moving the sheds. I brought up that they were mine and we showed them the contract. They admitted they didn't read it. Pam felt sorry for them as they were as good as broke. I told her I didn't want the sheds as such. We then told them they could still have them providing they were gone by Christmas. This gave them about 8 weeks after we were to move in.

Mr Carter showed me around the farm and Pam visited with Mrs. Carter. She told Pam how she had always wanted rainwater for her laundry. They never put it in as Roger had put in a bore and they used only the water from it, which was high in iron. It seems that he was not practical in a lot of ways and spent a lot of time getting others to do things for him. We were to learn as time went on that the place needed a lot of work and some of the work he had done was either not done properly or done without a permit. Our fun was yet to begin.

When the time came for the move, Pam's parents with their friends, the Chisholms, came up to give us a hand. They brought up some of our belongings that were in Palmerston North and helped move other belongings from their bach at Thornton Bay, over to the new place. Mr. Chisholm didn't say so at the time but felt we had taken on more of a project than we should have. The lawns were so overgrown and it bothered him so much, that he started cutting the grass with a small 2-stroke hand-pushed lawnmower, in an effort to try to give us some help. It was a busy weekend—even with the flat bed truck that I had borrowed from work to use during the move.

I did tell Mr Sutherland when I started working for him, that I had a little something to do the first part of November and would need about 10 days off. When the time came, Pam and I went down to Palmerston North for my vasectomy-reversal operation. We were to stay at her parents' place after I came home from the hospital. If it all went well, I would go in the morning and return that evening. After a few days of rest with my feet up, I would be ready for my return trip.

It all started off well enough at the hospital and I can remember being put to sleep. I could also remember starting to wake up at one point during the operation and some sort of rushing was going on. I wouldn't wake up again until I was in recovery, and then, again, later in my room where Pam was waiting. I had an extremely hard time coming out from under the anesthetic and started having cold chills. I had not urinated and they wanted me to try to but all I was worried about was freezing. They put one of those silver thermal covers on me and I finally felt I was starting to warm up. They became nervous and called for the urologist to return to the hospital. Not long after that I managed to urinate for them—at first with great difficulty. When the doctor arrived I was almost normal and any danger I might have been in had passed. They were worried I was going into postoperative shock but about an hour later we were on our way to the house. After taking it very carefully for several days around the house we were ready to return to Thames.

The doctor told me when he checked me over before we left, that the first side was not a problem and he was in and out in a very short time. When he started on the other side everything went wrong. The cord was too short and he had to rearrange and pull on me until I was "upside down and backwards". He told me I would feel unusual at first but in time I wouldn't notice it. It was during this time that it became necessary to switch the type of anesthetic they were using. That must have been when I started to wake up for a moment. It was now just a matter of time to wait and see if we had any success.

Pam told me she became scared when I was cold and they called for the doctor again. She told me she didn't know what she was going to tell the kids if something happened to me. She could just see herself trying to explain all of this and how I had died while trying to have an operation for her. But it was over and everything did turn out. After a miscarriage from working too hard (not even knowing she was pregnant), in less than a year she was on her way to motherhood.

In the years to come I would hear on and off from the kids. It was not always easy and we found ourselves thinking of them often. I learned that at some point Cecil decided to sell the strip center that at one point had my drug store in it. It seems he claimed it didn't bring much and kept the proceeds but it must have been paid for by then since a 10-year note would have been up about the time I left Boerne. At a later date, to my surprise, he sold the store in Boerne with some of the land. He and Henry had 6 million dollars to split this time. I can only hope that someday the kids will get a chance to see some of it—so far his promises haven't been worth much.

But the one main thing I did get out of the next number of years was the one main thing we came for. I would be able to spend each and every day with my new daughter, Amanda, who was born on the 18th of April, 1990. It gave me a second chance to spend the time with my own child that I had missed out on so much the first time and always regretted. One child can never replace another, as any parent knows, but Amanda gave me the opportunity to spend each day with her and watch her grow . . . to teach her and to watch her learn. To see the surprise in her eyes and on her face the first time she would see or do things . . . like taste chocolate . . . or see the stars. This is what I had missed before and was now given a second chance—even though at times it would make me sad when I would think about how this was what I had missed before.

This would be the start of our next big adventure that would consume our lives for more than a decade. It had many a surprise in store for us—some you wouldn't believe. We would learn a whole new industry and even win multiple awards in it. It would drive us to exhaustion and tears at times. It would introduce us to people from all over the world and all walks of life. It would be a continual challenge on numerous fronts—from the council, to government departments, the neighbors, repairs, competition, and the largest of all, the unknown background and history of the place itself that would become all-consuming and take over with a life of its own.

CHAPTER 76

THE FIRST OF MANY

Not long after we had purchased the place and moved in, we started to learn of many of the little-known hidden problems the place had. The first up was the fact that the water heater element was burnt out and we had no hot water. Then we were to learn that the water in the water tank was almost gone and it seemed that the well no longer provided the much-needed water.

We got a well-drilling company out and they originally estimated a thousand or two should fix it up. They weren't positive on just what was wrong but felt the well might have started to collapse or something. We had to go away to Pam's folks' place and when we called them back, we were told that now that they were into the well they could see a lot more work needed to be done. The well should be lined, and with new pipes and a new pump, it would be more like 4 thousand dollars.

I became very angry as I felt we were being taken advantage of but after Pam, her Mom and I talked it over, we decided to let them continue and complete the job as it would cost even more to get another company in at this late date. The well pump was left sitting on a concrete block in the side yard, almost falling over with a mess all around. It was evident that after the pump would be run for a short time, the whole set-up would fall over. The well company told us that this was not part of their job and it was up to us to sort this out for ourselves.

Alan suggested we get his friend, Don Forbes, to help do a concrete pad and at the end of it, we were put onto getting a man by the name of Peter Woolf, who was an older part-time builder who lived near their bach at Thornton Bay. He helped get the concrete pad down to bolt the pump onto, and later built a covering box to keep the pump out of the reach of people, so as to make the power company happy.

Just as we were starting to get over this last shock, having paid Mr. Woolf too, we got a bill in the mail from the drilling company. It wasn't for the $4,000 we had talked about—it was for over $7,000, almost $8,000 in fact. The more we started to get into checking the company out, the more we found they had a questionable reputation for this sort of thing. The good news was that after Pam checked it out with the Commerce Commission, we learned that since no other figure was talked about or agreed to since our last go round at the $4,000 mark, then that is all we were obligated to pay. After several letters and pointing the well drillers in the right direction, that was the end of it.

It was the end of that episode but only the beginning of the work that would need to be done to get the place in some sort of shape to open. It was decided that I should continue to work for Paul to try to make some money, while Pam and her family made arrangements for the work to be done. This would require a builder and as luck would have it, we were able to get Mr. Woolf to work on the project with us. Pam's Dad and their family friend Mr Chisholm, would do the electrical, and Pam would do all the rest that needed to be done including painting, wall papering, cleaning, and working with the council to get everything up to their standards so we could get our license.

It was during this time that Pam met a Mr. Mark Bridgman who was then with the council. He pointed out that Roger had done many things around the place with no permit and things such as the kitchen in one of the bedrooms, were illegal. It would also take more time than we would want to know about to get permission for it, as well as meet all the requirements. Pam had her long list of what needed to be done and was almost at the point she wanted to cry when Mr Bridgman told her that he would work with her on one issue at a time, to try and help her get this through as quickly as possible. He offered such solutions as getting the bathrooms permitted if the kitchen was taken out of a bedroom. It was a start and with his help, the task once again seemed to be conquerable.

We still needed a plumber and a lot of fixtures for multiple bathrooms. After some checking, Pam's Dad came up with some friends of his in Palmerson North who had a plumbing company. We would get them to come up for several days at a time when we needed them, and we would put them up with free room and board. After doing some checking with one of the local companies, one agreed to sell the materials we needed to us at a trade price as long as they were paid for each month.

It was hard enough just getting to this stage but once work actually started, it was one surprise after another. It seems that Mr. Carter had a tendency to just go for it and not worry about planning for electricity, outlets, and how to get items from one point to another—be it electrical or plumbing. We also found our share of old water lines that leaked, and a power box in a closet that had the entire load mainly on just one end.

After our experience in Texas at Mountain Ridge we shouldn't have been surprised. Maybe in a funny sort of way it was a training course for us for this place. I don't think we would have ever been game to take the place on if it hadn't been for what we had already been through on Mountain Ridge. It seemed as if there was no end to what needed to be done or redone.

We ended up putting in 4 new bathrooms and totally refitting 3 bathrooms. We added electricity for lights and fans in what was to be the restaurant, as well as windows and doors. A ceiling had to be installed as well as flooring. We needed a new oven for the kitchen and Pam agreed to buy the new one Pat had in storage, only to find after it was hauled up to Te Puru, that the mice and rats had gotten into it and had eaten most of the wiring and insulation. Mr Chisholm had his work cut out when he spent days rebuilding it before we could install the new unit.

Other items such as a washing machine, dryer, dishwasher, disposal, additional refrigerators, freezers, gas cook tops and Bar-BQ's, were but a few of the things we needed to buy and add to the place, as it had none or they were on their last legs. The items you don't think of but still cost money kept coming up—wash basins, water taps, mirrors, furnishings, decorating items, tables, chairs, television sets, microwave ovens . . . and then we needed cutlery, dishes, linens, beds, and the list went on and on.

It seemed no matter how hard Pam worked, we always had one more thing to do. It was during this time it became evident we were going to have a shortfall on the money we needed. When we first started on the project and we talked about it with Pam's folks, I told them the one thing we needed was their support and backing and that we would need it, with no holding back, until we were up and under control—or until we all agreed to get out. We let them know it might get scary along the way but that without their 100% support we should never start or we would be doomed from the outset. They agreed to this and over the next number of years did more and more to help us in every way they could. They sold their bach at Thornton Bay and gave us all the money so we could pay down the mortgage. They had some other money they had invested and again gave it to us to help pay for getting the place open.

We could see that we also had no choice but to sell the front lot for more funds. The plumbing bill was estimated to be around $10,000 when we started but no sooner were we into the job than we spent most of that on the supplies we needed. We agreed to put the front section on the market with the realtor who we had purchased the place through. He wasn't sure but wanted to put it on the market for around $50,000 until I reminded him that when we purchased the place he kept using a value of $65,000, so insisted we list the lot for that.

The out-of-town plumbers were told early on to get their bill in and keep us up to date on where it was up to. As we went along, we paid for the materials and finally after their work was done, we got a bill in the mail. It was for something like $13,000 and we had already paid for most of the supplies! We were in shock. As Pam went back and tried to reconstruct what the bill was from several months back, she noticed that a lot of the supplies we had already paid for were added on to the bill from Palmerston. Just on the items she could quickly identify and show we had already paid the people in town for, she came up with a figure of several thousand dollars of double billing. When she talked to the plumber about the bill he assured Pam that some mistake had been made and not to worry about it. They corrected the bill for the several thousand dollars but never reconciled their charges to our complete satisfaction. I always wonder what would have happened if Pam hadn't been so on the ball and been aware of what was coming from which supplier. We now definitely had to wait for the section to sell to get them the rest of their money.

It wasn't long, only a few weeks or so, and the realtor, Maurice Leonard, came to us with an offer from a Mr. White on the front section. We were able to get the $65,000 asking price but he had a list of questions and stipulations he wanted to have cleared up before he would close on the property. We were told they were at least several weeks away before the title would be through on the subdivision but saw no problem. Mr White's main concern centered on the Maori grave. He had a few other questions regarding the easements and rights-of-way but nothing concerned him more than the grave.

We told Maurice we would take the offer and signed the contract. He was to have about 4 weeks or so to get his questions answered and then either close on the property or back out. He went to the council, and wrote to the Maori Land Court. He talked to friends, relatives, and anyone he felt he could get an opinion from. They all told him the grave should not be a problem and as long as he left it alone then no one should bother him at all. During this time he was so sure he was going to buy the section he hired a man by the name of Dave Reynolds, to come and clear the section. It was during this time we got to know Dave Reynolds and then also had him come to work for us on a part-time basis, helping with the grounds.

Mr White kept coming up with more and more questions. We needed the money for the section and it was starting to look like he wanted to back out. I asked Maurice if he had ever picked up the deposit from Mr White as he was supposed to have done, to which he responded no. I then told him I was getting a letter ready for Mr White, giving him 10 days to put up the deposit and go forward with the purchase, or back out of the deal now as we did not want to waste any more time.

Maurice came to us to say that Mr. White was still nervous about the grave and the issues with the Maori people even though we had a "European Title" to the section. So he backed out. Maurice then told us his son was looking at moving up on the coast and that he would help his son buy the section from us. They agreed to pay us the $65,000. It was now just a matter of getting the title.

This was not an easy task and after a number of phone calls, and going by the office of a Mr. Dunwoodie, we finally got our subdivision through and the title in hand. By now we had gone past our first interest payment and owed John Armstrong an additional amount of penalty interest as well but once we closed on the section we paid the bills for the plumber, surveyor, and lawyers, and paid some of the principal and the interest owed to John Armstrong. This was the only time in 12 years we were ever late on a payment and it went back to depending on others to have their stuff in on time.

This wasn't the end of it—far from it. Only a few months went by and one day Maurice drove up with a realtor's sign and put it on the front section. It seems that his son had an offer to go into being partners at a trucking company and that was a better deal for him now with his money. With this in mind, he would need to sell the property to get rid of this debt. He wanted us to know that the reason he was listing the property for something like $95,000 only a few months after he purchased it from us, was because the markets had changed that much in just the few months since we had sold it to them. I guess he thought I had just fallen off the back of the last turnip truck that went through town but that was okay. It was what it was and we had needed to sell. He told us he would keep Dave on for now to have him cut the grass on the front section and keep it tidy. He did this for the next couple of years before he finally gave it up.

It had become increasingly evident to me that we needed to generate as much income as possible. We had never really talked about going into the restaurant business but at first, it was mainly an add-on for the people who stayed, if they wanted a meal. But I was afraid this was not going to be enough and that we needed to strongly consider opening the dining room to the public.

It was time for Pam to get back with Mark Bridgman to see what was needed. We had understood from the book of words that as long as we had a 'guesthouse' license we could open our dining room to the public on a space-available basis but as with most councils, they always see things slightly differently. They said no, not in our case. We were an "illegal" activity in a commercially-protected 'Coastal' (not residential) zone and that made us an exception. We tried to argue that since we already had the activity we should have all the associated rights but they would have none of it.

Mark Bridgman did finally work out that if we ran our ad in the paper for a hearing and did some of the fire and safety requirements, we wouldn't be far off what we needed for not only a public restaurant license but also a B.Y.O. liquor license. With this in mind Pam and Mark put a plan together and after having only one objection from a neighbor (who didn't show up at the hearing), it was all but certain the council would vote in favor of it. This they did, although they put a couple of other restrictions on us like no more than 32 at a time in the restaurant and some other such "wait and see" sort of things; but we had it. Pam had gotten us a public restaurant license as well as a B.Y.O. liquor license. There was no question now as to whether or not we could open to the public.

We had moved in on Labor Day weekend 1988 (late October) and were now coming up on May 1989 to open. It was after the season was over and at the start of winter. Very little business was around and the only hope we had was to get some restaurant business going. This was a business we knew very little about. What limited experience I had from the soda fountain days at the drug store was questionable as to whether it would even be of any help. Nevertheless we were willing to give it a go—and give it a go we did.

CHAPTER 77

A Restaurant

A restaurant is what we needed for now. It may be just as well we didn't really know what we were doing—just like the rest of the project—for if we had, we would never have done it. You don't really think about it until you have to do it—then it becomes overwhelming. It is enough to figure out the room with the tables and chairs, the decorating, and the needs such as glasses, dishes, linens, and reservations. A menu of what you are going to offer needs to be considered—not just from what you think the customer wants but also can you prepare it in a timely fashion, with consistent quality, at a price at which you can make a profit?

We started out with our own set of ideas and picked up on ideas from some of the people we hired. We learned that you must have communication between the front of the house, the dining room itself, and the kitchen. What they want, when they want it, and how they want it, must be communicated to the kitchen by those working the room. For whatever reason we decided to go with a Tex-Mex sort of menu. I think looking back, that this came from us coming from Texas and we knew the food was good; we knew how to make some of it; nobody else in the area offered it and it went with the looks of the place. This also goes back to the first name we came up with for the place. We started kicking names about and none of us were overly happy with any of them until, almost as a joke, I came up with something Dr. Joe would say to us all the time when we were at the ranch, "vamanos, la casa"—let's go to the house . . . 'La Casa'. All of a sudden Pam, Peg and all, thought it was a great idea. So we named it 'La Casa'. Unfortunately this would prove to be just one of our many early mistakes.

We had a menu done on a friend's word processor. It was a combination of Tex-Mex food, as well as steak, fish, shrimp, oysters, mussels, and so on. We had an oven-baked fish dish and everything was done from scratch in the kitchen. Oh, what little did we know then. We were at first associated with being a Mexican restaurant by the public and were perceived to offer nothing but hot Mexican food. This image, because of our name and a few dishes, was set for the duration that we used the name for the place.

Some would come because they wanted some different food that was hot. It was not hot enough for them since they equated the hotter with better and ours was not very hot. Others wouldn't come because they didn't want hot funny food. A number of people did come at first and that is when our learning began.

It seems that a certain portion of the population enjoys being a food critic. They enjoy going to a new place when they first open and before they have the problems worked out. They always want to come in a group of at least 8 to 12 people, and up to 20 if they can. Now, who in their right mind really expects you to be able to provide a dining experience when you are trying to feed 20 people all at the same time with a variety of dishes. You see, the other thing they enjoy doing so as to be able to try everything all at once, is to order just about one of everything and then try and share it around the table with everyone present.

They then demand extra cutlery and dishes for each, and if they can, they have you serve it up to each of them. This then takes the time and effort of one of the employees to do nothing but take care of this one group. They also don't understand that the mess and extra dishes, and work created so they can share a $5.95 dish does not make a warm spot in your heart for them.

Pam and Mr. Bridgman were right. If we didn't have at least a B.Y.O. liquor license, then we were not going to have a chance of getting enough customers to make any money in the restaurant. It is my understanding that the idea of B.Y.O.('bring your own') went back to England. It was when you went to all sorts of trouble and took on extra expense and responsibility that enabled you to then allow your customers to bring their own 'liquor' to the restaurant. Now this actually meant they could bring their own beer and wine. The beer was at times in a 'chilly bin' or ice chest, as I called it. It always amazed me how a table of 4 would bring two dozen beers and several bottles of wine and then feel obligated to drink it all before they could go home, as if they couldn't take it with them.

We took some advice from one of our employees at the start and did not charge any sort of corkage fee. He told us that he and a number of his friends would never go to a place that felt they had to charge for 'opening the bottle'. The fee was of course for a lot more than that—the glasses, the cleaning, the service, the cost of the license and the complying, and so on. During the first number of years we never charged and I never had so much as one person ever say thank you, or it was nice, or anything.

We started out with crystal glasses and soon learned that the people thought it was a funny sort of glass. They would bang them together, tap them with their knives, and knock them over on the table. One time when a customer knocked one over and broke it, he couldn't believe how easily it broke. So, he then proceeded to take some of the remaining glasses and gently knock them over on the table to see if they would also break. He, of course, felt he should not pay for any breakage.

One time when I did charge one of the customers for the broken glass as he was showing off and acting smart all evening long, he protested vigorously. I showed him on the back of the menu where it said we didn't charge corkage but did charge for breakage. He insisted he would never come back. This was something I should have learned sooner. Those customers that show off and become obnoxious and loud, only drive off your good customers. The sooner you get those that don't know how to behave out of the place, the better off you are.

We also learned that with groups you get a mob mentality going. Once-normal and well-behaved people change, when they become part of a group. After they start to drink and show off to the others, the others also feel the behavior is acceptable and start to participate as well. It continues to grow and if it is left unchecked, it can soon get out of hand. One time early on we had a respected group up for an evening and they decided they didn't like the tables set up as they were, and without asking or considering any others in the place, proceeded to rearrange the tables in the room how they wanted them. They, of course, left out any consideration of how the staff was going to get around the room to wait on people or clear dirty dishes—much less how they forced themselves on top of any others in the room. When they were asked to stop and given some explanation, they were indignant that they weren't going to get their way.

Another time with a group of school teachers—who we learned in time were some of the worst—came, and became very loud and started banging their fists on the table tops. Some of the tables had their extensions pulled out and for normal use were just fine but when they were pounded upon, broke. They also started leaning back in their chairs and rocking on just the back legs. The chairs in some instances also gave way. Again, the people didn't want to know about any damage—besides, they were having a good time and we should expect a certain amount of this, according to them.

You may have noticed that up to now I have not even commented on the food or what the customers had to say about it. In the early days we had a lot to learn and even though we put out a good meal, we were slow and our presentation left a lot to be desired. The Tex-Mex food and bar-BQ plates were much of a given on presentation, as they were what they were. However the regular dishes—fish, steak, lamb, and such—were at first presented more as a good home-cooked meal.

We never advertised or represented ourselves as fine dining. In fact, if anything, we said we offered a good night out and started with offering 3 courses for $20.00. This is a sure-fire way to go broke fast unless you make the three courses, soup, macaroni, and a cup of coffee. It became apparent very quickly that we needed to make some changes and make them fast.

The communication was at first the major problem. It was simple to solve once you knew what to do and to this day I have never seen a better system. Dave suggested we put a board up on one side of the room and we use a marker on it. We drew a cross sort of set up for the table and each seat had a number. Next to this number we wrote, going across the board, starters, mains and desserts, and put the table number by it. As the orders came in they were transferred from the pad to the board. At a glance you could see across the room who was next and what they needed. If you needed to skip or move an order up, you could call out and make a note. You could get set up for the next table and when ready, you could call go and each would start at a time so they would finish at the same time, and the food could be plated and sent in. After the food was sent in, the entry could be wiped off the board and everyone knew where we were up to.

The part that was always a continual learning process was the preparation, cooking and presentation of a dish. To do it in a timely and consistent fashion, and at a reasonable price, was a challenge. We learned you had to look at how much you could and needed to prepare in advance. You had to think about how much could you and did you need to do at the last minute. How long did it take from the time of the order to the time it left the kitchen? How long would it last? Could you do some of it now and carry it for three days before you lost quality and needed to dispose of it. Some items carried well and some didn't. The quality was always a consideration before health as an issue even came up. We carried over the philosophy I had learned in the drugstore days about things you take. You had to ask yourself if you would take it yourself or give it to one of your children. If you said yes, then fine, if not, then it was time to throw it out.

We did learn new methods and ways to do things. We eventually got it to where we could have an appetizer on the table in about 15 to 20 minutes, and the main course on the table in about 45 minutes. If a couple wanted to eat and just keep going, we could have them in and out in an hour and a half. People that wanted a little more time were usually about 2 hours and sometimes up to 2 and a half hours. Those that went to three hours and over were those who didn't want to go home and usually were the ones with a case of beer who felt they had to drink it all prior to leaving. These were the ones that created a problem when they didn't know when to go home. They would have maybe two courses and order coffee. They would bring their own liqueurs and put them into the coffee. [This was the only thing we were allowed to sell being a B.Y.O.] We would find ourselves standing around at midnight or one in the morning, wishing for these people to go that had come at 7 that evening and spent an average of $25 dollars each. They, of course, left only a mess and no tip, and could have cared less that for the last 2 hours that you were paying staff, they did nothing but visit and drink what they had brought with them.

If we had no houseguests we still couldn't get the place and the dishes cleaned and put up while we had staff available because we didn't want to be rude to the customers. This, of course, meant that the next day we would start behind where we needed to be and would have just that much more to do. We later got past this and after a reasonable time, we just cleared the table around them and if they didn't get the idea then, we let the music run out. If they still weren't sure and were the only ones left, then once or twice Dave went in and started stacking the chairs on the tables—something we didn't normally do but it was an attention-getter.

It wasn't until later on when we started to develop some accommodation business that we realized what a conflict we had on our hands. From the start, we began getting mainly overseas visitors who wanted a nice quiet place to come to enjoy the food and the scenery. They were not interested in hearing a bunch of drunks having a party until 1 AMin the restaurant up above.

We started going to various food industry seminars each year at the Food Service Association's annual convention and show. It was a wealth of knowledge for us and it was nice to find out that we were not alone. What we were experiencing was the same thing that other operators all over were also facing. We learned that you could not be sentimental about dishes, and that if they didn't sell or were not economical to make and sell, then they had no place in business. This came into full implementation later on when we decided we needed a change in direction.

The various incidents that came up in the restaurant were from one extreme to another. From the start, I made it a policy that each meal was to be checked with the customer, say within 5 minutes after it was delivered to them. I was happy to fix or replace any dish that a customer had a problem with. Over the years I replaced only one or two dishes when someone didn't like what they got because it wasn't what they expected. I cooked the steak more maybe a couple of dozen times over the years and all the rest said it was fine. Yet you would hear stories where people had told a friend it was too hot, too smoky, too cold, or something else but never told us—the ones that could have done something about it. One night I served a lady and she said it was fine. It was a Mexican plate with enchiladas made with flour tortillas. The next day she phoned me to complain as she could no longer contain her emotions. She told me they were the worst pancakes she ever had and then proceeded to tell me what may have gone wrong when we tried to make them. I told her they were tortillas but being the next day it was impossible to do anything about it then.

I had another lady one night give me all kinds of grief over the bar-BQ beef. She complained that it looked obviously overcooked and smelled of smoke. She was sure it was not worth eating and then asked her husband's friend what he thought of it, as he was the one who had ordered it—and ate it! He very sheepishly spoke up and told me it was quite good and he had enjoyed it.

On another occasion that sticks out in my memory, an older man came over to me at the end of the evening very upset and cussed me out. His complaint was how long he and his wife had waited for their meals and they had been quite hungry. They had come that night with a group of about 10 people for a birthday and each was to pay their own bill. When the orders were taken several, about 3 of them, ordered appetizers and the rest (including him) didn't. We sent the appetizers out in about 20 minutes and by the time they had finished and we had the 10 mains ready to go in, it had been about an hour since the orders had come into the kitchen. We actually felt we had done very well by delivering the several appetizers and 10 main courses in an hour's time. No matter what I said the man could not get past how it had taken an hour to get his meal and that he found it totally unacceptable. This is an example of how some are unrealistic and no matter what you do you will not make them happy.

By now I am sure you have an idea of what it was like in the early days when we first started the restaurant. This was an ongoing learning experience and whenever you thought you had seen it all, the public showed you that you ain't seen nothin' yet.

CHAPTER 78

GETTING GOING

We were lucky in one way, as we had opened at the start of winter of May 1989. We felt we were run off our feet at the time and we were learning as fast as we could; yet the next year when we compared our numbers, we had a significant increase in the number of people in the restaurant. It gave us a start and a chance to get our systems up to speed before the season really started.

We learned that we could handle only so much and that if we didn't have enough help, or if the bookings didn't work out at being spaced far enough apart, we knew we were in for a disastrous evening. We made a decision early on to turn down bookings. This was something that people could not understand—that they could get in on a reservation basis only. At times the place would be only half full, yet we would turn people away. We had decided to try to make half a room full of people happy and have a good reputation for quality and service, rather than take the money and let the stuff fall where it may. We tried this over the years and yet to this day, I don't think many customers really appreciated that we tried to do this for them.

We were no sooner up and going and then, of course, while she was not ever really sick, Pam was still in a state where she could hardly stand the smell of all the food cooking. This was a real challenge for her until Amanda was born the 18th of April, 1990, but she still managed to work 16 hour days, 7 days a week, through that whole summer high season (her final trimester), and service rooms as well as work the kitchen night after night, and do breakfast the next morning for the people that had stayed . . . along with all the general housekeeping and keeping the gardens tidy. It was a very active pregnancy.

We opened our restaurant at a time when a Chinese restaurant was re-opening, and over the next number of years, a parade of restaurants and cafes would come and go. The public would run from one to the next trying them out and as we learned more, we were able to guess just about how long they would last. The public wanted a place they could go and get outstanding service at a moment's notice. They wanted the 3 courses for $20 and to have the place B.Y.O. They also wanted to come at 7 and leave at 1 or 2 in the morning. Each new place tried this to varying degrees and each went bust.

We lost more during the first year or two after we opened than at any other time, yet we did more turnover during that period. It took us time to learn that the locals seldom went out in winter and then usually only in groups. When spring came you had some activity, and people geared up for the firm's Christmas party—once again, a group sort of thing; except this time the bill was paid by an employer so the people drank even more. We started to stay away from weddings, 21st's, and later the Christmas parties.

I felt lucky that over the years we came close to having a fight on our hands only a couple of times. Each really bad situation had to deal with groups that had too much to drink during our B.Y.O. days, where their behavior had gotten out of control. We had problems with them being loud and stealing things. We had a table of eight one time, steal all the appetizer forks. Another time we had one of our top quality steak knives stolen. After I phoned the two tables that we suspected, I received it back in the mail. I, of course, had denials and an ear full from both. After that we went to the cheap stuff.

The one that finally got to me and after which we swore we would never take another group or party again, was at Christmastime. We had several bookings coming up on the weekend and one was for a young group of 'Warehouse' staff, and the next night we had the 'Bank of New Zealand' from Whitianga with their staff and partners. We were afraid of the young ones, yet their Christmas party came and went without a problem and they were all well-behaved and polite. The next night was another story.

The group had done a 'pub-crawl' in a bus on their way over from the other side of the peninsula. I had understood they were in a small bus so no one would have to worry about drinking and driving. This was true but it is different when it is a pub-crawl. When they finished at the 'Royal Oak Hotel' up the road at Tapu, the pub owners called to warn us that they were on their way. They said this was the first group they had ever asked to leave over the years, and wished us luck.

As the bus pulled up in the parking lot, you could hear the yelling going on and one of the men was in the process of urinating out of the window. I ran down to the parking lot to show the driver where to park and pointed the way for the others to go to get to the restaurant. Some of the group was in the process of apologizing to the driver for some of the various antics of some of the others. I was deeply concerned about what we were getting into and when I returned to the restaurant I warned the others and told them we should try and serve them as fast as possible and try to get them out.

I never heard so much cussing and yelling, and running around the tables, in the whole time we had been open. I had to stop a couple of the guys from urinating on the herbs outside the window by the kitchen and point them to where the bathroom was. The younger ones, and mainly those that were the partners of the employees, were causing most of the trouble. The people from the bank could not get those in the group to behave and in fact the boss had all but given up and was letting them have their way. These sorts of functions were usually so much per head and they would give us a head count a day or two before they came. As usual the numbers were usually lower than we were told and of course they only wanted to pay for those that came. It was after this experience that we said no more.

We had learned enough to know we were still interested in quality. We entered the 'Taste New Zealand Awards' early on and were accepted on our first try. It was a quality assurance plan the New Zealand Tourism Board had sponsored. It seems that people from overseas complained that one of the biggest things against New Zealand was lack of service and value for money when eating out so they would send secret diners around, try your restaurant out and grade you. They were to look for quality of food, service, price for what was offered and so on. If you made it they would list you in a booklet that was published and distributed in overseas markets. We were happy and it gave us a real lift. The next time they had the polytech tutors go out and we were turned down. They didn't try our lamb or our fish or any New Zealand dishes. They ordered Texas Bar-BQ pork ribs and a Mexican plate, and then said it wasn't representative of New Zealand and therefore we didn't make the grade! They never did explain why they didn't order the dishes that were more representative.

We could see that it was necessary for us to get our accommodation up and with the two working together, we would have a chance at making enough money to get by. During this period we made enough during the summer to pay the bills but during the winter we had to get money to pay the mortgage from Peg and Alan, or from Pam's Aunt Joan and Uncle Kit. We knew we either had to get bigger or do something different—or we would be the next to go broke. We had worked in the trade long enough to know that on the Coromandel the way business went, was that you had only a few months of high season during the summer and if you didn't fill your pockets then, you were in trouble. To this day, that is still the way it is. You have your season from Labor Weekend in October to Easter Weekend in late March or early April, and that is it. The large push for us was the January through March period, and the other months were and are unpredictable from one year to the next. The rest of the year during the winter is predictable—very little to nothing.

The tourism organizations all say the shoulder season needs to be developed and then the off-season but you still need a reason for the people to come. It can be a food festival, an art show, a fishing contest, sunset photos, a boat race . . . it really doesn't matter as long as it is put together properly and it makes the people want to come and stay. We would laugh when some of those in the town would put together a one-day event and the outside people would come to town for a few hours and go home, and they then wanted to know why it didn't work.

We would get tired of the politics of the other operators and how they would take customers that were looking for you, or one of their friends would send them to a mate and tell the people that was the only accommodation left in town. On one of my daily outings to town I was getting some information about the peninsula to send to a travel writer and Amanda and I went into the Thames Information Centre to get some brochures. An older lady came over and asked if she could help. I told her I was okay and was getting some information on the various things the peninsula had to offer. I forgot how my American accent stands out like a sore thumb and she assumed that Amanda and I were tourists. She didn't have a clue who I was and proceeded for the next 15 minutes to try and send me to Dickson Holiday Park, a camp ground at the edge of town, to stay. I decided to ask her about a place either in town or near, that might have accommodation and a restaurant. I was assured that there wasn't any but if I stayed at Dickson Holiday Park I would enjoy it and would be only 10 minutes to town—and lots of nice restaurants.

At first I was angry but it again showed me how the locals still stuck together and that we didn't have a chance with them. I knew the manager who ran the centre and let her know what had happened—mainly so she would at least scare some of them for some period of time anyway.

We knew we would need to become a destination in our own right or we would have to get out. The one thing was for sure, it could not stay the same. I think by this time Pam and I were both worn out. We had both tried as hard as we could, and worked as hard as we could, for as long as we could. We did all the yard work and other things that needed to be done, and one year at the end of the season for a Mother's Day present, I bought Pam matching dishes for the restaurant. For the first time all the dishes would match and it would look like a real restaurant. We had received a letter from some guests who had stayed during the season and thanking us again for taking such good care of them. They also sent us a photo they had taken of us on the patio with the letter but while Pam and I could remember going out and them taking the picture, we could not remember their faces or them. That, we felt, was an indicator of how tired we would be by the end of the summer high season.

We felt we couldn't go on any longer like this and decided the only other thing to do was to sell. We felt we knew what needed to be done and didn't feel we had the energy or the money to continue on and relaunch the place. We had mixed emotions and at first Pam's father was upset and didn't want us to sell at all. But Peg knew what it had really been like for us and wasn't sure that maybe we weren't right and should get out.

We had all noticed that the place seemed to have a life of its own and when you came up the hill to the place, it was as if you went through a time warp. Time went by at a different rate and lost all meaning in relation to the rest of the world. Peg said she got to the point she quit putting her watch on when she came up. We always had more to do than time to do it in, and if you did something else other than what was planned, then something else would have to suffer for it. The lodge was so demanding that we could only ever do about one extra thing a day, outside our normal maintenance routine.

Pam and I decided we needed to try and sell. We wanted to spend time with Amanda and were tired of the place running us. We decided to take that winter and get the place up to speed, painted, cleaned, plants in the garden, the yard in shape and even provide the realtors with the information they needed to sell the place including marketing, background and history. We now put our major efforts into this with our goal being to sell. This too, proved to be a learning experience, once again, for us.

CHAPTER 79

SELLING

We weren't sure who we wanted to list the place with and so I went to several of the real estate offices in town and tried to get some information from each. Several of them wanted to come up and look at the place and the more I talked to them, the less confidence I had in them. It seemed that all they were concerned about was how much commission they would charge. I even talked to several companies in Auckland about selling the place, and then also went by and talked to them.

The more we talked to realtors, the more they all seemed to be selling real estate because they couldn't get a job doing anything else. They had no professionalism, no idea on how to sell or talk to me, much less a customer. We didn't want to sell it ourselves yet we felt we would need to do the work if anything was going to get done.

One day when I was reading the *'New Zealand Herald'*, I noticed an ad by a company in Auckland that I had seen several times before. It was an ad that claimed to help you sell your property yourself or with their help, at a reduced commission rate. They would come to your property and do an analysis, prepare a presentation with photographs, and help you set a price. You would then be run in their ads and inquiries would be passed on to you so that with their help, the property would be sold. I called and talked to them on the phone and they sounded like they were worth checking into.

The company called me back and made an appointment for one of their representatives to come and see us and go over the program. We had the place clean and everything ready, with all of the information on the place on the table at our fingertips. This girl, who was larger than the average person, showed up and she seemed to be distracted and in a hurry. As Pam and I tried to get her to look at what we had prepared and show her the property, all she wanted to do was go back to the table to sit down and fill out a contract.

I actually got very irritated with her and started to tell her about it, when I told myself we weren't going to do that. We then sat down and she told us she needed to get back to Auckland and if we wanted to get in with them now and for the next set of ads, we needed to give her a check now. It was something over a thousand dollars for the package they were to put together for us. She made a few quick notes and picked up a few things from us. She then took a few shots with her camera that reminded me of a disposable one, and left.

That week we were not in the ad and when I called them she explained they were just too busy to get it in. They then sent me their package that looked like something the kid's class put together for a project in elementary school. I couldn't believe it and called them to raise hell. The boss, a Mr. Knight, got on the phone and explained this was only a rough draft. He put me in touch with another of the men at the company and after we spoke to him, we agreed to send him more of the information we had already put together ourselves.

After several weeks we ended up with one mention in his ad that amounted to a few lines, and we had a presentation that was now up to about a junior high school level of presentation. Just as we were deciding what we were going to do about it, we sat down to watch television one night, when one of the consumer programs had a piece on a company that had just closed down in Auckland. It was our real estate company! It seems Knight was actually practicing real estate according to the courts, and did not have a license. His plans and help were what he was selling according to him, and many customers felt as we did that it was not value for money. According to the law, he did supply his plan and after being shut down he left hundreds of people holding the bag—we were just one of them. A number of times over the coming years, this man, Michael Knight, showed up on this television program for questionable business deals. By the late 1990's, he had a law passed against him in Australia, prohibiting him from running a business in one of states that had found him to be totally unreliable and a con man. I guess if you have to be taken, it might as well be by one of the best. He is probably still driving around somewhere with his "Y B Poor" license plates.

But this still did not get us out of our situation and after having the Harcourts' manager come out to see us with our local Harcourts' office manager, we decided to go with them. This was mainly on the basis of their being a national company and having national exposure in various marketing media. We agreed to their plan to put up $5,000 in an advertising budget which included various newspapers, as well as their national magazine. At the end of the period of about 6 weeks, we would have an auction at the lodge in the hope that it would sell for a good price.

Something we were not told at first was that around 90 % of properties do not sell at auction. They sell either before, or after, by negotiation. We had told Harcourts' agent, Liz Shaw, at that time that we would consider trades and offers, and were open to discussion. She said she was sure this wouldn't be necessary and seemed to discourage people from making offers to us.

As the day approached we noted that we had not had any of the people back through for a second look. Our lawyer, John Armstrong, gave us a number he could be contacted at if anything did come up but felt we may not sell as he knew that no one had run title searches to really check the place out.

We had several open days and even closed for business to make sure the place was clean and could be shown properly to prospects. This was a mistake. It was also a mistake from a business standpoint since as soon as the word got out in the community we were selling, business fell off. But we were not overly concerned as our objective was to sell.

A day before the auction we received a fax that was sent to the realtor from the solicitor of the Gavey's, our neighbors, on the farm block above. The Gavey's had never helped with the drive maintenance for years and only contributed the one time, to the original repair at the bottom that was put into concrete. We were unaware of any problem and with the noise about covenants being put on the place didn't know what was going on. We turned it over to John Armstrong to find out.

It seems that Roscoe, the lawyer, that was such a problem back when we purchased the property, had handled the easements and paperwork for the Carters and the Gaveys. When he put it through he did not get all of the easements recorded properly and had decided not to spend any more time or money doing it at the present time. He wanted to wait until some future date when the Maori land block would also need to have some issues taken care of. When the Gaveys heard that we were going to sell, they wanted assurances that the new lodge owners would honor the easements and sign any necessary paperwork at some later date. Rather than talking to us and getting this done in a friendly manner, they felt that by waiting until the 11th hour they could come in and threaten to disrupt the sale if we didn't agree. John Armstrong gave them assurances that we would make an announcement at the auction about the easements, and also make sure the papers would get signed. In fact the day of the auction, Jill Gavey even showed up to make sure something was done.

We had Dave Reynolds come on the day of the auction to park the cars in the parking lot and we served refreshments prior to, and after, the auction. We had no idea how many would come or if any buyers would be in the group. Our early day and first customers, Mr and Mrs. Kay, offered to come and look after Amanda for us so we would be free to deal with the auction as well. A few neighbors came, and several groups of people. One couple was a man and his wife who had previously had a motel in the area. Another was a couple who had already looked at the property. A woman on her own came—and turned out to be a girlfriend of the motel owner up the road, who also had his place on the market and wanted to see how we did.

Before the auction began, we sat down and talked to the auctioneer who was to run the auction for Harcourt's. We were to set our reserve and after much deliberation, set our reserve for what we felt was conservative at $650,000. I, to this day, think that the reserve was below market value. When the auction got underway, he fell back to something like $450,000 and then started to move forward up to about $550,000. He then said he was going to stop for a moment and talk to us. When we went in the next room he told us he did not have a single bidder—that he was pulling the numbers out of the air. He said we would be better off passing in at a low figure and giving people the idea they might still be able to buy. We told him to do it and get it over with.

After the auction about an hour went by and the people left. It was just us left at the place. We were both crushed. Not a single offer, not one bidder, $5,000 worth of advertising and people from all over (including overseas) asking for information on the place and not a single offer. Liz Shaw said she wouldn't get back with any suspect clients for about a week to ten days and then she would see if we had any interest. She didn't want to talk about those that had been interested in a trade early on, that were now gone.

After I put some more pressure on her, she got back with some of the people who had expressed some interest. A Mr. and Mrs. Cherry in Auckland, along with another couple, did finally put in an offer to us that was based on our taking in trade, two houses in Auckland. One was older and in a rougher part of town. It had been added onto about 3 times and showed it. They told us what their government valuation had been but when we checked into it, it was the previous one that was about $40,000 higher than the current one–and the next one due out soon, would drop again. The other house was a new house but small, located on the south side of Auckland. It would have been okay. We put our numbers together and counter-offered to them. They never responded as one of the couples decided to back out.

I told Liz Shaw I wanted the names and contact details of the people who had requested information or expressed interest in the place as I wanted to contact them, or at least write to them to see if any were still interested. She refused, claiming that it would be a violation of their privacy. I doubt that this was the real issue. When I even offered to write contact letters and let her address them to be sent out, she still refused. She didn't want to contact the people back is what it came down to. Pam and I knew we were at a dead end.

We decided to have a hard look at the place and the operation, and try to decide what needed to be done. We talked to the then-executive officer of Tourism Coromandel, Chris Adams, about the lodge. He would always give you his opinion and wouldn't hold back so we decided he might have something to offer. He told us that people coming halfway around the world to New Zealand didn't want to stay in a place with a Mexican name and eat Tex-Mex food. They were wanting to experience New Zealand. We should go more into the lodge market, and since we had only a few rooms fix them up and charge more, push a New Zealand theme and food, and market ourselves to become a destination.

He did have a point. People didn't know what to do with a guesthouse that had a Mexican restaurant attached to it. The restaurant people couldn't see how you would get enough people in, and the accommodation people who didn't see enough rooms, and with no kitchens or family facilities asked who we catered for? We already knew our numbers didn't stack up as we had always run the place for our own lifestyle and wanted to spend time with Amanda and our family we had moved across the world for. We always closed over Christma—-which cost us several thousand each year—but how do you get those years back once they are gone? We had also decided to stop the groups and the drunks. Chris Adams pointed out that people in the right market wanted to buy their drinks and didn't even understand the country's BYO liquor laws.

We knew that if we were going to sell we would need to do the work for the others so they could see it for themselves. So we would start over. We would come up with a new name that was more in keeping with New Zealand, and aim at food and wine that represented what people from overseas wanted. We would look at the lodge and see what we could do with the rooms and decor, to try and raise them to a new level. This was also true of the restaurant and the lounge, as the carpet was old and worn when we first moved in and time had not improved it any.

It was hard to accept this since we already had our minds made up that we were going to sell and would be gone but it also was not a choice and we knew it. We also knew that the sooner we got this done, the sooner we would be able to try and sell again—and, we hoped, with better results the next time. With this in mind, it was time for us to do some research and come up with a plan of changes that needed to be made and then put them into place.

CHAPTER 80

Doing our Research

It was not overnight that we came up with our new ideas. In fact, one of the first things we had to do was find the strength to finish the season and salvage what we could of it. We were in mid-February and had just known we were going to be leaving after the auction. It was very hard for us to get over the fact we didn't sell. We both felt like sitting down and crying. We were worn out.

I don't know how we found the energy and motivation—I guess it was out of necessity. We managed to get up and put one foot in front of the other. We knew we had to do what business we could before the season was over or we were going to be in real trouble. We had run up a $5,000 advertising bill with the real estate company we had to pay, and had less income for the season with our turning away business to make sure the place was neat and clean while we held open homes. It was time for the credit card again. It was our salvation, as we had no bank overdraft or ability to even get a loan at the bank.

During the next few months we worked, and used the time to think about what we had done wrong, what changes we might make, and who we might get some answers from. This took us back again to Chris Adams with our local tourism organization. He was somewhat abrupt but was more than happy to give you his opinion if you wanted it. He did hit the nail on the head on some of what he said as he told us what we already knew. He had previously told us to get rid of the name and upgrade the rooms to project a different image.

We knew we needed to be a destination in ourselves. We needed to have people who were coming to the Coromandel Peninsula, looking to stay at our place—not just find us (maybe) once they were here. We both had about all we could take of the cheap and cheerful restaurant market and knew that was going to be one of our changes. No more groups, weddings, 21st's, etc. Houseguests first, and we were going to look at a revised menu. Pam was going to get back with Mark Bridgman to see if there was any way we could now get a full liquor license as some of the laws had been changed over the last few years.

Pam found out that by working with Mark Bridgman she had developed a good relationship with him and from this led to Mark introducing her to Stan Blair, an ex-policeman and the liquor-licensing agent for T.C.D.C. at the time. We had a good reputation as a B.Y.O. place and had always stayed inside the law. Stan assured Pam that if she would leave it with him and stay out of it, he could make it happen for us. He believed that if we were going to be an "overseas tourist lodge", we needed to be able to serve drinks to our guests at all hours of the day or night. It was with his effort, along with Mark, they made a deal with the council for a variation. Since most of our people had their own room with a toilet, then the restaurant toilet could be used by the public if we kept the numbers down. They agreed to let us have our full liquor license if we cut back the number of people in the restaurant to 28. If we wanted more, then we would have to add another bathroom.

This was good news. Not only did Stan get us our license; he managed to get it put through with the unlimited hours he requested. Nobody seemed to look at the hours since they were so worried about the number of toilets. He got our hours listed as 24 hours a day, 7 days a week, anywhere on the property, as long as they were guests staying at the lodge. Restaurant guests were restricted to the restaurant during normal business hours when we took reservations for the restaurant. At the end of all the hearings, newspaper ads and so on, we spent around $3,000 for our full liquor license. It would come up for renewal in one year, and if we had been good and it was renewed, then it would be on a 3-yearly basis after that.

Now we were going to have to add several thousand dollars worth of stock to our inventory. We would need liquor, spirits, mixes, and a full assortment of wines. We also needed to learn a lot about wines. Just because you read it is a consistently top wine, does not mean you can get it on a regular basis for your restaurant. We had to find out who we could work with and who would work with us. We also needed to try to work with, and out of, the inventory of one of the liquor stores in town. If we could buy a bottle at a time, so to speak, each day I went to town, this would make it much more affordable for us to offer a selection by not carrying a large inventory on hand. Even then, when we carried 2 or 3 bottles of each wine and say 12 to 18 bottles of each kind of beer, the inventory went up $2,000 real quick, just for the drinks we offered.

The first company we made a deal with was 'Liquorland' in Thames. They were the only ones that would work with a small account and still get some of the special restaurant-only items in for us that we asked for. They would also give us a small discount on the purchases we made. It got us started as that one item for our new start was now off the list.

We had worked in town for the last several years mainly with one local butcher but his mother ended up winning 'Lotto' one year and he was out of the local meat trade. He had enough and they helped his family move back to Auckland. This left us with his replacement who was a joke. We started looking for another butcher in town and each one we went to, seemed worse than the last one. We somehow got started with a company named 'Fortex'; I think it was an ad in a trade magazine. At the time it was supposed to be the largest and most modern meat plant in the country. They had a division that would ship all over the country in 24 hours and their 'Gourmet Direct' division was a life-saver for us. They had us first as a private customer and then put us on their commercial accounts. It gave us a better price and free freight if the order was over 10 kgs. In the early days this was not a problem. The quality of the meat was the best we had ever had in all the years we had been in business. The price was as cheap as or cheaper than the local butchers and it was delivered to our front door usually in 24 hours. They had all the cuts of beef and lamb and as time went on, they offered salmon, turkey, rabbit, venison, and various other game. We now had a quality meat supplier.

Pam spent more time reading and talking to people, trying to see where everything was going. We had previously started going each year to the 'Food Service Show' in Auckland. The seminars were another place you could pick up on what was going on in the industry. More and more people were interested in other food dishes, with venison being the popular new kid on the block. We knew we needed to change our menu and add more New Zealand foods that people were looking for. We checked on the Coromandel Peninsula and found several suppliers that would provide us with fresh local oysters and mussels. It sounds funny but it was hard to get fish—that is any fish on a regular basis that was properly processed. Most all of it went to Auckland (or for export) and if you asked for some, the boat might have a mixed basket of fish with several varieties which may or may not have been cleaned. They would give you a price for the whole lot and you could take it or leave it. We found we needed to stay with a quality fish and buy it from one of the regular suppliers by whom it had been blast frozen and packaged. It would be in 10-kg boxes, skinned and boned. We found that Orange Roughy was a good mild fish that was consistent and cooked extremely well from frozen. It would cost around $175 per box with each serve costing about $3 to $3.50. We had learned this on our first go-round and after researching it again, found it could not be beaten, so stayed with it.

We still had not come up with a name for the place after the first few months and knew we would need it soon as our yearly advertising was coming up for renewal—as well as the name for the new licenses. We looked into names such as Pohutakawa Lodge (there were several already around the country), Coastline Lodge, Coat View Lodge, and many more. We didn't want to make a major mistake with a name this time.

We knew that a lot of the maps show Te Puru on them and when people look at a map to try and find the place they stay at, this would be a help—even if they didn't know the name of the place when they first started looking. They usually decide to look at maybe the North Island of New Zealand, then the Coromandel Peninsula, and then for places to stay on the peninsula. After talking to family, friends, and a few of our regular customers, we decided on Te Puru Coastline Lodge. Then a few days after we started to put this in place we realized this would cause confusion with Coastal Motor Lodge and the name maybe didn't make sense anyway. We then started to get it switched over to our other choice, Te Puru Coast View Lodge. We did have a view. That was one of the things our guest always commented on. So the name was chosen at last. It told where we were, what we had to offer, and the type of accommodation we offered.

Chris Adams, in working with the New Zealand Tourism Board, assured us that their major function was to get people from overseas into New Zealand. He worked, along with them, in promoting the area for their 'Visiting Media' program, as well as working with the inbound tour operators and wholesalers. These were the ones who organized the overseas visitors into places to stay, and things to do, in New Zealand. We were encouraged to get involved in the wholesale market but this didn't really get underway until later when we became more involved with his replacement. However, he did get us started with the visiting media and we hosted a number of writers at the lodge. They were from mainly the U.K. but some contact was also made with the U.S. and Europe. We didn't always get a write-up but sometimes we did. The main thing was to sell the Peninsula by getting them to come to our area.

We took more notice at the food show in Auckland and of what was going on in the trade magazines. We started getting a nice selection of wine for our guests and gradually changed over our menu to include venison, heart of lamb rump, scotch fillet, our own oyster and mussel dishes, as well as some of the standard New Zealand dessert dishes like pavlova. We knew we needed to get our credibility up so we decided to enter the 'Hallmark of Excellence Awards' for beef and lamb. Again this was not to be a competition as such but more of a quality assurance for the customer. We would have two sets of secret judges come to eat at our restaurant and they would score our beef and lamb dishes.

The first year we felt we had done a good job but maybe not enough and as luck would have it, one of the judges was from a competing restaurant on the other side of the peninsula. The night he came, he started questioning our guests in the restaurant and showing off. He assured them that he thought we were okay and buttered us up, yet he broke the rules by telling us and others in the restaurant, who he was. That year we learned that one set of judges gave us a passing grade and the other a failing grade that was just low enough to keep us out of the awards. No prizes for guessing who shot us down. We let the committee know we didn't think that was the best way to be graded but what was done was done. We did learn and the next two years in a row we entered and received high enough marks to receive the prestigious 'Hallmark of Excellence Award for Beef and Lamb' from the New Zealand Beef and Lamb Marketing Board. I don't know what our scores were—all I knew was we had the awards and hung them on the restaurant wall for all to see.

We still had the calls for the groups but we turned them away and started to build up a small local following again. It was somewhat as I had predicted—that we would need to make up for our lost income. I told Pam I needed to find some sort of job that was part-time or even full-time if it didn't conflict with the lodge, or we were going to be heading for trouble. It wasn't until the next winter that something showed up.

In the local paper ads I came across one that was looking for a rep for the Coromandel Peninsula area. The office was out of Tauranga at the time, which was about 120 kms away. It wasn't clear if I would need to be available every day in Tauranga or not. I told Pam I had nothing to lose as the last time I went out trying to get a job I ended up at an employment agency in Auckland, and the short story was that I was "too old"—being in my mid-40's. They couldn't say it by law but we had no doubt that is what the problem was. I had sent them my resume and they couldn't get me to Auckland fast enough for an interview. Of course I put nothing about my age on my resume and when they came into the interview room you could see the facial expressions change before a word was said. It was one of the shortest interviews I ever had.

This advertisement in the paper was already up to the deadline. I called the office in Tauranga and I was assured that it would be okay if I sent in my resume a few days late if they knew it was coming. This was in July, in the middle of winter. A man by the name of Alex Brodie called me back and wanted to come and see me for an interview where I lived. The ad was a bit vague and if it had said insurance sales I don't know if I would have answered it. This is what it was but with a twist. The company was looking for a new group of salespeople to train their own way and were willing to pay them a base salary and train them for a year before either giving them a contract or turning them loose. I didn't have a lot of choice and I told Pam I might as well give it a try. Alex seemed to be a nice sort of manager and if he was the one I needed to work with, I felt I could do it as long as the lodge wasn't a problem. The way it worked out, they cared about sales and customer service. They didn't care if I worked 10 hours or 2 hours a day, as long as I got the job done. The winter was usually their busy time and the summer was when they were going to training and seminars and not doing much business, so with that, it seemed it might work out. But this is the next year in the scheme of things; first it was time to launch our new lodge image.

This time we didn't run a big ad with an interview but we did get some of the suppliers to contribute to a mixed ad and gave the name a new launch at any rate. We had redone the menu, the name, the liquor license and on the strength that it looked like we were going to get a big new group of overseas tours in from Germany, borrowed money from John, our lawyer (and mortgagee), to put new carpet and flooring throughout the entire building. We also put new glass fronts on the front three bedrooms and did some redecorating. The restaurant was given a new look with color, and dividers made with plants and planters. The decor on the walls had more New Zealand pictures and some information on the area itself as well as the Pa site we were sitting in the middle of. As we became more involved in the area and the front section looked like it might sell, we became more concerned about it and what might happen. We had no idea at the time that this was going to turn into a major saga that would take over our lives for the next number of years.

CHAPTER 81

The Saga Begins

We always knew that someday the front section would sell although Maurice Leonard had done several things when he found out he couldn't sell it. He came up one weekend and took down the markers around the grave and with a shovel, lowered the burial mound of dirt. He stopped having anyone take care of the front section, thinking that if the grass grew up again the grave would 'disappear' and then maybe the lot would sell.

It wasn't long after he took the fence down that Pitau Williams showed up from Paeroa. He wanted to know what was going on and we told him what Maurice had done. He said that he would return with some white rocks and replace the fence with them, and the next day he returned to put down 6 white rocks. It wasn't long after this that Maurice came up again and saw the rocks. He came up to the lodge to ask us what was going on. We told him about Pitau coming up and he looked disgusted. He left and we felt he blamed us, although we had nothing to do with it.

The few potential buyers that had shown interest in the front section always became afraid of the Maori grave issue. The main issue was that no one knew what to expect, what could be done, and what couldn't be done. Maurice had been trying to negotiate to have the 'grave' removed and taken to Paeroa, offering to pay all expenses but the Maori family said no—this was where their ancestor wanted to be. We had originally been assured that as long as the grave was respected and the family could visit it from time to time, there would be no problems. Pitau had told us this as well. In fact, the Maori people had been up to visit the grave only about 2 or 3 times in the whole time we had lived there.

For whatever reason the interest in the front section picked up again. During the auction days we let interested people know that the front section might be for sale as well. It was a prime site for a house and these are few in the area. It just worked out that a young man had started looking at the section and I even went down to talk to him and answer his questions. He was aware of the grave but had no problem with it and felt he could work around it. He had been told about it by Chris Sharpe, a local builder we knew who had almost sold the section a couple of times himself by telling people about it who wanted to build a house. The young man later returned with Chris, and I helped them find the survey pegs so they could see if the house they were thinking about would fit.

Pam and I didn't like the idea of it selling as such but we knew someday it would sell and so we wanted to be friends with any new neighbors, feeling they should buy the place with their eyes wide open and not be deceived by anyone. After all, we would have to live next door to them every day from the time they moved in. It was in our interest, and theirs, if they knew everything about the property.

It was also during this time that an older bald-headed man started driving up on his own from time to time in his white Toyota car. Another realtor introduced John Hilhorst (a Dutchman) to me, on one of his trips up and I showed him the pictures of how the grave had looked in the past before Maurice leveled it. Again, we felt he should know the score as well. He told us that it didn't bother him and was sure he could put a little garden or something around it, and the family could still see it if he purchased the place. From no lookers to two. I was betting Maurice was glad to finally have so much interest.

At this time we were also looking at maybe adding onto the lodge. If we got all the necessary consents then, if we went to sell again, we could show it was all ready to be expanded without a lot of hang-ups. We had sketches drawn by an engineer and a cost estimate done by a building contractor. This was taken to the council representative for planning/building consents and he said that we would need to get the permission from the new owner of the front section if Mr Hilhorst did buy the property.

After the rocks were put back around the grave by Pitau, we were not on the best terms with Maurice so we felt that in some ways we may be better off if we did have to go through Hilhorst. Pam had gotten one of the forms from the council and the next time we saw Mr Hilhorst was when he came to ask us about what we thought about a Maori land occupation in the Whanganui. They were protesting and had set up camp and occupied the Moutua Gardens, saying they wanted them back. He wanted to know what we thought the local Maoris might do. We told him again it should not be a problem as long as the grave was respected and offered him Pitau Williams' phone number so he could talk to one of the family direct. He refused the number and left. Before he left Pam told him about our plans to enlarge the lodge so it wouldn't be a problem for him. He told us then that he would sign the papers if he purchased the front section. From what we understood, the next week he went and purchased the property and signed the papers on it. We were getting a new neighbor.

Then next time up he came to see us and told us he purchased the property, we had a cup of tea and Pam had him sign the council consent for our building extension. We offered to help him if we could and when he couldn't get a copy of the geotechnical engineering report from the council that we had to have done when we subdivided the lot, we provided him with a copy of ours. Other times he would want to get water from us and would drive his car and trailer up with a barrel on the back so we could then fill his barrel for him.

As they got the foundation started for the garage, he told us they were in no hurry as he and his wife were at odds with each other. She didn't think she wanted to move up on the coast as they had not sold their house in Morrinsville. So he had agreed to build the garage first so as to have a place to live if need be, while they built the house. He was up all the time and told us how he loved the view and the land. He was originally from Holland and had come out about the late 40's or so and now retired from farming.

As we started to get into our high season after Christmas and New Year, the problems started to surface. One night they worked late and had the car radio on all day so that when they went to leave that night they had a dead battery. In the middle of doing meals for the houseguests I had to stop and get the van and jumper cables, and go down to get him started so he could get home. It was an aggravation but was only the first sign of what was to come. It got to the point that each day they used our parking lot for a building staging area and when they left, it was always full of scrap building materials, sawdust, mud, and a mess. Pam and I would then have to pick up the place each day, so our guests would have somewhere to park–and would not track all the mud and clay into the lodge on their shoes. One time they had taken over the entire parking lot and when one of our house guests returned late in the afternoon, he purposely sat and waited for them to move their vehicles out of the way so he could park. I think he was trying to show them something as they never even realized—much less cared about—how disruptive they were to us and our guests.

One day, they came to us to say they were going to start building a house on the front section, as they may have their own house sold. They were going to start putting down the house foundation and put in the rainwater tank. They had also wanted to know if we could help fill their water tank to some degree. We told them we were sorry but being in mid—summer with guests, it was about all we could do to stay up with our own needs at present. We could do the barrel or so but that was it and you could tell this made them mad. John seemed to understand more than the rest of the family at first. In fact one weekend when he was digging on his own trying to follow the cables, he cut the phone lines by accident and we had no phone until Monday. I am sure we lost some business but when he offered to pay for it, we told him not to worry as no real harm had been done. We wanted to stay on good terms.

Another item in the original sale agreement that we pointed out to him, was that if any property owners damaged the shared driveway, it was up to that person to pay for having it fixed. He said they understood this but with some of their big trucks they could not help but destroy some of the sealing that had been done. We told them to get their truck drivers to go wide on the bend into his place and not to turn sharply, or turn while sitting still on the seal. We had done this with fair-sized vehicles with little or no damage. They soon got tired of running down to the entrance and getting the drivers to do as they should, so sure enough, the next thing you know what happens—they tore the seal in a number of places. When we asked them about it, they said they would pay for it after they finished construction. They had also decided to cut back a number of tree limbs that were over the drive so the trucks could get up. They did it on our property as well as their own, and made a hell of a mess as they didn't know what they were doing. I told him that after the trees lost their leaves I was planning on getting my trees topped and if he was interested I would get a price for him for his. He said that would be fine and to call him.

It seemed they were determined to try to get the place built in the next few months. It got increasingly worse with their mess and their starting work at 6.30 in the morning when our guests were still sleeping.

Then they said the deal had fallen through on their house sale but he still wanted to finish, as he was sure she would like it if she lived in it. If not, then he would put this property back on the market. One day they showed up with the heavy equipment operator, to do a lot of work in the front of the section and put the water tank in at the back of the house. This would make it necessary to work around the marker tree at the grave and either go around it, or take the tree out and go right through the marker tree area. As the day went on, the next thing we saw was a very tall pile of clay in the air and a road that had been cut down to where they wanted the water tank. This had required them to pull out the marker tree at the head of the grave. They had marked one corner of the grave with red tape and then proceeded to take the tank down and drop it in place. They then had to backfill the area they had driven down.

It was during this excavation that Pitau Williams was on his way back to Paeroa from some mussel farm hearings at Coromandel and saw this clay hill from the highway. He drove up and wanted to know what was going on. He talked to the Hilhorsts and they basically told him it was none of his business and to take off. He contacted one of the area's Maori leaders who was involved, a Mr Tai Turoa, who then came up with a representative from the Maori Claims group which was in Thames on some business. Tai couldn't even talk to the Hilhorsts and sat at our table by the window, where he held his head and cried. They were told the marker tree was dead and so they pulled it out. (It wasn't.) When the Hilhorsts put the dirt back they moved the markers for the grave to the side of the original burial site where it would be more convenient. From all our old photos you could see what they had done. They even put in a stake with the word 'tree' on it in the ground and Mrs. Hilhorst planted a handful of flowers.

The next thing we all knew was that Pitau and his Maori family group were going to have a meeting about this and we told Tai they could have it at the lodge. At this meeting they rededicated the grave and put the rocks back where they belonged. They then tried to decide what to do about it, going back over some of the history of the place.

It seems that the Pa site went way back before their ancestors lived there but in more recent times (the late 1800's) it was owned by the Tukukinos who had taken one of his cousin Taraia's wives and for compensation, had to repay him with this Pa site where Taraia had then moved in to live. As the generations went by, one of his granddaughters wanted to be buried there on the front section when she died and not at the Paeroa Marae, due to a family falling out. So she, Te Awhimate, was buried there. She was supposed to be the "keeper of the children" and as legend goes, several children are also buried there. She shows them the way so they can leave this world.

As time went on, the family that was in charge of taking care of the land-holdings in the area for the wider family, talked the mother (in charge) on her death bed, into making out a traditional type of European-style will. She left the land to one of her sons and he then proceeded to subdivide and sell off the land in the area to other people and spent the money at the TAB betting on horses. He lost all the money and now they all have no land and no money. The family still tries to oversee the land (as caretakers) in regard to the Resource Management Act of 1991, and the Treaty of Waitangi, under which they still have a say on land use in making sure its cultural aspects are respected.

When these issues were discussed at the meeting at our place and the history was brought out, we were to later learn not all that was known was told. It seems that Tai Turora was one of the surveyors who helped split the land up, and one of his daughters was married to one of the sons of Maurice Leonard. That is why he had always been so sure it wouldn't be a problem but as time went on, Tai was sorry for what he had done to his own family . . . and was starting to say no to Maurice.

At the meeting they agreed to have some meetings and contact with the Hilhorst family about the grave issue. T.C.D.C. had threatened to put a stop work order on the Hilhorsts if they didn't get this resolved. Pam went to the first meeting with the Turoa family and as Mr. Hilhorst told his side of the story, he denied ever knowing anything about the grave and said he was never told about it. Pam became very angry and told him he knew better and it became apparent things were not going forward at this time. Mr Hilhorst was told by the council to see about getting a plan drawn up for a garden or something to protect the grave area and if the Maoris approved it, then they could continue with the building.

I talked to both sides about this and John Hilhorst seemed like he was bending and considering doing as requested but they again had a run-in with Pitau and Jim Turoa later on. They were refusing to co-operate and some say Pitau put a curse on John at this time when the Hilhorsts told him where to go.

It was a couple of months later when we were getting our trees topped that I remembered I had told Mr Hilhorst I would give him a call when our people were here, to see if he wanted his done at the same time. I rang his place in Morrinsville and his son answered the phone. He was very hostile when I asked if I could please speak to Mr Hilhorst. It seems that just a couple of days before, Mr Hilhorst was by the roadside outside the church area in Morrinsville talking to a friend who was sitting in his car. As he was standing on the side of the road visiting, a car came by and accidentally hit him and killed him. The family felt that a curse had been put on him and we were to blame for bringing the Maoris into the conflict. The truth was that Pitau saw their pile of clay from the highway when he was returning from Coromandel. We never called them and we tried to help negotiate an understanding that would be acceptable to both parties.

It became apparent as time went on, that the wife and sons were very hostile. They refused to acknowledge that they had purchased a property knowing about the grave—even though they had put in the stake that said 'tree' and then planted flowers.They wanted to blame somebody else for their own mistakes and have them pay for the damage they had done. This is typical when you get some people who do not want to be held accountable for their own actions and then try to blame somebody else.

We were aware of the various stories that were going around; starting back when Roger Carter had the place and bulldozed the property, deliberately destroying any evidence he could of the old Pa site. It seems that the equipment operator also unearthed some skeletons and skulls. At a later date, one of these operators died in an accident on the driveway up to the site, and the other died of natural causes at an early age. Now Mr Hilhorst was dead. A few months after this, a roading crew down by the beach was working on a retaining wall by the sea and Pitau went down to tell them not to disturb the rock eel weirs near their work area. The crew had already moved some of the rocks and continued to do so but did not move all of them. These would have gone back to the time when the Pa site was heavily populated.

A few months later after they finished their work, the young driver who did that job was in a hurry going back to town with the equipment and went too fast around Windy Point, hitting a car head-on. He killed the woman driving and her infant son in his car seat. The only survivor was the little girl in the back. Was the man going to jail and paying a very heavy penalty for what he had done on the coast with his equipment—in more ways than one?

This saga goes on for years. Mr Hilhorst had some friends from Holland who had also moved out here when they did. They came up several times with them and after this all started, came up afterwards to tell Pam not to worry about Mrs. Hilhorst and her sons as they were bad people, as he put it. It was from them that Pam learned that back in Holland, they made their money from Mrs. Hilhorst's business—she had a brothel. Yet in New Zealand, she was always ready to condemn everyone else for what they did or said—and criticize us for always working and not going to church on Sundays!

CHAPTER 82

The Saga Continues

I think for the sake of continuity it may be easier if I take the statement I made for the council's lawyers in regard to this. This didn't take place overnight but over the next number of years. It may be easier to follow this story if it is presented on its own. It was something we had to continually work with, as we tried to do the lodge and work on developing and protecting the place as well.

It became more apparent as time went on, just what we were sitting on top of. Although it would have been much easier to ignore it and let it just disappear too, this was something that neither Pam nor I could do in good conscience. If it was truly as an important a site as the archaeologist said it was, then who were we to destroy it and not try and protect it for the generations to come.

As time went on and we were able to better understand the situation as well as from what Pam had picked up on in terms of 'Heritage Trails', it became apparent to us that by using the '1991 R.M.A.', there was no reason why this place couldn't be developed and protected if it was done properly. If it became part of a 'Heritage Trail' where people come to see the area's heritage and history, then this could be part of it, with some restoration and with exhibits in one of the outbuildings. Conducted tours could be given to explain the history and use of the place and the part it played in the history of New Zealand all the way back to well before the Europeans came.

It could be a sustainable business that didn't destroy the environment, its history, or its culture. In fact it would provide for a better understanding of where the Maori people were coming from and could be used to educate all of those who came to it, to learn from the past. This would also necessitate the employment of Maori to show and interpret, as well as working on the preservation of the place. After all, when you go to a place to learn about the history and culture of a people, you want to hear about it from them and not some other race that has come in and taken over. I would hope that a tour in Mexico would have a Mexican running the bus and not an Australian.

At this point in time the story is far from over. In fact we now have three stories all going on all at once. One is the continuing story of the lodge and the everyday work around the place. The second is the new story of trying to protect and develop the Pa site—and where and how to get not only money but also help, to do so. And thirdly, there is the story that still goes on, about the front section and all its unresolved issues.

But first I will bring the story of the front section up to date by using the transcript I gave to the lawyers, and then go from there on how we feel that it could be worked into a solution along with the overall preservation and development of the place.

LOT 1 PT TE APUTA (FRONT SECTION)

1988

October 1988 we purchased the property (Lots 1 & 2) from Roger and Karen Carter. At this time Lot 1 was already in the process of being subdivided off Lot 2 and the various easements and surveys were already in the process of being finalized by Thames surveyor, Mr. Morrie Dunwoodie. We found it economically necessary to continue with this subdivision, in order to continue with the development of the lodge. We also found out it was necessary to obtain a geotechnical report from an engineer in regard to Lot 1's suitability as a building site and we had this done by Thames engineer, Mr Max Bosselman.

During the early days as we were going through this process, a Mr Pitau Williams of Paeroa, came up looking for his "Nan's" grave and I took him through the long grass to show him where it was. This was the first time I met Mr Williams.

Lot 1 was then listed with Maurice Leonard of Harcourt's Realty in Thames—the same realtor we purchased the property through—who at that time had also indicated he himself might be interested in Lot 1 as a "spec" property if the subdivision was completed. During this time Mr Leonard presented us with a contract from a Mr Alvin White, of Ruamahanga Bay. Several conditions of sale/purchase were in this offer–one of which was checking out the Maori grave issue to his satisfaction. While he was researching this question, he had paid someone to clear the long grass from Lot 1, except for the grave area itself. During this time, as we still owned Lot 1, we contacted Mark Arnold then at Whakatete bay, and through him his late uncle Shu Tukukino, who was the Kaumatua at that time for our area. He gave us permission to clean up the long grass around the grave itself and replace the fence. This was done in one day before nightfall as requested, and Mark Arnold gave a blessing for rededication. It was during this time we came to understand that as long as the grave was respected and taken care of and the Maori people were able to come and visit if they wished, it would not be a problem for the landowners involved.

After a couple of months Mr White would still not go unconditional on his offer or put up a deposit as he said this was because he wanted a formal agreement for the shared driveway, or a trust set up for repair and maintenance. After several additional contacts, he was given the opportunity to put up a deposit or withdraw from the contract offer. He withdrew.

1989

We then placed Lot 1 back on the market with Mr Leonard. At that time he came back to us with an offer for the section from his son, Jeff Leonard. He explained to us that he was working with his son to buy the section, as he was considering moving to Te Puru. They then purchased the section at the asking price in June 1989, subject to the final title and easements coming through—which they did in August 1989. The Leonards were finally registered as owners in November 1989. Lot 1 was mowed and maintained during this time.

Feb. 1990

The Maori Land Court finished with legalizing the easements (through the Hauwai Block), around the same time the titles for Lots 1 and 3 (reserve contribution) came through. We had contact with the Maori landowners of the neighboring Hauwai Block during this period when the easements/right of way were created for access to both the Hauwai Block and Pt 2 Te Aputa. Shortly after this Maurice explained to us that circumstances had changed for his son and they would no longer be building a house and instead would be putting the section back on the market; which they did. He also explained that they would be asking a higher price as the market had changed considerably since they had contracted with us.

1990-1994

During this time the Leonards paid to keep the front section mowed and clean. It was listed with a number of local realtors during this time and shown by many of them. At various times the realtors would bring up clients to speak to us about the lodge, the Hauwai Maori Land block, and farm, which also shared our driveway access—and about the grave. We would show them the original pictures of the grave with its picket fence and tell them what we knew about it. Sometimes prospective buyers would come up on their own and ask questions, and at other times they would book into our restaurant to see what it was like, and then ask questions about the front section and grave. It became common knowledge in both the community and among local realtors, that the front section had a Maori grave on it and a lodge situated behind it, along with two other properties which shared the access.

After a period of time in 1991, Mr Leonard and his son Jeff felt the grave issue was preventing them from selling the section. They spoke to Tai Turoa of Thames, who was recognized now as the local Kaumatua since Mr Tukukino passed away. They offered to pay for the grave to be relocated but were told this was totally unacceptable and it would have to stay where it was—and that if it was disturbed, there would be a "war". (Both Mr Leonard and later Mr Turoa spoke to me directly about these negotiations—and the subsequent lack of resolution.)

As a result of their inability to have the grave moved, Maurice and Jeff Leonard eventually came back up to Lot 1 and took shovels from their vehicle and then proceeded to take down the fence around the grave and level the ground inside the fenced area. They then drove off. It was only a few weeks later that Mr Pitau Williams showed up again. He came to visit the grave and was upset and angry to find what had been done. He left and returned a few days later with rocks that were painted white that were about the size of bowling balls. He placed them around the grave area and then rededicated it.

I can only assume Mr Leonard was contacted by the Maori family as he soon returned to look at the white rocks. He seemed to blame us (for contacting them?) and explained he was trying to get the grave moved but was not getting any co-operation. He told us that as far as he was concerned they could "dig up their bones and bugger off". He also told us he could no longer justify the expense of keeping the section mowed and cleaned up. They left the rocks in place but they then allowed the section to become overgrown again with long grass.

During this time realtors would still bring clients to see the section. We would answer questions and show pictures as before. We would go down at times to the section to check and make sure the white rocks were visible. We did not clean up the gravesite but if the grass needed to be removed around the rocks so as to be visible, we did do that so the tapu area would still be marked for people to see so they would not walk on the grave area.

Because of our obvious 'involvement', we never wanted either the grave or our lodge business to be an issue with a purchaser. We wanted anyone purchasing this section to be fully informed of all these related issues and their ramifications for us all, before they bought it. This was in the hope of avoiding any problems in the future.

1994-1995

From about late 1994, the activity and interest in the front section picked up. During this time Mr John Hilhorst from Morrinsville, began coming up looking at the front section. He was working with a Coastline Realty realtor, Mr Graham Pickering of Thames. Again I answered questions about the section, the lodge, and the grave. I showed them the pictures from our album, of the section and the grave. I told him the grave had not been a problem as long as it was respected and worked with. Mr Hilhorst came back a number of times to look at the section on his own over several months and would spend time sitting smoking cigarettes and looking at the view. Occasionally he also brought Mrs Hilhorst with him.

Chris Sharpe of Focus Homes in Thames also came up here with a young couple who had looked at the section, to make some preliminary measurements. I helped answer questions about where the pegs were, about the grave (so they could work around it), and even helped hold the string as they set out house pegs. This buyer worked in maintenance at Goldfields Mall in Thames and he told me he had no problems with respecting the grave and working with it. They told me they had several things to work through and came back several times and to look at the section.

Mr Hilhorst came up to the lodge and talked to both Pam and I on several occasions both before, and after, he purchased the front section. He came to see us again around the time when the Moutoa Gardens occupation began (Waitangi Day, February 6, 1995) and expressed concern over Maori attitudes to land ownership as he was about to finalize the purchase. We again went over the grave issue and offered him Pitau Williams' phone number in Paeroa in case he wanted to speak to someone in the family. We also told him that we were in the process of applying for the necessary permits etc. for an extension on our lodge building so he would be aware of this before he purchased the front section. He told us then that he did not see why either the grave or the expansion should be a problem for him. He even discussed with us, making a feature of the grave as a landscaped garden area.

It was after this I was told that the young couple had conditions in their offer, whereas Mr Hilhorst would make an unconditional cash offer. Mr Hilhorst finally decided to purchase the property and did so on February 9, 1995.

1995-1996

After Mr Hilhorst purchased the property he came up a number of times and as we wanted to be 'good neighbors' and help, we provided him with cups of tea, water, and a copy of the geotechnical report from the engineer. He told us that Mrs Hilhorst was not sure she really wanted to move here but he hoped with time she would change her mind. During one of his visits on June 27, 1995, he signed the papers in regard to our expansion as requested by T.C.D.C., as an "affected person".

I also found our copy of the survey and helped him find the pegs for the property boundaries. This was so he could ensure he located his buildings within the property boundary and away from the grave. We helped provide water for his cement mixing and allowed him to use our parking lot continually as a staging and working area. I even left the restaurant one night and used my jumper cables to help start their dead car battery so they could go home. This was during the construction of the garage area and house foundation (mid-1995 to early-1996).

This construction eventually started to become a problem as our high season is summer when the Hilhorsts were busiest. The problems included early (noisy) starts at 6 AM(especially on weekend mornings when our guests complained), and the taking over of our parking lot with materials and vehicles (making parking difficult for our own guests), and leftover mess. Pam and I each day would have to pick up after them when they left. We warned them about large trucks and driveway damage in great detail, so as to prevent damage. We were ignored and were repeatedly assured that they would take care of it after they finished building. It was as if they had a fire under them to just get it done. The Hilhorsts had told us that the plan to build the garage first had changed when the sale contract on their home at 'Tasman Village' in Morrinsville fell through. They had originally been hurrying to complete the garage to store their belongings and live in while they built their new house. John Hilhorst then said his wife had changed her mind about moving to Te Puru and the house would be built as a "spec" home—with both he and the family hoping she would change her mind as the building progressed. The feeling appeared to be that the financial gain from a "spec" home would be better than just selling a section with plans if this did not eventuate.

In early 1996, they started the house foundation and installation of the water storage tank. Mr and Mrs Hilhorst and their son were working and supervising the bobcat driver. We could not believe the massive earthworks they were doing and were flabbergasted. They appeared to get tired of working around the grave marker tree after a period of time and proceeded to pull it out with the digger. They then excavated out by the grave to put the water tank in. They marked the grave location with orange tape. We were so surprised at the massive and unnecessary amount of earthmoving and obvious disregard for the grave site that we got our camera and took photos to send to Pam's folks, as we knew they would not be able to believe it either. After the water tank was put in and fill work done, they put a scoop of topsoil to the side and a stake with 'tree' written on it and Mrs Hilhorst planted flowers there. This was located to the side of the area of the grave—an area out of the way to be able to get to the house more easily for construction.

It was during this time of massive earthworks with the clay piled up—which could be seen far up the coast and from below—that Pitau Williams was driving along the coast road for a mussel farm hearing and saw this. He came up and was very upset. He retrieved the white rocks so he could locate and re-mark the grave in its original position. He then contacted Tai Turoa who also came by later. Mr Turoa's associate, John McEnteer, confronted the Hilhorsts and wanted to know what was going on and what had they done with the grave. Mr Turoa was so upset he sat at the table with us and could not even go down and talk to them himself. He just sat there and cried during these discussions. The Hilhorsts were advised to stop building after they finished using their hired compactor on the house foundation footing that day. Mr Turoa told us he felt sure that this was a misunderstanding, that they would reinstate the grave, and things could be worked out for all parties involved.

In mid-March 1996, we were invited by Mr Turoa, to a rededication of the gravesite by his family. We offered to have the meeting that followed at our lodge, as the ceremony was to be at the gravesite on Lot 1. Tai Turoa explained to the family at the meeting that we were involved whether we wanted to be or not, as we were affected by this and the outcome as well. He told them we were tangata whenua. The family set up a committee to pursue the various issues and were instructed to keep us informed. I was also appointed an ex-officio member of this committee.

I spoke to John Hilhorst on a couple of occasions after this, down on the front section when he was on his own. It became evident that the Hilhorsts blamed us for "calling the Maoris in". When I spoke to him I explained on more than one occasion that all they wanted at this time was the grave reinstated, as a garden, with a fence—using materials that would go with the house. They wanted it marked off and respected. The Hilhorsts told us that they really didn't want it at their back door and that in the Holland they dig up graves all the time . . . "When you are dead, so what!" However, we were still hopeful that something could still be worked out as Mr Hilhorst seemed to listen and I felt that he was considering working something out at the upcoming meeting that was scheduled with T.C.D.C. and the family representatives.

In April 1996, Pam was invited (by Tai Turoa) to attend the meeting at Mr Turoa's office at Te Korowai in Thames, between Bruce Baker, planning officer for T.C.D.C., Mr Turoa and his family, and Mr Hilhorst. We supplied photos of sequential events as requested. To our surprise at this meeting, Mr Hilhorst said he knew nothing about the grave and would not reinstate it, or retain it. He called Pam—in effect—a liar. The meeting got nowhere. Pam and I discussed this attitude and felt they were only out for themselves, with total disregard for the truth. We were concerned about the result of this attitude for us.

In April 1996, archaeologist, Nicholas Twohill of Thames, visited Lot 1 to investigate it from an archaeological point of view. We spoke to him at this time but he seemed totally disinterested in any information/history we might have had.

In May 1996, we contacted our lawyer, John Armstong at Davidson, Armstrong and Campbell in Waipukurau. At this point he suggested we write to T.C.D.C. and record our concern at this time regarding these issues that concern us, including the earthworks, the driveway, and the fallout effects this may have on us and others in the area.

It was around this time I called to speak to Mr Hilhorst at his home at Morrinsville, about cutting the tops out of some of the poplar trees below our driveway. We had discussed this before and he told me to call him if I had someone come to do some of mine, as he would like to have someone trim his trees too. It was then I found out he had been killed in an accident the day before. Pam and I then notified the Turoa/Nicholls family and out of respect, they said they would put everything on hold indefinitely.

In June 1996, our lawyer, John Armstrong, wrote to Ryan in Morrinsville, the lawyer we understood represented the Hilhorsts, regarding some of our concerns. This letter was returned saying Ryans no longer represented them. On 2 July 1996, Mrs Hilhorst came up to Lot 1 and had a look around. In August 1996, the power board came up and cut off the power, and 'Placemakers' came up and removed some of the building materials.

1997

Pam found out who was representing the Hilhorsts and John Armstrong sent a letter to them. We heard nothing. In December 1996, we heard the Hilhorsts had a stop work at T.C.D.C. as they had not resolved the issues on the grave. Jan and Feb 1997, there was finally some legal correspondence over our "blocking off" Lot 1 access because of their driveway damage etc. and we were asked by their lawyer Tony Coupe in Auckland, for help as who to contact. Pam talked to Tai Turoa (who was ill) and we provided his brother, Jim Turoa's name and number as advised by him.

Mr Tai Turoa had earlier delegated Pitau Williams to register the area as a Wahi Tapu, as he explained to us he could not do so himself because of a conflict of interest as a member of the NZHPT's Maori Heritage Council which had final approval of all registrations.

We eventually made contact with Dave Robson, head of Maori Heritage at the Historic Places Trust in Wellington, in an attempt to ascertain and resolve this impasse that we had become involved in, despite our best efforts to prevent any such occurrence.

On 12 November 1996, Mr Robson sent us copies of all the correspondence to date relating to Te Aputa Pa (i.e. between the NZHPT, Brake Rae & Co, Nicholas Twohill and Coupe, Davidson, Sweetman). He also sent a copy of Larryn Diamond's 1976 Thames Coast archaeological survey relating to the Pa our property is located on. This was the first time we even became aware of the existence of Te Aputa Pa.

After deciphering the meaning of the 1976 survey results we knew there was something wrong with Mr Twohill's identification of Lot 4 behind our property (purportedly the Hilhorst property), instead of Lot 1 which he had inspected. Following lengthy discussions/correspondence with Mr Robson, in July 1997, archaeologist Warren Gumbley spent 2 days surveying and mapping Te Aputa Pa, during which time we hosted and assisted him. This survey was commissioned by the NZHPT to assist in the (wahi Tapu) registration, future management, and interpretation of the site. It was then confirmed that Lot 4 had been mistakenly identified as Lot 1 by Mr Twohill—and that the whole front half of the Pa site had never even been recorded in 1976. This was also when the importance of Te Aputa Pa (including both Lots 1 and 2) was discovered.

Mr Twohill's mistake directly resulted in Mr Gumbley's October 1997 *'Te Aputa Pa Archaeological Survey and Assessment of Condition and Archaeological Values'.*

The May 1996 letter quoting Mr Twohill's findings also refers to a roadway created over part of the Lot 1 title. This in fact was the road that was (physically) created through Lot 2 and the Hauwai Block for access to Pt 2 Te Aputa. It did not physically involve Lot 1 as it only passed over the existing driveway through Lot 1, created by Mr Carter.

In his 12 November 1996 letter Mr Robson also requested our assistance with the wahi tapu registration of Te Aputa Pa, which Mr Turoa had told us was necessary to ensure future protection of the grave site. We worked with both Mr Robson and Mr Williams to register the Te Aputa headland on which our property is located. Te Aputa Pa was finally registered as a wahi tapu in December 1997, in an effort to ensure its future protection from irresponsible development.

While were concerned about what effects this would have on our land value, ability to build, develop, or even sell, we worked to make this happen anyway as we believed it was important to preserve and protect our country's history—especially such an important and relatively "pristine" site. We ensured this was now recorded at T.C.D.C. when Pam gave copies of report(s) to Bruce Baker for inclusion in property files for all 5 affected titles.

Steve Hilhorst met Jim Turoa again at the front section. I went at end of meeting to see Steve for a minute in regard to driveway repairs etc. He told me he had no intention of ever repairing the damage they had caused as he blamed us for all that had happened. I again reminded him they knew of the grave before they purchased the property. His response was still that they did not know—"And besides, who are they going to believe, you or a dead man!?" Pam called Tai Turoa to discuss some of this conversation and at that point he asked her whether we would be prepared to be "responsible" for Lot 1. She told him we would be. He told her he would call another meeting of "all the tangata whenua" to discuss this. Unfortunately Mr Turoa died in February 1998.

1998

In Feb. 1998, our resource consent for the lodge expansion was about to expire and we needed to renew it. We had been on hold ever since the front section issue started. Since Mr Tai Turoa had died, Pitau Williams and Jim Turoa were now mainly in charge.

In March 1998, T.C.D.C. hearing on renewal for 2 years was approved—except for portion the Hilhorsts ignored and refused to answer when papers and plans were sent to them.

On 20 July 1998, Pam and Pitau Williams spoke to Thames Mayor, Alasdair Thompson, in regard to a number of the front section issues. He offered to facilitate another meeting to try and resolve some of these issues. A letter dated 27 July was sent to Hilhorst lawyer, Mr Tony Coupe. This first letter and proposed meeting for 16 September 1998 were ignored. Another meeting was offered by the Mayor and Mr Coupe later set this for 12 October 1998.

At this meeting Pam, the Mayor, both Hilhorst sons with David Wilson their barrister, Jim Turoa, Tewi Nicholls, the Ngati Tamatera Iwi representative, and Steve and Ngaire Te Moananui attend. The Hilhorsts maintained they knew nothing about the grave before they purchased the property and started to build, and that none this problem was their fault. The Maori representatives said it was not possible for the Hilhorsts to build a house on Lot 1 anymore. Mr Turoa suggested that Lot 1 could become Council reserve—and the Runanga representative indicated that Maori ownership was not necessary. Mr Wilson then talked about suing various parties and asked Pam if he could call her for a statement. She agreed.

On 23 November 1998, David Wilson called Pam and said they would maintain they didn't know about the grave until work was stopped. Pam reminded him our photos showed otherwise. In his next call he then suggested they would say they didn't know about grave before buying the property and asked whether we had a diary or notes to establish our claim that we had told John Hilhorst before he bought the property? She told him she would talk to me and get back with him. She enquired as to whom to contact again regarding our driveway damage issues with his clients, and he suggested Tony Coupe. Pam and I discussed the issues. We had photos, phone bills, some notes in our daily diary-booking book, copies of letters to many of those involved as well as personal contacts and conversations with those involved. I told her I remembered Graham Pickering was the Realtor who sold him the property and I would call him.

I phoned Mr Pickering and he told me he remembered me talking to Mr Hilhorst about the front section and the grave when he first brought him up to look at it. He told me that Mr Hilhorst said he did not have a problem with the grave and that he had told him he had checked it out with both T.C.D.C., and the Historic Places Trust. He said he believed it was about 6 months from start to finish before he sold the property to the Hilhorsts, and that in fact it was so long he had just about given up on ever doing so. Mr Pickering was indignant that someone would insinuate that he would not fully disclose this, or would try to hide an issue such as a grave. He told me that he didn't need a commission that badly. He also agreed that it was common knowledge about the grave on the front section and that most people knew about it.

On 26 November 1998, I had previously left word for Mr Wilson to call me back and he called me back at 4.50 PM. I told him that John Hilhorst knew about the grave before he purchased the property etc. and that we had some notes and photos but did not keep a diary on every item. I then relayed the conversation I had with the realtor on the 23rd of November. I also told him that I was concerned about what the Hilhorsts had brought down on us and all our neighbors by their actions, and that I had a good mind to get together with all these neighbors and bring a class action suit against them for what they had inflicted on us all. I told him I had no sympathy for the Hilhorst family when they knowingly and willingly did something like this on purpose, and then tried to put the blame on someone else so they didn't have to pay the price for their own actions.

On 2 December 1998, (Started using Diary 23 Nov. 1998 as per suggestion). Steve Hilhorst came to pick up building material of any value from front section. Had a driver with him. Loaded truck 10.45 AM until 1.05 PM. I helped him open "gate" area. He left trash and mess on front section. Steve Te Moananui and his family came to help us tidy some of this up.

On 11 December 1998, letter to John Armstrong, gave overview of meeting and phone calls with Wilson.

1999

On 3 January 1999, at 11.45 A.M; Mrs Hilhorst and a friend drove up and checked out front section. Looked to see if any materials were left to be picked up.

I am quite clear that Mr Hilhorst knew about the grave before he entered into the sale and purchase agreement. He also knew the local Maori would not object to any building being carried out on the land providing they respected the grave site and allowed people to visit it. It was insensitivity to the situation and the eventual grave desecration, that led directly to the Hilhorst's inability to develop the site because of the ultimate protection afforded by the 1997 'Archaeological Survey' and 'Wahi Tapu Registration' necessitated by their actions.

It was after this we heard that Jim Turoa had become ill and died. We had also heard rumors, and we had our own suspicions, that he was taking a 'consultation' fee from the Hilhorsts to work this matter through. Mr and Mrs. Maurice Leonard had both become ill with cancer we heard through the grape vine and of course I had as well, which is why the lawyers wanted to get me on paper now and not wait until later. But I have been repeatedly assured by various local Maori people that mine has nothing to do with this place.

We had and have hoped, that the front section could be worked into a stepping stone and a starting place for a cultural heritage trail. The Hilhorsts do not deserve to get anything for what they did, before trying to blame all the others. However, the council is not totally blameless either as they had an obligation to work with local Maori on issues, and learn what and where land needed to be protected. When we asked the council they didn't know and didn't care. It has come out that Hilhorst also checked with the council and again it appears that the term "of no significance" came out. Yet the report done by Mr Diamond was in 1976 and had already established the place as a Class 2 category of national importance. We later learned again (at about the end of 1989) they were told this by another survey but the information was not documented or put into a useful form so it got lost in the mass of paper.

We have hoped that the council who were not without blame, would take some responsibility and try to purchase the place back from the Hilhorsts at a reduced amount—and then donate it to a trust or foundation as part of the heritage trail. This would then make some sense out of this, and protect and develop the area for future generations. This is the course we have tried to push forward from our point of view—even to the point of helping establish and become part of 'Toru Three Catchments Society Incorporated'. This group is to protect and develop the local area while using the local resources carefully so as not to destroy them or use them unwisely.

CHAPTER 83

THE STORY UNFOLDS

As if we didn't have enough to do already with trying to get the lodge off to a new start, this war with the neighbors in the front didn't help. We were trying to keep our minds on what needed to be done but that was a moving target and kept changing. At one point we could see this as a possible way to make this place a destination in itself. We knew we needed to take a number of different outcomes, both good and bad, and then extrapolate them out to a likely end. We didn't like the way some would end up but I think if you make plans you need to consider all possibilities and be prepared for various possible outcomes so as not to be caught off guard. We would then hope to influence events in such a way as to get the desired outcome.

None of this really hit us until after the events with the Hilhorsts at T.C.D.C. when John started to blame everybody else. That was why Pam went to the meeting—to make sure she knew what was being said. And she was very upset to see people act like this. She always had a soft spot for those she thought had been taken advantage of and this was the case with the Maoris. The more we talked to Tai Turoa and became involved with him, the more she wanted to help. It was through Tai she was introduced to Dave Robson at the Historic Places Trust in Wellington. He was to handle the registration of the Pa site as a historic site that needed protection. You could see that by doing this, it was like a knife for us—it cut both ways. If we helped protect the Pa then we would become completely subject to all the controls and conditions that the protection order would have for the Hilhorsts as well. It could affect the value and the ability for us to be able to ever sell the place. We knew that in the short term it was not a good move.

Most people don't like change and don't like the unknown. If they know what to expect, then they can cope and work with it. If we could show that other than having one more department to work with and do paper work for and be subject to their approval, then maybe it wasn't so bad. It would be a procedure to work through, to consult with the local Maori about the protection of the area and to develop only in ways they felt were culturally sensitive. The Historic Places Trust was to make sure you went through the correct procedure before they gave any approvals. It wasn't perfect but with all of us already being subject to the R.M.A. of 1991, it wasn't that much different as the Historic Places Trust was normally the only one left out of the loop. If we wanted their protection then we needed them to be part of the loop.

As part of the process the Historic Places Trust paid an archaeologist, Warren Gumbley, to come and do an update on the Pa. It also worked out that the Hilhorsts had commissioned a report by a different archaeologist that was to show there was nothing left to save. We learned during this time that Mr Twohill didn't know how to read the map and the area he assumed was the Hilhorst section in the Larry Diamond survey, was actually the area where the lodge is sitting. His report was worthless and it was up to Warren to show that the area was worth saving. We had Warren come and stay at the lodge when he did the survey and got to know him. I even went out with him on the field trips and helped him hold the tape as we remeasured the old terraces and marked the damage. As we did this, he explained to me what his interpretation of the place was. For one thing, he believed that each part was a piece of an overall big picture—at least in this case. Some people such as Twohill, saw each piece as a stand-alone issue and something that stood by itself without considering that which surrounded it. This is what was called the 'lumpers' and 'splitters', with Warren being a 'lumper' in looking at each thing in relation to what was going on around it.

This may not make a lot of "who cares" until an issue comes up as it did in our neighbor's case, that was off to the east side of the property. They wanted to sell and wanted a report in regard to the midden (seashell deposit) that was on their property. Mr Twohill had also looked at that and said it was significant and part of a Pa site on its own. When Warren and I looked at it, Warren showed me how the midden had washed down the hill in all the heavy rains over the years and was just some of the midden that had been transferred down from the Pa site above, higher up the hill. Warren could see no reason to place the property under a protection order and cause additional problems for the property owner who wanted to sell. If it wasn't for Warren, who knows where we would have ended up or where these neighbors would have ended up as well.

It was interesting going over the hillside with him through the bush and being shown what to look for and what things meant in the overall scheme. He estimated the site could be dated back to about 1350 AD from what he could see and from what Mr Diamond had put in his report in 1976. He wanted to see if money couldn't be raised to do a more complete archaeological survey of the entire area along with carbon dating. We told him we would like to help and work in this direction but as he noted, money was a problem—plus the fact that not all the neighbors were happy about this.

The neighbors that were mainly affected were the Gaveys up the hill on the so-called (original Carter) farm, the Bergersen family property that was between us and the Gaveys, and then the Hilhorsts down in front. Most of the others on the edge were out of the way, so to speak, and should not have any impact from the investigation and the Pa being protected.

Mr Bergersen was an older man who had a son that had served in the Navy with Pam's brother many years before. He was very much to the point and when we invited him to come and talk to Warren about the history of the hillside, he was more than willing. He explained how he in the early days, was one of the first buyers for the land when it went on the market. He had always wanted to build a house up on the piece behind us for his retirement. This didn't work out as Mr Carter purchased the farm and lodge property, after a subdivision deal had come unstuck with a developer.

According to Bergersen, he was going to get access through the Carter's place on the piece of land behind us, so he could build. For this, Bergersen was to put a fence in on the property across the boundary between himself and Carter. When it was complete, Carter then refused to let him have access. He claimed that he had put the fence one-meter inside of Carter's boundary on purpose. Carter had also filled in and leveled a lot of the ground in the area and told Bergersen at the time that he was destroying any significance so the Maoris wouldn't want it back at some later date. Bergersen never explained why he put the fence where he did—unless he felt it was easier. When we purchased the place and the survey was done, the fence was one meter inside the property boundary and still is today.

Bergersen went on to tell us how his kids would come up and play on the front section. One time they brought home a human skull from where the bulldozer had unearthed it. Bergersen told them to take it back to where they found it and leave it alone and stay away from the area. It was not considered a good thing to do and if you were not careful a lot of bad could befall you. He was one of the sources about the men who had done the original bulldozing that had come to such bad ends. Bergersen also pointed out where some of the old features were on the places that were now buried. Warren had come up with some old World War II recon photos of the area that had been done in case of invasion. From these it was possible to see a lot of the features that Bergersen talked about, which are no longer present.

By putting pieces of the puzzle together from the various sources, a picture of the place was starting to develop. We learned that it was possible for societies and trusts to get grants from organizations and the government for research into such matters, as well as the development and protection of such findings. On the surface it sounded very difficult at first but as we learned more and got information on how to apply to some of these places, it didn't seem so bad—that is, until you only got turned down. We could then see it was like most things, there was a certain way to get these applications approved.

Part of this was going to take time. Pam would need to develop new relationships with those who were in power at the right place. One time at Tourism Coromandel (once Lynn Banford had come on board with the new head, Jim Archibald), it was pointed out there was $5,000 available for work on a heritage trail. The European one had been done and most of the paperwork had been done on a portion of the Maori one but had not been completed. Pam became involved and this is when the importance of being a trust or such came out. She was assured that once she was at the correct stage she could get $5,000 a year for signs to be put up, according to the trust specifications. It was a start and Pam needed more backing so she went to work with the idea starting to develop, that maybe, with the help of the trust and a new organization, she could get this off the ground after all.

Pam spent more time doing stories and research on the Maori people of New Zealand and of the area. We started putting up displays and stories in the restaurant so people could learn more if they were interested. We started to push our place as sitting in the middle of a Pa site. We wanted and needed more Maoris involved. Pitau had worked with us some, as well as a few others since the front section had become an issue. Pitau was interested in doing tours or talking to tourists. He was a likeable enough sort of a person and came across well. Most people liked him and he was a good storyteller. In fact as we were to learn in time, his ability to tell a story was one of his trademarks that he was known by those that had been around him for some time.

Part of Tourism Coromandel's mandate was to help develop and promote Maori tourism in the area. Lynn was helpful and wanted to do what she could. As time went on we learned that Jim Archibald was the problem. He had Lynn doing all the work and paid only lip service to most things and would then let them fall over as he really didn't like working. Lynn assured us she needed to get his approval for things along the way but after that we should be able to do the work without any interference from him.

Unfortunately sometimes this too can be detrimental. A couple of years down this path and Pam had arranged to have a meeting here at the Lodge with the then-Mayor Alasdair Thompson, a planning consultant, an engineer, several other local responsible people and some representatives from the Maori group at Waiomu. The national CEO from the Heritage Trail Foundation was also here. She had driven that morning from Napier, about a 4 to 5 hour drive, just so she could attend and lend her support. The plan was to get the group to work with each other for the development of a cultural center at Waiomu. They needed some road works and road right-of-way issues straightened out, as well as some other permits. If the place could get off the ground, it would provide employment in the area and a place for the Maori to start to tell their history and culture. The cultural trail had already started around the country and a brochure was being produced that would link up such places for people to visit; thus helping develop Maori Tourism. Just as the meeting was almost over and had started to break up, Jim Archibald came in and made a joke out of his being late and in time for lunch as that was the best part of meetings anyway. We then learned from the head of the cultural trust that Jim was known in the industry as a joke—never on time, lazy, and useless. Today had been no exception.

CHAPTER 84

THE NEW LODGE

The transition went more smoothly than I had figured it would. Maybe it was because we planned to do it in the middle of winter so that when all the new books came out they would have our new name in it. It seemed like we had to explain to only a few—most of those were on the restaurant trade side of our business.

We did have one little hiccup at first but that lasted only about 6 weeks. We had started to allow B.Y.O. for wine only. Then we saw this wasn't working; and again it was the locals trying to abuse us. We decided that since they could only understand all or none, they could have none. We did tell our good customers, the Kays, that they could still bring their own but to slip it to me first and I would act as if they had purchased it from me, so as not to cause a problem.

This may seem petty at first but after you consider the hoops we had to go through and the several thousand dollars of expenses for getting the new license and then several thousand dollars worth of inventory, we were just protecting our livelihood. We didn't even charge outrageous prices. A lot of restaurants would buy a bottle of wine for say $10.00 at the store and then sell it for $20 to $30 at the restaurant. People knew what it cost and felt they were being taken advantage of. I told Pam that what I wanted to do was have a smaller markup but try to be fair. Chris Adams had suggested before he left that any decent place didn't have a bottle of wine below $20 on their wine list.

With this in mind we still wanted to offer some popular good wines that were not expensive. We learned with time that several of the major companies made a line each year that was directed at, more or less, a house wine level. We could sell their wine for $20 a bottle and make from $5 to $8 a bottle. If they purchased the house wine by the glass (and it was all bottle–not cask–wine) it was about $4.50 a glass at first. This gave us an equivalent price of about $27.00 per bottle but we had to serve it a glass at a time. In the mid-range we made about $5 to $8 per bottle profit, and in the top range we made usually about $10 per bottle, except on those of exceptional quality which were hard to get. Even then, the most we got was about $15 to $20—and this was something that cost us $20 to $25 dollars and was a gold medal winner and 'restaurant-only', i.e. not available at any price at the stores.

We wanted to make money with the new liquor license but we also wanted to control the amount people drank. You never realize just how drunk and stupid people can get until you have a B.Y.O. When we went to fully-licensed only, the people that used to drink 6 or 8 beers, now only had one or two—or even none. They might have a bottle of wine but that was it but at least we didn't have the drunks to put up with. I can still remember some of those that complained we wouldn't let them bring their own, when we sometimes had the same wine on the wine list for only $5 or so more. Corkage would have cost them that much. And the best of all were the ones who wanted to bring the really cheap and nasty cask stuff that no self-respecting person would be seen placing to their lips.

The new menu was not overnight and after about 18 to 24 months, I would say we had it pretty much worked out. I think now if anything, we offered too much. We do without a doubt, some of the best dishes around for quality and price. We still are not fancy but do a nice presentation. We provide good serves of food and use only top quality product in our dishes. We still use 'Gourmet Direct' even though they had many changes but still offer some of the best quality meat (and other food/drink products) around.

It seems that the man who put 'Fortex' in the spotlight knew it was going to work but the numbers weren't working for him so he did some creative bookkeeping and got in trouble. He didn't do it to take money and run; he did it to try and keep the doors of the company open and the jobs ticking over. At the end, the receivers came in and shut it down and sold off what they could. They took the most modern plant in the country with some great export ideas and turned it into junk. The employees of the gourmet division went together and purchased it from the receiver. They were out of business for about 2 months and during that time we purchased from 'Meat Cuisine' out of Auckland.

When 'Gourmet Direct' was up and running again they went forward and were backed by some of the big money players in the country such as 'Tower Investments'. Once they were able to make a nice profit out of their investment they sold out and not long after, a lot of the original employee owners did the same. It was sold to 'Richmond Meat Co'. They have so far kept up the 'good work' but I am not sure they will stay with the high quality, low price, low order size, that most of us small restaurants need. A lot of the restaurants in the country are small and do not do hundreds and hundreds of people each day. Only time will tell.

It just worked out that at the time we did our switch, the government got much tougher on drink driving and went on a big campaign around the country—especially in the rural areas where they felt nobody pays any attention. What this did was take the responsible diner and made him stay at home. The drunk still went out and got in trouble. The ones that were responsible wanted to have a drink with their meals—or maybe even one before, during and after—now felt that with the new penalty it wasn't worth it. If it was two couples, then sometimes one person would draw the short straw as the 'designated driver' and not drink at all. It wasn't that these people were drunks but they had learned to enjoy their going out and part of it was having several drinks during their evening.

Some of the places in town offered a courtesy bus where they would pick up and deliver in town. Well, that was okay if you were in town but we were up the coast. It was about $20 a trip each way by cab and we couldn't afford to put on an employee to drive people all over the peninsula for a meal out. As I remember, overnight, we had a decrease of about 1/3 in our business that must have been attributed to this factor. Another reason to get out of the local market as such.

The overseas people that stayed with us mostly ate with us and didn't care how much they drank, as all they had to do was walk to their room. When we had a few from the other area motels, again they were less worried as they felt they didn't have far to go. It was the local part of the market that this crackdown had an effect on.

Our average bill in the restaurant for a couple went from around $75 to $80, to more like $110 to $120 per couple. Some really enjoyed themselves and would come up and have a few drinks before dinner, then dinner and after dinner drinks. Some would have one or two bottles of wine during dinner. These were good for business and yet we didn't worry about them as all they had to do was walk to their room.

It seems like we got many more compliments on our food after we switched to our new menu but the main items the overseas people ordered were still the same: they still requested beef, fish, and lamb. The fish dish was the same Orange Roughy but the lamb was the heart of lamb rump, and the beef was either scotch fillet or filet mignon. The (farmed) 'Cervena' venison was a big hit and we did medallions from the Denver leg. This was about 1 ½-inch chunks of meat from the single muscle out of the leg. It was seasoned and cooked on the (extremely hot) barbecue for three minutes on each side and then placed into the oven to rest for about 5 minutes. The meat would be medium-rare and served with a spicy peach and plum chutney sauce. It was hard to beat. Many customers told us if we were in a major city, they would be lined up at the door trying to get in and we could charge a lot more than we were getting, without a problem.

These are the times you like to remember and the ones that gave you the ability to do it again the next day after a long hard night. Still, we knew we still had a seasonal business and no matter how hard we tried, that was not going to change for any of us overnight. Various ideas had come up over a period of time from different types of races to special events. It was a problem when the tourism organization was not consulted, as they were not seen as being an integral part of any special event. So many times people wanted to do an event in the middle of high season or on a holiday when you were already booked out. It was hard to explain to people outside the industry, that you needed to make the events in times when you need people to come—not when you already have more than you know what to do with. New Year's Eve celebrations were an example of this.

Another idea was the V8 boat race. Not a bad idea but they had the set up with the prize money, all in one day. The people in the race and the spectators could come and go all in the same day—usually a Saturday. Then they wanted to know why they didn't get any money out of it. First, they didn't have to stay overnight and secondly the shops were only open half a day on Saturday, or not at all. They also had the idea one time, of having a foot race down the main street to be a fundraiser on Labor Weekend. They would block off the main street and catch the tourists. Now this is the opening of the high season and the people are in a hurry trying to get to their bach and open them up. They don't need a traffic delay while runners come by the cars with their hand out asking for money. They put it together and raised some money for the high school but that was it; not a memorable experience.

Others that have worked again and again if they are done properly are cheese, wine or food festivals, fishing contests, and I think a photo contest would also work with prizes for different age groups and levels. Make it a special time of the year and do a subject or sunsets. The Pohutakawa Festival (we were involved in starting) has finally come to pass after many years. The Thames Coast area has an abundance of Pohutakawa trees that bloom usually from November to December and the first year was a success. With some help it could grow into a multiday event and this is before the high season when we still need help.

It is a shame but it seems that the different groups of people are afraid they are going to get left out and not get their share. This attitude you could see especially with Thames proper. The town is situated in a great spot and at one time was promoted as 'Gateway to the Coromandel Peninsula'. Then the people in town were afraid that gave the impression that town was just a place to pass through to get to the peninsula. They wanted this promotion stopped.

Another one was the promotions with Tourism Coromandel and the town name of Coromandel. A lot of complaints came in that the promotions of the Coromandel always sounded like they were for the town and not the peninsula. To some degree this is true in terms of confusion. Some people are hell-bent to get to Coromandel only to find a small town with a few attractions. They never realized the promotions were to experience the entire Coromandel Peninsula and what it had to offer as a whole.

To this day this sort of petty attitude still exists. Some people will spend more time complaining and trying to take something apart rather than try and build something. An example of this was when Pam and I were asked by Tourism Coromandel (by way of Lynn Banford) to do a reservation service. This came from the comments that had been made by Pam to one of those on the Tourism Board and others, about chain affiliation and inbound operators. It seemed that inbound operators would prefer to contact one central reservation point to make the needed bookings and be done. They would have confidence in the booking if it were a chain and was backed by more than just one operator.

Now our problem was that a lot of the places on the peninsula were too small to belong to a chain. The few that could usually did and you could see the big increase in business they got. This was true of the little motel at the bottom of our hill. It was a bit of an old sort of place but when he joined 'Best Western', you could see overnight, that the number of cars in his parking lot increased greatly. Our idea was to get a representative number of properties on both sides of the peninsula and then offer a central office for inbounds to contact for reservations.

This idea was put forward at some of the meetings with the operators and no one wanted to do the work. Finally we told Lynn that Pam and I would do it for a nominal sort of fee. We wanted $25 per month per property, plus an initial set up of about $100 per property. After this it would be 10% commission on bookings. This would be a pilot project and subject to revision at a later date.

A number of the other properties said they would join and we were off. We signed up about 9 properties as I remember. We packaged them up and worked with Tourism Coromandel promotions that they put together. One was a promotion that was a fly/drive, out of Australia. It was surprising how few inquires we had. I think it went to show again that the peninsula is not a primary destination for Australians. We are just too quiet for them, with only bush and beach walks.

The good news for us was the *'Friar's Guide'* that Pam had heard about from another operator. It was a most beautiful book being put together by a photographer who had travelled the country taking pictures for *'AA gardens'* book. He had come across places like ours in his travels and realized that no one made a guide book for them. We were able to get under the wire for his first edition, when he came and took some photos and we placed an advertisement. He made arrangements to send a copy to each travel agent inbound operator in Auckland, the New Zealand Tourism board to send to their offices overseas, and to shops overseas to sell.

The book was such a work of art that people would buy it just to show their friends where they had stayed around the country while they were in New Zealand. It was a big hit and for us it was an overnight wonder. We had more people calling for information and reservations from this one source than any other. It also hit the market we were looking for. Most of the people that we had out of his guide were aged in their late 40's and up, usually much better than average income, out of the U.K. or Europe, and wanted the relaxed view at the end of the day where they could get a drink, have a top-class meal, and never have to leave where they were staying. It was an answer that had been sent to us.

This made the upgrades we had done to our rooms and the building worthwhile. We would have never looked sharp enough for the *'Friar's Guide'* if we had not borrowed the money from John and put it on the mortgage. The rooms and bathrooms ran several thousand dollars each and the new flooring for the entire building was about ten thousand dollars. We had done it in anticipation of the German tours that had fallen over but Friars' saved our bacon.

Like all things, they change. In a matter of only a few years *'Friar's Guide'* got so big it started to look like a small phone book and we started to get lost in the pages. Then they decided to make two books; one that was just B&B, and one that was full service with meals—like us. I don't know that people will buy two books at about $25 each, to see where they will stay, or if they will just pick one and stick with it. School is still out. Now the talk is that they might split the books and do North and South Island editions. I am glad he has had such great success but I am only sorry that it has been somewhat at our expense. The increased competition, or dividing the market up into more places, means we have had a reduced share. We still do well with his book but not like the first few years. How many times do we say, the only thing constant is change? Now is the time to be looking for something else new for us.

CHAPTER 85

A New Job

We were pleased with the progress the lodge had made with the changes but we could still see we were not going to be able to pay the bills. This was especially true if we no longer did the local restaurant trade with its groups and all its problems. I told Pam the only choice was for me to try and find some sort of job that I could do, as well as the lodge.

I started reading the weekly paper and tried to have an open mind. I didn't have much faith in the jobs that were advertised that told you how you could make lots of money from home with no effort. I did run across one ad I told Pam about and that I was considering applying for it. She read the ad and was not impressed. She was afraid the job was in Tauranga and I might have to move there. She felt it also sounded like a sales job after training. I gave the number a call and the man that answered the phone told me the manager was out but to go ahead and send him my resume and he would tell him that it was coming. The cut-off was supposed to be in the next few days.

Pam was kind enough to help me rework my resume and get it to the point it sounded like something. Since we knew it wasn't in the automobile industry we played down the automobile part and pushed more on the education and other training in insurance and selling the oil well shares. Pam was good in how she could change the focus to what she thought the people were looking for.

A few days went by after we sent the resume to a Mr Alex Brodie at a P. O. Box in Tauranga. I then got a phone call and he wanted to know if it would be okay if he came by to talk to me about the job. It was a first interview but he wanted to have it where I lived. I guess he wanted some idea of what the person was like and what they lived in as well. I was afraid that if he found out about the lodge early on in the piece it might blow my chances for the job but there was not much I could do about it. I decided to assure him that if the job did go forward it would not be a problem as Pam ran the lodge.

Alex explained to me that Tower Financial Advisory Services was going through a number of changes. One change was they wanted advisors that were trained by their system in how they wanted things done. They would also teach you what products they had to offer and the 'ins' and 'outs' of each of them. The contract would be for one year where they would pay a flat $20,000 for the year on a bi-weekly basis. You would have a review at the end of each quarter and if your sales commissions were more than the base, then they paid you that. If not then you only got the base pay. At the end of each quarter if they didn't think things were working out they could let you go. They would also provide a customer base to work out of that was in the area. It just worked out that they were in the process of buying out the previous advisor, a woman by the name of Kay Berry. She had purchased the clients from the previous advisor on the Thames side so she was the only Tower advisor, or so I thought, on the Coromandel Peninsula. I later was to learn this was not completely true.

Alex ended up offering me the job. It was just as well Pam had played up my insurance side of things in my resume. This was in August 1995. I was to join a group in Auckland for training in a few weeks and I would also have on-going training with Alex. Alex was a real nice understanding guy and it seemed that he was willing to work with my situation as long as I did my job and produced. He appreciated it was not always that easy to get a good honest employee.

At first it was reading a book on the history of the company, 'Government Life', before getting familiar with what products they offered and what they were—the different kinds of life insurance, disability, and so on. I must admit a lot of it was left up to me to dig out of what he supplied and then ask questions. We did have our schooling at the head office in Auckland with several days of talks. This was after several short one-day meetings in the area. The company was in such a state of change that no one seemed to know what was going on. I learned early on that massive power plays were underway inside the company with people fighting for their jobs. 'Tower' was restructuring from the ground up. They were buying up companies and being approached themselves about being taken over.

The salesmen and the Advisors' Association were not happy and I was to learn over time, that they were at war with the company. The company wanted massive changes in the commission structure, as well as renewal commissions. They wanted to move to a fee-based system and do away with commissions. That is, they wanted us to charge a fee to the client for the work we did and the products they purchased would then have no commission. This was too new an idea for many people in the community and they were not about to pay me a consultation fee when purchasing life insurance or investments. All of these changes were coming in very fast and people were coming and going just as fast.

One of the people in the head office pointed out that if they changed the new advisor contracts to a lower salary and then added on reimbursement of motor vehicle expenses, it would be advantageous to them. So overnight, we had a new contract in the mail for $13,000 salary per year and $7,000 per year for motor vehicle expense reimbursement but the main thing I wanted to do, was to learn the job and make some money. I had to satisfy my new bosses first and they wanted me to learn how to do some of the things their way. This was fair enough and I was glad to learn how they did things, knowing we could then modify, each to our own style. I found the presentations they proposed very stiff and they took a long time. I also found that if you did everything they wanted on an appointment, you would be with a client at least 2 or more hours before you even got around to trying to sell him anything. This was part of what the advisors were complaining about.

It took months for the company to come up with approved forms of disclosure for the advisors to use. We then added in personal information and used them at the start of our introduction, as who we were and what protection the client had from us. It may sound funny but it did require you to report any convictions for fraud etc. so that people knew what they were dealing with. I found it a good tool to use as a starting place in the introduction and then move on to what we had to offer.

At first Alex wanted me to try and meet as many of the clients in the area as I could. The records showed we had about 450 clients in my area that covered the Coromandel Peninsula, part of the Hauraki Plains to Paeroa and over to Tauranga. The area was much too large and even the Coromandel Peninsula was hard to cover on its own because of the roads. It took 3 hours for a round trip to the other side at Whitianga. I did as Alex suggested and didn't worry too much about sales although I did make a few when I started out, as some clients were looking to add on to their cover or wanted to redo part of what they had. All in all, I did not do a lot of sales and consequently Alex caught it from the head office. We both decided I needed to try and make a few more sales for the home office and of course as soon as I tried, I couldn't find a sale for anything. But time did go by and sales did pick up.

I had learned a formula at the oil company that the number of calls, leads to the numbers of mail outs, and then to the number of sales. In the insurance industry they had a formula as well, that held pretty much true. If I was calling mainly existing clients, I could easily get 3 appointments for every 10 calls I made, if I wanted to visit. If I wanted to qualify them a little harder then I could get about 3 appointments for every 15 to 20 calls I made. I would usually get one sale for every 3 appointments. My average sale was low at first but started to rise and even then it worked out to something like $150 per sale as I remember.

During the middle of my training they had a motivational conference for the advisors. The new advisors were subsidized by the company and we were expected to attend. I enjoyed the first part of the conference but towards the end of the evening I learned something that I was unaware of—at least to its extent. We had a 'sour grapes' problem with some of the older advisors as they felt us new guys were getting a real 'gravy train' ride with the new training program and perks—including the salary. I was unaware just how bad it was until that night. As the evening was heading to a close I was called over to a table where some of the people were sitting who were out of the Tauranga office, and some were out of Wellington. The Tauranga people started to introduce me to those at the table and I guess as a joke one of them introduced one of the ladies as another man's wife, which she wasn't. This man right off the bat, had a chip on his shoulder and started giving me a hard time about who was I and who hired me. He became angry. As he became belligerent with me I told him I didn't know what his game was but I wasn't playing. I took my cup of coffee and turned it over in my saucer and got up to leave. As I did, he jumped up and his friend grabbed me from behind as he hit me.

Once it was over with and I returned to my room, my roommate wanted me to call the police and file charges on him. I declined as I felt this would only create problems and I still needed a job. The next morning I told Alex what had happened and with me having a black eye, I told him I would return to

Thames. It wasn't until later I found out he was a well-known advisor in the company—in fact one of the top producers and a known bully. As time went on, I heard more stories of how at a function in Wellington he became drunk and cussed his wife out in front of a room full of people. It showed me something I cannot stand in a company and that is if you are a top producer, they will tolerate almost any kind of behavior as long as you produce. This is wrong and shows where parts of Tower's morals were and are.

I was also to find out not long after this, that the company was also after Alex and wanted him to quit. He was a good, honest, hard-working man and the company had taken advantage of him once before when they closed down his agency and made him a manager. Now they wanted to close down the Tauranga office and not pay him hardly a dime. They kept on passing off that it was the last group that had made the promise and they were no longer there at the company and so it no longer mattered. I tried even harder to get my sales up and did so. I started to produce some figures, along with Alex's other advisors, that showed he had a top office. We no sooner got to Christmas and the New Year that Alex told us that the deal had been made to close the Tauranga office and he was out of a job. The head office relented and said they would keep the office open until the lease was up but the office would have no staff and the advisors would each have to pay a portion for the rent and utilities.

I then asked Alex about my contract and he said to wait until the new area manager contacted me about it. This was Trevor. He had been with the company almost all his life.

My cut-off date came and went on the contract and then Wellington woke up and told Trevor to do something. They did offer me a full-time advisor's contract. He started to spend more time with me and about once a month would come up the coast and set targets for me. He was reasonable most of the time and as the truth became known, the company was glad to get anything they could out of the Coromandel Peninsula. It was a large area and most advisors did not find it economical to service. For me it was fine, as I wanted to supplement my income at the lodge. Now it was up to me to keep the balancing act going between 'Tower' and the lodge.

CHAPTER 86

ON MY OWN

Trevor had his hands full with some of the advisors. It was unfortunate but several of them were not honest. A number of times the client was taken advantage of and the new advisor's pay was a little fatter. Trevor was busy trying to get proof of what had happened and make some sort of agreement with the client.

As I got out in my territory more and more I could see that the previous advisor Kay Berry, had also done several questionable deals with her clients. It was a funny sort of thing; some of the clients really liked her and hated to see her go, while others wanted to have her strung up. As part of my contract I was to get her client database, as well as Don McLean's—who had been the advisor for the Thames area. Kay had some sort of run-in with 'Tower' on how much they owed her but they finally agreed on a figure, and Alex and I went over to Whangamata one day to give her a check and pick up the records. (She had previously purchased Don McLean's, so we picked those up as well).

It was a real surprise when we found she had just thrown them all in a box. It took Pam and I the best part of a week to sort out the files, alphabetize them, and put them in boxes, in order. I started to make a few sales and had been given a laptop computer to use. It was only from having hours of experience at home that I didn't have a problem with it. The manager couldn't help and the service team in Wellington was very little help. The programs they were using left a lot to be desired, when you couldn't select clients by city or area. I came up with a way to do it after about a week working on it part-time. I showed Alex what I had done and with him being well-meaning, he told the head office as he felt it might be of benefit for them. The computer man called me and was a real smart a—on the phone. He wanted to know how I had done it. With his attitude as it was, I ran through it very quickly and skimpily. I wished him luck and got off the phone. It was some 6 months later that they offered advisors this ability; to sort by client address.

As time went on it became more and more apparent that this underlying attitude toward new advisors was getting worse. I talked to two of them who had been hired at the same time I was and they admitted that was part of the reason they quit. Trevor didn't want to hear any of this so I just left it alone and tried to make my sales quota each week and each month. In the wintertime it was less of a problem devoting time to 'Tower', as we had no lodge business. It wasn't uncommon for me once every several weeks, to make appointments too late in the afternoon on the other side of the peninsula. This meant it would be dark by the time I got home and a few times with the long drive, it was between 8 and 10 PM by the time I got home.

I started to build a friendship with a number of my clients and would stay in touch with them even if it were to just review what they had and have a cup of coffee. This would sometimes lead to additional business from them or a referral to a friend of theirs. Some worked out and some didn't. One day I was driving back from Paeroa on the road that goes around the base of the mountains. I had finished with my appointment and it was around midday. It was an autumn day with the leaves falling off the trees and the sky was blue. I looked up and to my right I saw a hawk flying in the distance along with me as I drove. I was approaching a curve and had slowed to 90 km/h. just as I entered the curve, I saw where a car had stopped in my lane. It was just about where the road went straight again. I hit the brakes hard and had smoke coming off all four tires. I saw wasn't going to be able to stop and with deep drainage ditches on each side of the road I would end up turning over. I looked up the road and saw a couple of cars coming, with a large truck at the front of the row. I decided to take my chances anyway and hit the accelerator, swerving out and around the broken-down car. The truck hit his horn and I went in the space between the car and the truck. I don't know how I made it through the gap to this day. I can only think that it was not my time to go; at least not then and there.

I told Pam my story after I got home that day and she didn't think much of it. We both agreed, and had for a long time, that the roads on the peninsula are dangerous. People don't drive on their side, they stop in curves, and they speed like crazy—just to name a few of the things they do.

The previous year had been good at the lodge and this year had been no exception. 'Tower' was starting to pay off, even though they had replaced Alex with Trevor. They had been pushing me buy the laptop computer but wanted too much for it. They were also pushing us to buy a new laptop, as they no longer would supply one. They also started changing the rules on the client base. When I went with them they told us if we serviced the clients for 3 years they were ours. We would get renewals off of them as long as we serviced them. After the 3-year mark they would place them in our client records as us owning them. They now said this wasn't so. They wanted us to buy them from the corporation. As I remember this would be about two or three times the amount of their annual renewals. The company would set up a paycheck deduction if this is what we wanted to do. Otherwise when later on we wanted to sell our register, these clients would belong to 'Tower'.

I told Pam we were looking at a situation where the renewals would do nothing for the next several years but pay the note off with 'Tower' and a fair chunk of my pay on new sales would go to paying off a new lap top computer. I would still make money but not as much since I was basically doing it part-time.

We had started to do a number of projects around the lodge and with our civil engineer friend Terry Goldsbury's help, we were able to move one of our parking lots up by the east end of the building. The one at the lower area was made smaller with a garden between it and the section below.

. . . And this is when Sam first went to the doctor with a 'sore back' (from his undiagnosed prostate cancer) . . .and probably why he stopped his recollections at this point. I suspect his story just got too painful for him to want to recount it from here on.

CHAPTER 87

All in a Name (Postscript)

The other day as I was reading my A.A. magazine that came in the mail, I came across an article about the names of cars—not only in the U.S. auto industry but also those in other parts of the world as well. It reminded me of many thoughts and feelings that spanned over the last 40-plus years.

It is obvious that the family has had varying degrees of relationship with and around the auto industry over this period of time. The article goes into great detail on the nomenclature that it claims began in earnest in the 1950's, and was in its heyday in the 1950's and 1960's. It was not just the names as I saw it but a real effort to conjure up emotions and feelings with a name plate that was attached to a new model. Each year or so, you knew a major change would take place as the industry would not allow the competition to get ahead.

The American auto industry was determined to supply what it thought the public wanted and if a little worked, then a whole lot must be better. The chromium-galore models, the fins, the horsepower and gasoline guzzlers, all hold a place in the industry's history. However, the name did not always match the models. In one picture I have Dr Joe getting out of the back of his 1959 Chevrolet Impala 4-door hardtop, The sleek, small, agile impala does not resemble the Chevrolet Impala. The Chevrolet was more like an aircraft carrier on wheels, in size and handling characteristics. I sometimes wonder now, that with the large back-swept wing-type fins, if only we could have gone fast enough, surely we would have lifted off and maybe even obtained orbit. This was especially true of the GM lineup in the 1959-1961 period. In this part of the world these larger-than-life American cars are known by the generic term of 'yank tanks'.

Other names in the article that I had forgotten about that it reminded me of, were used at different times to try to convey that special meaning . . . Chrysler's Imperial, De Soto's Diplomat, Rambler's Ambassador, Pontiac's Star Chief, the Nash Rambler, Mercury Turnpike Cruiser; and then with the space age . . . Galaxy, Satellite and Skyliner. Then there was the power . . . Cobra, Stingray—and what is a Starfire or a Superbird? The American marketing came up with names like Thunderbird and Plymouth Fury—while the British had the Morris Oxford and Austin Cambridge.

Other names from other parts of the world that are just as famous when they are at home, are the Capri, Cortina, Austin, the Mini, the Hillman Hunter and the Avenger. The cars were small and usually a 4-door model. In the rest of the world, cars have always been relatively expensive, and operating costs were a major consideration as well. As the Japanese came into the market they had several best sellers with names like Nissan Bluebird, Subaru Leone . . . and then some models they shot in the foot with a name like Mitsubishi Starion (seems it was supposed to be Stallion but that it hard to say with a Japanese inflection). This was in answer to the Nissan Fairlady (sort of like a 280Z). Why would you call it a Fairlady? It seems that for a period of time in Japan, this was a recognized problem and that is when we got the 120Y, 808, and the rest of the alpha numeric combinations.

They then moved away from this and we have the later Corolla, Corona, Accord, Prelude, Civic, City and many more. The variety of models made by the Japanese only became apparent to me after I moved to New Zealand. At first, it was some American GM, Ford and Chrysler remakes, with a number of British cars around. The Rover, the Mini, the MG, and various other makes. Then the Japanese used car market opened up here. For the first time in this country's history, a person could buy a car that was only a few years old, with things like electric windows, air conditioning, automatic transmission and so on. The interesting thing was that they all had between 45,000 and 53,000 kms on the clock, and were all priced from about $9,995 to $30,000 NZD at the time . . . if you could find one like it. The cars had front fender-mounted outside mirrors that looked like upside-down hockey sticks. This was a dead giveaway that they were 'used Japanese imports'.

At first, the number of models coming in seemed to be endless. As time went on, this became less of a problem as people realized there was a reason for the number of 'one-offs'. Nobody in Japan wanted them and so you could not get parts. Strange and unusual stories of a broken windshield a person would wait 6 to 9 months for (and then it would cost $1,000 or whatever the importer felt like charging) were not uncommon. The auto industry here protested and tried to get the imports stopped. Stories of unfit vehicles, speedos that had been spun, and false documentation (year, make etc.) all came up time and time again. At the end of several years, the government said it would watch more closely but the industry has been unable to stop these imports. The average New Zealander can now drive one of these—and does. Previously, he paid the same price but drove a 10 to 15-year-old British or American-made car that belched smoke and usually had a spun speedo and an expired inspection. It was a good $500 to $1,000 U.S. car—he just had to pay more for it here.

The industry has settled a bit more now. I have purchased two 'imports' since we came here. The first was a Nissan van that we drove for about 8 years until it was worn out. Now we have a Toyota van that is a 1990 Liteace model and it's still going strong with over 100,000 kms on it (that I know of). The names have settled down a bit more since the early days, with poor old Nissan falling on hard times and in a real financial mess at present. When things go wrong they really go wrong. They have one car named Nissan Laurel but how could they even sell it in Japan when most Japanese would find the word 'Laurel' unpronounceable? You surprised I speak your language?

Without a doubt, the industry has undergone many changes over the years. The changes have not always been easy for either the industry or the consumer and at times I am not sure if it was worth all this pain for either of them.

CHAPTER 88

AUNT LUDMA

Letters sent to us in New Zealand from Austin, Texas

(1988 to 1990)

MY BROTHER, JOHN by Ludma Kopecky.

I remember him when, as a child, I ran across the field to greet him on his return to school. Tom told me he was a prince (if at that time I knew of princes). He graduated with honors was Salutatorian at Sam Houston Normal Institute in Huntsville, Texas. At that same time, my brother, Joe, was graduated as Valedictorian. They were both bright, ambitious, intelligent—and sometimes, as little boys, partners in crime . . . such as hiding all the eggs they found before Mama got to them, in the bushes as 'nest eggs'. When they lived on the farm, John's further education was curtailed because of home responsibilities, and later, the sudden and tragic death of father (Papa). There were five of us—four little girls (d vu ki, as John affectionately called us), and then the 'blessed event'—a boy!—Laddie. Was he ever a dear, dear baby, all his spoiled life, but useful and intelligent. To his dying day, John loved him and affectionately called him "lada".

It was my father's dying wish that all of the younger children be educated, or at least have a go at it. John, being the eldest, 'ruled'—not with a rod, but he never spared the Chinaberry switch. But he was a teacher. He instilled in us five youngest 'criminals', the love and necessity of learning, of books. He never failed to keep us generously supplied. He fulfilled Papa's wish with the understanding that as teachers, we pay him back. We did—in a way—but we could never pay him what he sacrificed. He was always a bit partial to me, even when he gave me a two-way compliment. I was only seven years old when I was late carrying water to their parched throats in the hot, summer fields, and he said, "you'd be pretty if you were more thoughtful". Did I ever swing my black pigtails and smile with my black eyes! I never forgot that compliment and I'm 87 years old now.

He did not marry until we were all able to take care of ourselves. He married a lovely young woman who came also from an ambitious family . . . an only daughter in a family of boys. He and his wife Agnes, had three lovely daughtersand now I'll let them tell it all. L.K.

Texas,
August 12, 1988, 4 PM.

My dear Sam, In spite of the fact that I knew you mostly as a child with a very good appetite when at the ranch, I also remember you well; the last two times I had the pleasure of seeing what you had made of the tough little man who loved pinto beans that Grandpa Joe cooked over the open fire—so sleepy that Dr Joe punched you to wake you. Then suddenly, you were grown and quite capable to care for a handful of little Kopeckys. The littlest one as you held him (at a gathering at Grandpa's), was slowly drinking beer out of a bottle! Chip off the old block—and Grandpa. From that time on, I had not seen you until you and Pam came to visit—delightful, but too short. Your personality and easy manner, in spite of so much hair, reminded me so very much of your father as I knew him—the whimsical, dear Dr Joe Willis. He was always a delight—except when he wasn't—for he was all boy. Golda would say, "now, this time, I'm going to whip you Joe Willis!" And he gave that enchanting smile and would say "Oh Mama, you wouldn't; she didn't".

At the ranch, one day, he was reciting his heritage—what he got, from whom. From his father, the love of beer (he was drinking with me); from the Willis's, lack of potassium, and poor teeth and bones (Golda was furious)—"poor teeth Willises". Golda would hit him with the fly swatter! From Grandma and Grandpa, love of a large family. By that time he was out of breath and imagination—but full of good humor and appetite.

There are many stories I could tell of "JoJo" but I am inclined to take too long when I speak of someone I had loved so dearly through all of his life, so sadly and untimely ended but a blessed deliverance. My dearest love, Ludma Kopecky.

I had re-written the story of my brother Joe, about a week before I heard the sad news. Always it seems that I do not do it justice but if you think you could stand it, I'll mail it to you. Someday I may write "JoJo", Joe Willis. Send me a card of New Zealand. Aunt Ludma.

MY BROTHER JOSEPH (DR JOE) by Ludma Kopecky.

Almost from his childhood on, he was driven by a zest for knowledge—something besides the daily chores and duties on a poverty-stricken farm. Reach, he thought, for the stars and the moon, so beautiful seen from down on the farm—a challenge. So, with his parents' eager consent, he entered the Sam Houston Normal Institute and with the highest honors, received his certificate to teach school—especially, the country schools he knew best.

Good looking, with an abundance of shiny black hair, always neatly combed, he was very popular but he never forgot the stars and the moon (his goal).

University of Texas was next. He waited tables in the student houses and did other jobs until he became better known. He became an assistant teacher in the Blind Institute in Austin. He was popular there and when he came home he brought his little sisters ('The Quartet') gifts, that his patients had made—really lovely.

He did not have much time or money for romance but of course it did happen—a minister's daughter—so he joined the district church and for a time it seemed that he might choose to be a minister too. She was, of course, lovely, and knew how to make the most hard-to-stop-just-tasting candies, which she generously sent to Joe's little sisters. She commented on a picture she saw of me (I never forgot), she said, "You have a bewitching dimple in your chin!" (I think it's disappeared). But her name was Smith and Joe's was, oh dear, Kopecky. Too much for a Smith family. So they parted, and dear Joe entered medical school in Galveston.

The grind with the ever-present need to eat etc. had to be met but with the help of brother John and sister Amelia, a teacher, he made it again, with honors—and he still had all his beautiful hair.

Pinch of penury and all his duties, never seemed to deter him from some romance and social activities. He was devoted to his heritage and found time to make friends who felt the same, and spoke and sang in more than one language. Also, the lure of the good Czech pastries etc. and the very pretty brunette who came with it, was well—until here she came . . . Golda Willis.

It was in the Gulf, in the rolling waters in Galveston, one stormy evening that they met. As Joe can recall, Golda was near drowning and Joe was there to rescue—and so they met. She was then in training at the John Sealey Hospital.

So the romance slowly progresse—slowly? No. And then "the best laid plans of mice and men", Golda became ill—rheumatic fever—and her nursing career was never quite finished, and she had to return to her West Texas home. She wanted to give up any romantic plans but Dr Joe was adamant. For how long I do not know, until he brought her to our farm home. I was home from school for the occasion and it was love at first sight, as far as Golda and I were concerned—and it lasted, always. She had lovely black hair, and a beautiful smile and complexion—and she loved me. I was almost 16 years old, and then the war came—or was. Dr Joe enlisted as an M.D. and Golda was with us for a while. Then she attended the School for Women in Denton, Texas. Dr Joe served a great part of his service in Siberia until he returned to the U.S., bringing as always, gifts—from the Philippines etc. Mine was the 3 monkeys—can you imagine—"see no evil, hear no evil, speak no evil". What a gift to throw at me. Vlasta, my sister, got the pine cloth—it was like a dream. She made a dress out of it to wear at the U.S.T. He had a pet bear, which thank God, he kept at the Philippines.

So, at last Dr Joe and Golda had some time of their own, I think. They settled in El Campo, Texas and Dr Joe started that gruesome 'do everything' private practice medicine. He purchased a large car that was like his practice—everything. I can't quite remember its make. I think it was something "olds" mobile and it was always having trouble. That's when my baby brother became a mechanic and that's when my darling little Joe was born. Such a tantalizing smiling little package. The little girl called him JoJo and it stuck, even after he was grown. To me, he's still JoJo.

It was a rugged practice in El Campo but happy and then a call from The School of Medicine in Galveston came, as a request to join the medical branch then, under Dr Stone (not for long). So a new life—a busy one—and not too much financial boost.

I was then in nurses' training. It seemed that all my life I went to school where either a brother or a sister was a teacher, so I had to behave. Smile, but not show my teeth! Because it might seem that the relative was partial. So, when I found that my brother, Joe, was to be on the medical staff, I made the comment that if I had to have a course under him, I'd leave school. Somehow the word got out! And when Dr Singleton quizzed me in surgery, he really drove it in. Joe was on duty in the diet kitchen—tired and sweaty—and I threw the answers back in speed. He said, "I'm ashamed of you". I asked, have I failed? And he said "No, you made 80, but it should have been 100!" (So, "they always pick on me. They never let me be. I'm so very lonesome and so sad. It's a long time since I've been glad. I know what I'll do bye and bye. I'll eat some worms and then I'll die. And when I'm gone you'll wait and see. They'll all be sorry they picked on me.") That's what it costs to be born in a family of teachers. On State Finals I made 96—and Joe was proud of me.

After so long a time, Joe became head of internal medicine (over Dr Stone's almost dead body), and sassy blue-eyed Mary, was born. She was the darling of her Daddy's eye. Nothing she did was ever wrong—little Joe was "that mean and jealous", he broke his arm. Golda was under sedation when I was the attending nurse in the delivery room. Because she really loved me and always told me my nose was not big, she let the cat out of the bag when she drowsily said, "Is that my little girl a-crying? I hope she is like Ludma but I hope she doesn't have a nose like Ludma. Poor Ludma". (She always denied saying it.)

Since the Siberia days, the Kopeckys and the Reitzels were friends. Dr Reitzel too, had served in Siberia, and so was his very charming wife also on the staff, in her capacity while there. So, Dr Reitzel, through Dr Joe's recommendation, came to be on the medical staff in Galveston and succeeded Dr Joe when he resigned to private practice in internal medicine in San Antonio, Texas. But his destiny was not yet to be stilled. A call from the University of Mexico City came to invite him to teach medicine in Spanish (he had become quite a linguist), and so the Kopecky family, bag and baggage, Mary and Joe Willis, spent a glorious colorful year in Mexico City. Flowers, flowers—"Xochimilco" and all. They made many noted friends, and came home to find they had forgotten eggs in the refrigerator when they were hurriedly packing for Mexico. They almost had to leave again—never a dull moment in the Kopecky family.

Besides his professional achievements, he had other talents. Where he learned to play the piano, I do not know but he loved music, folk songs, national hymns etc. Still so busy in his profession, he organized an orchestra in which he had talented members of his staff. They specialized in folk songs, dances, the waltzes, one step—"put your little foot Mazurka"—all those beautiful, heart-warming dream dances, never to be forgotten. They practiced in Golda and Joe's home. Dear Golda, I don't know how she stood it. The families of different nationalities—mostly Czech—joyously attended those dances. They were really super. In good taste with wonderful music—especially waltzes, in which he proved his 'light fantastic', besides leading the orchestra. I adored to be his partner. I came to those dances from Austin, with my car full of U. of T. students who also loved the songs and dances. Then we had scrambled eggs, bacon and coffee at Golda's and Dr Joe's, before we departed for Austin.

The final chapters of Dr Joe's life were as full and interesting as the previous. He bought a 100 acre ranch in the very picturesque country just out of Boerne, Texas, only about a mile from the 'nameless cave'. The ranch was still in its natural wildness where wildlife, deer and, as the song goes, antelope play—plus other small animals and snakes. There were only shacks, country kitchen with equipment, and a large cistern for rainwater—clear, but oh, what a haven to come to, for rest. A cow and calves and a beautiful saddle horse (especially for me). There were also caves, caves, caves. A little slimy one, dark, and as far as I was concerned, a forbidding one I especially hated. I had only just, about a year before, had my first visit. Still limping from the compound fracture of my right leg at the ankle, which I sustained in a car wreck (plus a few other injuries), I did not want to go into that awful dark cavern with water up to my chin. But my bachelor brother who was tough and wiry, and whom everybody loved, just would not "let me lay". With only a lantern to light that awful dark 'hole', I carried on, my teeth chattering. It seemed that we had gone a mile. I said, "Jap, please is there some way so we wouldn't have to wade back?" He said cheerfully, no, but "just keep your chin up—come around this protruding stalactite and try to swim". I felt like dying in that cave and not have to go back. Jap was the beloved bachelor of the Kopecky family and caretaker of Dr Joe's ranch. We made it back to the cabin. It was wonderful to see the daylight, clouds, blue skies, and the heat of a summer's day.

That evening there were the guests, for it was a Friday, and the cave was adjoining Dr Joe's property. I had rested a bit and had just gotten over the nightmare of the cave and here came Jap, full of cheer and swinging a lantern in his hand to use on the short walk, and says he "we will now make a tour of the Nameless Cave". I almost jumped—but my leg wouldn't budge—and said "Oh no!" But you don't know my brother Jap, with a pipe in his mouth (I think he was born with it), "Oh yes, yes. You must!". So I picked up some courage and limped along with the rest of the smiling crew who had been there before. The entrance to the cave was lighted and the inside was unbelievable. I had never visited a cave before. The shimmering beauty of the formations was dazzling and so meaningful that it could never have been made by hand. It was celestial. I wanted to kneel down and pray, and dream (I did that nite).

That, among other things, was Dr Joe's contribution to the Kopecky family—and others too. The ranch was wonderful and perhaps the only relaxation that he and Golda ever had. Always there was someone on both sides of the family that needed more than just a home—and Joe and Golda were able to help.

Now, Dr Joe Willis Kopecky, Joe and Golda's precious son, was quite able to take over when Joe took off to the ranch. The fishing there was beautiful. Sunfish, perch, rainbow trout were almost tame. It was a delight. Deep, deep water, clear, yes clear water, but to reach it was a very rugged climb down the hill where there was some danger of skunks, rattle snakes and the almost-flying copper head. But neither Dr Joe or Jap were ever deterred. Sometimes they bounced down in a reluctant jeep—but it was worth it. When you were finally down, and the danger of the rugged tour climb was past, now a haven of nature and fishing.

Retirement for Dr Joe—"who needs it?" He came home from his daily professional duties, put on his frayed at the bottom shorts, an old shirt, tennis shoes, and with his beloved wife, was off to the Boerne far-from-civilization ranch. Here, his also devoted brother Jap (nickname from childhood) was ready, with tennis shoes, country attire, fishing tackle, worms for bait—or other morsels that fresh fish are gullible for—and to the beautiful clear running water, down the rugged hill they went. Golda sometimes shared in these excursions because she too, loved the peaceful country life and beautiful nature. She was at times, in her quiet way, able to catch more fish than the impatient Dr Joe. Jap was the unsurpassable expert in fishing—only bait the hooks and let them enjoy their catch. Never, but never, did the beautiful rainbow perch and trout, look and taste so heavenly. Shame so beautiful and lively a creature could also be so good to put on the table. But, so it was with the tantalizing freshwater watercress salad, too much—and beer to drink (the beer came from 'Osduse', the bartender in Boerne). Don't forget the beans that were slowly cooking over the open fire in the Mexican crock.

It makes me sad that it's all in the past now but what treasured memories of then can be now. That was Dr Joe's pleasure and relaxation after a life of service devoted mostly to humanity and others, until after almost the age of 91 years, he, in sleep, joined his beloved Golda who had for several years preceded him. My memory of Dr brother Joe, is just too much for Reader's Digest—just for his family and the loved ones who shared much of his life and generosity. Ludma, Ludmila Kopecky, with love.

P.S. Dearest Joe: I am now 88 ½ years old and so glad that these memories of you that I can still enjoy are, as the song goes "like a string of pearls" to me. I know you are glad that I have them to keep me happy and not alone. Ludmila.

Texas,
October 1, 1988; Lovely October.

Dear Sam and Pam, It's 3 PM and I have just re-read your letter. Was so glad to hear from you. You reminded me so much of Joe W—when you were here. Even tho' I had not seen him in many years, I felt very deeply, the loss of him no longer on this planet. That's how it is when loved ones go, even tho' for them as it were, it's a blessing.

On the 7th of September, my sister Lilly, 3 years younger than I, gave up–she had been off and on in the nursing home for a month or so, celebrated her 86th birthday at her lovely home on August 23—ambulatory but not always rational, now and then so funny in her flight fanciful imagination, that it was really too much. She was facing a dreadful going by those who loved her—so it is a blessing that she has left us. To spare you further details, I'll mail my story of her that I had written before she died—except the P.S.

Can you believe that leaves me the only Kopecky of the first generation, still in circulation? Alba is in a nursing home, 91 years old—deaf and nearly blind, mentally lucid—wanting to go. I pray and pray that she be released but can you imagine me, of all the Kopeckys, still here able to drink beer, when as a child I was so frail, they fed me wine because I couldn't eat. Boy, I've fooled them all. How my darling JoJo would laugh with me about this situation—maybe we'd have a drink or two over this. I'll always miss him, and remember him as he sang, with a few dance steps—Cervana Vino "bila kolace" (red wine and fruit rolls).

The first drink of whisky I ever had, I took when Dr Joe poured me a glass of 'Johnny Walker'. I was then in nurses' training at John Sealey. And that nite I was off duty and babysitting with JoJo, while Joe and Golda were partying. I had put JoJo to sleep and then drank my glass of 'Johnny Walker' while I took a bath. I have never had such a merry time in just a bath. Lilly and Alba never drank anything but milk and coffee—but here I still am.

I hope you like my stories—I need a bit of inspiration. I have Jap and three others to write. Will sometime write Joe W—as Golda would say "macprice" (much work). You see how easy it is to write to you—"a tie that binds". Love and best wishes—and do let me hear. The lone Kopecky of the 1st generation . . . Ludma—Ludmila.

P.S. I hope you can read my writing (my brother never could) and sometimes my spelling is bad (I can't reach my dictionary).

Love to you both again,
Ludma.

LILLY by Ludma Kopecky.

The youngest, tallest, and most aggressive one of the Kopecky Quartet family. She really should have been a boy when there were three 'females' ahead of her and in those days, the male addition on a farm was needed. So, when she arrived, the fourth girl of the Kopecky Quartet, there wasn't any particular celebration. I am sure my father looked at her and took a drink or two. She was not a beauty then, all wet, no dazzle, in every way it seemed, she should have been a boy!

As a child she had a vivid and fantastic imagination. At times it was more than my mother could understand. She thought that Lilly was a bit addled or without all her marbles. That's because my mother never had any time for any flight of imagination and daydreaming, which Lilly had. Such as the young man who carried her books to school and told her she looked just like her grown-up sister, Theresa (she longed to be like Theresa, who made her dresses and dressed her long hair with ribbons etc.). Actually she looked less like Theresa than did father. She loved animals "great and small".

As she grew older, her pets were not always so small—cows that were not like the docile 'Blue Bell' type. She could train to "lay low" while only she could milk—that cow, we named her Lilly. That cow could never be trained to be docile. She kicked, stomped her hooves, snorted etc. We named the cow Lilly because she liked Lilly.

And there was a horse who loved jumping fences. Only Lilly rode him. His name was Charlie. One day Charlie decided to jump a closed, high gate, with Lilly astride. She went flying over Charlie's head. It could have been a tragedy but the hired hand was standing nearby and caught Lilly in his arms—only chance he ever had.

She seemed to grow more, or faster, than I, so our dresses were nearly always alike (we looked like twins), our hair (long) dressed alike too. Our teacher sister did them beautifully, much like the hairdos of now, swept back and tied with a ribbon on top of the head, and tied with a ribbon below. I guess we were quite striking.

Because we had grown-up sisters and brothers who were also teachers, we had to be pretty well behaved. So much of our school days were where either a brother or sister were teachers, so goodbye any mischief or pranks—not even a whistle or whisper "during books"—it was not fair!

In spite of the horses and other wild escapades, Lilly became quite a tall, dazzling beauty—no 'pimples', fair complexion, and lovely blue eyes—a dare-devil, mixed with 'come-hither' looks. She went away to "seek more learning" at the age of 15 or 16, and fell in love. He was dark (not colored), tall and handsome, an athlete, and a catholic—"dyed in the wool" kind—and she a Methodist—also "fast dye". The parents on both sides said NO, so the two young scholars parted. He became a national basketball player and Lilly went off to teach school.

Teaching had its problems but Lilly made good at it, and then came Johnny—Oh, Boy!—he had joined the navy when World War I broke out. He was very young but the sound of clicking heels, uniforms and all the glory and promise, was just too much for his imagination and duty, so "they just couldn't keep him down on the farm". The best laid plans of mice and men fouled Johnny's military ambitions. He became very ill with meningitis and after many months, had to give up military life for good. However, in his zest for living and making the most of what he was spared in the severe attack of meningitis (he had lost the vision of one eye), he found Lilly. It took more than a little persuasion but finally Lilly took the plunge—and a plunge it was, for Lilly knew very little of what changes to her life this decision would make—still a teenager and bred in the old-fashioned way of what a young bride didn't know until after the ring was on her finger, and a lot thereafter. She had a lot to learn and overcome. As far as I know, she "took the bull by the horns" and courageously, with Johnny's undying love, decided to make the marriage "until death do them part", and so it did.

It was far from an easy life for both of them but the amazing strength, courage and ambition, and the old-fashioned "tie that binds", made a home for the four children that they will always remember with pride as "the home that Lilly and Johnny built". Joy and tears, hard labor, and often the "pinch of penury". Lilly still lives there, with visits to the hospital or nursing home—often necessary. Johnny preceded Lilly a good many years ago but I think she knows he's looking and saying "well done, my honey", as he often called her.

The two sons survived the ruggedness of World War II in its most severe action but came back almost unscathed. The ravages of war, especially in the days of unbelievable ravages of destruction, these are not always seen or known to passers-by.

So J.B.—John Bryce—and Robert, are sons that both Lilly and Johnny can be proud of, and so are the younger daughters, Josephine and Marianna—both a few years younger than their brothers. Josephine knew some of the war too—with two children, she joined her husband in Tokyo, but their stories are theirs to do with what they may. Ludma Kopecky; September 1, 1988.

All I will now say of the four of them (two sons and two lovely daughters) is "well done, Lilly and Johnny. I am proud to have known you, and do take care Lilly. I am hoping that after you have rested, you'll be back in your home that you and Johnny built". With love, Ludmila.

On the 7th of September, 1988, Lilly finally gave up trying. She had celebrated, somewhat, her 86th birthday with a few friends and relatives on the 23rd of August, and from then on she gave up. She will be remembered by many for her love of gardening, cooking, sewing and sharing rare herbs and spices which came from her hothouse and garden, graced her table—especially at club meeting seasons or any special day. Don't forget the kolaches, now so popular—her baking knew no limit.

She spoke two languages and was not afraid to use them both—English and Czech—especially in song. Her voice was very special. She was the alto in the Kopecky Quartet. Now her voice is stilled. I am just going to say "Vaya con Dios, dear sister, vaya con Dios Lilly-Lilly". Forever in wonderful memories, Ludma (Ludmila) September 9, 1988.

Texas,
March 7, 1989; 4 PM.

Dear Sam and Pam, my story of your Dad really does not do him justice but I was a bit slowed up with allergies—especially cedar (I could not go to the ranch during cedar time—it laid me low until spring). Then I came down with something everyone else is having.

Anyway, as you read it, you will know he was a wonderful blessing to the family, even as a child. Children, those days of large families, were somehow more special and cherished than now. No, I am sorry, it's just now they do not always have the country, and so many unattached aunts and uncles!

Why was he "JoJo" until he was a bit embarrassed when already a doctor?

It was Easter Sunday yesterday—so different from the Easter Sundays I knew as a child. The home-made nests of wild and garden flowers, filled with colored real bunny eggs—but I wondered how in the world did Peter get all those colors—and not a trace of the one who laid them? Just plain magic—or a miracle? When it rained and we feared there would not be any, sure enough, there were nests made with rope and filled with wonderful color. Who needs flowers when it rains and there is imagination! That's how I knew Easter. Joe Willis would love my story—I hope you do too, Sam and Pam.

"Tell me", as the little girl said, "will there be any little ones to share your Easter, or is it all in the past?" You are such a wonderful couple and I'm ever glad you looked me up . . . the <u>only</u> Kopecky of the first generation, still in circulation. Who would have thought it—guess the "One up above, loves me" or I would not be here now. I was 89, December 8th.

Let me hear,
Aunt Ludma.

P.S. Shake well and hope you can read it. Would you do me a great favor and send me some New Zealand stamps? I would love it. L.

<u>JOE WILLIS—JOJO.</u>

The third in the second generation, he was the adored, most welcomed little male child. His mother was lovingly bathing him in a basin when suddenly, wide-eyed, he was feeling himself and discovered that he was . . . a boy. Not that it truly mattered to him, but why or where was that extra something that he had not noticed before? It was so very funny that his mother broke out in a laugh and told it! That's the first vivid story of him when he was just a bassinet baby, and there were many more. Always smiling and seemingly happy. I honestly can't remember that he was crying for anything unless there was a very good reason.

No matter, it was enough that he had not only his loving parents, but 5 still unmarried uncles on the Kopecky side, and 6 aunts, also on the Kopecky side. Teachers, teachers, teachers–all ready to help, or give a helping hand whenever they were in reach. He had two rivals or pals. These two older members of the second generation, and young Joe Willis, JoJo, were somehow always pals. They, Annie See and Joe Miller, lived on a farm with "creatures great and small", and all the other wonderful ways that so fascinate children. Before they recognized the labor, they loved the feathered hens and chickens, and the docile cows with their supply of milk for the table. Even the pigs fascinated him, with their grunts, mud, and stuff they chose to bathe in.

So from his early childhood on, he never forgot the charm as he saw it, in that farm. His Uncle Armin who played a mouth harp after the chores were done, and his wonderful Aunt Theresa, who was only about four foot-plus high, but could bake the most mouth-wateringly lovely sweets, that sometimes were decorated with different kinds of fruit or sugar, inside and out. Sometimes she put him in the highchair so he could watch her stir and mix all those goodies. When he was a bit older, it was wonderful; she let him stir some of those wonders that came out after baking. He could never forget even after years later, what life on that farm, Aunt Theresa, Uncle Armin, and the children, meant to him.

That was Joe Willis, JoJo, always. While still a child, his father joined the medical staff with its personnel in Galveston, Texas. He was then about 3 or 4 years old. Before he was born, his father, Dr Joe Kopecky, had joined in World War One, the medical staff, which took him to Siberia. In that service was also another doctor of medicine who had a son about the same age as Joe Willis. The two became very close friends in fun, and sometimes 'crime'. Their mischief knew no bounds. Joe Willis Kopecky and Bok Reitzer. It was a very good thing that their fathers were doctors. So often there were accidents and broken bones that they sustained in play or fights. Young Joe seemed almost at home with his arm in a sling, but always a smile and heart-warming laughter—"oh Mama, you wouldn't!". That was when she threatened to "whip" him—I don't believe she ever did. Winning ways that heal—way had without an effort.

Joe Willis loved his grandmother Kopecky. Sometimes they almost had fights in play but she adored him and he well knew it. He was a poor eater—good food like what makes Uncle Cyril, who had wonderful arches on his feet, and could fight most anyone who crossed him. But he liked sweets—who needs teeth anyway? Grandma took hers out every night and could during the day.

But in spite of his accidents and his delightful childhood, he grew up to be quite a handsome man—never outgrew his whimsical outlook and sense of humor. Delightful company wherever his almost dedicated schedule took him. He was a very good scholar—never a problem there. It just seemed natural to be like his father—a doctor—"no problem". He took his Premed. School at the Rice Institute of Houston, Texas—no trouble—and fun too. He took an interest in the athletic activities of his school, and often joined me, Aunt Ludma, who was a member of the University of Texas Health Service. To see him walking across the campus, all handsome, in front of him a bottle of 'Johnny Walker' in his hand, and a promise of a good time was "held by all". I was as proud as an aunt could be, to sit there with the rest of the Rice boys and sneak in a highball too. Then after the game, the Rice boy Joe Willis, and I, went to my apartment where we had barbecue and Aunt Theresa's sauerkraut, beer, and loved it. Really it was a wonderful clean way to spend a Saturday. That was because Joe Willis was just that kind of gay person . . . fun, easy to be with and self-effacing, and I was always proud to be his aunt. We were pals always.

One of those Rice boys drank his beer almost in one easy gulp. Later on he was in World War II. Friends, friends, all of them.

Joe Willis took his internship in Sealey Hospital, Galveston, and later joined his father in Internal Medicine in San Antonio, Texas. He married a Galveston girl, a teacher, and responsibilities as per carte grew. But except for his hair which seemed to grow elsewhere, he looked almost like Yul Bryner, except much taller and better looking, and spoke better English. When he started a family it seems he forgot to say when and they just kept coming. Boys, boys, and then the very blessed event, at last a girl. I was visiting in San Antonio when Dr Joe Willis came bringing 6-months-old little Beulah Ann. She already had a ribbon in her black hair and he proudly sat her in my lap. She looked lovely, like her lovely mother, the Galveston Beulah. Four boys and Beulah Ann—never a dull moment.

So for Joe Willis and his lovely wife, life became quite wonderful but like the "little peppers", the family with accidents and such, grew and grew, and I did not see much of them anymore. But for Joe Willis and me, it was a tie that still binds—we still had our laughs when we met.

For the rest of my story of my beloved Dr Joe Willis, I shall leave to his children. Joe Willis, JoJo, may be where he had a clear call but to me, I can still see him taking a dance step or two, singing "Cerervino Belakolace"—in Czech. I believe that was the only Czech song he ever knew—the wine song. But he sang and danced it with his usual flair and whim. I just don't know why he had to shed his hair so soon. Such a nice head and such a dear person to remember. "Hasta la vista, vaya con Dios", Aunt Ludma.

P.S. I had not forgotten. Last but not least, Joe Willis was not an only child—far from it. "Forget me not" Mary. Vivid, blue-eyed, curly-haired little tyrant—but that's another story. Both had a heritage—super, on both sides of the family. Cousins, cousins from both sides of Dr Joe's family, to live by—music and dancing, and family lore.

Joe Willis loved it all. He loved to recite at family gatherings, what all he had in heritage and from whom. With his keen sense of humor he brought forth laughter, and some he sent so I dare not mention it here. Poor memory, poor posture, poor teeth etc. etc. He knew and loved them all, especially after a few dance steps and beer. He enjoyed these "carefree" weekends at his parents' ranch, away from his professional duties, in which he so ably assisted his father, Dr Joseph Kopecky.

Dr Joe Willis and Mary in their adult years were dyed-in-the-wool brother and sister—gifted, talented, wonderful people, and I have lived from their childhood on. So forgive me if I don't spell it right, for my nostalgia. The only one left still in circulation of the first generation of the Kopecky family.

Goodbye Joe Willis. I am going to remember Mary next. I hope you are at peace—wings should become you. Aunt Ludma.

Texas,
April 2, 1989, 3 PM.

Dear Sam and Pam, it just occurred to me as I was reminiscing through some of the papers I was trying to throw away (memories etc.) and remembered Sam—the beautiful, interesting and loving . . . by everyone who knew him. Sam—Sam Kopecky—and I wondered if you knew anything much of Sam, for whom you were really named. Someday, if I can ever catch up on chores etc. I am going to write for his mother. She is 90 years now, a little troubled with arthritis (especially hands) but mentally alert. We visit often. She was a great favorite of the K. family—and <u>good</u> looking. The boys were lucky, and so was I.

Joe Willis and Sam were very close friends, as well as cousins and partners in childish prank—sometimes almost crime—and sometimes having to put up with their tough outdoor fathers. When on a fishing trip, after Joe and Sam just had their tonsils removed, they came home after a day or 3, pale and starved, to a wonderful spread from the Golda and Edith kitchen. Both mothers were eager to serve the poor boys, turkey, fresh fish etc. and all that Sam and Joe wanted (throats still sore) was sardines! They remained partners—after time of college and later. But that's another story.

So, to Jo Willis. I do not feel that I have done him a good story—or one that he deserves—but hay fever slowed me up. He was always such a vivid personality as I knew him—from a child on. But I shall send what I have, on. All my stories I hate to do over again because of time, and self care of me and my interests. So please do know that I wrote with undying love and memories. Joe Willis, lovable, loving, whimsical and carefree (sometimes). I still remember him when he came to take me to the Rice-Tex football game, with a 5th of 'White Horse' in his hand. Let me hear. I tried.

Love,
Ludma.

Texas,
December 10, 1989, 5 PM.

Dear Pam and Sam, the 8th was my "happy" 90th birthday—and I don't mind bragging when I say that I had many remembrances, and dressed up to celebrate it—in a very beautiful outfit that Annie had sent. You know, she and Johnny escaped the Californian quake just 18 miles from their home. They felt the tremors over several days but no harm otherwise. Their daughter had damage to her home but otherwise escaped. Annie, she was in the garden and wondered what made her so suddenly dizzy—Johnny was holding the door open for her to hurry and come in. Those two wonderful people have lived a charmed life. Through war—the war years—and now the quake. I guess I'll maybe live to see it in a movie.

I was very glad to hear from you. Shared your report with the Rowena people, Edith and Jack. Made the trip to Rowena with Joe Miller. He's such a dear and wonderful to take a trip with. Survivor of WWII, Annie See's brother—remember?

It is amazing how much I do remember at the age of 90—just days past—but don't ask me what I had for supper last nite. The past, it seems to have been so much more interesting than now. Tho' I must say that I am now, far from dull. I have made a memories garden in which I am trying to represent all of my dear ones. The mountain laurels are for Dr Joe etc. etc. It is a wonderful pastime. I don't know how it happens that I should be the one of eleven children, still in circulation. My sister Alba, is 94, but is in a rest home 5 years—and in a wheelchair—fairly lucid but not able to really enjoy anything. So . . . I hope I can be spared! J.D., Lilly's son who lives here, brought me a beautiful poinsettia plant, a huge box of compost, and a large can for rainwater, for my garden. Even though I was 15 when I left the farm to go to school, I never forgot the joys of the country—like Dr Joe, God love him, and Golda. They shared with all of us, the many blessings. How we enjoyed the blessings of their ranch. The nameless cave, water cress, Irish bean stew and venison! Such wonderful <u>sharing</u> people. Golda with her never-ending conversation. Remember how you, Sam, chastised young Sam finally—after he pulled your leg to come on home—at Golda and Joe's 50th anniversary. He finally turned on his grandma and said "Shut up". You spanked him and took him to the car—it was past midnight! That young Sam was, as I remember, a very alive, interesting young one. I wonder how they all are now?

Mary writes an interesting letter, when she writes one. Even sent stamps and cards for my birthday—but only a note. She stays busy. I do not hear from many of the others. Tommy was a dear, when a child. I do not know much about his escapades after he became an adult—or did he ever?? I never got the boat ride with him when he was Robinson Crusoe—on the Boerne ranch. He was an adorable child.

Your youngest two children, I did not know well. I remember the little boy, still in your arms, drinking beer out of the bottle! Chip off the old block—Dr Joe. Yes, say what you will. The Kopeckys and Golda were at home—in town, ranch, or what have you—with dear, dear Golda, and her sense of humor and love of life. All the blessings I've lived to enjoy . . . so if I am 90, life will have to go on. A very happy Christmas and New Year. Let me hear.

Love and memories,
Ludma.

Texas,
December 11, 1989 (card).

Always a lift to hear from New Zealand! Memories come flooding fast to me at this time. Have a special Christmas.

Love, love,
Ludma.

Texas,
January 20, 1990; 7 PM.

Dear Pam and Sam, What delightful news. A Kopecky to be born in beautiful New Zealand! I felt glad for days. A boy, girl . . . nevertheless. All my very best wishes and fingers crossed. I wont say why or what—secret.

It was dear of you to share your news as Christmastime. How was Christmas in New Zealand—snow or heat? I mailed your card to Edith and Jack in Rowena. Had a delightful visit with them in October. Joe Miller, my oldest nephew—Mama's 1st grandchild—delightful to take a trip with, and so were Edith and Jack. Don't know whether you, Sam, knew them. Their Sam and Joe Willis, were as children, great partners in fun and crime. Never a dull moment with those two, when I took them to the city in my rumble-seat car. They had purchased some funny masks at the S.A. Curio Shop (I didn't know, I was the driver), and almost stopped the traffic–horns blowing! They put those masks on at the Czech folk dance when I was dancing with the very clumsy, no-rhythm, Mr Bucek. I wanted to hit them and Mr B. too. But they loved me, both of them. After they were both in college—Joe in med. School and Sam in U. of T.—they met during a holiday in Houston for a ball game. Later they purchased a fifth of Bacardi and on a rainy night, slipped on the sidewalk, and so did the Bacardi. No more dinero and no more Bacardi! So they sat down in the rain and cried—so the story goes. They were a lovesome pair when small, and ever after.

I do not believe that I sent you my C.W. story before—so I'll send it to you now. It was among my first, so I hope the spelling is not too bad. I am the one K. whose spelling was poor—don't know why. C.W., Cyril, as I knew him in childhood, was a very handsome knight. So was Sam, only not as rough as his Dad. I missed them in Rowena. Jack is over 6ft tall and still handsome but not curly-haired any more. I always loved him—so I hope the new one inherits both looks and daredevil from the two I knew so well, and loved. And my heart goes out to both of you.

Love,
Ludma.

MY BROTHER, CYRIL—C.W.

As a child, I knew him only as a rough, tawny-haired villain who took pleasure in taunting his four little sisters—especially Alba—whom he scared to death with his new air gun. He and she were at variance with each other—I was too small but he caught me on a cold day when I was trying to get warm at the family heating woodstove in the bedroom. I lifted my dress like a ballerina when—ouch!—a big-headed nail was pressed to my dancing leg. The scream woke my father who was sleeping nearby. He didn't get punished because he was a boy and I shouldn't show my legs. To my grown-up days I had the scar. He called it his 'brand' on me.

Time and change from the ruggedness of farm and country—like a magic wand, had changed our ruffian to an ambitious and handsome young man. His blond hair curled softly around his classic face. He had a year at the State Normal Institute Houston (S.H.N.I.). He was now ambitious for his four younger sisters and devoted to the youngest in the family, baby, and I mean 'Baby'. Dear, dear brother. Where he learned to play the organ (Monarch, which we had) and how to teach music, I do not know. But he had the gift—and nightly it was almost a ritual. We were lined up at the organ and sang the many hymns, folk songs etc. that he taught. There wasn't a national anthem that we didn't know. That's why we four sisters were invited to sing in churches—funerals, all voices—in the county.

He loved animals and had a veterinarian's soft touch with them. In those days, there came periodically a man with wild horses from the mountainous regions. My brother John, who did not have that usual gift with horses, brought those horses for Cyril to train. Cyril was just not afraid of anything wild (including women). John fled into the blacksmith shop to hide when Cyril tried to break Mike—the biggest—I mean biggest, clumsy white horse that ever walked the plains. He pitched and kicked, and pitched—we all ran to hide—terrorized, but not Cyril. He stayed on the beast until he had him tamed. I can't remember whether or not Mike was good for anything. He was just too big (a big, white horse).

He also had a wonderful dog, white and grey—Ponto—which we all loved dearly. One day a rabid dog (which was not unusual in those days) came, and he and Ponto had a fight. Both had to be shot. Cyril was away at school. I cried and cried for days. He just loved all things great and small—my brother Cyril—after he grew up.

Times and the rumbling of a distant war, seemed to bring many changes at home and abroad. Germany was at war with France and England—or whom, as it seemed to me, to find to attack in our peace-loving communities. Even the animals went rabid. That's why Cyril's beloved Ponto had to be put to death—rabies. So I cried and cried. No movie star did it better—not even Norma Shearer. Our home was in a state of chaos—Cyril enlisted into the Air Corp. Wouldn't he just—he was might to fly. He stayed long enough to get the hang of it but it seemed not to be his destiny. A defect in his hearing was found and he came home dejected and a bit hard to live with. I was away at school—homesick and scared, and crying puddles in wartime movies.

I lost touch with C.W. My teaching days began, and C.W. stayed at home to help keep the home fires burning—especially his temper. He was never really a farmer. He had a classic vision of what a farm should be—like raising rare vegetables—celery, broccoli and such, but cotton and corn were just not his dish. He did odd jobs such as raising white-faced cattle, selling—and to my grief, selling and butchering them for sale at the Saturday market where I kept 'books'. It was amazing how he knew the choice cuts without any 'learning' from college. You can't imagine what those choice cuts were, for less than 25c. I only ate grape nuts and jelly when that day was done but C.W.'s pockets did jingle. He always seemed to have ready change, come what may, and the girls were ready to share what he had to offer. I held my breath for fear he'd choose the wrong one. In my adoring eyes he was a Prince, and not to be taken lightly—at a very young age I was very particular—and the females he sometimes brought home just didn't seem—at least to me—to be the right choice. Too loud, too ready, and not my choice for lovely C.W.—and then low and behold, he came one day and brought home his bride, Edith. It was, as far as I was concerned, love at first sight. He valued my opinion but this time he did not even have to ask me. She was and still is to me, beautiful—lovely brown eyes, olive clear complexion, hair to match, and a smile and voice to match it. Dear Edith. I guess she really didn't know what she was getting into when she saw the girl Quartet and baby brother—all still at home, almost in judgment. But her charm invaded us—and especially my mother who, to her dying day, was devoted to our blessed sister Edith.

Edith Crouch. She was a great influence on Cyril and perhaps vice-versa. They tried rice-farming at first but it didn't seem to fill in their style, so they moved to West Texas and started teaching school—first in San Angelo, Texas. Then later they moved with their two beautiful sons, Sam and Jack, to the historic and unique town of Rowena—a place where "men were men". The doctor was known by all, and food was rare and plentiful. With Sam and Jack, who could ask for more. How "Mother Kopecky" loved them, especially Edith. "Mother Kopecky" really loved her, and shared their joy and problems. Problems there were but there was a sort of sharing element or love, in that small town, that seemed to be a gift and quite rare. I spent a lot of my vacations there—usually tired and worn out from my professional duties. Edith and Cyril's home and what they had to offer, was a haven to me. I liked their friends. The wonderful air—none other like West Texas with its wildlife. Tang in the air and hospitality. To Cyril, I am afraid I was a great disappointment—even if I sat in the sun all day, hoping the crappies would surely bite. He knew me only as the youngster who sprained both her thumbs trying to catch his fast balls. But I was tired—after 24-hour duty at the U. of T. it was sometimes hard to respond to the ruggedness of country living. My apologies Cyril, I know I was, at times, a disappointment—not the eager youngster you used to box with. To him, I was no longer the favorite sister but to Edith I was always the same, and my memory of those classic days I spent in Rowena, will never die. I love you Edith and Jack, Ludmila.

CHAPTER 89

CANCER

**"Life is a test. It is only a test.
Had this been your real life it would have come with further instructions."**

(from American Cancer Society Prostate Cancer website)

Excerpt from American Cancer Society Prostate Cancer Resource Centre:

(a message from Sam—who was not high risk—for all the Kopecky males . . .

Prostate cancer is now the leading cause of cancer among men and the second most frequent cause of death from men's cancer. Its incidence has increased by 50% since 1981 and mortality from this disease has continued to increase. Previously most men died of other illnesses or diseases before dying from their prostate cancer. We now face increasing morbidity as men live longer and the disease has the opportunity to progress.

Screening for prostate cancer in men without any symptoms of prostate disease can help detect cancers at an earlier stage when, on average, they are smaller and have spread less than cancers discovered because of the symptoms they cause. These tests can often detect prostate cancer at an early stage when treatment is most likely to be successful and for men appropriately treated for cancer that has not spread beyond the prostate gland, the five-year survival rate is 100%.

The American Cancer Society recommends that both a PSA (prostate-specific antigen) and DRE (digital rectal examination) should be offered annually, beginning at age 50 years (to men who have at least a 10-year life expectancy), and to younger men who are at high risk. The latter group are defined as those with two or more first-degree relatives (father and a brother, or two brothers) for whom it is recommended, screening begin at a younger age—45 years, for example. While it does not provide a definite answer, it is by far the best screening test available for prostate cancer. The society recommends this blood test, to measure PSA—a protein which is made by prostate cells—as the higher the PSA level (results under 4 ng/ml are considered normal), the more likely the presence of prostate cancer.

Most cases of early prostate cancer cause no symptoms and are detected by a screening examination, which is why screening is so important. Some cancers may be found because of symptoms (often involving urinary function) but these symptoms are not specific, can be benign, or present with other diseases. Although many prostate cancers have spread beyond the prostate by the time a man notices any symptoms, putting off getting these checked out by a doctor can allow the cancer to grow and spread further, making treatment more difficult and less effective.

A Cancer Sufferer's Creed

Cancer is so limited . . .

It cannot cripple love.

It cannot shatter hope.

It cannot corrode faith.

It cannot eat away peace.

It cannot destroy confidence.

It cannot kill friendship.

It cannot shut out memories.

It cannot silence courage.

It cannot invade the soul.

It cannot reduce eternal life.

It cannot quench the spirit

It cannot lessen the power of resurrection.

(Contributed by John Clark)

Summary from Sam's statement to N.Z. Accident Compensation Commission's Cover for Personal Injury (as a result of Medical Misadventure); and Health and Disabilities Commission (under the Medical Practitioners' Act):

Sam first went to our GP in August 1998. After examining him she ordered tests and referred him to urologists in Hamilton, who then performed a prostate biopsy. Five of the six biopsy samples taken were positive, with a recorded PSA of around 120. At the first urology appointment in September, it was decided that correct staging was one of the most important factors at this time before any treatment should be agreed upon. Additional tests were ordered—x-ray, ultra sound, blood tests and a nuclear bone scan.

At a second appointment for prognosis and staging, these latest results confirming a positive bone scan, were reviewed in November 1998 but x-rays and ultrasound still showed nothing. At this point Sam told the urologist about symptoms in his legs and side, as well as his back, and requested additional tests/ scans be run on his spine, to help determine how far the cancer had spread and thus be able to properly stage his condition before starting any treatment. Sam told the urologist he would consider palliative treatment including localized x-ray on his spine, once test results and staging were complete, as he did not want to start any treatment for the cancer until this staging process was complete. The Urologist, Dr Patrick Bary, did not examine him (on either appointment), did not appear to take notes of symptoms, and no other tests were ordered.

This urologist told Sam it was very rare to have spinal tumors and that, as far as he was concerned, it was a waste [of money] to order any more tests. The only course of treatment, he believed, was hormone therapy (HMT), as radiation and chemotherapy were not helpful in this situation. He also did not believe in continual monitoring of PSA levels to follow the cancer's progress. Sam was finally told that if he did not want to start hormone therapy immediately, without additional tests for staging (to see whether it was already present in various organs), he could take the 'watchful wait' approach and see what happened. When asked about local radiation therapy for his bone pain, Sam was told that the urologist did not believe in radiotherapy for this, as such, and felt that HMT was the only way to go—and that he could only have palliative radiotherapy if he did the HMT, as they were only offered tied together.

When Sam left at the end of this second appointment he also asked the urologist, specifically, about his spine and tumors. He was told these were "rare"; paralysis was never mentioned; nor was there any acknowledgement of his (detailed) symptoms in relation to spinal compression. While Sam had been able to research his prognosis and staging on the internet, he had been unable to find the time—while working the lodge summer (high) season—to uncover the extensive information on spinal compression for prostate cancer patients. He was therefore, relying on his health-providers to inform him of potential problems involved in his treatment (albeit palliative care only). He was not in favor of Hormone Manipulation Therapy at that time, as his overall quality of life was good and he did not want to have to contend with an untold number of side effects, if it was not absolutely necessary. He again stated that he was interested in quality, rather than quantity, of life.

Sam visited his GP to discuss what had transpired and she offered to help monitor his 'watchful wait' case, but said her hands were tied and that she could not order an MRI or other additional tests. If he did change his mind about hormone therapy, it could still be started later. [Much later, she admitted to me, that she felt Sam had been "a victim of the health system".]

Up to this time he had still been able to work. Three months later, at the beginning of the second week of February 1999, the numbness in his side and legs increased. Our GP was away at that time and the symptoms worsened while Sam waited for her return. By Friday 12th February (4 days later) he was unable to walk or stand. A locum doctor came to the lodge and arranged to have Sam transported to the Emergency Room at (regional) Waikato Hospital in Hamilton (90 minutes away) to have an MRI done on his spine, as she suspected spinal compression. This showed compression and injury—and additional involvement—of the spinal cord. Sam was started on high-dose IV steroids and hoping to get some movement back in his legs, oncologists ordered localized radiation over the next few days but the spinal injury was permanent, with paralysis from the waist down and permanent loss the use of both legs. He was sent back to (local) Thames Hospital by ambulance and released a few days later. [As his full-time caregiver, I could then also no longer work either.]

At Thames Hospital the following month, a locum consultant oncologist, reviewed Sam's history and examined his condition. He was then diagnosed as being permanently paralyzed from the waist down, with numbness and only some deep touch. The injury done to his spinal cord was found to be permanent and irreversible with the permanent loss of the use of both legs, along with the loss of his bladder and bowel function. With this spinal injury he could no longer work—a situation which would remain a permanent condition. His PSA was found to be increasing rapidly. The oncologist reported that Sam was aware that hormone manipulations would potentially prolong his life was that he was "quite correctly" in his opinion, not prepared to undertake this treatment. He explained to Sam that if the thoracic pain in his spine persisted, he could have further radiotherapy to it since the cord was already irreparably damaged by the tumor. He concluded that Sam was being well looked after by his GP who he stayed in close touch with, and that he was aware he could attend clinics at either Thames or Waikato Hospital.

Sam felt that the urologist who was originally involved had made a number of mistakes and violated a number of his rights under the 'Code of Health and Disability Services Consumers' Rights'. Because of his concerns for future patients in the community, he filed a complaint with them accordingly. The commissioner reviewed it, having been unable to reach a direct outcome under mediation. The contracted Urology Services health providers involved, maintained that the only recourse was approach the Accident Compensation Commission. Sam believed that his request to be treated symptomatically was valid—and a patient's right. "I also did not want to suffer in pain and sickness," Sam wrote to the Commission. "I felt strongly that, as we are all going to die, when it is my time I would rather go, than drag it out and suffer. Even at this stage when I have my days of pain and sickness, I ask myself, why would I want to prolong this? Because of my unnecessary paralysis, I feel I have no quality of life and I am nothing but a drain on the family," he continued. "I would rather let them go on with the life they have left in front of them. How much extra burden and expense has now been placed on me and my family?" he asked. "This has also affected their quality of everyday life as well. Long-term, I do not want to make the situation at home any harder for the family than it has to be. With the stress of everyday life, bills, workload and now me, why drag it out for an extended period and put the family through just that much more? Is not an important part of the treatment, the quality of the patient's life and wishes? What has the system saved on investigative tests for staging, by now having to take care of my paralysis?" Sam asked.

In spite of an objective medical legal opinion from an Orthopedic Surgeon who "believed we did have reasons to pursue our complaints", both commission processes failed to find there was a case to answer as there were no witnesses at either of the crucial prognosis and staging urology appointments. The recorded notes of the urologist concerned were at odds with those of the complainant, and since no one else could say with any certainty, which were correct, Sam's case was dropped.

December 1999,
E-mail from Dr Craig Kopecky:

Dear Dad, I'm sorry it has taken so long to reply—I've been working nights (4 PM to 10 AM) and have been mainly sleeping otherwise.

Unfortunately, the issue of steroids is a catch-22; something I think you have already found out. That is, the side-effects can be as troublesome as the benefit you receive. Originally the steroids were to reduce the swelling in the spinal cord, as a temporizing measure. The radiation therapy was to treat the locally advanced disease at those sites in the spine that were causing the problems. Usually this is effective and the steroids can be tapered (to off at times). I do not know if you have received the max dose of radiation at this point (I tried to read the file you sent but I'm having trouble opening it). It is possible you have reached the full extent of treatment with regard to those areas, and that it did not completely arrest the tumor's progression, thus making continuing steroids necessary. On the other hand, because the steroids cause water retention, osteoporosis, hyperglycemia, and thus can be neurotoxic, they may, at least, be partly to blame for your current problems. Also steroids make the connective tissue weak and that, as I'm sure you know, is the reason for the very fragile skin. It sounds like you are trying to wean off the steroids at present. I think this is worth trying but I am concerned that it is being done with dexamethasone. In general, we usually wean off steroids using prednisone, as it allows for smaller dose adjustments, and thus less risk for side-effects from adrenal insufficiency. Dexamethasone is about 5 times more potent than prednisone. Physiologic doses of prednisone are 10mg in the morning and 5mg in the evening.

With regard to your previous question about prognosis/progression of the disease, I am afraid you were correct when you asked me if it is a waiting game. Bone mets are painful and cause neurologic problems, as you are all too familiar with at this time. However, it is generally not disease in the prostate bed or bone mets, that lead to death. The grim truth is that the final farewell is brought about by organ failure after the cancer has spread to the organs in question, and fully infiltrated them. This usually means liver failure, encephalopathy, and then no longer able to eat or drink. If there is any bright side (poor choice of words on my part), the person with encephalopathy is in a dream-like state and no pain. Other sites of metastasis that may lead to death, include the lungs (rarely fatal in and of itself but may lead to needing O2 to breathe comfortably), and the brain (again, usually leading to a dream-like state that prevents eating and drinking). The last common cause of organ failure is renal failure due to obstruction at the bladder outlet, from the primary tumor itself. The most common cause of death overall, is infection.

I wish there was some way to pass this information to you that did not sound so cold and unattached. The best I can do is tell you how much I love you, think of you, and pray for you. I wish we had been more in touch over the last decade but I assure you I think of you often, and you have helped make me who I am. I hope the above information helps you.

I know the unknown is the most unbearable part. Keep writing, whether you have questions, answers, or notes about your day. We all love you.

Love
Craig, Elizabeth, Brittany and John.

December 1999
E-mail from Dr Charles Kopecky:

Sam . . . I looked at the lab reports you sent. You may be more knowledgeable about prostatic cancer but here are a few thoughts . . .

Appears the MRI shows "slight improvement" from 2/99 (not sure what is "improved")

L3-L4 vertebrae has more tumor involvement (increased lower back pain radiating into leg? Source of increased edema?) Any discussion of treatment/radiation?

Cervical area "ok".

Some T4 involvement, but minor.

Refers to continued involvement of T10 and L3-L4 with spinal compression. Is there more compression? (increased numbness, weakness in lower extremities?) Any discussion about radiation?

Labs look good (would expect some increased liver activity because of medications/ steroids . . . but they are in acceptable range). K+, Na+ . . . etc. fine (Renal function good). PSA as expected. Still no thoughts of hormonal treatment?

How is your blood count—WBC, RBC . . .anemia, immuno suppression?

Possible causes of cramps, weakness, numbness etc. in arms are compression (sleeping on your arm; esp. if you have some muscle wasting), steroid myopathy or Lambert-Eaton myasthenic syndrome (disorder of the neuromuscular junction caused by antibodies in some cancer patients. Characteristics include fatigue without muscle-wasting, ptosis, proximal muscles of the lower extremity more commonly involved, and dry mouth).

Again, sorry, not my area of expertise. Will get back with any other thoughts.

Otherwise, Mrs. Lincoln, how was the play?

(Hope everyone is doing well and anticipating a Merry Christmas). Will give an update soon on the Houston Kopeckys. Really not much to say but I will give it some thought and try to be creative.

Love to you, Pam and Amanda—
Charlie, Heather, Cassie and Lexi.

December 1999,
Response to the Dr's Kopecky from Sam.

I received your input on the various aspects of my reports. I appreciate you and Craig both giving me straightforward information and comments. I really do understand that things keep changing and a lot of this is not 100% black and white. I guess part of the problem is that no one out here really wants to feel like they are sticking their neck out or being too negative about the situation.

I am not negative. I am just trying to be realistic about what the situation really is, and try to adjust my life and time accordingly, as best I can. Dr Josh Dass, the last oncologist I saw, is a nice guy. He has a different (cultural?) outlook toward life in that regardless of what or when, or what you do, you die when it is your time. Thus, regardless of what treatment is used, when your time is up, it is up—so the best you can to make yourself comfortable for as long as you have to last. Then he goes into the standard speech about CHT and getting off steroids etc. (He is working under the first oncologist I saw who was a bit disgusted I wouldn't do CHT.)

The short story is that the standard treatment uses some form of hormone therapy (one or a combination), an operation, or a combination of both. Yet in a number of 'studies' and comparisons, the bottom line is, none of the above combinations—including watchful waiting—are superior to another (including any evidence on comfort or quality of life). "Each patient has to be evaluated on his own basis." Some did do better after surgery or CHT. Some did not. In my case, I have had very little in the way of side-effects or problems with my treatment and they agree that I would surely have some degree of side-effects with CHT.

So why do CHT? Some studies have shown . . . start early, start late, before surgery or treatment . . . it makes no difference in the "effectiveness". Others say it does. They really don't know. Does CHT extend the 'time' you have? I have been told YES and been told NO. I have been told it will make you feel better without the steroid side effects (including pain). Yet they do not want to go into the side effects of CHT that I may experience, and talk of the pros and cons.

At the start of this about 15 months ago, my symptoms on my arms, legs, voice and such, were all present before treatment of any kind. That is part of what makes me angry.

All of the side, leg etc. symptoms were text book for spinal compression. (T10 etc) and my urologist refused to order additional tests when I did request them (MRI etc) when we were supposedly still doing staging. He told me to do CHT, and "maybe" he would consider doing some local radiation on the spine—although CHT was a good general treatment regardless of where it was. I feel if he had proceeded with the MRI and local radiation, it would have prevented or at least postponed, my paralysis, and I would not be unable to work today.

I sleep on my back only; since the treatments as it is the only comfortable position. I have had little or no numbness etc. in arms, except when I previously reduced my dexamethasone. My voice and arm numbness are still a bit of a mystery. My T's and L's are not. The T radiation area is "better" than before radiation on the compression area. The other areas have "grown"—especially the L4 and L5 (no treatment areas). No discussion of additional radiation—only, how about some CHT? I am, at present, trying to reduce my dex. I am down to 1mg per day total now. Will try and hold it at this level until after the New Year. I have also reduced a little, with my diet, and I am trying to reduce the use of the Lasix.

Well, that is about it for now. Do have a good holiday season. Drop a note when you can.

Love to all,

Sam, Pam and Amanda.

P.S. Charles: Other than that, Mrs. Lincoln did enjoy the play, I think!

January 2001,
E-mail from Dr Craig Kopecky:

It has been quite a while since I have had a chance to write an email. Life stays forever busy and there is always some demand on our time. I work long hours to make up for the lack of foresight on the military's part . . .

I did receive your email with all of the specific questions. I know how I would have handled things but I did not want my personal practice style or emotions to influence my answers to the questions you posed. I will try to be as open and frank as I can in my response. I know that you believe there is a single best approach for any problem, given a set of circumstances—a very pragmatic ideal that has long impressed me. Unfortunately, in dealing with cancers of any sort, but especially in prostate cancer that is metastatic when diagnosed, that is not exactly the case.

You, as I'm sure you're aware, are very young to have been diagnosed with such advanced disease. This is one of the factors that likely delayed your diagnosis. Non-specific complaints of low back pain in someone who is very active doing yard work, renovating their home/business etc. would be treated conservatively. That means a few days of rest, followed by back and stomach—strengthening exercises and an NSAID like ibuprofen for 3 to 4 weeks is the standard of care. Without weakness or numbness, or bony tenderness on exam, x-rays would not be taken until the follow-up appointment at 3 to 4 weeks. If things had gotten worse during that time, or even just not improved, a more complete exam, x-rays, and lab work (most likely to include a PSA) would be done. It is likely that the x-rays would be normal. The lab tests would be back in a week. When the result was unusually high, a biopsy would be taken and the results of the path would be returned in a total of about 2 weeks. In addition, the abnormal PSA and back pain would lead to a more sensitive test (most likely a bone scan done by nuclear medicine—again in the same time frame). Once the positive bone scan results and the biopsy were back, a treatment decision would have to be made—either to treat the symptoms or go for full-scale treatment.

Once metastatic, it is Stage D cancer (non-respectable). The best chance at long-term survival is full hormonal manipulation (orchiectomy and flutimide—an anti-androgen) and a platinum-based chemotherapy regimen on one of the newer agents like topotekan. In patients that have underlying illnesses that have a shortened life expectancy based on their other diseases, hormonal manipulation alone is used because it has the fewest side effects and slows the course of the disease considerably. A patient's wishes, in terms of what they want or are willing to put up with in terms of treatment, is always discussed and different parts of the treatment plan are used with some degree of effectiveness.

Radiation therapy is used for pain control from bone lesions. At any time, if anyone comes in with acute onset of weakness, numbness, change in bladder/bowel habits, or "saddle anesthesia"—especially if it is known or suspected they have metastatic cancer (but really, anytime)—they get an MRI that day (or night) and are started on high dose IV steroids.

When diagnosis of cord compression is made (the same day) they have emergent radiation therapy (that day/night) or emergent neurosurgery if the cord compression is from something other than metastatic disease. [Of note, the Gleason score of cancer does not really come into the treatment of the cancer. It is used for prognostic purposes—in other words, it can help predict who is likely to respond the best to the treatment plan. But metastatic disease is metastatic disease.]

I think of you most every day and enjoy wearing the watch you gave me. I wish things didn't happen to you the way they did. I believe that if you had not started off paralyzed, you would have been more willing to consider treatments to prolong your life. I love you and understand we must all make the choices that are best for us, and I know that you must also think of your family. When I get overwhelmed with the things I am asked to do, and start to feel resentment to those who entrust their care to me—because they are making me stay and work harder—I think of you. I do the best I can. I hope things are well. Please write me again to let me know how things are going and I will be more focused.

Give Amanda and Pam a hug for me and give everyone my love, Craig.

January 2001,
From Sam Kopecky to Dr Craig Kopecky:

I have just finished up with the first [Health and Disabilities Commission] hearing with the urologist and I have put down some questions and thoughts on how things went and where they were going.

The main point the doctor and his group made was, that since I turned down hormone therapy, everything that happened was my fault and a result of that decision. They say that this is the treatment—and the only treatment. My argument was that this was but one choice—one of the other choices being radiotherapy for back pain and control of the problem, at that point. They refuse to acknowledge this as an acceptable option on therapy. (In other words, I wanted to treat as little as needed, for the pain, and try to keep side—effects etc. to a minimum).

They even went so far as to say they knew the "outcome" was inevitable when I refused hormone therapy—although they did not tell me or offer any options, as hormone therapy was it. They also inferred that hormone therapy would have been given in an effort to head off spinal compression.

After having heard some of these comments, I decided to try and find out what, if any, other recognized options would or should have been given at some other hospital. I still believe that my request for an MRI and more tests was not unreasonable or that my request for radiotherapy for the pain on a local spot on my back, was unreasonable either.

I feel that with the urologist never giving me any examination, and by not listening to all the symptoms, he missed the spinal compression signs—or did not recognize them for what they were. He still maintains that hormone replacement therapy was the only choice. I am trying to get some doctors to state what they think the choices really were, and which ones were reasonable. (I realize I could take herbs at full moon and sing, but it might not be considered reasonable.)

If you have any additional comments or if you have anyone at the hospital that would like to tell you what they think and pass it on, please let me know.

Love to all,
Dad.

February 2001,
Response from Dr Craig Kopecky:

Hormonal therapy (either surgical or medical, or both) is the cornerstone of treatment. However, your choice to be treated symptomatically is valid—and a patient's right. As a right, no one can withhold other treatments (or fail to mention them) because they don't agree with your decision.

There is NO DOUBT that the doctor that was seeing you was AT THE LEAST providing substandard care, and in my opinion (based on what you have told me of your encounters with him early in the disease) was gross malpractice.

Furthermore, if an MRI was not offered within 24 hours of your onset of symptoms consistent with cord compression, and radiation therapy was not performed—and IV steroids not given within 24 hours of diagnosis by MRI—you would be a millionaire in the States. (THAT IS STANDARD OF CARE!)

Specifically, with regard to recognized treatment options for metastatic prostate cancer, this includes radiation therapy for control of pain in bone mets, and at the prostate bed to control tumor size and associated problems with obstruction—VERY EFFECTIVE for those types of problems. In addition (curative) chemotherapy (not hormonal) is used with approximately 75% partial or complete remission.

I will also ask several friends who are oncologists.

Love,
Craig.

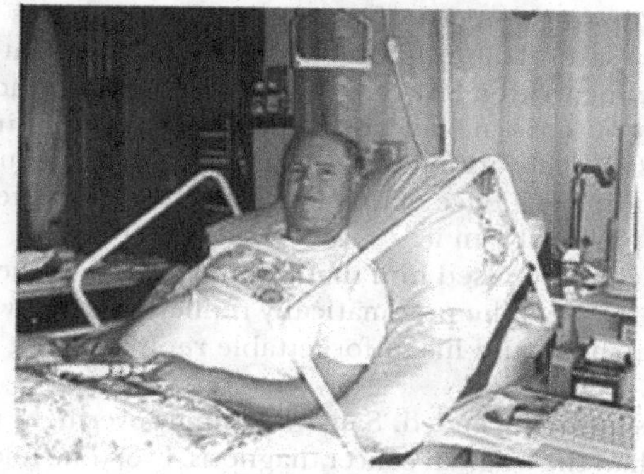

Sam in bed at home after paralysis

Adjusting to living with Cancer

When Sam's cancer was first diagnosed, we knew we had to learn to live with it and somehow not let it dominate our lives. Once he got used to the idea, he was quite philosophical—especially after attending his first hospital oncology clinic where he saw a little girl and her family (babe in arms), dealing with the same issue. He told me then, that he'd had a good life and lived a lot longer than her—or even someone like my own sister who died at only 31 when we were still living in Texas.

Sam's cancer brought us close together again as we made room in our hectic working lives to again share all our feelings. We made peace with each other for any misunderstandings we had had over the years. We found the time to toast the sunsets together again, each night, as we finally learned how to live daily . . . and how precious our lives were. My Dad, who was incapacitated with congestive heart failure, was so distraught at this turn of events that he insisted on getting out of his own bed to come to us (for the last time), and we had a memorable Christmas with my family and our friends. It was a magical time.

We talked about the practicalities of dealing with the progress of this disease, alongside his teaching me to single-handedly run a property/business that was not at all 'user friendly'. His enduring concern throughout the long illness preceding his death was that I was "not ready". He began working on "improvements" to make it all easier for me. He drew plans of all of the lodge's reticulation and maintenance systems, and tried to teach me accounting. But I still would never have been prepared . . . no matter how long he hung on to help me. It was a precipitous learning curve as there was still so much for me to learn even after he had finally gone but as Amanda has since reminded me, her Dad was "superman". He could do anything . . . and everything! I know we'll both always remember the sheer courage and indomitable determination he showed when, so angry and frustrated at his inability to accomplish what he wanted to do to help me, he got me to help him out of his room so he could work on the electrical systems around the lodge, while I lifted and supported him. Then again—ordering us to stand back in case he fell—when he somehow got himself up the stairs to our own dentist's first floor office, when the local ground-floor dentist proved to be inept. After that, our dentist came to the lodge with portable equipment, to work on Sam there—and even did a tooth extraction, with Amanda holding the bedside light for him when I got too 'faint' to help.

Operating on the premise that "you have to be cruel to be kind", almost immediately after his diagnosis, Sam pragmatically confronted me with a letter he'd written to the U.S. Social Security administration office in Baltimore, informing them of his advanced terminal cancer and enquiring about death benefits for his "dependent daughter" and "surviving spouse". He then wrote letters and made phone calls to their Manila office in the Philippines (responsible for expatriate Americans in the Southern Hemisphere), trying to communicate the urgency of this matter to Filipino staff who barely spoke English—before finding out he had to already be dead before they would listen.

Ignoring my tears, in his determination to make me "get real", next he sent me to the local undertaker to choose his coffin and find out minimal prices so he could budget for his own funeral arrangements . . . and when I arrived home with the details (still in a state of shock) he then called them back and renegotiated—and locked in (for three years)—a better deal. He got all the personal information together (birth certificates, ID numbers, divorces etc.), that I would need for his death certificate (in both countries), and wrote to New Zealand's Inland Revenue Department to have our business partnership changed to a sole proprietorship so I would not have any future tax issues. And then at the time I went to fill in his last U.S. tax return, several months after his death, I found that he had photocopied the one from the previous year, and having written SAM KOPECKY—DECEASED across the top, highlighted the parts I would need to copy out onto the next year's form, when it arrived in the mail. Albeit sometimes unconventionally, Sam never stopped working towards helping Amanda and I prepare ourselves for life without him! I have kept on finding evidence of this ever since but I still often struggle with the difficulty of living my life without him (physically) in it.

I will never forget that, having promised him that I would keep him there at home with us, whatever happened, Sam then shocked me when he pragmatically replied that "he would die as fast as he could". Aghast, I told him that was harsh . . . and his unforgettable reply was that "sh—is still sh—, even if you sugar coat it!"

The magic suddenly and shockingly ended. Sam's seemingly-overnight paralysis several months later was much harder to deal with than the original cancer diagnosis. Everyone told me I could/should not bring him back home to live with us, as the two-storied hillside lodge was an impossible place in which to take care of a paraplegic. But aside from my own emotions which would not have let him go anyway, I also knew I had promised to keep him with us "no matter what". Sam was very frustrated and angry, and it took some time for him (and us) to adjust and come to terms with his having lost total control of his life and now having to live with paralysis—something that was the absolute antithesis of his planned "quality of death". In order to cope with the physical realities of his condition (which centered around bodily functions), at the insistence of our holistic district nurse—who was concerned about the health and emotional wellbeing of the whole family—we were finally forced to move him from the inaccessible inside master bedroom, into the lodge's purpose-built disabled access bedroom with its paraplegic ensuite bathroom and outside ground-floor entrance looking out over the coastal scene below.

With this sudden downturn in his medical condition, our GP told us it was time to "send for Sam's family" as he was not expected to live for much longer. He had not wanted his own Kopecky family told about this turn of events but for the only time in our almost 20 years together, after many sleepless nights, I finally went behind his back and let his siblings know through a friend—one of Sam's Oldsmobile salesmen in Texas, who had just stayed at our lodge. I did not believe that this should be just Sam's decision to make, as he did not have to live with the consequences of a lifetime of regrets for things said and unsaid. I know he was glad I did this, as he, quite unexpectedly, then saw and heard more from his family over the next couple of years, than he had for many years.

These were the worst of times . . . and yet the best of times. I could write my own book on them—with its message of facing up to what life hands you and dealing with it, as Sam did! But instead, I will just recount a couple of my favorite memories of Sam's unique sense of humor . . . and grace under fire. He never lost that sense of humor . . . right up to the end. One day towards the end of his life, I went out to his room and he was lying there in an angelic repose . . . eyes closed . . . holding his breath . . . with his arms crossed on his chest. As I leaned over to look at him more closely, suddenly his eyes flew open, he grinned at me and said, "gotcha!" Another time, I went to see him and he was lying in bed with the sheet pulled completely over him, covering his face and head. I pulled it back to look at him and he just smiled up at me . . . "just practicin'", he said.

And, having traded me in and out of many vehicles during our years together, Sam still had not forgotten his automobile sales background. In his last weeks, his growing concern that the van we had been driving for a couple of years needed to be replaced, led to him making a telephone deal with a vehicle wholesaler he knew. Still trying to provide for us, he felt Amanda and I would no longer need a van (to transport him and his wheelchair) and would be better off with a car, to start out on our new life together. So, after watching the newspaper advertisements and looking unsuccessfully around the local car yards, I then drove him to Hamilton to have the van appraised and negotiate a trade-in.

When he could not find a suitable replacement vehicle, he worked with this wholesaler/importer to specify what he wanted from Japan and our Mitsubishi Galant was finally delivered to the lodge during the week he died. Sam got our friend Tom to check it over for him since he could no longer move and could barely even see from his bed. Once he was satisfied that the car was just as he had specified, he only just managed to shakily sign the papers and the dealer took our van back with him. It was his last car deal.

I would like to believe that when my turn comes to pass over, I will be able to muster Sam's qualities of—albeit unconventional—caring, humor, courage, honesty, integrity and dignity. As one of the most important mentors in my life, while he was just as flawed as all of us, he will always inspire me as I live my life, mindful of, and consciously emulating, the consistent example he set. He taught me so much . . . and gave me the beautiful daughter I had always longed for. He is part of me now and will always be with me. I will never tell him to go. Sam challenged me in ways that I could never have dreamed of—sometimes, even in my worst nightmares! Many times during our years together I had wished that Sam was less volatile but the hardest thing for me at the end, as I watched his death steadily approaching, was seeing his 'fire' go out as he became almost saintly. Be careful what you wish for, you might get it!

My other enduring memory of this time was his own practice of the Kopecky medical tradition. For three years, our understanding GP and head district nurse also recognized this and let him run his own care as they called in periodically to confer with Sam, who (like the head doctor on hospital ward rounds), would show them his meticulously-monitored medical charts, discuss his symptoms and possible treatments, and then give them his orders. Knowing his background and real need to manage his own care, we all tried to empower him as he researched, analyzed, recorded and controlled every aspect and stage of his illness—right up until his death, when he reluctantly had to let me take over his medications and (input and output) fluid level recordings, finally realizing that his increasing morphine pump delivery was affecting his own ability to do so.

While there are some lessons in my life that I don't care to repeat, I have absolutely no doubt that, if I ever had my life to live over, I would love and marry him all over again . . . in a heartbeat. I wouldn't have missed the adventure of loving—and being loved by him—for all the world!

CHAPTER 90

LEARNING TO LIVE

Florida,
March 11, 1999.

Dear Pam and Sam, Charlie and I are discussing coming over and helping out for a while. I don't know for sure when Charlie can get away but taking off from his job is not a problem. I thought I could help Pam get through with the tourist season which you said is around Easter. We promise not to be a burden but we do want to help. Besides, Tommy said if I went, you might give him your secret barbecue sauce recipe. I have talked to the travel agent and am looking to leave here around the 24th of March and return whenever.

Think seriously about us coming. No brave soldier, or I don't want them to see me like this. We want to hug your neck. Anyway, just think of the money I'll save by bringing you that second volume [of '*Letters*']! Talk with you soon.

Love,
Beulah.

Texas,
March 12, 1999.

This is your cousin, Denny, and my prayers are with you. Remember that as long as people are thinking about you, that you will not be suffering alone. My summer memories in San Antonio will always make happy thoughts of you. You shall live forever in our hearts and minds.

Florida,
March 15, 1999.

Dear Pam, Sam and Amanda . . . I understand Sam needs the time to finish his projects. I'm not sure how I would prioritize if I was in the same situation. I am here for you and can move on pretty short notice. I have contacted a travel agent so if you can decide on a time that is good to come over, let me know so I can book in advance.

Pam, if you find you can use some help, I am willing to do any job you need done. Please ask. We are all devastated by the news. You are all in our thoughts, constantly.

Sam, you are a good man. Everyone talks about your positive attitude, your laughter and wonderful outlook on life. We hope you have the time you need and as little suffering as possible. My heart breaks for all of you.

On a lighter note, Mom has been visiting me again, so I sent her to be with you. She always does weird things to my electrical appliances. You know she believed Rena would come visit her. Dad and I made a deal that he wouldn't come back and visit me because I told him it would scare the sh—out of me. He has kept his word.

Uncle Gene and Aunt Jeannie have asked if Pam's parents have been told. I hope you are not upset with Charlie and me for telling the family about your cancer. You need to know that even though we are a wonderfully dysfunctional family, we all love you.

Vaya con Dios (from Paw),
Beulah.

Florida,
March 22, 1999.

Sam . . . I know you may not have agreed on telling your children but in some strange way, you have been blessed. You all get the opportunity to make peace. This way your children won't spend the rest of their lives wondering what they did wrong that you couldn't tell them.

We all love you. I think of Pam and Amanda each day.
God bless.
Beulah.

Charles and Beulah in New Zealand, April 1999

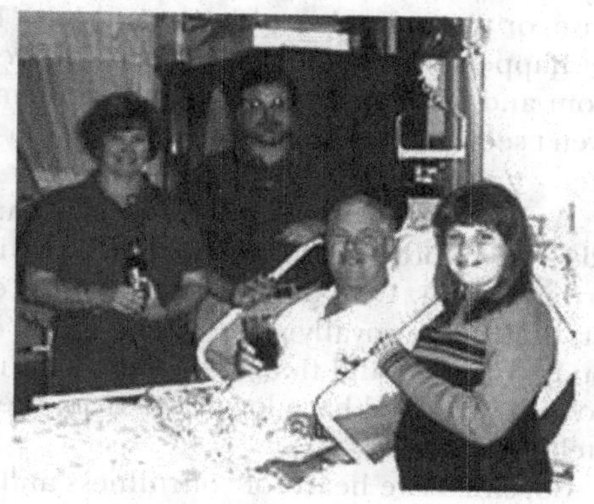

Beulah and Charlie, with Sam and Amanda

Texas,
March 21, 1999.

Dear Sam, I was very saddened to hear that you have cancer and it is now a part of your life. So many people I know have had the same disease; it almost seems like an epidemic.

While I know from others that there is considerable pain associated with prostate cancer, I also know your Kopecky genes will serve you well in coping. Even as a young kid, maybe age 2, you fell about 30 feet from an oak tree in your grandparents' yard. Your only comment was "ouch".

Not long afterwards, in the same yard, you nearly cut off the tip of your nose and it was hanging by two slivers of flesh. The inside of your nostrils were clearly visible. Your Dad stuck your nose back in place, holding it there until the blood clotted so he could reattach it with a band-aid. I don't remember that you even cried but you probably still have the scar.

Then as a young father, you fell from a tree on the chainsaw you were using to cut limbs. I recall your telling me the saw was still running and that you had nearly amputated your foot. Those are only some of the things I remember about your ability to absorb pain, macho man.

I hope you know how much your Aunt Mary loved you; she always thought you were very special. She was pleased with your achievements and sad when things weren't going your way. She and Golda shared many laughs about your bizarre activities as a teenager, and you evidently supplied them with plenty of things to laugh about. You were very dear to both of them.

You need to know that you are on the prayer list at my church, and that you, Pam and Amanda, are in my thoughts and prayers. The following quote may give you comfort . . . "The struggles you're going thru now—don't discard them. Listen to God as he teaches you so that you can teach others. You see, a time of suffering teaches us something that we never knew before and may prepare us for a time of counsel that we will give someone for years to come. When we cannot understand, help us to trust".

Peace be with you, Pam and Amanda.

Love,
Uncle Gene.

Texas,
March 30, 1999.

Dear Sam, I have been at a loss for words, having received the news of your cancer and paralysis. I spent several days walking around awash in memories of Boerne, of you and Joey corralling us younger kids into dragging logs to the cliff to create that funky little house, or playing poker with you and John Dietle (you guys always beat us), of the wreck that happened at Olmos Park when you were driving me and Susie home from Golda's (Mom and Dad used the insurance settlement to take us to Port Aransas). Though we haven't seen each other in years, we are kin nevertheless, knit together come hell or high water.

As Mom was dying, it was very clear that your Dad came to visit her. She'd talk to him and to Dad's brother Billy (who died in a flight training accident as an Air Force enlistee during WWII). One day I told her that I expected her to come for me when I die. In fact, that I'd be royally pissed if she didn't show up. Those eyes—which had been pretty cloudy—cleared and flew wide open. I think she figured out that the party wasn't over. I also told her she'd have lots to do from the eternal side of things, praying for us all and watching over us.

So, since I've heard of your illness and pain, I've been telling Golda and your Mom and Dad, to get their butts in gear. Golda, in particular, seems to have much experience in the midwife task of being born to eternal life, aka dying. I also thought it might be good if Ludma showed up with her armadillo purse, just to give you a laugh and let you know for sure you were in the company of the wondrous, strange and eccentric clan of Kopecky.

Much of what I do as an Episcopal priest is work with those who are dying, who are dealing with a terminal diagnosis. As you may be discovering, while there is much grief, there are also many opportunities for the giving and receiving of gifts beyond measure. May you and yours have opportunity for that gifting, may you grow increasingly aware of the community that waits to receive you, and may there be healing in the midst of grief.

You are daily in my prayers. I'm including a picture of Golda, whose ancestry (as Beulah Ann has discovered) includes a heavy dose of Irish (Leary, O'Neill, etc.). So I am also sending along a prayer from the Irish/Scots/Welsh tradition, knowing full well that the women of your lineage will be reaching forth hands to receive you.

Be each saint in heaven,
Each sainted woman in heaven
Stretching their arms for you,
When you go thither
Over the river hard to see;
Oh when you go thither home
Over the river hard to see.

May your time with your children be tender.

With love and lots of memories,
Mary Beth.

Texas,
April 5, 1999.

Sam . . . I guess at this time you are a little under the weather and I have a very heavy heart—not only when I was told about your illness but each time I think of you. I have a very heavy heart for where you are both physically and mentally, but also for your lovely wife and children.

I have always felt especially close to all of you—especially you, Joe and Tom—perhaps because I grew up with y'all and through the years have felt your joy and sorrow with the many changes and chapters we have all gone through. I want you to know what a great and wonderful person you are and how very much I have always felt a closeness to you that I have not felt towards the others. Maybe it goes back to U.T. Austin, the time I lived in San Antonio, and the fact that our first-borns are only a few days apart. I will always remember you and Pam sitting in my gazebo after Cecil died, your making me laugh and the wonderful outlook you had on life in general. I will always remember the card you sent me after my Mom died, and the kindness you shared with me. You were the only one out of all the Kopeckys that acknowledged the pain when you lose a Mother. I do not know if any of y'all know that your Mom and Dad were my godparents and what a special place they always had, regardless of their imperfections.

I pray that you get my email and know that my love and prayers are with you. I always wished that God would give me that special power to be his messenger and help take away my loved ones' pain and illness—but then I suppose that is selfish of me. Always remember Sam, that God loves you and has a very, very special place for you, for he knows what a wonderful person you are and always have been. Your wonderful sense of humor, your loving and caring ways, your sensitivity. God knows how very special you are and has another plan for you. You are loved by so many and please don't ever forget that.

This is for Pam: I feel your pain and sorrow, and I am so sorry. You are very lucky as I am sure that you know God sent Sam into your life to love and be loved. What a wonderful person, husband and friend you have but I know I am telling you something you already know. We, however, do not get to decide how long we will have this special person. Be grateful that you have been given the time to say special things to Sam that only a husband and wife can say or share with each other, as we don't all get that opportunity. While I know and understand your anger with what is happening, for whatever it is worth, only my faith has sustained me—and only after I got past the total anger of Cecil being taken from me.

Cecil was 49 and I didn't have the chance to say any of those special things. I must believe that when we leave this earth, that is the end of life as we know it here on earth—but it is the beginning of a new life such as we have never known, with no pain or sorrow. I am quite sure you don't want to hear this but I truly can relate and I understand your anger and pain. As I keep reminding myself as I go through each day, I was so blessed to have Cecil in my life for the 12 short years we spent together, for so few people have ever found or experienced that true love that was Godsent. That doesn't mean that I still don't get angry that I am alone, especially when I am trying to fix something that has broken, or when I get up at 5 AMeach morning when I go to work. But then I think about the happy and glorious times we shared and yes, I was blessed. If, at any time, you need a shoulder or just to talk, perhaps we can get this email to work both ways.

Sam, I love you very much. I pray for you daily and know you made a difference in my life for the positive, and in so many other lives. You are truly a wonderful person and yes Sam, God loves you and has a special place for you. You are in my prayers constantly and perhaps God will hear me and give me that power of healing I ask for each day. I hope this reaches you and I will receive a reply from you. I would tell you a joke but unlike my Mom, I can never remember any. And no, after reading this, I have not become a religious fanatic and have not ordained as a minister. I am still the same person with the same imperfections. However, at the same time, I know someone, or a greater power than I can explain, has sent me a guardian angel or I would not still be here.

I will close and hope to hear from you,
Ena.

Texas,
April 23, 1999.

Sam, I don't know if my mother or father ever told you this story but it is true. I know because I was there and my mother actually has 8mm film of the incident. It seems that Nan, Papa, my mother and father, and your mother and father, were all at the ranch at Boerne. They all decided to go down to the creek and take a boat ride. My Dad, your Dad, your Mom and Papa, all got in that flat bottom boat you guys had there. My Dad was in the front rowing and they were all in the back. They tooled around the creek for some time and after a while, decided to head back to the bank. Nana, my mother and I stayed on the bank watching them. My mother was taking the movies. Anyway, when they got back to the bank, someone stood up to get out of the boat (I think it was Papa) and of course, over it went and they all hit the water. When your mother hit that cold water it must have taken her breath away because she began to have real difficulty. My Dad saw her, got behind her and got her back up onto the bank. She was in real trouble as no one else saw her, as they were all trying to get their own bearings.

Finally, I remember seeing Papa treading water and spitting. I don't know if you remember but Papa always trod water with his lips just above the water and spat like some kind of porpoise. When Nana saw him come up from under the water, her first words were classic. "Freddie, do you still have your wallet?" Can't blame her for having her priorities in order.

Later, they were all safely back at the ranch house, and I think my Dad was still a little shaken and had the adrenaline still pumping. Your Dad, with his dry, dry wit, came up to my Dad and asked him "Lloyd don't you like me anymore?" My Dad looked at him kind of puzzled and said "Sure Joe, I like you". To which your Dad replied, "Then why did you save Beulah?" It broke my Dad up and he still talks about it today. So just a little family anecdote for your archives.

Take care and write,
Lloyd (Jr)

Sam and Laurie, in New Zealand, April 1999

California,
April 27, 1999.

Dear Dad and Pam . . . I've talked to Allen a little bit about my trip. I find it difficult to get really deep with him on it—maybe because he doesn't know you guys and can't really appreciate what it was like to see you again. He can't hurt with me. I know he would be understanding and supportive but that just doesn't do in a situation like this.

I've been thinking about the things that make you so unique to me Dad and why I enjoy listening to you talk and talk, when other people wear me out with their talking. When you talk it's about something profound—or at least useful. You soak in information and wind it together with meaning for the rest of us that hear it but don't always understand its importance. You don't give advice unless we are obviously asking you for it. I will miss you playing devil's advocate; even though at times it irritated the hell out of me. You made discussions worthwhile and thoughtful. And afterward, when you drove us back home, whether we ended up agreeing or disagreeing, you always gave me such big hugs. Sometimes I thought you were going to squish me to death! How I didn't realize how much I would end up missing those hugs only a few years later. I always thought that someday, eventually, I would hear Arthur complain about you squishing him.

I have come to think of you more as my mentor. You taught me tolerance and logic in those years after the divorce. I remember nights being up at 1 AMdiscussing topics (familiar to you I'm sure) with my best friend in college, and citing some of our talks as support for MY view (so what hasn't changed?). Those talks were my first step towards being an excellent teacher. Now I avoid supporting MY views on a topic in class and instead play devil's advocate for my students . . . a disorienting experience for them of course, since teachers usually just tell them what to think. Suddenly in my students I see fervor and passion because they matter—and I have you to thank for tempering me. How I would have crushed them if I were still the same person I was back then, with only one way to think and feel! As I struggled with my beliefs long after college, I remembered the arguments that Pam and you would both raise. I could no longer deceive myself and I had to eventually deal with the facts that the two of you showed me. My life changed. Thank you both for freeing my mind.

Dad, you're not getting out of mentoring me! You'll no longer have the excuse of being miles away! I suppose even spirits can't be in two places at once, and you should dwell beside Amanda and Pam. But I am hoping that that uncanny sixth-sense of yours that proved to be unnervingly correct in this life, will continue into the next. Visit me whenever you can. As for the here and now, I'm going to talk to you while I KNOW you can still hear me (forgive me for my skepticism). I won't waste the chance to talk to you today, by waiting for tomorrow. You're going to get sick of me! Just consider it training. And you'd better get your two cents in while you can! Then again, maybe you'll be skilled at using our dreams.

Love,
Laurie.

Texas,
April 29, 1999.

Dear Sam, I just got your email address from Beulah Ann. I thought, given your Maori connections, that you might enjoy this story . . . I have a friend, Dr Patty Chandler, who is a physician who has become very interested in Native American healing practices. She is now head of the family practice department at the University of Texas Health Science Center in Dallas.

Several years ago she began attending conferences sponsored by the Roman Catholic Diocese of Arizona that brought together Native American shamans and physicians. She made friends with several Hopi shamans, right off the bat. When she returned the next year to the conference, one of her Hopi friends was not present. She asked about him and discovered that he had died. She was puzzled. He was a younger guy, in good health. As she was ranting a bit about his death, one of the other shamans looked at her and said matter of factly, "He had work to do from the other side".

The older I get and the more I am with those who are dying, the more convinced I am of the truth of that statement. We do have work to do from the other side, beyond the limits of space and time. Your Maori friend may have similar perspectives.

Lastly—here is a little confession. When I was about 10 or 11 years old, I had a full—blown schoolgirl crush on you. No doubt you did not notice, for such is the way of teenage guys. (As the mother of sons, believe me, I know.) I remember having a conversation with Mom about whether or not it was okay to marry your first cousin. She very tactfully explained why that wasn't okay and then told me she'd been very attracted to a cousin of hers who had been killed in WWII. Now I see she read the whole thing perfectly. From the perspective of 50 years, I see that crush as a sense that in many ways you are like Daddy—and I can't give you a higher compliment than that. It doesn't mean you are perfect. I have no use for perfect people because they are usually dead. What it does mean is that you have something gutsy and real, also playful, about you. My oldest son Bryan, reminds me a lot of Dad and they have a great relationship. You three have some of the same feisty passion.

Bryan, who is now 24, spent the fall back-packing in Europe. For some reason the Kopecky blood is really calling to him, and his main destination was Prague. Before he left on the trip, we had a family dinner. Doug and I had written up a series of blessings—things like, "May you taste every beer in the Czech Republic; may you meet many intriguing women; may you taste a new food every day". The last blessing was: "May you stand in the square in Prague and be surrounded by your Czech ancestors giving you their blessing".

When he was in Prague, one crystal clear day he was crossing Wenceslaus Square. A single cloud was in the sky. As he stood in the middle of the square, the cloud opened up and snow fell on the ground around him. When he called us that night, he was speechless.

So all of this is to say, that I am praying that the ancestors will come to you, that vast community of souls in Christ; and may they be ready to teach you the work you have to do from the other side. And may we who will be the recipients of that work, have the wit to recognize your presence.

Love,
Mary Beth

Florida,
May 24, 1999.

Promise to write soon . . . Susie and I have talked many times about the ranch and have tried to remember stories and names of places on the ranch. We remembered the big hole and what we think was called Depugh's (first fishing hole on the creek). Do you remember the names of the other areas? Like the area by the waterfall. I took a writing course a couple of years ago (children's writing) and one of the stories I wrote was based on a fishing adventure that I had with Marybeth and Susie.

We were all fishing and I wanted to go swimming but Marybeth insisted that we continue to fish as long as the fish were still biting. Susie and I fixed that . . . we stopped baiting our hooks and those darn fish just weren't interested in our bare hooks.

Give my best to Amanda and Pam . . .

Love,
Beulah.

Texas,
May 24, 1999.

Dear Sam, thanks for taking the time to write. I suspect that just watching the world, being with Pam and Amanda, and paying attention to life is your primary focus, as it ought to be. I am keeping you in my prayers daily, especially hoping that you are not in pain.

As you know, May 30 is Golda's birthday. I always observe it as a feast day—the celebration of the life of a family saint. I wrote this little piece about her that is going to be in a book about grandmothers. I thought you might like it since, if nothing else, it evokes her sense of wonder and her amazing playfulness. Sometimes Daddy, Susie and I, get to telling Golda stories and end up giggling. I think she is the one who instigates the story-telling. Here's proof she was magical: she convinced us all that peanut butter and onion sandwiches were absolutely delectable. Here's the little story. Take care.

Love,
Mary Beth.

"GOLDA"

She was Texas born and Texas bred. She survived the Galveston hurricane of 1900, the Great Depression and over 50 years of marriage to my grandfather. This was no small feat. Golda Willis Kopecky was a maverick. She took off for Galveston in order to become a nurse, leaving behind a conventional life. She fell in love with and married, a man who was a Bohemian. She went where her heart led, even when it was risky, even when that was against the grain.

She was a mystic in her own way—not the sort of mystic of whom weighty hagiography is penned. Not the sort of mystic whose feats of sanctity leave the rest of us wondering if the person were really human. The wonder of life and the mystery of love were at the center of Golda's living. Early on I became aware of her ritual. She would traipse across the grass, hose in hand, to water the plants. To the casual eye this appeared to be a chore. To some of us, it was revealed to be an act of worship. Her presence showed us what prayer looked like; we children saw reverence and delight in this daily connection to earth. Golda would stand in the garden, blessing the dripping leaves, noting the changes, rooting herself and her family in what Marge Piercy has called "the common living dirt"—the earth that is our home and our mother.

Golda taught me to feed the earth worms. Every morning, she would put coffee grounds, banana peels and other vegetable bits, in the garden by the back door. Those worms, well-fed and tended, created rich soil, dark and aromatic. The toads that lived under Golda's back stoop were equally treated; she made sure there was fresh water for their drinking. The "common, living dirt" was home—home for worms, for toads, for vegetables. This earth home was dear and sacred.

Once, when I was about six, several of us grandkids were gathered at Golda and Joe's ranch near Boerne in the Texas hill country. We were playing underneath the water tower, dancing around in sheets of water cascading as the pump pulled water up from the creek. Suddenly Golda emerged from the cedar trees at the lip of the canyon. She emerged radiant and astonishingly beautiful. Her hands waved in the air. She searched for words. "I have been given such a gift! I saw two king snakes doing their dance!" The air around her pulsed, quivered. We grandchildren became mute. Now I know that we were beholding that age-old, bone-deep knowing; fall down and worship. Take off your shoes. Keep silence, Keep watch. The dirt is common, the dirt is living. Yet there is more.

I was beholding ecstasy. From that moment on, I began to awaken to the truth that the earth is holy ground.

Florida,
May 29, 1999.

Dear Sam, I truly enjoyed reading Marybeth's letter about Golda. I think that is why we all have such a connection to the earth. I know that there are many times that I say I have to go dig and move earth. The outdoors brings a peace to me but digging in the sand is not as much fun as dirt. Golda gave us all a love of flowers and nature. Maybe that is why we all wish for the ranch.

Sam, you may not have realized that you have been instrumental in bringing this wayward family back together. Maybe not all of us, but at least the ones who want to be part of the family. These past few weeks have been exciting. Hearing about all of our family, past and present. I know I have cried and laughed more over the stories and memories, and it feels good. Thank you for letting us be part of your life.

By the way, do you think Amanda's cheese and onion sandwiches have any connection to Golda's peanut butter and onion sandwiches? Maybe a stray gene. I think they are yummy!

Love,
Beulah.

Texas,
May 31, 1999.

Dear Sam and Beulah, happy feast of ST. Golda—today being her birthday! She woke me up yesterday morning with a head full of memories.

The older I get, the more I laugh at this: you know how she would bring lunch down to us at the creek and we felt like we were treated royally? Well, I also now understand this: while we were down at the creek running around, she was up at the cabin mostly by herself, humming little songs and doing whatever she was doing. In other words, she was a master at getting a little time out from her grandchildren.

Does this ring a bell? "Fools' names and fools' faces, always seen in public places". We probably had the singular claim to having a shack with its own graffiti.

One time when I was around 10 or so, still with a little girl body, I got into seed ticks at that first fishing hole. Golda made me take off every stitch of clothing (because they were in the cloth), and then I rode back up to the shack in the front seat of the Buick, with Charlie giggling and making remarks all the way up the hill. I had to get out of the car stark naked, get slathered with kerosene, then go shower. The nurse in her could be straightforward and very task-oriented. I will tell you this—I've managed to avoid seed ticks (and being naked in front of Charlie) ever since.

Love,
Mary Beth.

Florida,
May 31, 1999.

Dear Sam, one of my favorite memories of Golda was when she was peeling apples in her kitchen on Lamont. She would make long ribbons of peel and then tell me to throw them over my shoulder. Then I would pick them up and she could tell my fortune from them.

I sent Charlie the stories of the ticks from Marybeth. I still enjoy bathing in flea soap to this day! HA!

Love,
Beulah.

Texas
May 31, 1999

Dear Beulah and Sam, I remember the apple peel but not the part about telling your fortune.

One of the ongoing discussions we have is this: which of Mrs. Schneider's cookies tasted the best? I contend that the valentine hearts were the best, especially because Golda served them with strawberries and powdered sugar. To this day, when strawberries begin appearing in February, I think about going to her house for tea and strawberries with powdered sugar.

She also used to just show up all the time with one of those wire baskets full of hot kolaches. She'd just walk in the back door and that yeasty aroma would fill up the whole house. One day after Daddy got his boat, and was spending every possible minute out on the water, she showed up with kolaches and *'The Wind in the Willows'*. She made us all sit down while she read to Daddy (and us) the part about Ratty, saying, "There's nothing I like so much as messing about with boats". I'll never forget that—kolaches and *'The Wind in the Willows'*.

Love,
Mary Beth.

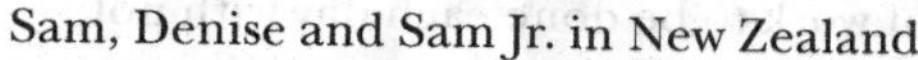

Sam, Denise and Sam Jr. in New Zealand

Sam Jr. Sam, Amanda and Laurie

Texas,
June 2, 1999.

Dear Dad, look how fast the days fly by. It's already June—almost 6 weeks since we left to come home. Happy birthday!!!! Yours, Craig's and Joshua's, all this month. What a party!!! I hope you had a great day. Since you are all a day ahead I guess it has come and gone already.

We got all the notes you sent . . . Mary Beth's letter about Golda, and Beulah's too. I really enjoy hearing stories about Sam's family. Sam is still a little down—he wishes he knew more about the Kopeckys—Golda, great-grandfather and grandparents. I think aunts, uncles and cousins too. Hopefully Sam will sit down and write—I guess he thinks it has to be a college-level letter with perfect grammar, to send you! I figure you could care less as long as you get to hear from us every once in a while, instead of once a year or so!!!!

Tell everyone hello from us! Amanda we love you! Pam too! Take care and happy birthday.

All our love,
Denise and kiddos.

Texas,
July 4, 1999.

Sam, just read your email. I have been out of town on a short vacation. Me, my wife, and my oldest daughter (Kaci—15), took a short jaunt up to the hill country. We went camping in Pedernales State Park, just outside of Johnson City. We also went into Fredricksburg to let the women get in their shopping fix. Fredricksburg is now a tourist center with antique stores, specialty shops, restaurants and motels, up both sides of the main street. It is a far cry from the little town we knew as kids.

Funny you should mention coming up for your Mom's birthday. We always looked forward to coming to San Antonio so we could go to the ranch in Boerne, as much as you looked forward to coming here to the coast to swim in the gulf. Anyway, those visits as a child sparked a lifelong love of the Texas Hill Country that makes me return at least 2 or 3 times a year. It is still as beautiful as ever.

Recently I asked my mother what happened to Papa's movies. She said Uncle Freddy had them. Since he died I don't know where they are now. Yes, I do remember that we all had to leave the room when Papa put on his "adult" movies.

Just read an article in today's newspaper about the appointment of a new economics advisor here in the U.S. His main objective (he says) is to convince the American people of the need for free trade and open markets without tariffs. He states that is what is keeping the U.S. economy strong. Sounds like maybe in you guys' case, he speaketh with forked tongue. Lastly, don't let Nostradamus scare you. I think he was a communist. Hope you find a chunk of meteor and keep on writing.

Lloyd, Lisa, Kaci and Kellye.

Texas,
July 8, 1999.

Dear Sam, thinking of you and as always, you are in our prayers. Summer is here in Texas for sure. Hot and dry with plenty of dust here in Tyler. However, you know the old Texas saying—just wait and the weather will change. Extremely high temp. so towards the end of the day there is a good chance of thunderstorms with plenty of lightning as witnessed today. Besides the above, just plenty of work to be done each day with not enough time to do it. Again Sam, you are always in my thoughts and prayers. We can witness the mental toughness and spiritual peace you display thru' your letters. We continue to pray for you all. Keep up the good fight Sam—you too, Pam and Amanda. Take care and let me hear from you soon.

Love to all,
Tom and Lisa.

Craig, Sam and Brittany, in New Zealand

Texas
July 19, 1999.

Hi everybody . . . I am glad things remain stable currently. Brittany continues to pray for you every night (and of course you are in our prayers as well). You are a great example for a courageous spirit, and I hope you may find comfort in the fact that you have helped me in understanding and helping my patients and their families, who are dealing with similar issues and problems. I think of you every time I look down at my watch. It reminds me of the good times we got to share together when Brittany and I were there in New Zealand. It is also a constant reminder that time is not mine to hoard but only mine to give to those who are important to me.

As I have said before, I am beginning the application process for fellowship (and considering applying for Chief Resident), I will let you know when I am further into the process. Well, I'm post-call, so I guess I need to get off but I just couldn't wait any more to at least make a brief contact.

Love,
Craig, Elizabeth, Brittany and John.

Texas,
July 23, 1999.

Dear Sam, Pam and Amanda, you have been very much in my thoughts for the last several weeks so I was glad to read your emails to Mary Beth. I had no idea that you had been struck by a meteorite.

Our newspapers are so concerned with local and national events that things that occur elsewhere, get very little coverage. I have often wondered what it would be like to live in a country not so preoccupied with being No. 1—countries like yours, Portugal, Scotland and the like. I suppose there's a big difference in priorities and suspect there's considerably less frenzy. But maybe that's not the case at all.

You spoke of your early memories of Galveston. Mary, Mary Beth and I, lived in Houston in 1949 and 1950 when Joe was doing his internship at Galveston. Often, we drove there on weekends. We had a small dog that had survived distemper, and inadvertently became the mother of a motley group of pups. Wanting to see all of you but not knowing what to do with this bunch of dogs, we drove with all of them to your Galveston house one weekend. That night, the mother, while nursing her pups, went into shock (Joe thought from calcium deficiency) and nearly died. Joe diagnosed the problem and went to the pharmacy for help—just like a good vet. He brought her round immediately with a shot. We were very impressed with his medical skill, and so was the mother. The evening went on without skipping a beat.

On another weekend—New Year's Eve as I recall—we were again at Galveston, joining Golda and Dr Joe. New Year's morning, you, Sam, and Joey, woke Mary and I early—too early—by crawling into our bed with very dirty, smelly diapers. That's very hard to take on New Year's morning, before coffee. But I suspect you may know that, from personal experience. Golda came to the rescue, bless her.

A few months ago I drove to Rowena (near San Angelo) to visit Mary's favorite aunt, Edith Kopecky, widow of C.W. and mother of Sam Kopecky, for whom you were named. Edith is now over 100 years and still sharp mentally, although not too quick physically. She lives alone in their old house and has daily help. She was interested in knowing about your family and other news of the Kopecky clan. You may remember her from the ranch and from holidays.

Mary was such an eloquent writer. I wish she was here to send you a note. You were very special to her, although she loved all your siblings. She probably would send you a letter that would bring a belly laugh and then paint an accurate word picture prompting great memories. I wish she had completed the book she began. Fictitious characters? Yeah, right.

Given the limitations of my primitive computer, I think I'm writing beyond its capacity. However, please know that you are much in my thoughts and prayers.

Much love,
Uncle Gene.

Texas,
July 24, 1999.

. . . I don't know if I truly remember seeing the first moon walk on TV, or I just remember the film clips I later saw growing up. However, I do remember getting up out of bed to see something no one had ever seen before. And I remember my Dad wanting to share a special moment in time with me, despite not usually getting to see him after a long day at work, since I was usually asleep in bed. It made a difference.

John is still too young to appreciate "special events" but often it's the time I make a point of including Brittany in 'milestones' of our country, and those rare episodes of human achievement these days. I hope I make lasting memories for my kids too, as I often think of the times we spent together.

Not much else going on here, so I'll sign off for now.

Love you guys!
Craig.

Texas,
August 8, 1999.

Dear Sam, it's hotter than hell here. We are flirting with 100 every day—but then it's the first half of August in San Antonio. I am ready for some rain. It gets old, looking at the brown grass. Somehow I can't imagine New Zealand being brown and dry.

Pawpaw Joe's birthday is coming up soon—August 12. I always think of boisterous parties at 627 Lamont with Czech oompah bands in the front yard and a rock band in the back, with lots of Michelob playing, Mrs. Riebe's dumplings growing to monstrous proportions in the refrigerator, Czech relatives showing up with Mason jars gleaming with canned peaches, tomatoes, pickles, and kolaches and sausages galore. And Golda, in the kitchen, somehow not batting an eye with all that Czech goofiness swirling around.

Oh and lest we forget—Paw peeing off the balcony for good measure.

Don't you love this heritage? Someone once said to me when I was telling them family stories, "Well, at least you don't suffer from the curse of being normal". No shit!

Love,
Mary Beth.

New Zealand,
September 16, 1999.

Must be coming up on Labor Weekend. The end of summer, back to school, and all those things.

I can remember when I was in elementary school and each year my grandfather would take us to the Kendall County Fair as our last event of summer. We would go and ride a hundred rides, eat and drink until we almost got sick, and try the games until we almost broke him.

One year he was bound and determined to win one of those $5 bears. On and off during the late afternoon and into the evening, he would go back and try, then he would have a beer and again return. The good news was he finally won the bear—the bad news, I think it cost him about $50!!!

In later years I found that about half the games are rigged by the way they are set up, and using tricks of the trade. We also used to get the glass dishes with the 5 and 10 cents being thrown. I understand that a lot of these are now becoming collectors' items.

At the end of the evening we would leave and no sooner get in the car to head to the ranch at Boerne, that we would be asleep by the time we hit the main road. We would fall into bed; sometimes we would get undressed, sometimes not. The next day always looked different; the sun wasn't as bright, the air smelled different, and the outlook wasn't the same. It was the last weekend before school and fall, and summer was over for another year. It seems a lifetime ago, yet I can remember it as if it were yesterday.

Have a good Labor Weekend, and enjoy fall and winter that are yet to come.

Love to all,
Dad, Pam and Amanda.

Florida,
October 18, 1999.

I just had a visit from Tom and Lisa and wanted to send a picture of them. Tom has turned out to be a kind, caring person and Lisa is the best thing that ever happened to him. It is hard to believe that they have been married for 16 years. Tom still has more energy and moves faster than anyone I know. His memory is unbelievable and it was fun talking with him. They are both happy and a pleasure to be around.

Love,
Beulah.

Tom and Lisa Kopecky

New Zealand,
November 8, 1999.

I guess it is time to check in, or check up, on how everyone is doing. I have had things up and running again for a while. Just been busy. All much the same here for now.

Time does seem to fly. The Great Pumpkin has come and gone, and Guy Fawkes this last weekend, has come and gone. Thanksgiving is just around the corner, then the fat man in the red outfit. That does make me depressed.

Oh, you don't know about Guy Fawkes? Well, in the English side of things, it seems he was some sort of protestor, or patriot, who had a run-in with the English and blew up parliament or such. The good news is for kids and retailers each year. They sell fireworks and displays are set off at city parks, schools and the like. Each year here in Te Puru, the school has its 'Gala Night' with food booths, fund-raising, and of course a bonfire with fireworks. From our place you get a good view of the fireworks on the beach below. That is usually . . .

This year, Amanda was lucky enough (with Pam stuck here) to have a neighbor take her, with her own daughter, to all the fun and festivities. You could hear the loud speaker and all the voices, up on the hill, from down below. The auction of items, gift certificates, food booths going—and all waiting for dark. Then, as luck sometimes has its own way, just as it was getting dark enough, the promised ("some possibly heavy") thunderstorms that may move through, did just that. For about 15 to 20 minutes, the rain poured down . . . the old cow over the flat rock . . . the old frog strangler. By the time it was all over, almost all the cars were gone. Only a handful of folks left on the beach, with $20 fireworks packs, left to watch. At least 5 or 10 minutes worth anyway.

Next year is another year and in every life a little rain must fall. If only we could say when. As the old song goes . . . "How come a heartache always has to get you when you're down?" Amanda was not a happy camper. Stay in touch.

Love to all,
Sam, Pam and Amanda.

Texas,
November 17, 1999.

"Effective Immediately–My official RESIGNATION:

I am hereby tendering my resignation . . . as an adult. I have decided I would like to accept the responsibilities of an 8-year-old again.

I want to go to McDonalds and think that it's a four-star restaurant. I want to sail sticks across a fresh mud puddle and make a sidewalk with rocks. I want to think M&M's are better than money because you can eat them. I want to lie under a big oak tree and run a lemonade stand with my friends on a hot summer's day. I want to return to a time when life was simple and all you knew were colors, multiplication tables, and nursery rhymes. That didn't bother you because you didn't know what you didn't know, and you didn't care. All you knew was to be happy because you were blissfully unaware of all the things that should make you worried or upset.

I want to think the world is fair. That everyone is honest and good. I want to believe that anything is possible. I want to be oblivious to the complexities of life and be overly excited by the little things again. I want to live simple again. I don't want my day to consist of computer crashes, mountains of paperwork, depressing news, how to survive more days in the month than there is money in the bank, doctors' bills, gossip, illness and loss of loved ones.

I want to believe in the power of smiles, hugs, a kind word, truth, justice, peace, dreams, the imagination, mankind, and making angels in the snow.

So . . . here's my check book and my car keys, my credit card bills, and all my statements. I am officially resigning from adulthood. And if you want to discuss this further, you'll have to catch me first, 'cause . . . Tag! You're it."

Sam Jr.

New Zealand,
November 22, 1999.

. . . I do know exactly what this is saying. We didn't move to New Zealand for that reason as you know . . . Pam's Dad's situation—and all the rest. But, having said that, we also knew if we stayed we could make more money and live the life to resign from. If we moved and gave it a chance, we could always leave and move back. We would never make 'lots' of money here but what we would do, is tag the rest of the world, and go and live in a place for a lifestyle, to live again and enjoy all of the other things.

As you know, it is not perfect here but the lifestyle in the areas like we live—not the big city—is very much intended to be spent with school on the beach, the creek up the valley, the firth, the marine (oyster, mussel and scallop) farms, and mostly time together as much as possible. (There is no money.)

So, I'm sorry we couldn't have spent more time with each other in this environment. It is something I wish we all could have shared with each other over the years. But don't give up! There are still rainbows!

You can't tag me. I'm already—and have been—living, the resigned life. Remember we love you all.

Love you,
Dad, Pam and Amanda.

New Zealand,
November 23, 1999.

First of all, thank you all—I got the tape. I cannot tell you how much it means. We really have enjoyed it. I will write more a little later but wanted to get this to you to let you know. I am still the same and hanging in—or on?

Is it that time again? Happy Thanksgiving!! Enjoy the turkey and have a beer for me! Or should I say, have a Bud for me.

Love to all,
Sam, Pam and Amanda.

PS. Ena, I think the 44 may be overkill but you are looking good and time has been much kinder to you than the rest of us!

New Zealand,
December 1999.

It seems as if the other day was the start of the New Year and I was needing to organize myself for what was to come. No sooner did we get into the high season and my problem with the paralysis in mid-February decided to present itself. It took several months for us all to work out the changes that needed to be made.

We are now in a stable mode holding pattern. At the present time we are just trying to decide how we are going to make it through this high season, so we can make it through the winter. Who knows what may be ahead for us? With last year's luck, I could undo my belly button and my butt would have fallen off.

That would not necessarily be all bad; I could stand to lose some weight right now. With the edema from the steroids and all, I weigh the most I ever have (240 lbs.). I am actually doing some dieting at present and have considered watching some of those fitness videos, although I still don't understand how watching them is going to help. Pam is the one who has benefited from this. Running from upstairs to downstairs, from inside to outside the building, bringing me my meals, has had her exercise level up to where she has actually lost weight and is back to about her (pre-Amanda) weight of years ago. But I have not been able to convince her that I am actually doing her a service.

This year for the first time since we have been here, Pam's folks will not be coming up for Christmas. Last week, Pam and Amanda went to Palmerston North for a few days to see her Dad and family. Alan's health has deteriorated to the point he shouldn't travel. We decided that while things were quiet for a few days, they should take the time and go and visit. With a few friends and neighbors being able to check on me and bring me meals, I was able to hang in on my own for the several days. It was a good visit for them even though it wasn't long enough; but then it never is.

It's not all bad. I am actually better now than I have been in the last several months. If one good thing has come out of this last year, it is without a doubt having heard from so many family and friends. It seems that something like this makes us all really think about what really counts in the long run. I have spent a fair amount of time trying to get some of the old facts and pictures of family together so it can be passed on to those who want it. In day to day living we never have time for doing that sort of thing, so I am glad to have some time to do it now.

I have had to spend a fair amount of time looking back into the past to try and gather some of the facts to put on paper. I don't think any of us want to live in the past; I dont. However, after looking back over the years, I must say I feel I have had my share of really good times, friends and most of all, family.

So, who knows what this Christmas, New Year and Millennium will bring. I can only hope that it brings you as much happiness and love as you have all brought to me this last year and in the past.

God bless and love to all,
Sam, Pam and Amanda.

Texas,
December 24, 1999.

Dear family, well, our presents are wrapped, sermons are written, food in the refrigerator. I have been wondering how in the world Golda managed to buy presents for nine grandchildren, fix kolaches, deal with Pawpaw and be kind at the same time. Here's one thing I remember—after all the presents were opened, standing in wrapping paper up to my waist. And then one year, Joey or Sam, losing silver dollars in the middle of all that paper and fishing through it for the treasure.

I thought I would make kolaches for the first time in some years—then I got out the recipe. It calls for butter AND crisco. Post pancreatitis, crisco is definitely not permitted. I have to figure out how to make low fat kolaches. Hmmmm.

May this Christmastide be filled with blessings for one and all.

Love,
Mary Beth.

Texas,
December 28, 1999.

Dear Sam, what a great Christmas gift—to receive this story [on Misha—Siberia] AND the photos. I copied it out to put in my 'Pawpaw Joe' folder.

. . . Our oldest son Bryan went to Prague last fall—he has an almost mystical sense of connection to the Kopeckys, though he never knew Golda and was only two when Pawpaw died. (Though Bryan swears he remembers playing with Pawpaw's medical bag.) When Bryan was in Prague, he went to the Holocaust Museum. On the huge memorial plaque, the name Kopecky is listed with three different spellings. Some years ago, when I was doing graduate work in Mexico City, a Polish friend there told me the name is Jewish. Pretty interesting stuff. Thanks once again.

Love,
Mary Beth.

Texas,
December 31, 1999.

Dear Sam, this is a really ambitious undertaking; I hope we all get a copy.

. . . RE Paw's contacts. When I was newly ordained in 1987 and sent to be vicar of St. Matthias Episcopal Church in Devine, Texas (on IH 35 on the way to Laredo), there was an uneasiness about having a woman priest. (I was the third woman ordained in this diocese, so it wasn't common.) What made the difference was this: the matriarch, Roberta Hundley, had been one of Paw's patients for years. When she found out whose granddaughter I was, that sealed the deal. No problema. And what Roberta said carried for the rest of the little congregation.

Just before Christmas I took communion to a 90-year-old woman I'd not met before. (I am now part-time at St. Mark's, which is the big downtown parish, and no one on staff can possibly know all the parishioners.) We visited for a bit, and she said, "I wish I had a doctor like the one I used to have". "Who was that?" I asked. "Joseph Kopecky. He saved my life. I had lumbar pneumonia and didn't know it but he diagnosed it and saved my life." So we had a long conversation about all that. There are also several older members of St. Mark's who dearly loved Golda. I mentioned her in the first sermon I preached there (the story about her telling the chickens "and you call yourselves Christians!") and some of these people who knew her (they are more or less Dad's age) came to tell me how much they'd loved her.

RE the Moravians—I didn't know that they had Asian origins. This is getting very interesting.

I hope you all have a joyous New Year celebration.

Love,
Mary Beth.

P.S. Bryan loved having pictures of Pawpaw and Misha. I'd told him that story since he was little but it's all the better because now he's got the photos.

Texas,
December 31, 1999.

Dear Sam, here's the chicken story . . . At one point during the 30's, Golda was raising chickens in the backyard on Lamont. There was one chick that was pretty much of a runt and she, of course, took a liking to him. So she was trying to feed him a little extra etc. One day she looked out to see that the chickens had reverted and gone into pecking order behavior, ganging up on the little runty. She is said to have torn out the back door, flapping her apron and hollering, "AND YOU CALL YOURSELVES CHRISTIANS!"

Mom and Dad told me this story over and over. In our branch of the tree, it's one of the major stories of the oral tradition.

I never got to see Golda's homestead. I don't know about the Cherokee connection but would guess you are on the right track when you look at where her people came from. Dad's line (his Dad—the Colberts) were linked to a Choctaw chief named Levi Colbert whose fellow Choctaw fought with George Washington. Pretty amazing. Dad's aunt and uncle, his Dad's siblings, had very strong Indian features.

By the way—Claire Colbert, my brother Bill's daughter, who will turn 16 in April, looks very much like Golda in her early years. There is a portrait that Mom kept from the Lamont house, a pastel rendering of a photo taken of Golda in nursing school. Claire looks extraordinarily like her great-grandmother in that pastel.

. . . I look forward to reading these files. This is great stuff. I just had a little book published, *'Praying with the Celtic Saints'*, which I co-authored with Sylvia Maddox. And now here are these Celtic tribes yet again. It's a substratum for a lot of history.

The map is great too—you know, Gaelic and Sanskrit have a lot in common. I am not a linguist so I can't draw a decent family tree about all of this but the connections are really fascinating. Many, many thanks.

Love,
Mary Beth.

CHAPTER 91

LIFE GOES ON

Texas,
January 11, 2000.

Dear Sam, Pam and Amanda (not to mention Carmen the cat), it was so good to get this card, with photos. I am particularly impressed with this cat that appears to be bigger than any of you . . .

. . . Sam, I don't know if you are aware that in '95 and again in '96, I had acute pancreatitis. I don't recommend this ailment for fun and games. Apparently a combination of high triglycerides and a virus caused the initial attack, and then a year of wasting because my body seemed unable to appropriate the nutrients that were in my food. To make a long story short, I am in pretty good shape but that sequence of hospitalizations and learning to live anew, made all the difference in the world. It was like a shake-down cruise. An intensive course in "What do you think life is really all about? And why are you spending all your time doing some of this stupid stuff?" I also had a round of malignant melanoma (no chemo, no radiation, just excision) when I was 33. My take on all of this is that I am so stubborn that I need all of this to keep the focus clear. And in a very peculiar way, I am grateful for all the health problems.

When I was first diagnosed with the melanoma, a seminary prof said to me, "You are lucky. Now you know you will die. The rest of us have forgotten". That woke me up.

So much of what you wrote in your letter rang very true. Odd that paralysis could be a source of so much freedom. Or that, in my case, so much pain could result in so much release. Life is just plain wonderful and strange. That's all there is to it.

One thing for sure, I hate it that you have the damn cancer. And I am grateful for the fact that it has caused the family to begin to knit back together, bit by bit.

Best wishes to you all and prayers for life in the midst of all the mess. Amen.

Love,
Mary Beth.

California,
March 5, 2000.

Hey there Dad, I'm sorry to hear you feel so terrible. I guess good news from the lab at least brings some comfort in the midst of pain. I also remember them saying that they didn't think you'd last the summer—and look! A whole year is coming up! It brings me some joy because I know that very soon we will be making enough money to come over there as a family. I guess you're not too excited about meeting new people when you feel like crap—I know I wouldn't—but maybe things will get better? Who knows, maybe you'll be doing well enough that you can take car trips out and show us around.

. . . I love you guys. Please stay in touch and tell Pam and Amanda hello.

Love,
Laurie.

Texas,
April 2, 2000.

Dear Sam, I am VERY glad to hear that you are still kicking! May you kick as long as you want to. Thanks for this transcription and the photo. I am always surprised by the elegance of that generation's written correspondence—the varied vocabulary, the wonderful variety of diction, the images. And I always get a kick out of reading this teasing between Golda and Joe.

When Doug and I were engaged, one night we stopped by to visit Golda and Joe. He had gone to bed already but she was up for conversation. She started reminiscing about their first week of marriage and she got giggly telling us about Joe being too long for their marriage bed. She said (and I'll never forget this description), "He just hung over the end, with his big scoopy feet off the edge. So finally he lifted up those big scoopy feet and pulled the sheet up and out". We laughed and laughed. I'll have to admit that at 22, I had a hard time believing that Pawpaw ever rollicked around in bed playing, but now (for some reason) it seems a whole lot more plausible.

She reminisced with us for an hour or so. Sadly, I don't remember the other details besides the scoopy feet. What I do remember is her obvious delight in their first days together as a wedded couple. The letter you sent brought all this to mind because she turns out to be such a FLIRT. Here is this competent, independent nurse out on her own in 1916, and she is flirting her head off in these love letters. Don't it make you want to shout???

I hope you are pain free. Dad seemed to think that you are not in a lot of distress physically. May that be true. Thanks again.

Love,
Mary Beth.

Texas,
April 16, 2000.

Dear Dad, I'm sorry I have not spoken to you for so many years and did not come to see you when everyone else did. I have had a hard time dealing with my feelings about our relationship and the changes we have both had in our lives. Grandma's death has been very hard on me, and at the same time, opened my eyes. I was able to spend some time with Grandma the day before she died and it was important to me that I spend that time with her to let her know that I loved her.

I know that you are in a very delicate state with your health, as well. I pray that you will get better. I think of you more often than I would like to admit but the truth is that I love you, and miss you. I'm sorry I was not able to spend more time with you. Take care.

Love,
Scott.

New Zealand,
April 16, 2000.

Dear Scott, I am sorry to hear about Grandma Tindall. Sambo and Craig told me how she was doing along the way. I wasn't sure she was going to make it to Christmas last year. I always liked her and dropped her a note a few times. I wrote to her when I heard about her cancer, to tell her how sorry I was about her situation. I guess we should be thankful for the time we did all have with her. At least now she won't be suffering. She had it a lot worse than I do and I know how tired I am of being sick and feeling bad—not counting being tired of being in this wheelchair all the time. Never mind, hopefully it won't be for a long time.

I am glad to hear from you. If you send me your mailing address, I will send your cards etc. to your address instead of to Zornia. I am sorry you have felt for so long you could not communicate with me about how you felt about things. Many a time I wished to hear from you; even if it was nothing but a note to call me a son of a bitch. At least then I would have known how you felt and that you were thinking of me. I am glad you want to try and work some of this out. I think in the long haul it will be best and I think this will give us both some peace of mind.

I will be in touch. Take care of yourself and tell everyone hello.

Remember we love you all,
Dad, Pam and Amanda.

California,
April 17, 2000.

Dear Dad, thanks for the note back. Personally I think you have it worse. I can only imagine what it must be like but I feel strange running down a checklist of things I can't imagine, that I know you are going through. That's not exactly a 'pick me up letter' for you to get. Besides, our family hasn't dealt with death much until now, so I think we really don't know how to handle talking about it, and all that. On one hand I just want to come out and say what's in my head, and on the other hand I don't want to sound callous and unmoved. So often I say nothing, which maybe seems just as callous and unmoved.

. . . I would like to create as website in memory of you too. I know it may not be your kind of thing but it helps me deal with death. I have some things but I know that Pam has most of the stories that have come in . . . I love you and hope you accomplish all you want and don't suffer long. The hardest thing about saying that, is that I feel like I'm giving up on you but it seems selfish to want you to stay alive (and therefore suffering) just so I can feel better. Talk to you again soon.

Love,
Laurie.

New Zealand,
April 17, 2000.

As someone once said, "I don't mind dying; it is being dead so damn long that bothers me".

I think death is part of life, in a funny sort of way. It is part of what is going to happen to all of us. I have more fear and dislike for pain and suffering than I do for death itself. (I could use a good rest.)

The first statement would bother me from the standpoint that I will not be able to do all I would like to while here—and see, and be with, the ones I love. And yet hopefully, it will be a while before I see them on the other side.

If I can watch over or send a sign to you all, you know I will.

Maybe I am, and always have been, an optimist. There must be something on the other side. There are too many amazing and beautiful things on this side for there not to be.

In my family, the funerals were always a time of loss, sorrow, storytelling, and party. It is sorrow and loss for not being able to see them again until after your own death. It is the stories and times we remember them with. It is the party we have to celebrate their life, their presence, and the gifts they have made to us in so many ways—be it wisdom, understanding, guidance, or love. We should be thankful for the time we had with them, and remember and celebrate this.

As far as the website goes, I do not know a lot about it. I like lighter colors. I like blue. I don't care much for black or dark backgrounds. I like whatever you do. You know you do not need to do it for me. Don't put a burden on yourself, please. A good party and storytelling session will do just fine.

I am still working on a lot of the Kopecky history and stories. I hope it will give you a better idea of who you all are, and who I am, after it is done. A number of stories are entertaining, some have lessons in them to all of us, and some help us understand why we are like we are.

I hope this helps.

We love you all,
Dad, Pam and Amanda.

California,
April 17, 2000.

Dear Dad, yes, that does help . . .

I understand your sentiments. I have told Allen before, that I would rather die suddenly than slow and painfully but then I guess one never really knows what one would prefer if given a choice. Children certainly change the whole thing.

I love you and I hope to God you are right about the Afterlife.

Love,
Laurie.

Texas,
April 18, 2000.

Dear Down Under loved ones, thanks for the email. I talked to Beulah today and heard you had a long phone conversation with her yesterday. She said you sounded "real perky".

I remembered a little story about Golda's childhood. You may recall most of her brothers and sisters were much older. She was talking to a sister, about Golda's age, about an aunt who both sisters agreed was extremely ugly. Their mother overheard the conversation and told them "Beauty was only skin deep". One of the girls, probably Golda, said "Then let's skin her".

I drove Golda to a funeral in Graham, Texas, to the old homestead, back in the mid—50's. Her relatives were a typical ranch family who looked and acted the part. Some of her brothers were Homer, Claudus, Virgil (a very tall cowboy with a very tall cowboy hat), and others whose names I don't remember. I think the ugly aunt's name was Lottie. I don't think there were 14 children but it was a big family.

They were a good family, very close, but not as rambunctious as the Kopecky clan.

Happy birthday to Amanda.

Love,
Gene.

California,
May 1, 2000.

Dear Dad, the hardest part was the funeral. Ironically it was the most cathartic part too . . . The next day Mom and I went to get Grandma's stuff . . . It was very difficult to be in the house without her. She was the house! Since we were children, that is where we went to see her, where we colored in coloring books, ate her spaghetti and her doucha (crepes), cakes and ice cream bars. It's where Scott and I played back the tape of her cussing at us in the car about an hour earlier, and she started laughing about it. It's where I climbed in bed with her and Grandpa when I was scared, or I had pee'd in my underwear, and where Grandma would get up at 5 AMto play Parcheesi with me because I couldn't sleep. It's the only place that all of us always came together to be with each other. And now the house will be gone, like her.

. . . I was sleeping with the lamp on every night after the funeral because I was afraid she might visit me. The idea didn't bother me until Mom said that she doesn't think there are ghosts. She believes that any visitation like that is really a demon. Well, even though I'm agnostic, it's hard to shake those words out of your head at 1AM. That's the biggest reason I was so terrified all my life of the dark. I believed that all the unexplainable phenomena were caused by demons lying in wait. Perhaps part of the reason I am agnostic now is to escape the fear. If you don't think there is a God, there can't be a Devil either. If there is no Devil, then there are no demons and therefore you only need to fear other people, not the dark. Of course, that meant giving up all hope for the afterlife too—thus making me agnostic. I want to believe in an afterlife but I don't think there is one. And so I found myself trapped in my fear again. On one hand I wanted to have a visitation from Grandma—even if she was a demon—so I could know there really was a spirit world, but on the other hand I was terrified of it being a demon and wanted no visitation at all. So I slept with the light on. Sometimes I try to relate this to Mom but she's just a broken record with no desire to examine her beliefs or consider other possibilities. So, I don't tell her any more. She read my '*Discussion about Religion*' which outlines my reasons for not wanting to believe in the God of the Bible, citing the Bible itself, but I think all it did was upset her. I told her she didn't want to read it and she insisted. But that is another story . . . I haven't had any more dreams since then about Grandma. Part of me is saddened by it and part of me is relieved. I still wonder if any of it is at all real. I am such a skeptic that it would take something indisputably unexplainable to make me consider it real. Maybe you will have the strength to reach me. Maybe Grandma lacked something, I don't know.

. . . I have never had dreams of men that died though, only females, so I hope that doesn't mean you have a hard time reaching me because of some weird rule or something. But I have never dreamed of Golda or your mother. In my case, I am torn about your death. Part of me looks forward to it so that you might come to me and show me it is all real; that there is an afterlife. But there is the part of me that dreads it. I hear songs in my head and see foggy scenes of you when I was a child. It makes me very sad to realize that you will be so completely out of my reach after that. I remember the day a song came out, called "The Living Years" by Men at Work. When I heard it the first time I couldn't stop crying. Nothing has changed. When I hear it you are already gone. It is about you, though when it first came out I never thought you would be dying so soon after I first heard it.

I think the thing I will most miss about you are the years ahead that I will never have. When I was a child I could not know or understand how quickly you would be gone from me through the divorce. The weekends with you were wrought with turmoil (religious, or because of Walt, or because of your new family). We never really communicated because I was like Mom back then—I could not see beyond my own little world. My awakening happened in college and of course, you were gone then. But I had hoped that one day I would be able to sit with you and discuss life and philosophy, science and the world's politics, taxes and death. I wanted to have you with me to meet your new son Allen, and to be a Grandpa with Arthur. I never got to know your Dad or Mom but I thought that could be different since I was the Mom now. At least Arthur would get to know you like that, even though I did not have that with your Dad. I just had to wait until we were making enough money to see you, to fly to New Zealand every year at least. And now it is only two months away and you are dying. It's just not fair! I have waited for so long and now it's in my grasp, and you are slipping away. I will miss the years we will never have.

These are the things I don't think I am supposed to say because I'm not sure if it's proper. But that is the truth. A lot of sadness, some anger, and the emptiness that comes from happiness that slips right off your fingertips. I have much to deal with where you are concerned, and now I must do it without you. If your spirit needs a second residence, I hope it is with me. I love you Dad, and you will never know how much, but I do love you desperately.

Love forever,
Laurie.

New Zealand,
May 3, 2000.

Dear Laurie, first of all I would like for you to understand that these are some of my observations and thoughts. Some give me more questions than answers. Also when I make comments, I am trying to stick to facts that were at least valid back at the time the observations were made.

It was once said that a mind is a terrible thing to waste. I think this is true and is one of life's miracles—at least for those who have one and use it. We have different levels of awareness and some of us have the ability to sense things more than others. You remember when I ran you down, trying to get in touch with you. I called your Mom and Walter to try and get phone numbers, got Craig's, and finally yours. I had told Pam that I had bad feelings in regard to you for some time, and they got stronger and stronger. I finally decided not to try and ignore them, and that I must get in contact with you to see what it was, and if I could help or at least understand. This is one thing that has come and gone with me at times.

Another time was when my Aunt Gerri was killed and when my mother came to tell me about it, I told her I already knew who it was. I was also very close to my grandmother Golda, that I grew up with. Before she died, she came by one day to see me at the drugstore. She picked up a few items, and we walked around the store and talked at the same time. I don't remember any of the conversation but I knew then, and shortly after, that the reason she came by was to tell me goodbye. The whole time she was there it was unreal and the whole episode was very unreal. It was as if we both understood why she was there, without a word being spoken. I never saw her alive again.

When I was little and growing up in an older house in San Antonio (in Alamo Heights), sometimes at night I would see things outside my window (2 storey's up). I know I was awake and I feel I know what I saw but I never talked about it to anyone then.

Many other items you are aware of, such as the book (I think it is) '*Chariots of the Gods*', which was about strange things. Pyramid power, pyramids, ancient civilizations, Stonehenge, the Venetian calendar in the Mayan—or was it Aztec—civilization. And much more. The point is, the more you learn about the wider human knowledge and what we don't know about it, the more the mind finds out there is to know. The standard answer is that they don't know what they're talking about. It is all made up. This may be true in some cases. However, even in our more recent times, if a person opens their mind and takes a more open approach and even explores things like the beliefs and legends of Indians and other indigenous people such as Maori, a whole new world opens.

The Maori people go back several thousand years. They are part of the Polynesian group of the Pacific. Some say they originated in Southeast Asia, some say South America. They sailed their dugout-type canoes around the Pacific and found New Zealand—navigating by the stars, while those in England were in the dark ages and everyone was still sure the world was flat.

The reason I bring this up is because of both you and Amanda. You are the only two of my children that I have seen this extra sense in. You both can feel you have either seen or felt the presence of something you cannot explain. Amanda was sure she had sensed and seen the Maori woman from the grave on the front section. She said she kept coming to her. She was supposed to be the protector of children and the granddaughter of the chief that was here. This is an ancient Pa site, which we didn't know when we bought it, and the spirits of the people that were here sometimes appear in a protective manner for the land. The Maori spirits (by legend) after death and the tangi (funeral) are released and leave via Cape Reinga, at the northern tip of New Zealand. From there they go back to their original land. (A legendary place? A place on earth? The stars? No one is sure.)

The Maori were not Christian until converted in the early 1800's. When I say converted, I should explain that they had a whole set of religious beliefs before we showed up. They saw that being Christian could fit in and work with their beliefs. Until this day, many still believe in both. This brings up such things as a Tohunga—the Maori equivalent of an Indian shaman. He is like a priest but not as we think of it. It is a combination of teaching, foretelling the future, medicine, spells (and originally, even curses). The curse part was so widely believed that the government/churches here passed a bill in the 1800's, outlawing the teaching of Tohungas. The Tohunga who foretold of the forthcoming Mt Tarawera eruption that would bury a town near Rotorua, was blamed by the townspeople and persecuted, in the late 1800's. Our Maori friend Tom Winitana, who stays here now, on and off, helping with the local treaty claims, is in his 60's. He grew up with his grandparents in the Urewera mountain ranges. His Tohunga grandfather taught him many of these things and he's told me that a lot of the black magic part has now been 'lost', which he feels is just as well. (Back in the States we learned to burn witches from the English. Anything to it?)

Here in the local community, some (Pakeha—European—and Maori) feel the front lot—and all this land—has a curse on it. This is partly due to the fact that the first (Pakeha) owner who purchased it, destroyed a lot of the Pa features on purpose, and desecrated several graves on the lot in front. As the story goes, later after leaving here, within a couple of years, the two bulldozer drivers that put the first road in, were killed in accidents. Roger Carter, the previous owner (to us), went broke—a fate worse than death for him. The Dutchman who desecrated the grave after being told (by us) not to, was hit by a car while standing by the roadside, talking to a friend—and killed. And now I have come down with cancer—although the local Maori have told us this cancer has nothing to do with this, as we have always been friends, and is just a disease. Tom has gone around all this land and cleared it, by assuring the spirits of the ancestors that we are friends, and here to help and protect. To this day, whenever a Maori goes to a grave or graveyard, they wash their hands with water as they leave. This is to cleanse and protect them. (Then in the church we use water to wash away sin at baptism and have other such ceremonies as well.)

First we have to open our minds. We must not be put off by those who close theirs. The church used superstition, curses, demons and the like, to control its followers. They still do. Some people just cannot understand any of this and they close off and rebel against it. They know; they have made up their minds. Your mother (and I am not trying to start a fight) had a limited education. She took the standard girl education at Robert E. Lee High School. She went for about a year to U.T. for a basic business degree but her grades were very poor and she was not passing all of her subjects when she quit going. She never opened her mind to much. Whenever I read such a book as '*Chariots of the Gods*' she could not understand why. When I would try and relate some of the really interesting things in science—be it chemistry or physics or such—I might as well talk to a wall. (Is space flat? Is it warped? Now they think it is flat. Is time the fourth dimension? Are black holes just portals to transport us to different distant locations in both place and time? A gate to other places?). Your mother was originally a Lutheran via her mother Elizabeth. We were married in the Lutheran Church. Elizabeth did not have the greatest open mind, I am sorry to say, and both she and your mother would close things out and rubbish them, rather than try to consider or understand them. It is just the way they were. (You said Grandma came back at the funeral and was mad. Was it because she was at the Baptist Church?) I think you found this out with the demons; first control, and second block things out and rubbish them. I am sorry I didn't know about this demon issue. Like I told Amanda, there must be both good and evil as we see both. If you are good and try to protect and not destroy—like the front grave—why would they want to hurt you? Checks and balances on the other side? I hope so.

Like I said at the start, I have more questions than answers. I do feel there must be more to life after death. Not just Christians believe this. Many other religions and people have believed this, over the millenniums. You take even a good, healthy body of an animal or human and kill it. Why can't we start it up again? It is all there. That extra little force, life spirit . . . where does it go? Does it just disappear? Or does it just transform into a spirit? Look at all the amazing things around us; from mountains, space, microscopic, the mind, you name it . . . all by accident? Well, I don't think so. Something after death, I hope so. There must be. We will all find out.

I have never understood why your mother tried so hard to poison all you kids against me after the divorce. I fought like hell to stay as a family but she wanted it; I fought it for years because I knew that the ones that suffer are the children. She got all she wanted . . . and more. In the long run with the way things were, it was best to go on our own way but that doesn't mean you all didn't suffer with all the games and manipulating, and on and on. I took all the bills and gave up all the rest. I was always there to take you—firstly, if she didn't want you; secondly, if they couldn't care for you; and lastly, if they were ever mean and abused you, I would take you. She knew this, and was told this was part of the deal. When Sambo was too much and almost split she and Walter, this is why he went to live with me. Craig asked once and I told him to try and work it out one time. It was not a get-along issue and I told him if he ever left, it would be one way—and he would catch hell for it. He decided to work it out and stay. I used to call on the phone every week to talk to you all. I was told a number of times that she would give you the message. I would always try and get you every other week but sometimes you had plans for church camp or skiing, so I said fine, I would get you next time. Sometimes this was okay, sometimes she said no, that was their weekend. I always sent birthday cards, Christmas, Easter, Valentines . . . I don't know if you ever got them all or not. I did not want to get you into the middle, to choose, and cause more upset.

No other kids can ever take any of your places, just as you cannot take theirs. We always wanted all of you to come and spend time with us. We wanted to talk, get to know each other better, answer questions, who knows . . . we may have found the meaning of life! You all were never a pain and we both wanted you to come. [The big mistake of course was Sharon. I listened to Cecil . . . "She will be good for Sambo" . . . "She will take care of things". She was hell. In the year we were married, we knew we could not work it out, and that we should get out and did. This was mainly both our personalities and we did not see many things the same way. It was a mistake. It had nothing to do with you kids at all.]

When Pam and I got married, we both knew the situation with me. I always felt I got cheated out of my kids and had nothing against having more. I always loved you all and wanted to be with you. We held off for about 8 years for a number of reasons. As you know since you now have a kid, now that we have Amanda, we wouldn't take anything for her—and I wouldn't take anything for any of you kids. I think you can understand this better now that you have one of your own.

I have never known what all your mother has said to you, and what stuff she has filled your heads with. (Craig told me once that when he was going to move in with Pam and I to go to U.T., his mother said "She won't want you there, they will want to have kids". He said back to her . . . "Mom, don't you remember, Dad had a vasectomy?". Was this a game, and why? Was it her business? Why should it be a problem?) I am sorry to say but for whatever reason, I think she has always wanted complete control and has feared losing it. Maybe I'm wrong. I just don't understand why anyone would put grief in all your lives.

Scott sent me an email—the first contact in over 10 years!! Do you mean to tell me he grew up in a helpful, guiding environment? I don't think so. Why? I don't like this.

I know my parents were not perfect. I used to not get along with my mother at all. We did later make peace. I learned to accept them for what they were. I learned to recognize and ignore some things about them. I learned to like and enjoy other things about them. I still don't like some of the things they did. We learned to accept each other as, and for, what we were, and leave some of it alone. I feel they made mistakes but I feel they tried to do what they thought was best for me. I feel like they loved me.

I want all of you kids to know that I have always loved you and still do, and will. I know I've made some mistakes. I didn't mean to. I never wanted for any of you to get hurt and be like pawns. I tried to avoid this to the point of getting out of the way at times. I wish I could have done more along the way.

No, I still don't have all the answers. I still don't understand. I doubt I ever will. I just hope that with time you will all be okay.

With love,
Dad.

California,
May 5, 2000.

Dear Dad, I read your letter from May 3rd and have been thinking about it all. I want you to know I didn't mind you getting remarried. It really didn't bother me. I know Scott feels different about that but I can't blame you for wanting to share your life with someone.

I thought your having more kids was kinda exciting whenever that subject came up about you. I didn't really grasp what a vasectomy was for a while . . . on one hand I was excited about babies but on the other I saw myself becoming non-existent . . .

There is no doubt that Mom and Walt poisoned our minds against you, as you well remember . . . Walt did straighten us out as far as our ability to deal with other people and our emotions. I mean you can just about handle anyone and not get angry after you've had to grow up with Walt in charge! He certainly wasn't, and isn't, open-minded, considerate, fair, insightful, curious, empathetic or particularly nurturing. He was a trial by fire that Scott and I lived through, and even blossomed after. Oppression does that I suppose. I used to think that you couldn't have done the same job, raising us into the responsible individuals that Walt did, but that was unfair. How can I know what you would have been like? I certainly remember Craig complaining about you not paying for this or that, or not doing something or the other (as children do) and how Mom and Walt would jump on that and shake it to death! "How unfair!" "How stingy!" "How callous!" It never occurred to me at the time to turn the tables. I don't know how much of what they told me was lies but I have always loved you anyway. I just didn't realize the importance at that time. I think about all the wasted hours on those weekends when we came to see you and watched cable instead. I know it upset you too. Pam told us one time after you came home and we hardly noticed you. I'm so sorry about that. I think I was a little scared to talk to you and Pam back then. It was easier to watch TV and ignore it. I wish I had gotten closer to you back then.

I won't claim that you being in New Zealand doesn't bother me. Sometimes it makes me upset but most of the time I don't think about it. I think Amanda is wonderful!—and I'm glad that you and Pam have her. Believe me, I can totally understand Pam wanting to have a baby . . .

I really had no idea who you were (or are, I guess). It seems silly to me to think I do when I can count the number of times you and I have really talked heart to heart, on my hands! But I don't blame you, Dad. I don't see you as the problem or the evil man that destroyed a marriage. I've been married now for nine years and I know a hell of a lot more now than Mom led me to believe back then! . . . to threaten to leave Allen or divorce him, would be like telling Arthur I hate him and never want to see his face again. You just don't do that to a family member. Allen is part of my soul, so I also understand how you feel about Pam and Amanda too.

If I had to choose some words to describe you I suppose they would be ones like genius, down-to-earth, pensive, hot-headed and mystic. You wear your heart on your sleeve but God help the person who tries to poke at it! Scientist or soothsayer, meditative or volatile, who will you be and how will you react when I ask you something? You are a contradiction and a mystery. To me when I was a little girl, you were God. Your mind was the vast night sky, unfathomable and laden with amazing stories like treasures. Your anger and your love were equally great but knowing you was like chasing the wind. I thought perhaps now I finally knew enough to fly with you instead of chasing after your thoughts. I suppose this sounds bizarre but it's quite true. Fear and awe were things I associated with you (and still do). I was looking for you when I wanted to be a missionary. I was looking for you when I found Allen. I am looking for you now in myself. (This all sounds so trite—that's why I don't usually say it but I may never get to otherwise).

Perhaps you still are God for me and I am facing the death of my Creator—and hoping that your power truly does reach beyond the grave. As a matter of fact, these emails remind me a lot of my prayers as a teenager. Hmmmmm, maybe that's why I started to drift from faith when you moved away. My belief in God faded without visits to you to stoke the fires? Interesting. After all, I have never claimed there is no God . . . but science and God have never been a conflict for me.

. . . I know you love me and your family both. I know you always had open arms for me. No, I don't think I got all the letters you sent until I moved away. I half expect to find them all when Mom dies. Most of all, I took you and your letters for granted. I am sorry. I love you Dad.

Love,
Laurie.

New Zealand,
June 22, 2000.

Dear Beulah, I have been trying to get some dates and things in the right order. What was the date, or about when was it, that Dad had his accident? I think it was in 1976. I know it was before Paw died in February 1977. I was thinking you and Dad went with us to Papa's funeral in Hitchcock in March 1977, when the motor home broke down. I would think this would have made his accident early 1976.

How's everything going for you? All is still a muchness here. I have a doctor's appointment at the clinic tomorrow afternoon. I have been stable so long they are afraid I might live a long time. This scares me and Pam both. Have you any room at your place?

Better go for now.

Love to all,
Sam, Pam and Amanda.

Florida,
June 22, 2000.

Lots of room. I live in 4000 sq. ft with 2 dogs and visits from Tommy and Sean . . . Dad had his accident in April 1976. I remember because of the Red Cross call we received telling us to come home. We were due to PCS back to the US in July '76. I stayed with Dad until late May and then returned to Okinawa to pack. He moved in with us in August of '76. I remember the trip to Papa's funeral but I don't remember Dad being with us.

I read your attachments and enjoyed them. I find parts of them painful to read. I don't think they should be excluded but it stirs old memories and feelings that I have tried hard to forget. Some of those times bring mixed, and even guilt, feelings. I know as teenagers, we hated seeing Mom and Dad drunk but if they were sober, we lost part of our freedom. I wonder sometimes how different our lives could have been if they would have handled their lives differently. Maybe it made us all stronger. I know I forgave them a long time ago.

. . . Anyway, let me know how your appointment goes and send more stories.

Love,
Beulah.

Texas,
October 26, 2000.

Oh my God! I'm so glad to hear from you! I was so worried. Aunt Beulah told me that you were going to have some treatment in Hamilton. I hope it was for the better! I didn't know what they were going to do. I hope that you are not suffering too much. I know that now is the time that everything gets really tough. Pam and Amanda must be going through a lot. Please let me know day by day how you are feeling. Sarah is very concerned about you too! We all want you to be comfortable. It seems like you aren't taking very much painkiller? I know you are tough!!

I'm sorry that things are so bad! We think about you all the time!!! Our prayers are with you! Dad I love you and know that things can only get better! You give me inspiration! . . . Sarah is with me now and she wants you to know that she loves you! All of us feel the pain even though we are so far away. Please know that we are all praying for you! It's all I can think about. I hope that I haven't been too depressing but you know that you are the most important person in my LIFE!

Love you,
Sam Jr.

Texas,
October 28, 2000.

I just got a chance to re-read your email. Glad to see you still have your sense of humor. I am glad you're back home and that things are at least somewhat better. Hopefully some of the lingering side effects of the treatments will fade. I did have to laugh at your observations of the hospital stay and the nursing staff. In fact, I would like to share it with the nurses I work with, to give them a little appreciation of the pt's point of view (if that is okay with you). You would be surprised at the number of calls I get at 3 A.M., asking if they can give a patient Tylenol for their headache, only to remind them that there is a prn order for the mediation already! Oh well, I guess that is why they call it practicing medicine . . .

Love,
Craig.

Texas,
November 25, 2000.

Dear Sam, re:. "I sometimes think we all need reminding that we have a lot to be proud of when it comes to who and what we are. So this is your reminder for now."

Amen to this; Susie and I have been having somewhat the same conversation. Yes, there was a lot of drinking and craziness (there were Christmas Eve gatherings when I tended to hide in the little back hall at Golda's). There is also genius, creativity, incredible generosity, a deep desire for gusto, and amazing ability to respond to family need in times of trouble (cf. all the help Golda and Joe gave extended family during the Depression and after the war. Daddy remembers courting Mom and coming to Golda's late, only to have to step over sleeping bodies of relatives who were there because of the generous hospitality). Not to mention a real penchant for storytelling and embellishment, and the most incredible ability to simply engage life. Kopeckys do NOT sit back and watch. They live, and because of that, they make mistakes. I am convinced that those genes are full of genius, stubbornness, healing vocation, humor, and a taste for excess—which causes both grace and pain.

Bryan, our oldest (he's 26), is very much drawn to the Kopecky line. After visiting Prague, he has tried to learn Czech and is hoping to return to the Czech Republic in the spring. (Jason, the younger son, age 23, is in France teaching and they hope to team up for some adventures). He also has the same hyperlipidemia I have, that led to my acute pancreatitis—which came from the Kopecky line. Who knows how much is encoded in our DNA?

I will look forward to reading what you have sent—many thanks for preparing the book for us, and for our children, grandchildren and great grandchildren. Take care.

Love,
Mary Beth.

New Zealand,
November 27, 2000.

Dear Laurie, I got your last 2 emails and I must admit you have been busy updating the web pages with stories and all.

I am not sure that your popularity will hold up with some of the stories. I didn't realize that Grandma called you all such names. I am sure I was guilty of it from time to time as well. I have become more aware of the fact that this does not do a lot for a kid's self esteem and have tried to remember this when I get angry. I guess it is like we have said before, none of us are perfect and we all make mistakes.

I like to remember her in my own way I guess, and remember how much she had to put up with over the years, and how many times she had been taken advantage of in so many ways. It was a wonder she wasn't more bitter than she was.

I have tried to keep a lot of this out of my second book but as you say, both sides do need to be told if a true picture is to be given.

I do know that you grandchildren were very important to her and she loved you all very much. I only wish that when she died, she would have left everything she had to only the grandchildren. That is where the true love was a two-way street.

Take care I will write again later.

Love to all,
Dad.

Colorado,
November 29, 2000.

Thank you for your support with my family web site. I really do enjoy writing the stories. I look forward to your books! Does it include the diary information from several Grandpa's back? I remember sitting for hours reading that diary when you guys still lived in Austin. Allen finds all the stories interesting too. He actually wanted to get a copy of the diary but I told him that was next to impossible. He will be as excited as I am to read your books! . . . Anyway, I know so little about you, really. I really do want to read those books.

Take care of yourself and I will be writing again soon.

Love,
Laurie.

New Zealand,
December 12, 2000.

Dear family and friends, another year is almost over and it is time to write another one of those group letters. I guess one of the reasons is that I don't really have a lot new and things are much the same.

I had some radiation treatment in October, on three areas, over a 10-day period. It was on my lower spine, neck and pelvis. The pain in these areas is now much better but the nausea I have is almost all the time. But overall I am doing okay and much the same.

Pam has been busy with the lodge, looking after Amanda and me, and working on some of her projects. She is trying to work on some of the native and conservation issues with our Maori friend Tom Winitana, who we got to know over the last year and a half. They, along with Terry Goldsbury (who some of you have met) have been trying to put a plan together with the district council, to map out which areas on the peninsula are under the jurisdiction of the 10 local tribes. I am helping by drawing the maps on the computer. Along with this, they are also identifying who the spokesman is in each of these areas. At present this is a big unknown and yet when anyone wants to buy/sell, or do some sort of work on their property, the council always wants to know if they have consulted with "local Iwi" (tribes) on any issues. Most people don't even know who to talk to, much less whether there are any issues.

This really got started back in 1990 when the (national) 'Resource Management Act' became law out here. Part of the act was for people to consult with the Maori people on any issues that might affect them in terms of tradition, cultural values, heritage, and various other interests they might have—such as in our own case with Pa site/neighboring Maori grave. The local council runs into problems with such things as when they want to put a trash dump in an area, and then finds out it was a site of special significance to local Maori, and it would not be appropriate for such use. A lot of times the reasons given are vague, and on a number of occasions a conflict does not surface until a project is underway. The council has been known to negotiate an agreement with one group, only to find out they have been talking to the wrong tribe. It is not uncommon for more than one tribe to claim an interest in one area. This is because it may have changed hands among the tribes via wars, trades, gifts etc. in years gone by.

Some of the Maori involved are out to make what they can out of it. Others are trying to protect and preserve areas of true importance. We became aware of this problem through unknown issues on our own property. The Iwis in the past, in our area, have so far mainly been out for what they can get. It is often the older generation that want to try and protect real sites. It has gotten to the point that most people have had enough and it is time for the council to decide if they want it to be business as usual, or whether they want to set up this group to define areas with spokespeople. That is the first step. Next step will be for Tom to then work out, with the people in that area, "what, if anything, needs to be protected".

Tom is a very well-respected Maori from tribes in the upper half of the North Island. Before coming to our lodge he was Chief Adviser/Ministerial Aide to the New Zealand Government's Treaty of Waitangi Minister, in charge of nation-wide negotiations with its indigenous Maori people. He is also Maori 'royalty', as first cousin to the Maori Queen. He has worked all over New Zealand with numerous tribes in trying to get their settlements under the Treaty of Waitangi—originally signed with England's Queen Victoria in the 1840's. It was during these and various other negotiations, that a lot of the tribes got to know him. It has been impossible for the locals to work out some of the issues themselves and that is how Tom became involved in working in our area (and becoming a guest at our lodge). He is a sort of respected third party who is trying to work with the tribes, through some of these issues from the past. Because of her own interest in indigenous history, Pam works with him on local knowledge, ideas, and does the everyday work. Terry is working mainly on the map side of things, to get the information in the right place on the maps I have drawn, and make sure the computer file types are compatible etc. This is while Sam and Amanda mainly watch and try to stay out of the way.

It is unfortunate but now the council is not sure if they even want to go forward with the project and fund it. They spend thousands every year trying to get this information on a piece by piece basis and now they have a chance to put a system in place, they are not sure they want to put the money out for it. Should know soon.

Amanda has been doing really well and has made good grades in school. For her, this is the end of the school year and when she goes back at the end of January, it is the start of the new school year, and the time to start in the next grade up. I fear that she is fixing to start going into her adolescence as early as she has done everything else. One advantage is she is tall, and has been able to help serve people in the restaurant. Pam has been taking people in the restaurant, as long as they are staying here. Before the season started, Amanda asked if she could get a paper route. We asked what for and she said she wanted to make some pocket money. We told her to wait and try working with Mom. Over the last number of weeks Amanda has been getting tips and this keeps her happy. Some give her 2, 3 or 4 dollars, which makes her happy as she feels she has done a good job. Then about once a week, some of the guests spoil her and give her a $20 bill. This has happened several times now. She has now decided this is better than a paper route.

I have finished up the writing I was doing on the first part of the family history. It turned into a book and is very different from what I had set out to do. As more people saw it and read parts of it, they felt that it would be of broad interest and that I should see about getting it published. We have started to send off some excerpts from it to some publishers and hope that we may be able to get a publisher interested in it. We are hoping to know something in the first half of the New Year.

Well that is about all for now. I hope that you and yours are all doing okay and are all well and happy. Drop us a note and let us know how you are.

Love to all,
Sam, Pam and Amanda.

Texas,
December 23, 2000.

Dear Sam, Pam and Amanda, best wishes to all of you for a peaceful Christmas with some satisfaction that a trying year is nearly over.

Your collective determination in facing adversity is inspiring. I think you have set a standard for all of your relatives to try for. Your work with the Maori people, the effort that's gone into the book, Amanda's service to your dining customers—all speak well for each of you. We onlookers are proud. I'm sure that includes your parents, grandparents and, God bless her, your cheerleader, Mary K. Colbert.

Thanks very much for your Christmas card and the letter you enclosed. It was a good account of your interaction with the tribal people and the mutual respect you have gained working with them. It could be a pattern that might be useful elsewhere, including the U.S. where opinions are so divided now.

Thanks again for your message and I hope the nausea soon lightens up. Your family remains in our thoughts and prayers.

Love,
Gene.

Texas,
December 27, 2000.

Dear Sam, Pam and Amanda, Merry Christmas to you all! On this second day of the season, we are freezing our fannies off. Winter weather has come to Texas big time! Tomorrow they are predicting ice, sleet and/or a little snow.

We had a jolly gathering at Dad's on Saturday. Bill and Karen came in from Austin with their two children, and Tom had the week off from Luby's, so he and Amy, the twins and Paige, were all there too. I think that this Christmas has been a little easier for Dad. Since Mom died four years ago on Dec. 28th, this season has been bittersweet for all of us. For some reason, this year, things have been much more light-hearted and easy. A real gift.

Dad came here on Christmas Day, as did Doug's Mom. Dad brought a letter he'd written to Mom on Christmas Day, 1944, from the Battle of the Bulge. He was so homesick. He wrote with much longing for the hospitality of 627 Lamont, and said he knew Dr Joe would give him something to help him warm up! Dad and Mom were not yet engaged at that point, and he was referring to Golda and Joe as "Mrs. K" and "Dr K".

I hope this season and the coming year bring you and yours much joy and contentment at being here. Dad shared your Christmas letter with us; I so admire your work with the Maori. As you well know, the story of what happened to the Indian nations of the U.S. is a terrible one.

Blessings and love,
Mary Beth

CHAPTER 92

LONG STORY SHORT (VOICES FROM THE PAST)

Texas,
September 20, 2000.

Dear Sam, well, it has taken some 20 years but I have finally tracked you down. I was working at an Albertson's Pharmacy (I work a little relief from time to time) when I took a prescription from a Dr Craig Kopecky. You must be very proud to have a son follow his grandfather and great-grandfather into medicine.

It seems only last week that two young pharmacists were eagerly anticipating their new careers with University Drug Store. Man, how the weeks became years and the careers changed; first here, then there, then back again . . . until now, it's 31 years since last week.

I guess the last time we spoke, you were in Austin, in the car business, and I was in Cotulla, in the banking business. I believe you told me at that time you were remarried and moving 'Down Under'. That must have been about 1981 or '82. Well, since that time I have divorced, remarried, raised my kids (Georgann left us), got out of banking, and opened a new pharmacy. I sold the pharmacy to Albertsons' in 1998 and retired to a little ranch in the Texas Hill Country, near a town called Pipe Creek.

My daughter, Jackie, and her husband, live in Conway, Arkansas. They are both computer folk, and work for a company that makes school buses and U.P.S. trucks.

Jason, my son, and his wife, are both marines, and stationed in Twenty nine Palms, California. Cynthia, my wife, is still working full-time in the banking business.

Now that I have bored you with my life and family, IT'S YOUR TURN! Honestly, I would really like to hear about your family and adventures. Were there 2 boys and a girl—or more? I remember working for you at Zipp's one night when one of your kids was born. Right? So give with the details. Whuzzzz-up!

Sam, Craig shared with me your current health problems. I cannot imagine the frustration you must feel in dealing with this challenge. Suffice to say, that you and yours, are in our thoughts.

Please take the time to bring me up to speed on your situation, knowing that my concern for you, and my interest in your life and family, is real.

With warmest personal regards,
Jim Pollock.

New Zealand,
October 3, 2000.

Dear Jim, I must admit it was a real surprise to get your letter the other day. It seems so many things have happened since I last spoke to you. You are right about one thing for sure, nothing eventuated as planned.

It's hard to decide just when things started to go to hell—maybe right after birth, I'm not sure. As you may have been aware, Cecile decided she was being treated unfairly as she was responsible for the house and kids. She wanted 'out' and started to work in the store, but was jealous as hell. She even got to the point where she would measure the girls' dresses to make sure they were not too short. It got worse and worse. Eventually she started running around on me while I was working my butt off all the time. She ended up taking up with the boys' football coach, and after several years of being told "she wasn't seeing anyone", "it's over between us" etc., she wanted a divorce.

It wasn't until this hit the fan that I found out her father had known what she was up to for at least a year or more, and had kept it quiet. She helped bust me by always needing more money for her business (the bookkeeping one), and a secret apartment, she and Walt were sharing. She never paid our bills, and when we split, I took all the bills—to get my credit under control again. I left with the clothes I had, a few personal effects, and the bills. She got the rest—the house, car, business etc.

It was during the time of going broke, before the divorce, that I went to work for her father at the dealership. It was to be until I got a job. I interviewed with several drug companies, and even took a number of their aptitude and personality tests. I was told I did real well on them and should continue to apply. I had one offer from Eli Lilly to go with them, but I needed to move to El Paso. Cecile wouldn't do it. The job fell over and I was left working for her Dad. I didn't know at the time that the reason she didn't want to move was because of Walt.

I never got along with her brother and out of necessity worked with him at the dealership. Cecil, her father, knew I could help him and after a few years, had a number of the departments running okay at the dealership, and was a big help. He came to me one day and told me he had a chance to get another store, but he wanted to know if I would stay and do it with him. The deal was that I would work 7 days a week and do everything to get it off the ground. This included dealing with the factory for new plans, and getting approval along the way. I got an insurance license so we could sell insurance at the store, and did everything from sales, advertising, factory claims, customer complaints, ordering vehicles—you name it, I did it . . . yes, including washing cars and the bathroom, in the early days. He paid me $1500 a month from the time I went to work for him, until I left about 5 years later. The deal was, if I did all this and the store got going, then I would get paid an average amount but the store would be for my kids, Sam, Craig, Laurie and Scott. Henry, his son, would have no part of it. He would have the San Antonio store. Well, I went for the deal and that is how Cecil Tindall Chevrolet-Oldsmobile in Boerne, got going. He purchased it from Epperson, along with the land on the highway. I did the work and he got the money.

During this time I met a girl that I think may have gone to school with you—a Sharon Ferguson. I knew her for about 6 months and everybody said I should marry her as it would be good for Sam, since he had come to live with me from the start. I wasn't sure but after a while, gave in. This was a case where once the ring was on the finger, everything changed. It was hell. She claimed to be women's lib, and tried about 6 religions in the 6 months we were together. We were divorced in less than a year. What a mistake.

It just happened that, one day, I was filling out reports for the factory and needed a copy of the numbers of shares, and holders thereof, for the corporation. Cecil had it in San Antonio and had it sent up to me. He even said that he didn't remember why he had it instead of me. The box came up, with the seal, the papers etc., and guess what? Henry Tindall, his son, owned 25% of the shares. I was busting my butt and putting up with hell, to make his son that much better off. I had been taken advantage of and knew I was gone, as soon as I could find a job.

I had built up a reputation with some of the people in the automobile business over the previous five years, and had done a good job for Cecil. When I put the word out, I was told to contact Doug Maund at Charles Maund Oldsmobile-Cadillac in Austin. I talked to the son, and got a job with them for the next 6 years. The old man, Charles, was the best employer I ever had. I could not have worked for a better place. They paid extremely well, left the managers to do their job, and were usually easy to get along with. My mistake was company politics. We had a sales manager who worked for them for a couple of years who they hired from Capitol Chevrolet. He spent his time soaping up the boss and looking for another job, as he felt we worked too many hours, and that was not going to change. When the stuff hit the fan in the late 1980's, the sales went down and everyone got nervous. The son, Doug, listened to Hank on how he could do it all, so, without consulting me, decided to keep Hank and let me go. The funny thing was, I was the one doing all the work. They hired an advertising agency and put on some other support staff, after I left, to do part of my job. I still wonder if they weren't nervous about my new wife, Pam.

When I moved to Austin, I met a girl called Pam. She was from New Zealand and to save you a long story, we were married about a year after we met. We have now been with each other almost 20 years. The word around the store was that I was going to move to New Zealand anyway. This was one of those 'someday' things we talk about. Her Dad was in poor health and most of her family had passed away. We always said that someday we might go and live there before she had no family left. When everything hit the fan, it really did. About 2 months later, her Dad had a stroke and before it was over, had to have open-heart surgery. I had a chance to, maybe, go to work at a Honda store for a friend of Charlie Maund, but we felt as long as we were going to have to move, and her folks weren't doing very well, it might as well be time for that 'someday', after all. So we moved to New Zealand.

We had a good time in Austin but when it was over and done, we had saved very little money. We had not planned on pulling the plug just yet. We came across a half-finished place that was up for sale on the Coromandel Peninsula, near Thames. This is about 1 ½ hours from Auckland International Airport. We spent the best part of the next 12 months finishing the place, and fixing it up enough to open as a combination restaurant and accommodation facility. Today it is known as 'Te Puru Coast View Lodge'.

We have had one battle after another and, to this day, still have a battle going on with the local council and Iwi (Maori tribes), about certain rights regarding this land. We found out that it was one of the largest (fortified) 'Pa' sites in the area. Most likely it was inhabited around 1350, and had a very large tribal settlement. The archaeological studies have been very superficial but enough to create great interest. This presents us with a unique opportunity. We could possibly do a partial restoration of the site with displays and interpretation for the tourists that are interested in the Maori history and culture. It could help protect the site for those in the future, and educate those in the area and from overseas, on the past. This is much easier said than done.

Along the way, Pam wanted a family. You came and covered the store for me when Laurie was born. After Scott was born, Cecile insisted I have a vasectomy. It was 16 years before I tried to get a reversal. Once I was here in N.Z., I went to a urologist and micro—surgeon. We had no odds, so we just went for it. It worked out, and after postoperative shock and a few things, I was fine. After Pam had one miscarriage (because of all the painting etc. she was doing), within the year, we had Amanda on her way. Amanda was born on April 18, 1990.

We have been broke most of the time we have lived here in N.Z. and have worked harder than we ever have. But the one thing I did get that I didn't have before, was a wife and a child I could spend time with. With the type of business we have, I was able to spend a lot of time every day, with both. This is the one thing I treasure from the last 10 years or so. I did finally get a wife that I can't say enough for, and another chance with my kid. They are all precious and the big difference is that I was able to spend time with this one.

I am proud of Craig. His grandfather told him he couldn't do it. His mother wanted him to do bookkeeping, so as to help her. But Craig's wife encouraged him and her family helped support him in his idea of medical school. He graduated at the top of his class, and along the way has been given honor after honor. It gets almost embarrassing to tell you how well he has done. He is presently at Ft. Hood.

Sambo, I am very proud of as well. He dropped out of university with one year to go. He was actually making good grades but was talked into going to work for his grandfather, Cecil, who took advantage of him for years. He is working now (and for the last several years) for D. Howard Aircraft at S.A. International Airport. He is with a department that makes some sort of steering stabilizer for big trucks and motor homes. He is a good kid and a down-the-middle family man.

Laurie ended up running away after her mother gave her a bunch of crap, along with Cecil. She was going with a guy at Baylor and they found birth control pills in her purse. They took the car and everything away, so she ran off with the guy and got married. They have had some rough times. He has now finished up with a PhD in chemistry; she has a BS in biology and is working on a Masters in chemistry. She is teaching at present and he works for a drug company in Colorado.

Scott is a C.P.A. He works for some firm in San Antonio and got married a year or so ago. I heard from him for the first time in 10 years, just 5 months ago. He still doesn't say much or contact me much at all. It seems that his mother and Walt did a real number on him.

When I was still in Austin, Cecil sold the San Antonio store for $3 million. He and Henry then spent most of their time in Boerne. Since I moved here, they sold that store to Cavender for a reported $6 million. They have some store now on the south side of town, I've been told. The kids have never seen a dime from any of this. I had a feeling they never would. It got to the point that Cecil was mean and I could no longer trust him. Their grandmother died this last Easter, and that was the first time they were given anything that amounted to much. I heard that Cecil is not in all that good a health, and I can only imagine the fight when he goes.

In the meantime . . . I had a backache from working in the yard, moving bark and making a new garden area in the parking lot. I waited a few weeks and it didn't get better. Then over about a 6-week period, my amount of fluid that I produced when we had sex went from a normal amount, to almost nothing. I wasn't sure if some sort of problem had come up with scar tissue or something, so I went to the doctor. Everything was fine except for the above, and I had started to get pains in my legs and feet. I also had a funny feeling going on around one side and it felt numb or something at times. The lab came back with a PSA of 76. I was sent for a scan and a biopsy. They were both positive with nice high numbers, and over a couple of months I went from backache to advanced terminal cancer—primary prostate and secondary bone cancer. The doctor I had, a urologist, said he wanted me to do hormone therapy, and I told him I wanted to know the full extent of how far it had spread before I did anything, as my understanding was that it was terminal and therefore treated with palliative therapy only, once it had gone to the bone. He said he was not worried about the positive spots in my spine and didn't want to run an MRI etc. I could do the old 'watchful waiting'.

In February 1999, I cut the grass on the weekend. I had more pain in my back and took more aspirin. I then got shooting pain in my legs. By Friday, I was in the hospital emergency room, paralyzed from the waist down. When I went and looked it up, the literature says that in my situation, you have a 30% chance of getting paralysis as a complication. It is recommended to do localized radiation on the tumors, to reduce the chance of damage and paralysis. I have had a painful and slow partial recovery. I have been unable to work and been a burden on the family, in this state. I have filed a complaint on the doctor—a year ago—and if it goes through, with the piece of paper and $2.50, you can get a cup of coffee.

It seems that after being in remission for the last 10 months, things are now on the move again. I have another bone scan and radiation scheduled for 11th October in Hamilton. This is a slow, painful, way to go. It is also a problem with being nauseous, and the paralysis has also caused problems with my guts and bladder. The next time I have another doctor ask me about hormone therapy and trying to last a while longer, I think I will cut theirs off and push them down their throat, for my therapy. Why would I want to last longer? I feel like hell, and hurt. I am not doing Pam and Amanda any favors either.

Don't misunderstand me. It is what it is. I have accepted that. It was like the lady they talked to, that was terminal, who said "It is like waiting around at the airport, with all the commotion going on, that is the bother; once you are on your way, it's not so bad". I have been very lucky. I have had great kids. I love them all very much. I have been fortunate to spend the last 20 years of my life with someone that I love and feel is my soul mate; that person that you find yourself looking for approval from, trying to do things for, working with, enjoying things, and just being with.

I hope you have found as much peace and happiness as I have. It has been good to hear from you. Asked if I could do it again? Only if we can leave the parts out where it hurts.

Love to all,
Sam R. Kopecky.

Texas,
November 7, 2000.

Dear Sam, I received your letter a couple of weeks ago. I have read it several times and reflected on it, and am still at a loss on what to say in this letter. I showed your letter to my wife; her response was "Wow—what a life!" I guess my take is; Wow, what an adventure! I am proud of your determination and your devotion to your kids. I trust your October 11th date was positive. So enough of this.

So, how did you all get involved in a B & B business? Sounds like a lot of hard work. The finishing of the lodge and the building of this type of business must have been very exciting. I am somewhat of a Native American history buff, so now I must learn more about the Pa or Iwi (help me with this). I assume these are the native peoples of New Zealand. Is your lodge in a destination location or is it more of a transition facility ie. overnight and then on to other places? Send me some info—who knows . . .

I gathered from your letter that Craig was, or is, in the Army. Does he anticipate relocating to San Antonio? My son is a career Marine and will be stationed in Australia at some point. That will be my excuse to travel to your side of the world.

As I sit here on a cloudy, cold day watching TV coverage on the election today, I am totally ignorant of how your country elects its leaders. This campaign has cost—according to the press—one billion dollars. That would be a pretty big budget item for your country—and it would certainly go a long way in this country, to fix some of our problems, instead of for plastic buttons etc.

Will you send us your lodge info and get me started on the Iwi's. Hook em!

Pam, take care of that good man you have!

Warmest regards,
Jim

Texas,
January 2, 2001.

Dear Sam and Pam, it has been many years since we have heard from each other. Hope you two are doing well and living large.

I retired from the remodeling business. I am a manager at IRS with a group of 22 examiners working for me. Lynda and I are still together. We celebrate our 19th anniversary, January 9. As you can see from the attached picture of the Florence family, Lynda and I have three wonderful boys. Lorin, 15 (yes, that tiny little boy, the remodel of your Austin house helped feed); Thaddeus Jay (T.J.) 12; and a late life surprise, Quinn Alon (who will be 17 months old on Jan. 10).

I think of you two often, as I recall the feast or famine days of my remodeling. I still have all my tools and stuff but IRS has offered me security, great benefits, and a healthy retirement plan, that I just couldn't seem to find being self-employed. The vagaries of the construction business here in Austin, made it awful tough to feed a family; unless you were willing to work multiple jobs at the same time. That was never my style. I cleaned up too many half-finished jobs the fly-by-nighters had left unfinished.

In 88/89, I spent all of my spare time building my parents a 3,200 sq. ft. home on 14 acres of land, 25 miles SE of Austin. They have both retired and spend most of their days on the 16'X38' screened-in porch, drinking 'Keystone Light' beer and watching the grass grow.

Lynda still works. After my next promotion, we plan for her to retire and be a stay-at-home Mom. My personal take on that, is that it will last all of a month and she will bail out and go back to work. I love her dearly but she is not the stay-at-home type.

Well, I am enjoying a day off. Quinn is here with me and I enjoy the time he and I have together. I missed a lot, working two jobs and long hours, as Lorin and T.J. grew up. I will not have to say that about Quinn.

My love to both of you. You both have a special place in my life. I learned much from each of you.

Dayne.

PS. The picture was taken in May of last year before Quinn had surgery. Lynda and I were not sure he would live through it and wanted a family picture of all of us. Yes, I am sure you will think that is me in the back but actually that is Lorin and I am the old geezer in the hat.

New Zealand,
January 4, 2001.

I must admit Dayne, I don't think I would have recognized you with the beard and hat. I still remember you with the nail bags and tools around your hips, and your saying that you would need to get out of that line of work as it was too hard on you.

I don't blame you for getting out. Pam and I still talk about our time in Austin. We always said if we ever went back, it would be to Austin. I know things have changed a lot. I had a salesman that worked for me that was married to an Australian. He left Charles Maund several years ago and they came to see us when they went to Australia to see her family. He told me how the whole area has grown.

We, too, have lots of memories of those days and tell many a good story from them. I think Pam's favorite is when she was frustrated and got you to take over and talk to some of the sub's, and you explained to them that you were the HMFIC. When they didn't understand, you told them what it stood for—she has never forgotten.

You have a nice-looking family. I am glad things have turned out better for you. You deserved it. Pam and I had a little girl, 18 April, 1990. Not so little any more—she is 10 ½ now. Amanda has been a real joy for us both.

We didn't know what we were going to do when we first got to N.Z. We were going to just take some time off at first, then one thing led to another, and we ended up buying a half-finished, half-done tourist lodge. The first thing was to get enough of the place done, so we could open. It has been a 12 year project. Still needs lots of work. We have had to learn the tourist trade, and have run a restaurant, along with the accommodation. Here you have 6 months of business and 6 months with very little—that is when you do repairs or travel. We have been on the repairs, as what little money we had each year, needed to go back into the place.

I took a second job with 'Tower Corporation' here, selling insurance and investments. I started with them in 1995 and it worked, as the 'seasons' were opposite from the lodge. Then in late 1998, I was diagnosed with prostate cancer and it had already spread to the bone in my spine. By February 1999, I had a problem with spinal compression and have had paralysis from the waist down. At first they were thinking I had about a year to go. Now they are not sure—maybe 2 or 3, maybe 4. I have good weeks and bad. I told Pam, it was my Dad getting back at me for making me use a walking frame like he had—except I can't get around as good and usually need a wheelchair.

Pam is doing okay and Amanda is old enough to be a help. Pam's folks are just hanging in. Her Dad is very ill with his heart and we feel like it could be any day. But he got his 10-plus years they promised him with the open-heart operation back in Austin. Pam's mother is getting worn out trying to take care of him. She has day care nurses that help but it is still a strain on her.

Well, that is the short and sweet summary about us. I have been writing a family history and finished the first volume last December. I have done most of the second one as well now, and that included Austin and moving out here to N.Z. It was good to hear from you, and stay in touch.

Love to the whole family,
Sam, Pam and Amanda Kopecky.

PS. Whenever we had a problem with the repairs here, we would make reference to Dayne and Root and wish you were here!

Texas,
January 4, 2001.

Sam, was thrilled to hear back from you. And greatly saddened by the news of your illness. I don't often pray these days but when I do, you and your family will be mentioned. Please keep me posted on how you are, and let me know if there is anything I can do for you, Pam or Amanda.

I am thrilled you and Pam have had a child. I just hope she got your brains and Pam's looks. Haw haw! Actually, since you and Pam were both attractive and smart, I am sure Amanda will be a success at anything she wants to do.

Yessir, I had to get out of construction. I worked both my business and IRS full time for almost two years, then at 39, had a heart attack that nearly killed me. Didn't learn well, and had a second one about eighteen months ago. The cardiologist said I wouldn't be able to have sex for at least six weeks after that one. Quinn proved he was wrong. I told Lynda we should go to court and see if he could help support the boy. Haw haw! I have cleaned up my lifestyle some and hope to see all of my boys grown and off on their own paths.

We still tell the tale of Lynda getting in the jacuzzi at your house when she was pregnant with Lorin, and how he kicked and shoved her tummy like something out of "Close Encounters".

You said you were writing your family history. Are you going to have it published? I have been dabbling at writing a novel but it seems these days are so full I have little time to devote to it. My "spare tome" seems to be eaten up by my children. I don't really mind that.

Need to close as I have a load of oak in the back of the truck I need to get unloaded. I bought a huge New Braunfels grill/smoker this past summer and will barbecue even if it IS freezing cold. We eat a lot of grilled lean meat. Lorin, being a type 1 diabetic and I, with a tattered ticker, have to eat healthy.

Dayne.

New Zealand,
September 21, 2001.

Dear friends and family, just a quick note to let you all know that Sam passed away peacefully at home this morning, at around 7am. It was exactly a month since he had been admitted to hospital with spinal compression again and became paralyzed from the chest down. We brought him home to die—and as usual, he confounded all the experts by refusing to comply with their predictions.

I will get back to you all individually but just wanted to let everyone know ASAP. I am glad he is finally at peace but will miss him so much. Amanda is doing well—especially since we had a practice run just 2 months ago, with my Dad. Maybe now they can finally go fishing together again, as they had always wanted to do.

Love,
Pam

Texas,
September 26, 2001.

Dear Pam and Amanda, I, and my family are greatly saddened by Sam's passing. The world is a bit smaller.

The words I would put into this email have weighed heavily on my mind since I received your message. I would give anything to be near so I could give you both a huge hug and maybe recount a few of the great moments we shared. They were some of the best times, even though we faced more than a few challenges. Through my more tempestuous moments, Sam was the voice of reason. And Pam, you were the one that always said something that made me feel better about myself. The true payment I received for the work I did was never the money. It was your friendship.

Should there come a day when I can come to New Zealand, I will deliver the hugs I send now, in person. Please write when you can.

God bless you both,
Dayne (a.k.a. HMFIC), Lynda, Lorin, T.J. and Quinn.

CHAPTER 93

THE END IS NIGH

Texas,
February 5, 2001.

Dear Pam, Sam and Amanda, our dear Aunt Edith passed away this morning at 6 AM. She would have been 102 this August and has been in poor health for about 1 ½ years. She was a favorite of Mary's and I was very fond of her too. One of her former students has been taking care of her in Rowena, Texas, for several months and a call from her this afternoon informed me of the passing.

Her eldest son, Sam, lost his life in an airplane training accident during WWII and as you know Sam, you were named for him. The entire Kopecky clan considered young Sam a favorite, so you were honored to bear his name.

I'm sorry to bring this news but I knew you would want to know.

Best wishes and much love,
Gene.

Florida,
February 22, 2001.

Sam, I just returned from Texas and did a whirlwind tour. I went to the rodeo three times, Austin twice and Leaky twice. I viewed 8 ranches and have pretty much decided on the Sabinal Canyon. There is one property we are interested in but it is expensive so we'll have to see what happens. The ranch is in Utopia and has 6,000 feet of river on it. Want to open a B & B on the river?

I saw Scott, Craig and Elizabeth and kids at the rodeo. We didn't talk long but did promise to email once in a while. Scott probably thought I was nuts because I know he doesn't remember me. They looked great and it was a pleasure talking with them.

I took your book chapters to U.T. Press on 15 Feb. The editor who handles Texas history is William Bishell. He was not there but I talked with his secretary. Let me know what you hear. Have to go unpack and see if there is anything to eat in this house. Tommy has been gone while I was in Texas and gets back Friday. It sure is different when Sean isn't here. He called me every day in Texas. Talk with you soon.

Love,
Beulah.

Texas,
March 26, 2001.

Hello! It's been awhile so I wanted to tell you what was happening here . . .

How is everything going? I've been contemplating coming back over and the fares I've looked at are reasonable but they are for May at the earliest. If I came, it would be just me and I would stay for a week or so. I've been thinking that it would be nice to see you all again and I want to help out any way I can (fixing things up or projects).

I hope you are feeling well (as well as can be expected). Please give me some details on what's going on. I think about you all the time and wish I could be there for support. Tell everyone hello from all of us! Even short emails are fine, just short notes. I'm sorry it's been over a month since my last confession—I mean email (ha ha). Please know that anything I can do to help, all you have to do is ask. I LOVE YOU ALL! Better go. Bye.

Love,
Sambo.

New Zealand,
May 7, 2001.

Dear Laurie . . . it's a shame if we feel we have gaps that are not being filled at home. I guess that is one thing I finally found with Pam. We share a lot, talk a lot, and do a lot of things together. We talk and work with each other on projects.

When we were in Austin we shared an interest in Trans Designs, as well as doing up the properties and houses with each other. Out here it has been the property, the lodge, the restaurant, and now all of these other various projects she has become involved with. She has admitted that this is one of the things that will be hardest for her when I go. We see each other every day and share what is going on, with what we think and what we do. I am sure she will find herself talking to the room at times after I am gone but who knows, I may still be around.

I think that it is one thing with this relationship that has been different. The caring, the sharing of interests, and communication. At times it has not always been easy but I think she still sees me as her best friend, and that is what has made this relationship for us both, very special. It is something we both wanted. A person to come home to that would always be in your corner, that would share ideas, interests, projects, you name it. We have really enjoyed our time with each other and all the things we have done. I think that is part of the difference. I hope with time you have all found this as well. It makes a difference.

Take care.

Love to all,
Dad, Pam and Amanda.

New Zealand,
May 25, 2001.

Hi Sam!

I've felt rather submerged at times recently by events that have poured themselves on top of me and felt disappointed that we haven't made contact.

Tuesday, I talked to the latest class of American students, here for only a few weeks: a half credit. The usual theme, touching on the Treaty of Waitangi but more concerned with dispelling the images of both "noble" and "ignoble" savages, and presenting a highly adaptable people with a holistic world view, a spiritual ecology, responding to market forces, reaching out eagerly and successfully for new technology.

I shot my mouth off for a long time but was disappointed not to tell them about the "head factory" at Whangaroa. Dried, smoked heads of important friends were apparently placed with their bones in highly tapu caves. Thus their mana was recognized. But dried heads of enemies were put on display to be reviled so that their mana/tapu was destroyed. Such was the demand from European traders for such curiosities that entrepreneurial Maori set up a head factory where slaves were taken, tattooed elaborately to look like chiefs, and then parted from their heads. Of course, surplus protein would not be wasted. Maori tattooing was a lengthy, painful process of carving into the flesh with tiny bone adzes. Healing had to take place, so the subjects had time for contemplation. How to improve the product? The entrepreneurs arranged for glass eyes to be imported from Europe. These embellishments identify as commercial jobs, some of the heads recently returned from overseas collections.

You probably knew that Sam.

But I am re-reading a book that impressed me a couple of years ago: "Te Tangata"—the Human Person, by Michael Shirres. I found it so good that I thought someone would steal it from the local library. They did. The local library put it on order at the beginning of the year without success. The copy I am reading now is borrowed short-term from the

Waikato Library Service. I am impressed by the section which speaks of everyone and everything having mana/tapu (intrinsic worth?) which should be respected but can be attacked disastrously. I remember feeling offended when a (local) Ngatimaru person from this side of the range spoke disparagingly of Whitianga's Ngatihei. I quote Shirres: "This "trampling" on the tapu of another is itself seen as a way of increasing one's own tapu, while diminishing the intrinsic tapu of the other. With the weakening of the intrinsic tapu there is a weakening of the power of the restrictions, the extensions of tapu. The other person becomes "noa" or "free from restriction" in a negative way and able to be treated as "otaota", as rubbish."

At base, I find a profundity, a mana, a tapu, in Maori spirituality which enables me to understand why Kendall, the first Anglican missionary priest wrote to the Church Missionary Society, that he was so taken with the sublimity of Maori ideas that he had almost turned from a Christian to a heathen.

Better dash—I'm due at a function in ten minutes.

Best wishes Sam, Pam
and Amanda,
John [Clark].

New Zealand,
June 11, 2001.

Hi Sam, hope that transfusion's still kicking in.

I'd hoped to see you last Tuesday and still have in my hip pocket, a printout I'd hoped to hand over but I felt a bug coming on, and thought that I'd better not hand out samples.

Heard this one?

Two bees ran into each other. One asked the other how things were going.

"Really bad," said the second bee, "the weather has been wet and damp, and there aren't any flowers or pollen, so I can't make any honey."

"No problem," said the first bee, "just fly down five blocks and turn left, and keep going until you see all the cars. There's a Bar Mitzvah going on, and there are all kinds of fresh flowers and fresh fruit."

"Thanks for the tip," said the first bee, and flew away.

A few hours later, the two bees ran into each other again and the first bee asked, "How did it go?"

"Fine," said the second bee, "it was everything you said it would be."

"Uh, what's that thing on your head?" asked the first bee.

"That's my yarmulke," said the second bee, "I didn't want them to think I was a WASP."

Probably an old one Sam, but new and funny to this New Zealander.

Best wishes,
John.

Texas,
June 21, 2001.

Dear Pam and Sam,

Thanks for letting us know of Alan's passing. There is relief and sorrow at a time like this and all of his family and friends are now experiencing both. It's too bad some folks have to suffer so much before leaving this life and I suppose we'll never understand as long as we are among the living.

The good part has to do with memories collected when our loved ones were in good heath, and enjoying and loving life.

You and Peg are in my thoughts and prayers and I'll send a snail mail card to Peg.

Love,
Gene.

New Zealand,
July 21, 2001.

Not a lot new. I have just come home from the hospital after being in the Waikato Hospital for the last 4 days. I had low dose radiation on my lower neck (1 ½ minutes on each of the 4 treatments). I also had treatment on my chest area below my breast area, sort of, on each side for 5 minutes, for my ribs. They also did some ribs on my back on my right side, sort of the area as if I had been shot in the front and this is where it came out.

I know we missed the Fourth of July but if anybody needs some ribs I am sure mine are done by now!

The main reason for the treatment was continual pain. I also was showing signs in my neck of loss of use of my two lower fingers of my right hand. We had some fear that this might progress to paralysis at a higher level if not treated. They told me to wait and see what it is like in 1 or 2 weeks and we should have a better idea on how effective the treatment was.

It is good to be home now, I can catch some naps and rest, take my medication, and wait for the pain to go away. I will be in touch, do the same.

Love to all,
Sam.

New Zealand,
August 18, 2001.

Hi everyone, Amanda and I have decided to outvote Sam and let you all know what is happening here now.

Sam went into Waikato Hospital in Hamilton nearly a month ago for radiotherapy as a combination of pain relief and to prevent further possible spinal compression which was beginning to affect his right arm. There has not been an obvious benefit from this yet and he began having more pain higher up his spine (between his shoulder blades) last week—which reminded him a lot of his original tumor which caused the spinal compression, resulting in his partial paralysis. His morphine had to be increased to stop him from climbing the walls, and he gritted his teeth and tried to ride this out. Obviously it affected his bowel with the result that by Wed. PM he had gone 9 days without anything happening. We tried (unsuccessfully) suppositories and enemas, and ended up at Thames Hospital A & E on Thursday A.M., as it had obviously got past us here at home—even though he had got to 8 or 9 days in the past. X-rays show there is nothing in the lower bowel—it has all stopped in the top half and cannot be reached by enemas etc. I imagine that the onset of spinal compression higher up his spine—along with the increase in morphine—has a lot to do with this. Tomorrow is day 12 . . . and so we wait.

In the meantime, he can no longer transfer from chair to bed etc. as his legs have started to go again. His oncologist from Hamilton came to see him yesterday and told him radiotherapy was not an option for the spinal compression now (as he has already exceeded the maximum in that area), or even for pain relief. In desperation he finally agreed to hormone therapy—to escape the excruciating pain—but that is still under review as he is now on a morphine pump and if that proves to be a better form of delivery, the other may not be necessary.

This morning when I got to the hospital I found that not only can he no longer even wiggle his toes any more but the paralysis has spread up his spine, with the result that he now has no sensation from the mid-chest down. His upper body strength is going and his arms are not what they were. His sore neck (which was radiated last November) is worrying him, along with increasing difficult in swallowing—and he is afraid he is heading for quadriplegia.

He does not feel I can take care of him at home any more but I have told him that as soon as he is sorted out in hospital, I will get him home by ambulance (I took him there in the van—by myself—only 2 days ago!) to be with us. The district nurses will come and help me with him morning and night (if not during the day as well) and we will get an electric hoist so I can lift and transfer him safely without causing injury to either of us. The transfer board we got so good at using in the beginning is no use at this stage.

I wish I had better news for you all. We knew this was coming one day but I prayed it would not be this way, as he tells me he is already almost a vegetable—hence his reluctance for me to tell you what is happening now. However, once again I do not feel this is his decision. I believe that you all need to be informed so you can make your own choices—they are not his to make for you. He is upset because he feels that I am not ready but the reality is, I never will be. I love him dearly and to see him reduced to this state is indescribable. It has all been so sudden and while he has come back from crises before, I am not sure this time that he will as he is now losing his will to live.

I am not happy about the hormone therapy if he does not need it for pain relief, as his original argument is now stronger than ever—and that is its side effect of lowering his PSA and slowing down the progress of the cancer. The oncologist has admitted that it is very unlikely it would alter the effects of the spinal compression now as he has likened this to a vascular event such as a stroke. However, he insists on going on about quality of life when he promotes its implementation—while I keep looking at Sam with his near total paralysis now and wonder what that really means. His quality of death may be a more relevant term now. Anyway, for the doctors amongst you, he has been started on Androcur (sp?) to stop any testosterone flushes caused by the monthly hormone injections he is to begin on Monday. He is thinking hard about this now as the morphine pump seems to have got the pain under much better control and he too is wondering about the wisdom of risking prolonging the agony, when he feels his quality of life is so minimal. He has not been able to have a drink (even one) for months now, he hardly eats, and now if he cannot move and is not very aware of things because of his medication, he is not sure that this is quality of life.

The nurses have been wonderful because we have a friend there who is one of them. He is being well cared for and they are doing whatever they have to, to make sure he is sleeping etc. I am not sure what I will find when I go in tomorrow morning but I will keep you all posted as we continue our journey. I have not done this much before as I wanted him to keep going (and communicating) for a long as he could but I will now take over from him. He is being well cared for at Thames Hospital—they even found him a brand new electric pressure mattress like he has at home, and all the other mod. con.'s he has got used to. We will get him back as soon as possible and just take one day at a time. I will make sure he knows how much he is loved and supported, and he will not be alone. I have told him to have us called if he needs us during the night and we will come to him.

I will send you another message when I get back from the hospital tomorrow night . . . maybe I will have better news. There will be another conference on his condition on Monday, so will definitely know more after that—although he cannot come home again I'm sure, until his bowels are working again.

Amanda and I are thinking of you all too at this time. We love and miss you.

Love always,
Pam and Amanda

Colorado,
August 19, 2001.

Dear Pam and Amanda,

Thank you for letting us know what is happening with Dad. Allen kept asking me about him and I kept telling Allen that you can never really know with Dad, just exactly what is going on. I will continue to pray for you guys and if you need any help, let us know.

Since this summer, incredible things have been happening in our lives and we are greatly blessed. If you have need of money, or things, or companionship, or whatever, tell me. I know I have been rather distant the last few months but a great spiritual battle was going on in my life and it consumed my time, thoughts and energy. I am now ready to turn outward again. Let Amanda ask too. She is my sister and I care about her deeply. We are all family.

Love,
Laurie.

Texas,
August 19, 2001.

Dear Pam and Amanda,

Thank you so much for your very informative though very sad transmission. I'm sure you and Sam will be much in our thoughts, on our minds and in our prayers as you pass through this time of deep concern. I know we would all like to be there to share your burden if it were possible, but sadly, this is not the case.

May the Lord be with you as Sam is called to enter into peace with those loved ones who have made this journey earlier.

Love,
Gene.

Texas,
August 19, 2001.

Dear Pam, even after a decade in oncology nursing, I am at a loss for anything to say to you and Amanda, that doesn't sound patronizing or trite or just plain stupid. I don't "know just how you feel" because I've never had to go through anything quite like this, and it would be presumptuous of me to even speculate on what this has all been like for you. I guess that I am just writing to thank you for your devotion, and to tell you that I am sorry that there is nothing I can do to help.

It has long been my observation that the truest grace of a lingering death, at least for those who are blessed to be surrounded by loving family and friends, is that there is time to say everything you want to say, and time to show all of the love that you feel for the person whose death is approaching. I am thankful that you and Amanda will not have to know the torment of a sudden death, but I also know that there is never a way to "be ready". I truly hope that, as the years go by, you can both look at the roles you have played in Sam's life, and death, with all of the pride and satisfaction you deserve to feel. You have taken a tremendous burden and turned it into a life's lesson for all of us who have had the privilege to know of your long, tough journey.

We are thinking of you and you are in our prayers. Tell Amanda that her Dad was always one of my idols too.

Love,
Susie.

Texas,
August 20, 2001.

Hi, we received your message about Sam, and Joe is upset like he always gets. Please keep us informed and I will respond if Joey can't. Sam, and Joe were like best friends growing up and his illness has an effect on Joe, like it does us all. We are praying for you, Sam and Amanda.

Love,
Gail.

New Zealand,
August 20, 2001.

Hello, today Dad (Sam) came home by ambulance right at about 4.30 PM. He is feeling a bit better now I think, because he is at home and around us all again. But is still pretty much the same. Just wanted to let you all know.

Love from us all,
from Amanda.

Texas,
August 23, 2001.

As I care for my sister Sharon, with her cancer, I truly appreciate what you are all going through and my heart breaks each time I think about what you all have been, and are, going through. Please tell Sam I love him, and pray for him and all of you, daily. May God keep you all close and give you the strength for his will.

Love to you all,
Ena.

New Zealand,
August 24, 2001.

Hi everyone, sorry I have been so long getting back to the computer but it has taken us a while to get re-organized now that Sam has come back home again. When I went back to the hospital on Monday, the nurses and I decided it was time to bring him home—especially as it had been decided that any further real intervention with his bowel situation was too cruel and invasive, and will not change the outcome anyway. He still has not had any really meaningful bowel motions for over 2 weeks because of the paralysis stopping anything from moving down to the lower bowel. They were all very supportive and conspired (behind the doctors' backs) to get an ambulance organized, along with an electric hoist to lift Sam (as we can't move him any other way now), and everything else we needed—district nurses, caregivers etc.

I went ahead, and called one of our Maori friends and quickly got some of the surplus furniture in his room moved so we could have enough space for this new regime—and then Sam came home by ambulance (only a few days after leaving here with me, in his wheelchair) and was transferred from a stretcher to his electric bed, with its electric pressure mattress—where he will now stay (except for showering etc.) to prevent bedsores etc. from not being able to move. Because of the sudden onset of this latest paralysis, it has been a big adjustment. The paralysis is now total from his chest down, with increasing difficulty in breathing and swallowing, and decreasing function of his arms, and especially his hands.

However, we are all relieved that he is home again and he is much happier to be here than he was in hospital. He is now relatively pain-free—thanks to the morphine pump—and he finally has to let go enough to trust me to look after his medications. The district nurse comes every morning and with 2 helpers, showers him etc. and gets him ready for the day. He will probably not be on the computer again—as a result of decreased mobility, coupled with increasing lack of concentration (due to the morphine, I imagine). It is not perfect but better than last week when he was climbing the walls with pain etc. They are still trying (gently) to stimulate his bowels—so far without success.

We rebuild him every morning with his medication, get him ready for the day, and then he drifts in and out all day until night-time. Tonight is the first night we have decided to get him a night nurse, as his deterioration is obvious. He is as pragmatic as always, and quite philosophical about his situation. He has asked that we don't grieve for him as he does not want to linger like this for any longer than he has to. All we can really do is keep him as comfortable as possible now, look after him, and let him know how much we care.

My mother and her younger sister (my Auntie Joan—who has brought her own invalid husband, Kit Ellis), have come up here to support us, and are doing all the cooking, laundry etc. so I can focus on Sam. They are intending to stay for a while to help. So here we are—finally almost at the end of this long journey. Sam is right—I am still not ready though. I think (like Amanda) I was starting to believe we would go on like we were indefinitely. The speed of this was quite shocking—and we didn't even see it coming. I guess nothing really prepares you for that.

I will try to write a short note every day to let you all know what is happening with Sam. While he is still relatively lucid, if you would like to talk to him the phone # is 64 (7) 868 2326. He will not get any better, so it is probably the best time. I can rouse him if he is asleep—which he is for much of the day now. No one is game to predict how much time we have left with him—except for our district nurse who knows him pretty well after 3 years, and thinks maybe 2 weeks. However, there are days now when I feel that is probably optimistic. I guess we will see. I will also make sure we read him any messages that you send him, and even try to get responses if possible—although I haven't been very successful lately in holding his attention for too long.

I wish there was something more cheerful I could tell you all—but I guess we can only be thankful for the time we have had, and hope for his sake that he will find peace soon, with the minimum of discomfort. I think he feels loved and supported at this time and we will all do everything we can here, to ensure that this is so. We are thinking of you all too, at this time especially.

Love as always,
Pam and Amanda.

Texas,
August 24, 2001.

Pam, this is Sam's cousin Lloyd. Please tell him we are thinking of him and our prayers are with him. Tell him as I see him in my mind's eye, that my memories of him will always be those of our youth. I will always see him laughing, with a smile on his face, and I will always remember him that way. My mother and I always said that when Sam smiled, he always looked exactly like Papa Rayner.

Our best to you both,
Lloyd.

New Zealand,
August 25, 2001.

Hi Beulah, I have been thinking some more after your call earlier today. If you would like to come back to say goodbye to Sam, I want you to know how welcome you are. We would love to see you again—but I do not want you to feel obligated!!

Sam would probably say you would only get to watch him sleep but he is awake throughout the day—he just keeps nodding off.

My mother and aunt told me to tell you they are here to run everything upstairs—to keep the food up to the troops etc., so I can forget about day to day routines right now. They have come to support us in the most practical way they can think of. While they pop in and out to say hello to Sam, neither of them are up to much more than that now—since after 3 years, Joan is still doing this for her own invalid husband, Kit, and my Mom has just finished her own three years of hands-on nursing/care giving with my Dad, who just passed away 2 months ago.

Aside from that, Amanda and I would love to have you here but please note, I am only telling you this in case you feel you would be intruding because my family are here now. They would love to meet you too, and we have lotsa room for more family yet. I do not want you to feel though, that you must come—it needs to be about what you would like to do.

I intend to have Sam's funeral service videotaped so I can send it over to the family there, so there can be a family service (or something) for closure. I also would like to include any messages from family members, so you can all become direct participants in this too. Sam and I talked about this originally but I put everything on hold when he got better, so will have to start thinking about it soon again, I guess.

Anyway, if you do decide to come, I could get you from Auckland airport and take you back of course, so you wouldn't need a rental car. We can always find room here too. I just wanted you to know though, that you are so very welcome to come if you feel you would like to. You told me when you left that Amanda and I would always be Kopeckys!!! On that basis, you are my family too!!

Love,
Pam.

Texas,
August 26, 2001.

Dear Dad, this is probably the hardest thing I've ever had to do, but here goes.

I've always been a person who keeps my emotions to themselves most of the time but I wanted to say, with all of my heart, how much you have meant to me. You have had the most impact on my life and I'm proud to say Dad, that I'm just like you. I'm proud to be your son, I'm proud of my Czech heritage and the family name, especially the fact that I'm a Jr.

Even though it has been many years that you and I have had apart, I still remember the times when we lived together. You taught me right from wrong and though I didn't always agree with you at the time, I've come to learn that you made the right decisions for me. You taught me respect, honesty and integrity. I will pass these lessons on to my kids and even though I make mistakes, I always try to live my life by these principles.

I only now realize how much pressure and stress you were under to make ends meet back in the 70's. I myself now know what it's like to have all the bills and wonder how to afford not only the luxuries but also the necessities. I appreciate all the late hours and weekends you worked at the pharmacy. The effort you put in is to be admired. Mom has even said that when you lost the pharmacy is when she thinks you lost your dream (at the time) for the family. Things don't always go the way we plan, no matter how hard we try. I want to say thank you, and that I have forgiven you a long time ago for some of the things that happened. I now am dealing with the same problems with my kids, and Denise and I are trying to keep our family together the best we can but we argue and have a hard time keeping a level head sometimes also.

Speaking of Denise, I credit meeting her and having my kids also, to you. If it hadn't been for you I wouldn't have moved to Boerne and wouldn't have met Denise, or had the opportunities that I had, like getting to play football. It made a big difference in my life and still does to this day. I decided to be assistant football coach this year for Chris' team in Pop Warner. We are the Canyon Lake Cowboys and are in our second year in the tough league and are always playing catch up to all the other teams, in terms of our development. I have very fond memories of those days in Boerne, and you wouldn't believe how much the town has grown since you and I lived in the house on Schweppe St. Sometimes when I'm driving through Boerne and I hear a Willie Nelson song, I think about you and going to the Kendall County Fair, and the times we had in what used to be a small German community. Speaking of Willie Nelson, I've found I like his music more and more, all the time. I download a lot of older country from that time period when you used to listen to the likes of Waylon Jennings and others. I think about those days very fondly now and it makes me happy to be able to listen to those songs.

I promise you that I will stay close to Pam and Amanda, and stay in contact with them to see how they are doing. I hope to travel back again in the future, back to your wonderful place, and I hope I can bring the kids next time. You and Pam have put a lot of hard work into your place and it's a testament to your work ethic, which you have always had. I'm glad you got the chance to do something you loved, and got a chance to live in a beautiful place and raise a child the way you probably wish you could have the first time around, when you had more quality time and didn't have to work so hard. I understand now that things didn't work out the way you planned and I wish too, that you could have come back to visit us in the States more often. I'm proud to say now, that when people ask how many siblings I have, I can say that I have two brothers and two sisters.

I wish things could have been different when it came to the diagnosis and treatment of the cancer. I know Craig feels some responsibility for the way things turned out but again you impressed me with your courage and humor when it came to such a grim reality. I hope I can face my mortality with the same dignity you have. You impress the hell out of me Dad.

I'll never forget the times we had, the good and the bad, and every time I see a '67 GTO I think of you. My dream car is to someday own a car just like you had. I want to keep a piece of the past in my life. Thanks for the things you provided for me and I hope this is enough to repay you for all that you did for me.

I wish now that I had moved to Austin with you and attended the University of Texas.

You will never be forgotten and I keep the pictures you sent to me when we came to see you, right above my computer. I'll always treasure those photos for as long as I live because it was the last time we were together.

I hope you can understand all of this now and I pray for you that you won't be in pain much longer. If you could let me know via email when the best time to call is, I would like to speak to you after you receive this. I'll check my email every day to hear from you Pam. Thanks Pam and Amanda for taking such good care of Dad for so long. I can't even begin to imagine what it has been like for you two all this time. You are both saints!

Goodbye, maybe for now, maybe forever.

I LOVE YOU ALL AND KEEP YOU IN MY PRAYERS. YOU ARE, AND ALWAYS HAVE BEEN, THE BIGGEST PART OF ME, DAD. THANK YOU, AND GOD BLESS YOU AND TAKE YOU TO A BETTER PLACE WHERE YOU DON'T HAVE TO LIVE WITH ANY MORE PAIN.

LOVE, YOUR SON,
SAMBO.

New Zealand,
August 26, 2001.

Hi Sambo, your Dad is reading your message now. It is around midday here and looking up his time zone program, I think it is around 5 PM your time—yesterday.

This is a good time to call. He has a shower/sponge bath, shave, teeth etc. at around 11 AMevery day. He is more awake after that than at any other time. So, if you give him an hour-ish to do that, it's a good time. Shower days (Monday, Wednesday, Friday—until it gets too much—we review daily) take much longer. more like 2 hours. So I guess 5 to 6 PM your time, is about the best we can do right now.

He is still trying to make jokes but his confusion I find harder to take than his bodily changes. For someone as sharp as him, to be losing the plot now seems especially cruel. He is slowly trying to read your letter himself—but I will read it to him again later as well, to make sure he understood it.

We love and miss you,
Dad, Pam and Amanda.

Texas,
August 27, 2001.

Dear Pam, Sam and Amanda, Doug and I have been in Scotland for several weeks so I am just now reading these accounts of Sam's last few weeks. Please be assured of our continuing prayers for him. As these things go in the spiritual life, one morning at a B & B we had a chat with a couple from New Zealand. Of course we talked about all of you, though they live on the other island. That did prompt me to sense there was occasion for more prayer, so I have been "travelling" with you from afar, without concrete details, yet somehow sensing something had turned.

Pam and Amanda, you are very much in my prayers as well. As my Mom was dying several Christmases ago, after an acute turn for the worse somewhat like Sam's, I remember the same sense of surprise and numbness which you describe. She had coped for a couple of years with dialysis and pretty much held her own. Then suddenly things just fell apart. I am glad to know that you do have support, and hope that you will all have occasion to communicate to Sam, and to one another, whatever is needed.

May you all be enfolded and encompassed by ministering presences, earthly and heavenly. We hold you close.

Love,
Mary Beth.

Texas,
August 27, 2001.

Dear Pam . . . I wanted you to know that I am praying for you, Amanda and Sam. I am so thankful that Sam found you and that you have had a wonderful life together.

Sam is so young. It is too soon to be saying goodbye—no one is ready to say goodbye to him. Sam, Craig, Laurie and Scott want to call and talk to him but are having a difficult time trying to formulate what to say. They want to thank him for all he has meant to them and done for them.

I ask that you and he forgive me for any wrongs that I have done to you; and I forgive also . . . in Christ's love . . . Cecile.

New Zealand,
August 29, 2001.

Dear Mary Beth, I visited Sam yesterday. He's now paralyzed from the chest down. Pam says he could go at any moment for he's been sent home from hospital to die. Since knowing Sam, I have been conscious of your prayers and your vocation. In fact, your letter of 24 May, 1999, is in front of me now. Yesterday I read your latest, and knowing that we were united in prayer for Sam, Pam agreed that I might make contact with you. Your love is precious to them.

More than two years ago, I visited Sam. He was paralyzed then but so vital. Since then we've spent time together often and I've sensed the currents of love, anguish, protest, support etc. that have moved the little family. I've been "in" on the book and know about Golda and Joe, enjoying Joe's letters to Golda. Sam writes well. There are so many things about Sam that move me with both indignation and compassion that such a splendid guy should be cut off so miserably.

My tie to you—not just that we both grieve and pray for Sam, Pam and Amanda—but I share your vocation and your prayers. I'm a senescent priest of the Anglican Parish of Thames, feeling sad that I fly out on Sunday for Russia, knowing that unless he dies today or tomorrow, I shall fail Sam by not being on the spot to celebrate his life in the funeral service we planned together. However, in a way he'll fly with me.

Shalom,
John Clark.

Texas,
August 30, 2001.

Hi Pam, thank you for the update on Dad's health. Craig is out in the field in California until September 3. Unfortunately I have no contact with him. I know there is nothing he could do, he doesn't even have access to a phone.

I will be praying for you guys during this difficult time. You are so strong, I can't even imagine what you must be going through. If there is anything I can do please let me know.

Love,
Elizabeth.

Texas,
September 1, 2001.

Dear Pam, Sam and Amanda, many thanks for taking the time to give us updates; it does help just to know how you are all doing.

I loved the note from John. It was very dear of him to write. I was struck by how well he has come to know Sam, and by his tenderness for the whole family. I am sad though, that your pastoral care isn't present at the moment, though I'm sure they keep you close in prayer.

Tell Sam that I am going through pictures of Golda today, in preparation for another project. As I am looking at her face in so many different poses, she and I are having a tender visit about Sam. It helps to picture her, Mom, Beulah, Pawpaw Joe, Lily, Ludma, C.C., Jap, Teresa, John and all the others, gathering to surround your family during this passage. May you have a sense of being upheld by familial presences and prayers, on both sides of the veil.

Love,
Mary Beth.

Texas,
September 4, 2001.

Just wanted to touch base with all of you and see how it's going. I wanted to tell you how good it was to talk to you and hear your voices . . .

. . . Denise and I have been reminiscing about the days when you and I, Dad, lived together, and some of the funny things that happened back then when I was in high school. That's been almost 20 years ago now. (I'll be sending some of these stories to you, Pam, when I've decided which ones I want to send.)

We have been thinking about you a lot the last couple of days and want you to know how much we love all of you. The kids and I have been talking about you and how much you mean to us.

. . . It's back to work tomorrow and both of us wish we could be there with you all. Please remember that you are in our prayers and that we love you very much.

Stay in touch.
Love, Sambo.

New Zealand,
September 9, 2001.

Dear Mary Beth, I am hoping you will be able to help me—or rather, Sam. Sam has been receiving both emails and phone calls lately, asking him about being "saved"—and promising hellfire and damnation (or the Baptist equivalent) if he does not repent before his death. I have tried to stay out of all this—and even bit my tongue the other morning when I received a (deliberately timed, so I was told) 3.30 AM phone call, to follow these up. It's hard enough for all of us to sleep at night right now, without intentional interruptions!

The result of all this, of course, is that I believe, in his morphine-induced confusion, it has undermined Sam's confidence about the validity of his own spiritual faith. This was compounded yesterday when a "born again" hairdresser friend (?) came up to cut his hair as he requested (he's folding his tent), and then—unbeknown to me until I saw her coming out of his room with her Bible—spent another hour or so haranguing him, and doing this same thing.

The great thing about all these "Christians" is that they have discovered the ONLY answers to life's great mysteries and are arrogant enough to believe there is only their way . . . and the wrong way. There is no room (or respect) for anyone else's faith or beliefs. I have always seen Sam as a very spiritual person—rather than a religious one. He made the comment to me once (after some experiences with new-found 'born-again' piety), that he was somewhat dubious about the established church, in case he forgot what it meant to be a Christian. He always felt it was more important how he lived his life every day of the week—and not just on Sundays, as many hypocritical people seem to do. He is a good man who has spent much of his life trying to help others wherever he could. I have always loved him for his kindness and generosity, his courage, his high principles and values, his honesty and integrity, and all those other things that have made him the kind of man he is.

He told me several days ago that he was now afraid to die. I tried to help him but since my own faith is somewhat questionable too right now (under these present circumstances), I accepted help from our "new" minister, David North, an ex-navy chaplain from the Anglican/Episcopalian Church—in which we were both confirmed. After visiting Sam for most of the 3 years of his illness, our minister friend, John Clark, now sadly cannot be here as planned, and has asked David [who John told we were "unconventional Christians"], to fill in for him. While I have made sure Sam's physical needs have been attended to, I wasn't so sure about his spiritual ones. Our Maori friend Tom, who could also talk to him about this (from a very similar perspective to your own), is not due back here for several days, so David came to us on Friday morning and the three of us took communion together. He talked to Sam about death and was very good. He anointed him and told him that, while this wasn't the last rite, it would double as that if he didn't see him again. I really felt Sam was at peace with things after that—until everyone started up again.

Yesterday he told me he would go in two more days—and looked like it . . . again. This morning he was recanting and asked the district nurse about blood tests etc. to see how to fight back. He has now accepted, again, that he is going (and has even had his hair washed to be ready) but is still afraid. I cannot get either John or Tom here to talk to him now, and you are the only other person I trust who might get through (the morphine) to him. I will stay with him as much as I can but since my own family had to go home after 2 weeks here, I am on my own again, dealing with all the day-to-day things that keep going on around us.

Your letters have always touched me so deeply and made me tune into my own spirituality. I have tried telling Sam the things you have said about those who have gone before, waiting for him, but he is not sure. I do not want him to die being afraid. Maybe I cannot change that but I am having such a hard time encouraging him to let go, when all my instincts are telling me I don't want him to let go and leave us. I'm not sure I can help him with this now too. I don't have the right words.

He is more lucid right now than I have seen him since this started back at the hospital. I have discontinued all but the essential (to keep him comfortable) drugs—as he is having a hard time swallowing. His edema is increasing (the diuretics are not working now), his respiratory function is getting worse, and his body is slowing down. I wish he wasn't so sharp mentally at this time—although that could change again at any time too. He is pain-free now though, thanks to 2 morphine pumps.

I'm not sure if you have any ideas of how to help him in his struggle to find peace so he can finally let go, but if you have any ideas, please do. I will read him anything you send—or even if you would like to talk to him direct by phone, he is pretty good right now (especially if you don't call at 3.30 AM!!)

I will try and write a note to everyone tonight, to catch up on where he is. Meantime, take care. We are thinking of you all too.

Love,
Pam.

Texas,
September 10, 2001.

Dear Pam, Sam and Amanda, I told Sam that I hoped he could see the prayers being offered for him, and for Pam and Amanda, as a sort of hammock. This image comes from my own experience when I was terribly ill in '95 and '96. I was very weak, and one night when I couldn't sleep I "saw" this delicate, tensile webbing that was holding me up. I knew intuitively that was the webbing of prayers being offered on my behalf. Because I have been working in interfaith dialogue for some years, these were prayers from Christians of various sorts, Jews, Muslims, Hindus, Buddhists and not a few people who are as unconventional as all get out. The image has remained with me, and I think that is because it somehow disclosed a spiritual reality that is for all of us, not just for me.

Here is the encircling prayer that I prayed for Sam over the phone:

My Christ, my Christ, my shield, my encircler,
Each day, each night, each light, each dark,
Be near me, uphold me, my treasure, my triumph,
My Christ, my Christ, my shield, my encircler.

This comes from the Scots tradition of the Outer Hebrides, and the English is translated from the Gaelic. It's an old, old prayer, probably with roots in pre-Christian practice of making circles to recall the divine presence. To this day the people in the Hebrides pray the prayer by extending their right hand and circling slowly sun-wise (Son-wise in Christian tradition). I use it all the time in pastoral situations and I prayed it for Mom by making a circle around her bed. It helps me remember that divine mercy and love encircle each and every one of us. Mercy within mercy within mercy.

I called Dad and Susie to let them know how things were going. You will probably hear from them later or tomorrow.

Know that this brings our love. The gracious webbing of the prayers of many (some known to you and others unknown, some in this earthly life, and most in the throngs of all the company of heaven) holds you. You can begin to let go and let the prayer support you.

Love,
Mary Beth.

New Zealand,
September 14, 2001.

Dear family,

Just a quick update to let you know what is happening here now. Sam, as usual, is confounding all the experts—and doing this his way too. I have given up even trying to guess where he is up to now. I can see that he is getting weaker daily. His eating and drinking are minimal now, his breathing is getting more labored, and he has increasing congestion. He is not as lucid as he was earlier this week but then he is on more medication again at the moment, so that may well account for that. He is sleeping more because of that and appears to be less anxious again so I believe that all the kind thoughts and prayers you have all been sending, and all the reassurance we have been trying to give him on this end, are working.

He is very upset (as everyone is here) about what has been going on in the States over the last few days (9/11), and has been following it all on TV cable news. Nothing else is penetrating much though right now.

His first caregiver has just arrived to take care of his ablutions this morning (after I've been here with him all night), so I will close and get out of her way. Will get back to you all soon.

Love,
Pam, Sam and Amanda.

Texas,
September 14, 2001.

Pam, please give Sam a kiss for me, and tell him I love him and think of you all every day. Know that my prayers are with you all for you are certainly travelling a long and arduous road. I keep a plaque of "Footprints" by my bed as I know I certainly cannot "walk alone" . . . just as I know God is walking with you. I appreciate your updates.

Love,
Ena.

New Zealand,
September 15, 2001.

Dear Mary Beth, thought I would fwd email and show you what is still going on re Sam's "eternal destination". I will not even try to show this to him. What really gets me is the presumption that we need help and that this way is the only one!!!! Or that we don't even own a Bible!!!! They obviously don't see Sam as the good man he is—and always has been. Since this seems to be more about someone else's needs than Sam's, I hope it makes them feel better at least.

Sam is calmer now and your last email is by his bed. I read it to him when he is more cognizant. His caregiver brought him a copy of "Footprints" too—so I think those can counter all this other 'stuff'.

Thank you for your input. One day when Amanda and I come back to see everyone again, I would love to spend some time with you. I believe it is you who has taken over Grandma Golda's role as the family saint, and sad as I have always been that I was too late to know her, I am grateful to have had the opportunity to have read the things about her that you have written. As a journalist, I probably read more in the written word than many. I will stay in touch.

Love,
Pam.

Texas,
September 15, 2001.

Dearest Pam, that message gave me chills. From the context of our present catastrophe, it just looks like the same stuff as Bin Laden, only sugar-coated with pseudo-Christian crap. As you can see, this sort of thing provokes a lot of ire in me.

I am so relieved that you are not passing this along to Sam. It is a form of poison, I think. Our younger son is gay, and has been subjected to some of this ridiculous tripe. As the woman in whom he took flesh, from whom he nursed, and who raised him, I have no doubt that he has been, from the beginning, a fine and genuine person. Yet to people of this ilk, he is an abomination. Again I note how very much the dynamic has to do with projection, fear, anger and anxiety. Herbert O'Driscoll, who is an Irish Anglican in Canada, is fond of saying "We live in apocalyptic times, and in apocalyptic times, fear and anxiety get together, make love, and then have a bastard child called fundamentalism".

It's almost as if this person has formed a little terrorist cell and they are lobbing their message your way. You might just want to start deleting them without reading. You can always claim that the computer networks are fouled up as a result of the heavy internet traffic due to the terrorist attack.

Many thanks for the comparison of me with Golda. I would hesitate to claim that I am the family saint . . . Susie is probably more qualified in that respect. What I do agree with is that she taught—by her life, more than by a lot of yammering at us—that all people deserve respect, courtesy and kindness. She never stopped learning, and she was never afraid of looking at her own behaviors, and desiring to be a more genuine and merciful person. When *"Look"* magazine came out with the term 'WASP' for the first time in the 60's, and raised the issue of racism in a very public way, I remember her saying, "I guess I am a WASP".

I also have a very clear memory of being at her house for some family gathering when Sam and Joe were in high school. They came busting into the kitchen, furious with one another as only testosterone-laden males can be. One of them pulled a knife on the other and started spouting off. She, with a spatula in her hand, shook the spatula at them, told them they were being ridiculous and to get out of her kitchen if they wanted anything to eat. Ah, the power of a good grandmother. They were like puppies who had been swatted with a newspaper. The knife was put down and they shuffled out, ashamed because they had defiled Golda's kitchen. (You can remind Sam that Golda is quite capable of that sort of spatula-shaking when it comes to this. She would have no truck with this idiotic (as in the original Greek, meaning turned in upon oneself) message.)

And, you are the one who is being Golda-like for Sam at the moment. You are the bearer of ordinary grace, of a down to earth sense of humor, of a simple human touch when things are their hardest! Golda understood what you understand: what matters ultimately is how we are with one another, particularly when we are not in public, when our guard is down, when the stress is high. I hope you get some rest, and that you will be kind with yourself in the days ahead.

If you don't get to the States, maybe we will head to New Zealand. One never knows about these things! Until then, this brings my love and continued prayers. Now to light a candle, that I won't lose it and bonk someone over the head with Golda's iron skillet.

Love,
Mary Beth.

Florida,
September 18, 2001.

Dear Pam,

Thanks so much for keeping us all up to date. Know that we are all thinking about all of you and you are in our prayers. Let Sam know how proud we all are of him for the admirable way he has handled his life. He has been an inspiration for me. In the future when he is watching over us, it will be hard to live up to the standards he has set. Pam and Amanda, thank you for your strength in loving and taking care of him.

Love,
Beulah.

Texas,
September 18, 2001.

Just wanted to say hello and let you know we are all okay, even though we are still reeling from the recent events. I hope you are all getting by okay. Things are trying to get back to normal . . . if you can call the changes we are all going through, normal . . .

. . . I wish everything had a cure that was that easy. I think someday they will have a lot of the answers to the diseases that trouble us all so much now. Hope and faith is what gets us all through the most difficult times in our lives. It's not easy for me, by any means, to just say to pray but I don't know what else is a viable option any more. Hope that things will be better. Hope that all suffering will be relieved and love for all of us who are here in this world. These are the days I will remember for the rest of my life.

I'm always wondering what all of you are doing right at this very moment. You are in our prayers. I love you all very much and am thinking of you always. Peace to you.

Love,
Sambo.

Texas,
September 20, 2001.

Dear Pam,

I woke up this morning with Sam very much "present". I have been remembering a story that came to mind as I read of your following the Maori advice.

My former physician, a woman named Patty Chandler, became a professor of family practice medicine at the Univ. Of Texas Health Science Center in Dallas. She has also had a long interest in native American practice. So, when the Roman Catholic archdiocese of Arizona convened a conference for practitioners of medicine of both indigenous groups and of standard US professional schools, she went. She made friends with several shamans from the Pueblo people of New Mexico. The conference ended, and they all resolved to return the following year.

When Patty arrived, she discovered one of her friends from the Pueblo community was missing. She asked, and was told that he had died several months before. She was stunned, for he seemed healthy and was not that old. The shaman who was telling her said, "Don't you see? He had more work to do from the other side". I keep thinking that Sam may need to know that he does have work to do from the other side, whatever that may look like. If you think this is something he might want/need to know, please pass it along. If not, just delete the message.

Having been present at many deaths, I do have a very real sense that the Presences, both familial and heavenly, show up. And I also firmly intuit that in some way, shape or form those who have been "gathered unto the ancestors" (as our *'Book of Common Prayer'* puts it), do continue to help those of us in earthly pilgrimage, through prayer, companioning, and who knows what.

I hope that you are able to get some rest, and that as the final hours draw near, the time may be sweet, gentle and deeply peaceful.

Love,
Mary Beth.

Deep peace of the running wave to you,
Deep peace of the shining stars to you,
Deep peace of the gentle earth to you,
Deep peace, deep peace of the Son of Peace to you.

New Zealand,
September 21, 2001.

Today on Friday the 21st of September at 7:15 AM Dad/Sam passed away very peacefully. Pam and I (Amanda) were there holding his hands, as he went. It wasn't as bad as I thought it would be and you could tell that he wasn't in any pain. I am glad that he is out of his misery but I will always dearly miss him.

We will stay in touch, and we love and miss you all.

Lots of love,
Pam and Amanda.

P.S. It is very sunny and peaceful here today.

Notes found beside Sam's computer, after his passing:

Dear Pam,

I have kept putting off writing a note—if I wait too long, it will be too late.

I was thinking the other night, about all the things from the time we first met in Austin, thru Buda, Austin, the trips, and then here. Except for the misunderstandings, I wouldn't change anything.

We had some good times and a beautiful little girl. Well, I wouldn't trade the two of you for anything. One wife, and five children, are keepers.

I don't really know what else to say—other than I love you. I will try and watch over you until you tell me to go.

With all my love,
Sam xoxo

P.S. I guess I will get the last word this time. I love you. Don't let "them" get you down.

Amanda,

You are my dearest little sweetheart and always will be. I am so glad we had you.

I have always been very proud of you and always will be. Remember I'll always love you and try to watch over you until you want me to go.

Listen to Mom. She will always be your best friend.

I love you very much,
Dad xoxoxox

Texas,
September 21, 2001.

I feel your pain and sorrow. Please know my prayers and thoughts are with you all. Another precious member of our family has left us but we must take comfort in knowing Sam is in God's hands with the rest of our loved and departed family.

Love,
Ena.

Texas,
September 22, 2001.

Dear Pam and Amanda, blessings on you both as you begin this phase of the journey together. We all give thanks for your tender, faithful, gracious care of Sam. I know that he was blessed by your tender attention and loving presence in a way that few of us are as we die.

"May his heart and soul ring out with joy to You, the living God and the God of the living."

Much love,
Mary Beth.

Texas,
September 22, 2001.

Dear Pam and Amanda, I was sorry, but somewhat relieved, to get your news. I know it has been a difficult time for all of you and I admire your courage. Sam is now at peace.

Amanda, your note was very touching and I was glad you and your mother could be there when he passed. I am sorry I can't be there but want all of you to know we are praying for you.

Pam, what can we do to help? I am sure you are very busy and emotionally (and physically) drained. I don't really know what to say (I am not as eloquent as Amanda), but want you to know we are all here for you.

I haven't called yet because I thought you might be busy and need some time but was planning to call this weekend if that is ok.

Love,
Charlie.

Colorado,
September 23, 2001.

I, also, am glad to hear that Dad is finally at peace. It was a little shocking to read the news yesterday, even though I knew it was coming. Let me know what I can do to help or whatever. Please don't ever hesitate to ask.

Love,
Laurie.

Texas,
September 24, 2001.
Dear Pam,

I hope you and Amanda are doing ok. Writing Dad's eulogy has been very hard for me. I didn't want to make it too long but I wanted to say some things about Dad and what he meant to me. I'm sure this has been very hard for you too. Just as the loss of life here in the States has been very sad, it is the time to begin a new chapter in all our lives.

I appreciate all that both of you have done. Please know that if there is anything that I can do, please let me know. My prayers are with you and I know that Dad is in a better place, free from any suffering. God bless you and please stay in touch.

Love,
Sambo.

For Dad

You were a good father,
You were smart and a hard worker.
You liked to have a good time,
Someone who enjoyed the good things in life.
You liked fast cars,
You liked to bar-b-que.
You loved country and western music,
You were proud of our family heritage.
You were an urban cowboy,
You stood up for what and who you believed in.
You were always your own man.
Though times will be tough without you,
I'll draw from what you taught me.
Certain characteristics that you lived your life by:
Honesty,
Integrity,
Courage,
Commitment and Humor.

Even in your darkest hours, Dad, you had the ability to laugh and make the others around you laugh with you. I remember a saying in reference to funerals, "Why do they always throw the best party for you when they know you can't come?"

You always encouraged me to strive to achieve. You always told me, "You can do whatever you want to in life." And I think I understand now why you would get so angry with me when I made a mistake. It was because you cared so much about me.

I look back and remember the years we had together in Boerne. I'm thankful for those times.

I recall the picture that hung in our apartment in San Antonio when we first lived together. It was a picture of a sun through the green leaves of a tree. You would ask me, "Is that a sunrise or a sunset?" It's funny that it stuck with me all these years.

I remember how you used to tickle me when I was very young. Out of breath, I fought to tell you to stop even though I didn't want you to.

I wish I could have written and spoken to you more over the years.

I'll never forget the last time I hugged you when I visited your beautiful home in April of 1999.

You always made me feel loved when I was near you.

You deserved the love you found with Pam. I'm glad you had the chance to be the father you always wanted to be, to Amanda.

You didn't die lonely Dad; you knew how much you were loved.
Even though your life has expired, you inspire me.
I know now I will not take any of these things for granted.
I have always been proud to be your son.
Yes, you did good Dad,
You were a good Father.

Love, your son,
Sambo.

New Zealand,
September 24, 2001.

I wanted to write you all a short note to let you know where we are up to now. Sam's funeral service will be at 11 AM (NZ time) tomorrow, Tuesday, September 25th, here at our home at Te Puru. We will bring Sam up from his room shortly before that, to the lodge restaurant which has been decorated with flowers and family photos. Our new (substitute) minister will officiate and we have tried to make the service as relevant as possible to all our cultures. We are filming it all so if we can get it all worked out, will be able to email you all a copy so you can share in our goodbyes.

Amanda's school here in Te Puru observed a minute of silence on Friday and flew the American flag at half mast for the day, so Sam's passing has not gone unnoticed in our small community. The support has been tremendous and my Mom and aunt are back here again, along with my niece and nephew, and a friend or two.

After the service, our friend Tom and I will take Sam to Auckland to the crematorium as he wished, as he did not want to go with strangers on his "last ride"—and Tom will say a final karakia (prayer) for him there, to farewell him. We will eventually hold another service to scatter his ashes here, as he wished.

I will write again when this is over. We are thinking of you all too and will make you a part of this day.

Love to you all,
Pam and Amanda.

Sam's casket in the lodge room set up for his funeral

Samuel (Sam) Rayner Kopecky

1945-2001

Pam and Amanda
(New Zealand)

Sam, Craig, Laurie and Scott
(United States)

Welcome friends and family to a service of remembrance,
to celebrate the life that is Sam (Snr)—

Father,
Husband,
Friend

Order of Service . . .
'Amazing Grace' Willie Nelson

Introduction:
Greetings—Prayers David North
'Ave Maria' Soloist: Paddy Ronaldson

Eulogies:
Sam Jr's Email Peg Fowles
Reading David North
Speaker Alex Brodie
Reading David North
Speaker Tom Winitana

Prayers of Thanks: David North
'Amazing Grace' Steve Te Moananui

Prayers of Comfort: (for the Family)

Announcements: David North
'Immortality' Celine Dion

Committal:
Words and Prayers David North
Tom Winitana
'America the Beautiful' Barbara Streisand

E koro, E koro, E koro
Whai atu i tekowhai tapuwae
O Tipuna. He Huarahi e Kore e hoki mai
He mata Ngaro, ma te Kowhai ka kitea.

My friend, My friend, My friend,
follow the pathways trodden by
your ancestors—the path of no return.
Your face will not be seen again,
but when the beautiful Kowhai
is in bloom it will be
to your memory forever.

Pall Bearers:

Ben Ellis	*Tom Winitana*
Alex Brodie	*Paul Gurnick*
Peter Fowles	*Steve Te Moananui*

Florida,
September 24, 2001.

Today has been a hard day for some reason and I have thought a lot about Sam. I will really miss him. He became a good friend in the last couple of years. One of the last times I talked to him he was showing self doubt about what he had accomplished in his life. He meant so much to me, and I tried to point out the accomplishments that most of us never come near to, in our lives. Be proud of him. He was a wonderful, generous, dear man and a good friend to most of us.

Love,
Beulah.

Texas,
September 24, 2001.

My deepest sympathy to you and Amanda. I will miss Sam. He was always a good man as I knew him, and I loved him. My prayers are for you and I hope that you are well. I know that you are exhausted and have suffered so much. Again, my prayers are for you.

Love,
Joe.

Texas,
September 24, 2001.

Joe is having a hard time expressing the grief he feels for the loss of his brother. I knew Sam many years ago when Joe and I were married before and he was a good man then. What we really want to say is that family is family, and that Sam will always be in our hearts and in Joe's funny stories of Sam. He didn't want me to mention this but one of his funniest memories is them getting into trouble for using the word kaka, which means poop. He grins at this. They fought like brothers and loved as brothers. He will be missed dearly! Please just say that Sam's life was good and that he was loved by all.

Gail.

PS. Please let us know how you are and keep emails to keep in touch.

Texas,
September 25, 2001.

Dear Pam and Amanda,

Bless you for sending us this message; it does help those so far removed. The beauty and tenderness of this parting are so moving; again I am deeply grateful for the ways in which you have honored Sam as the unique and remarkable human being that he was, and the unique and remarkable spirit he now is. I am keeping you all especially in prayer as these final arrangements for the service take place; lighting candles and incense.

Mom was cremated, and we all spread her ashes in the courtyard at the Episcopal Church of Reconciliation, where Doug and I were then serving (this is the custom for many in that parish). It was the Feast of the Epiphany, when we remember light shining in the darkness, and a roaring icy north wind caught the ashes and played with them. It felt like a deep release for Mom, and for us.

I know that given Sam's life and spirit, there will be moments of surprise and connections in these next days. May your grief know also the lightness of Sam's ongoing presence, and the gathering of the ancestors, all shining and resplendent in the light of Glory.

Love,
Mary Beth.

Texas,
September 25, 2001.

How wonderful of you to keep us updated. Thank you. May God continue walking with you through all your difficult days, especially the ones ahead of you.

Love to all,
Ena.

New Zealand,
September 29, 2001.

Dear family,

I will start to send some things as I get myself organized again. It has been a difficult week—we miss Sam so much. I will write more as I can but we are still in the process of getting the video tape sorted out so we can email a copy of the service to you.

Amanda and I are back on our own again now and everyone has gone. We have Sam's ashes back here with us again, the house is full of flowers and photos, and we are both wandering around trying to find a new routine. His presence is everywhere—but upstairs especially, in the lounge, dining room and restaurant, which is strange since he had not spent much time up there for nearly 3 years. His bedroom feels very empty and next week I will probably try to put it back together, now that all the hospital equipment has gone. Amanda tells me his spirit is most likely happier upstairs with us, than in the room he was sick in for so long!!

Please bear with us—it may take a while to be able to talk about all this. We will stay in touch.

Love to you all,
Pam and Amanda.

E koro, E koro, E koro
Whai atu i te kowhai tapuwae
O tipuna. He Huarahi e kore e hoki mai
He mata Ngaro, ma te Kowhai ka kitea.

My friend, My friend, My friend,
follow the pathways trodden by
your ancestors—the path of no return.
Your face will not be seen again,
but when the beautiful Kowhai
is in bloom, it will be
to your memory forever.

Samuel (Sam) Rayner Kopecky
1945-2001
Husband
Father
Friend

Thank you.

The thoughtfulness and support of our family and friends
has been a great source of comfort to us.
It is difficult to express in words,
our gratitude for these expressions of love,
sympathy and support.

CHAPTER 94

LIFE KEEPS HAPPENING

Texas,
September 30, 2001.

Dear Amanda and Pam, I have no doubt [re Sam's spirit being happier upstairs] that this is true. Sam is newly alive and is celebrating that ongoing life with you both. It will be interesting to see if you sense his ongoing capacity for humor. Mom continues to come up with ways to make me and Susie laugh.

Go slow. Do not rush yourselves. Enjoy the flowers. Just let yourselves savor what you can, grieve when you can, breathe as much as possible. Grief is like the waves of an ocean . . . it comes of its own rhythms and pattern. I am convinced that grief is as particular and unique as the person who has died.

You two are in my prayers all the time. For some reason the hummingbirds (which are here in droves this fall) are the prompt for prayer for you and Sam.

Love,
Mary Beth.

Texas,
October 1, 2001.

Dear Pam and Amanda, thanks for your recent mail. I really wish some of the family was there to give you a shoulder to lean on. Grief is so exhausting. You're so glad the pain and suffering have stopped and yet it's hard to realize that the one you loved is not in the house any longer.

Someone told me after I lost Mary, that grieving was very hard work and that made very little sense to me at the time. However, I found after some passage of time, the words were accurate. If you have a library nearby you may find some writings to be very helpful. Also, a support group, if available, could offer some comfort.

Memories of the good times when there was no sickness and much laughter, helped me immensely and maybe that would be useful to you as well. There is no getting around the fact that there is a lot of pain that you will have to endure and we really wish we could be there to offer some comfort.

Sam had many friends in this area and I would be glad to have an obituary published in the local paper if you wish. With your talent for writing, the words in such a notice would be more meaningful if they were yours.

Our prayers and thoughts are with you both and we thank you for your messages.

Love,
Gene and Susie.

Texas,
October 2, 2001.

Dear Pam and Amanda, I know exactly how you feel and what you are going through. Yes, your life has changed and you are all on your own, with the exception that God is carrying you through each minute, each day, as he has all of your life—but even more so in the painful times of watching your husband and father fight, struggle, and fade away. You absolutely must focus on the fact that you all were extremely blessed to have had the short time with Sam that God granted you, for it is obvious that he loved you all very much and that you returned that love. Not many people can attest to having that kind of love in their entire lives. It doesn't make your pain and loss, and feeling as if part of you has gone but in time it will bring you comfort, for Sam may have left you physically but just when you are least expecting it, you will feel his presence and I know you may think this sounds silly but, as in the movie "Ghost", there will be little things that you will know he is truly "there" with you.

Do things in your own time, when you are ready, not when others tell you what is best for you, and only when you know you are ready to "go on". You must do what is best for you and Amanda, and know, as time passes, there will only be a few people that will genuinely care "how you are doing" and whether they can help you with anything. I do not mean to sound cynical but people get on with their own lives. While their words of "let me know if I can do anything for you" are sincere when they say them, perhaps because they don't know what else to say.

You have lost your best friend, your confidante, your father etc. I am an ocean away but only minutes by email. While I may not be able to provide any comfort, I will be here for you to talk with if you need to. I don't have any solutions or answers but know my thoughts and prayers are with you each minute of each hour. God will provide you strength. The pain will never go away but will be easier to deal with, in time. To this day, I miss Cecil even when I get mad at him for leaving me to handle everything (especially getting through life and getting through each day) by myself. Take care of yourselves and rely on your family. God bless and keep you.

Sincerely,
Ena.

New Zealand,
October 6, 2001.

Hi Beulah, I have spent days looking for Sam's CV/resume so I can give you some details as you suggested for San Antonio/Austin papers. I cannot seem to find one anywhere. I have been looking again since Uncle Gene offered to handle obituary too but it is still eluding me—and I am having trouble finding all kinds of things on Sam's computer . . .

. . . I miss Sam so much—Amanda has been good but the days are so long now without him here with us. I know it is supposed to get better than this . . . but it doesn't feel like it ever will, right now!!

I will keep looking for the relevant info. and send it ASAP. I just wanted you to know that I haven't forgotten.

Love,
Pam.

Florida,
October 7, 2001.

Pam, I will look on disks Sam sent me, today. The original letter and chapters were given to the UT Press.

I know you must feel lost and hopefully a new routine will set in for you, shortly. I miss him also and am thankful that we got to know each other again in the last couple of years.

Hang in there. You know he would make some stupid joke about the whole situation if he was around. I picture him in heaven going 90 miles an hour and talking a blue streak. I feel he is at peace and happy. Thank you again for taking care of him.

Love,
Beulah.

Texas,
October 11, 2001.
Dear Pam, thank you for the well-written, thoughtful obituary which has been sent to the *"San Antonio Express"* in its entirety and without amendment. It will be in this Sunday's paper and a copy will be sent to you by snail mail. I know it is very hard to be dealing with these matters but they must be attended to.

Bless you and Amanda. Our hearts go out to you.

Love,
Gene.

KOPECKY

Samuel Rayner Kopecky, age 56, died (peacefully) at his home in Te Puru, New Zealand, on September 21, 2001, following a long battle with prostate cancer. He was educated at Douglas McArthur High School, San Antonio; San Antonio Junior College; and the University of Texas, Austin, where he was awarded a B.Sc. Pharmacy in January 1969. He was then associated with both the pharmacy and automobile industries in San Antonio and Austin, until his relocation to his New Zealand-born wife's home in 1988. A multi-cultural Memorial Service was held at his home, "Te Puru Coast View Lodge", on September 25, 2001, where tributes were paid to this well respected 'Texan' by members of both the New Zealand Maori and European local communities. The American flag was flown at half-mast at the nearby Te Puru School. He is survived by his wife, Pam and daughter, Amanda, of Te Puru, New Zealand; as well sons, Sam Kopecky Jr., Dr Craig Kopecky and Scott Kopecky, all of San Antonio, TX; daughter, Laurie Thomas of Longmont, CO; six grandchildren; brothers, Joe Kopecky, San Antonio, TX, Tom Kopecky, Plano, TX, Dr Charles Kopecky, Houston, TX, and sister, Beulah Hughston, Niceville, FL.

Texas,
October 17, 2001.

Dear Pam,

Yes, I will get the death notice to the *"Austin American Statesman"* since you two did have many friends there. Mary Beth Earle scanned the notice and sent it to all the relatives addressed by you in some of your previous email. I assume she sent you a copy.

You and Amanda continue to be in our thoughts and prayers.

Love,
Gene.

Texas,
October 15, 2001.

Just wanted to drop a quick note and see how you and Amanda are doing. We are all fine even though there have been a lot of scary things going on around the U.S.

. . . I just received a copy of Dad's obit. forwarded to me from Mary Beth and unfortunately, it is a bunch of jumbled up mess. I can make out about every 4th or 5th word at best.

I wonder sometimes how you guys are doing. It must be tough, considering. He was so much of your lives and now he is gone. Please understand, it is just as tough for me but

I can't begin to deal with it as much as you two have to. I miss him too and wish so much, that his life didn't have to end like it did. He was a very proud man and sometimes a very private person but the disease brought him to a point, I know personally, he didn't want to have to be in. Thank you both again for caring for him and giving him so much. I know you would've loved for things to be different but it wasn't to be. I know he was in the best hands and he was comforted by you two, more than anyone else in the world.

It is a different world in so many ways.

I remember little things, all the time, about Dad. I think of when we would watch the TV show M.A.S.H.—he always reminded me of Alan Alda. He was a very complicated man in some ways and a very simple person in others.

I just wanted you both to know we are still here for you and know it must be the hardest thing you have ever had to face. Please let me know if you need to talk to someone and drop a note when you can. Until then, God bless you, and remember we are all here for a reason; it just depends on us, what we decide to do with our lives. Take care and know one thing, we feel your pain too.

We love you,
Sam Jr. and family.

Texas,
October 23, 2001.

Dear Pam and Amanda,

I hope you are beginning to get some rest and take some deep breaths. I remember feeling somewhat disoriented after Mom died. Her hospice care had been the main focus for us and when that ended, we were sort of at loose ends and not quite sure what to do with ourselves. I also hope that you are aware of the gracious gift that you gave Sam by your constant and open care, and willingness to invite him to be true to himself down to the last moments of his earthly existence. I have no doubt that he is blessing you with prayer, and giving thanks for your mercy, faithfulness and real tenacious love.

Take good care of yourselves; we are keeping you in prayer.

Love,
Mary Beth.

New Zealand,
November 5, 2001.

Dear Uncle Gene,

I have finally got myself mentally prepared to finish dealing with all kinds of things relating to Sam's death. In going through and deleting his emails etc. I realized I hadn't really replied to this one. No, I never did receive copy of scanned obituary—and Sam Jr. told me he could not download it properly. I hate to be a nuisance but would it be too much trouble (retrospectively) to snail mail a newspaper copy? I have collected all kinds of things—including emails—for Amanda (and anyone else in the family) who may want to look at all this, in due course.

My next job is to follow up on Laurie's offer to take over the responsibility of publishing Sam's book—I can do so little from this end. I would like to bring Amanda over to meet everyone but I do not see this happening before the end of next year.

I also, finally, have received the recording of Sam's funeral service here. Unfortunately, it could not be put onto disk as first envisaged as no one was able to load it onto computer because of the length of the recording. I guess they could not access a large enough system. So, it is on a VCR tape. I have been thinking about how to do this and as you are the Patriarch of the family, decided to ask you. The tape is on NZ system, which is different from U.S. (PAL vs NTSR, I think from memory) but these days newer VCR's are multi-standard here in NZ, so I assume they will be there too. If not, it is probably possible to hire one that is. I thought some of the family may wish to play this at a memorial service (or something similar) for Sam, there in San Antonio, where most of the family are. It would probably help the kids a lot to have real closure. I believe it is a fitting tribute to Sam—and I know I found it very emotional. Sam Jr, Laurie, Craig, Charlie and Beulah, will all find it more familiar, having been here where it was filmed. Maybe it will just get passed around the individual family members—but either way, I thought I would send it to you first since I believe it is you that still holds everything together. Outside of the Kopecky clan, it also needs to be available to Aunt Jeannie and Uncle Lloyd, Lloyd Jr and Ena, in Galveston. What do you think? If I airmail it, it will be there in about a week or so.

I understand what you meant about grieving being hard work. I am finding it so much more difficult than I anticipated. I thought I would have been more prepared, having known it was coming for 3 years, but there was still something shocking about the finality of the end, and I think the very real adjustment problems I am having relate to the ongoing nature of the 3 years of care giving. I am trying to work through everything though. I will try to stay in touch more now. Take care.

Love,
Pam and Amanda.

Texas,
November 17, 2001.

Dear Pam,

Sorry to be so long in answering your email and thanking you for sending the funeral service card, dedicated to Sam. I know you and Amanda are going through some very trying times and finding it hard to adjust to Sam's absence. Please know that it will become easier, although likely later, rather than sooner.

Some excellent advice passed on to survivors has to do with decision-making, that is to say, the making of major decisions. If you have done any reading about this, you'll find that it is in your best interests to defer any major decisions for at least a year, and possibly longer. Day to day routines are taxing enough and anything of importance deserves clear thought which is hard to muster.

Emotions are another thing altogether but I found it helpful to try mentally, to relive the good times through music, pictures and visits to places you enjoyed. This helped me. Maybe it will be useful to you. Staying occupied is also a way to keep your mind off your sorrow. You might also consider visiting with the priest you and Sam had come to know. Remember too, you are in our prayers.

I have checked on the VCR conversion to use in the U.S. and there is a company here in town that does that work. So please send the NZ tape and I'll have it "translated" to operate in any VCR. If you have the mailing addresses of Lloyd and Jeannie, and Ena, please send them to me. I have addresses for most of the other family members.

Best wishes to you. I'll be expecting the tape thru snail mail.

Love,
Gene.

Colorado,
November 19, 2001.

I will be more than happy to take on Dad's book project. It will allow me to feel like I am somehow part of his will to finish this for him. I have a lot of time now, since I am home—schooling Arthur.

And BTW, I gave everyone a copy of the letter sent to us by your aunt, Joan Ellis. It was very nice of her to write such a long and thoughtful letter to us. Tell her thank you, if you get the chance.

I hope things get better for you two. I have found it much easier than I thought. Most of my grief took place when we first heard about Dad's condition, and when I came to see him. Allen and I pray for you two almost every day. Thank you for letting me get do this for him—and for you. If you need any other help, of ANY kind, let me know. We will do whatever we can.

And also, I want you to know that I don't harbor any ill feelings about everything. Really, about the strongest one can ever say my feelings got about it, was "piqued". I am glad that Dad was supremely happy for those 14-odd years he had with you and Amanda. What was there for him here? Our lives were so busy that even if he had been here in the States, I really don't think anyone would have seen him that much more—well, maybe Sam or Craig might have, these part 3 years, if he had lived in Texas but he still would have had to be dying before any REAL efforts were made. You can't live your life for everyone else's approval and Dad made the right choice. It is what you needed and he was able to discover new things about himself that he might never have done otherwise. I hope things start to get easier for you two, soon.

Love,
Laurie.

New Zealand,
December 2, 2001.

Hi Beulah, I have been meaning to let you know the sequel to this saga of Sam's book. Laurie will take it over so I am in the process of gathering up all the info. I can find to snail mail it to her, so she can see where Sam got up to with it. How have you got on with the disks? Uncle Gene contacted me back right after we talked and said to mail him the VCR tape—which I did about 10 days or so ago. So you should be able to see it when you are ready.

Amanda and I went back to work properly over the weekend and had our first real guests since last summer. It went well but I felt sorry for Amanda since they were Yankees and too cheap to tip. It wouldn't have mattered if it was only $1 but since she busted her ass for them 2 nights and 2 mornings, she was somewhat disappointed. Sam would have told her that the only tip she will get from people like that, is not to bet on Dallas in the playoffs!!

He had a saying for every occasion and Amanda and I often laugh about them since they are too politically incorrect to share with almost everyone else. I am so proud of Amanda, she really is doing well. All this has made her grow up faster than I would have preferred but as well as loving her, I like her a lot too, as a female—she'll never be a bitch like most of her peers at school. She's even got our combined senses of humor which is also a big plus. She has her moments but overall she really is doing ok with everything that has happened.

I'd better stop procrastinating and see if I can figure out how to check these guests in and out of our reservation system now—the moment of truth!! It should be a 5 minute job but I'm sure it won't be. Take care. Thinking of you.

Love,
Pam and Amanda.

Florida,
December 6, 2001.

Pam, I got your message and will send Laurie the disks . . .

Glad to hear you are getting back into the swing of things. I am so glad Amanda is such a help to you. I know the two of you are strong and together, will get through the loneliness. I will be in touch.

Love,
Beulah.

New Zealand,
December 22, 2001.

Merry Christmas y'all, I have been sitting here on my own, watching a NZ TV program on Christmas in New York (after WTC events) and it seems the appropriate time to send you our own Christmas greetings. Amanda has been away for a couple of days since school finished for the year, camping with some girlfriends in the bush behind their parents' house, about 30 mins. from where we live. Of course, it is summer here at this time of the year and I decided it would be good for her—they can't get into too much trouble—and I can get myself (and her) organized to go to my Mom's for Christmas, Sunday (our time) until Boxing Day. Our last couple of Christmas's have not been great but I thought it would be good for both us and my Mom, to be together for this one . . . so I am locking all the doors and leaving, and hoping everything will still be here when I get back.

We have been working some with the lodge and have reservations for Jan/Feb/March when we get back, so will be back to work very soon. Will probably bring my Mom back with us until New Year, and then put her on a plane home. The first holiday will be the worst for all of us.

Sitting watching the New York program I kept thinking of Sam . . . and Christmas . . . and all the things he used to talk about. He had Christmas early this year in September—courtesy of his caregivers who did not want him to miss it—but I have so many memories of Christmas's past. When I heard the various renditions of 'Silent Night', I kept thinking about him laughing at Beulah singing "sleep in heavenly peas" when she was little; of his Mother loving listening to Elvis singing "Blue Christmas" every year; and Pawpaw Joe's "Christmas in Siberia" stories. I guess his Christmas's (like many things he talked about) always seemed more colorful than my own. I still miss him so much and always will.

On a brighter note—Amanda has the same teacher again for the third year (the one that Sam finally got to thank just before he died) for the next school year—her last one at local junior high equivalent, before high school. From her school report, I am pleased to say that she has inherited the Kopecky genes as regards intellectual ability, as, in spite of everything, she is doing really well at school academically. She is having more problems socially it seems, as she is so independent but that is also not inconsistent with her genealogy, as she seems to have a distinct lack of tolerance for mind games, politics and BS!! I have not managed to raise a 'pleaser', Beulah and Charlie—in spite of my best endeavors!! Between her teacher (who has always reminded her of Sam), and our Maori friend Tom who works with me (and you will see in the tape of Sam's funeral service), Amanda has continuity and strong male role models who both identify with, and subscribe to, all the same principles that he did. Sam told us all many times, that he was relieved to be able to leave her in their care too.

Now that Uncle Gene has the tape of Sam's service, I hope it will help those of you who want to see it, find some real closure. I know from my own sister's death when I was in Texas, how difficult and unreal it is to grieve from such a distance, and have always wished that such things had been easier then. I brought the tape of my Dad's service back here for Sam to watch in June, and I know it brought him some peace, since he was so upset at not being able to be there to say goodbye to one of his best friends (who, in turn, regarded him "as the brother he never had").

I had thought about sending everyone a précis of the year as Sam always did, but his illness and passing seems to have eclipsed everything else. So, instead all I will do is tell you all that we love you and think of you often, we are grateful to have been part of Sam's (and your) life, and that we will always remember him with love, and strive to live up to the standards he set us by his own example. We are planning on coming to the States at the end of 2002 for an indefinite period, if everything goes to plan. I will spend the next year getting the lodge ready to sell—as I am too tied to it otherwise, to leave. I hadn't really appreciated how much Sam was still doing for me on the computer, until he stopped—between reservations, book keeping/bill paying, advertising, and other general office functions.

I thought I would have had more time once I was no longer looking after him but that has been cancelled out by the contribution he was still making to our everyday lives. Hopefully we will finally be able to catch up with everyone when we do make it back to the States. Until then, I will keep in touch.

Take care everybody—we love and miss you all,
Pam and Amanda.

Kuwait,
December 22, 2001.

Dear Pam and Amanda, it was good to hear from you. I am sorry I haven't been in touch. I have been deployed to Kuwait since early November, and will be here at least until late May. I am here in support of Operation Enduring Freedom (the Afghan War and war on terrorism). Needless to say this is not where I wanted to spend Thanksgiving and Christmas, much less New Year's, Brittany's birthday, my anniversary etc., etc., but this is where my country needs me right now (Freedom is never free). I suppose I will have my own Christmas stories about being away from home as a doctor in the Army, fighting the latest world evil. (That sounds a bit grandiose, forgive me.)

I know this must be a hard time for you both. Just when things seem to be inching back to some normalcy, the holidays can bring back so many memories of what we have lost. I remember the Christmas mornings of my youth. Waiting as long as I could to come down and find the presents and all the goodies. And I remember Dad, usually quiet and pensive in those days, with the smile of a child. I think he enjoyed watching us open the gifts that he got for us, almost as much as we enjoyed getting them. And then those holidays later in life, when we got to be together, slowing down for a while, enjoying getting to know each other better as adults; these are some of the best times. Dad will be missed by all of us.

I hope and pray that this season can bring a measure of peace and joy as well. I know Dad wanted this to not just go on but to continue to get better—he was always striving for the best.

Please tell Peg Merry Christmas from me. I hope you all get to enjoy your vacation away from the lodge. Remember that you both are in my heart and prayers. You are always welcome at our home when you do make it to the States. Merry Christmas and Happy New Year.

Love,
Craig.

Texas,
December 24, 2001.

Dear Pam and Amanda, you are so dear to take the time to write us, and the mail card is quite a treat. I especially love the cats and dogs that show up. We live with a menagerie (the yellow cat is sleeping under the Christmas tree just to drive the border collies crazy).

I am sure that this Christmas is hard. There is something about walking through those holidays for the first time, without a beloved family member, that is so tender. Both Golda and my Mom died right after Christmas, and still I have moments of feeling the ebb tide of grief. It's not overwhelming; it's just there from time to time. So I can imagine that this year will be especially tender for both of you.

I loved hearing about Amanda's independence. I would say that as much as I am sure that Sam's genes play into this somewhat, I am also sure that Pam's own genetic makeup contributes to this spunk. Sam would not have married a pleaser or a wimp. That's for darn sure.

Those Kopecky genes ARE strong though. Our oldest son Bryan was a psychology major in undergraduate school but was very clear that he did not want to become a practicing psychologist. Instead, he has become a massage therapist and is now attending the Utah School of Massage where he is getting a national certification. Here's the kicker: he loves anatomy, and has discovered this real and ancient wonder about human physiology. He has to do work with cadavers, and tells us that mainly it is a lesson in how little we know. We are glad to have both of our sons home. Bryan (who is 27) lives in Austin. He came in on Friday so that he could meet his brother Jason (who is 24) when he arrived from France late last night. Jason's flight was uneventful, though long. He was unaware of the American flight that was disturbed by the man with explosives in his shoes, though Jason did notice that, by the time he arrived at Chicago's O'Hare airport, the security was more stringent than it had been in Europe. I am glad he's not travelling today.

Dad had Little Sam over to the house the other day. He looks so much like Sam, and talks a mile a minute, just like his Dad. Daddy had some photos of Sam that he gave to Little Sam. We heard some funny stories, and Dad told us some as well, so Sam was well remembered and no doubt got a kick out of being the center of attention. (When Sam was very much into photography, he had a habit of posing the subjects, then readjusting everything, posing again, etc. One day when he was five or six, Little Sam grew tired of being posed. He bolted from his position, went over to his Dad who was crouching to take the photo, put his hands on either side of Sam's face and said (moving Sam's head from side to side), "You tell us you are going to take the photo and we WAIT and we WAIT and we WAIT". We all got a good laugh out of that. We retold that story to Little Sam, amongst others.)

I keep you in my prayers. May 2002 bring you both a tender sense of Sam's ongoing life in the Spirit, and gentle healing of the grief.

Love,
Mary Beth.

Texas,
December 25, 2001.

Merry Christmas Pam and Amanda, hope this email finds you both very well. Sorry, it's so last minute a greeting but we are just now getting caught up on our emails.

I got the video tape of Dad's funeral and just now had a chance review it. It made us both laugh and cry. It was the closure I needed. Thank you so very much for taking the time and effort to make it for us. I will make 3 copies to send to Craig, Laurie and Scott. It was a little hard to understand what people were saying at times but I was able to make out most of it. The music was especially good. It was a great tribute to Dad. I hope you are both getting on with your lives now. I know that's what Dad would have wanted you both to do. The best you can.

At this time of the year I seem to really appreciate what I have, and come to understand what is the most important thing to me. Love is the most powerful thing in all our lives. Faith has been the thing that helps us all get through the tough times. It is most important now to realize how lucky we all are, when you look at what's been going on in the world we live in. As you probably know, Craig was shipped off to Kuwait and it's hard to say for how long. We saw Elizabeth, Brittany and John this last week for dinner, as they are off to Naples, Fl., for a holiday. They are all well.

We are all fine and are just getting over a brief cold. There have been a lot of people suffering from it. The weather has been back and forth. Very cold to moderate, and at times just downright beautiful. We both think of you often and wish you much happiness and good health. Please shoot us off an email when you can and remember we love you both!

Love,
Sambo.

Colorado,
December 30, 2001.

Got the forward! I plan to dive into this at the beginning of the year. I got the disks from Beulah last week and will be loading the info on both computers soon. I will keep everyone updated as we go. Pray the Lord blesses this endeavor. Only by His hand can we accomplish all we hope to!

Love,
Laurie.

Texas,
December 31, 2001.

Dear Pam and Amanda, and a very Happy New Year to you and yours as well. Thanks so much for staying in touch. Your email is always very interesting. I'm so glad the books Sam worked on so diligently are going forward. I know he invested huge amounts of time and his fading energy into them, but was only aware of the one book.

We have a "Texas Institute of Culture" here, that was established in connection with our World Fair in 1968. Among other exhibits there is one that is devoted to Czechoslovakian families that settled here in our early days. The staff there might be interested in seeing Sam's final product. When you are ready to publish, I'll get the names and addresses that are appropriate.

Best wishes to you during the coming year,
Gene.

New Zealand,
December 31, 2001.

Dear Laurie, just a quick note to let you know that I airmailed a package to you today. It should take about a week by airmail. I ended up putting it all together as a package, as it turned into a nightmare trying to send it at letter rate in smaller lots. It is all the electronic and printed info I could find, that Sam had put together regarding publishing his book and it may pay to follow some of this up again now. It includes info/correspondence on commercial/subsidy/ self publishing (you can also see where he got to on most of that), author's instructions and bibliographical documentation. The disks Beulah sent you are the book itself—in its entirety.

I believe the book is at the publishable stage now but may be too long to be commercially viable (it would have to be two books from what we could ascertain) so may have to be subsidy or self-published. I could not bring myself to edit it (other than spelling and grammar) as it is also in either Dr Joe's, Golda's or Sam's words—and I hated to impose my own over any of theirs, which always felt right. The project also kept growing as his research extended to include subjects that explained some of the background events to the letters and diary—such as Czech history, Mexican history, the Russian Revolution/ Trans Siberian railway, the civil war, prohibition etc.—topics Joe and Golda alluded to, but that he felt that his descendants may not know a lot about. The book is like a thesis—all of the correspondence and diary contents, plus Sam's comments of these at different points, with intro. and summary, and then all the appendices, photos, maps, and a lengthy bibliography. (His 2nd book is not at all scholarly—except for the Rayner genealogy!)

I helped Sam by proof reading (although I know I didn't get everything—like the "foreword"—would you please correct that for me) but I was loath to change anything else. Since it was your Dad's book, I didn't ever feel like I wanted to change anything much. I will probably do more myself with the second one I will carry on working on over this next year or so. It is as long again!!

It seemed obvious to me originally that the Czech connection would work but the rejection from UT Press made me wonder about that—I had high hopes that they would be interested for that reason too, as well as the Kopeckys' association with the university. However, I also have TX Highways info. on Czech Museum being set up. That was also why we had high hopes that UT would be interested in the project—Dr Joe set up first Czech infrastructure there for language, culture etc. (Kopeckys were written about in *'Czech Pioneers of the Southwest'*, amongst other publications). I had also thought as ex-UT professor—and first exchange professor to University of Mexico—that they might get involved. All told, he and his siblings taught for something like 149 years (collectively) in the TX school system.

There's also a huge amount of medical interest, I would have thought, in the letters between Joe and Golda, comparing notes on patients etc. It is like a window in time . . . medically and socially. But I'm not sure where to start from that angle—maybe Charlie or Craig would have some ideas. And I believe the book has value in terms of earlier TX history—which is why I can't do much from this end. It will not find the market in NZ to be published commercially, and it will only be affordable to self/subsidy publish in the States, where rates are more competitive. In the end it may have to be self-published, with those wanting copies having to buy them in advance, to get it printed. I imagine that the 2nd book will be self-published but only immediate members of the family would ever be interested in that one. Sam got this first book all the way to publishing stage though, so now it is up to us to make sure this Kopecky family history sees the light of day, so his work was not in vain.

The easiest place to start might be just to print out the book as I had to (it was too hard to read on the screen) and just read it all and take it in. Then you will have a better feel for the whole thing. Our Anglican Priest friend here, John Clark (an intellectual and a scholar), was so blown away by Sam's book that he thought UT should give him an honorary doctorate or similar, for this work. Not bad for a dyslexic!!

I guess if he hadn't had cancer and been paralyzed, there would never have been the time to do something like this—so that is why it seems so important now. It is the product of the last years of his life—i.e. how he chose to spend them, on what he thought was his priority. Take care.

Love,
Pam.

Texas,
December 31, 2001.

Dear Pam, thanks for letting me know about this; I can't imagine reading all that he'd written at this particular time. I also think it will be a great gift to his family and friends to have this writing see the light of day. All will unfold in its own good time.

I am hoping that you are having some time to just be still and let yourself breathe. One dear friend of mine here, who lost her husband to cancer, said that she felt as if she were standing at the edge of the ocean, and every once in a while a huge wave of grief would just come up and knock her down. At the same time she was always feeling the movement of grief about her feet and ankles, sometimes rising higher, sometimes ebbing. All of that takes its own toll. I do think the Christian language about a married couple becoming "one flesh" makes sense. And when one of the two dies, there is such a ripping of heart, soul and body. Sam would want you to take very tender care of yourself. Furthermore, if you don't he will probably start finding ways to get your attention.

We are having a spell of really cold weather here, and it is supposed to last all week. We are actually having fires in the fireplace daily. St Mark's (the parish where I serve part-time) is downtown, and is an old stone building. It was so cold this morning. It's taken me all afternoon to warm up again. Supposedly we may get ice and sleet on New Year's Day.

I hope that you and Amanda will encounter gentle blessings in the year ahead as bit by bit, day by day, your lives take on their new shape. Be under the Mercy.

Love,
Mary Beth.

Colorado,
December 31, 2001.

Good morning Pam, yes, I am eager to read the history he has put together. I know it will be amazing and sobering. I just recently started having dreams with him in them. They aren't lucid yet but I am hoping they might become real visits from him . . . Thank you for your offer of help and if I run into snags, I will certainly seek help. I plan to treat this as a professional endeavor and personal mission.

Love,
Laurie.

Colorado,
January 21, 2002.

Hello again! Yes, I will send the CD right way to you guys. The disks were confusing at first but once we got the files restored it was a piece of cake. I knew that most people would probably have trouble opening the disks so the CD's have been a nice alternative.

I did get the publishing information that you sent. If it appears that Protea will be prohibitively expensive or they won't go with it, then I will try the other company Dad had going.

I had already warned everyone that the second volume was about Dad's life and that he didn't pull any punches. I told my brothers that probably there were things in there about all of us too, that they might not like . . .

Love,
Laurie.

Texas,
January 19, 2002.

Dear Pam and Laurie, the CD of Sam's book arrived in today's mail. Laurie, many thanks, it opened perfectly.

There is something so profoundly, joyously moving, about reading Sam's words. I think the foreword from your Maori friend sums it all up. This is such important connective spiritual and genealogical material for all of us. My sons will be delighted by having this CD; Doug is at this moment burning one for each of them so we can put the CD's in the mail today.

Many, many thanks to both of you for keeping this flame alive for it allows us all to participate in Sam's ongoing life and gift, and to give thanks to those who have gone before, throughout all the generations. (In a way it is like writing the Kopecky family subtext of Genesis!).

Much love,
Mary Beth.

Colorado,
March 6, 2002

Dear Pam and Amanda, I, too, am very glad that we are going to get to move forward on the book! I know there will be some publishing costs but some of the family have said they will help . . .

It is so good to know that Dad meant so much to you. I think I would have found his temper unbearable, myself. I loved sitting and talking with him about science and philosophy, eating his bar-b-que, and smelling the beer and cigarettes on him. Those things always make me think of him now but he was always so angry as I remember. You are a stronger woman than I, to be able to love him so deeply and dismiss his anger.

I did finally have a good dream about him about two weeks ago or so. He was showing me all the different things I made for him over the years as a child. I kept taking his face in my hands so he would look at me and I told him I loved him . . . he kept moving through his gallery of stuff to show me. I say it was good because it is the first one that was not dark and scary. And he was young—about 30 or so. Funny thing is, I never had dreams about him before he died—even when I heard he had cancer and I was very upset . . . For me, homeschooling Arthur has been the perfect answer to the problems that were surfacing . . .

I am so very happy that I have decided to stay home and do this! I know that Te Puru is much better than the public schools here and that you have Amanda helping you out a lot. That is wonderful. I envy Amanda's oneness with you now . . . she will have a place like no other in your heart because of all this. And I am sure you learned much patience and love by dealing with Dad for so long and with such gentleness. Amanda is a lucky young woman . . .

Good luck with getting ready to sell. I know this makes the most sense . . . stay strong. I pray for the both of you.

Love,
Laurie

Colorado,
April 30, 2002.

Dear Pam, do you happen to have an unedited version of Dad's manuscript? The publisher believes it will have greater historical value if all of the original material and pictures are included.

This is pretty exciting to me—that means all the information Dad originally intended to be there may very well end up getting published! It will most likely be two volumes but I would rather do that than leave out the most important details that will give the books real value as time marches on.

Attached are the publisher's request and insights.

Love,
Laurie.

Georgia,
April 29, 2002.

Dear Laurie, I have spent many hours completing the layout of the manuscript and illustrations as Sam Kopecky had presented them. The layout comes to a 719 page count in 6x9 book size.

During the process I have had an opportunity to closely read a large portion of Dr Joe and Golda's correspondence. I have some reservations that the material is incomplete from the perspective of public readers who are best moved by emotions expressed through characters in a work, and from the view of academics who are best moved to recommend a publication by the historical value of the work.

When I first corresponded with Sam Kopecky on the project, I commented from a cost-savings' perspective, on the large page count of the initial manuscript submitted. Sam set about pruning the material doing a good editing job—but with too sharp a set of clippers, I fear. It seems advisable to retain the original material even if the publication should be divided into two volumes—the pre World War One years and World War One.

My interest in this project is to serve the 'public'—as in 'public-ation'. To this end, there are valuable attributes to the letters, deserving of full treatment. There are glimpses of rural life, and family relations and travel problems in turn of the 19th century Texas and historic towns such as Galveston, which was probably the case in all the 'frontier States' of pre WWI—a condition not resolved until after Roosevelt's New Deal and WWII.

There appears a vivid portrayal of organized nursing at its infancy in rural communities. Also illuminated are the uncertain and difficult circumstances of establishing a country practice for practitioners of the Hippocratic Oath as opposed to their big-city brethren, and a good account is given of the transition of country doctor from horse-and-buggy to the first fruits of Mr. Henry Ford's assembly line, the automobile.

There is also the beginnings of the 'medical corps' in General "Black Jack" Pershing's notational army with the advent of World War One, to become a permanent institution in the federalized army of the USA in WWII. (Organized medical and nursing services were almost completely lacking with tragic consequences, in the American War between the States of 60 years before Dr. Joe and Golda's correspondence.)

Lastly, and most valuable in the extensive body of correspondence, is the much medical discussion that occurred because of the fortunate coincidence of one party being a trained nurse and the other, a doctor, and the happy result of their eventual union in marriage—a rare first-hand account of the strains and hardships of a country nurse, country doctor and WWI veteran from humble origins.

As the first two decades of 20th century America steadily recedes into the distant past, many details of daily life during that pre-depression period in America, fade from the public conscience, leaving an increasingly abstract perspective, void of the feeling so aptly brought to life in the correspondence of a loving couple.

Further, the imagination of 21st century readers is revived, instilling appreciation for daily life in "Frontier States" of turn of the 19th century south western United States, where disease and sudden death continually stalked young and old. Not until the conclusion of the New Deal of the 1930's—early 40's and the demands of WWII, can one say that the great advances in medicine and nursing care achieved in hospital of the north eastern United States, had reached all corners of this great country.

The Kopecky correspondence is sure to awaken in readers, an understanding of just how much is taken for granted today, and to what extent values of pre-depression generations have eroded.

I am well familiar with the publication histories of such famous diarists as Samuel Pepys Esquire of 17th century London, England; James Boswell Esquire of 18th century England; and others. These landmark diaries in English literature had achieved their fullest value to the public and academia, only after several editions, touched by the hands of many editors, eventually resulted in full and complete publishing, with minimal editing. The greatest value of diaries are in the minute details of everyday life, often thought insignificant by editors closer to the time of the writings, or closer in relationship to the authors. Yet, the details became more important as the distance in decades between readers and the correspondence, increased.

I would welcome an opportunity to review all the material, and photos and illustrations available to Sam Kopecky, to determine the fullest scope for the publication that I believe Sam originally envisaged.

Regards,
Johan du Toit (Protea Publishing).

New Zealand,
April 30, 2002.

Dear family, I thought I would forward Laurie's email and publisher's attachment to you all—firstly, so you could see where Sam's *'Family History'* book is up to, and secondly, to ascertain how you feel about my letting this material go 'outside' the family . . .

I am thrilled that someone else sees this work Sam did; the way I always did. I always knew when the rejections came back to him saying that it wasn't "commercial" enough, or of wide enough public interest, that it would take a different kind of publisher to see the value of this project. While Sam began to doubt this, I couldn't believe that I, Tom (who wrote the foreword) and others who all read parts of it, were so wrong about this too, when we were all moved to care so much about Dr Joe and Golda, while we only got to know them through their writing. Right now, our G.P. is reading her way through my only hard copy—having been aware of its production from the sidelines. And there are several other unrelated people who have asked me about its possible publication, who have already asked me about buying a copy for themselves!!

Anyway, the bottom line (in terms of the publisher's query) is that there is no unedited manuscript. Sam did it as he went. When I asked him once, he told me the main editing was the "mushy stuff" which I too, always thought was a shame to leave out of what was, in effect, a love story. How do you feel about this?

I feel a real tie to this project but because of my loyalty to Sam and respect for his judgment and consequent decisions on his grandparents' story, am probably not objective enough to do this editing the publisher has requested. The problem is that there is only what Sam produced—or the raw material. I have to leave this decision to you as grandchildren, rather than to any of Sam's children who will barely remember their great-grandparents. You will all know how Dr Joe and Golda would have felt. Sam always believed there must have been a reason his grandfather gave the diary etc. to him and it made his enforced 'time out' easier in that it gave him a purpose he believed in—until it got to the publishing stage. He knew he would never have found the time otherwise and wondered how Dr Joe could have sensed this. Take care everyone.

Love,
Pam.

Florida,
May 2, 2002.

Pam, I just returned from Texas . . . I had the opportunity to go to the (Boerne) ranch and see the property, and walk around the old homestead and creek area. Tom Colbert did the same a few weeks ago. There is a new house built where the woodpile used to stand and the old road cuts in back of the new house. The water tower is still there, as are the old cement steps that came up the back porch to the shack.

We went because the house and the 8 acres around the house and down to the creek, are for sale.

Tommy had never been to the ranch and said it was an opportunity that he wouldn't have missed because of all the stories he had heard about the place for so many years. I have been looking at a lot of hill country in the last year and the view from where the pagoda used to stand is probably the most beautiful that I have seen in that area. Having said all that, I think that the memories that are associated with Golda, Joe, and the ranch, are some of the best that we all have had in our lives.

I know that we all hope that the book is published some day but have reservations about the diary, volumes and pictures being sent to someone outside the family. When I sent the 2nd volume of letters to Sam I had reservations about sending it through the mail for fear of it being lost but I knew it was important to him, so I sent it. Paw was a great historian and I believe he entrusted us with this history so that we would pass it on to our families but I do not have good feelings about letting any of the original items out of our care. I hope you will understand.

Love,
Beulah.

Georgia,
June 29, 2002.

Dear Pam, thank you for your positive response. My interest is as keen as ever. I have an endless line-up of manuscripts and move from one to another as the moment dictates. Eventually they all make it to the press. I might not think of one for some time until an author alerts me to it . . .

I understand the concerns about letting the original material out of the family. Photo copies of letters and diaries would work fine I think, and high resolution scans of photographs saved to CD's will work.

The text I have in the current digital file consists of letters, interspersed with commentary and passages from diaries. In working from copies, if originals are not available, my approach would be to match the source material with the corresponding parts in the digital file, and add what is missing. Sam's commentary can be left as is.

I think "soppy" stuff is what is what makes life real—and makes family members real to posterity.

Regards,
Johan.

New Zealand,
June 30, 2002.

Dear Beulah and Mary Beth,

Please find attached email I received yesterday from publisher who Laurie finally got to take up the challenge (Sam started with him) of doing something with Sam's book . . . that could be one answer to this dilemma.

I am intending to return all these originals to you as soon as I can, as now everyone in the family has access to everything as Sam intended—in addition to all the research work he did. Sam felt strongly that he had also been given the responsibility of carrying the (wider) tradition and so when he was finally given the time and opportunity to do something to honor his grandfather's wishes, chose to spend his last days in this tribute to his grandfather and wider family. I think he always had the feeling that this was 'unfinished business' which he was supposed to do something about one day, so when he knew he was going to see your grandfather again, thought he had better do something about it so he could look him in the eye.

When he started the project it was just to make sure that everyone had copies of what he had, but the project kept growing as time went on and finally metamorphosed into a much bigger mission than he had originally foreseen. The fact that you, Beulah, sent him the 2nd volume of letters (that he must have left at Zornia), kept him going, along with photos from Uncle Gene, the 100-year-old encyclopedias (for Bohemian history) that I had from my own grandfather etc. The bibliography says it all. He spent days just reconstructing the original Czech flag—using written documentation from several sources.

Sam was driven by completion of this project for over 2 years, through sickness and pain, and made himself get out of bed every day to finish what he had started. Now I feel I owe it to him to keep trying to find a solution that accommodates everyone. I believe books are written to be read, rather than just sitting in collections—and while I am not related by blood, feel, I suspect, like most of those who have married into the Kopeckys, that I wish I had been. You all have such a sense of your own heritage and history to be proud of.

Because of his interest in recording and teaching history (especially Czech), I have to believe that Pawpaw Joe would have welcomed this opportunity to tell his story to an even wider audience. Having come to know him so well through all his writings, I believe that he would have been gratified to find such a receptive publisher—even if he was not sure it would ever be possible. What I do suspect now from his work (and from Sam's stories about their 'discussions'), was that Sam was the 'hard-headed' grandson he saw as being just like him, so that if anything was ever possible, he would make it happen.

After Sam died I heard indirectly from the mortician that he was in the worst condition (as in, most "fragile") they had ever seen. Unbeknown to me, they gave instructions that under no condition was I to touch him anywhere other than his face and hands—because they had such a terrible time trying to prepare him for me. I can only surmise that he outlived all the medical predictions to this extent because he was a man on a mission and would not rest until it was completed.

I am grateful that Sam achieved what he initially set out to do—and that, thanks to Laurie, this history is now available to everyone in the family in electronic form. But I would love to see its wider dissemination handled professionally, as a living memorial to these people. I know from the reaction of the people around us, the positive reaction to this work from outside the family. It is of immense value, as Johan said in his last email.

I will be away next week as I am taking Amanda (during her school vacation) to stay with a friend on a farm during the next few days. With any luck the lambs will start arriving while we are there . . . We have just had a 'weather bomb' along the Thames Coast with widespread flooding etc . . .

Bit daunting on my own but still working towards selling . . . with any luck we will get to see you before too long.

Love,
Pam and Amanda.

Texas,
July 8, 2002.

Dear Pam, we too are having severe flooding. Maybe New Zealand and Texas are closer than we think! Nothing like this has ever been recorded. Dams are overflowing that have always been sufficient to hold the water, and catastrophic flooding is taking away whole houses. It is very sobering.

. . . I was so touched by what you wrote concerning the condition of Sam's body upon death. Clearly he was an inheritor of the Kopecky strong will. We saw something akin to that in Mom's dying. Susie, who is an RN, could not believe that she kept going as long as she did after the dialysis was discontinued. There is something in that line that does love life—though sometimes that exuberance went into addiction. Nevertheless, I am convinced that Sam manifested that genius and resilience and sheer tenacity. I am hoping that you and Amanda have had many encounters with new born lambs and are being refreshed by the appearance of new life. No doubt heart and soul and body are still needing replenishment and refreshment.

Peace to you both,
Mary Beth.

Georgia,
July 14, 2002.

Pam, I believe you have sound and valid reasons to see the work published in as full a manner as possible, particularly considering what it obviously meant to Sam.

My early feeling was that we might divide the publication into two standalone volumes. One, the early 'country doctor' period in Texas, and then the World War I experience.

Your plan to complete the project sounds good . . .

Regards,
Johan.

New Zealand, July 2008.

At this time, I sent copies of everything I could to this publisher on the understanding that he and I would, between us, undertake re-editing Sam's book. However, between the ongoing turmoil in my own life, and obviously his too, there was minimal communication or progress on Sam's manuscript over the next few years.

After 'losing the plot' in the interim, I finally re-contacted him in late 2007, when he emailed back to tell me that he no longer published but had my manuscript package safe and had referred it to a publisher friend. This publisher had helped several Protea authors follow through on publication of their pending works after he had to quit the business. This material was finally returned to Sam Jr. but although this new contact asked to still be considered as a publisher for Sam's book, this also proved to be a dead end.

With Beulah's help, I also followed up other possible publishing options including the Texas Czech Genealogical Society, the Association of American University Presses and the Writers' League of Texas without any real positive resultst at that time.

However, I am still cautiously optimistic that we will again find a publisher for Sam's book but now that I have written one of my own and knowing how I would feel if anyone arbitrarily changed it, I have decided that Sam's original *'Family History' (Part 1)* should for the most part, remain as he originally intended. I have gone back through it and reinserted the detailed historical sections of Dr Joe's diary into this manuscript and reformatted this text accordingly but unless I can be convinced of the need to do otherwise, out of respect for Sam's own perception of his grandparents' sensibilities, it will now remain just as he wrote it. I believe he knew just what he was doing . . . and why.

In the meantime I will get his second *'Family History' (Part 2)* manuscript published for the family, knowing that wherever he is, Sam will be watching over us and that as long as I keep faith with him by keeping on 'knocking on doors', I just have to trust that his ongoing legacy to us all will unfold however it is meant to.

Since Sam's death as the first of the third American-born Kopecky generation, the family has now also tragically lost two of the precious members of its next fourth generation—Dr Joe and Golda's great grandsons, Bryan Earle, on December 26, 2005 and Sean Hughston, on May 19, 2011.

On both occasions, emailed words from Bryan's mother, Sam's cousin, Mary Beth, once again touched me deeply, reminding me of our ongoing connection to all those Kopeckys who have gone before . . .

Texas,
January 14, 2006.

Dear Pam, thank you for your message and prayer; Bryan is already making his ongoing presence known in many creative ways. This morning I woke up to the smell of brewing coffee (his favorite indulgence was expensive coffee)—and the coffee maker was cold and quiet. He is following in Golda's footsteps—she used to let us know she was around because we would catch the scent of her cologne . . . Yardley's 'Red Roses'. I have no doubt that he and Sam are having quite a time getting to know each other. He matched/matches Sam in feistiness—so be on the lookout. Lord only knows what mischief they might cook up in true Kopecky fashion.

These are some of the last photos of our Bryan—the first one was taken in Prague by Jason. We scattered most of Bryan's ashes here last Sunday at Reconciliation Episcopal Church where Mom's ashes are, and Dad's will be when that time comes. And Jason, Doug and I, will take a small portion of Bryan's ashes to Prague next summer. He had a phenomenally mystical experience the first time he visited that city; it was a deep and stunning sense of his Czech ancestors gathering around him.

I hope that you and Amanda are finding those steps towards a new life; if you come this way we would love to see you. Many thanks for your prayers and your kindness.

Love,
Mary Beth.

New Zealand,
July 26, 2006.

Dear Mary Beth, thank you so much for sharing the family photos with us. I was so thrilled to hear this good news. Your father deserves to be happy again—and is much too nice (and too much fun) to have remained on his own!!! Amanda was so pleased to hear he had remarried too.

I have—this week—finished my part of the writing on Sam's second book and have now ONLY to proof read the whole thing (c 550 pages) and import the relevant graphics I need to add . . . and it's finally done! I should get this done in the near future. Am still waiting to hear about the financial future of the Lodge and then I will have a better idea of where to go next. I have boxes of Kopecky family things (including your grandfather's original diary) I want to hand-carry back to you all—and some things of Sam's that I need to give to Sam, Craig, Laurie and Scott. They belong in Texas, not in New Zealand. So, maybe now I am finally being allowed to move on with this part of my part. Time will tell . . .

This second book of Sam's is too long for me to print out for everyone so will give everyone who is interested, CDs, to do so themselves. In doing this for him (and you all), I have had to retrace every single step of our journey together so it has been very bittersweet. But I feel a sense of relief to have done so—and my favorite aunt tells me she is "looking forward to seeing the albatross drop off my shoulders". While I had an overall sense of where I had wanted to go with this, it has turned out in a way I did not foresee as, like much of what I write, it seems to have a life of its own.

Please give my love to everyone—especially your father! I am just so happy for him. I won't write directly now though as I know he will be busy. I will never forget his love and support during Sam's illness and after his death. I still have all the *'Texas Highway'* magazines he sent us—and the prayer he sent me (about trust) when Sam was first diagnosed, continues to help me 'keep the faith'. I used to go back upstairs from putting Sam (who was paralyzed by then) to bed some nights, in a state of total despair, and would take that out and read it once again, and weep. But it helped me so much!

I guess these are some of the things I wanted to write about—the positive things within that particular negative.

Take care. It was lovely to hear from you again. I think of you all so often (especially lately) and your own family especially, with all that has been happening to you.

Love,
Pam and Amanda.

Texas,
July 29, 2006.

. . . I had a lovely dream in Prague the night before we scattered the last of Bryan's ashes in the Moldau River. In it, Sam appeared to me, healthy and funny. He told me not to worry about Bryan. "He's with us" he said, which I took to mean with the Kopecky clan . . . He also came to me in a dream after we got home, and in this one, he brought Bryan to see me.

I thought that while Bryan was in hospice, for all that I knew, Sam was among the presences who would receive him. I often thought they would really have liked each other. They were both so darn funny and smart, and also men with a lot of spiritual depth. And neither was inclined to suffer fools gladly. At any rate, it has been a blessing to have Sam show up in these ways, and to imagine he and Bryan together, tending all of us and raising rumpus.

Love to you and Amanda,
Mary.

Texas,
December 21, 2006.

. . . We will be marking the one-year anniversary of Bryan's death on Dec. 26; it is a very different Christmas—which, I guess, goes without saying. I have this rather surprising sense of Sam's tending Bryan in eternal life. They would have loved each other, had they the opportunity to be close geographically. Bryan had a huge dose of that Kopecky blood.

Mom died Dec. 27 and Golda died Dec. 26. The Celtic tradition says that those who die during the twelve days of Christmas have an easy transition into eternity . . .

All the blessings of the season to you and Amanda.

Love,
Mary Beth.

Texas,
May 20, 2011.

Pam, I don't know any nice way to deliver bad news but Sean committed suicide last night. I thought you would like to know that our beloved, sweet boy is gone. Please tell Amanda. He really cared about her and said she was one Kopecky that seemed to have sense.

Love,
Beulah

For Sean

There are very few people in life that can touch you to the core and change your life forever but, Sean, you were certainly one of these people and I was blessed to have had you in my life at all.

I first met you when I was thirteen and never expected that you would become a best friend, and essentially a brother, to me. I can say for a fact that I would not be where or who I am today, if it wasn't for you, and your Mom and Dad. You were what I felt was the first person to actually understand me; through the good times and far-too-frequent bad times when we would sit up late at night and talk (even on Facebook over the last couple of years). Your unique and wicked sense of humor always had me in stitches—whether it was your "Oedipus" joke; sitting up with me late at night drinking beer while brutally making fun of bad zombie movies; or just your constant wit and take on the world. Through your large, kind heart, you taught me that it is a gift to love and care about people—not something to be ashamed of, even if you get hurt; that you should always be who you are and never apologize for that; that you should stand up for what you believe in, and last but not at all least, how to make a frozen Margarita late at night without making any noise and waking the whole house up (because you were supposed to be asleep hours ago and you both will get in BIG trouble if you're caught) . . . followed closely by how to make the perfect grilled sandwich.

I wish that we had been closer recently and that I had told you how much you actually meant to me, instead of just talking about when I would be able to come back to visit and how we would stay up late catching up . . . you would teach about mythology; we would drink many beers and listen to music such as the Doors ("because it must genetic to have an identical good taste in music").

Whatever type of pain it was, if I could have, I would have taken it all away—or at the very least tried to share your burden. I'm sure the many people that love you would agree. There have been lots of times when I have wished that we weren't on opposite sides of the world but not nearly as much as I wish right now. I know that you would tell me that it doesn't matter that I'm not there to say goodbye; that what really mattered were the times that we spent together but I would give anything to be there right now, for you and the family. Both my mother's and my hearts are with all of you in Texas and we are both there in spirit. There is not even a second when you all of you, or Sean, aren't in my thoughts and heart.

Sean, you will forever live through my heart and actions every day. I promise that I will live every minute of my life for you.

I love you my dear friend and I'll see you at the next whisky bar.

Your cousin,
Amanda xo.

Homily for Sean Michael Hughston

How we wish we were not here today. How we wish we were listening to Sean tell a joke, were listening to his laugh, were watching his smile. What we would give to watch him walk into a room, full of questions and ponderings.

How we wish we were not here today.

And yet, because we love Sean, and because we love Beulah, Tommy, Tommy II and Maxine and Amanda, we are here. We are here to walk together through this grief. We are here to accompany one another through this sadness. We are here to help one another simply absorb the shock that Sean took his own life.

A word of advice to all of us—let us not get stuck in the bog of asking "Why?" We labor with the illusion that if we could just figure it out, the pain would diminish. We won't know the answer to "Why?"

We do know this: the very minute that Sean departed this life, he was received into God's mercy. The very Moment Sean began his journey Home to the God from whom he came, he was enfolded in Love. That infinite Mercy embraced him, held him, received him. We know that the Love that knit Sean together in his mother's womb (Psalm 139:12) is the same Love that welcomes him Home. We know that the Love that receives Sean into the arms of Mercy is the love of Christ: stronger than despair, steadier than human happiness, far more creative than we can ask or imagine. Even now, Sean's wounded spirit is being healed and made new. Even now, he is restored to the community of those who have gone before.

As many of you know, Sean decided over a year ago to register for organ donation through the Texas Organ Shared Alliance. This is a commitment over and above what we do when we sign the back of our driver's license, thereby signaling that we would permit organ donation upon the event of our death.

When Sean was 26 years old, he made a clear and conscious choice to share himself in the most concrete, embodied fashion. Today someone lives because Sean's heart beats within his or her chest. Today someone thrives with a new liver. Today two people are being given new life by Sean's kidneys. His decision tells us something profound about this young man: he knew that life is for sharing, not hoarding. He knew that we are here for one another and not only for ourselves. He knew that each step we make along this path of life is only truly possible when we uphold one another.

On Sean's Facebook page he had posted many pictures of his trip to Europe and his time in Rome. It is so telling to see his beaming face among ancient ruins. And it is so telling to see what he chose to photograph, and even more so to note what he chose to comment upon.

One photo comes from a fourth century fresco in the Basilica of San Clemente in Rome. ("Clemency", as you know, means a disposition to show mercy.) The fresco is an ancient depiction of Christ harrowing hell. Sean noted that the fresco shows, (and these are his words) "Christ going into the underworld to rescue souls in limbo. It is hard to see but Adam's foot is being held by a gnarly looking demon." Sean knew that gnarly demon. He knew what it was to be held back by addiction. And Sean knew something of the strength of the grace that now pulls him out of the grip of the gnarly demon. Now he knows more fully. Now he sees from the perspective of eternity. Now he beholds with a spirit set free from every bond.

An ancient Christian homily from the second century tells of Christ descending among the dead, and going in search of "our own first parents," Adam and Eve. The Risen Lord seeks them out and proclaims, "Arise! Awake! I did not create you to be a captive in hell!" Not one of us was made so that we might be a captive in hell. Certainly not Sean. This very Moment, the Risen Lord, the one through whom we are created, gazes at Sean, gazes at each of us, outstretches the hand of Life and draws us from our own captivities to a life of freedom–freedom to love, freedom to serve. Sean saw a glimpse of this truth in that fresco, both the truth of the gnarly demon and the more resplendent, stunning, reverberating truth: "I did not create you to be a captive in hell."

You who are his friends and family have witnessed to Sean's ability to help you be freed from the grip of the gnarly demon. As we go forth this day, we are presented with the possibility of honoring Sean's life in our lives. Some of you are here because Sean talked you out of your own suicidal Moment. Some of you are studying at the university level because Sean told you to go for it. Some of you are pondering travel abroad because Sean said in his life: "Let's go see."

In the days ahead, honor Sean in clear and steady ways. Choose to help one another. Choose to be honest about your own addictive tendencies—and believe me, in this society we all have them—and seek help. Choose to honor someone who needs a leg up. Choose to remember that every single day there are people who need to be set free from whatever hell they are living. And when you discover the right Moment to act in honor of Sean, let Tommy and Beulah know. Send them a note saying, "I read a new book in honor of Sean and made a donation to a literacy program." "I decided to get clean and am going to meetings in honor of Sean." "I am planning a trip to Rome and am going to tell that gnarly demon that he lost the battle."

When the grief seems too big, do something to honor Sean's life. When the sadness strikes, remember the persons who are literally walking around giving thanks to God for Sean because they received an organ from him. When the days seem too long, light a fire in the backyard, sing one of Sean's favorite songs, and remember: Sean has been received into the arms of Mercy. Receive the words of the Risen Lord echoing through your very cells, throughout the entire magnificent universe: "I did not create you to be a captive in hell." Amen.

The Rev. Mary C. Earle, St. Paul's Episcopal Church, May 24, 2011

Celtic prayer for grief

Do not hurry
As you walk with grief
It does not help the journey

Be not disturbed
By memories that come unbidden
Let God support you

Be gentle with the one who
Walks through grief
If it is you,
Be gentle with yourself.
Swiftly forgive
Walk slowly
Pausing often

Take time, be gentle
As you walk with grief.

CHAPTER 95

LEARNING TO BE BI-CULTURAL

Sam has made many references to New Zealand's Maori culture in which we unwittingly became caught up, when we bought our historic Te Puru property. Of all the challenges we ever faced together, this was by far, the greatest . . . on every imaginable level!

Having been born into the monocultural New Zealand of the early 1950's, my own contact with my country's indigenous people had been minimal. Raised and conventionally educated in the 1950's and 1960's co-educational school system of the provincial city of Palmerston North, with its relatively urban Maori population, I believed as most Pakeha (non Maori) of that era were encouraged to do by the patronizingly self-righteous governments of those times, that the race relations between New Zealand's two cultures were exemplary. I simplistically accepted that the only difference between myself and the few Maori children I went to school with, was that they had a better suntan than I did. I had no other contact with Maori culture and so what little exposure I had, was only tokenism. My impressions were formed entirely by the mainstream Pakeha assimilationist concepts of those times.

Even in my job as a journalist through the 1970's, my contact with Maori culture was not great, as New Zealand's provincial newspaper coverage was still concentrated only on the mainstream Pakeha worldview. However, it was during this decade that the status quo first altered as the Maori people began to go through a renaissance of their own culture and New Zealand's racial/political climate started to change. While I supported this change, I was still somewhat unaware of the cumulative effect of these changes as I had left New Zealand—and my first husband—in 1980, to return to Canada where I had lived with him the previous year, while he was studying for a Masters in Journalism at Carleton University in Ottawa. On my return to Ottawa, I found a position as Press Secretary for the New Zealand High Commission but in order to process the required immigration procedures as a New Zealand national, I then had to leave Canada. There was a Canadian Consulate in Dallas, and while staying with friends in Austin, I met Sam. Having also fallen in love with the Texan culture in which I instinctively felt more at home than I ever did in Canada, I decided that I would stay in Texas with him, rather than return to Ottawa.

Moving back to New Zealand with Sam in 1988, I found a different country to the one I had left, eight years before. The country's liberal left-wing reformist political system had changed the structure of its whole society, with widespread and far-reaching economic and social reforms designed to produce a "user pays" system. The racial climate had also altered but as I had already become sympathetic to the Maori 'cause' during the previous decade, I was pleased to see this growing cultural awareness and resurgence taking place. Not only was there increasing recognition of the institutionalized racism (and its consequent disparity gap) which earlier last century, had almost resulted in this culture and its people dying out, but also some acknowledgement that protection of the rights and aspirations of New Zealand's indigenous people was long overdue in order to help lift them from their current socio-economic position to one of greater equality.

Having intended to live a much simpler life in New Zealand with no lawns and no mortgage, Sam and I then did exactly the opposite when we bought an unfinished large property at the (northern North Island) Coromandel Peninsula seaside village of Te Puru, just north of Thames, with the intention of using its existing commercial use rights to establish an up market tourism lodge business. In 1990, our long-awaited daughter, Amanda, was also born and while we both saw this as a real blessing, this additional complication also created another everyday challenge for us to balance and overcome, without sacrificing either our precious family life or our demanding lifestyle business. This was the steepest learning curve of our lives.

Not only did we have to build this business but we also then became caught up in an ongoing seemingly insoluble situation involving reputed cultural issues surrounding the headland on which our lodge had been built by its original owners in the late 1970's. Adjacent property owners constructing a house in the mid-1990's, desecrated a known Maori burial site (urupa) on their land in front of our lodge. Eventually, in order to gain some clarity into the ramifications of this situation for our own property and reach resolution for all parties concerned, having suddenly become increasingly aware of the whole headland's now obviously significant historical and cultural value, we were forced to begin to investigate this issue ourselves.

It proved to be a time-consuming, expensive and often emotionally painful education. We began this journey from a position of total ignorance of the Maori cultural issues involved. Sam was very conversant with the original history of his own land with its numerous still-visible signs of early American Indian and Hispanic settlement, and subsequent early European settlement. But like many Pakeha New Zealanders, I had absolutely no idea of what a Pa (fortified village) site even looked like—much less, any recognition of the now-obvious signs of its original habitation such as its living and defensive terraces, and sea shell deposits.

Finally, in 1997, we discovered through New Zealand's Historic Places Trust, that the land we now lived on, was part of the previously well-known ancient Te Aputa Pa. On hearing this we had mixed feelings . . . elation to have been involved in making this re-discovery of New Zealand's real history which could now be preserved and passed on; along with some trepidation as to what this development could mean in our now unknown future. But although he was not a New Zealander, Sam was excited to learn of our connection to this especially significant land, commenting to me at the time that he now felt like he had just bought the Alamo. But we both suspected that if we had known of this history before we bought the property, we would probably not then have had the courage to purposely do so.

However, our overwhelming feeling was one of vindication . . . in knowing that we had been fighting for something worthwhile, as we both felt that if this was not Pakeha history too, then we did not really have any to call our own. We felt fortunate to have stewardship of this heritage resource and consequently worked with tangata whenua (the people of the land) to register the lodge and its surrounding properties with the Historic Places Trust, as a waahi tapu protected site—in order to save its remaining archaeological remains. We believed that it was possible to make an educational heritage statement by balancing the historical and cultural realities of the area, with an ethically-conscious commercial development.

We fought many complicated issues—and sometimes even both cultures—in our continuing efforts to protect this land that we now felt so connected to and responsible for. During the last half of the 1990's, the block of land containing the burial site at the front of the Te Aputa headland, finally became tied up in litigation between its owners and the local council. This situation remained at an impasse for five years, in spite of our best efforts to help resolve it.

One of New Zealand's most respected Maori leaders, Maori cultural consultant, Tom Winitana, became a regular weekly guest at our lodge in late 1999, when he was working on the local Maori land claims arising from the 1840 Treaty of Waitangi (New Zealand's founding document) signed with the British monarch. Historical injustices from these obligations collectively agreed to, are now being addressed through reports to Waitangi Tribunal hearings as this process makes public, tragic stories and injustices previously kept private. Many Pakeha New Zealanders do not want to address Maori grievances and would prefer there were no Maori claims but it has become abundantly clear since this process first began, that the Crown breached/breaches its obligations under the Treaty of Waitangi, in many ways. Increasing awareness of the injustices of the past, along with a growing Maori population whose culture is also going through a social, cultural and economic redevelopment renaissance, means that Maori agitation for the rights affirmed to them from the beginnings of Pakeha settlement in New Zealand, will not stop now.

Through no fault of our own, Sam and I had become almost completely isolated and surrounded by Maori issues, and under attack from both cultures because of the on-going environmental vandalism of neighboring property owners. Once he was confronted with the situation we had so unwittingly become involved in, Tom felt he had no choice then but to also become involved in, and then committed to, helping us to sort out this complex situation—as only he, because of his standing in the Maori world, had the skills and influence to do. He had great respect for Pakeha he believed had committed "commercial suicide" over the courage of their convictions and knowing I was trying to resolve these related issues alone while running a business, and looking after a paralyzed husband and young daughter, he decided he had to help. While his initial relationship with us was that of a lodge guest, it soon evolved into one of a very close family friend, and through him we finally began to understand the Maori culture he always epitomized so simply . . . and the real differences between his Maori culture and our own Pakeha one. The unwavering strength of Tom's ongoing support and friendship helped us all endure through this difficult time.

I remember once (some time before Tom's arrival on the scene) when my Auntie Joan's husband Kit 'read me the riot act' over my continuing involvement in Maori issues . . . and the practical necessity for this to stop when Sam became paralyzed. Sam unequivocally vetoed this. Instead of agreeing and selfishly demanding all my attention for himself now, he pragmatically defended this perceived distraction, explaining to my very concerned and well-meaning uncle that this work with the Maori people was my only "escape" from the sheer hard work of our seemingly endless, depressing life that otherwise centered mainly around his bodily functions. Sam believed that contrary to everyone else's view, my work (and his) with the Maori people was mutually beneficial as, in addition to any altruism, it actually filled a need for us too, by helping to keep me balanced and sane.

Sam and I had always hoped that the land in front of the lodge could be worked into a stepping stone and starting place for a cultural heritage trail along the Thames Coast. We felt that its developer owners did not deserve to be reimbursed for the damage they had knowingly done, before lying about it and then trying to blame everyone else for the repercussions of their actions. However, we also knew that the local council was not totally blameless either, as it had a statutory (if not moral) obligation to work with local Maori on land issues through learning what and where this needed protection. Because of the part they had also played in this environmental vandalism, we always hoped they would eventually take some responsibility by trying to purchase this land back from these owners at a reduced amount—and then donate it to a trust or foundation as part of the region's heritage trail. This, we both felt, would then make some sense out of all this desecration and destruction, in order to protect and develop the area sustainably, for future generations.

However, after Sam died in late 2001, having already unsuccessfully attempted to help us resolve the legalities of the adjoining land situation with the local council, my lawyer/friend decided at this point, that I should now buy this contentious land block as part of the legal settlement with the local council, since its litigation process had finally reached New Zealand's Environment Court. Once I had achieved this outcome in 2002, it was then possible to begin to resolve this situation through a bi-cultural partnership that benefitted everyone involved. I had found it impossible not to personalize our shared history as I became increasingly aware of its inequalities and was forced to re-examine my own (fifth generation colonial) family history, in the light of these discoveries. This helped give me my own sense of responsibility as a New Zealander, to try to do something to make a difference in today's increasingly intolerant racial climate. A friend and colleague recently wrote to me that what Sam and I had done at Te Aputa was an achievement in many ways—"not the least of which is that you chose, or were chosen, to build a beacon of hope for a sustainable future for this great country of ours".

I have realized that I really started to learn to be bi-cultural from Sam, when I lived in Texas with him for almost ten years, amongst some of the most culturally-aware people anywhere in the world. I realized then that it is your strong sense of identity that even threatens other Americans—hence all the 'Texan' jokes. Sam taught me that because Texas was originally its own country, it was a cultural melting pot from the outset as the ferocity of the Commanches and other tribes, coupled with the harshness of the environment, made much of the state untenable for extensive colonization—either by the United States or Mexico. This diverse cultural mosaic was formed by a synthesis of Tex-Mex and Hispanic, Cajun and Black, German, Polish and Czech, Gaelic and Britannic, the antebellum Southern model (through which, slaves brought in African and Caribbean influences), and the cowboys and vaqueros. And I also found that Texans are not precious . . . I did not have to have arrived on the "Mayflower" to feel as if I was accepted and belonged. As I was told, "Texas is a State of mind". Living there, away from my own country, gave me an appreciation of multi-cultural history, and regret that I did not feel as connected to my own. I loved the real, larger-than-life heroes of your culture and found I had gradually become aware of what it was to have a history and culture to be proud of—quite unlike our 'New Zealand Land Wars' history of that same (mid to late 1800's) period! As a New Zealander, I found that like much Maori culture, Texans had a strongly intact sense of identity which made them inclusive, rather than exclusive, towards other cultures.

Living overseas also taught me that it is only our indigenous Maori culture that is truly unique in the world, and ultimately differentiates and defines us (as distinct from Australians) as Aotearoa New Zealanders. On our return to my own country, I missed living amongst people with 'attitude', who were inclusive in sharing their culture with anyone who was secure enough to not be threatened by it. And so, as a result of my experience of living with Sam in Texas, it was probably a natural progression for me to then relate more naturally to the Maori culture than my own European Pakeha one. Sam pointed out to me when I came back to live in my own country again, that (unlike the Maori people) most Pakeha New Zealanders did not have that same real sense of who they were or where they had come from. And when Sam became paralyzed and began writing his first *'Family History'* book, it finally dawned on me that you do not have to be colored to be indigenous! Having always known this, our Maori friends were highly amused when I told them of my surprised revelation. I eventually discovered that the real history of my own country had been 'hidden' because of the 'cringe' factor that only its indigenous people have been honest about.

I believe that the motivation behind Sam's actions was very similar to my own. He, too, had always had a very highly developed sense of fairness and championship of the 'underdog' causes on which we invariably found ourselves on the same side. We both had always had a 'soft spot' for people we thought had been taken advantage of and this was the case with New Zealand's Maori people. And as a 'culturally intact' Texan with a very real sense of his own Czech heritage, he was also very open to, and accepting of, other cultures. While it would have been much easier to ignore all this background Maori history that, at times, threatened to overwhelm and consume us, and take over with a life of its own, it was something that neither Sam or I could do in good conscience. Sam felt that if Te Aputa was truly as important an archaeological site as was claimed, who were we to destroy it and not protect it for the generations to come. We both knew that in the short term this waahi tapu registration was not a good move as we were well aware that our protection of the Te Aputa Pa site was "like a knife for us . . . it cut both ways". If we helped protect the Pa then we would also become completely subject to all the controls and conditions of its protection order—which could affect the value of our own property adversely, as well as our ability to even ever sell it. But the principles involved here were absolute and immovable for us.

However, maintaining that our lodge could also be a sustainable tourism business that did not destroy the environment, its history, or its culture, Sam believed that it could provide for a better understanding of where New Zealand's Maori people were coming from, by being used to educate all those who came to visit and learn from the past. Sam knew too, that this would also provide some economic assistance as it would necessitate the employment of local Maori people to show and interpret the Pa site, as well as work on its preservation. After all, he would say, when you go to a place to learn about its history and culture, you want to hear about this from the indigenous people and not some other race that has taken over . . . and that he hoped a tour in Mexico would have a Mexican running the bus, and not an Australian!

Although still relatively young, our wise Maori friend, Steve Te Moananui (who the visiting Kopecky family members met in 1999) became close to our whole family here when he tried—unsuccessfully—to help us resolve the Maori 'issues' relating to our property, before Tom eventually came into our lives later that year. Knowing of Sam's deep sense (and awareness) of spirituality, he also recognized Grandma Golda's disclosure to Sam, of her Cherokee Indian heritage, and accepted Sam as a "brother". On learning of Sam's cancer diagnosis in 1998, I remember going to Steve, totally distraught, seeking an answer on how to deal with this destruction of our lives which had totally blindsided us. I told him then, that I did not even know how to help someone to die . . . to which he calmly replied that my role was actually to help Sam find peace. I understood this concept better and was less afraid as I felt that I could do that. When I then asked him why this was happening to Sam, his answer was that Sam had now done his job here by bringing me back to my own country to do what I needed to do next . . . and that he was now being freed to go (to do other work). I also remember him showing Sam's family where Sam would one day be buried, when a lot of important people would be present. I had no more idea what he was talking about at that time than Sam's family did but although I still don't understand how Steve and many of his people can 'see' the future, I do now accept this phenomenon. At Sam's funeral, Steve finally apologized for his people having taken so much from him and thanked him "for being sent to us" . . . "to show us the way".

The events in Steve's prophetic words eventually all came to pass—including his (then) incredibly unlikely later prediction that our friend Tom had come to us to find his next wife. I was aware that Tom had discussed this with Sam before his death as, in addition to his Maori view of Sam as 'tapu tapu' (doubly prohibited/sacred) because of his combined paralysis and advanced terminal cancer, they were both the same kind of honorable men of their word who would never do anything hypocritical or underhanded to each other. On his return from talking to Sam, Tom told me only that he had told Sam he loved his taste in women—to which Sam had replied that he had "had to look under a lot of rocks for this one". Tom did not volunteer anything further and realizing I had unintentionally challenged his innate code of honor, I did not ask, as while the three of us spent time together regularly, these two unusual men also maintained their own one-on-one relationship, independent of mine with either of them. However, I did sense that they had reached some form of understanding which I decided not to question. Tom told me later—on the return drive from taking Sam to the crematorium—that he had on that day, told Sam of his eventual intention to marry me and asked for his permission to do so. He told me that Sam had been startled at his honesty but that he had then nodded, acknowledging the practicality of this solution as our own relationship was in effect over and he knew I would need to go on with my life. However, Sam had requested that as men of honor Tom would agree not to discuss this conversation until after he had died. Tom never did and I was so grateful to Sam for his generosity of spirit as someone who I came to realize, knew how to love as an action and a practice, and not just a concept. He loved me enough to set me free and not imprison me in our dying relationship, dragging me down any further with him. Tom later always observed that Sam had been a bigger man than he could have been under those circumstances. But I was glad I had not known of what really passed between them that day, as we constantly endeavored to maintain Sam's dignity and self-respect. This knowledge that Sam was completely aware of Tom's eventual intentions and had given his blessing to this relationship, would have made the situation impossible for me.

After three years of living with paralysis, Sam finally finished the books he was writing on his family history and died at peace, knowing that Tom was with Amanda and I, and had promised him he would look after us both as his own. Tom had assured Sam that while he would never try to replace him as a father, as her stepfather he would be whatever kind of father our daughter wanted him to be. Sam would even sit Tom and I down sometimes and worry about our future together. These two men—my real-life heroes—became very close during this last two years of Sam's illness, which also had the effect of bringing Tom and I even closer too, in our shared grief for our courageous and unselfish friend. We were all dedicated to each other and this also became a story of aroha (love) and manaakitanga (caring) between the three of us.

An incident I recall that illustrates the unusual depth of this relationship occurred when a foster son and namesake grandson of Tom's, were both killed in a car accident. I had told Sam this news and on his return to us following their tangi (funeral), Tom went downstairs to Sam's bedroom as usual, to pay his respects to him. He later told me how it had touched him when Sam had asked him to come closer to his bed, and then reached out and hugged him to show him how sorry he was about this loss. Sam, too, believed that his actions spoke louder than his words.

Another time, when Tom, himself, became ill with pneumonia while staying with us, he spent a few days at the local Thames Hospital. When I brought him back home to the lodge, Tom immediately went to pay his respects to Sam who immediately told him that his "family" had been there, while he was in hospital . . . looking for him. I could not work out why they did not know he was in hospital, rather than at the lodge but Tom immediately understood what Sam was saying and acknowledged this accordingly. While I knew that Sam was also very aware of the forces around us, it was only afterwards that I realized he had been talking about Tom's spiritual 'protectors', who he later described to me just as Tom already had. I realized then, that part of this unique connection between these two men was spiritual. Tom attributed this to the fact that although only small, part of Sam's Texan bloodlines—as he was originally told by his paternal grandmother who had raised him—went back to the Cherokee people in the north of Texas.

Tom, in turn, had helped Amanda and I support Sam through a 'medical misadventure' legal dispute caused by his unnecessary paralysis, and assisted me each time I had to take him to Waikato Hospital for radiation treatment for pain relief and to prevent quadriplegia. He also became his alternate caregiver and companion—often nodding off himself in the reclining chair alongside Sam's bed—so his friend would not be alone as the cancer progressed, in order to free me to take care of other essentials I could not deal with when I was alone. Sam even asked Tom to represent him by standing beside me at my own father's funeral when Sam was too ill to travel and directly support me himself, as it occurred only weeks before his own death. Tom then helped me organize and recover from Sam's funeral at home where he had finally died with us around him, and later get through and recuperate from my own subsequent major surgery.

When the local Maori community knew Sam was dying, we were asked—through Tom—if we would like to have his tangi (lying in state/funeral service) at their Marae (traditional meeting place) . . . a rare honor for a Pakeha (non-Maori). Knowing what Sam had done to try to protect the land during his years at the lodge, they wished to acknowledge him accordingly, as a Rangatira (chief). Sam and I decided to decline this option (and instead do this at the lodge) because of the unfamiliarity and resultant additional stress that this scenario could cause for Amanda and other family members. Instead, our closest Maori friends, Tom Winitana, Steve Te Moananui and Hakaraia Gurnick (all of whom have been Te Aputa

(Reserve) trustees) paid their respects—and those of their people—to Sam at his funeral, where they were pallbearers along with my own family.

It was typical of their unusual relationship that when Sam died, Tom spoke so movingly of this "Texan . . . who taught me what patience was all about". While he had read some beautiful stories about patience, Tom said in this public tribute, that the way he had seen Sam practice it had made him realize what the word really meant. He also spoke of Sam's other quality of caring for people . . . right up to the time when he had said his own final farewell to him the previous week, both knowing it was the last time they would say goodbye to each other. Sam had told him then, to take care until they saw each other again—to which Tom had responded that he knew they would meet again one day. Tom told our family and friends that Sam was a very spiritual man which he attributed to his American Indian bloodlines, and that they had "that sort of relationship". Because of this, he said, it was fitting that his tangi was held on an old Pa site, and in farewelling his friend from his own Maori value base, Tom reverted to type and became the teacher he always was.

In telling his friend to go, Tom reminded Sam that according to the Maori genealogy viewpoint he had often spoken to him of, the trees were the first, with Ngaio being the first breath of his God, Io. His people had always understood that they needed the trees to keep the air clean. Go tell my people that the trees are being regenerated again to keep the air clean, he told Sam. Next he told him that it was such a pity he did not ever have the time to get out fishing in New Zealand as he had wanted to do, because the fish were second in this order of descent. His people understood that the biggest octopus in the world lived here, he said, and knew that Kupe had fought one of the very big ones that was 80 feet long from the centre to the tip of its tentacles. Remind them when you get up there that they are still here, Tom told Sam, and that they are still healthy and still trying to keep the water pure and fresh. And he also told Sam to remind the tipuna (ancestors) that the kowhai were just starting to bloom on the Pa site when he had said his goodbyes to us—that there were kaka there again, along with the tui and bellbird whose song was so beautiful to listen to, and that they would all keep on propagating the kowhai trees. Every time the kowhai is in bloom it will always remind me of you, he told him. Though they had known each other only a short time, Tom said, Sam had taught him the meaning of sincerity, patience, tolerance and above all honesty . . . the most profound he had ever known.

Tom was planning on eventually moving to Te Puru permanently and some time after Sam's death, he asked me if I would marry him. We agreed then, that this would not happen until Amanda was ready to accept it. Tom finally knew when he came to Te Aputa, that the work we had been brought together to do was to record, full time, his oral tradition value base of the old Maori . . . "for the generations yet unborn". He had never been interested in doing so before but in his 'twilight years', felt the time was finally right. Tom had intended to set the record straight—in terms of finally recording his Tohunga (Maori name for experts—or original equivalent of today's university professors—in "all things") oral tradition value base, in written form.

I was always humbled by the whole concept of what we were doing together and struggled not to be overawed by the magnitude of it all, as the many catastrophic events in both our lives appeared to have been designed to bring us together at this point. When I would question Tom as to why, as naïve and ignorant as I was, I had been chosen for him to channel this knowledge through—as his "scribe"—he told me it was because I was so open and uncontaminated by any prior knowledge of 'things Maori'. Therefore I had no preconceived ideas for him to overcome. Consequently I was completely accepting of all he taught me as what he described as his best pupil, and was only interested in the profoundly moving purity and sublimity of the cultural knowledge—and not the political aspects of any perceived power around this.

I had always sensed that my purpose in life was not just to have a job and had instinctively sought out a way to give something back that I was passionate about. Through Sam and Tom I had now made the inner discovery of the spiritual value of my life . . . to create from the soul. I also finally reluctantly accepted that I was never going to be allowed to leave my responsibilities at Te Aputa until this work was done. But I now wanted to make the most of whatever time we had been given, rather than putting this off until we were free to leave and live our own life together without all these shared responsibilities to his people. We decided to focus on the present, having both finally realized that Te Aputa had become our turangawaewae . . . our place to stand . . . together.

Before I came to Te Aputa, I realized that as a Pakeha New Zealander I had always been homeless in my own land, without the Maori sense of identity and security that comes from having a place to belong to, where I had a past, a present and a future. While I am still not sure I really understand it, I now hear the heartbeat of this land where I can somehow feel the history beneath my feet. This is why I had to create the Te Aputa Reserve as the place where Sam, Tom and I all stood together and fought back-to-back . . . otherwise I would still not really feel as though I could stand anywhere at all.

Unfortunately, we were only just beginning to 'paint the picture' of life at Te Aputa Pa but I have now recorded this work Tom and I did do together, following his mantra that the best way to learn is to teach. At least now this small part of his vast store of priceless knowledge of the 'old Maori' oral tradition value base handed down to me is retained, and has not disappeared with him too. Tom's car accident and resulting death just 18 months after Sam's passing, seemed such a senseless way to lose such a 'Taonga' ('living treasure'). A Maori friend urged me at that time, to "hold strong . . . as while the pathway may seem insurmountable at that moment, it is still there, as is the dream". While I despaired that I would ever be able to see this concept again, one year later when the Te Aputa land reservation process was formalized, I realized that this was true. Our bi-cultural vision continues through the Te Aputa Trust, with its Maori and Pakeha trustees, who are all still working together on this ancestral kaupapa (plan). It was not an option for me to give up on our dream and while we could not do it all without Tom's knowledge and inspirational leadership, there is still a resolve to salvage what we can of this and do the things we can, working together bi-culturally as originally intended. It is the only acceptable outcome after so much sacrifice.

While both Sam and Tom have now passed on, I find my extraordinary bi-cultural journey continues—even without my mentors alongside to guide me now. They continue to prove to me that our love has not died but in fact stay with me . . . and that my future has already been shaped by my past. They helped teach me the meaning of my life . . . to open my eyes . . . and live with their spirit of acceptance, relinquishing myself to the natural order of things. I know that these two uniquely courageous and resilient men who recognized and appreciated in each other these qualities they both shared with unmistakable mutual love and respect, will always be part of me now because of this amazing life journey we went on together.

Trust

The struggles you are going through now—
Don't discard them.

Listen to God as he teaches you, so that you can teach others.

You see, a time of suffering teaches us something we never knew before and
may prepare us for a time of counsel, that we will give someone else for years to come.

When we cannot understand—help us to trust.

(Much loved and read prayer sent to me by Uncle Gene—when Sam's
advanced terminal cancer was diagnosed)

CHAPTER 96

My Father Would be Proud

Texas,
February 16, 2006.

To the new hosts, my name is Sam Kopecky Jr. and I live at Canyon Lake in Texas, USA, and Te Puru Coast View Lodge was my Dad and Pam's dream. I know it must have been hard for Pam and Amanda to sell the place but you have to move on.

It looks wonderful. My father would be proud.

I was there for a brief week in April of 1999, before my father's passing, and even though it was his pride and joy, it was a lot of work.

He was a proud man, full of integrity, and that is what I'll remember most about him.

Keep the dream alive!

Sincerely,
Sam Kopecky Jr.

P.S. The plans for the new rooms look great!

New Zealand,
February 22, 2006.

Dear Sam and Denise, as you can see, the Te Puru Lodge owners forwarded me your email and I was so touched to hear from you again in this way. I am so sorry we have lost touch and I would so like to re-establish more regular communication with you all again. Like you, my most enduring memories of your Dad are his pride and absolute integrity. It is because of these—and many other—unique characteristics of his, that both Amanda and I have been struggling ever since his death, to pick up all the pieces and move on again with our lives. He will always be irreplaceable for us and I know we will never stop missing him.

I would like to explain some of what has transpired here since we last talked and will try to keep it short . . . Not too long after you all came and stayed, one of this country's best known Maori leaders (a paramount chief and Maori royalty, as first cousin to the late Maori Queen) came and stayed at the lodge and 'adopted' us—and began to help resolve all the cultural issues relating to our land. He became a lodge guest (as part of his consultancy company's work) every week from then until your father died—which was why then, he spoke at your father's funeral. Tom eventually just became part of our family and your Dad finally died at peace, knowing that Tom would be there for Amanda and I, to help us after he had gone. The three of us developed a remarkable friendship—which was only possible because of the similar kind of men Sam and Tom were. Your Dad asked us both to take him on his "last ride" as his "two best friends", and we were then able to support each other in our shared grief over the loss of our friend. It was not a situation many people could get their heads around but we all loved and were there for each other.

It was a very special time and I was so privileged to have been part of it. I will always love your father and appreciate his courage and pragmatic unselfishness in making me go on with my life.

When your father died, I discovered I was ill and needed major surgery and I spent much of the next year recuperating from this. At the start of 2003, I finally felt like I was ready to move on with my life and Tom then said he would move to Te Puru permanently, to be with us. He was to be with us by my 50th birthday in May . . . but leaving the lodge in late March, he was involved in a car accident and died in hospital unexpectedly 5 days later, from undiagnosed and untreated kidney failure. I was with him at the end in the Intensive Care Unit but it didn't help much as he died during a scanning procedure with medical staff oblivious to what was even happening. After dealing with your father's paralysis (medical misadventure) and death, and then this unnecessary death, it was all too much. I had lost my Dad two months before Sam, and then my Uncle Kit (Joan's husband), two months before Tom. In less than two years we lost all the men in my family . . . the past, the present, and the future, all at once. I had had no time to grieve before Tom so it hit me all at once. Amanda was badly affected too.

I found—like your Dad—that the only way I could find to begin to heal myself, and make any sense out of all this loss, was to write. It is a very lonely process though and so I became quite isolated for the next couple of years. Throughout the rest of 2003 I also worked on $60k worth of deferred lodge repairs and maintenance—finally selling it at the end of 2004. I moved up the coast to Tapu on the understanding that I would return when the new owners built Amanda and I a new townhouse there as part of their development plans for the lodge. It was hard to sell but there had been too much sadness there for me to find the energy to rebuild the business on my own. I then also had to leave money in as a 2nd mortgage, in order for the sale to go through. I retained freehold ownership of the lot at the front of the headland the lodge is on—where the grave is—and after forming a Charitable Trust (for funding purposes) signed a Protected Private Land Agreement with the Minister of Conservation, making that land block a Private Historic Reserve. Since then, that land has been archaeologically restored and the trust is working on public interpretation/education initiatives associated with the cultural history of the land. In due course, your father's ashes—along with some of my father's—will be placed there, where the grave is. (Remember Steve telling you all that one day there would be some important people up there when that happened? I don't know how he 'saw' all that but it is happening!) In due course, I may well end up there too and the land will eventually be gifted to the nation as a living memorial to all the people who have been associated with its—ancient and modern—history. There will be some specific acknowledgement of both Sam's and Tom's roles in saving this land.

I have written the story of what has happened since we arrived at the lodge. You were right. It was our dream and the only way I can find for it not to be a total waste now, is to write about what I learned there—and these amazing men who shared that humbling experience with me. My first book [as the background to all this] is primarily about [the Maori history and culture of] Tom [and his people], and my discovery of what it really means to [see things through Maori eyes and] be a bi-cultural New Zealander. Of course though, it is also about Sam and I too. My second book—which I have already started as part of this first one—is my own story [about being a Pakeha (European) New Zealander]. This is why I have not finished working on your father's writing yet as I had to do my own first. Now maybe I will be able to handle going back to his project again. It has not been forgotten but I had to heal myself some, first.

My professional author/editor friend and mentor, who lives here in Te Puru, wrote a précis of my book for the publisher, which I thought might help you understand the scope of what I am talking about . . .

['*Sharing the Cloak / Te Korowai Atawhai . . . a bi-cultural journey*' is] "a book tracing the development of Tame. His early childhood mentored by his grandfather in the ways of the old Maori, his forced acceptance of the ways of Pakeha New Zealanders, his foray into the wars of the wider world, his return to his people and his determination to help them develop as Maori New Zealander—culturally, politically and commercially.

Interwoven in the story of Tame are the general background history of colonial New Zealand, the development of Maori influence in many spheres of government, and his growing friendship with a Pakeha New Zealander and her American husband who made great sacrifices to restore and return to the people of New Zealand, an historical Pa site—an aim probably not achievable without Tame's help."

As a journalist, I had never seen myself as a writer but these past events seem to have shaped my future. I am hopeful that I will find a publisher soon.

Meanwhile . . . my landlady at Tapu decided they would move back there (from Auckland) by Xmas, so I had to move suddenly and ended up back at Te Puru, down below the lodge. It was only supposed to be temporary until our townhouse was built but now the lodge is going into foreclosure and a mortgagee sale seems inevitable. This puts me in a difficult position as second mortgagee, so life is a bit stressful right now. It will be hard for me to move on if I cannot get my money out of the lodge. My lawyer is working on it with me so I'm not entirely alone on this. It's complicated though as the lodge owners now see themselves as close friends.

BUT . . . whatever happens up there, the dream will still always live on through both the reserve and what I have written. Our dream is bigger than just the lodge and I will always keep it alive and not let it die too. And we will always be able to go up there to where your Dad will finally be laid to rest on the land he grew to love. He will never be alone there, as there are many others there with him. Chances are too, that Sam and I will be at peace there together one day, as he always hoped.

As for Amanda . . . her time in the States gave her the break from all this sadness, that she needed and me some time alone to try to begin to heal. I will always be so grateful to Beulah, Tommy and Sean for giving her a home with them, as well as the rest of the Kopecky clan who gave her a sense of her roots there. She was angry for a long time (for all kinds of reasons) but is now more at peace with all that has happened, and tells me how much she misses both her Dad and Tom. Unfortunately her education has suffered as she opted out of high school to do Correspondence School (with inconsistent results). This grieves me too as she has the Kopecky intellect but I just have to trust that she will get her act together when she is ready as I can't do it for her. We have had lots of bumps in the road and I anticipate there will be many more yet. She is so like her father in so many ways!! He would have known how to deal with her better than I do—although she admits he would probably have killed her by now!

Anyway, I guess before we get to book length, that gives you some idea of where we are up to now. I wanted you to know though, that we haven't really moved on . . . neither has the dream died. I will not let it, as it will always belong to Sam, Tom and I. While I could no longer stay at the lodge on my own, I will always carry the responsibility of doing whatever I can to ensure that all this hard work, sacrifice and sadness, were not for nothing. Your father will ultimately be part of changing this country's (modern) history, and will be recognized as such.

I would like to come back to Texas and catch up with you all again but have not been able to, either before or since I sold the lodge, as my capital was still tied up there. Once I am totally out of there financially, I will finally be able to look at that option . . . before all Sam's grandchildren are Amanda's age. Sam, could I please ask you to fwd this to Craig, Laurie and Scott, as I am not sure my contact details for them are up to date. It's too hard to keep writing this out so, maybe under the circumstances, they will forgive me for not writing to them individually. It's complicated to explain this story but I wanted to try before any more time went by. You have all been on my mind so much over all this time—I love and miss you all!! Sam, Craig, Laurie and Scott, please know that your father will never be forgotten. I will claim his place up on the reserve we all fought so hard to preserve and wherever I move on to eventually, I will always carry him with me in my heart. I would love to hear from you all.

Our love to you all,
always,
Pam and Amanda.

Texas,
February 23, 2006.

Dear Pam and Amanda, it has been too long! I am so encouraged to hear that things are getting better for you both. I have to admit, I never fully appreciated the heartaches and struggles that you have both endured in the time since my Dad's passing. It is hard to believe it has been almost 4 ½ years. They say, "time heals all wounds" but sometimes it takes a lot longer for some to heal than others. The other really significant man in my life, my grandfather Cecil, passed away in June of 2004. He is someone I think of almost every day also.

Some quick catch up on us . . . It just goes to show you, what people say and what they do, can often be different. That was one thing that Dad really made an impression on me, "Do what you say you are going to do!" I've found myself in the last 2 months, when I'm on job interviews, recalling what Dad instilled in me and the words honesty and integrity, have some quite significant relevance, evoking memories of Dad. I remember when he and I were living in a rent house in Boerne TX, when we first moved there because he was to operate the newly-acquired dealership for my Grandfather. We would butt heads over things, as I was challenging his authority because I was the same age Christopher is now—14 years old. I thought I knew enough to make good judgments but as I learn almost every day still, that I don't . . .

I feel I'm at a crossroads in my life. I just turned 42, and I really want to find my "calling", and find the job that not only I love and want to go to, but also feel challenged and reap the rewards of knowing you've done a job well. I wish I would have completed college like my siblings and have a degree . . .

Please feel free to write as I know it is the most economical way to communicate but can be time-consuming. I'm very interested to know how you are doing and if I can help with anything, please let me know. I look forward to the day when you two will be back in Texas.

Peace be with you two and hopefully this year will be the best of all our lives. (God knows, it has to get better sooner or later!.

Love and miss you!
Sambo and family.

PS. I found the book excerpts very interesting. They do help to provide insight. Bye, and stay in touch!

New Zealand,
July 13, 2006.

Hi Sam and Denise,

I am so glad we finally caught up by phone—I will not let that connection go again now. Amanda was so pleased to hear we'd talked again—and sorry she missed you. We will have to call again sometime when she is here.

I won't make this long as I've attached so much for you to read, as it is. Thought I would let you see draft of where I am trying to go with all this. I think it is timely—and that it might be a good thing for all of your siblings to also have it when you do. I think we have to trust your Dad's instincts as I know he gave it a lot of thought . . . and left a lot out. Maybe it would help them all deal with any issues—and in a funny way, reconnect them to their sense of who they are as Kopeckys, once they have been reminded by him about the importance of family. This seems to get lost nowadays with the everyday pressures of just surviving in today's world.

Just a quick catch up on us. After we last emailed, when it became obvious that lodge had no future with current owners (in spite of their having just refinanced again) I decided I needed to finally get a place so Amanda and I at least had a home again. We bought a townhouse in Thames, as without the lodge money (which is tied up until end of this year), I couldn't afford to stay on the coast. But at least we are no longer renting.

I had just bought property and got back from going to spend Easter with my widowed mother and aunt, when Amanda announced that she REALLY WAS going to live in Auckland on her 16th birthday, later that month. She wanted to do her Correspondence School work there. Knowing how early her father had left home—and that legally she could do so on that date without my permission—I could not oppose this move since I wanted to maintain our relationship after all that has happened, and ensure that she knew she could always come home again to me if things did not work out as she planned. She'd been telling me she wanted to do this but I had kept hoping it wouldn't eventuate. She definitely has the headstrong Kopecky gene—as well as the stubborn one from my side, if I'm honest.

Long story short . . . she did move—with my eventual support. If I had opposed her going, I think all I would have done is lose her and it has been too hard a journey for us to find our way back together again, for me to risk that now. Odd as it sounds, this may be a much better solution for us all. Only time will tell. It is not the way I would have liked everything to happen (one more time!) . . . but we had finally come out of all the turmoil our relationship had been through and were friends again. Maybe this was our lesson in not taking each other for granted! Strange way for this to resolve itself but I have had to learn to let go (much earlier than I'd planned) and let Amanda find her own path. It is lonely at times on my own but I console myself that her Dad will be watching over her! And now, while I am waiting to hear back from my publisher(s), I have no excuse for not getting back on to his book(s). Amanda is finally happy again though, for now, and achieving—which gives her self-esteem—and that is all I have ever really wanted for her. I guess we all have to find our own way in the end . . . however unconventionally.

I should know more on lodge situation soon—either when next quarterly (1st) mortgage payment is due (late August) or my 2nd one, in November. With any luck I will get something back and can then finally come back to Texas to see you all again. Anyway, that's a quick catch up on where things are now. Enough already . . . talk soon.

Love y'all,
Pam and Amanda.

New Zealand,
July 15, 2006.

Sam, just a quick note to tell you I remembered name of "Once were Warriors" sequel. It is "What becomes of the broken-hearted". You might also like to check out Jane Campion's "The Piano" and Vincent Ward's "The River Queen". If you liked "Warriors" and "Whale Rider", I think those would interest you too, as they are both also set in NZ and deal with (real) Maori culture. Another well-known, much older one is "Utu".

Your Dad used to love it when our friend Tom would tell his people (when he got most frustrated with them—for acting like Pakeha) that "once were warriors—now just wankers!" In spite of its fierce Hollywood portrayal, it is a culture of honesty, integrity, spirituality and humor, that I have become more drawn to over time, as I had never really appreciated that until after I lived in Texas—and with your Dad. Texans are not too different! They have that same warrior mentality still—or at least your Dad did!

I am still working on his 2nd book—now writing out letters (and Kopecky family stories—which even include you) we got from Aunt Ludma, after we moved to NZ. Sam had been told for years to stay away from her (she lived in Austin) but finally we went to see her, when we were leaving TX. We were so sad we hadn't done so sooner. We had a beer with her (she was 88!) and they reminisced, and she then wrote to us until her death a couple of years later. I guess it was our reminder that we both knew better than to let other family members make up our minds for us! She was the only one of the 1st generation of Kopeckys I met—and if she was anything to go by, they really must have been something else! But at least we do still have the stories. Most families don't have anything like this.

Yesterday I typed out the notes that your Dad left Amanda and I (beside his computer) before he died. We finally read them the morning he passed. This has been somewhat of an emotional treadmill for me to do all this but I am hoping it will help y'all—then it will be worth it. After hundreds of hours spent on this, I have only a couple of chapters left to finish, will insert graphics, proof read and then copy it all on to CD's for you. I don't believe it will make things worse for anyone as along with your telling me you need this input from your father now, I feel it may also be what Craig, Laurie and Scott all need to remind them of who they really are. I believe you already know—just as you know who your father really was. This will just confirm that for you—and maybe make you realize that in emulating his example, it has made you that same kind of man that I am so proud of!

Any parts that can be perceived as negative (like your father's perspective of some of your mother's and grandfather's actions—the Tindall observations are the main ones) should not come as a total shock anyway. I guess one of the first things that happens when we grow up, is that we realize that the people we love are flawed and not perfect—but that that does not need to affect how we feel about them. Love isn't blind—or stupid. Your father deals with a lot of issues from your own childhood(s) that may help—including apologies!—as well as being very honest about his own life, which may help you all overcome your own challenges. Overall, I think it's quite inspirational in dealing with issues of life and death, spirituality etc . . . but most of all, family . . . and love. These are the connections between us all now—and I think ones that we may all need to be reminded of again. I believe this is your father's reminder to us all again now, that we are still all connected by him (including his own siblings and cousins) even though we may still feel lost and disconnected. I would like to believe that he may still have the power to bring us all back together again now, just as he did when he was ill and dying.

Stay in touch.

Love,
Pam

Texas,
January 13, 2007.

Pam, just a quick note since we spoke. I have received and burned copies of the CD to give to my brothers and my sister. I plan to give them theirs tonight at dinner . . . I did explain that you wanted to include a letter with an explanation that it was my Dad's will, and that you and I think he wanted to not "drop a bomb on people" but I think they understand the situation . . .

I'm on page 314 or so and have laughed and cried several times over so far and I just want you to know how much I appreciate, and how much this book means to me! It brings back so many GOOD memories! I hope my other siblings will understand as I have, that a lot of what happened is in the past and was a long time ago.

As I was telling Denise last night, the book gives me such a feeling of "who I am and who my father was" and makes me proud—and also a confidence as I face the challenges of everyday life, that I didn't have before.

I truly want you to know how much I am thankful for all that you did for my Dad, and that I look forward to seeing both you and Amanda again soon! Denise and I will do whatever we can to help you two come back to the States (if she so chooses) . . .

Please stay in touch and I'm sure as I near the end of the book I will be back in touch with you.

Love,
Sambo.

Update—June 2008 . . .

I have realized that as hard as it is to let go of these last things that were so important to Sam at the end of his life, it really is now time for me to finally also put this book of his to rest. His 63rd birthday has just passed . . . 10 years from his original cancer diagnosis and paralysis . . . and 7 years on from his death. Amanda and I have not fully recovered from these events—and maybe never really will.

I still seem to be struggling to work our way through all the ongoing lodge issues that were part of his legacy as the future of the lodge (and my resulting financial position) has not yet been resolved . . . and may never be now. But work on the Private Historic Reserve I still own in front of it, is nearing completion with only the explanatory information panels left to be installed. We have finally put Sam's name on the grave there where his ashes are buried and I feel he would have been proud of what we have all achieved there now. In time, I will join him there and we will finally be reunited.

While I still miss Sam as much as ever, I feel as though I am running out of energy now and must finish up these last projects while I still can do so. Once this second manuscript is finally 'off my desk' and dispatched to his family as he intended, I should be able to focus better on finding another publisher for his first one as he also wished me to do. Then, maybe, I can get on with my own life again and discover just what it is that I am now meant to do with the remainder of it. Amanda is still trying to complete her education so she can also get on with whatever the future holds for her.

Over these last few years I have sorted through most of the remnants of our life together and it is over 6 months now since I went back to Texas to return some of Sam's Kopecky possessions to the family. It was very hard coming back to Texas without him and I found the whole experience quite surreal and overwhelming. It felt like losing him all over again but I was very moved by the family's hospitality and generosity, and intend to bring Amanda back before too much more time passes—when, hopefully, we will be able to catch up with all her siblings and wider family.

I was also overwhelmed by the very real physical, emotional and spiritual connection I still feel to Texas . . . I guess it really is "a State of mind". Having believed that the worst of my grief was behind me, I was overwhelmed by an inexplicable sense of loss when I was back in Texas with Sam's family, that made me so overcome with conflicting emotions that it was difficult at times, to even communicate. Those feelings have never left me again and I find I am still struggling with this same sense of numbness today. Living there with Sam changed me irrevocably and as far away as I find myself living again now, I know that part of my heart will always still belong in Texas. It will be difficult for me to ever find that sense of peace and belonging anywhere—or with anyone—else now.

I know that Sam would be devastated by the difficulties Amanda and I have had—separately and together—since he left us, as well as the fact that all these years later, neither of us have truly got over his loss. Sam, unintentionally, left such a gap in our lives but we are both still struggling to find new paths and will no doubt, one day, find our own new directions . . . just as he always wished.

Tommy II, Tommy, Beaulah and Sean Hughston, Thanksgiving 2007

Mary Beth (Colbert) Earle, Tommy Hughston, Scott Kopecky, Sean Hughston and Jason Earle, Thanksgiving 2007

Joe Kopecky, Aunt Jeannie (Deauquier), Ena (Hughes) and Beulah, Thanksgiving 2007.

Scott, Chris, Pam, Lisa, Evan, Sarah and Michael Kopecky, November 2007

CHAPTER 97

Rest in Peace

Sam had always told me that he wanted to be cremated and have his ashes buried down in front of the lodge where we had lived, because it was the only place he had ever lived in New Zealand. When I asked him about my returning his remains to Texas to be buried with other Kopecky family members, his reply was that it had taken him his whole life to finally find out where he belonged. I then suggested splitting them—to which his answer was that, if I did this, with his luck, when he got to wherever he was going he would be missing all the parts he needed! Instead, he wanted to be buried where he could watch the sunsets forever—and then I could take him a beer occasionally, to toast them with him. I will follow those wishes accordingly.

After the Pa site had been completely restored to its original contours, Sam's ashes were interred at Te Aputa on May 15, 2006. Unbeknown to us, the following writing by the late Tom Winitana, would be read out on this occasion by our Anglican Priest friend, (now also the late) John Clark. John, who after visiting Sam for almost three years, was overseas in September 2001 when Sam died and had been unable to take the original funeral service that we had all planned together. At Sam's 2006 interment more than four years later when the grave was to be rededicated, although I knew he must also be nearing the end of his own battle with terminal cancer (to which he succumbed only 3 months later) I had asked John to be present, to speak to, and on behalf of, Sam, Amanda and I (and unexpectedly Tom, too, through his 'Taha Wairua' reading—below); along with our Maori friend who some of you met (and one of Sam's pallbearers), Steve Te Moananui (now also deceased), whose own ancestor—his 'Nan'—is also buried at this gravesite. The Te Aputa trustees were present, along with Department of Conservation personnel, and Maori whanau (family) of Tom's, who 'adopted' Amanda and I after his death. We all 'broke bread' together afterwards up at the lodge, our former home. It was a very special day and felt very 'right' because of the uniquely interwoven circumstances and relationships of the people involved with this land.

Taha Wairua—or the Maori Dimension of Spirituality

Taha Wairua is the greatest gift given by Io, the Supreme Being, to mankind.

Listen to these word pictures, see the conceptual sketches and behold the mural thoughts.

Taha Wairua is: the timeless twinkle of celestial lace in a crystal-crisp night sky, the warm open smile of an innocent child, the calm caring touch of a faithful friend, the denial of pleasures to give to another, and the protection of basic principles for the families of Nature and Human-kind.

Taha Wairua is also: the gleeful joy of the roaring surf, a half-halo rainbow on a clouded wind-swept sky, the pristine gold of an untrodden beach, the hypnotic quality of natural masterpieces, the spiraling beauty of Bird and People song, and the fractured reflections of a mosaic raindrop.

It is the unforgettable cry of birth, the magical Moment of natural death and the sobering hallowed anguish from crucified Humanity.

Taha Wairua allows each person, in time, to see their true inner selves and to amend any deficits in a more enlightened and positive way.

Everyone has some Taha Wairua, but it is rarely used, all day and every day.
Some people deny its existence and endure a life-time of spiritual emptiness.
Others mis-use it and are denied further riches to their lives.
Taha Wairua is the God-force that transcends all man-made boundaries.

It can be found behind a grotesque facade, in a wretchedly deformed container or tragically mirrored across a brutally shattered window.

It is the most difficult gift to receive but the easiest to use.

It is the only gift that is indescribably beautiful with a magnificent purity that beautifies the environment.
It also shows as a quiet incandescence in the eyes of those so afflicted.

Taha Wairua makes the intolerable, tolerable; the biased, objective; despair, hopeful; and mankind, God-like.

It is the seed for World PEACE, the power for brotherly and sisterly LOVE and the crucial element for the MATURITY of mankind.

(Tom Winitana—1985)

Alongside Sam's ashes, we also buried some of the ashes of my own father, who loved Sam as "the brother he never had". Both being ill and unable to visit each other in person, they would often do so, and reminisce by phone . . . at which time Sam would always tell him to "wait for me, Alan . . ." It seems fitting that they will now be together in perpetuity on this special land they both came to love so much—looking out over the spectacular views of the sea, coastlines, and surrounding bush-covered hills. It must be one of the most beautiful burial sites in the world! This Kopecky who finally came to find his place on the side of a hill, has now been buried on that same hill. I know Sam has finally found peace there and is happy he is not alone. Eventually, I expect that I, too, will join him there on this land where we have all shared so much joy and pain . . . the best of times . . . and the worst of times. May 15, 2006, was a very special day of peace and closure but one that Amanda and I will never forget. Later that day, after everyone else had left, Amanda and I went back to the reserve to watch the sunset, and share a bottle of his favorite 'DB Export Gold' beer with her father and grandfather—as Sam had always requested.

'Interpretation' specifically identifying expatriate Texan, Sam Kopecky, and his pivotal role in the modern history of New Zealand's Te Aputa Pa, was erected and appropriately dedicated once the Reserve was finally opened to the public. The significant date of the commemoration of the signing of New Zealand's founding document, the Treaty of Waitangi, was chosen to formally open Te Aputa Reserve. This Waitangi Weekend dawn ceremony on February 3, 2007, was hosted traditionally by the Hauraki Maori people who welcomed former Treaty of Waitangi Minister (and Tom Winitana's former 'boss'), the Rt. Hon. Sir Douglas Graham—and other distinguished guests—onto Te Aputa Pa, to formally unveil the carvings and open its reserve.

In order to ensure its ongoing future protection and preservation, Te Aputa Reserve is now under the conservation of the Department of Conservation—on the specific understanding that my own ashes will be interred in due course, alongside those of Sam.

Sam's dedication plaque

Te Aputa Reserve urupa with Te Puru township (and sunsets) below

Te Puru sunset photographed by Sam Kopecky from Te Puru Lodge, 2001

Te Aputa Historic Reserve (with Te Puru Lodge behind)
at front of bush-covered Te Aputa Pa headland. Sam's grave is centre left

View of Te Aputa Pa Reserve (with Te Puru Lodge behind) from Te Puru township below

CHAPTER 98

TE APUTA RESERVE

Funding application document (used to raise around $200,000)

Aerial Postcard showing Thames Coast (and Te Puru Lodge) on New Zealand's Coromandel Peninsula

Background history of Te Aputa Pa:

The Coromandel Ranges of Hauraki's mythical waka float in Tikapa Moana or the Hauraki Gulf where they cast a shadow over the Hauraki lands, according to the local traditions of the Marutuahu tribes of the Tainui waka. In terms of the Hauraki ancestral landscape, their waka is said to extend from its prow at Mt. Te Aroha to the stern at Mt. Moehau near Cape Colville. The middle of the canoe rests on Puke-O-Raka ('Gentle Annie') near Thames. Within that larger picture each hapu has its own ancestral landscape of heritage places and features, and names left behind by their chiefly ancestors. According to the 'old Maori' traditions recounted by Tohunga Ahorangi, Tom Winitana, Te Aputa Pa at Te Puru on the Thames Coast has real significance in this historical context with Te Aputa being the opening for Te Puru, the drainage plug of the canoe into Tikapa Moana (the Firth of Thames). A relatively-recent discovery of the large rock 'plug' in Te Puru's Te Tuta Stream south of Te Aputa Pa—which then disappears underground at this point—could support this argument. The recorded history of Te Aputa tells of Ngati Huarere who were of Te Arawa extraction, in occupation possibly pre-dating 1350. And one version of the naming of both Tikapa Moana and of Te Aroha is attributed to Tama Te Kapua, captain of the Arawa Waka, who was interred on Mt. Moehau. According to the Tainui traditional view of their own world, Hauraki forms the eastern boundary of the mythical Tainui waka domains which stretch from Mokau on the West Coast of the North Island, to the Tamaki area in the north. In this context, the Coromandel Peninsula is the figurative outrigger or ama of this legendary Tainui waka.

One of the reasons the ancient Te Aputa Pa is of significance is because it is easily the largest archaeological site recorded by the New Zealand Historic Places Trust (N.Z.H.P.T.) on the Coromandel Peninsula's West Coast and one of the largest in Hauraki. In addition, it had been occupied by successive tribal groups over a long period of time. It originally covered the area from the sea up to the top of the ridge above. The recorded section of the Pa is located on the north western-most spur of the ridge which forms the south side of the Te Puru Valley. It overlooks the Te Puru Delta which is the largest on the Thames Coast and the Firth of Thames. The southern aspect of the spur is very steep and clad with regenerating coastal Pohutukawa forest. The northern aspect is gentler, tending to flat on the crest (Lots 1 and 2), with the slope becoming steeper as it descends. The spur terminates on Lot 1 at its western end in a cliff approximately 10 meters high above the Thames-Coromandel S.H. 25 Road below.

One of only eight or nine waahi tapu ("prohibited places") in Hauraki which are registered with the N.Z.H.P.T., the Te Aputa Pa site is a unique archaeological area in that it has a small hospitality business, Te Puru Lodge, located in the middle of it. Fourteen years after the lodge's initial development, a scheme plan application for subdivision of the front part of the headland was prepared by the original land owner and approved by the Thames Coromandel District Council (T.C.D.C.) in 1987. The previous owner of the lodge bought the property with its commercial Existing Use Rights in October 1988—nine years before the rediscovery of the site's historical significance. Lot 1 with its frontage to S.H. 25 below, was legally subdivided from Lot 2 (Te Puru Lodge) in 1989, to help defray the lodge's significant development costs as it was brought up to the required local authority licensing standards. This subdivided Lot 1 section was then sold to the realtor who had initially handled the lodge sale and it subsequently changed hands again in 1995.

In 1996, developers building a 'spec' house on Lot 1 ran into problems with the T.C.D.C. when their building permit was withdrawn pending consultation with local Iwi as required under the Resource Management Act, over reputed cultural issues surrounding the land. Massive earthworks had accompanied their construction, with T.C.D.C. allowing the site to be interfered with in an irresponsible manner from both environmental and cultural perspectives—including the desecration of a known burial site. Eventually the building site was abandoned and the area became an eyesore for the local community, with its resultant noxious weed problem impacting on Te Puru and beyond through distribution by wind and birds.

Te Puru Lodge:

The then-Te Puru Lodge owners became increasingly aware of the historical and cultural value of the site—which erection of their premises by the original owner had disturbed. They began working with local kaumatua, the late Tai Turoa, and the N.Z.H.P.T. After their discovery in 1997 that Te Aputa had originally been recorded by the N.Z.H.P.T. as a Thames Coast archaeological site back in 1976, the decision was finally made by the lodge owners at that time, to register the whole headland with this Trust as a Waahi Tapu in order to protect what remained of part of the real history of New Zealand. They had come to realize that all New Zealanders and not just Maori, have a moral responsibility to exercise a guardianship role in preserving, conserving and protecting New Zealand's non-renewable natural and physical heritage, using modern advocacy tools and strategies to manage these taonga. They felt fortunate to have stewardship of a heritage resource and believed it was possible to balance the waahi tapu and historical realities of the area with commercial development.

Earthworks on the subdivided land had destroyed the central Pa terrace and also substantially damaged the one above where the grave was thought to be. The Lot 1 land owners had refused to 'consult' with local Iwi as required under the Resource Management Act and T.C.D.C. were consequently involved with them in a five-year long litigation process which was not resolved until March 2002. To help resolve this impasse, the adjoining Lot 2 Te Puru Lodge owner then bought back Lot 1 as part of the T.C.D.C. settlement in the Environment Court.

The initial rehabilitation of the area began with weed eradication—a combined tangata whenua and Environment Waikato contribution. It was eventually decided to re-establish the seaward aspect of the Pa as recommended in the 1997 N.Z.H.P.T. archaeological assessment. In addition, information was gathered and collated which provides an educational statement acknowledging the former inhabitants, as well as the importance of promoting the significance and conservation of Maori heritage values and sites.

This "stake in the ground"—in legal, physical, historical and spiritual Maori value terms—now represents an extended settlement area where the spirit of former inhabitants still lingers. The mana of this whenua is again acknowledged by the area now being registered as a Private Historic Reserve. Remembrance of those who have been associated with the land and who have now passed on, has been "woven" into the overall development, giving the land status be-fitting the mana of the people who are remembered there.

It is felt that further value has been added to this area by redefining, protecting and preserving this lower part of the Pa site, which is of archaeological and historic significance for local Maori especially. People can now be educated about the presence and significance of this Pa site, raising the profile of the Te Aputa area as a heritage icon. The establishment of the Te Aputa Private Historic Reserve is the first site on The Coromandel's West Coast to be formally recognized in this manner. It has set the stage for a restoration project which is invaluable in terms of both potential learning and teaching, since the prevalent perception in the community is that 'history' only began locally with the (European) gold mining and kauri timber harvesting, which has been the traditional heritage focus for the area. There is now an additional opportunity to realize any tourism potential and at the same time, to ensure that this cultural heritage place is preserved for all time for future generations.

The historic movements of the region's Maori people, their way of life and technologies, have often been overlooked in the public domain. Information regarding these activities exist in official records and in oral histories passed down from generation to generation, rather than in forms that are accessible to all. It is possible to make this wealth of knowledge available through a bicultural partnership—an exercise that could be mana-enhancing for all.

Te Aputa Trust:

Following the 1997 N.Z.H.P.T.-funded *'Archaeological Survey and Assessment of Condition and Archaeological Values'*, initial funding for Te Aputa came from the Community Employment Group (CEG) in 2000. This support made it possible to 'kick start' evaluation and research, and progress development of the 'Te Aputa Pa Restoration and Information Project'. The CEG funding support enabled a *'Conservation Plan for Te Aputa Pa'* to be produced by Heritage Resource Management Consultant Warren Gumbley in 2001. Subsequently an authority was granted by the N.Z.H.P.T. in 2002 to Te Puru Lodge owner, Pam Kopecky—"to modify or damage part of an archaeological site (Te Aputa Pa) for the purposes of restoration".

Maori Cultural Consultant, the late Tom Winitana, had become involved in leading the project during this period, and part of this CEG funding allowed him to carry out extensive background historical research into the Te Aputa land records and to work towards the preparation of a Maori Values Assessment. This work was also supported by other agencies including New Zealand Landcare Trust and the Department of Conservation, with the intention of working co-operatively towards the eventual archaeological restoration of Te Aputa Pa. Learning and teaching educational programs with specific aims of training young people in restoration of our past heritage, were planned for the Thames Coast area. The original vision was also to create employment opportunities as a Community Employment Organization through the development of joint venture ecological and cultural tourism, which would utilize the existing Te Puru Lodge hospitality infrastructure. While this was envisaged as being primarily environmentally-oriented, this project was also expected to address long-term Maori unemployment and family issues, in turn reducing the decile ten poverty rating of the local community.

After an original application for a Tindall Foundation funding grant in 2000, the Compass Community Foundation in Tauranga became involved in the project in 2002—as the Tindall Foundation's Funding Manager for the Thames/Coromandel area. Compass CEO Peter Wyatt and General Manager Martin Steinmann, facilitated the creation of the Te Aputa Trust through the Companies Office with its IRD charitable exemption in September of that year and also worked on related funding initiatives. The Te Aputa Trust was specifically formed for the purpose of creating a Private Historic Reserve under the

Reserves Act, over part of this registered archaeological site (and waahi tapu) on the Thames Coast Te Aputa Pa at Te Puru. The Te Aputa Trust comprised Tom Winitana, then-Te Puru Lodge owner Pam Kopecky, Department of Conservation Hauraki Area Manager John Gaukrodger, and local Ngati Tamatera iwi representative Steve Te Moananui.

Compass confirmed the initial Tindall Foundation grant of $15,000 towards phase one of the project in August 2002. However, the proposed payment dates from late 2002 through to early 2003 did not eventuate as anticipated. And then in early April 2003, project leader Tom Winitana tragically died from injuries received in a car accident. The remaining trustees again met with the Compass Community Trust in late May when it was decided to downsize the Te Aputa project from the proposed renovation of Te Aputa Pa and its related educational aspects, to the reservation and restoration of the front part of the headland only. A Private Historic Reserve was to be created over part of this waahi tapu as a community initiative with an Iwi Maori focus, led by the Hauraki area Department of Conservation office. It was agreed that the original $15,000 Tindall Foundation matching funding grant could still be used for this revised plan as its criteria had not changed, with the project still encompassing both archaeological and 'natural' restoration work and eventual interpretation of the overall site. Representing an early iwi group of settlers on the block, Hakaraia Gurnick took Tom Winitana's place on the Trust.

Payment was to be made at the start of the new funding year in August but the Trust was then notified that the Tindall Foundation was no longer giving Compass funding for matching grants from that date forward—"due to the Warehouse having a not so good year". In September, the Compass Community Trust gave Te Aputa Trust $5,000 as a community investment from its own Acorn Foundation Fund to which the Tindall Foundation was a major contributor. This contribution towards the establishment of an environmental area on the Te Aputa Pa site was made by Compass "in recognition of the work to date by trustees, and also in recognition of Tom Winitana", founding chairman of the Te Aputa Trust. Compass is no longer the funding manager for the Tindall Foundation in the area.

This initial $5,000 Acorn Foundation grant was used to complete the Protected Private Land Agreement process under the Reserves Act in February 2004, between then-lodge owner Pam Kopecky and the Minister of Conservation. The land agreement was made with the department on the basis of the natural, scenic, historic, cultural and archaeological qualities the site possesses which are desirable in the public interest to warrant protection. The landowner specifically purchased the land for this purpose with no intention of selling and under this agreement, its title must now either remain in private ownership or be taken over by the Department of Conservation. But this agreement also stipulates that the Minister of Conservation must also have first option to purchase the reserve (for a 'token' amount) in the event of its sale or disposition—providing surety of its ongoing reserve status protection for funding agencies. The land's planning designation has now been permanently changed from Coastal Residential to (Historic) Protected Private Land status. The Thames Coromandel District Council has now granted rate remission under the Local Government (Rating) Act, on this basis—thereby permanently destroying the commercial value of this land as a building site. It has now been re-valued accordingly at the standard 10 percent formula of its original market value.

This 'seeding' funding was also used to obtain the Maori archaeological and historical input necessary for any physical work to be done. A significant 60-plus page historical report was produced by Hauraki historical researcher Dawn Danby in November 2003, from the extensive Te Aputa Native Land Court records. Her report—produced at a reduced rate as her own contribution to this project—was envisaged as the foundation for this restoration work as well as any future interpretation. Archaeologist Warren Gumbley re-surveyed the site in November 2003, drawing up a site plan (February 2004) for site modification and restoration work. This was also used by local Department of Conservation volunteers who contributed their own relevant environmental expertise towards the creation of this private reserve, in determining its landscaping and access issues.

A $4,000 Environmental Initiatives' Award funding grant was then received from the Department of Conservation for this 'historic site reclamation' and as a result, in June 2004, the Te Aputa Trust passed the threshold of no return when the primary basis of the restoration work was completed. Utilizing this DOC grant, landscape construction machinery (at a contributory reduced rate), was brought onto the site to restore the original three Pa terraces under the archaeologist's supervision. While Native Land Court records indicate that Te Aputa's urupa was originally more extensive, its only known 'lost' burial site from the more recent past was also specifically identified without disturbance and marked for future protection and 'interpretation'. This work was all monitored in accordance with accepted archaeological practice under the Historic Places Act, adhering to the original *'Te Aputa Pa Conservation Plan'* already prepared three years earlier.

The Te Aputa Trust then sought other funding options to progress this physical restoration phase of the work which was to include track construction for public access, hard and soft landscape construction and planting, with appropriate acknowledgement of the burial site, and a concept plan and graphics for historical interpretation purposes. The carving and placing of the Te Aputa kaitiaki pou whenua as originally envisaged by Tom Winitana, to represent the "stake in the ground", was also seen as a key component of the site's restoration and interpretation.

Te Puru Lodge on Lot 2 of this Te Aputa block was sold in December 2004, with its new owners also being prepared to support the Lot 1 historic site reclamation. As their support as neighbors was seen as crucial to this ongoing restoration project, they were then also represented on the Te Aputa Trust accordingly, through Te Puru Lodge owner Beverley Gausden (Ngati Tuwharetoa). However, Lot 1 was not sold along with the lodge and the former lodge owner retained ownership of the adjoining Te Aputa Private Historic Reserve on the (Lot 1) front of the headland on which the lodge also sits.

In March 2005, the Department of Conservation made a further grant of $11,500 towards the reserve's restoration from its Community Conservation and Tikanga Atawhai Funds. This funding was specifically targeted to cover the costs of completing the site reclamation, protection of the specific waahi tapu burial site, formation of public access to the site, landscaping issues, and interpretation for visitors to the area. The next stage of the initial landscaping component of the site restoration scheduled for March-April 2005 was delayed because of the unusually late onset of the damper autumn conditions required for lawn germination. The topsoil was finally spread over the terraces in early May when grass seed was sown over this site. The formally-identified waahi tapu burial site was also separated off at that time.

The Te Aputa Trust then explored options to fund the reserve's carving for which its trustee, John Gaukrodger and Moera Hughes of Ngati Rereahu (Maniapoto), had already donated a heart totara log for the kaitiaki pou whenua, as their own koha for this project. Even in its raw form this log has special significance, representing a time and place in this nation's history for both Maori and Pakeha. It whakapapas back as part of a ngahere that survived the Taupo eruptions of 2,000 years ago, having spent all of its life—even after its demise—on Maori land. It has been logged over, burnt over and planted with exotic trees, and logged over again. And while its outer skin has suffered considerably from these actions and age, the heart is still pure red Pureora totara that has enabled it to endure like a true warrior. This log was taken from the Pureora Forest to the nearby King Country workshop of Maniapoto Ngati Paretekawa Tohunga Whakairo Samuel Roa, who was finally commissioned to begin its carving. He has consulted on this project with mandated Te Aputa tangata whenua representative and newly-appointed Te Aputa trustee, Apanui Skipper, whose Ngati Tamatera Te Kiriwera hapu most recently occupied this site. When completed, it was intended that this three meter-high pou whakarei would be housed in a 17.28 m^2 Whare Ruruhau traditional Maori-style protective shelter on the reserve, specifically designed to minimize elemental damage to the carving and its related interpretation panels. This 4.8 x 3.6 meter interpretation centre—funded in August 2005 by Trust Waikato—was to be decorated with a whakapapa carving of Taraia Ngakuti Te Tumuhuia, a renowned ancestor of great significance to the Hauraki Maori people, and, as former rangatira of Te Aputa Pa, particularly to the Thames Coast tangata whenua. This structure was also designed to protect and present the interpretation panels relating to this more recent history, as well as that of the ancient Te Aputa Pa itself, going back to its earliest recorded Te Arawa Ngati Huarere inhabitants pre-dating 1350. Helping tell the story of Te Aputa—past and present—for the benefit of future generations, both the tekoteko for this whare and the waharoa entryway, were also to be carved by Samuel Roa and his team.

In July 2005, a further five-year N.Z.H.P.T. Authority was granted to reserve owner Pam Kopecky, to modify part of the archaeological site at Te Aputa Pa, Te Puru, for the purposes of restoration, under continuing archaeological supervision. And later that month, the Pa's original lowest lateral defensive terrace was again uncovered when it was cleared of undergrowth as work began on the public access to Te Aputa Reserve. In September 2005, above-ground box-type steps were put in from the road (S.H. 25) below, up to this lowest terrace where an existing informal benched track then gives further access to the main part of the reserve. A spoil slip was also cleared from the lower lateral defensive Pa terrace, enhancing the previous archaeological restoration work. The traditionally-carved waharoa gateway with appropriate signage denoting and explaining the special waahi tapu nature of this historic reserve was not erected at the roadside entrance to the foot track until after its official opening, as it was intended that this project proceed through to its completed state without significant fanfare. The landscaping, planting and fencing (pallisading) of Te Aputa Reserve were also not to be completed until after the opening, along with the waahi tapu burial site 'interpretation'.

Te Aputa Reserve opening:

A traditional-style native timber batten pallisade surround (in keeping with the reserve's planned pallisade fencing) was researched and then purpose-built for the burial site, in order to separate this urupa as a specific waahi tapu within the reserve. According to Hauraki Maori historian the late Taimoana Turoa, this was the burial site of Te Rauoriwa Pereniki, widow of Taraia's grandson Ngati Tamatera chief Haora Tareranui, the last rangatira of Te Aputa Pa. Also re-named Te Awhimate after Taraia's daughter (and only surviving issue) of the same name, she was reputed to have died in 1959 at the age of 96 and been buried—according to her wishes—at Te Aputa Pa where she had lived. Significant effort went into the urupa's design criteria imposed by the Trust—including the fact that no treated timber could be used. This pallisade surround was finally put in place at the urupa re-dedication on May 15, 2006, when the ashes of former lodge owner, the late Sam Kopecky (who had facilitated the original Te Aputa waahi tapu registration), were also finally buried at this site. An important stage in the overall restoration of Te Aputa Pa, this event took the Trust's effort well beyond the restoration of the "form" of Te Aputa, originally recommended by archaeologist Warren Gumbley in order to rehabilitate the values of this urupa area and restore some integrity to the whole Pa by re-establishing the form of its seaward aspect. The emotion that was present in the people attending this rededication ceremony, identified that the redefining of the urupa contributed significantly to the restoration of the dignity that is an integral part of Te Aputa.

In July 2006, building plans for the Whare Ruruhau interpretation centre went through the Thames Coromandel District Council's Planning Consent process and construction approval was obtained. This 17 sq.m. whare is significantly bigger than initially envisaged as its size was determined by the height of the pou whenua carving, in order to keep its visual balance in proportion. There was also a desire to retain traditional building lines as the original concept for Te Aputa included the construction of original-style whares on site. Cost aside, this larger structure now presents a wider range of opportunities, including some seating, and an ability to house and present the interpretation. For water tightness, the whare roof has been lined with treated construction ply and butanyl, and then covered with a natural woven fern material. After completion of the main roof structure, the rear wall of the building was lined with ponga logs to blend with the surrounding native bush. This last major part of the site's physical development was led by Paul White, the VETEL Contractor who built both the boxed access steps and the urupa palisade surround, and who once again, made himself available to continue this specialized construction. Paul White contributed significantly to this project—not only with his construction expertise and experience but also his 'feel for the job', and ultimately his volunteer effort and contribution of materials to the construction of the whare.

The traditional dawn carving unveiling and opening ceremony for the Te Aputa Private Historic Reserve at Te Puru (funded by the Thames Coromandel District Council), took place on February 3, 2007, when it was officially opened to the public. This significant time of Waitangi Weekend was chosen by the Trust as an appropriate celebration of biculturalism in Hauraki. Organized by Te Aputa Trustee and Ngati Kiriwera hapu representative Apanui Skipper, it took the form of a Ta-i-te-kawa ceremony led by the tangata whenua, which commenced at the waharoa before proceeding up the steps to the marumaru, the pouwhenua, and the tekoteko on the ridge of the whare ruruhau. The karakia were followed by a powhiri and opening ceremony. This coming together of Maori and Pakeha was also represented by the significant presence of former Treaty Negotiations Minister, the Rt. Hon. Sir Douglas Graham (a direct descendant of the founder of Grahamstown, Thames), who, along with his former Justice Department Chief Advisor/Ministerial Aide and Te Aputa trustee, the late Tom Winitana, helped establish the Treaty of Waitangi Claims process. Their colleague, the former Chief Historian and Crown Negotiator from this time, historian and Director of Victoria University's Treaty of Waitangi Research Unit, Professor Richard Hill, also spoke at this ceremonial opening. Many tributes were paid to the founding Te Aputa Trust chairman, Tom Winitana, who had helped initiate this project. This event, in its entirety, was the defining moment in bringing Te Aputa back into focus as a site of cultural and historic heritage significance. It also gave the community in general a greater appreciation of the purpose of the Te Aputa Trust both within the physical reconstruction aspirations of the project, along with the primary purpose of the Trust's objective of re-defining the cultural value and historic heritage of Te Aputa.

The dominant feature of the whare ruruhau is the kaitiaki pou carved by Waikato carver Samuel Roa, in a heart totara log from the Pureora Forest. Both traditional and contemporary patterns and figures appear on the pou which give a brief history of the land and people. The Kaitiaki Atua are carved in Hauraki style in acknowledgement of the tangata whenua. The traditional Kaitiaki figures on the right-hand site are Tumatauenga, the God of War; Rongo Maraeroa, the God of Peace and Cultivated

Food; and Haumiatiketike, the God of Uncultivated Food. The kaitiaki figures on the left-hand side are Tangaroa, the God of the Sea and Seafood; and Tane (as the Totara pou), the God of the Forest and Birds. Tane is also the God of Nga kete o te Wananga (the knowledge taught in the Whare Wananga), represented by the rauru (3 spirals), Aronui, Tuauri and Tuatea. Carved in Waikato (Tainui) style called 'Taura' (rope pattern) used and made famous by the late Maori Queen's carvers, this style has been used in acknowledgement and support of the Kingitanga movement and the unity of the Maori people. The kohatu (stone) represents the rivers and streams in the area, as well as the drainage plug (te puru) of the mythological waka, spoken of by Tom Winitana. The paua represents Te Aputa's springs. The Taniko pattern around the base of the pou represents the connection of all things back to Papatuanuku. The pou as a whole is symbolic of the Korowai—a cloak of protection over the land, the sea, and the people.

The contemporary carvings of the opposing tuatara and weta kaitiaki are also very powerful ancient Maori symbols with many layers of meaning, as a fundamental belief in the reciprocal concept of kaitiakitanga originally governed Maori custom. The tuatara lizard carved on this pou, stands upon the mythical outrigger of the Tainui waka. As the benevolent kaitiaki, it represents the keeper and protector of the genealogies. The larger lizard represents all those who have passed on. The great chiefs were once also known as lizards—and even referred to as tuatara—because of this inherent responsibility associated with their iwi, hapu and whanau . . . from time immemorial and the beginning of creation with Ranginui, Papatuanuku and their descendants, and on down through the ages to them. The whole concept of the people associated with these realms was embodied in the tuatara—just as the Ariki was—and when Maori saw a tuatara representation they knew this genealogical knowledge was protected. The weta, carved inside the pou, represents the malevolent kaitiaki which lives inside dark places such as rotten logs, caves, manuka and other trees. Delving inside living things in order to sustain itself, it eats from the inside out.

A journey of several hundreds of years for a totara from Rerahu, ended with this Pou Whakarei being set upon its stand at Te Aputa. The creative skill of Sam and Nathan Roa and their team, is superbly demonstrated in the pou, tekoteko and waharoa at the public entrance to Te Aputa Pa. Their skill and experience, along with gentle hands, was also central to the safe mounting of all three carvings on the day. The tekoteko at the entrance to the Whare Ruruhau represents Taraia Ngakuti Te Tumuhuia ('the shredder of palisades') with his favorite patiti (hatchet) battle weapon. Taraia, who regularly resided at Te Aputa Pa from around 1840 until his recorded death in 1872, was the great Marutuahu leader of his time, as the acknowledged paramount chief of Ngati Tama-Te-Ra and Ngati Maru. The waharoa entrance gateway to the reserve represents the three related Ngati Tamatera ancestral figures of Haora Tareranui (Taraia's grandson and last rangatira of Te Aputa Pa), the rangatira Ahiataeawa Tukukino (Taraia's cousin), and the chieftainess, Kiriata. Symbolizing the three states of existence—the past, present and future—this gateway entrance to Te Aputa Pa, marks the transition from the present into the past. And walking back out from under the waharoa, one passes again from the past, through the present and back into the future.

With the second funding grant of $10,000 received from Trust Waikato in August 2006, all the necessary interpretation information from amongst the extensive Te Aputa research already undertaken, was finally brought together. This design process was necessary in order to enable the key message and relevant historic information to be compiled into a concise artistic, pictorial and factual form for presentation on the on-site panels, which sit alongside the carved pou whakarei in the Trust Waikato-sponsored whare ruruhau interpretation centre. Based on comparable Department of Conservation information panels, the information produced is presented on six 800 by 600 mm panels at an estimated $10,000 design cost. A further funding grant of $5,000 made by the Department of Conservation's 2006 Community Conservation Fund in November 2006, contributed towards the cost of their production and installation, in order to help bring this development stage to completion. Three interpretation/orientation panels with pictorial pointilism recreations of the original pre-European Te Aputa Pa site were produced as Puriri artist, Rick Fisher's impression of what Te Aputa might have looked like some 200 years ago. Bringing all the Te Aputa archaeological and Maori historical information together, the Pa structures and real life scenes portrayed, are in keeping with the extensive original ground excavations surveyed by archaeologist, Dr Warren Gumbley, in 1997. Other panels include pre and early European history, as well as photographic displays of the changing Te Puru landscape—caused by fire, kauri logging, gold mining, farming, urban development, and introduced animals and plants—from the early 1900's through to the present time.

In addition to these information/orientation panels, the Te Aputa whare ruruhau interpretation centre also provides an opportunity to house an explanatory background brochure (written by historical researcher, Dawn Walton), which highlights the importance of promoting the significance and conservation of Maori heritage values and sites. Along with other records, it also publicly acknowledges the significant sponsorship provided by the Department of Conservation, Trust Waikato, Environment Waikato, New Zealand Landcare Trust, and other Te Aputa Reserve funders.

Further development has also been planned to enhance the natural heritage component of this landscape. Vegetation currently consists of ancient pohutukawa with kowhai native shrub, hardwood species and a significant mix of exotic weed species. Initially funded by 2005 Environment Waikato Environmental Initiatives and Transpower Landcare Trust Grants Programs, work has been already been undertaken which includes ongoing removal of existing plant pests by a variety of actions including both hand and chemical methods. This action will eventually be followed by restoration plantings compatible to the existing forest cover and coastal environment. In addition to rehabilitating the vegetation cover of this private historic reserve, an associated objective is to capitalize on past and proposed pest control operations. Native bird life in the area is significant and establishing a food source for native birds will be a particular focus of this initiative.

The ultimate destruction of the Te Aputa Pa terraces that have now been restored was an event that was recorded through photography, as was the restoration process. What is not easily evidenced is the contribution made by a variety of individuals and organizations who have contributed significantly to the restoration initiative. In 2009, the sudden and unexpected death of Steve Te Moananui, a founding trustee with direct links to Te Aputa, was a major blow to the overall initiative. Steve's direct 10 year involvement in the protection and restoration of Te Aputa was crucial as it even predated the 2002 registration of the trust. His ongoing support as the original tangata whenua representative was key to this project's inception and his contribution critical to enabling the somewhat dramatic but necessary restoration work to proceed. Steve's mana lives on within the spirit of the land that is Te Aputa.

Te Aputa, originally protected as a Private Historic Reserve with full public access, came under the stewardship of the Department of Conservation in December 2009 to be managed as an Historic Reserve under the Reserves Act 1977. This will ensure the continuity of lasting protection of this historic site. Linking cultural, historic and natural heritage into a single entity, the Te Aputa Reserve marries together Maori and Pakeha into one identity within an all-encompassing natural community. Te Aputa Trust members and supporters share a belief in the need to develop a Maori cultural education programme as part of the Thames-Coromandel region's overall economic development programme, to sit alongside mainstream Pakeha economic development opportunities. Through this cultural and historical educational resource, they envisage a coming together of Maori and Pakeha cultures based on this sharing of the region's real history. In addition to creating an ongoing harmony between all the region's residents, it is hoped that this could also lead to the empowerment and ultimate creation of employment opportunities for tangata whenua, through the development of their own initiatives centered around interpretation of this history.

Further construction of the interpretation centre recommenced in July 2010, as part of the already-funded Stage 6 interpretation. VETEL Contracting's Paul White replaced the temporary seaweed roof cladding with more permanent rough-sawn macrocapa planks donated in part, by Te Puru resident, John Antonovich. Seats have been added, along with timber frames on which to hang the adjoining interpretation panels. The water supply (diverted from the spouting on the interpretation centre) has also been completed, to enable the collection/replacement of a continuous source of clean rainwater for hand washing at both the upper and lower reserve entrances/exits.

In December 2010, additional funding grants of $5,000 and $3,300 were also received from Environment Waikato and the Department of Conservation respectively, now that all possible land movement has come to an end, following the significant earthworks required to restore the Te Aputa Pa headland. Follow up maintenance work was required to cut out the (formerly buried and now exposed) concrete foundations, and to fill and re-level the main terraces. Along with the addition of new topsoil and grass resowing to tidy up Te Aputa Reserve for easier maintenance and more effective weed control, this has ensured that any of the necessarily buried projections remain well below the newly-regrassed surfaces. This work was then followed up by further site clearance and replanting from the roadside entrance up to the original lower level of the reserve.

This initiative has, since conception, been a planned process . . . planned steps in a journey. However, the project is not yet finished. While we can be proud of our combined efforts in setting the stage, we have yet to tell the story. The role of the Te Aputa Trust will be ongoing alongside the Department of Conservation, in terms of both site administration, and for the development of Te Aputa's public educational and historical interpretation aspects. As the location of this 2ha area is a prominent headland within the Te Puru township on the Thames Coast, immediately adjacent to S.H. 25—the 'Pacific Coast Highway' tourist route of the Coromandel Peninsula—there is the opportunity to further enhance this natural asset within an urban environment that will be fully accessible to the public. The possibility also exists that extensive ongoing archaeological restoration work could be done around the surrounding site if further funding becomes available in the future—building on this initial "stake in the ground" at Te Aputa Pa . . . a symbol which continues to motivate the forces behind this project. The Te Aputa journey has touched a number of people along the way and there are few projects where willing contributions have been so freely given.

"If you have built castles in the air, your work need not be lost;
that is where they should be.
Now put the foundations under them."

Henry David Thoreau, *'Walden: Or, Life in the Woods'*

Te Aputa Private Historic Reserve

(On-site public brochure)

Around 70 million years ago the Coromandel Peninsula was born in a violent volcanic upheaval of the earth's crust. Great hills arose above the shallow Firth. In time, trees grew and covered the hills, streams slipped through the valley. And then, sometime around 1350, the people came in their great waka to explore the coast.

Later, around 1600, more people came. They built fish traps and gathered the abundant fish, made nets and caught mackerel, harvested the berries and birds in the forest. There was a constant movement of people as the area became a focal point at which to gather for seasonal fishing. Later many fortified Pa were established on the surrounding hills. Most of these Pa were originally founded as a sometime residence for the chief and tohunga.

This was an ideal area, sheltered and defensible with streams and springs for fresh water. The people planted their crops on the fertile flat land by the sea and established kumara pits on the hill above this site. They caame and went with the seasons. Eventually a palisade was erected around the buildings on this land and a permanent Pa, Te Aputa, was established as the largest Pa on this side of the Coromandel Peninsula.

Among the earliest occupants were Ngati Huarere whose ancestry was from the Te Arawa waka. Gradually through a combination of conquest and intermarriage the mana over the land was assumed by the Marutuahu tribes who originated from the Tainui waka. In more recent pre-European times the Te Puru area had been a major settlement for the various Ngati Tamatera iwi of the Marutuahu tribes.

What do we know about the individuals who lived here in times past? For most of the 19th century there was widespread tribal warfare in both the North and South Islands. During the first two decades of the century there were several invasions of Hauraki by Hongi Hika and Nga Puhi. In 1821—while Taraia and his kinsmen were fighting alongside Ngati Toa in the lower North Island and upper South Island—most of the Hauraki people fled to re-establish themselves at Horotiu near present day Cambridge. Taraia Ngakuti Te Tumuhuia became one of the outstanding warriors of his time and was, for twenty-five years, closely associated in warfare with Te Rauparaha throughout the North and South Islands. Between 1830 and 1831 the Hauraki contingent of several thousand returned to re-possess their lands. By 1840 Taraia and his people were in residence at Te Aputa and had strengthened the Pa fortifications to withstand the expected retaliation from Ngaiterangi with whom Taraia had been carrying out 'tit for tat' acts of hostility.

Taraia was not only a brave warrior but he was also the great Marutuahu leader of his time. He worked to preserve his people's survival and integrity through political means. Neither he nor many of his people had signed the Treaty of Waitangi, believing that its relevance was to regulate the behavior of Europeans. In the years after 1860 Taraia and the other great Marutuahu leaders became adept at negotiating and administrating on behalf of their people. When he died in 1872 (allegedly in his nineties) Taraia left a proud legacy. None of his sons survived him but he did leave a grandson, Haora Tareranui.

Why did the inhabitants of the Pa leave their home? Probably because with the introduction of modern methods of warfare, the defensive Pa became obsolete. The people could more safely live in their kainga down on the flat land by the river from where, should they be threatened, they could escape by way of the sea in their waka.

The land on which you are now standing eventually became the property of Taraia's grandson Haora Tareranui, then passed to his widow Te Awhimate (II) who, on her death, left her estate to the cousin who had cared for her for many years. He sold the land to Europeans in 1968 who on-sold it a year later. The second European owner of the land built a large residence on the upper portion of the block, intending to create a centre for the treatment of drug and alcohol addiction, a purpose which raised objections from the then-neighbors.

In 1988, a two acre parcel in three lots, on one of which was the building which then became the Te Puru Lodge, was bought by Pam and Sam Kopecky who then on-sold one lot which ended up in the possession of a couple who started to build a house on the land. It subsequently became this Reserve.

To ensure that areas of historical significance are protected and preserved the Resource Management Act requires consultation with local iwi before major development of such sites can be undertaken. Unfortunately in this instance the necessary protective steps were not followed before massive earthworks had caused considerable damage. The worst of this was the desecration of a known burial site—that of Te Awhimate (II) who, legend has it, was in death, placed on the site to guide to Cape Reinga, the spirits of those who may have died on this land where she had lived. The environmental vandalism caused by these earthworks led directly to a rediscovery of significance—the ancient Te Aputa Pa site. The resulting litigation was not resolved until 2002. At that time Pam Kopecky bought the land back with the intention of preserving the rediscovered historical significance of the land and making it accessible to all people by creating a private Historic Reserve. In 1998 the land had been registered as a Waahi Tapu "a place sacred to Maori" . . . (and hopefully, to all New Zealanders) by the Maori Heritage Council of the New Zealand Historic Places Trust who had commissioned Warren Gumbley to prepare an archaeological report on Te Aputa Pa. Subsequently the Community Employment Group funded Warren to produce a Conservation Plan for the site.

Remembering the spiritual significance of the land we ask that visitors to this site observe its significance. Please do not leave rubbish on the land nor behave inappropriately. It deserves your respect.

Two people in particular—Pam Kopecky and John Gaukrodger—have contributed to the preservation and restoration of this site. They have been and are tireless in their efforts to create and maintain this Reserve that provides a unique example of our early history. Without their dedication and determination to overcome the many and various difficulties, and to show by example that we are capable of respecting and preserving our history, this reserve would not have been available to us.

In 2002 The Te Aputa Charitable Trust was formed. The Compass Community Foundation who administered the Tindall Foundation provided the initial funding. The first trustees were the land owner Pam Kopecky, the late Tom Winitana, (whose place was subsequently taken by Hakaraia Gurnick), John Gaukrodger of the Department of

Conservation, and local iwi representative the late Steve Te Moananui of Waiomu, who was joined later by Apanui Skipper (Ngati Kiriwera) of Te Puru and then-Te Puru Lodge owner Bev Gausden. The Trust has been grateful for the support of local kaumatua, Kemara Tukukino (Ngati Kiriwera). Others who have contributed to the ongoing development of Te Aputa Reserve are the Department of Conservation, Trust Waikato, Environment Waikato and New Zealand Landcare Trust.

The dominant feature of the whare ruruhau is the kaitiaki pou carved by Waikato Carver Samuel Roa, in a heart totara log from the Pureora Forest, a koha (gift) donated by Moera Hughes of the Maniapoto hapu, Ngati Rereahu. Both contemporary and traditional Maori patterns and figures appear on the pou. They give a brief history of the land and people. The Kaitiaki Atua are carved in Hauraki style in acknowledgement of the tangata whenua. The traditional Kaitiaki figures on the right-hand site are Tumatauenga, the God of War; Rongo Maraeroa, the God of Peace and Cultivated Food; and Haumiatiketike, the God of Uncultivated Food. The kaitiaki figures on the left-hand side are Tangaroa, the God of the Sea and Seafood; and Tane (as the Totara pou), the God of the Forest and Birds. Tane is also the God of Nga kete o te Wananga (the knowledge taught in the Whare Wananga), represented by the rauru (3 spirals), Aronui, Tuauri and Tuatea. Carved in Waikato (Tainui) style called 'Taura' (rope pattern), this style has been used in acknowledgement and support of the Kingitanga movement and the unity of the Maori people. The kohatu (stone) represents the rivers and streams in the area while the paua represents its springs. The Taniko pattern around the base of the pou represents the connection of all things back to Papatuanuku. The contemporary figures are the Tuatara which represents the benevolent kaitiaki (and keeper of the genealogy), and the lizard, those who have passed on. The Weta, inside the pou, represents the malevolent kaitiaki. The pou as a whole is symbolic of the Korowai—a cloak of protection over the land, the sea, and the people.

The tekoteko on the entrance to the Whare Ruruhau represents Taraia Ngakuti Te Tumuhuia, the Marutuahu Ngati Tama-Te-Ra leader. The waharoa gateway symbolizes the three states of existence—the past, present and future. Walking under the three Ngati Tamatera ancestral figures of Haora Tareranui, Ahiataeawa Tukukino and Kiriata, you make the transition from the present into the past. And walking back out from under the waharoa, you pass again from the past, through the present and back into the future.

The New Zealand Historic Places Trust (Pouhere Taonga) has, for the last 50 years, recognized, protected and promoted New Zealand's heritage places saving our past for our future through its role of preservation and advocacy. The New Zealand Historic Places Trust meets the challenge implicit in its vision . . .

"Keep the treasure handed down by the ancestors
for descendants yet to be born in Aotearoa."

"Puritia nga taonga tuku iho a nga tupuna hei tiki huia ma nga uri
Whakatupu o Aotearoa"